Data Privacy and Cybersecurity in Mobile Crowdsensing

Data Privacy and Cybersecurity in Mobile Crowdsensing

Guest Editors

Chuan Zhang
Tong Wu
Weiting Zhang

MDPI

Basel • Beijing • Wuhan • Barcelona • Belgrade • Novi Sad • Cluj • Manchester

Guest Editors
Chuan Zhang
School of Cyberspace Science and Technology
Beijing Institute of Technology
Beijing
China

Tong Wu
School of Computer & Communication Engineering
University of Science and Technology Beijing
Beijing
China

Weiting Zhang
School of Electronic and Information Engineering
Beijing Jiaotong University
Beijing
China

Editorial Office
MDPI AG
Grosspeteranlage 5
4052 Basel, Switzerland

This is a reprint of the Special Issue, published open access by the journal *Electronics* (ISSN 2079-9292), freely accessible at: www.mdpi.com/journal/electronics/special_issues/5Y6R6N9ZX8.

For citation purposes, cite each article independently as indicated on the article page online and as indicated below:

Lastname, A.A.; Lastname, B.B. Article Title. *Journal Name* **Year**, *Volume Number*, Page Range.

ISBN 978-3-7258-4540-8 (Hbk)
ISBN 978-3-7258-4539-2 (PDF)
https://doi.org/10.3390/books978-3-7258-4539-2

Contents

electronics

MDPI

Editorial

Data Privacy and Cybersecurity in Mobile Crowdsensing

Chuan Zhang [1,*], Tong Wu [2] and Weiting Zhang [3]

1 School of Cyberspace Science and Technology, Beijing Institute of Technology, Beijing 100081, China
2 School of Computer and Communication Engineering, University of Science and Technology Beijing, Beijing 100083, China; tongw@ustb.edu.cn
3 School of Electronic and Information Engineering, Beijing Jiaotong University, Beijing 100044, China; wtzhang@bjtu.edu.cn
* Correspondence: chuanz@bit.edu.cn

Mobile crowdsensing (MCS) has emerged as a pivotal element in contemporary communication technology, witnessing substantial growth recently. The advent of 5G [1], the Internet of Things (IoT) [2], and edge computing [3] has propelled MCS to achieve enhanced sensing efficiency and broaden its application spectrum across various domains such as environmental monitoring [4], traffic management [5], and healthcare [6].

However, despite these advantages, MCS confronts significant security and privacy challenges due to its open and diverse nature. Critical concerns encompass data leakage [7–10], unauthorized access [11,12], data tampering [13,14], and cross-network attacks [15,16]. These issues can severely compromise the stability, privacy, and security of MCS systems. Furthermore, the dynamic mobility of users and devices within MCS introduces additional complexity to conventional security measures, particularly concerning communication and cross-domain access control [17,18].

To tackle these challenges, researchers have devised several strategies aimed at bolstering the security and privacy of MCS systems [19–21]. These novel protection mechanisms offer distinct benefits over traditional approaches. They are capable of securing data even with constrained computational and communication resources, enhancing system flexibility, and effectively thwarting sophisticated cyberattacks. These strategies provide both theoretical and practical underpinnings for fortifying MCS security and lay a robust foundation for the field's future evolution.

As concerns over data privacy and cybersecurity increase [22,23], numerous researchers have proffered innovative solutions in the realms of mobile sensing, the Internet of Things (IoT), and federated learning, with the aim of safeguarding data privacy and bolstering system security. Regarding the protection mechanism for UAV network task chains, Contribution 1 introduces a UAV network mission chain protection mechanism grounded in vulnerability analysis and topology reconfiguration. By employing the multi-indicator node vulnerability assessment algorithm and the node importance-based topology reconfiguration algorithm, this research can effectively pinpoint critical nodes and optimize network topology to enhance both reliability and security. In the domain of recommender systems, Contribution 2 advances a differential privacy-based federated recommendation framework that safeguards user privacy while preserving recommendation accuracy through the addition of noise to model updates. The study substantiates the efficacy of the framework across various datasets experimentally. In Contribution 3, the authors propose an innovative federated recommendation framework that integrates differential privacy techniques to protect user privacy without compromising recommendation accuracy. To fortify privacy protection further, the authors also devise a specialized differential privacy algorithm for ensuring that individual user information cannot be inferred from the global model by meticulously calibrated noise added to aggregated data updates. Moreover, addressing privacy protection challenges within the Internet of Vehicles [24,25], Contribution 4 puts forth a consensus mechanism based on proof-of-multiple-state. This mechanism leverages blockchain technology to resolve data security and privacy issues in vehicular networking while optimizing communication efficiency among mobile nodes. The PoMS mechanism utilizes vehicle driving state predictions and machine learning models to dynamically adjust node weights and select optimal relay nodes, thereby enhancing both the efficiency and security of network communications.

In the realm of affective speech generation, Contribution 5 introduces a method for generating high-quality affective speech data by integrating affective embedding and phonological style embedding. Utilizing the Mel spectrogram as an input, this method generates affective speech through a diffusion process. Addressing challenges in mobile sensors and localization problems, Contribution 7 proposes a multi-source sparse inverse localization technique based on mobile sensors. This approach targets signal source localization issues within long-distance mobile sensor networks. Additionally, a long-range localization method grounded in the block sparse model is presented, along with a unilateral branching ratio decision algorithm designed to adaptively control the iterative process amidst unknown sparsity levels. Building upon these advancements, Contribution 6 presents a swell neural network algorithm tailored for resolving time-varying path query problems while considering privacy protection. The algorithm efficiently identifies multiple paths, including the shortest path, while safeguarding user privacy. It also designs an encrypted indexing scheme to effectively prevent the leakage of user information. Targeting concerns related to privacy breaches and malicious disruptions in electronic voting systems [26,27], Contribution 8 proposes an efficient e-voting system leveraging homomorphic encryption. An enhanced HSE-Voting system is designed, which fortifies system security by incorporating signatures and partial proof-of-knowledge protocols, simultaneously reducing computational costs for proxies. This improved system ensures the accuracy and verifiability of election outcomes while preserving voter privacy.

To tackle the escalating issue of copyright infringement in models [28,29], Contribution 9 introduces a framework named PTFCP. This framework is meticulously designed to counteract the burgeoning threat of model copyright infringement. By leveraging cryptographic technologies, PTFCP facilitates privacy-preserving similarity assessments between victim and suspect models without disclosing sensitive details. In genomics research, Contribution 10 presents MLPPF, a method for the multi-tagging prediction of piRNA function. MLPPF demonstrates its efficacy by efficiently identifying mRNA-associated and lncRNA-associated markers of piRNA function, thereby revealing pivotal elements within piRNA sub-sequences. Regarding WiFi gesture recognition, Contribution 11 addresses cross-domain challenges through an innovative combination of knowledge distillation and Jensen–Shannon scattering techniques. Within the domain of mobile sensors, Contribution 12 proposes a secure certificate signing scheme tailored for resource-constrained devices. This scheme innovates with a novel public key structure that obviates the need for pairing operations. Furthermore, Contribution 13 unveils a pioneering IoT intrusion detection scheme. This scheme harnesses a cutting-edge neural network algorithm to adeptly manage large-scale, heterogeneous, high-dimensional, and time-dependent IoT network traffic data. Lastly, addressing the key management conundrum in identity-based cryptography, Contribution 14 advances a new certificateless signature scheme. This scheme extends the SM2 algorithm into a certificateless context, effectively resolving key management issues while enabling the batch verification of multiple signatures.

In the realm of big data management for IoT, Contribution 15 advances a novel strategy dedicated to safeguarding privacy across extensive networks of systems. This approach ensures the robust protection of both data and model privacy through the synergistic integration of distributed model training and secure model aggregation. Addressing multiple ciphertext equivalence testing, Contribution 16 introduces a certificateless encryption concept that facilitates multiple ciphertext equivalence testing with agent-assisted authorization. The proposed scheme fortifies security by enabling concurrent equivalence tests on numerous ciphertexts while incorporating an innovative agent-assisted authorization mechanism. Within the Internet of Vehicles, Contribution 17 unveils an efficient and secure blockchain consensus protocol. This protocol integrates a trust assessment mechanism, node partition strategy, and Dynamic Unique Node List to significantly enhance reliability and adaptability within IoV environments. Furthermore, it presents dynamic K-medoid practical byzantine fault tolerance—an optimized practical byzantine fault tolerance algorithm—designed to minimize latency and boost throughput efficiency.

In terms of energy efficiency and privacy preservation, Contribution 18 combines a federated learning framework with a pulsed neural network and differential privacy techniques to significantly reduce energy consumption and enhance privacy preservation for large-scale cross device learning. Regarding blockchain-based privacy protection [30], Contribution 19 introduces privacy-preserving rewritable blockchain. This innovative approach supports flexible policies through an enhanced identity encryption scheme, batch policy support, and improved accountability traceability via a proxy re-encryption mechanism. For privacy protection within mobile crowdsensing applications, Contribution 20 presents PRBFM—a privacy-preserving blockchain framework grounded in thresholded linear secret sharing. By optimizing privacy protection and efficiency through sophisticated policy matching and task delegation mechanisms, this framework sets a new standard in secure data management.

In addressing the challenge of task allocation in spatial crowdsourcing [31], Contribution 21 introduces PKGS—a privacy-preserving hitchhiking task assignment scheme. Leveraging the Paillier cryptosystem, PKGS enables secure computation over encrypted data to safeguard the privacy of both workers and task locations. This innovative approach incorporates a privacy-preserving travel distance calculation protocol and a privacy-preserving comparison protocol to facilitate efficient task assignment while maintaining strict confidentiality. Within the domain of federated learning, Contribution 22 unveils FRIMFL—a fair and reliable incentive mechanism rooted in reverse auctions and reputation trust. Designed to ensure robust client participation and equitable reward distribution, this mechanism incentivizes truthful bidding through integrated reverse auctions. Additionally, it employs a trust-based reputation system to assess the quality of contributions. The proposed method features a weighted trust assessment technique for reliability measurement and utilizes the Shapley value method to allocate rewards fairly based on marginal contributions. Simultaneously, Contribution 23 presents EPTA-T, an advanced task assignment scheme that amalgamates temporal access control with attribute-based encryption. By harnessing an attribute-based encryption framework enhanced by function integration, EPTA-T supports granular and time-bound access control. This ensures effective protection of data privacy during task allocation and significantly enhances overall efficiency. Lastly, tackling the issue of privacy-preserving frequent itemset mining on cloud servers, Contribution 24 proposes PPFIM—a verifiable privacy-preserving frequent itemset mining protocol. Through a dual-cloud architecture and encrypted databases, PPFIM mitigates data leakage risks and fortifies system security, thereby providing a robust solution for preserving privacy in large-scale data analysis tasks.

Funding: This work is financially supported by the National Natural Science Foundation of China (Grant Nos. 62202051 and 62232002), the China Postdoctoral Science Foundation (Grant Nos. 2021M700435 and 2021TQ0042), the Open Project Funding of the Key Laboratory of Mobile Application Innovation and Governance Technology, the Ministry of Industry and Information Technology (Grant No. 20231FS080601-K), the Beijing Institute of Technology Research and Innovation Promoting Project (Grant No. 2023YCXY010), the Beijing Institute of Technology Research Fund Program for Young Scholars, and the Young Elite Scientists Sponsorship Program by CAST (Grant No. 2023QNRC001).

Data Availability Statement: No new data were created or analyzed in this study.

Conflicts of Interest: The authors declare no conflicts of interest.

List of Contributions

1. Yue, Q.; Li, J.; Huang, Z.; Xie, X.; Yang, Q. Vulnerability Assessment and Topology Reconstruction of Task Chains in UAV Networks. *Electronics* **2024**, *13*, 2126. https://doi.org/10.3390/electronics13112126.
2. Li, J.; Yue, Q.; Huang, Z.; Xie, X.; Yang, Q. Vulnerability Analysis of UAV Swarm Network with Emergency Tasks. *Electronics* **2024**, *13*, 2005. https://doi.org/10.3390/electronics13112005.
3. Xu, Z.; Chu, C.; Song, S. An Effective Federated Recommendation Framework with Differential Privacy. *Electronics* **2024**, *13*, 1589. https://doi.org/10.3390/electronics13081589.
4. Zhao, F.; Cheng, R.; Li, C.; Su, Z.; Liang, G.; Yang, C. A Proof-of-Multiple-State Consensus Mechanism for Mobile Nodes in Internet of Vehicles. *Electronics* **2024**, *13*, 1553. https://doi.org/10.3390/electronics13081553.
5. Kim, Y.-J.; Lee, S.-P. A Generation of Enhanced Data by Variational Autoencoders and Diffusion Modeling. *Electronics* **2024**, *13*, 1314. https://doi.org/10.3390/electronics13071314.
6. Zhao, M. A Swell Neural Network Algorithm for Solving Time-Varying Path Query Problems with Privacy Protection. *Electronics* **2024**, *13*, 1248. https://doi.org/10.3390/electronics13071248.
7. Ren, J.; Qi, P.; Li, C.; Zhu, P.; Li, Z. Multisource Sparse Inversion Localization with Long-Distance Mobile Sensors. *Electronics* **2024**, *13*, 1024. https://doi.org/10.3390/electronics13061024.
8. Zhan, Y.; Zhao, W.; Zhu, C.; Zhao, Z.; Yang, N.; Wang, B. Efficient Electronic Voting System Based on Homomorphic Encryption. *Electronics* **2024**, *13*, 286. https://doi.org/10.3390/electronics13020286.
9. Wei, D.; Wang, D.; Wang, Z.; Ma, Y. A Privacy-Preserving Testing Framework for Copyright Protection of Deep Learning Models. *Electronics* **2024**, *13*, 133. https://doi.org/10.3390/electronics13010133.
10. Liu, Y.; Li, R.; Lu, Y.; Li, A.; Wang, Z.; Li, W. MLPPF: Multi-Label Prediction of piRNA Functions Based on Pretrained k-mer, Positional Embedding and an Improved TextRNN Model. *Electronics* **2024**, *13*, 92. https://doi.org/10.3390/electronics13010092.
11. Geng, H.; Deng, D.; Zhang, W.; Ji, P.; Wu, X. Personalized Federated Learning Based on Bidirectional Knowledge Distillation for WiFi Gesture Recognition. *Electronics* **2023**, *12*, 5016. https://doi.org/10.3390/electronics12245016.
12. Wang, G.; Shen, H.; Chen, L.; Han, J.; Wu, G. Mobile Sensoring Data Verification via a Pairing-Free Certificateless Signature Secure Approach against Novel Public Key Replacement Attacks. *Electronics* **2023**, *12*, 4865. https://doi.org/10.3390/electronics12234865.
13. Liu, Y.; Lan, Y.; Yang, C.; Ding, Y.; Li, C. A New DSGRU-Based Intrusion Detection Method for the Internet of Things. *Electronics* **2023**, *12*, 4745. https://doi.org/10.3390/electronics12234745.
14. He, C.; Zhang, B.; Zhang, L.; Xi, Z.; Fang, Y.; Wang, Y. Improving Throughput of Mobile Sensors via Certificateless Signature Supporting Batch Verification. *Electronics* **2023**, *12*, 4700. https://doi.org/10.3390/electronics12224700.
15. Karras, A.; Giannaros, A.; Theodorakopoulos, L.; Krimpas, G.A.; Kalogeratos, G.; Karras, C.; Sioutas, S. FLIBD: A Federated Learning-Based IoT Big Data Management Approach for Privacy-Preserving over Apache Spark with FATE. *Electronics* **2023**, *12*, 4633. https://doi.org/10.3390/electronics12224633.

16. Dong, S.; Zhao, Z.; Wang, B.; Gao, W.; Zhang, S. Certificateless Encryption Supporting Multi-Ciphertext Equality Test with Proxy-Assisted Authorization. *Electronics* **2023**, *12*, 4326. https://doi.org/10.3390/electronics12204326.
17. Si, X.; Li, M.; Yao, Z.; Zhu, W.; Liu, J.; Zhang, Q. An Efficient and Secure Blockchain Consensus Protocol for Internet of Vehicles. *Electronics* **2023**, *12*, 4285. https://doi.org/10.3390/electronics12204285.
18. Han, B.; Fu, Q.; Zhang, X. Towards Privacy-Preserving Federated Neuromorphic Learning via Spiking Neuron Models. *Electronics* **2023**, *12*, 3984. https://doi.org/10.3390/electronics12183984.
19. Xu, Y.; Li, Z. PIRB: Privacy-Preserving Identity-Based Redactable Blockchains with Accountability. *Electronics* **2023**, *12*, 3754. https://doi.org/10.3390/electronics12183754.
20. Guo, H.; Liang, H.; Zhao, M.; Xiao, Y.; Wu, T.; Xue, J.; Zhu, L. Privacy-Preserving Fine-Grained Redaction with Policy Fuzzy Matching in Blockchain-Based Mobile Crowdsensing. *Electronics* **2023**, *12*, 3416. https://doi.org/10.3390/electronics12163416.
21. He, P.; Xin, Y.; Hou, B.; Yang, Y. PKGS: A Privacy-Preserving Hitchhiking Task Assignment Scheme for Spatial Crowdsourcing. *Electronics* **2023**, *12*, 3318. https://doi.org/10.3390/electronics12153318.
22. Ahmed, A.; Choi, B.J. FRIMFL: A Fair and Reliable Incentive Mechanism in Federated Learning. *Electronics* **2023**, *12*, 3259. https://doi.org/10.3390/electronics12153259.
23. Song, F.; Liu, Y.; Ma, S.; Jiang, Q.; Zhang, X.; Fu, Z. Enabling Efficient and Privacy-Preserving Task Allocation with Temporal Access Control for Mobile Crowdsensing. *Electronics* **2023**, *12*, 3016. https://doi.org/10.3390/electronics12143016.
24. Zhao, Z.; Lan, L.; Wang, B.; Lai, J. Verifiable Privacy-Preserving Outsourced Frequent Itemset Mining on Vertically Partitioned Databases. *Electronics* **2023**, *12*, 1952. https://doi.org/10.3390/electronics12081952.

References

1. Wang, Z.; Cao, Y.; Jiang, K.; Zhou, H.; Kang, J.; Zhuang, Y.; Tian, D.; Leung, V.C. When Crowdsensing Meets Smart Cities: A Comprehensive Survey and New Perspectives. *IEEE Commun. Surv. Tutor.* **2024**, *early access*. [CrossRef]
2. Liu, K.; Peng, S.; Gong, W.; Zhang, B.; Li, C. Hybrid user based task assignment for mobile crowdsensing: Problem and algorithm. *IEEE Internet Things J.* **2024**, *11*, 19589–19601. [CrossRef]
3. Deng, L.; Gong, W.; Liwang, M.; Li, L.; Zhang, B.; Li, C. Towards Intelligent Mobile Crowdsensing With Task State Information Sharing over Edge-Assisted UAV Networks. *IEEE Trans. Veh. Technol.* **2024**, *73*, 11773–11788. [CrossRef]
4. Yu, Z.; Zhao, L.; Cui, H.; Song, Y.; Liu, Y.; Luo, Y.; Guo, B. CrowdKit: A Generic Programming Framework for Mobile Crowdsensing Applications. *IEEE Trans. Mob. Comput.* **2024**, *23*, 10584–10597. [CrossRef]
5. Jiang, Z.; Zhu, H.; Zhou, B.; Lu, C.; Sun, M.; Ma, X.; Fan, X.; Wang, C.; Chen, L. CrowdPatrol: A mobile crowdsensing framework for traffic violation hotspot patrolling. *IEEE Trans. Mob. Comput.* **2021**, *22*, 1401–1416. [CrossRef]
6. Wang, W.; Yang, Y.; Xiong, Z.; Niyato, D. Footstone of metaverse: A timely and secure crowdsensing. *IEEE Netw.* **2023**, *38*, 171–178. [CrossRef]
7. Zhang, M.; Chen, S.; Shen, J.; Susilo, W. Privacyeafl: Privacy-enhanced aggregation for federated learning in mobile crowdsensing. *IEEE Trans. Inf. Forensics Secur.* **2023**, *18*, 5804–5816. [CrossRef]
8. Zhao, B.; Li, X.; Liu, X.; Pei, Q.; Li, Y.; Deng, R.H. CrowdFA: A privacy-preserving mobile crowdsensing paradigm via federated analytics. *IEEE Trans. Inf. Forensics Secur.* **2023**, *18*, 5416–5430. [CrossRef]
9. An, J.; Ren, Y.; Li, X.; Zhang, M.; Luo, B.; Miao, Y.; Liu, X.; Deng, R.H. Privacy-preserving user recruitment with sensing quality evaluation in mobile crowdsensing. *IEEE Trans. Dependable Secur. Comput.* **2024**, *22*, 787–803. [CrossRef]
10. Wu, A.; Luo, W.; Yang, A.; Zhang, Y.; Zhu, J. Efficient bilateral privacy-preserving data collection for mobile crowdsensing. *IEEE Trans. Serv. Comput.* **2023**, *17*, 865–877. [CrossRef]
11. Yu, R.; Oguti, A.M.; Obaidat, M.S.; Li, S.; Wang, P.; Hsiao, K.F. Blockchain-based solutions for mobile crowdsensing: A comprehensive survey. *Comput. Sci. Rev.* **2023**, *50*, 100589. [CrossRef]
12. Agrawal, A.; Choudhary, S.; Bhatia, A.; Tiwari, K. Pub-SubMCS: A privacy-preserving publish–subscribe and blockchain-based mobile crowdsensing framework. *Future Gener. Comput. Syst.* **2023**, *146*, 234–249. [CrossRef]
13. Cheng, Y.; Ma, J.; Liu, Z.; Li, Z.; Wu, Y.; Dong, C.; Li, R. A privacy-preserving and reputation-based truth discovery framework in mobile crowdsensing. *IEEE Trans. Dependable Secur. Comput.* **2023**, *20*, 5293–5311. [CrossRef]
14. Zhang, S.; Li, Z.; Liang, W.; Li, K.C.; Bhuiyan, Z.A. Blockchain-Based Hybrid Reliable User Selection Scheme for Task Allocation in Mobile Crowd Sensing. *IEEE Trans. Netw. Sci. Eng.* **2024**, *11*, 6494–6510. [CrossRef]

15. Wang, T.; Shen, H.; Chen, J.; Chen, F.; Wu, Q.; Xie, D. A hybrid blockchain-based identity authentication scheme for Mobile Crowd Sensing. *Future Gener. Comput. Syst.* **2023**, *143*, 40–50. [CrossRef]
16. Zheng, Z.; Li, Z.; Huang, C.; Long, S.; Shen, X. Defending Data Poisoning Attacks in DP-Based Crowdsensing: A Game-Theoretic Approach. *IEEE Trans. Mob. Comput.* **2024**, *24*, 1859–1876. [CrossRef]
17. Liu, Y.; Yu, Z.; Cui, H.; Helal, S.; Guo, B. SafeCity: A Heterogeneous Mobile Crowd Sensing System for Urban Public Safety. *IEEE Internet Things J.* **2023**, *10*, 18330–18345. [CrossRef]
18. Zhao, G.; Wang, X.; Wang, J.; Liu, J. Task recommendation for mobile crowd sensing system based on multi-view user dynamic behavior prediction. *Peer-Netw. Appl.* **2023**, *16*, 1536–1550. [CrossRef]
19. Zeng, H.; Xiong, Y.; She, J.; Yu, A. A Task Assignment Scheme Designed for Online Urban Sensing Based on Sparse Mobile Crowdsensing. *IEEE Internet Things J.* **2025**, *early access*. [CrossRef]
20. Peng, S.; Zhang, G.; Zhang, B.; Yao, Z.; Liu, C.; Li, C. A Stable Task Assignment Mechanism for Multi-Platform Mobile Crowdsensing. *IEEE Trans. Veh. Technol.* **2025**, *early access*. [CrossRef]
21. Guo, Q.; He, Y.; Li, Q.; Liu, A.; Xiong, N.N.; He, Q.; Yang, Q.; Zhang, S. PPAT: An effective scheme ensuring privacy-preserving, accuracy, and trust for worker selection in mobile crowdsensing networks. *Future Gener. Comput. Syst.* **2025**, *163*, 107536. [CrossRef]
22. Kim, J.W.; Edemacu, K.; Jang, B. Privacy-preserving mechanisms for location privacy in mobile crowdsensing: A survey. *J. Netw. Comput. Appl.* **2022**, *200*, 103315. [CrossRef]
23. Suhag, D.; Jha, V. A comprehensive survey on mobile crowdsensing systems. *J. Syst. Archit.* **2023**, *142*, 102952. [CrossRef]
24. Wang, N.; Yang, W.; Wang, X.; Wu, L.; Guan, Z.; Du, X.; Guizani, M. A blockchain based privacy-preserving federated learning scheme for Internet of Vehicles. *Digit. Commun. Networks* **2024**, *10*, 126–134. [CrossRef]
25. Al Sibahee, M.A.; Nyangaresi, V.O.; Abduljabbar, Z.A.; Luo, C.; Zhang, J.; Ma, J. Two-Factor Privacy Preserving Protocol for Efficient Authentication in Internet of Vehicles Networks. *IEEE Internet Things J.* **2023**, *11*, 14253–14266. [CrossRef]
26. Haines, T.; Mueller, J.; Mosaheb, R.; Pryvalov, I. Sok: Secure e-voting with everlasting privacy. In Proceedings of the Privacy Enhancing Technologies Symposium (PETS), Lausanne, Switzerland and Online, 10–15 July 2023.
27. Shankar, A.; Pandiaraja, P.; Sumathi, K.; Stephan, T.; Sharma, P. Privacy preserving E-voting cloud system based on ID based encryption. *Peer-Netw. Appl.* **2021**, *14*, 2399–2409. [CrossRef]
28. Zhang, X.; Li, R.; Yu, J.; Xu, Y.; Li, W.; Zhang, J. Editguard: Versatile image watermarking for tamper localization and copyright protection. In Proceedings of the IEEE/CVF Conference on Computer Vision and Pattern Recognition, Seattle, WA, USA, 16–22 June 2024; pp. 11964–11974.
29. Zhang, X.; Xu, Y.; Li, R.; Yu, J.; Li, W.; Xu, Z.; Zhang, J. V2a-mark: Versatile deep visual-audio watermarking for manipulation localization and copyright protection. In Proceedings of the 32nd ACM International Conference on Multimedia, Melbourne, VIC, Australia, 28 October–1 November 2024; pp. 9818–9827.
30. Ferrag, M.A.; Shu, L. The performance evaluation of blockchain-based security and privacy systems for the Internet of Things: A tutorial. *IEEE Internet Things J.* **2021**, *8*, 17236–17260. [CrossRef]
31. Wang, L.; Yu, Z.; Wu, K.; Yang, D.; Wang, E.; Wang, T.; Mei, Y.; Guo, B. Towards robust task assignment in mobile crowdsensing systems. *IEEE Trans. Mob. Comput.* **2022**, *22*, 4297–4313. [CrossRef]

electronics

MDPI

Article

Vulnerability Assessment and Topology Reconstruction of Task Chains in UAV Networks

Qingfeng Yue [1], Jinglei Li [1], Zijia Huang [2,*], Xiaoyu Xie [1] and Qinghai Yang [1]

[1] The School of Telecommunications Engineering, Xidian University, Xi'an 710126, China; 21181214312@stu.xidian.edu.cn (Q.Y.); jlli68@xidian.edu.cn (J.L.); xiexy96@chinaunicom.cn (X.X.); qhyang@xidian.edu.cn (Q.Y.)

[2] The 20th Research Institute of China Electronics Technology Group Corporation, Xi'an 710068, China

* Correspondence: beiyouhzj@163.com

Abstract: With the increasing complexity of environments and the diversity of task chains, individual unmanned aerial vehicles (UAVs) often struggle to satisfy the demands of task chains, including load capacity improvement, information perception, and information procession. In complex task chains involving various UAVs, such as area reconnaissance and fire rescue, any attack on critical UAVs can greatly disrupt the execution of the entire task chain by causing equipment damage or connectivity disruption. To ensure network resilience post attack, identifying vulnerable nodes in the UAV network becomes crucial. In this paper, a Vulnerability-based Topology Reconstruction Mechanism (VUTRM) is proposed to rank the importance of nodes in task chains and formulate a topology reconstruction. It consists of two parts: the first part is a Multi-metric Node Vulnerability Assessment Algorithm (MENVAL) used to rank the importance of nodes in task chains, and the second part is a Node Importance-based Topology Reconstruction Algorithm (NITRA) used to reconstruct the UAV network with the obtained node ranking. Finally, simulations carried out with simulation software demonstrate that our proposed method accurately identifies network vulnerabilities and promptly implements effective reconstruction measures to minimize network damage.

Keywords: UAV swarm network; vulnerability analysis; topology reconstruction; task chains

1. Introduction

Unmanned aerial vehicles (UAVs) were initially predominantly used to track targets in complex environments [1]. Subsequently, their utility has expanded into civilian domains, permeating various facets of everyday life. These civilian applications encompass real-time monitoring, provision of wireless connectivity, remote sensing, search and rescue operations, cargo transportation, precision agriculture, and the surveillance of civil infrastructure locations [2]. With the growing complexity of task requirements, it has become difficulty for the independent operation of a single UAV to meet demands. To solve this problem, UAVs are employed for execution and data exchange through communication links.

The interconnectivity, communication capabilities, and interoperability among diverse types of UAVs empower them to undergo agile reconstruction as the need arises, thereby significantly bolstering the reliability and resilience of the overall system. However, due to malicious interference and complex flight scenarios, UAVs may lose connection with neighboring nodes, rendering them unable to execute tasks and causing node failures in task chains [3]. Given the limited network resources, it is crucial to find the key UAVs in the network and apply topology reconstruction. Therefore, the vulnerability analysis and topology reconstruction within task chains have constituted pivotal research challenges in recent years.

Vulnerability analysis is crucial prior to rational allocation of limited network resources. Highly important UAVs are usually assigned critical or urgent tasks, ensuring a swift and efficient response during pivotal moments [4]. This ranking facilitates optimized resource allocation, ensuring that these UAVs receive the most dependable network resources available. Such rankings often rely on relevant parameters within the UAV network topology. Nodes with high degrees in the network typically connect to more nodes, making them pivotal points for information dissemination and task coordination [5]. In addition to the topological importance of UAVs within the communication network, we also need to consider their functional importance. Nodes play different roles in the task chain, and their importance is influenced by multiple factors, including the number of UAVs of the same type, the number of different types of connected UAVs, and the number of task chains they participate in. Some nodes may not be highly important in terms of communication topology but play crucial roles in task chain execution. However, in existing research papers, there are few studies that analyze the vulnerability of nodes based on their functional attributes.

Despite the protection measures in place for UAVs within the network, the issue of node disconnections may still arise in complex scenarios, highlighting the importance of promptly implementing repair measures for networks experiencing node failures. Topology reconstruction is one of most effective repair measures, which involves adjusting the network's connectivity structure to enhance overall robustness and adaptability. When one or more nodes fail, topology reconstruction allows the network to rapidly adapt to changes, redistributing resources and paths, thus minimizing the impact of failures and ensuring the network's stable operation and communication efficiency. In a constantly changing environment, such dynamic adjustments are crucial for the sustained effective operation of complex network systems. However, there is often a risk of excessive adjustment, leading to wastage of resources.

In this paper, we propose the Vulnerability-based Topology Reconstruction Mechanism (VUTRM), which comprises two key components: the Multi-metric Node Vulnerability Assessment Algorithm (MENVAL) for ranking node importance based on communication and functional attributes and the Node Importance-based Topology Reconstruction Algorithm (NITRA) for rebuilding the network considering node vulnerabilities. MENVAL combines metrics like node degree, betweenness centrality, and closeness centrality with functional attributes in order to assign importance scores. NITRA employs different reconstruction strategies for vulnerable and non-vulnerable nodes, optimizing network resilience and energy efficiency during failures.

The rest of the paper is organized as follows. Section 2 delves into relevant research on vulnerability node detection and reconstruction algorithms. Section 3 introduces the system model and problem formulation discussed in this paper. Section 4 details the VUTRM. Experimental results and evaluations are presented in Section 5. Finally, the entire paper is summarized in Section 6.

2. Related Work

Early research mainly focused on communication transmission between UAVs, aiming to ensure the normal operation of the network through more efficient data transmission methods. Researchers such as Mahdi Asadpour have proposed the concept of a multi-hop micro-aerial vehicle network, which focused on addressing the primary challenges of data packet forwarding in practical applications [6]. With growing concerns about secure transmission between UAVs, researchers like Bin Li introduced physical layer security into UAV organizational networks, which has become a common method to address the transmission characteristics of wireless channels [7]. Simultaneously, the identification of vulnerable nodes in UAV networks has also become a key research area, which aims to identify key UAV nodes in the network and provide them with special protection.

Typically, methods for identifying vulnerable nodes primarily originate from communication topology attributes, focusing on a node's position in the network and its connectivity with other nodes. Among these methods, degree centrality [8] is the most commonly used approach in vulnerable node identification, which primarily considers the number of a node's neighbors and has been proven effective in identifying vulnerable nodes based on neighbor relationships [9]. Poulin et al. introduced the K-shell decomposition method, addressing the issue that a node's degree does not necessarily indicate its centrality. Additionally, identification methods based on closeness centrality [10], which measures a node's vulnerability by calculating the average shortest distance between the node and the remaining nodes in the network, have been proposed. Katz centrality, proposed in Ref. [11], is based on closeness centrality and considers other paths between nodes. Betweenness centrality takes into account the number of shortest paths passing through a node in the entire network, and a node's vulnerability is proportional to the number of paths involving that node. Ref. [12] extended betweenness centrality to directed networks, verifying its effectiveness under the same network topology. Additionally, Refs. [13,14] addressed the randomness issue in betweenness centrality by introducing a random walk-based centrality metric for identifying important nodes. In addition to discussing the communication attributes of UAVs, we also need to consider the operational characteristics that UAVs undertake during task execution. In certain task scenarios, UAVs often play diverse roles, which are typically based on the concept of the OODA (Observe, Orient, Decide, Act) loop. The method in Ref. [15] combines the concepts of betweenness and information functional chains to measure the importance of nodes and links but does not consider link integrity. On the other hand, Ref. [16] evaluates UAV network nodes and loops at the OODA loop level by considering the network diffusion (ND) and influence in the loop (NIO) of nodes. However, the algorithm's complexity is relatively high, making it challenging to meet real-time requirements in rapidly changing scenarios. Ref. [17] abstracts the elements in the operational system and their information connection relationships, constructing the network structure of the operational system. This paper assesses nodes based on aspects such as the node's substitutability, local connectivity, and operational effectiveness, providing a node ranking.

Once vulnerable nodes in the network are identified, selecting an appropriate network reconstruction strategy becomes crucial. Network vulnerability reconstruction algorithms are generally classified into two categories: large-scale and small-scale topology reconstruction algorithms. However, considering the relatively small scale in modern UAV task scenarios, large-scale recovery algorithms are less applicable. Therefore, we mainly focus on studying small-scale network topology reconstruction algorithms, especially targeting scenarios with a small number of UAVs in the network and individual node failures. Topology reconstruction algorithms, such as the Redundant Node Movement algorithm [18], the MCDS (Minimum Connected Dominating Set) algorithm [19], and the RIM (Resilient Information Matrix) algorithm [20], do not include the step of evaluating node importance. While they can reduce message transmission overhead to some extent, they also involve many unnecessary repairs. Subsequent research began to consider the importance of nodes. In the DARA (Degree and Relative Distance Aware) algorithm [21], reconstruction algorithms are selected based on the degree of neighboring nodes and the distance from the faulty nodes. However, this algorithm is prone to excessive substitution, and each node requires a substantial amount of network information. The PADRA (Partition-Aware Dominating Set-based Recovery Algorithm) [22] classifies nodes into two categories using the minimum connected dominating set, reducing total movement distance and energy consumption. However, it introduces a depth-first algorithm, leading to longer iteration cycles. The LeDiR (Least Disturbance Routing) algorithm [23] takes repair measures only after node failure, relocating the minimum number of nodes to restore the network through block movement measures. In conclusion, existing reconstruction algorithms lack discussion of node importance and fail to propose differentiated allocation schemes to proactively prevent node failures.

We propose the Vulnerability-based Topology Reconstruction Mechanism (VUTRM) to rank nodes and formulate a topology reconstruction. It consists of two parts: the first part is the Multi-metric Node Vulnerability Assessment Algorithm (MENVAL) used to rank the importance of nodes in the network, and the second part is the Node Importance-based

Topology Reconstruction Algorithm (NITRA) used to reconstruct the UAV network by the obtained node ranking. The main contribution in the VUTRM is summarized as follows:

- In MENVAL, we consider both the communication and functional topological attributes of nodes to obtain their network importance. Communication attributes encompass node degree, betweenness centrality, and closeness centrality, evaluating a node's connectivity significance. Meanwhile, functional attributes assess a node's role in task chains. By combining these attributes, MENVAL assigns an importance score to each node.
- In NITRA, we implement distinct topological reconstruction strategies for vulnerable and non-vulnerable nodes, aimed at addressing node failure issues in UAV networks. For vulnerable nodes, a relatively complex reconstruction strategy is employed to minimize their impact on the network when they fail. Conversely, for non-vulnerable nodes, a simpler strategy is used to reduce unnecessary energy consumption. This differentiation ensures effective functional recovery in case of node failures while minimizing network resource utilization.

3. System Model and Problem Formulation

Before conducting vulnerability analysis on UAV networks, it is necessary to model the system and formulate the problem. System modeling is divided into three parts: UAV nodes, communication links, and task chains. Additionally, an analysis of the primary issues related to node failures is conducted to facilitate the development of subsequent research content.

3.1. System Model

(1) UAV Nodes

In the context of UAV network nodes, we categorize the nodes according to the OODA theory into 'Observe', 'Orient', 'Decide', and 'Act'. As shown in Figure 1, four types of UAVs play different roles in the scenario, collectively forming the entire task chain. The functionalities of the four categories of nodes are as follows:

- **Observe**: These nodes are responsible for collecting data and information from the environment. They gather sensory data and observations from their surroundings.
- **Orient**: The Orient nodes process the information collected by the Observe nodes. They analyze and interpret the data to gain a better understanding of the current situation and context.
- **Decide**: Decide nodes make decisions based on the information provided by the Orient nodes. They evaluate the available options and select the most appropriate course of action.
- **Act**: Act nodes execute the decisions made by the Decide nodes. They carry out the chosen actions, which may involve controlling the movement or operation of unmanned aerial vehicles or other tasks.

We use V^S, V^I, V^D, and V^J to respectively represent the sets of Observe, Orient, Decide, and Act nodes, with V representing all the unmanned aerial vehicle nodes in the network: $V = V^S \bigcup V^I \bigcup V^D \bigcup V^J$.

(2) Communication Links

In the context of a UAV network, edges in the network represent the communication links between UAV nodes. During UAVs' flight, the communication range between UAV nodes is calculated, and it is defined that two UAVs can only engage in wireless communication if they are both within each other's communication range. After modeling the nodes, UAVs are deployed. Subsequently, the UAVs undergo a specified number of motion iterations. In each iteration, the generated network topology is recorded. The connection status $E_{ij}^{n_t}$ between nodes i and j at the n_t-th iteration is defined as follows:

$$E_{ij}^{n_t} = \begin{cases} 1, & \text{when there is a connection and } i < j \\ 0, & \text{otherwise.} \end{cases}$$

Figure 1. Scenario for a UAV task chain.

(3) Task Chains

In the OODA, task chains consist of four types of UAVs. If we study the functional connections between each set of two UAVs, the types of edges could amount to 16. However, if we study every possible connection among UAVs, the number of connection types involved will be extremely vast, leading to a significant workload. To focus more on the research emphasis of this paper, we primarily studied five types of directional connections within the UAV network: Perception–Collection Edge (T^S), Perception–Control Edge (T^S), Collection–Control Edge (T^I), Command–Control Edge (T^D), and Control–Execution Edge (T^J). The Perception–Collection Edge involves communication links from Observe nodes to Orient nodes, where Observe UAVs transmit collected information to Orient nodes ($T^S : V^S \rightarrow V^I$). The Perception–Control Edge represents direct communication links from Observe UAVs to Decide UAVs for decision-making and assessment, without going through Orient nodes ($T^S : V^S \rightarrow V^D$). The Collection–Control Edge signifies communication links from Orient nodes to Decide nodes, where Orient nodes forward gathered information from Observe nodes after computation and processing ($T^I : V^I \rightarrow V^D$). The Command–Control Edge represents communication links between Decide nodes with a hierarchical relationship among them ($T^D : V^D \rightarrow V^D$). Lastly, the Control–Execution Edge denotes communication links from Decide nodes to Act nodes, where Decide nodes transmit decisions to Act nodes, and Act nodes arrange tasks accordingly based on received information ($T^J : V^D \rightarrow V^J$).

These five types of communication links can be combined to form a complete task chain, and the combination method is illustrated in Figure 2. It can be observed that the composed task chains mainly consist of four types: $V^S - V^I - V^D - V^J$, $V^S - V^D - V^D - V^J$, $V^S - V^D - V^J$, and $V^S - V^I - V^D - V^D - V^J$. Their corresponding links are represented as $T^S - T^I - T^J$, $T^S - T^J$, $T^S - T^D - T^J$, and $T^S - T^I - T^D - T^J$.

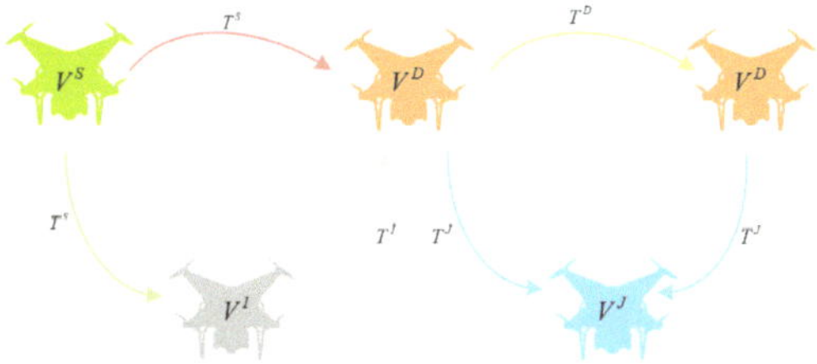

Figure 2. An example of communication links.

(4) Network Topology

The network topology matrix, denoted as E^{n_t}, is used to represent the connection relationships in the UAV network, specifying that two UAVs can only transmit information when they are within each other's communication range. Table 1 illustrates the communication connections in the network shown in Figure 3 using this matrix. The figure depicts a network composed of five UAVs, including one Observe node, one Orient node, two Decide nodes, and one Act node. Information transmission between UAVs is only possible when they are within each other's communication range. For example, Node 1 has communication connections with Nodes 2 and 3, so the values in the first row of the table are 1 for columns 2 and 3 and 0 for other columns. The situation is similar for other nodes. The topology matrix effectively reflects the communication topology in the network.

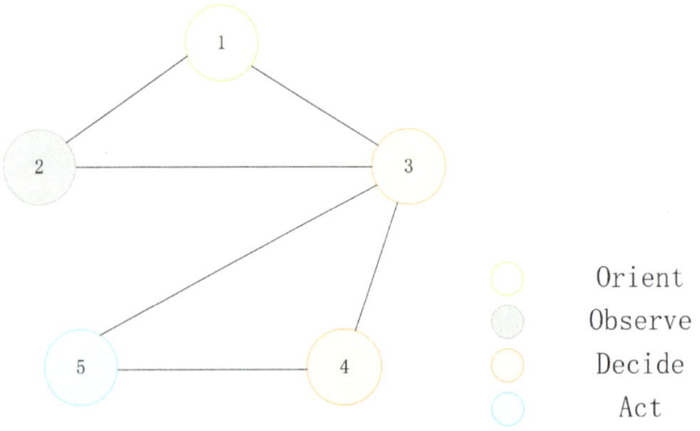

Figure 3. A software-generated network topology diagram.

Table 1. The upper-triangular conditional adjacency matrix E^{n_t}.

Node	1	2	3	4	5
1	0	1	1	0	0
2	0	0	1	0	0
3	0	0	0	1	1
4	0	0	0	0	1
5	0	0	0	0	0

3.2. Problem Formulation

Task chains play a crucial role in distributed systems, consisting of a series of interdependent tasks or operations aimed at achieving specific objectives. In such systems, topology connectivity is paramount, as it ensures communication and collaboration among the nodes within the task chain, ensuring smooth execution of tasks. However, task chains are vulnerable to various attacks or disruptions, such as network attacks, node failures, etc., which may lead to interruptions or abnormal execution of tasks. Therefore, conducting vulnerability analysis and topology reconstruction is essential for identifying and addressing potential issues, thus enhancing the reliability and stability of task chains. Through these measures, the resilience and robustness of task chains can be effectively strengthened, ensuring their smooth operation in complex network environments.

The main goal of this study is to explore how to ensure maximum remaining task integrity after node failures in UAV scenarios. To address this issue, we divide it into two steps: assessing vulnerable nodes and reconstructing network topology. The former step is aimed at assessing the importance of the failed nodes within the network, meaning they play crucial roles in the network and their failures could have a significant impact on the entire network. The latter discusses how to reconstruct connections and communication paths in the network when node failures occur in order to ensure that the network can still effectively carry out its tasks.

In the first step, we aim to identify important nodes within the network. To test whether the nodes identified by the algorithm are vulnerable, we will remove them and calculate the remaining task integrity of the network after their removal. The remaining task connectivity R is defined as the ratio of the number of task chains in the network after node failures to the initial number of task chains, which is expressed as follows:

$$R = \frac{1}{l_0} \sum_{i=1}^{N} l_i^{n_t}, \tag{1}$$

where $l_i^{n_t}$ represents the number of task chains passing through node i at the n_t-th iteration in the network after each topological update, and l_0 represents the number of all task chains in the network before the node attack. Generally, the larger the importance of a node, the greater the impact on network task execution when the node fails, resulting in lower remaining task chain integrity.

In the second step, we also use the network remaining task chain integrity to represent the repair effectiveness of the algorithm and use the movement distance to indicate how far candidate UAVs have to move for topological reconstruction. The greater the distance a UAV flies, the more energy it consumes, and conversely, the shorter the distance, the less energy is consumed. Therefore, the objective of the reconstruction algorithm is to minimize the energy consumption of the swarm while maximizing the network's remaining task integrity after reconstruction.

4. Vulnerability-Based Topology Reconstruction Mechanism

As described above, the VUTRM algorithm consists of two parts: MENVAL evaluates the importance of nodes by assessing their communication topology attributes and functional topology attributes, while NITRA maintains the stability of the UAV network by employing different topology reconstruction strategies for vulnerable and non-vulnerable nodes. This section provides a detailed explanation of these two algorithms.

4.1. Multi-Metric Node Vulnerability Assessment Algorithm

MENVAL evaluates the importance of nodes based on both their communication topology attributes and functional topology attributes. The former focuses on the geographical significance of nodes within the network, while the latter emphasizes their importance within the entire task chain.

4.1.1. Importance of Communication Topology

The importance of communication topology focuses on the significance of a node's topological position within the network and the extent of its connectivity with other nodes, without considering the node's functionality. The topological importance of nodes in the network consists of three components: node degree, node betweenness, and node closeness.

(1) Node Degree

Node degree is the most fundamental metric for identifying important nodes: the more neighbors a node has, the higher its degree centrality is, indicating its greater importance. In a UAV's network, it is only necessary to count the number of nodes connected to a particular node in the directed adjacency matrix E^{n_t}. The node degree $K_i^{n_t}$ of the node i at motion iteration n_t is represented as follows:

$$K_i^{n_t} = \sum_{i<j} E_{ij}^{n_t} + \sum_{i>j} E_{ji}^{n_t}. \tag{2}$$

After normalizing $K_i^{n_t}$, we obtain

$$K_i^{\prime n_t} = \frac{K_i^{n_t}}{K_{\max}^{n_t}}, \tag{3}$$

where $K_i^{\prime n_t}$ represents the normalized node degree, and $K_{\max}^{n_t}$ represents the maximum node degree among all nodes at iteration count n_t.

(2) Node Betweenness

Node betweenness is a key metric in network analysis that quantifies the importance of a node by measuring the number of shortest paths passing through it. The higher the betweenness centrality of a node, the more influential it is in controlling the flow of information or resources within the network. As shown in Figure 4, it represents a UAV network with a total of 13 nodes. According to the node degree formula, we can calculate the degree of each node, where $K_2^{\prime n} = K_3^{\prime n} = K_4^{\prime n} = \frac{1}{6} > K_1^{\prime n} = \frac{1}{8}$. From the perspective of node degree alone, Nodes 2, 3, and 4 are all more important than Node 1.

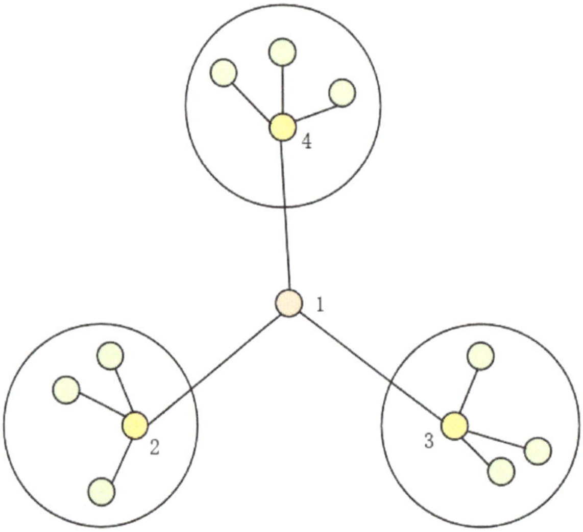

Figure 4. Illustration of node betweenness.

However, it is evident that Node 1 is the hub of the entire network. In practical networks such as UAV networks or social networks, hub nodes are often the most crucial. Therefore, we calculate the number of shortest paths in which each node participates to analyze the importance of nodes in the entire network. The node betweenness $B_i^{n_t}$ of the node i at iteration count n_t is represented as follows:

$$B_i^{n_t} = \frac{g_{ist}^{n_t}}{g_{st}^{n_t}}, \tag{4}$$

where $g_{st}^{n_t}$ represents the number of shortest paths from node s to node t at the n_t-th iteration, and $g_{ist}^{n_t}$ represents the number of shortest paths passing through node i. After normalizing $B_i^{n_t}$, we obtain the following:

$$B_i^{\prime n_t} = \frac{B_i^{n}}{B_{\max}^{n_t}}, \tag{5}$$

where $B_i^{\prime n_t}$ represents the normalized node betweenness, and $B_{\max}^{n_t}$ represents the maximum node betweenness among all nodes at iteration count n_t.

(3) Node Closeness

Closeness centrality is a measure in network analysis that quantifies how quickly a node can interact with other nodes in the network. It is calculated based on the average shortest path length from a node to all other nodes in the network. Nodes with higher closeness centrality are considered more central and have shorter average distances to other nodes, indicating their greater accessibility and influence on the network. Assuming $d_{ij}^{n_t}$ represents the number of hops from node i to another node j at iteration n_t in a topology network, and the average distance from this node to all remaining nodes in the network is denoted as $\mathrm{d}_i^{n_t}$, it can be represented as follows:

$$d_i^{n_t} = \frac{1}{N}\sum\nolimits_{j=1}^{N} d_{ij}^{n_t}. \tag{6}$$

It is obvious that when d is smaller, the average distance from node i to all other nodes in the network is closer. To some extent, it indicates that the topology of node i is of greater importance. Therefore, the reciprocal of d, denoted as c, is defined as the closeness centrality of node i in the network, and the formula is expressed as follows:

$$C_i^{n_t} = \frac{1}{d_i^{n_t}} = \frac{N}{\sum_{j=1}^{N} d_{ij}^{n_t}} \tag{7}$$

$$C_i^{\prime n_t} = \frac{C_i^{n_t}}{C_{\max}^{n_t}}, \tag{8}$$

where $C_i^{\prime n_t}$ represents the normalized node closeness, and $C_{\max}^{n_t}$ represents the maximum node closeness among all nodes at iteration count n_t.

According to the assigned weights for the three evaluation metrics α_K, α_B, and α_C based on task execution, the normalized topological importance $\beta_{\mathrm{i}}^{n_t}$ of node i at iteration n_t can be represented as follows:

$$\beta_{\mathrm{i}}^{n_t} = \alpha_K K_{\mathrm{i}}^{\prime n_t} + \alpha_B B_i^{\prime n_t} + \alpha_C C_i^{\prime n_t}, \tag{9}$$

where three weight coefficients satisfy the following conditions:

$$\alpha_K + \alpha_B + \alpha_C = 1. \tag{10}$$

4.1.2. Importance of Functional Topology

For the evaluation of node importance in task chains, it is necessary to consider the functions of UAVs. In task chains systems, not all paths are meaningful; only those that form the OODA task chain can reflect the efficacy in task chains. Therefore, the importance of functional topology comprehensively considers three key aspects of elements, including substitutability, node connectivity, and efficiency importance of nodes. Through these measurements, we are able to provide a comprehensive assessment of the importance of elements in the network, offering valuable guidance for optimizing and enhancing the task chains.

(1) Importance of Substitutability

The substitutability of a node indicates whether other UAVs in the network can replace its functionality in case of failure or attack. The substitutability is related to the number of nodes in the network: the more nodes of the same type, the higher the substitutability; conversely, the fewer nodes of the same type, the greater the system's dependency on that UAV. Therefore, substitutability can be represented as follows:

$$\gamma_i^{n_t} = |V_X|, \quad i \in X \text{ and } X \in \{S, I, D, J\}, \tag{11}$$

where V_X represents the set element of X-type UAVs when the iteration count is N; $|\cdot|$ denotes the quantity of UAVs in the specified set; and S, I, D, and J represent the sets of

UAVs for Observe, Orient, Decide, and Act, respectively. The normalized node's importance of substitutability can be represented as follows:

$$\gamma'^{n_t}_{i} = \frac{|V_X^{n_t}|}{N}, \quad i \in X \text{ and } X \in \{S, I, D, J\}. \tag{12}$$

(2) Importance of Connectivity

Importance of connectivity is used to describe the degree of connectivity between a node and other types of nodes in the UAV network. The higher the degree value of a node, the greater its level of interaction with other nodes. Taking an example, the connectivity importance $d_i^{n_t}$ of observation UAV node i at the n_t-th network iteration is defined as the number of nodes in three categories: Orient, Decide, and Act, that are connected to node i. Since the matrix is an upper triangular matrix, it can be expressed as follows:

$$d_i^{n_t} = \sum_{j\in I} E_{ij}^{n_t} + \sum_{j\in I} E_{ji}^{n_t} + \sum_{j\in D} E_{ij}^{n_t} + \sum_{j\in D} E_{ji}^{n_t} + \sum_{j\in J} E_{ij}^{n_t} + \sum_{j\in J} E_{ji}^{n_t}, i \in S. \tag{13}$$

The normalized node's importance of connectivity can be represented as follows:

$$d'^{n_t}_{i} = \frac{d_i^{n_t}}{d_{\max}^{n_t}}, \tag{14}$$

where $d'^{n_t}_{i}$ represents the normalized importance of connectivity, and $d_{\max}^{n_t}$ represents the maximum importance of connectivity among all nodes at iteration count n_t.

(3) Importance of Efficiency

The more task chains a node participates in, the more significant its impact on the overall network's task implementation effectiveness. Therefore, we analyze the number of task links each type of node participates in. For links of the Observe node and Act node, because each task chain always includes both of them, the task chains involving both can be discussed together and represented by the following formula:

$$\mathrm{b}_{ij}^{n_t} = T^S T^I T^J + T^S T^J + T^S T^D T^J + T^S T^I T^D T^J, \tag{15}$$

where $\mathrm{b}_{ij}^{n_t}$ indicates that there are $\mathrm{b}_{ij}^{n_t}$ task chains from Observe node i to Act node j at the n_t-th iteration as follows:

$$l_i^{n_t} = \sum_{j=|V^S|+|V^I|+|V^D|+1}^{N} b_{ij}^{n_t}, i \in \{1, \ldots, |V^S|\}. \tag{16}$$

The total number of task chains passing through the task execution node j is given by:

$$l_i^{n} = \sum_{j=1}^{|V^S|} b_{ji}^{n_t}, i \in \{|V^S| + |V^I| + |V^D| + 1, |V^S| + |V^I| + |V^D| + 2, \ldots, N\}. \tag{17}$$

For links passing through Orient nodes, they mainly involve two types of edges, which consist of $T^I T^J$ and $T^I T^D T^J$, and they can be expressed as follows:

$$c_{ij}^{n_t} = T^I T^J + T^I T^D T^J. \tag{18}$$

The quantity $c_{ij}^{n_t}$ represents the number of links from the Orient node i to the Act node j at the n_t-th iteration: $i \in \{|V^S|+1, |V^S|+2, \ldots, |V^S|+|V^I|\}, j \in \{|V^S|+|V^I|+|V^D|+1, |V^S|+|V^I|+|V^D|+2, \ldots, N\}$. The number of links passing through the Orient node is:

$$l_i^{n_t} = \sum_{j=|V^S|+|V^I|+|V^D|+1}^{N} c_{ij}^{n} \times \sum_{j=1}^{|V^S|} E_{ji}^{n}, \quad i \in \{|V^S|+1, |V^S|+1, \ldots, |V^S|+|V^I|\}. \tag{19}$$

For links of the Decide node, they mainly involve three types of edges, which are T^S, $T^S T^I$, and $T^S T^I T^D$. The number of links passing through Decide nodes can be expressed as follows:

$$d_{ij}^{n_t} = T^S + T^S T^I + T^S T^I T^D, \tag{20}$$

where d_{ij} represents the number of links from the Decide node i to the Act node j at the n_t-th iteration: $i \in \{1, 2, \ldots, |V^S|\}, j \in \{|V^S|+|V^S|+1, |V^S|+|V^S|+2, \ldots, |V^S|+|V^S|+|V^S|\}$. The number of links passing through the Orient node is:

$$l_i^{n_t} = \sum_{j=|V^S|+|V^I|+|V^D|+1}^{N} c_{ij}^{n_t} \times \sum_{j=1}^{|V^S|} E_{ji}^{n_t}, \tag{21}$$

$$i \in \{|V^S|+|V^I|+1, |V^S|+|V^I|+2, \ldots, |V^S|+|V^I|+|V^D|\}$$

After normalizing the node's importance for functional topology, it can be represented as follows:

$$l'^{n_t}_i = \frac{l_i^{n_t}}{l_{\max}^{n_t}}, \tag{22}$$

where $l'^{n_t}_i$ represents the normalized importance of efficiency, and $l_{\max}^{n_t}$ represents the maximum importance of efficiency among all nodes at iteration count n_t.

Based on the performed task, we allocate weights to three evaluation metrics, α_γ, α_d, and α_l. From iteration $n_t - 1$ to iteration n_t, the functional importance $W_1^{n_t}$ of node i can be represented as follows:

$$W_i^{n_t} = \alpha_\gamma \gamma'^{n_t}_i + \alpha_d d'^{n_t}_i + \alpha_l l'^{n_t}_i, \tag{23}$$

where three weight coefficients satisfy the following conditions:

$$\alpha_\gamma + \alpha_d + \alpha_l = 1. \tag{24}$$

4.1.3. Comprehensive Importance

Considering the importance of communication topology and functional topology of each node, the comprehensive topological importance ρ_i of node i at iteration n is obtained as follows:

$$\rho_i^{n_t} = \varphi_1 \beta_i^{n_t} + \varphi_2 W_i^{n_t}, \tag{25}$$

where φ_1 represents the weight coefficient for communication topology importance, and φ_2 represents the weight coefficient for functional topology importance; the sum of these two coefficients satisfies the following:

$$\varphi_1 + \varphi_2 = 1. \tag{26}$$

By calculating the arithmetic average of the accumulated comprehensive importance form the previous equations, we obtain:

$$\rho'^{n_t}_i = \frac{1}{n_t} \sum_{n=1}^{n_t} \rho^n_i. \tag{27}$$

4.2. Node Importance-Based Topology Reconstruction Algorithm

In Section 2 of this paper, we discussed the significance of studying network reconstruction algorithms that discern node importance. Additionally, we provided an in-depth background of the specific algorithm examined, outlining its theoretical basis and relevance in network analysis. Before introducing the algorithm, we made some prerequisites in our scenario that each node in the network has a unique ID obtained through technologies like GPS, ensuring that the failure of a particular node does not affect the unique IDs of other nodes. Furthermore, each node stores information about nodes within a two-hop range, including details such as distance, type, importance, and other relevant node information. Additionally, nodes possess the ability to move freely. In the event of a UAV node becoming inactive due to an attack, the network can be repaired by relocating other nodes. However, this process is constrained by the limited energy of each node, with activities such as data transmission and network maintenance consuming energy. Notably, the energy consumption for moving to reconstruct the network is much higher than for the first two activities, leading to the adoption of moving reconstruction only in essential situations.

In current research on UAV topology reconstruction, the MCMA (Minimum Cascade Mobile Algorithm) is commonly employed [24]. MCMA consists of two steps: cut-point detection and node movement reconstruction. When a node in the network fails, the algorithm performs cut-point detection.

This algorithm combines cut-point detection with node movement reconstruction, to some extent addressing the problems of excessive substitution and excessive movement distance . Based on the algorithm, we have implemented the following modifications. UAVs are categorized into distinct types, allowing only UAVs of the same type to substitute for one another. In the mobile reconstruction strategy, we prioritize the importance of failed nodes and candidate replacement nodes to ensure post-reconstruction network robustness surpasses the pre-reconstruction state, avoiding unnecessary reconstruction and repair for every failed node. While MCMA primarily focuses on reconstructing and repairing cut-points, we have recognized the potential benefit of having UAVs move shorter distances to enhance network robustness. Thus, we have designated different topological reconstruction strategies for non-vulnerable and vulnerable nodes, with the former requiring fewer system resources for scheduling compared to the latter.

Inspired by the modifications made to MCMA as described above, we propose NITRA. The process of NITRA is shown in Figure 5, and its pseudocode is shown in Algorithm 1. In this algorithm, we define the set of nodes with the same type and smaller comprehensive importance within the selected range of the failed node as the candidate node set. Before each iteration, we check whether there are nodes that have failed in the network. If there is a failed node and the node has its candidate node, we perform a movement reconstruction, which is the replacement of the least important node in the set of candidate nodes for the failed node. If there are no nodes meeting the criteria within the one-hop range of the failed node, we then determine whether to expand to the two-hop range based on whether the failed node is a vulnerable node. If the failed node is a vulnerable node, we search for candidate nodes within the two-hop range. If there are nodes that meet the criteria, we perform a movement reconstruction, and this process continues until the maximum number of iterations is reached. The time complexity of this algorithm depends on the number of edges in the network and the maximum degree of nodes, which is $O(|E| \cdot d_{\max})$. In the algorithm, iterations are performed for each failed link and for each neighboring node of each node. For each node, the algorithm requires retrieving its set of neighboring nodes, followed by calculating additional data allocation and updating data quantity based on a specific formula. Overall, the complexity of this algorithm increases with the scale of the network but is also constrained by the maximum degree of nodes.

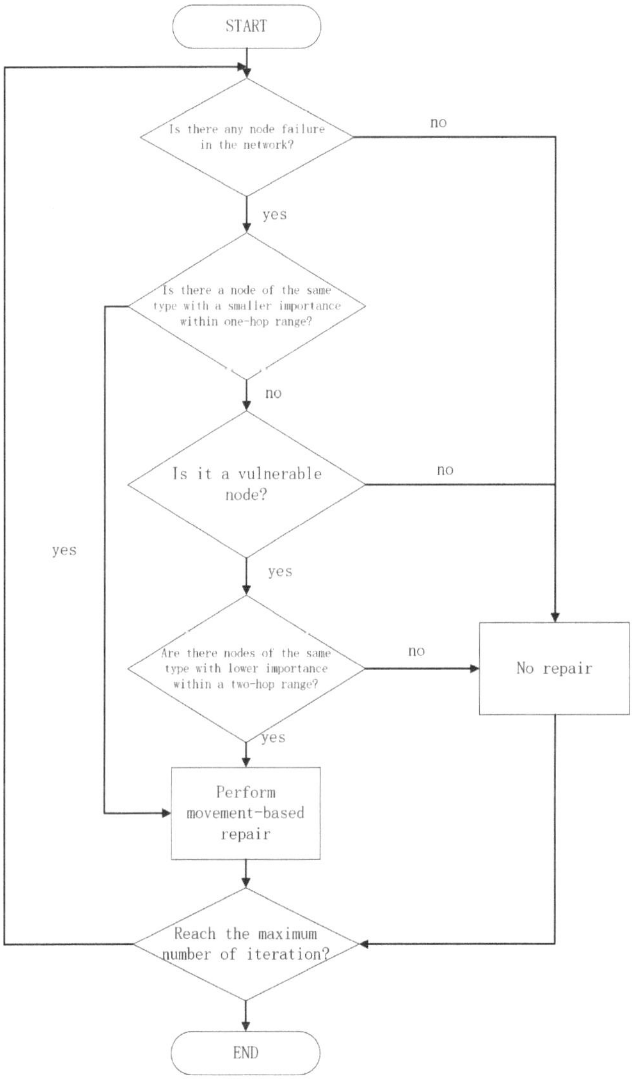

Figure 5. Process of NITRA.

As an example, the topology structure of the UAV network generated in a single simulation is shown in Figure 6. Assuming Node 23 fails, and since it is a non-vulnerable node, we only search for candidate nodes within the one-hop range. From the graph, we can see that, within the one-hop range of Node 23, Nodes 22 and 24 are present, but they are not of the same type as Node 23. Therefore, no reconstruction operation is performed for the failure of Node 23. If Node 15 fails, within its one-hop range, we find Nodes 14, 8, and 16. Since these three nodes are not of the same type as Node 15, we expand the range to two hops. Within the two-hop range of Node 15, we find Nodes 13, 9, 20, 9, 4, 7, 17, 21, and 22. Among them, Nodes 4 and 17 are of the same type, and since the importance of Node 4 is relatively lower than that of Node 17, Node 4 becomes a candidate node to replace Node 15. Node 4 is then moved to the position of Node 15. Although in this iteration, Node 2 loses Node 4 and becomes an isolated node, the dynamic nature of the network allows Node 2 to join the network in the next iteration. If no candidate nodes are found within the two-hop range, other methods should be considered to reconstruct the network, such as adding nodes of the same type, utilizing intermediate nodes for forwarding, and so on. This specific case is not discussed in this paper. Thus, we prioritize timely reconstruction measures for nodes with higher degrees to maximize the integrity of the remaining task chains.

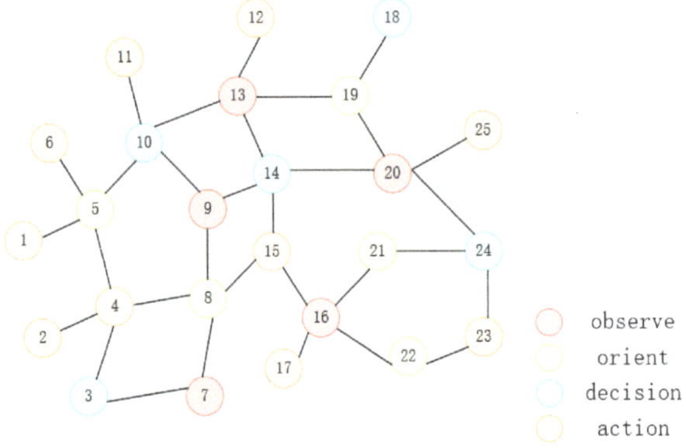

Figure 6. The topology structure of the UAV network.

Algorithm 1 Redistribute Data After Link Failure

procedure REDISTRIBUTEDATAAFTERLINKFAILURE(linkFailureList)
  Input: *linkFailureList* ▷ List of failed links with data and capacities
  Output: remaining *taskintegrity* ▷ Data redistribution after link failure
  Initialization:
    $\Gamma_i \leftarrow$ getNeighborNodes(linkFailure.node$_i$) ▷ Neighboring nodes of node v_i
    $\Gamma_j \leftarrow$ getNeighborNodes(linkFailure.node$_j$) ▷ Neighboring nodes of node v_j
  for each e_{ij} in linkFailureList **do**
    for each e_{ik} in Γ_i **do**
      $\Delta L_{ik} \leftarrow L_{ij} \times \frac{C_{ik}}{\sum_{a\in\Gamma_i} C_{ia} + \sum_{b\in\Gamma_j} C_{jb}}$ ▷ Calculate extra data allocation
      $L_{ik}^{\text{new}} \leftarrow L_{ik} + \Delta L_{ik}$ ▷ Update data carried on link e_{ik}
      if $L_{ik}^{\text{new}} > C_{ik}$ **then** ▷ Check for communication congestion
        handleCommunicationCongestion(e_{ik})
      end if
    end for
  end for
end procedure

5. Simulation Results

For the simulation, we consider an area of 5×5 km with 25 UAVs that are located uniformly in this area. As for the quantities of various types of UAVs, to avoid an excessive number of UAVs of the same type, we have decided to specify a range of values while still maintaining the total sum as a predetermined value. Additionally, based on the experimental findings in Ref. [25] and the various operational requirements for firefighting in real-life scenarios, we have determined that there will be a higher probability of having a greater number of UAVs dedicated to firefighting compared to other types of UAVs. The UAV can communicate with other devices with their communication range and move at a fixed speed in random directions within the scene range. We have used MATLAB (R2023a) for the simulation model, and the initial simulation parameters are given in Table 2.

Table 2. Parameters of the simulation.

Parameters	Values
Size of area	5 × 5 km
Time of iteration	2 s
Number of iterations	20
Number of Observe nodes	1–10
Number of Orient nodes	1–10
Number of Decide nodes	1–10
Number of Act nodes	5–10
Maximum UAV speed	20 m/s
Number of vulnerable nodes	5
Node mobility	Random way-point model

5.1. Vulnerability Analysis

Before conducting a vulnerability analysis on the network, we first need to determine the weights of various indicators in UAV communication attributes and functional topology attributes. It is not feasible to experiment with every possible value, so we compare network vulnerability performance under two types of weight proportions (emphasizing a certain indicator and relative balance) to assess the network's vulnerability.

In Figure 7, a series of experiments were conducted where the weights for node degree, node betweenness, and node closeness centrality in the communication topology were set as (0.2, 0.2, 0.6), (0.2, 0.6, 0.2), (0.6, 0.2, 0.2), and (0.3, 0.3, 0.4), (0.3, 0.4, 0.3), (0.4, 0.3, 0.3). Different node communication topology importance rankings were obtained based on these weight settings. Then, according to the ranking order, the most important nodes were iteratively removed from the current network, and the remaining task chain integrity was calculated. The experimental results show that, when there was a significant difference in weights among the three indicators, the rate of decline in network task chain integrity was relatively slow. It required removing 9 to 98 nodes to completely reduce it to 0. However, when the weights of the three indicators were close, the average decrease in remaining network connectivity after removing nodes was 0.13 compared to the previous group. Only 5 nodes needed to be removed to reduce the remaining task chain integrity of the network to 0. This suggests that weight allocation for communication topology attributes should be as evenly distributed as possible.

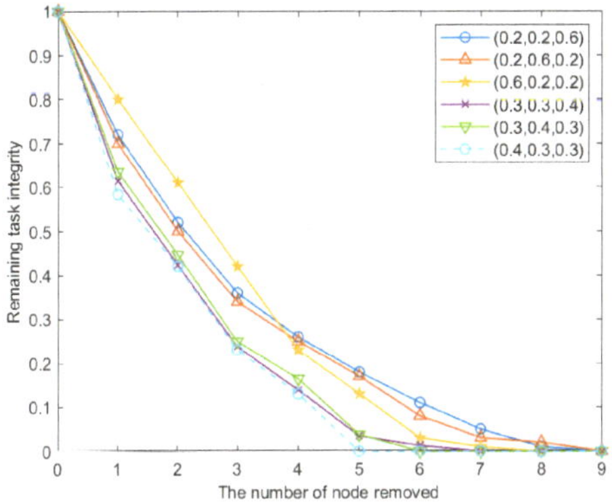

Figure 7. Effect of Topology Attribute Proportions on Vulnerability Analysis.

Similarly, in Figure 8, this experiment also set the weights for substitutability, connectivity importance, and efficiency importance in the functional topology as (0.2, 0.2, 0.6), (0.2, 0.6, 0.2), (0.6, 0.2, 0.2), and (0.3, 0.3, 0.4), (0.3, 0.4, 0.3), (0.4, 0.3, 0.3). Different UAV importance rankings were obtained based on these weight settings, and then the most important nodes were sequentially removed. By observing the results, it was found that, when the allocation ratio was (0.3, 0.4, 0.3), the removal of a single node had the greatest impact on the remaining task chain integrity of the network, and only 4 nodes needed to be removed to reduce the task chain integrity of the network to 0. Therefore, this weight allocation ratio became the default proportion for subsequent experiments.

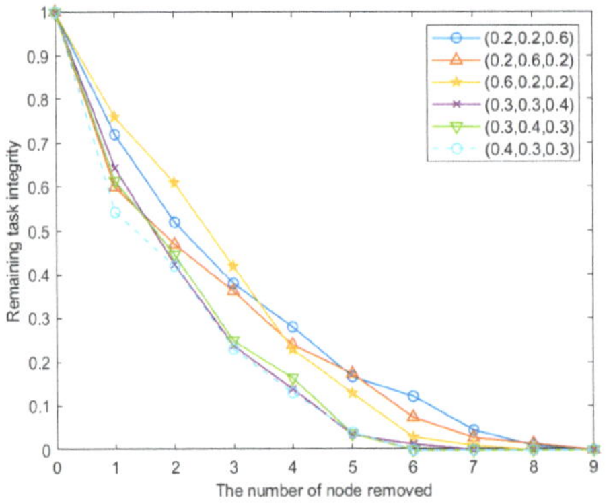

Figure 8. Effect of Functional Attribute Proportions on Vulnerability Analysis.

Finally, this experiment mainly deals with the impact of the ratio of functional topology attributes to communication topology attributes on the effectiveness of vulnerability analysis. Based on the results of the previous two experiments, this experiment sets the weight distribution of indicators within the communication topology attributes as (0.4, 0.3, 0.3) and the weight distribution of indicators within the functional topology attributes as (0.3, 0.4, 0.3). Then, by adjusting the weights of the two types of attributes, the importance ranking of nodes is obtained, and the most important nodes under the current weight distribution are removed to obtain the remaining task chain integrity of the network. In Figure 9, it can be observed that, when the weight coefficient of communication topology attributes ϕ_1 is 0.55, and when the weight of functional topology attributes ϕ_2 is 0.45, removing the most important nodes under this weight distribution causes the greatest decrease in network task chain integrity. Therefore, this weight allocation ratio is used for subsequent vulnerability analysis experiments.

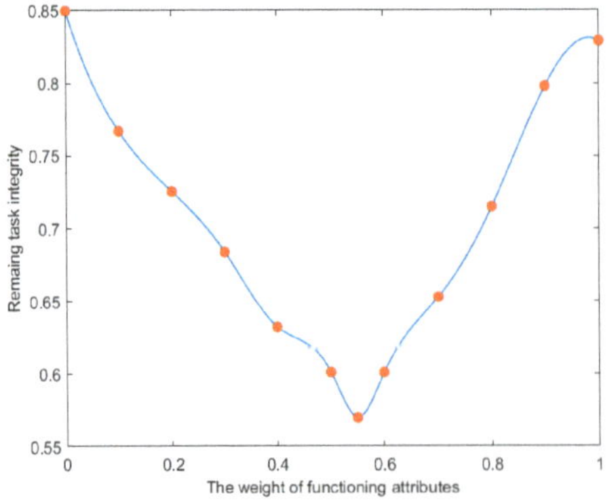

Figure 9. Vulnerability Analysis Effectiveness under Different Importance Weightings.

After confirming the weight values, in each iteration, we obtain the vulnerability node importance ranking through MENVAL. At the same time, we also use the traditional topological analysis method (NVA(Node Vulnerability Algorithm)), in which the selection of important nodes is completely based on the importance of communication topology. For the UAV network topology depicted in Figure 6, the node importance rankings obtained through MENVAL and NVA are shown in Tables 3 and 4.

Table 3. Importance ranking through MENVAL.

Number	Node ID	β_i'	W_i'	ρ_i'
1	9	0.68	0.76	0.72
2	14	0.70	0.63	0.67
3	10	0.69	0.64	0.66
4	8	0.68	0.60	0.64
5	20	0.65	0.59	0.62

Table 4. Importance ranking through NVA.

Number	Node ID	β_i'
1	14	0.70
2	10	0.69
3	8	0.68
4	9	0.68
5	20	0.65

We sequentially attack the identified vulnerable nodes obtained from both methods by removing all communication links of each node. The vulnerability of nodes is then assessed by evaluating the integrity of the remaining task chains, and the simulation results after the attack are shown in Figure 10.

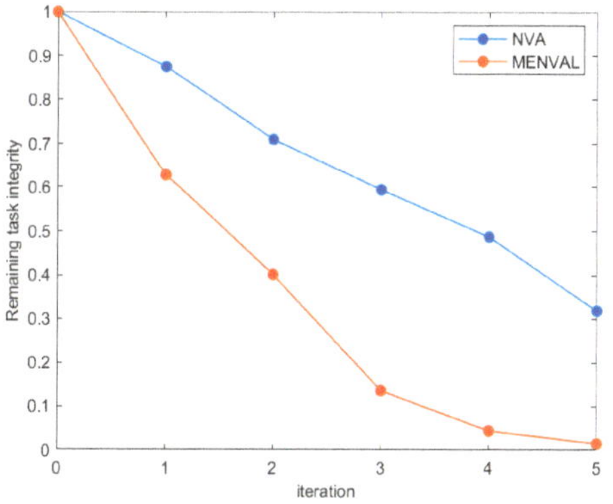

Figure 10. Different Algorithm-Derived Node Vulnerability Effects

The horizontal axis represents the number of iterations, and the vertical axis represents the remaining task chain integrity of the network. In each iteration, we remove a vulnerable node and then calculate the remaining task chain integrity in the network. In Figure 11, we can observe that, with the removal of each node, the network vulnerability decreases accordingly. However, it is evident that the removal of vulnerable nodes obtained by MENVAL has a significantly greater impact on the network. By the fifth iteration, the network connectivity is almost zero. In contrast, attacking the vulnerable nodes obtained by the NVA method results in a relatively slower decrease in network metrics, and the remaining task chain integrity at the end of the last iteration is also higher than that of the first method.

Then we set the node scale to 25, 50, 75, and 100, and the number of various types of nodes increases proportionally to the corresponding numbers. In each iteration, we remove vulnerable nodes obtained by MENVAL in order of importance and compare the impact of removing vulnerable nodes on the UAV network at different node scales.

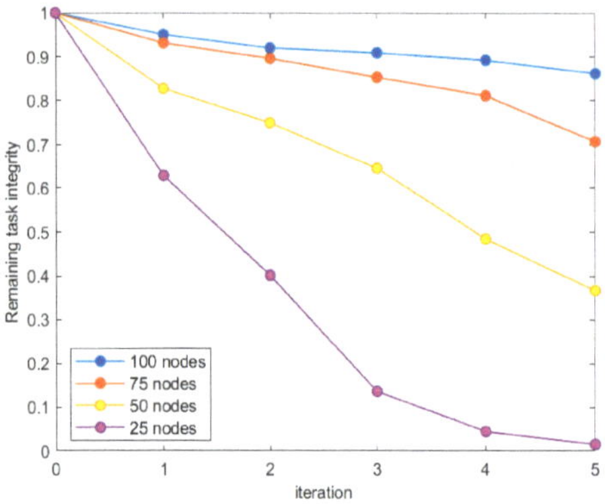

Figure 11. The network's remaining connectivity change curve on a multi-scale network.

In Figure 11, we can observe that, as the scale of the UAV network increases, the impact of removing individual key nodes on the remaining task connectivity in the network gradually decreases. This occurs when there are a larger number of UAVs and a greater number of task chains, where the removal of individual nodes has a weaker impact on the entire network. Conversely, in networks with fewer UAVs and a relatively smaller number of task chains, the impact of the removal of individual UAVs on the network becomes more pronounced.

5.2. Topology Reconstruction Strategy

Based on the vulnerability analysis results, we proceed with experiments related to the topological reconstruction algorithm NITRA. Taking the example of Node 9 failure on the generated topology network shown in Figure 6, we sort the importance of the one-hop range nodes from small to large in Table 5.

Table 5. Importance of the one-hop range nodes through NITRA.

Number	Node ID	Function	$\rho_i^{'}$
1	8	Orient	0.64
2	10	Decide	0.66
3	14	Decide	0.67

Within the one-hop range, there are no nodes of the same type as Node 9. Since Node 9 is a vulnerable node, according to the algorithm rules, we need to continue searching for candidate nodes set within the two-hop range, which is represented in Table 6.

According to Table 6, within the two-hop range, both Node 13 and Node 20 are of the same type as Node 9. Additionally, the comprehensive importance of Node 13 is less than that of Node 20 and Node 9. So, Node 13 is considered a candidate node for Node 9. Using the same method, candidate nodes for other vulnerable nodes can be determined.

At the same time, we also use the traditional topological reconstruction strategy MCMA, in which the selection of candidate nodes is completely based on the degree of the nodes. Obviously, by using MCMA, the candidate node for Node 9 is Node 8 because of its smallest degree and the lowest index number.

Table 6. Importance of the two-hop range nodes through NITRA.

Number	Node ID	Function	$\rho_i^{'}$
1	11	Act	0.64
2	7	Observe	0.66
3	5	Orient	0.67
4	4	Act	0.67
5	15	Act	0.68
6	13	Observe	0.70
7	20	Observe	0.71

We conducted 20 experiments to compare MCMA and NITRA, with parameters consistent with Table 2. Each experiment generated a different initial network topology, and a random vulnerable or non-vulnerable node was removed from the network. Subsequently, various topological reconstruction methods were applied to the network after removal. After the simulation concluded, we compared the integrity of the remaining task chain and the distance moved by the candidate UAVs under both algorithms. The average values of the evaluation metrics obtained by the two methods were then calculated. The experimental results are shown in Figures 12 and 13.

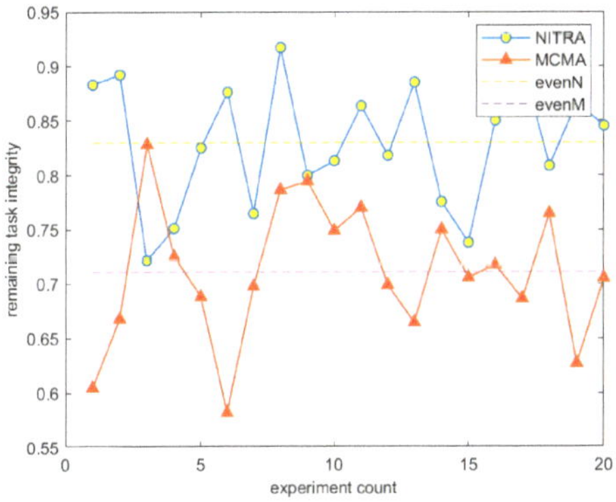

Figure 12. Removing a random vulnerable node in generated networks.

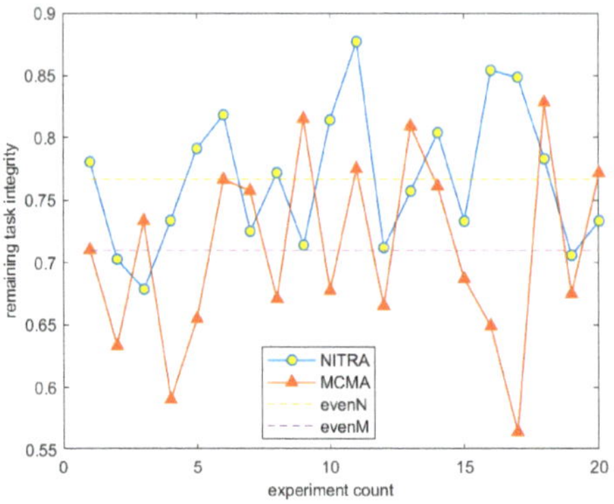

Figure 13. Removing a random non-vulnerable node in generated networks.

In Figure 12, each experiment randomly removes one vulnerable node from the generated network, and then different reconstruction algorithms are used to repair the network topology, represented by dashed lines indicating the averages. Through observation, it can be noted that, although in a few experiments the MCMA method slightly outperforms the proposed NITRA method in terms of remaining network connectivity, overall, networks reconstructed using NITRA are superior to those using MCMA. The residual task chain integrity of NITRA is 0.83, whereas the MCMA's average is 0.71, indicating a 17% improvement over MCMA.

In Figure 13, each experiment randomly removes a non-vulnerable node from the network. From the experimental results, it can be observed that, compared to the removal of vulnerable nodes, in overall performance, NITRA has an advantage in restoring network connectivity over MCMA. The average residual task chain integrity of networks reconstructed using NITRA is 0.77, while using MCMA for reconstruction yields a value of 0.70. Although the repair effect is not as pronounced as in the case of vulnerable node failure, it still represents a 10% improvement over MCMA. This indicates that, in ensuring the integrity of the remaining task chain during network reconstruction, NITRA is superior to MCMA, thus better maintaining network task execution performance. Both sets of experiments demonstrate that, in UAV task chain networks, NITRA surpasses MCMA in ensuring residual task chain integrity, thereby better restoring network task execution performance in the event of node failures.

In Figures 14 and 15, experiments were conducted to compare the movement distances of candidate UAVs after removing random nodes using two different reconstruction algorithms. It can be observed that, in most experiments, compared to MCMA, NITRA results in shorter average travel distances for candidate UAVs, reducing them by 26%. Particularly noteworthy are experiments 7 and 15 in Figure 15, where, because the algorithm did not find candidate nodes within the two-hop range of failed nodes, NITRA did not perform topology reconstruction. Although MCMA achieved higher residual task chain integrity relative to NITRA in experiment 7, the improvement was not significant. Even in experiment 15, the obtained residual task chain integrity was not as good as that of NITRA. This confirms that NITRA, compared to MCMA, can reduce the movement distance of candidate UAVs, thereby lowering the energy consumption of UAVs and prolonging the operational time of UAV networks.

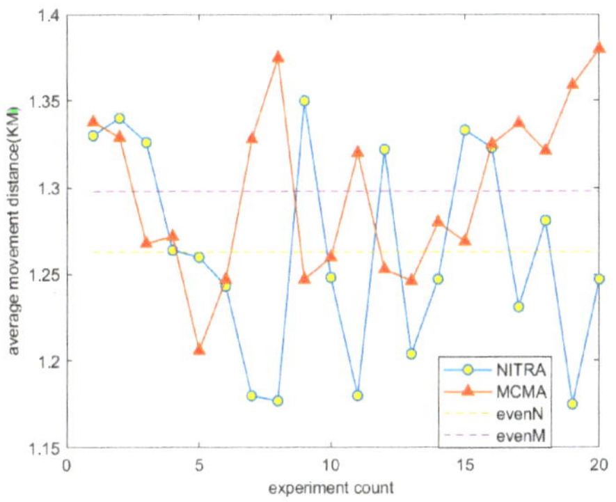

Figure 14. Average movement distance change curve upon removing a vulnerable node.

In Figure 16, we compare the time taken for network recovery to a steady state under different topology reconstruction strategies using NITRA and MCMA after node failures occur in the network. It can be observed that, within 0.6 s after node failure, the remaining task integrity of both algorithms rapidly decreases. After 0.6 s, the network under the NITRA strategy reduces its rate of decline and reaches a steady state around 1.7 s, with a remaining task integrity of approximately 0.75. The network under the MCMA strategy declines more rapidly, reaching a steady state around 2.3 s, with a remaining task connectivity of 0.63. Therefore, NITRA can restore network stability faster than MCMA, maximize the remaining task integrity after node failures, and improve it by about 19%.

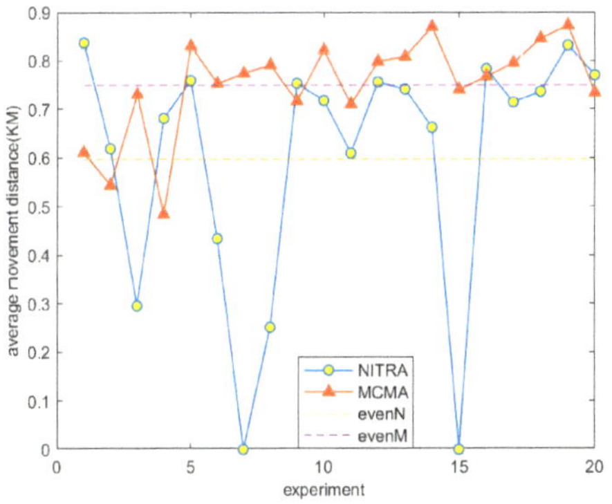

Figure 15. Average movement distance change curve upon removing a vulnerable node.

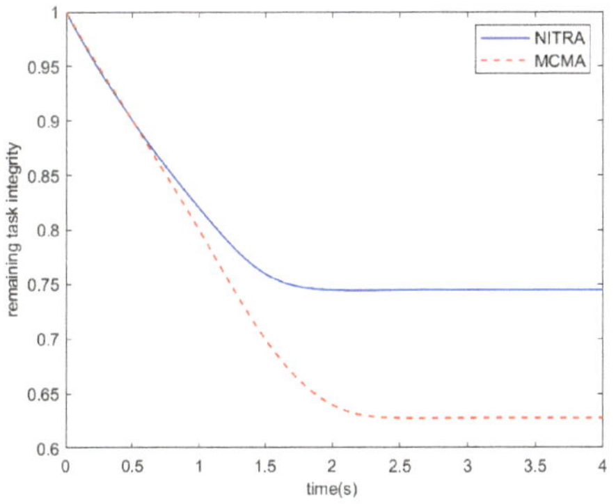

Figure 16. Average movement distance change curve upon removing a non-vulnerable node.

6. Conclusions

In this paper, we propose the VUTRM algorithm to address node failure issues in UAV task chains. The algorithm comprises two parts: MENVAL and NITRA. For MENVAL, an innovative multi-metric node evaluation method is employed to comprehensively consider both communication and functional importance of nodes, thereby enhancing the accuracy of ranking vulnerable nodes in the network. NITRA, based on the obtained node importance ranking, adopts different reconstruction strategies for vulnerable and non-vulnerable nodes. Experimental results indicate that, in small-scale networks, the vulnerable nodes identified by MENVAL have a more significant impact on the network task chains, necessitating targeted protection. Furthermore, in scenarios of single-node failure, compared to MCMA, NITRA demonstrates improvements in ensuring the connectivity of the remaining task chains and reducing the movement distance of candidate nodes, thus enhancing the robustness of UAV networks.

Author Contributions: Conceptualization, J.L. and Z.H.; methodology, Q.Y. (Qinghai Yang); software, Q.Y. (Qingfeng Yue); validation, X.X.; writing—original draft preparation, Q.Y. (Qinggfeng Yue); writing—review and editing, J.L. All authors have read and agreed to the published version of the manuscript.

Funding: This research was supported in part by the Natural Science Basis Research Plan in the Shaanxi Province of China (2023JCYB555) and by the National Key Research and Development Program of China (2020YFB1807700).

Data Availability Statement: Data are contained within the article.

Conflicts of Interest: Author Zijia Huang was employed by the company The 20th Research Institute of China Electronics Technology Group Corporation. The remaining authors declare that the research was conducted in the absence of any commercial or financial relationships that could be construed as a potential conflict of interest.

Abbreviations

The following abbreviations are used in this manuscript:

UAVs	Unmanned Aerial Vehicles
VUTRM	Vulnerability-based Topology Reconstruction Mechanism
MENVAL	Multi-metric Node Vulnerability Assessment Algorithm
NITRA	Node Importance-based Topology Reconstruction Algorithm
MCDS	Minimum Connected Dominating Set
RIM	Resilient Information Matrix
DARA	Degree and Relative Distance Aware
PADRA	Partition-Aware Dominating Set-based Recovery Algorithm
LeDiR	Least Disturbance Routing
ND	Network Diffusion
NIO	Influence in the Loop
NVA	Node Vulnerability Algorithm
MCMA	Minimum Cascade Mobile Algorithm

References

1. Ding, G.; Wu, Q.; Zhang, L.; Lin, Y.; Tsiftsis, T.A.; Yao, Y.-D. An amateur drone surveillance system based on the cognitive internet of things. *IEEE Commun. Mag.* **2018**, *56*, 29–35. [CrossRef]
2. Sahu, A.; Davis, K. Structural learning techniques for bayesian attack graphs in cyber physical power systems. In Proceedings of the 2021 IEEE Texas Power and Energy Conference (TPEC), College Station, TX, USA, 2–5 February 2021; pp. 1–6.
3. Liu, X.; Abdelhakim, M.; Krishnamurthy, P.; Tipper, D. Identifying malicious nodes in multihop iot networks using diversity and unsupervised learning. In Proceedings of the 2018 IEEE International Conference on Communications (ICC), Kansas City, MO, USA, 20–24 May 2018; pp. 1–6.
4. Allodi, L.; Banescu, S.; Femmer, H.; Beckers, K. Identifying relevant information cues for vulnerability assessment using cvss. In Proceedings of the Eighth ACM Conference on Data and Application Security and Privacy, Tempe, AZ, USA, 19–21 March 2018; ser. CODASPY '18; Association for Computing Machinery: New York, NY, USA, 2018; pp. 119–126. [CrossRef]

5. Akkaya, K.; Thimmapuram, A.; Senel, F.; Uludag, S. Distributed recovery of actor failures in wireless sensor and actor networks. In Proceedings of the 2008 IEEE Wireless Communications and Networking Conference, Las Vegas, NV, USA, 31 March–3 April 2008; pp. 2480–2485.
6. Asim, M.; Mokhtar, H.; Khan, M.Z.; Merabti, M. A sensor relocation scheme for wireless sensor networks. In Proceedings of the 2011 IEEE Workshops of International Conference on Advanced Information Networking and Applications, Singapore, 22–25 March 2011; pp. 808–813.
7. Zhao, Z.; Li, Z.; Guo, H.; Yang, M. Research on vulnerability of space information network based on interdependent networks. In Proceedings of the 2018 IEEE Third International Conference on Data Science in Cyberspace (DSC), Guangzhou, China, 18–21 June 2018; pp. 302–309.
8. Asadpour, M.; Hummel, K.A.; Giustiniano, D.; Draskovic, S. Route or carry: Motion-driven packet forwarding in micro aerial vehicle networks. *IEEE Trans. Mob. Comput.* **2017**, *16*, 843–856. [CrossRef]
9. Li, B.; Fei, Z.; Zhang, Y.; Guizani, M. Secure uav communication networks over 5G. *IEEE Wirel. Commun.* **2019**, *26*, 114–120. [CrossRef]
10. Poulin, R.; Boily, M.-C.; Mâsse, B.R. Dynamical systems to define centrality in social networks. *Soc. Netw.* **2000**, *22*, 187–220. [CrossRef]
11. Howell, N. Applied network analysis: A methodological introduction. *Can. J. Sociol.* **1985**, *10*, 209–211. [CrossRef]
12. Freeman, L.C. Centrality in social networks conceptual clarification. *Soc. Netw.* **1978**, *1*, 215–239. Available online: https://www.sciencedirect.com/science/article/pii/0378873378900217 (accessed on 22 May 2024). [CrossRef]
13. Zhao, M.; Wu, M.; Qian, L.; An, Q.; Li, S. Evaluation of cross-layer network vulnerability of power communication network based on multi-dimensional and multi-layer node importance analysis. *IEEE Access* **2022**, *10*, 67181–67197.
14. Dolev, S.; Elovici, Y.; Puzis, R. Routing betweenness centrality. *J. ACM* **2010**, *57*, 1–27. [CrossRef]
15. Osinga, F. Getting'a discourse on winning and losing: A primer on boyd's 'Theory of intellectual evolution'. *Contemp. Secur. Policy* **2013**, *34*, 603–624. [CrossRef]
16. Diaz, D.O. An Optimization-Based Approach to Measuring Robustness in Command and Control Networks. Ph.D. Thesis, Naval Postgraduate School, Monterey, CA, USA, 2019.
17. Cao, Y.-Y.; Liu, R.-R.; Jia, C.-X.; Wang, B.-H. Percolation in multilayer complex networks with connectivity and interdependency topological structures. *Commun. Nonlinear Sci. Numer.* **2021**, *92*, 105492. [CrossRef]
18. Kenett, D.Y.; Gao, J.; Huang, X.; Shao, S.; Vodenska, I.; Buldyrev, S.V.; Paul, G.; Stanley, H.E.; Havlin, S. Network of interdependent networks: Overview of theory and applications. In *Networks of Networks: The Last Frontier of Complexity*; Springer: Cham, Switzerland, 2014; pp. 3–36.
19. Akram, V.K.; Ugurlu, O. Detecting the most vital articulation points in wireless multi-hop networks. *IEEE/ACM Trans. Netw.* **2023**, *31*, 2389–2402. [CrossRef]
20. Younis, M.; Lee, S.; Gupta, S.; Fisher, K. A localized self-healing algorithm for networks of moveable sensor nodes. In Proceedings of the IEEE GLOBECOM 2008–2008 IEEE Global Telecommunications Conference, New Orleans, LA, USA, 30 November–4 December 2008; IEEE: Piscataway, NJ, USA, 2008; pp. 1–5.
21. Abbasi, A.A.; Younis, M.; Akkaya, K. Movement-assisted connectivity restoration in wireless sensor and actor networks. *IEEE Trans. Parallel Distrib. Syst.* **2008**, *20*, 1366–1379. [CrossRef]
22. Senel, F.; Akkaya, K.; Younis, M. An efficient mechanism for establishing connectivity in wireless sensor and actor networks. In Proceedings of the IEEE GLOBECOM 2007—IEEE Global Telecommunications Conference, Washington, DC, USA, 26–30 November 2007; IEEE: Piscataway, NJ, USA, 2007; pp. 1129–1133.
23. Abbasi, A.; Younis, M.; Baroudi, U. Restoring connectivity in wireless sensor-actor networks with minimal topology changes. In Proceedings of the 2010 IEEE International Conference on Communications, Cape Town, South Africa, 23–27 May 2010; IEEE: Piscataway, NJ, USA, 2010; pp. 1–5.
24. Hao, W.; Wenbai, C.; Cui, H.; Hang, M. A minimum cascade mobile repair method for wireless sensor networks. *Microelectron. Comput.* **2021**, *38*, 31–37.
25. Wang, K.; Yuan, Y.; Chen, M.; Lou, Z.; Zhu, Z.; Li, R. A study of fire drone extinguishing system in high-rise buildings. *Fire* **2022**, *5*, 75. Available online: https://www.mdpi.com/2571-6255/5/3/75 (accessed on 22 May 2024). [CrossRef]

electronics

MDPI

Article

Vulnerability Analysis of UAV Swarm Network with Emergency Tasks

Jinglei Li [1], Qingfeng Yue [1], Zijia Huang [2,*], Xiaoyu Xie [1] and Qinghai Yang [1]

1 The School of Telecommunications Engineering, Xidian University, Xi'an 710071, China; jlli68@xidian.edu.cn (J.L.); 21181214288@stu.xidian.edu.cn (Q.Y.); h578960@163.com (X.X.); qhyang@xidian.edu.cn (Q.Y.)
2 The 20th Research Institute of China Electronics Technology Group Corporation, Xi'an 710068, China
* Correspondence: beiyouhzj@163.com

Abstract: With the rapid development of Unmanned Aerial Vehicle (UAV) technology, UAV swarms are used for emergency tasks in various scenarios such as area detection, fire rescue, logistics, and transportation. However, for complex scenarios, UAV swarms are prone to environmental interference that damages their equipment or disrupts their communication links, affecting the normal execution of tasks. In this paper, an information–communication interdependent network model is designed for the vulnerability analysis of UAV swarm networks with emergency tasks. Firstly, from the perspective of network functions of a UAV swarm, we introduce the theory of interdependent networks to abstract the relationship between the UAV swarm's communication network and its information network, where the communication network represents its communication topology and the information network is related to the function of each UAV individual in the UAV swarm. Then, the vulnerability of the UAV swarm is analyzed according to the relationship between network construction costs and network connectivity under environmental interference. Finally, the effectiveness of the vulnerability analysis method is verified through simulation.

Keywords: UAV swarm network; vulnerability analysis; emergency tasks; interdependent network model

1. Introduction

Unmanned Aerial Vehicle (UAV) swarms, composed of interconnected UAVs coordinated through communication and control systems, efficiently achieve specific tasks or goals. When UAVs fly individually, their limited energy supply constrains their flight distance and operational range. Furthermore, they are susceptible to various interferences, and their communication reliability is relatively low. UAV swarms can achieve collaborative interaction among all nodes through advanced open communication networks, enabling fast and efficient task completion while possessing strong scalability and robustness. For instance, they are used for emergency tasks in various scenarios, such as area detection [1], fire rescue [2], and transportation [3]. For emergency tasks, the quality of communication between UAVs can be disrupted by different environmental factors, such as electromagnetic interference, adverse weather conditions, and geographical obstacles, hindering coordination and information exchange among UAVs. Environmental interference in emergency tasks poses significant challenges to the communication networks of UAV swarms. Meanwhile, the diverse functionalities of individual entities within UAV swarms play distinct roles in emergency tasks, collectively impacting the overall task. Therefore, we need to analyze the vulnerability of UAV network links to ensure that they can work with maximum efficiency in the case of a link failure.

In the early network vulnerability analysis models, all the nodes in the network were classified into one class. The vulnerability assessment method based on expert experience is mainly through the common vulnerability scoring system to assess network vulnerability [4]. Model-based vulnerability analysis methods mainly include the fractal mechanism-based vulnerability analysis method [5], the general attack tree model-based vulnerability analysis method [6,7], the Bayesian network-based vulnerability analysis method [8], and the cascading failure model-based vulnerability analysis method [9,10]. However, in the real world the composition of many networks is very complex, so it is not appropriate to describe them simply as a single isolated network. Therefore, we need to discuss the classification of UAV nodes in the network and analyze it from the perspective of interdependent networks.

Interdependent networks have been applied to various application scenarios. Zhao studied the vulnerability of a space information network coupled with a communication network and a function network and proposed the concept of the task component [11]. Chen proposed a novel model to investigate the cascading failures in interdependent power grids and communication networks and identified the vital nodes from the perspective of network robustness [12,13]. Reference [14] introduced interdependent networks into scenarios of network cascading failures and studied the effect of degree heterogeneity on the structural vulnerability of interdependent networks when they suffer targeted interference. Building upon this, Liu constructed a two-layer asymmetric dependent network model for unidirectional dependent UAV network physical systems, but did not consider interdependent decision making among clusters [15]. Xing attempted to combine weight analysis methods with interdependent networks, constructed a double-layer dependent network with weights, proposed a cascading failure model, considering node overload and node repair, and constructed three improved strategies based on the weight-based load redistribution strategy [16]. This framework is efficiently applicable to time-dependent multiplex networks. Jia began to analyze networks from the perspective of node and link connectivity. Jia studied the effects of the interdependency characteristics of cross-layer nodes, the connectivity characteristics of intra-layer nodes, the interdependency characteristics of intra-layer nodes, and attack strategies on cascading dynamics [17]. Yang studied interdependent networks based on physical networks and logical networks and analyzed the cascading failure of the model [18]. Zou designed different key fragile dependency links removal strategies based on the assessment of links [19]. And reference [20] presented a method for evaluating the robustness, vulnerability, and efficiency of multi-layer infrastructures using various probabilistic evaluation measures to tackle cascading problems in interdependent critical systems. In general, these studies mainly focused on vulnerability prevention, and did not conduct targeted research on the vulnerability analysis of the network after cascading failures.

In this paper, to effectively convey the functions of UAVs in executing emergency tasks, we combined interdependent networks with UAV networks for our research. According to the network characteristics of the UAV swarm network, in addition to the communication ability between network nodes, situational awareness and the information sharing of the UAV swarm are other major features of the swarm network. For a UAV swarm, a single UAV in the swarm networks is both a network node for communication and a node for information perception and processing [21]. The network can be divided into two layers: a communication network and an information network, where the communication network represents its communication topology influenced by the UAVs' motion trajectory, and where the information network is related to the function of each UAV in the normal execution of emergency tasks. Aiming at the network vulnerability analysis of a UAV swarm with emergency tasks, we have designed a network model of information–communication interdependence, and a link redistribution rule is proposed.

The rest of paper is organized as follows. Section 2 introduces the system model and problem formulation discussed in this paper. Section 3 details the information–communication interdependent network. Section 4 describes the whole network vulnerability analysis process. Experimental results and evaluations are presented in Section 5. Finally, the entire paper is summarized in Section 6.

2. System Model and Problem Formulation

The primary aim of this section is to model the UAV swarm network and its link data capacity, as well as formulating the corresponding problem. This will enable further research on cascading failure and simulation experiments.

2.1. System Model

2.1.1. UAV Swarm Networks

In rescue scenarios, for a UAV swarm, an individual UAV within the system serves not only as a communication network node but also as a node for information perception and processing. In communication networks, the communication links between nodes form the network's topology, responsible for data transmission across the entire network. And in information networks, nodes are responsible for sensing, processing environmental information, and sharing it with other UAVs, primarily tasked with executing network tasks. Information network nodes have faster information processing speeds and stronger task execution capabilities, providing input information for the network. Communication network nodes have a broader communication range and higher-quality communication, serving as intermediary nodes to assist information network nodes in information exchange. The mutual dependence between the two networks forms the information–communication interdependent model of UAV swarm networks: the lower layer constitutes a communication network consisting of UAV nodes and communication links, while the upper layer forms a functional network composed of information perception and processing nodes carrying task payloads and their information-interaction relationships.

As shown in Figure 1, fire rescue is a common emergency task scene. In complex environments like high-rise buildings and outdoor settings, safely implementing firefighting measures has always been a global challenge. UAVs, due to their rapid deployment and flexible operations, can execute multi-UAVs coordinated firefighting strategies for different fire scenarios [2].

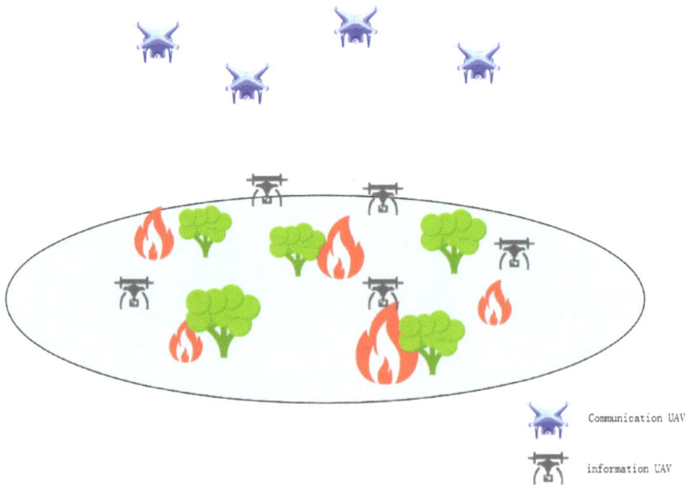

Figure 1. UAV swarm fire rescue scenario.

The communication topology structure of a UAV swarm network is represented by undirected graph G_P, which is composed of the UAV nodes set V_P and the communication links set E_P, and G_P can be expressed as $G_P = (V_P, E_P)$. If the undirected graph G_P contains n nodes, $V_P = \{v_i | i = 1, 2, \ldots, n\}$. E_P is the set of communication links in the UAV swarm network, and it can be expressed as $E_P = \left\{e_{ij}^P | e_{ij}^P = (v_i, v_j), v_i, v_j \in V_P\right\}$. There can only be at most one link between two communication nodes in a communication network. The information network of a UAV swarm system can be expressed as $G_F = (V_F, E_F)$. The information nodes are mapped from UAV nodes according to different functions, indicating the different functions of the UAV nodes due to the different task load equipment. If the information network G_F contains m nodes, $V_F = \{v_j | j = 1, 2, \ldots, m\}$. The information node has certain information-interaction and information-sharing relationships, which can meet the task requirements of the UAV swarm network. The information interaction between UAV nodes with different functions can be represented by information links, denoted as $E_F = \{e_{ij}^F | e_{ij}^F = (v_i, v_j), v_i, v_j \in V_F\}$.

2.1.2. Link Capacity Model

Motter proposed a cascading failure model, also known as the ML (Motter–Lai) model [9]. He applied it to a scale-free network and a uniform network, respectively. In this model, the initial load L_i is defined by the global characteristic variable betweenness B_i. The initial load of node i in the ML model is formulated as

$$L_i = B_i \tag{1}$$

where B_i is node v_i's betweenness and L_i represents the node i's initial data transmission capability. The two variables exhibit a strong positive correlation. For example, the connecting hub of two subnetworks may be a node or a link, although the number of nodes or links connected to it is relatively small. If the node fails or the link is interrupted, connection failure between two small networks may ensue. Therefore, the node plays an extremely important role in the network. The interface number reflects the influence and force of a node or link in the entire network, and it represents the traffic volume of a node or a link. In task execution, communication UAVs, due to their higher computing capabilities, are responsible for calculating the load capacity of various links, and there is a periodic update of the computation results for each UAV in the entire network by communication.

However, in the UAV swarm information–communication interdependent network model, due to the coupling links between the two layers of the network, the initial data transmission capability of the network link needs to be redefined. Firstly, it is assumed that the coupling strength ω_{ij} on the coupling link e_{ij} of the dependent network is related to the node number of UAV nodes at both ends, and the formula is

$$\omega_{ij} = (B_i B_{ij})^{\alpha} \tag{2}$$

where B_i is node v_i's betweenness, B_{ij} is link e_{ij}'s betweenness, and α is the weight that controls the coupling strength.

The node betweenness B_i is defined as the number of shortest paths through node v_i in the network; it can be expressed as

$$B_i = \sum_{j \neq i, k \neq i} \frac{\theta_{jk}(i)}{\theta_{jk}} \tag{3}$$

where $\theta_{jk}(i)$ is the number of shortest paths passing through node v_i in the shortest paths between node v_j and node v_k, and θ_{jk} is the number of shortest paths between node v_j and node v_k.

The link betweenness B_{ij} is defined as the number of shortest paths through link e_{ij} in the network; it can be expressed as

$$B_{ij} = \sum_{k \neq i,j, l \neq i,j} \frac{\theta_{kl}(e_{ij})}{\theta_{kl}} \tag{4}$$

where $\theta_{kl}(e_{ij})$ is the number of shortest paths passing through link e_{ij} in the shortest paths between node v_k and node v_l, and θ_{kl} is the number of shortest paths between node v_k and node v_l.

Taking node 4 in Figure 2 as an example, this network consists of seven nodes. Assuming that this network is a communication network, its adjacency matrix E_P is as shown in Table 1. There are three shortest paths between node 1 and node 6, with one of them passing through node 4. Similarly, there are three shortest paths between node 2 and node 6, node 1 and node 7, and node 2 and node 7, all of which pass through node 4. After calculation, the node betweenness centrality of node 4 is found to be 1.33. Likewise, for the link between node 2 and node 4, there is one shortest path passing through this link between node 1 and node 6, and another one between node 1 and node 7. After calculation, the B_{24} is found to be 0.67.

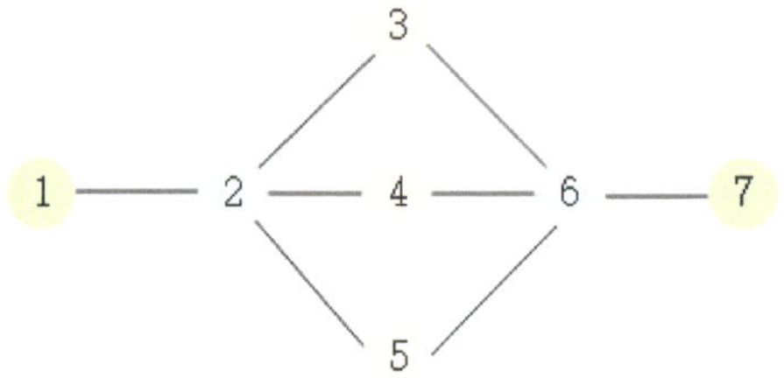

Figure 2. The information–communication double-layer interdependent network model of a UAV swarm.

Table 1. The adjacency matrix E_P

	1	2	3	4	5	6	7
1	0	1	0	0	0	0	0
2	0	0	1	1	1	0	0
3	0	1	0	0	0	1	0
4	0	1	0	0	0	1	0
5	0	1	0	0	0	1	0
6	0	0	1	1	1	0	0
7	0	0	0	0	0	1	0

Due to the coupling link between the two layers of the UAV swarm information–communication network, the initial data transmission capability of a link in a network is not only related to itself but also related to the coupling strength of the coupling link between two nodes on the link and the corresponding node of another network. In other words, this means that when a node communicates with nodes of the same type in the same network layer, it always ensures communication with the nodes of another layer with which it is coupled. In the information–communication interdependent network model, the node v_i in the information network is coupled with the node v_m in the communication network, and the node v_j in the information network is coupled with the node v_n in the communication network. The initial data transmission capability L_{ij} of link e_{ij} in the information network is associated with three factors: the betweenness centrality of the link itself and the betweenness centrality of the coupling links e_{im} and e_{jn} at both ends of the link. The initial data transmission capability L_{ij} is influenced by three factors: the betweenness centrality of the link itself, as well as the betweenness centrality of the connecting links e_{im} and e_{jn} at both ends of the link. It can be defined as

$$L_{ij} = B_{ij} + \frac{B_i}{B_i + B_m}\omega_{im} + \frac{B_j}{B_j + B_n}\omega_{jn} \tag{5}$$

Since the data transmission speed of a link is related to the link's transmission capacity, the data capacity of link e_{ij} can be represented as

$$T_{\text{ij}} = (1 + L_{ij})T_0 \tag{6}$$

where T_0 represents the minimum data transmission speed of the network, and T_{ij} represents the maximum data transmission speed of link e_{ij}. Once the data transmission range is exceeded, there is a probability that the link will fail.

2.2. Problem Formulation

In the context of UAV swarm networks, interdependent networks play a crucial role, facilitating efficient collaboration and communication among UAVs, enabling the cluster to execute complex tasks in a coordinated manner. The transmission capability of links is pivotal in maintaining such collaboration, ensuring timely data transmission and the stability of communication links. However, interdependent networks face various challenges, including susceptibility to different attacks and disturbances. Risks such as malicious attacks, network congestion, or node failures may lead to cascading failures within interdependent networks, significantly impacting system stability and reliability. Therefore, conducting vulnerability analysis and implementing appropriate measures, including reallocating network links, is imperative. This helps enhance the system's resilience against disruptions, thereby reducing the risk of attacks or disturbances and ensuring the stable operation of UAV swarm networks.

Generally speaking, the ability of each link in the UAV swarm network to transmit data is limited by the network cost, so it is impossible to endlessly undertake the transmission of a large number of information flows, otherwise it will cause communication blockage or even link interruption. Therefore, we assume that the data transmission capability of each link in the network is directly proportional to the initial data transmission capability L_ij of the link. Based on the ML model and other related research definitions, the adjusted data transmission capability $L_{ij}^{'}$ of the link e_{ij} is represented as

$$L_{ij}^{'} = (1 + \beta)L_{ij} \tag{7}$$

where β is the capacity parameter, indicating the ability of the link to process additional data. The larger the value of β, the stronger the ability of the link to process data and the ability of the network to resist attacks.

When we choose the value of β, the construction cost and link transmission capacity should be considered. In real life, the link cost consumption of UAVs is influenced by various factors, such as materials, scenarios, and technologies, making it difficult to define the amount of cost consumption. When the value of β is relatively large, the ability of data transmission in the link of the UAV swarm information–communication network is stronger, and the ability to cope with cascading failures is stronger. In a fire rescue scenario, the interruption of some network links due to high-temperature radiation or the isolation of a burning building only causes a partial failure. The entire network cannot be paralyzed. However, the larger the value of β, the higher the cost of network construction and the more difficult it is to implement. Considering the limited technology and cost, the value of β generally has a certain threshold, and the ability of the whole UAV swarm network to resist cascading failure can be expressed by its threshold β_c. The larger the threshold β_c is, the more the network is vulnerable to cascading failure, and the smaller the threshold β_c is, the more the network is robust against cascading failure. In other words, when $\beta > \beta_c$, the interruption of any link in the network due to fire will not cause the interruption of other links. When $\beta < \beta_c$ is used, the data transmission capacity of links in the network is limited, and the interruption of some links in the network will increase the data transmission volume of other links, which may cause the failure of other links or even the collapse of the whole network. Therefore, in this paper, we studied the impact of the value of β on the vulnerability of links, providing a reference for builders of UAV network links.

3. Information–Communication Interdependent Network of UAV Swarm

In a UAVs network, communication nodes and information nodes are coupled in a one-to-one or one-to-many manner, with each pair mapping to each other. Information nodes are mapped by communication nodes, meaning each information node uniquely corresponds to a communication node, but one communication node can correspond to multiple information nodes. This is because within a certain range, to ensure the accurate and error-free transmission of information from each information node in the information network, each information node must designate a communication node to receive the information it obtains during operation. This enables personnel to retrieve information through the corresponding communication node when checking the operational status of each information node, facilitating effective management and monitoring of information transmission. Figure 3 is an information–communication double-layer interdependent network model of a UAV swarm. The upper layer is the information network, and the lower layer is the communication network.

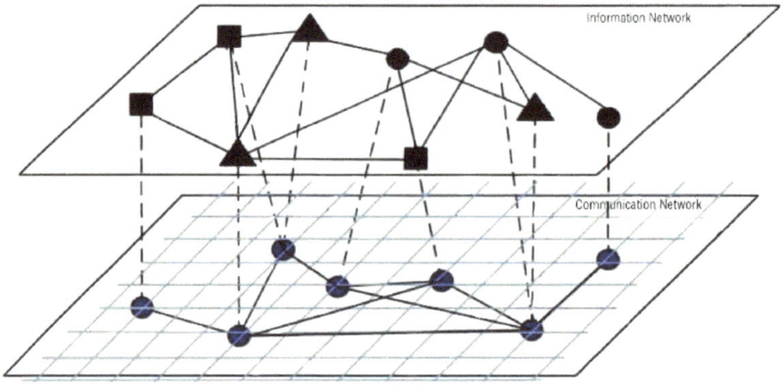

Figure 3. The information–communication double-layer interdependent network model of a UAV swarm.

The communication topology and the information network of a UAV swarm network are interdependent, forming the interdependent network model of the UAV swarm. Nodes in the communication network are mapped to information nodes in the information network in a one-to-one or one-to-many manner. This means that information nodes rely on communication nodes to interact with other nodes in the network, transmitting their perceived and processed data. Similarly, communication nodes need to perceive and process scene information through information nodes to implement corresponding functions. Generally, due to the limited energy of UAV nodes, each UAV typically carries only one task payload, leading to a one-to-one mapping relationship between UAV communication topology and the information network. However, there are rare instances of one-to-many mapping, where each UAV carries multiple task payloads. The information–communication double-layer interdependent network model of a UAV swarm is represented by $G_{P-F} = (G_P, G_F, E_{P-F})$. This representation includes a dependency matrix E_{P-F} that indicates the dependency relationship between nodes in the communication network G_P and nodes in the information network G_F. If there is a dependency between node p_i in the communication network G_P and node q_j in the information network G_F, it is expressed as $E_{P-F}(i,j) = 1$; otherwise, $E_{P-F}(i,j) = 0$. Supposing $n = |V_P|, m = |V_F|$, the dependency matrix E_{P-F} can be expressed as

$$E_{P-F} = \begin{bmatrix} e_{11} & e_{12} & \cdots & e_{1m} \\ e_{21} & e_{22} & \cdots & e_{2m} \\ \vdots & \vdots & \ddots & \vdots \\ e_{n1} & e_{n2} & \cdots & e_{nm} \end{bmatrix} \quad (8)$$

4. Vulnerability Analysis of UAV Swarm

The focus of this section is to investigate the cascading failure process of UAV networks and propose a link re-allocation rule based on interdependent networks to address this issue. Additionally, two vulnerability evaluation indicators are defined to assess the effectiveness of the reallocated network.

4.1. Process of Link Cascading Failure

For a UAV swarm network, because different UAVs carry different task loads, UAVs with different functions share data information through information interaction to complete the tasks of the whole system. Therefore, network function has a certain impact on the vulnerability of the UAV swarm network. Due to the complexity of the task scenario, the communication link between UAVs can easily encounter environmental interference leading to link interruption. For instance, UAVs equipped with various communication and imaging devices may lose connection with other UAVs in high-temperature environments or in areas with potential electromagnetic interference. Additionally, they might be unable to operate effectively in the presence of physical obstacles. In such cases, other UAVs need to take on the tasks and the link transmission of the failed UAV [22]. Once a communication link is disconnected, the information exchange between the UAVs will be affected to some extent, or cascading failure will even occur, resulting in other communication links being affected. Therefore, this paper builds an information–communication interdependent model of the UAV swarm, introduces the cascading failure theory, and analyzes the vulnerability of the UAV swarm network under different task loads.

In the UAV swarm information–communication interdependent network, failures can be categorized into intra-network failures and inter-network failures. Intra-network failures refer to the interruption of a network link, leading to the redistribution of load to other links in the network and potentially causing cascading failures. On the other hand, inter-network failures primarily result from the coupling mapping relationship between different networks. When a link in the network is interrupted, one node at each end of the link is removed, potentially causing fragmentation of the entire network. According to percolation theory, nodes in the largest connected subgraph of the network can still function normally, while nodes disconnected from this subgroup may fail, leading to the disconnection of coupling connections.

In a fire rescue scenario, the normal work of the rescue UAV needs the data information support provided by the positioning UAV, the surveying UAV, the reconnaissance UAV, and the monitoring UAV that constitute the most basic functional subgroup. The whole UAV swarm network is composed of multiple functional subgroups interleaved with each other.

However, if the communication link of a reconnaissance UAV is interrupted and the location information sent by the positioning UAV cannot be accepted, the location of the fire site cannot be accurately found and the investigation of the fire area cannot be completed. Thus, the UAV is not in the functional sub-group and cannot play its function, which is equivalent to a fault. The area that should be investigated by this UAV naturally also needs to be investigated by other UAVs. The positioning UAV needs to transmit the location information of the fire area to the other UAVs, which increases the burden of the link. Figure 4 shows a flowchart of the cascading failure of a UAV swarm network information–communication interdependent network.

Figure 5 shows the cascading failure process of the links in the information–communication interdependent network of a UAV swarm: $\{a1, a2, a3, a4, a5, a6\}$ represents a node in the communication network; $\{b1, b2, b3, b4, b5, b6\}$ represents a node in the information network; the solid line represents the communication link or information connection within the network; and the dotted line represents the dependent link between networks.

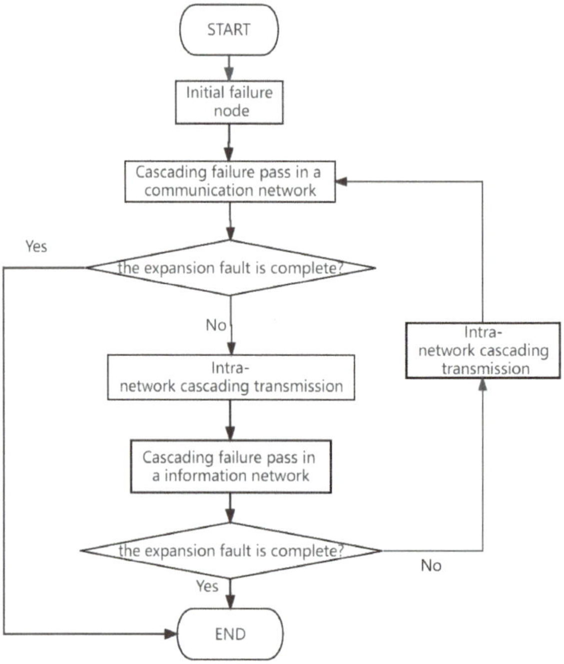

Figure 4. Process of cascading failure of UAV swarm information–communication interdependent network.

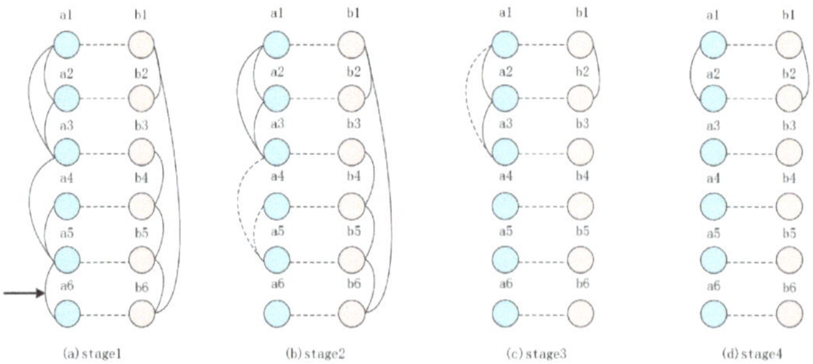

Figure 5. Cascading failure process of information–communication interdependent network link of UAV swarm.

Originally, the network is in a normal and stable operation state. At the initial moment, the link $a5a6$ in the communication network is interrupted, due to the influence of high-temperature thermal radiation. In stage 1, the data carried by link $a5a6$ are redistributed to the adjacent links $a4a5$ and $a3a5$ according to the redistribution rule. If the total amount of data on link $a3a5$ and link $a4a5$ exceeds their carrying capacity after re-allocation, another round of re-allocation will occur. In stage 2, adjacent links $a1a3$ and $a2a3$ receive the allocated data information. We assume that link $a1a3$ also fails due to the total data volume exceeding the carrying capacity. However, link $a2a3$ has strong load capacity and can withstand excess data without failure. Then, turning to the information networks, in stage 2, because links $a3a5$, $a4a5$, and $a5a6$ in the communication network of the previous stage fail, the information nodes $b3$, $b4$, $b5$, and $b6$ cannot normally interact with the other information nodes through communication links. Therefore, the information links $b3b4$, $b4b5$, $b5b6$, $b1b6$ are faulty. At stage 3, although there is still a communication link between node $a2$ and node $a3$ in the communication network, the information node $b3$ corresponding to the communication node $a3$ has no information edge connection and no longer has information interaction with the other information nodes, so the communication link $a2a3$ is invalid. Finally, the connectivity map is composed of communication nodes $a1$, $a2$, communication link $a1a2$, information nodes $b1$, $b2$, and information link $b1b2$. The remaining functional subgroup in the information–communication interdependent network of the UAV swarm is formed.

4.2. Rule of Load Distribution

The load distribution rule is the core mechanism of intermediate link failure propagation in the load capacity model, which determines the load transfer method and load transfer amount. Because the coupling link in the information–communication interdependent network of a UAV swarm only plays the role of node coupling mapping between the two layers of networks, it cannot transmit data and cannot accept the data information distributed on the interrupted link. Therefore, after a link is interrupted, the data transmitted on the link flow only on the network layer where it resides. Using the low/mid/high-tier airborne wireless network mechanism from Reference Paper [23], we applied it to the two-tier UAV network in this paper and adjusted it based on the UAV-based scenarios. In this paper, the load distribution rule is defined as the optimal allocation according to the capability of the adjacent links of the interrupted link, and the redistribution rule is

$$\Delta L_{ik} = L_{ij} \frac{C_{ik}}{\sum_{a \in \Gamma_i} C_{ia} + \sum_{b \in \Gamma_j} C_{jb}} \quad (9)$$

where ΔL_{ik} is the extra data allocated on link e_{ik} receiving interrupted link e_{ij}; a represents a neighboring node of node i, while b represents neighboring nodes of node j; Γ_i represents the set of all neighbor nodes of node v_i; Γ_j represents the set of all neighbor nodes of v_j.

Figure 6 shows a schematic diagram of link data redistribution in a fire rescue scenario after the communication network in the information–communication interdependent network of the UAV swarm is interrupted. The link e_{ij} in the network is interrupted by high-temperature radiation and cannot synchronize the information perceived by one UAV to the other UAVs, so as to normally perform tasks. The data transmitted on this link are allocated to intact links in the network using the preceding method. As a result, more data are transmitted on other links and the load becomes heavier.

The rule of redistribution begins by identifying neighbor node sets Γ_i and Γ_j of the UAV node v_i at both ends of an interrupted link e_{ij} due to high-temperature radiation or fire isolation. Then, it reallocates the data flow originally transmitted on the interrupted link to the remaining intact link e_{ik} based on a proportional allocation formula $\Delta L_{ik} = L_{ij}C_{ik}/(\sum_{i\in\Gamma_a} C_{ia} + \sum_{j\in\Gamma_b} C_{jb})$. After updating the data carried on the link e_{ik} by the formula $L_{ik}^{new} = L_{ik} + \Delta L_{ik}$ and judging whether $L_{ik} + \Delta L_{ik} > C_{ik}$ is true, if yes, the data on this link exceed its data transmission capacity, resulting in communication congestion and failure. Finally, when a new faulty link occurs, the process loops back to identifying new faulty links until none remain. The pseudocode for this algorithm is shown on Algorithm 1:

Algorithm 1 Redistribute Data After Link Failure

```
procedure RedistributeDataAfterLinkFailure(linkFailureList)
    Input: linkFailureList                        ▷ List of failed links with data and capacities
    Output: None                                  ▷ Data redistribution after link failure
    Initialization:
        Γ_i ← getNeighborNodes(linkFailure.node_i)    ▷ Neighboring nodes of node v_i
        Γ_j ← getNeighborNodes(linkFailure.node_j)    ▷ Neighboring nodes of node v_j
    for each e_ij in linkFailureList do
        for each e_ik in Γ_i do
            ΔL_ik ← L_ij × C_ik / (Σ_{a∈Γ_i} C_ia + Σ_{b∈Γ_j} C_jb)   ▷ Calculate extra data allocation
            L_ik^new ← L_ik + ΔL_ik                   ▷ Update data carried on link e_ik
            if L_ik^new > C_ik then                   ▷ Check for communication congestion
                handleCommunicationCongestion(e_ik)
            end if
        end for
    end for
end procedure
```

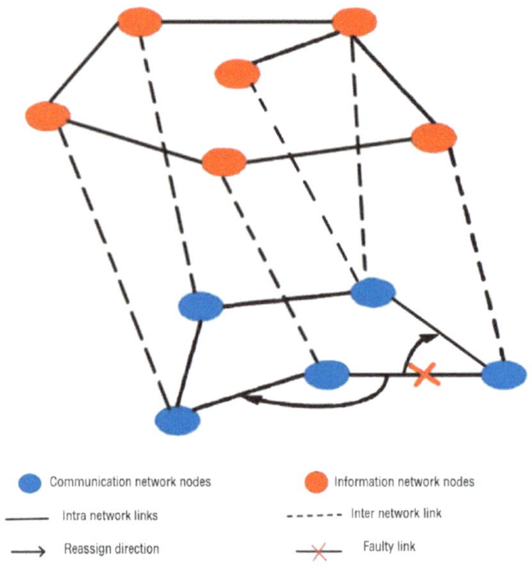

Figure 6. Diagram of redistributing data flows after a communication network link is interrupted.

4.3. Vulnerability Measurement Parameter

After the network status is stabilized, the vulnerability of the UAV swarm interdependent network after link interruption due to complex environment interference is reflected by evaluation indicators. This paper mainly evaluates the vulnerability of UAV swarm networks through the following three evaluation indicators:

(1) The threshold β_c.

When the capacity parameter β is large, the network links have a strong capacity to carry data information. If other links are interrupted due to environmental interference, cascading faults will not occur, but the cost of building a network is correspondingly high. If the capacity parameter β is small, partial link disconnection will cause partial network crash or even the whole network to crash. The threshold value β_c is the phase transition point where the network cascades, which can measure the vulnerability of the network.

The smaller the value of β_c is, the more vulnerable the network is. The larger the value of β_c is, the stronger the network robustness.

(2) The connectivity indicator P_∞

This is an important indicator to measure the connectivity of the UAV swarm network. It means that after the network cascading failure (caused by the interruption of link e_{ij} in the network due to high-temperature radiation or a fire barrier) ends, one link is randomly selected among the remaining links, and there is a possibility that this link exists in the maximum functional subgroup. Let us break this down for clarity:

We assume the number of links in the information network is k and the number of links in the communication network is l. After the disconnection of link e_{ij} and the subsequent restoration of the network to a stable state following the cascading failure, let M_{ij} represent the number of links in the remaining maximum functional subgroups of communication networks P and information networks F. The larger the value of P_∞ is, the more likely a link is to be in the maximum functional subgroup after the cascading failure is stabilized, and the stronger the network robustness is. The P_∞ is expressed by the formula

$$P_\infty = \frac{\sum_{e_{ij} \in P \cup F} M_{ij}}{(k+l)(k+l-1)} \tag{10}$$

(3) The proportion of faulty links ϕ

We assume that the number of links in the information network is k and that the number of links in the communication network is l. In a complex environment, link e_{ij} is interrupted due to complex environment interference, resulting in a network cascading failure. After the network is restored to a stable state, the number of faulty links in the communication networks P and the information networks F is ϕ_{ij}. The larger the value of ϕ is, the smaller the number of remaining links in the maximum connected subgroup after the cascading failure is stabilized, indicating that the UAV swarm network is more vulnerable. The proportion of faulty links ϕ is expressed in the formula

$$\phi = \frac{\sum_{e_{ij} \in P \cup F} \phi_{ij}}{(k+l)(k+l-1)} \tag{11}$$

5. Simulation Results

The default network parameters for the experiment were initially established for this section. Subsequently, a vulnerability analysis of the network was conducted, following link failures. Finally, experimental results were observed under different network environments by varying the number of link failures and link construction parameters.

5.1. Parameters Setting

Based on the settings of the UAV parameters in Literature [13] and Literature [18], combined with the experimental conditions achievable by the user, for this section we set simulation parameters for the UAVs. Our experiments constructed a UAV swarm network consisting of 50 UAV nodes, among which there were 25 information nodes and 25 communication nodes, each having a one-to-one coupling relationship with each other. It was assumed that the task scene was a 1000 m × 1000 m fire rescue scene. We used MATLAB for the simulations, to generate the network topology structure, and the default simulation parameters are given on Table 2:

Table 2. Paramater of simulation.

Parameters	Values
size of area	1000 m × 1000 m
flying altitude of information UAVs	20–80 m
flying altitude of information UAVs	100–300 m
number of information node	25
number of communication node	25
number of action node	10
communication range of communication UAVs	30 m
communication range of information UAVs	15 m
speed of UAVs	10–40 m/s
duration of time slot	0.2 s
minimum link transmission speed T_0	2500 bps

5.2. Vulnerability of UAV Swarm Information–Communication Interdependent Network after Links Failure

We defined a communication rule: the default communication range for information UAVs was 50 m, while communication UAVs had a default communication range of 100 m. If two UAVs were within each other's communication range, they could establish a communication link. The nodes between the two networks had a coupling mapping relationship, and the coupling weight was $\alpha = 1$. We used MATLAB (R2023a) software to generate the initial network topology, allowed UAVs to operate for 20 time slots within the specified range based on the listed parameters, and randomly generated data on their links within the range of their own maximum transmission capacity. During the UAV flight, we recorded the network topology positions of the UAVs for each experiment, preparing for subsequent experiments. We used green nodes to represent information nodes and blue nodes to represent communication nodes, and an example of a generated network topology is shown in Figure 7.

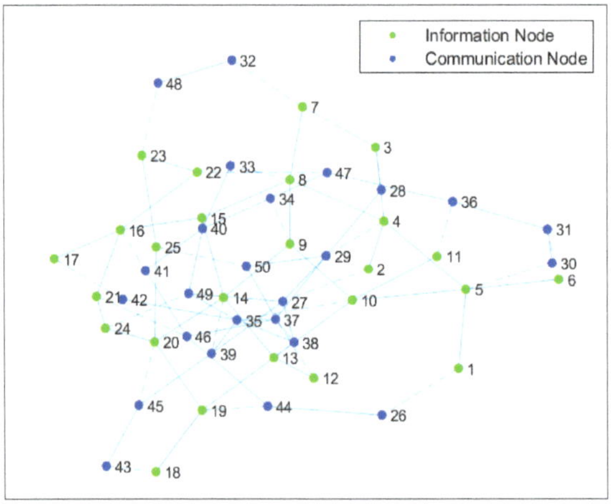

Figure 7. An example of a generated network topology.

After the network topology was generated, 10 links in the communication network were interrupted randomly by high-temperature thermal radiation in each experiment. The data from these damaged links would be re-allocated to other undamaged links according to the method mentioned above. We recorded the values for each experiment, calculating the final average. Through simulation experiments, we used the threshold β_c, connectivity indicator P_∞, and the proportion of faulty links ϕ as metrics. The simulation results are depicted in Figure 8.

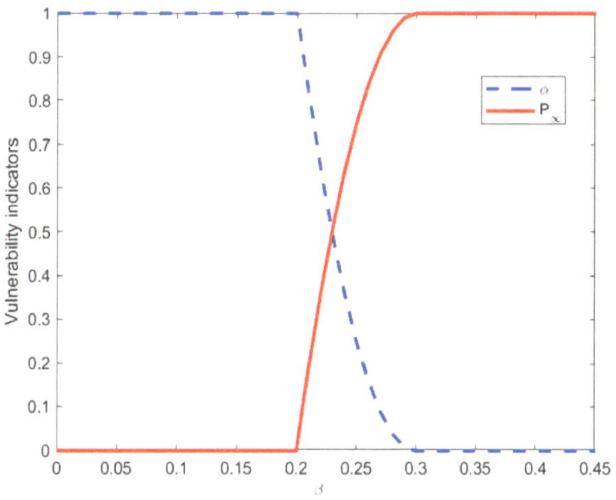

Figure 8. Vulnerability indicator change curve with capacity parameter β.

As shown in Figure 8, when the value of the capacity parameter β was between $[0, 0.2]$, the connectivity indicator P_∞ was a constant 0, and the proportion of faulty links ϕ was 1. When the capacity parameter β exceeded 0.2, β continued to increase, and the connectivity indicator P_∞ increased continuously from 0 and reached the maximum when $\beta = 0.3$, P_∞ approaching 1. The proportion of faulty links ϕ decreased with the increase of β and reached the minimum when $\beta = 0.3$ and ϕ approached 0. Later, as the capacity parameter β continued to increase, the connectivity indicator P_∞ and the proportion of faulty links ϕ remained stable and unchangeable.

According to the curve trend analysis in the figure, the vulnerability of the network was highest when the tolerance parameter $\beta \leq 0.2$, the connectivity indicator $P_\infty = 0$, and the proportion of faulty links $\phi = 1$, which can be denoted as the lower-limit threshold of the capacity parameter β_{min}. That is, if $\beta \leq \beta_{min}$, 10 links in the network were interrupted by high-temperature radiation, the network would completely collapse, due to cascading failure. With the increase of the capacity parameter β, the degree of damage brought about by cascading failures to the whole network was gradually weakened, and the robustness of the network against successive failures was gradually enhanced. But, correspondingly, the higher the cost of network construction, the less the possibility of network implementation. When $\beta = 0.3$, the robustness of the network reached the maximum. Then, when the capacity parameter β was added, the robustness of the network no longer changed, but the cost was still increasing. Therefore, $\beta = 0.3$ was the critical point at which the vulnerability of the network changed, the point at which the network changed from unstable to stable, namely, the threshold value $\beta_c = 0.3$. Furthermore, from the graph, we can observe that the rate of change of the curve varied from fast to slow. We speculate that there were not many portions of the communication links that exceeded the capacity threshold. Only a small increase in the transmission capacity of the original link would be needed to restore it to normal status.

5.3. *Influence of Parameters on Vulnerability Analysis*

Due to high-temperature heat radiation, we assumed that 1, 10, 20, and 30 links in the communication network were interrupted, respectively. To ensure authenticity, we chose these links randomly. Taking the network connectivity indicator P_∞, the proportion of faulty links ϕ, and the threshold β_c as indicators, this paper studied the cascading failure changes of the UAV cluster information–communication interdependent network model, and compared the network vulnerability under different link failure scopes. The simulation results are shown in Figures 9–12.

These figures illustrate the variations in the curve of P_∞ and the capacity parameter β when 1, 10, 20, and 30 links in the communication network were disrupted by high-temperature heat radiation, respectively. The variation trends of the three curves are similar. The general trend was that when the capacity parameter β was small, the vulnerability of the network was high. With the increase of the capacity parameter β, the robustness of the network against successive failures was gradually enhanced.

It can be seen that β_{min} and β_c gradually increased with the increase of the attack degree, which indicates that the connectivity of the network decreased with the increase of the link fault range. That is, the ability of the network to resist cascading failure decreased with the expansion of the attack degree, and the network became more and more vulnerable. This is because when the degree of network faults is large, more network links fail at the same time. As a result, the ratio of reassignment of data received by intact links increases, and the spread of successive network faults is faster.

Additionally, from these graphs, we can observe that the range of curve variation gradually expanded as the number of interfered links increased. This is because with the increase in the number of interfered links, the probability of a single link carrying interfered traffic increases, requiring a greater increase in transmission capacity to adapt to high-load scenarios.

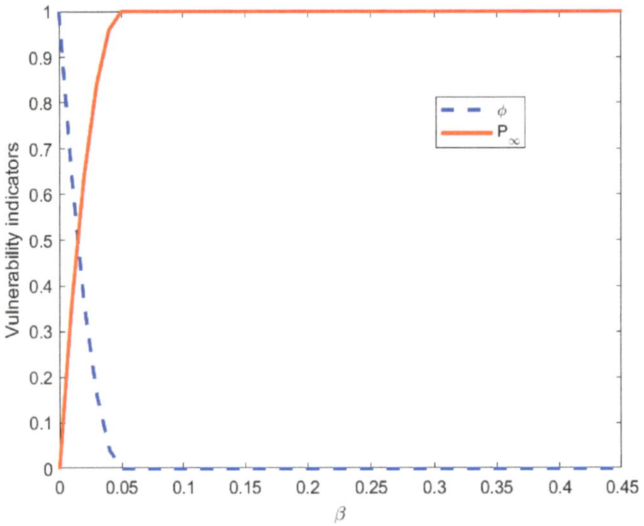

Figure 9. One link in the communication network is interrupted.

Assuming 10 links in the communication network were interrupted, we studied the cascading failure of the UAV swarm information–communication interdependent network model and compared the network vulnerability under different coupling link weights. The simulation results are shown in Figure 13.

As can be seen from Figure 13, if $\alpha = 0.4$, the vulnerability of the network is highest when $\beta \leq 0.3$. With the increase of β, the robustness of the network gradually becomes stronger, and the threshold of the network from unstable to stable is $\beta_c = 0.4$. If $\alpha = 1$, the vulnerability of the network was highest when $\beta \leq 0.2$. With the increase of β, the robustness of the network gradually became stronger, and the threshold of the network from unstable to stable was $\beta_c = 0.3$. If $\alpha = 1.3$, the vulnerability of the network was highest when $\beta \leq 0.1$. With the increase of β, the robustness of the network gradually became stronger, and the threshold of the network from unstable to stable was $\beta_c = 0.2$. And, with the increase of coupling link weight α, the lower threshold β_{min} and threshold β_c of the capacity parameter gradually decreased, and the vulnerability of the network gradually weakened. This was because when the coupling weight increased, the corresponding coupling strength also increased. According to the load setting rules, the larger the coupling strength, the more initial data transmitted on the link, the stronger the link data transmission capacity, and the more information it can carry during the link data information reassignment. If this does nothing more than to bring the construction cost of the network and the β value of the network topology composition as close as possible to β_c, it will reduce vulnerability and the network will be more robust.

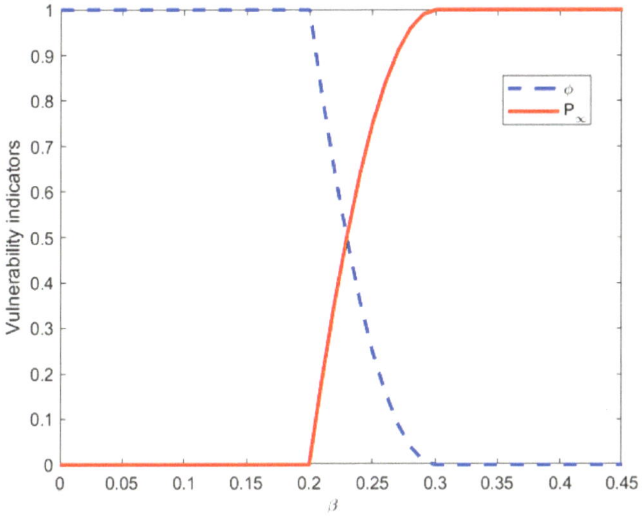

Figure 10. 10 links in the communication network are interrupted.

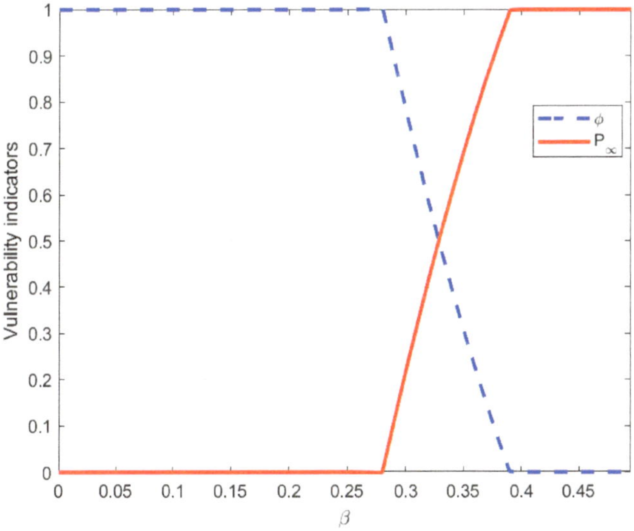

Figure 11. 20 links in the communication network are interrupted.

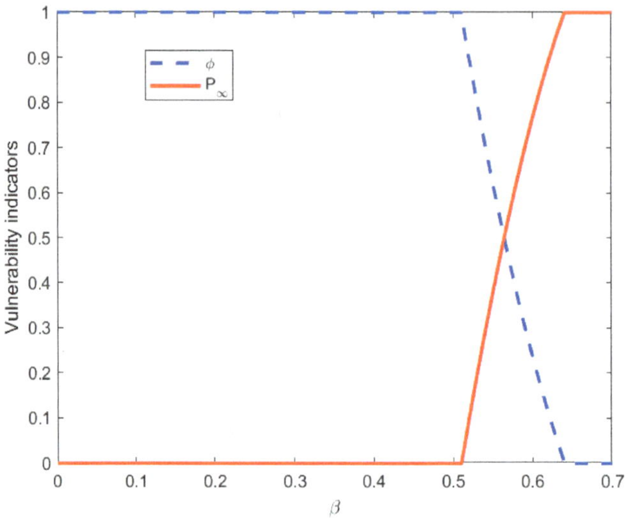

Figure 12. 30 links in the communication network are interrupted.

To continue studying the impact of the coupling link weight coefficient on the overall system performance, we varied the value of the coupling link weight coefficient to observe its effects on the low threshold β_{min} and the threshold β_c.

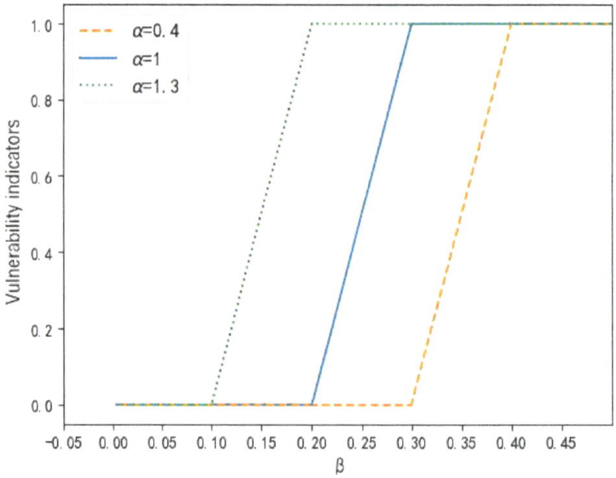

Figure 13. Vulnerability indicators change curve with capacity parameter β.

In Figure 14, we can observe that as α increased, the values of both curves decreased, reaching zero at $\alpha = 2$. Additionally, as α increased, the difference between β_c and β_{min} gradually decreased. At $\alpha = 0$, the difference between them is 0.2, while at $\alpha = 2$, the difference decreases to zero. This was because with the increase in the coupling coefficient, the link transmission capacity of the two UAV networks also increased, and their connection became tighter. Therefore, adjusting the transmission capacity of one link also increased the overall impact on the network.

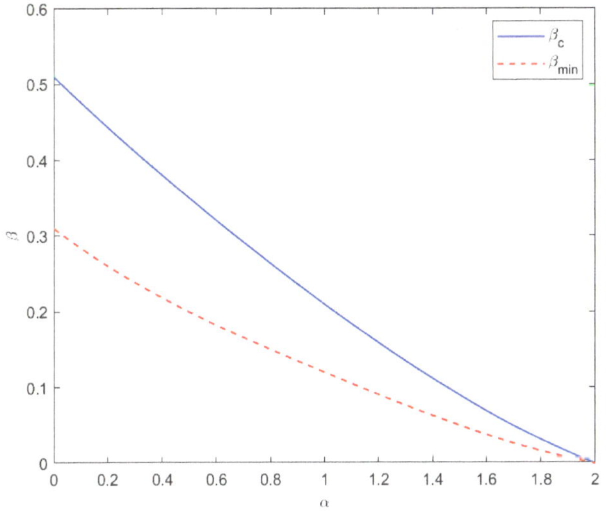

Figure 14. Threshold β change curve with α.

6. Conclusions

This paper proposes a vulnerability assessment method for UAV swarm networks with emergency tasks. Taking the UAV swarm network under a fire rescue scenario as an example, the UAV swarm network can be abstracted as a communication network and an information network. A UAV swarm information–communication interdependent network model with coupling mapping relationship was constructed to simulate the UAV swarm network with emergency tasks. On this basis, considering the successive failures of the interdependent network, a cascading failure model of the information–communication interdependent network of the UAV swarm was constructed, and the vulnerability of the network was analyzed by evaluating the cascading failures of the network. Finally, the vulnerability of the UAV swarm information–communication interdependent network under complex environment interference was analyzed by a simulation experiment, the influences of the fault range of the link in the information–communication interdependent network and of the coupling link weight on the vulnerability of the UAV swarm information–communication interdependent network were compared and analyzed, and the feasibility of the method was verified. In future work, from the perspective of network functions, we will explore the changes in network vulnerability after node failures of different functions in the UAV swarm network, and further explore the vulnerability characteristics of the UAV swarm network.

Author Contributions: Conceptualization, J.L. and Z.H.; methodology, Q.Y. (Qinghai Yang); software, Q.Y. (Qingfeng Yue); validation, X.X.; writing—original draft preparation, Q.Y. (Qinggfeng Yue); writing—review and editing, J.L. All authors have read and agreed to the published version of the manuscript.

Funding: This research was supported in part by the Natural Science Basis Research Plan in Shaanxi Province of China (2023JCYB555), and by the National Key Research and Development Program of China (2020YFB1807700).

Data Availability Statement: Data are contained within the article.

Conflicts of Interest: Author Zijia Huang was employed by the company The 20th Research Institute of China Electronics Technology Group Corporation. The remaining authors declare that the research was conducted in the absence of any commercial or financial relationships that could be construed as a potential conflict of interest

Abbreviations

The following abbreviations are used in this manuscript:

UAVs	Unmanned Aerial Vehicles
ML	Motter–Lai

References

1. Memari, M.; Shakya, P.; Shekaramiz, M.; Seibi, A.C.; Masoum, M.A.S. Review on the advancements in wind turbine blade inspection: Integrating drone and deep learning technologies for enhanced defect detection. *IEEE Access* **2024**, *12*, 33236–33282. [CrossRef]
2. Wang, K.; Yuan, Y.; Chen, M.; Lou, Z.; Zhu, Z.; Li, R. A study of fire drone extinguishing system in high-rise buildings. *Fire* **2022**, *5*, 75.
3. Cvitanić, D. Drone applications in transportation. In Proceedings of the 2020 5th International Conference on Smart and Sustainable Technologies (SpliTech), Split, Croatia, 23–26 September 2020; pp. 1–4.
4. Allodi, L.; Banescu, S.; Femmer, H.; Beckers, K. Identifying relevant information cues for vulnerability assessment using cvss. In Proceedings of the Eighth ACM Conference on Data and Application Security and Privacy, Tempe, AZ, USA, 19–21 March 2018; pp. 119–126.
5. Liu, Y.; Xu, S. Design and simulation of an algorithm for assessing the vulnerability of communication network topology. *Comput. Simul.* **2022**, *39*, 201–204+326.
6. Huang, B.; Qin, Y.; Liu, Y.; Ji, D. Vulnerability assessment and risk probability study based on generic attack trees. *Inf. Netw. Secur.* **2022**, *22*, 39–44.
7. Yang, Y. Vulnerability assessment model for government network topology based on attack tree model. *Autom. Technol. Appl.* **2022**, *41*, 116–119.
8. Wu, Y. Vulnerability assessment of power information physical systems based on bayesian attack graphs. *Electr. Power Electr. Eng.* **2022**, *2*, 6–13+55.
9. Motter, A.E.; Lai, Y. Cascade-based attacks on complex networks. *Phys. Rev. E* **2002**, *66*, 065102. [CrossRef] [PubMed]
10. Wang, B.; Kim, B.J. A high-robustness and low-cost model for cascading failures. *Europhys. Lett.* **2007**, *78*, 48001. [CrossRef]
11. Buldyrev, S.V.; Parshani, R.; Paul, G.; Stanley, H.E.; Havlin, S. Catastrophic cascade of failures in interdependent networks. *Nature* **2010**, *464*, 1025–1028. [CrossRef] [PubMed]
12. Zhao, Z.; Zhangyuan, L.I.; Guo, H.; Yang, M. Research on vulnerability of space information network based on interdependent networks. In Proceedings of the 2018 IEEE Third International Conference on Data Science in Cyberspace (DSC), Guangzhou, China, 18–21 June 2018; pp. 302–309.
13. Chen, Z.; Wu, J.; Xia, Y.; Zhang, X. Robustness of interdependent power grids and communication networks: A complex network perspective. *IEEE Trans. Circuits Syst. II Express Briefs* **2017**, *65*, 115–119. [CrossRef]
14. Liu, F.Z.; Xiao, B.; Liu, J.J.; Wang, H.R. Robustness of asymmetric dependent network under cascading failure. *J. Natl. Univ. Def. Technol.* **2021**, *43*, 49–56.
15. Gao, J.; Buldyrev, S.V.; Havlin, S.; Stanley, H.E. Robustness of a network of networks. *Phys. Rev. Lett.* **2011**, *107*, 195701. [CrossRef] [PubMed]
16. Xing, J.; Chen, C.; Zhu, Z. Cascading failure of double layer networked command information system. *Control. Decis.* **2020**, 35, 3017–3025.
17. Jia, C.; Li, M.; Liu, R. Percolation and cascading dynamics on multilayer complex networks. *J. Univ. Electron. Sci. Technol. China* **2022**, *51*, 148–160.
18. Shen, D.; Li, J. Research on military information grid cascading failure model and robustness strategy. *Syst. Eng. Electron.* **2015**, 37, 310–317.
19. Zou, Q.; Ding, L. Research on key fragile dependency links removal strategies in interdependent power and communication networks under cascading failures. In Proceedings of the 2023 3rd International Conference on Neural Networks, Information and Communication Engineering (NNICE), Guangzhou, China, 24–26 February 2023; pp. 565–570.
20. Huynh, P.K.; Rahman, M.M.; Yadav, O.P.; Le, T.Q.; Le, C. Assessing robustness and vulnerability in interdependent network infrastructure: A multilayer network approach. In Proceedings of the 2024 Annual Reliability and Maintainability Symposium (RAMS), Albuquerque, NM, USA, 22–25 January 2024; pp. 1–7.
21. Li, P.; Mao, P.; Geng, Q.; Huang, C.P.; Fang, Q.; Zhang, J.R. Research status and trend of uav swarm technology. *Aero Weapon.* **2020**, *27*, 25–32.
22. Roldán-Gómez, J.J.; González-Gironda, E.; Barrientos, A. A survey on robotic technologies for forest firefighting: Applying drone swarms to improve firefighters' efficiency and safety. *Appl. Sci.* **2021**, *11*, 363. [CrossRef]
23. Wang, D., Al-Alumed, S.A.; Shakir, M.Z. Optimized link distribution schemes for ultrareliable and low-latent communications in multilayer airborne networks. *IEEE Trans. Ind. Inform.* **2020**, 16, 5866–5873. [CrossRef]

electronics

Article

An Effective Federated Recommendation Framework with Differential Privacy

Zihang Xu [1,2], Chiawei Chu [1,*] and Shiyang Song [3]

1 Faculty of Data Science, City University of Macau, Macau 999078, China; d21092100110@cityu.edu.mo
2 Aliyun College of Data Application, Zhuhai College of Science and Technology, Zhuhai 519041, China
3 Faculty of Innovation Engineering, Macau University of Science and Technology, Macau 999078, China; 2240002754@student.must.edu.mo
* Correspondence: cwchu@cityu.edu.mo

Abstract: This paper proposes a novel federated recommendation framework that incorporates differential privacy to safeguard user privacy without compromising on the accuracy of recommendations. Unlike conventional recommendation systems that centralize user data, leading to potential privacy breaches, our framework ensures that user data remain on local devices. It leverages a federated learning approach, where a global model is trained across multiple devices without exchanging raw data. To enhance privacy protection, we integrate a specially designed differential privacy algorithm that adds carefully calibrated noise to the aggregated data updates. This mechanism ensures that the global model cannot be exploited to infer individual user information. We evaluate our framework on two real-world datasets, one from the e-commerce sector and another from the multimedia content recommendation domain. The results exhibit that our framework achieves competitive recommendation accuracy compared to traditional centralized approaches, with minimal loss in precision and recall metrics, while significantly enhancing user privacy. Our work stands as a testament to the feasibility of creating recommendation systems that do not have to choose between privacy and performance, paving the way for more ethical AI applications in sensitive domains.

Keywords: privacy protection; machine learning; federated learning; recommendation system

1. Introduction

In the era of digital transformation, recommendation systems have become indispensable tools across a myriad of platforms, enhancing user experiences by personalizing content, products, and services. These systems leverage vast amounts of data to predict and suggest items that are most likely to be of interest to users based on their past behavior, preferences, and interactions. While the utility of recommendation systems is undeniable, their reliance on personal and sensitive user data has raised significant privacy concerns. The aggregation and analysis of user data, if not properly managed, can lead to unintended privacy breaches and the exploitation of personal information.

Federated learning emerges as a promising solution to this privacy conundrum. It is a distributed machine learning approach that enables model training across multiple decentralized devices or servers holding local data samples, without exchanging them. This paradigm not only helps in safeguarding user privacy by keeping the data localized but also utilizes collaborative learning to improve the model's performance. However, federated learning itself does not guarantee absolute privacy, especially against sophisticated inference attacks that can deduce individual data points from shared model updates.

Enter differential privacy, a mathematical framework designed to provide strong privacy guarantees by adding randomness to the data or algorithms, thereby making it difficult to infer information about any individual within a dataset. Integrating differential privacy into federated learning, especially in the context of recommendation systems, presents a viable pathway to achieving a balance between personalization and privacy.

Despite its potential, the application of differential privacy in federated recommendation systems poses unique challenges. The primary concern revolves around the trade-off between privacy and utility. Excessive noise can protect privacy but may degrade the quality of recommendations, whereas minimal noise may compromise user privacy for the sake of accuracy. Moreover, the decentralized nature of federated learning complicates the uniform application and management of privacy-preserving mechanisms across different nodes.

This paper seeks to address these challenges by proposing a novel architecture for a differentially private and effective federated recommendation system. Our research aims to explore innovative approaches to integrate differential privacy into federated learning frameworks without significantly compromising the system's recommendation capabilities. We delve into optimizing the privacy–accuracy trade-off, ensuring that the system remains robust against privacy threats while maintaining high levels of personalization and user satisfaction.

Through this work, we contribute to the burgeoning field of privacy-preserving machine learning by offering insights and practical solutions that can be applied to federated recommendation systems. Our goal is to pave the way for the development of recommendation systems that not only respect and protect user privacy but also maintain the quality and effectiveness that users have come to expect.

To summarize, this paper makes the following contributions:

- We introduce a novel framework that combines federated learning with differential privacy mechanisms. This approach decentralizes data processing to keep user data on local devices, enhancing privacy without significantly compromising the accuracy of recommendations.
- This paper details the implementation of a specifically designed differential privacy algorithm that adds calibrated noise to model updates. This ensures the privacy of individual user data in the aggregated model, offering a robust privacy guarantee while maintaining the utility of the recommendation system.
- Through extensive experiments on widely recognized datasets like MovieLens and Amazon Product Reviews, this paper validates the effectiveness of the proposed framework. It demonstrates that the system achieves competitive recommendation accuracy and privacy preservation, establishing a practical balance between user privacy and personalized recommendation quality.

This paper is organized as follows. Section 2 introduces related work. Section 3 presents preliminaries of our work. Section 4 gives our method to achieve a privacy-preserving recommendation system in federated learning. Section 5 presents our empirical evaluation results and Section 6 concludes our work.

2. Related Work

2.1. Recommendation System

Recommendation systems are pivotal in navigating the vast amount of content available in today's digital age, enhancing user experience by personalizing content delivery based on user preferences and behaviors. The evolution of recommendation systems has been marked by significant advancements, from basic collaborative filtering algorithms to complex deep learning-based models [1,2].

Early recommendation systems relied heavily on collaborative filtering techniques [3,4], which make predictions about the interests of a user by collecting preferences from many users [3]. This approach was further refined through matrix factorization techniques, which decompose the user–item interaction matrix into lower-dimensional matrices, capturing latent factors associated with users and items [5,6].

With the advent of deep learning, recommendation systems have seen a paradigm shift. Neural network-based models, such as the Neural Collaborative Filtering framework [7,8], have demonstrated superior performance in capturing complex user–item interactions.

Moreover, the incorporation of contextual information, such as time and location, into recommendation algorithms has further improved their accuracy and relevance [9,10].

However, the effectiveness of these systems often comes at the cost of user privacy, as they require access to sensitive user data [11]. This has led to an increasing interest in developing privacy-preserving recommendation systems. Differential privacy has emerged as a promising approach to safeguard user privacy in recommendation systems by adding noise to the data or the algorithm's outputs, ensuring that individual user data cannot be inferred [12,13].

2.2. Federated Learning

The concept of federated learning has emerged as a groundbreaking approach to address privacy concerns in machine learning and artificial intelligence [14,15]. Initiated by McMahan et al. [16], federated learning enables model training across multiple decentralized devices or servers holding local data samples, without needing to exchange them. This approach not only helps in preserving the privacy of user data but also reduces the communication overhead associated with traditional centralized learning paradigms [17,18].

The implementation of FL has been explored in various domains, ranging from mobile keyboard prediction to healthcare and financial services, demonstrating its versatility and effectiveness in privacy-preserving data analysis [19,20]. Konečný et al. [21,22] further extended the federated learning framework by introducing optimization strategies that enhance model convergence speed. A number of recent studies also focus on reducing the required communication rounds between the clients and the central server [23,24].

In the context of recommendation systems, the adoption of federated learning is relatively recent. Pioneering studies [25,26] first applied federated learning to collaborative filtering, illustrating its potential in creating personalized recommendation systems that respect user privacy. Their work demonstrated how FL could be adapted to recommendation systems, ensuring data remain localized while achieving comparable accuracy to traditional centralized approaches.

Moreover, the integration of differential privacy within federated learning frameworks, as proposed by [27–29], has set a new standard for privacy-preserving machine learning. By adding noise to the model updates in a controlled mannver, differential privacy ensures that the trained model does not reveal sensitive information about the data on any specific client's device [30,31].

We introduce a pioneering federated recommendation system that seamlessly integrates differential privacy to ensure user data privacy while maintaining high recommendation accuracy. Distinguishing itself from existing approaches, this work leverages federated learning to process data locally on devices, thus mitigating central data collection risks. A key innovation is the implementation of a differential privacy algorithm that injects noise into aggregated data updates, safeguarding against the inference of individual user information. Through rigorous evaluation on real-world datasets from the e-commerce and multimedia sectors, the framework demonstrates a practical equilibrium between privacy protection and the quality of recommendations.

Our work differentiates itself from previous works by introducing a novel federated recommendation framework that integrates differential privacy directly into federated learning, enhancing privacy without compromising recommendation accuracy. Unlike prior approaches that primarily focused on theoretical models or specific aspects of privacy, this work presents a comprehensive solution with a custom differential privacy algorithm and empirically validates its effectiveness using real-world datasets like MovieLens and Amazon Product Reviews. It effectively addresses the critical challenge of optimizing the privacy–accuracy trade-off, offering both practical implementations and demonstrating superior performance in privacy preservation compared to earlier methods.

3. Preliminaries

3.1. Differential Privacy

Differential Privacy is a framework designed to ensure the privacy of individuals' data within a dataset while allowing for the analysis and extraction of meaningful insights. It provides a quantifiable way of protecting individuals' privacy by adding randomness to the data or the outcomes of algorithms applied to the data. The core idea is to make it mathematically improbable for anyone—even those with access to the output of a differentially private mechanism—to infer the presence or absence of any individual's data in the dataset.

A randomized mechanism $\mathcal{M}$ satisfies ϵ-differential privacy (ϵ-DP) if for all datasets D and D' that differ by at most one element (these are called adjacent datasets) and for all S within the range of $\mathcal{M}$, the following inequality holds:

$$\Pr[\mathcal{M}(D) \in S] \leq e^{\epsilon} \times \Pr[\mathcal{M}(D') \in S]$$

Here, ϵ is a non-negative parameter that quantifies the privacy loss, with lower values indicating stronger privacy.

The sensitivity of a function f, denoted as Δf, is a measure of how much the output of f can change by altering a single individual's data in the dataset. For a function $f : \mathcal{D} \rightarrow \mathbb{R}^d$, the sensitivity is defined as

$$\Delta f = \max_{D,D'} \|f(D) - f(D')\|$$

where the maximum is taken over all pairs of adjacent datasets D and D'.

The Laplace Mechanism adds noise drawn from the Laplace distribution to the output of a function f to achieve differential privacy. The scale of the Laplace noise is determined by the sensitivity of f and the desired privacy level ϵ. The probability density function of the Laplace distribution with mean 0 and scale b is given by

$$\Pr(x|b) = \frac{1}{2b} \exp\left(-\frac{|x|}{b}\right)$$

To achieve ϵ-differential privacy, the scale b is set as $\Delta f / \epsilon$.

The Exponential Mechanism is used for differential privacy in cases where the output is not numerical. It selects an output with a probability proportional to the exponential of the privacy loss parameter ϵ, divided by twice the sensitivity, times a utility function $u(D, r)$ that measures the usefulness of result r. The probability of selecting a particular outcome r is

$$\Pr(r) \propto \exp\left(\frac{\epsilon \cdot u(D, r)}{2\Delta u}\right)$$

where Δu is the sensitivity of the utility function u.

Differential privacy also provides composition theorems that describe how the privacy parameter ϵ accumulates when multiple differentially private mechanisms are applied. Sequential Composition states that if a series of k mechanisms, each providing ϵ_i-differential privacy, are applied to a dataset, the total privacy loss is bounded by $\sum_{i=1}^{k} \epsilon_i$. Parallel Composition asserts that if multiple mechanisms, each providing ϵ_i-differential privacy, operate on disjointed subsets of the dataset, the overall privacy guarantee is governed by $\max(\epsilon_i)$.

The concept of a privacy budget is crucial in differential privacy. It refers to the total amount of privacy loss (ϵ) that is allowable over the course of multiple queries or analyses. It is essential to manage and track the privacy budget to ensure that the cumulative privacy loss does not exceed a predefined threshold. By employing these principles and mechanisms, differential privacy ensures that the privacy of individuals in a dataset is protected while still allowing for valuable data analysis. This balance is crucial in a wide range of applications, from statistical analysis to machine learning, where the use of personal data is often necessary to generate insights and make decisions.

3.2. Recommendation Systems

Recommendation systems are pivotal in personalizing user experiences across various digital platforms, using algorithms to suggest items, such as products, movies, or articles, that users are likely to be interested in. These systems can broadly be categorized into three types: content-based filtering, collaborative filtering, and hybrid systems. Each employs distinct methodologies to analyze and predict user preferences.

Content-based filtering relies on item features and a profile of the user's preferences. The recommendation score, s, for a user u and item i can be calculated as

$$s(u,i) = \mathbf{p}_u \cdot \mathbf{q}_i^T$$

where $\mathbf{p}_u$ is the preference vector of user u, and $\mathbf{q}_i$ is the feature vector of item i.

Collaborative filtering makes recommendations based on the past behavior of users in the system, without requiring item metadata. User-based collaborative filtering computes the similarity between users, for instance, using the Pearson correlation coefficient:

$$sim(u,v) = \frac{\sum_{i \in I}(r_{ui} - \bar{r}_u)(r_{vi} - \bar{r}_v)}{\sqrt{\sum_{i \in I}(r_{ui} - \bar{r}_u)^2}\sqrt{\sum_{i \in I}(r_{vi} - \bar{r}_v)^2}}$$

where r_{ui} and r_{vi} are the ratings of users u and v for item i, respectively, $\bar{r}_u$ and $\bar{r}_v$ are the average ratings of users u and v, and I is the set of items rated by both users.

Item-based collaborative filtering computes similarities between items, often using the cosine similarity:

$$sim(i,j) = \frac{\mathbf{r}_i \cdot \mathbf{r}_j}{||\mathbf{r}_i|| \, ||\mathbf{r}_j||}$$

where $\mathbf{r}_i$ and $\mathbf{r}_j$ are the rating vectors of items i and j, respectively.

Matrix factorization techniques, such as Singular Value Decomposition (SVD), are commonly used in collaborative filtering to predict unknown ratings:

$$\hat{r}_{ui} = \mu + b_u + b_i + \mathbf{p}_u \cdot \mathbf{q}_i^T$$

where μ is the global average rating, b_u and b_i are the user and item bias terms, and $\mathbf{p}_u$ and $\mathbf{q}_i$ are the latent factor vectors for user u and item i.

Hybrid systems combine collaborative and content-based methods to improve recommendation quality, addressing limitations such as the cold start problem and data sparsity. The combined score might be computed as a weighted sum:

$$s(u,i) = \alpha \cdot s_{\text{CBF}}(u,i) + (1 - \alpha) \cdot s_{\text{CF}}(u,i)$$

where s_{CBF} and s_{CF} are the scores from content-based and collaborative filtering, respectively, and α is the weight that balances the two.

To evaluate the performance of recommendation systems, metrics such as Mean Absolute Error (MAE) and Root Mean Square Error (RMSE) are used:

$$\text{MAE} = \frac{\sum_{(u,i) \in T} |r_{ui} - \hat{r}_{ui}|}{|T|}$$

$$\text{RMSE} = \sqrt{\frac{\sum_{(u,i) \in T}(r_{ui} - \hat{r}_{ui})^2}{|T|}}$$

where T is the set of user–item pairs in the test set, r_{ui} is the actual rating, and $\hat{r}_{ui}$ is the predicted rating.

By employing these methodologies and metrics, recommendation systems aim to enhance user satisfaction and engagement, tailoring content to individual preferences and interests.

4. Method

This section outlines our novel method for a privacy-preserving recommendation system leveraging federated learning and differential privacy. The system model enables private, client-specific model updates using calibrated Gaussian noise to maintain a balance between user privacy and recommendation accuracy. The recommendation algorithm combines collaborative filtering and deep learning within this privacy-aware federated framework, optimizing for personalization and accuracy. Through advanced aggregation techniques and privacy budget management, the system effectively mitigates privacy risks while preserving the quality of recommendations. A general pipeline of our proposal is given in Figure 1.

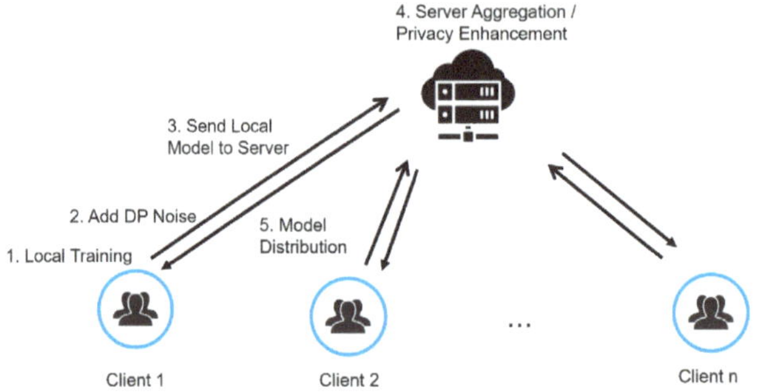

Figure 1. A general pipeline of our proposal.

4.1. System Model

Our proposed system model intricately weaves differential privacy mechanisms within a federated learning framework to construct a recommendation system that not only respects user privacy but also delivers personalized content with high precision. Operating over a distributed network, this model empowers a collaborative yet private learning environment, significantly mitigating the privacy and security concerns associated with traditional centralized systems.

The cornerstone of our model is the local model update, a process that enables individual clients to contribute to the collective learning objective without exposing their private data:

$$\Delta w_i = \nabla L(w, D_i) + \eta_i, \quad (1)$$

where Δw_i denotes the update computed by client i, derived from the gradient of the loss function L with respect to the model weights w over the local dataset D_i. To safeguard privacy, noise η_i is introduced, adhering to the principles of differential privacy. This noise is meticulously calibrated, following a Gaussian distribution $\mathcal{N}(0, \sigma^2 I)$, to balance the trade-off between privacy and the utility of the aggregated model:

$$\eta_i \sim \mathcal{N}(0, \sigma^2 I). \quad (2)$$

Secure aggregation is the next pivotal step, where updates from all participating clients are amalgamated to refine the global model. This process is encapsulated in the following equation:

$$w_{\text{global}}^{(t+1)} = w_{\text{global}}^{(t)} + \frac{1}{N} \sum_{i=1}^{N} \Delta w_i, \quad (3)$$

ensuring that the synthesis of updates enhances the model without compromising the confidentiality of individual contributions.

Client participation is inherently probabilistic, governed by their respective privacy budgets, ensuring a democratic and equitable learning environment:

$$P_i = \frac{\exp(\epsilon_i)}{\sum_{j=1}^{N} \exp(\epsilon_j)}. \tag{4}$$

At the heart of personalized recommendations lies the recommendation score, a measure that determines the relevance of items to users based on the insights gleaned from the global model:

$$S(u,i) = f(w_{\text{global}}, u, i), \tag{5}$$

where f denotes a sophisticated function that meticulously analyzes user preferences and item characteristics to generate precise recommendations.

Model convergence is a testament to the efficacy of the learning process, marked by the stabilization of the global model across successive iterations:

$$\lim_{t \to \infty} \|w_{\text{global}}^{(t+1)} - w_{\text{global}}^{(t)}\| = 0. \tag{6}$$

The differential privacy guarantee assures that the introduction or alteration of a single data point negligibly affects the outcome, which is a foundational pillar of privacy protection:

$$\Pr[\mathcal{M}(D) \in S] \leq \exp(\epsilon) \cdot \Pr[\mathcal{M}(D') \in S] + \delta. \tag{7}$$

The update frequency of the global model inversely correlates with the learning rate, highlighting the dynamic nature of the learning process:

$$\tau = \frac{1}{\gamma}. \tag{8}$$

Adjusting the learning rate is crucial for optimizing the convergence rate, ensuring the model rapidly adapts to new data insights:

$$\gamma^{(t+1)} = \beta\gamma^{(t)}. \tag{9}$$

4.2. *Privacy Mechanism*

Differential privacy provides a quantifiable guarantee that the privacy of an individual's data is maintained, even in the aggregate. This is achieved by introducing a calibrated amount of noise to the data or model updates, effectively obscuring individual contributions. Differential privacy is applied by adding noise to the model updates computed on client devices before they are aggregated by the central server. The noise-added update can be represented as

$$\Delta w_i' = \Delta w_i + \mathcal{N}(0, \sigma^2 \mathbf{I}), \tag{10}$$

where $\Delta w_i'$ denotes the privacy-preserving update from client i, and σ^2 is the variance in the Gaussian noise, which is a critical parameter in balancing privacy and utility. The calibration of noise is based on the sensitivity of the function computing the updates and the desired privacy level, formalized as follows:

$$\sigma = \frac{\Delta f \sqrt{2 \ln(1.25/\delta)}}{\epsilon}, \tag{11}$$

where Δf is the sensitivity of the function, ϵ is the privacy loss parameter, and δ is the probability of exceeding this privacy loss. This equation ensures the noise is calibrated to provide (ϵ, δ)-differential privacy.

The privacy budget, ϵ, is allocated to each client to manage the total privacy loss over multiple interactions. The allocation is adjusted dynamically based on the client's activity level and the overall system's privacy requirements:

$$\epsilon_{\text{total}} = \sum_{i=1}^{N} \epsilon_i, \tag{12}$$

ensuring that the cumulative privacy budget across all clients does not exceed the system's predefined threshold.

To mitigate the impact of noise on the aggregated model, we employ advanced aggregation techniques that enhance the utility of the noisy updates. One such technique involves weighted averaging, where updates are weighted based on their variance:

$$w'_{\text{global}} = \frac{\sum_{i=1}^{N} w'_i/\sigma_i^2}{\sum_{i=1}^{N} 1/\sigma_i^2}, \tag{13}$$

where w'_i is the noise-added update from client i, and σ_i^2 is the variance in the noise added to client i's update. To ensure the quality of recommendations, algorithms are designed to be robust against the noise introduced for privacy preservation. This involves adjusting the learning algorithm to account for the expected noise, thereby minimizing its impact on recommendation quality:

$$\hat{S}(u,i) = S(u,i) + \alpha \cdot \text{Err}(\sigma), \tag{14}$$

where $\hat{S}(u,i)$ is the adjusted score for recommending item i to user u, $S(u,i)$ is the original recommendation score, α is a scaling factor, and $\text{Err}(\sigma)$ represents the error introduced by the noise, which is a function of σ.

By integrating these advanced techniques and carefully managing the privacy budget, our federated recommendation system achieves a balance between preserving user privacy and maintaining the efficacy of personalized recommendations.

4.3. Recommendation Algorithm

The recommendation algorithm at the heart of our federated recommendation system leverages collaborative filtering and deep learning techniques, adapted to operate within the constraints of differential privacy and federated learning. This subsection outlines the algorithm's core components, including model training, personalization strategies, and the integration of privacy-preserving mechanisms.

The foundation of our recommendation algorithm is the federated averaging (FedAvg) process, which aggregates model updates from multiple clients to improve the global recommendation model. The training process for each client's local model can be expressed as

$$L_i(w) = \frac{1}{|D_i|} \sum_{(x,y)\in D_i} \ell(f(w;x),y) + \lambda\|\omega\|^2, \tag{15}$$

where $L_i(w)$ is the loss function for client i's model given the weight w, D_i is the local dataset of user–item interactions, ℓ is a loss metric (e.g., mean squared error for rating prediction), $f(w;x)$ is the predictive function of the model, y represents the true preference values (e.g., ratings), and $\lambda\|\omega\|^2$ is a regularization term to prevent overfitting. After local training, the model updates are aggregated to update the global model:

$$w_{\text{global}} \leftarrow w_{\text{global}} + \eta \sum_{i=1}^{N} \frac{|D_i|}{D} \Delta w_i, \tag{16}$$

where η is the learning rate, N is the number of clients, $|D_i|$ is the size of the local dataset, D is the total size of all datasets, and Δw_i is the update from client i. To personalize recommendations, the global model is fine-tuned on individual clients' data, allowing for tailored recommendations. The personalization step for client i can be represented as

$$w_i^* = w_{\text{global}} - \alpha \nabla L_i(w_{\text{global}}), \quad (17)$$

where w_i^* is the personalized model weight for client i, and α is the personalization learning rate. For generating recommendations, a prediction score for each user–item pair is computed using the personalized model. The score indicates the likelihood of a user's preference for an item:

$$\hat{y}_{ui} = f(w_i^*; x_{ui}), \quad (18)$$

where $\hat{y}_{ui}$ is the predicted preference score for user u and item i, and x_{ui} represents the user–item interaction features.

Based on these scores, the items are ranked, and the top-N recommendations are selected for each user:

$$R_u = \text{rank}(\hat{y}_{ui})_{i=1}^{M}, \quad (19)$$

where R_u is the ranked list of recommendations for user u, and M is the total number of items. To ensure that the recommendation process adheres to differential privacy standards, noise is added during the aggregation of model updates and the personalization step. In this way, the recommendations are generated in a manner that respects user privacy while maintaining the effectiveness of the system.

5. Experiments

To validate the efficacy and privacy guarantees of our federated recommendation system, we conducted a series of experiments focusing on various aspects, including recommendation accuracy, privacy preservation, and system scalability. This section delineates the experimental setup, the datasets employed, the evaluation metrics, and a detailed discussion of the findings.

5.1. Experimental Setup

The experiments were carried out using a simulated federated environment consisting of a central server and multiple client nodes, each with its dataset simulating user interactions with items. The client nodes were configured to represent different data distributions, mimicking real-world scenarios where user preferences and item popularity can vary significantly across clients.

5.1.1. Datasets and Evaluation Metric

We utilized two benchmark datasets widely recognized in recommendation system research:

- **MovieLens Dataset.** A collection of movie ratings by users, facilitating the evaluation of the recommendation system's ability to predict user preferences accurately.
- **Amazon Product Review Dataset.** Comprising user reviews and ratings of products, this dataset allowed us to assess the system's performance in a more diverse and sparse data environment, which is typical of e-commerce platforms.

5.1.2. Model Configurations and Privacy Settings

We implemented the following three recommendation models:

- **Collaborative Filtering:** This model is based on the assumption that users who agreed in the past tend to agree again in the future. It uses user–item interactions (ratings, likes, etc.) to predict preferences. The model structure can be user-based, item-based, or a mixture of both, employing similarity measures like cosine similarity or Pearson correlation to recommend items.
- **Content-Based Filtering:** This model recommends items based on the features of items and a profile of the user's preferences. It uses item attributes (e.g., genres, tags,

descriptions) to recommend other items similar to what the user likes, based on their past interactions. The model structure involves creating item profiles and user profiles, then matching these profiles to predict preferences.

- **Matrix Factorization techniques:** This approach decomposes the user–item interaction matrix into lower-dimensional matrices, capturing latent factors associated with users and items. The structure involves finding two lower-dimensional matrices (for users and items) whose product approximates the original matrix. Techniques like SVD, ALS (Alternating Least Squares), and SGD (Stochastic Gradient Descent) are used to optimize the factorization.

Our experiment incorporated a Gaussian noise mechanism tailored with a differential privacy parameter ϵ ranging from 0.005 to 0.05 to achieve varying levels of privacy assurance. Model training parameters included a batch size of 128 and a learning rate initially set to 0.005, which was adjusted using a decay factor of 0.99 per epoch to accommodate the diminishing gradient issue over 100 epochs. Each client processed a subset of data, typically around 10% of the total data pool, ensuring substantial data diversity and representation. Noise calibration followed the sensitivity of the data, calculated based on the maximum change observed in the user–item interaction strength, with a privacy budget (δ) set to 1×10^{-5}. Secure multi-party computation protocols were employed for aggregating updates securely, ensuring no individual client's data could be inferred from the shared updates. These parameters were validated on real-world datasets, demonstrating their effectiveness in maintaining a robust balance between user privacy and recommendation accuracy. In particular, DP was implemented in our federated recommendation system using the Gaussian mechanism. The process involved the following key steps:

1. **Noise Addition:** Gaussian noise was added to model updates from each client. The noise's standard deviation, σ, was determined based on the sensitivity of the update function, Δf, and privacy parameters ϵ and δ, as follows:

$$\sigma = \Delta f\left(\sqrt{2\ln(1.25/\delta)}/\epsilon\right).$$

2. **Privacy Parameters:** Parameters ϵ (privacy loss) and δ (probability of exceeding privacy loss) were carefully chosen to balance between privacy protection and model utility.
3. **Secure Aggregation:** Noisy updates were aggregated to update the global model securely, ensuring the final model complied with (ϵ, δ)-differential privacy.
4. **Performance Evaluation:** The trade-off between privacy protection and recommendation system performance was quantified by evaluating accuracy metrics under various ϵ and δ settings.

5.2. Results and Discussion

5.2.1. Recommendation Accuracy

Table 1 presents the accuracy metrics of a collaborative filtering recommendation system tested on two datasets, MovieLens and Amazon Product Review, with various numbers of clients (1C to 200C). The metrics include precision, recall, F1 Score, mean average precision (MAP), hit rate (HR), reciprocal rank (RR), and diversity score (DS). The selection of 200 clients (200C) as the upper limit in our experiments was based on a balance between computational feasibility and the representation of a realistic federated learning environment. This upper limit allowed us to simulate a sufficiently large and diverse network of devices, capturing the challenges and performance dynamics in a distributed learning scenario without exceeding practical resource constraints. It ensured that our findings were scalable and applicable to real-world federated systems, where the number of participating devices can vary significantly. For MovieLens, precision, recall, F1 Score, and all other metrics gradually decreased as the number of clients increased. The highest scores across all metrics were observed with the lowest number of clients (1C). A similar trend was seen with the Amazon Product Review dataset, albeit with lower scores across all metrics compared to MovieLens. The decrease in performance metrics as the number of clients increased suggests that the model may be more accurate with fewer clients or needs adjustment to scale effectively.

Table 1. Recommendation accuracy of collaborative filtering under different numbers of clients.

Dataset	Configuration	Precision	Recall	F1 Score	MAP	HR	RR	DS
MovieLens	1C	0.86	0.81	0.83	0.87	0.92	0.95	0.88
	5C	0.85	0.80	0.82	0.86	0.91	0.94	0.89
	10C	0.84	0.79	0.81	0.85	0.90	0.93	0.87
	20C	0.83	0.78	0.80	0.84	0.89	0.92	0.86
	50C	0.80	0.76	0.78	0.81	0.86	0.89	0.83
	100C	0.78	0.73	0.75	0.79	0.84	0.87	0.81
	200C	0.74	0.69	0.71	0.75	0.80	0.83	0.77
Amazon Product Review	1C	0.71	0.66	0.68	0.72	0.77	0.80	0.74
	5C	0.70	0.65	0.67	0.71	0.76	0.79	0.73
	10C	0.69	0.64	0.66	0.70	0.75	0.78	0.72
	10C	0.68	0.63	0.65	0.69	0.74	0.77	0.71
	50C	0.66	0.61	0.63	0.67	0.72	0.75	0.69
	100C	0.64	0.59	0.61	0.65	0.70	0.73	0.67
	200C	0.60	0.55	0.57	0.61	0.66	0.69	0.63

Tables 2 and 3 present the recommendation accuracy of three different filtering methods across two datasets (MovieLens and Amazon Product Review), with varying numbers of clients (from 1 to 200). Each method is evaluated based on precision, recall, F1 Score, mean average precision (MAP), hit rate (HR), reciprocal rank (RR), and diversity score (DS).

Table 2. Recommendation accuracy of content-based filtering under different numbers of clients.

Dataset	Configuration	Precision	Recall	F1 Score	MAP	HR	RR	DS
MovieLens	1C	0.82	0.73	0.77	0.82	0.85	0.91	0.81
	5C	0.80	0.74	0.76	0.80	0.85	0.93	0.83
	10C	0.80	0.72	0.75	0.77	0.86	0.88	0.84
	20C	0.81	0.74	0.79	0.78	0.86	0.91	0.82
	50C	0.75	0.69	0.73	0.75	0.80	0.78	0.77
	100C	0.73	0.65	0.68	0.76	0.79	0.84	0.77
	200C	0.72	0.67	0.67	0.71	0.73	0.78	0.72
Amazon Product Review	1C	0.67	0.61	0.61	0.64	0.70	0.74	0.71
	5C	0.64	0.60	0.62	0.67	0.73	0.74	0.67
	10C	0.65	0.57	0.58	0.64	0.73	0.69	0.66
	20C	0.62	0.57	0.58	0.63	0.69	0.72	0.65
	50C	0.60	0.56	0.58	0.63	0.69	0.71	0.62
	100C	0.59	0.52	0.57	0.62	0.66	0.71	0.62
	200C	0.52	0.51	0.52	0.57	0.60	0.63	0.58

For collaborative filtering, the highest precision, recall, and F1 Scores on the MovieLens dataset are observed with the smallest client configuration (1C). The scores generally decrease as the number of clients increases. In content-based filtering, similar to CF, the performance metrics tend to decrease with more clients. However, the starting precision and recall values for 1C are lower than those for CF. For matrix factorization, the trend of decreasing metrics with increased client numbers continues. However, the starting precision and recall for 1C are lower than those for CF but similar or slightly higher than those for content-based filtering. All methods show a trade-off between the number of clients and recommendation accuracy metrics across both datasets.

Table 3. Recommendation accuracy of matrix factorization techniques under different numbers of clients.

Dataset	Configuration	Precision	Recall	F1 Score	MAP	HR	RR	DS
MovieLens	1C	0.79	0.70	0.74	0.79	0.82	0.88	0.79
	5C	0.76	0.71	0.74	0.78	0.83	0.90	0.79
	10C	0.77	0.70	0.71	0.74	0.82	0.86	0.82
	20C	0.78	0.70	0.76	0.74	0.83	0.87	0.78
	50C	0.72	0.66	0.70	0.72	0.77	0.75	0.73
	100C	0.69	0.62	0.65	0.73	0.76	0.80	0.74
	200C	0.69	0.63	0.64	0.67	0.70	0.75	0.69
Amazon Product Review	1C	0.65	0.58	0.58	0.61	0.67	0.71	0.68
	5C	0.62	0.58	0.59	0.64	0.69	0.71	0.64
	10C	0.62	0.54	0.55	0.61	0.69	0.67	0.63
	20C	0.59	0.54	0.55	0.60	0.66	0.69	0.62
	50C	0.57	0.53	0.56	0.60	0.66	0.68	0.58
	100C	0.56	0.49	0.54	0.58	0.63	0.68	0.60
	200C	0.49	0.48	0.49	0.55	0.57	0.60	0.55

5.2.2. Privacy Preservation

Our system maintained robust privacy guarantees across all experiments. The differential privacy parameter ϵ was adjusted to explore its impact on recommendation quality, revealing a manageable trade-off between privacy and accuracy. We used Membership Inference Attack to evaluate whether the model can defend against such a privacy attack.

Tables 4–6, each displaying the Membership Inference Attack (MIA) accuracy of a collaborative filtering system under a range of differential privacy budgets for two datasets: MovieLens and Amazon Product Review. The tables show the effects of varying levels of ϵ (ranging from 0 to 0.2) on the recommendation accuracy for different numbers of clients (from 1C to 200C).

Table 4. MIA accuracy of collaborative filtering under different numbers of clients and different scales of noise.

Dataset	Configuration	1C	5C	10C	20C	50C	100C	200C
MovieLens	$\epsilon = 0.0$	0.79	0.75	0.72	0.70	0.68	0.65	0.60
	$\epsilon = 0.001$	0.77	0.73	0.70	0.68	0.66	0.63	0.58
	$\epsilon = 0.002$	0.76	0.72	0.69	0.67	0.64	0.61	0.57
	$\epsilon = 0.005$	0.74	0.70	0.67	0.65	0.62	0.59	0.54
	$\epsilon = 0.01$	0.72	0.68	0.65	0.63	0.60	0.57	0.52
	$\epsilon = 0.2$	0.70	0.66	0.63	0.61	0.58	0.55	0.50
Amazon Product Review	$\epsilon = 0.0$	0.65	0.63	0.61	0.59	0.57	0.54	0.50
	$\epsilon = 0.001$	0.64	0.62	0.60	0.58	0.56	0.53	0.49
	$\epsilon = 0.002$	0.63	0.61	0.59	0.57	0.55	0.52	0.48
	$\epsilon = 0.005$	0.61	0.59	0.57	0.55	0.53	0.50	0.46
	$\epsilon = 0.01$	0.59	0.57	0.55	0.53	0.51	0.48	0.44
	$\epsilon = 0.2$	0.57	0.55	0.53	0.51	0.49	0.46	0.42

The accuracy metrics presented are precision, recall, F1 Score, MAP, HR, RR, and DS. These metrics evaluate the performance of the recommendation system, with a particular focus on the system's resilience to (Membership Inference Attack) MIA under varying levels of privacy. The accuracy of a Membership Inference Attack (MIA) measures its effectiveness in correctly identifying training data samples and is calculated using the formula Acc $= \frac{TP+TN}{TP+TN+FP+FN}$. In this formula, TP (True Positive) and TN (True Negative) count the correctly identified training and non-training samples, respectively, while FP (False Positive) and FN (False Negative) account for the incorrectly identified samples.

Table 5. MIA accuracy of content-based filtering under different numbers of clients and different scales of noise.

Dataset	Configuration	1C	5C	10C	20C	50C	100C	200C
MovieLens	$\epsilon = 0.0$	0.77	0.73	0.69	0.67	0.65	0.63	0.58
	$\epsilon = 0.001$	0.75	0.71	0.67	0.65	0.63	0.61	0.56
	$\epsilon = 0.002$	0.74	0.70	0.66	0.64	0.62	0.60	0.55
	$\epsilon = 0.005$	0.72	0.68	0.64	0.62	0.60	0.58	0.53
	$\epsilon = 0.01$	0.70	0.66	0.62	0.60	0.58	0.56	0.51
	$\epsilon = 0.2$	0.68	0.64	0.60	0.58	0.56	0.54	0.49
Amazon Product Review	$\epsilon = 0.0$	0.63	0.61	0.59	0.57	0.55	0.52	0.47
	$\epsilon = 0.001$	0.62	0.60	0.58	0.56	0.54	0.51	0.46
	$\epsilon = 0.002$	0.61	0.59	0.57	0.55	0.53	0.50	0.45
	$\epsilon = 0.005$	0.59	0.57	0.55	0.53	0.51	0.48	0.43
	$\epsilon = 0.01$	0.57	0.55	0.53	0.51	0.49	0.46	0.41
	$\epsilon = 0.2$	0.55	0.53	0.51	0.49	0.47	0.44	0.39

Table 6. MIA accuracy of matrix factorization techniques under different numbers of clients and different scales of noise.

Dataset	Configuration	1C	5C	10C	20C	50C	100C	200C
MovieLens	$\epsilon = 0.0$	0.74	0.70	0.67	0.65	0.63	0.60	0.55
	$\epsilon = 0.001$	0.72	0.68	0.65	0.63	0.60	0.57	0.52
	$\epsilon = 0.002$	0.71	0.67	0.64	0.62	0.59	0.56	0.51
	$\epsilon = 0.005$	0.69	0.65	0.62	0.60	0.57	0.54	0.49
	$\epsilon = 0.01$	0.67	0.63	0.60	0.58	0.55	0.52	0.47
	$\epsilon = 0.2$	0.65	0.61	0.58	0.56	0.53	0.50	0.45
Amazon Product Review	$\epsilon = 0.0$	0.60	0.58	0.56	0.54	0.52	0.49	0.44
	$\epsilon = 0.001$	0.59	0.57	0.55	0.53	0.51	0.48	0.43
	$\epsilon = 0.002$	0.58	0.56	0.54	0.52	0.50	0.47	0.42
	$\epsilon = 0.005$	0.56	0.54	0.52	0.50	0.48	0.45	0.40
	$\epsilon = 0.01$	0.54	0.52	0.50	0.48	0.46	0.43	0.38
	$\epsilon = 0.2$	0.52	0.50	0.48	0.46	0.44	0.41	0.36

As the ϵ value decreases, implying stronger privacy constraints (more noise added), the accuracy metrics tend to decrease for both datasets across all configurations. This trend illustrates the trade-off between privacy and utility, where increasing privacy protection generally leads to lower accuracy of the recommendations.

The decrease in metrics is consistent across all three tables, showing a systematic degradation in model accuracy as the privacy budget becomes more stringent. Additionally, as the number of clients increases, there is a general trend of decreasing accuracy, reflecting the complexity of preserving privacy in a more distributed environment.

5.2.3. Impact of Differential Privacy

The experiments highlighted the nuanced balance between privacy guarantees and system performance. By fine-tuning the noise-addition parameters, we established an optimal setting that preserves user privacy without excessively compromising the quality of recommendations.

We present the privacy and model accuracy trade-offs in Figures 1–3. Multiple lines in the Figure, each representing different client configurations from 1C (single client) to 200C (two hundred clients), show that as the noise level increases, the accuracy for each configuration decreases. The decline is more pronounced with a lower number of clients; the 1C configuration starts with the highest accuracy and shows a sharp decline in performance as noise increases. In contrast, the 200C configuration begins with lower accuracy, which decreases more gradually with added noise. These visual data suggest that models with fewer clients are more sensitive to the addition of noise, while those with more clients are somewhat more resilient but start at a lower accuracy level.

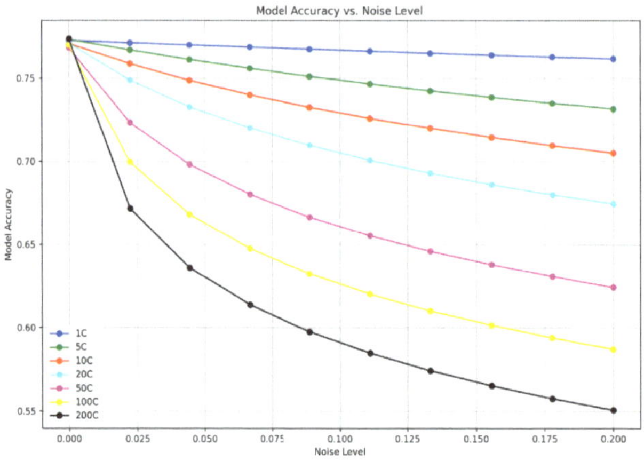

Figure 2. Trade-off between model accuracy and noise added for collaborative filtering.

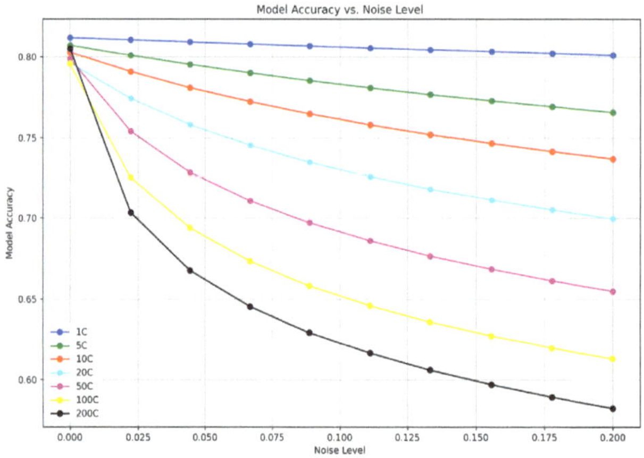

Figure 3. Trade-off between model accuracy and noise added for content-based filtering.

For content-based filtering, the first graph shows a series of curves for various client configurations (1C to 200C) where each curve markedly dips as the noise level rises from 0 to 0.2. This illustrates that even a small addition of noise can significantly lower the accuracy, with configurations that have fewer clients being the most sensitive to noise increase. Figure 4 details the effects on matrix factorization techniques, where the initial accuracy rates are generally higher across all client configurations when compared to content-based filtering. However, similar to the first graph, an increase in noise correlates to a decrease in accuracy. The decrease is more uniform across different client configurations, indicating a certain robustness in matrix factorization techniques against noise when compared to content-based filtering. These results highlight the inherent challenge in balancing privacy with utility: as the system becomes more private (through increased noise), the ability of the model to accurately recommend items diminishes. This is a critical consideration for the design and deployment of privacy-preserving recommendation systems.

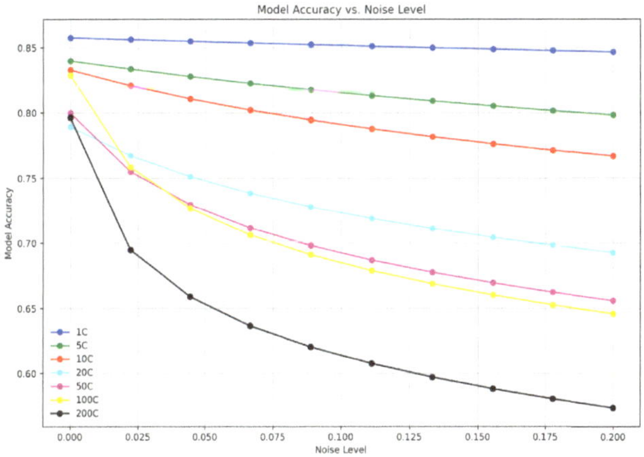

Figure 4. Trade-off between model accuracy and noise added for matrix factorization.

6. Conclusions

This paper presents a comprehensive federated recommendation system that effectively integrates differential privacy to ensure user privacy without significantly compromising the quality of recommendations. Through extensive experimentation with real-world datasets, the system demonstrates a commendable balance between privacy preservation and recommendation accuracy. The innovative integration of differential privacy mechanisms within a federated learning framework addresses the critical challenge of protecting user data while maintaining the utility of the recommendation system. The system's scalability and efficiency in handling varying numbers of clients and dataset sizes further underscore its potential for real-world applications. This work contributes significantly to the field of privacy-preserving recommendation systems, showcasing the feasibility of achieving high-quality recommendations alongside robust privacy guarantees.

Author Contributions: Conceptualization, Z.X.; Methodology, C.C.; Validation, C.C.; Formal analysis, C.C.; Investigation, S.S.; Writing—original draft, S.S. All authors have read and agreed to the published version of the manuscript.

Funding: This research received no external funding.

Data Availability Statement: Data is contained within the article.

Conflicts of Interest: The authors declare no conflicts of interest.

References

1. Tang, H.; Zhao, G.; He, Y.; Wu, Y.; Qian, X. Ranking-based contrastive loss for recommendation systems. *Knowl.-Based Syst.* **2023**, *261*, 110180. [CrossRef]
2. Sun, J.; Gao, L.; Shen, X.; Liu, S.; Liang, R.; Du, S.; Liu, S. Separated Graph Neural Networks for Recommendation Systems. *IEEE Trans. Ind. Inform.* **2023**, *19*, 382–393. [CrossRef]
3. Zhang, Z.; Patra, B.G.; Yaseen, A.; Zhu, J.; Sabharwal, R.; Roberts, K.; Cao, T.; Wu, H. Scholarly recommendation systems: A literature survey. *Knowl. Inf. Syst.* **2023**, *65*, 4433–4478. [CrossRef]
4. Zhu, Y.; Chen, Z. Mutually-Regularized Dual Collaborative Variational Auto-encoder for Recommendation Systems. In Proceedings of the WWW'22: The ACM Web Conference 2022, Lyon, France, 25–29 April 2022; Laforest, F., Troncy, R., Simperl, E., Agarwal, D., Gionis, A., Herman, I., Médini, L., Eds.; ACM: New York, NY, USA, 2022; pp. 2379–2387. [CrossRef]
5. Hou, D.; Zhang, J. BFRecSys: A Blockchain-based Federated Matrix Factorization for Recommendation Systems. In Proceedings of the IEEE International Conference on Big Data, BigData 2023, Sorrento, Italy, 15–18 December 2023; He, J., Palpanas, T., Hu, X., Cuzzocrea, A., Dou, D., Slezak, D., Wang, W., Gruca, A., Lin, J.C., Agrawal, R., Eds.; IEEE: Piscataway, NJ, USA, 2023; pp. 2283–2292. [CrossRef]
6. Shen, X.; Yi, B.; Liu, H.; Zhang, W.; Zhang, Z.; Liu, S.; Xiong, N. Deep Variational Matrix Factorization with Knowledge Embedding for Recommendation System. *IEEE Trans. Knowl. Data Eng.* **2021**, *33*, 1906–1918. [CrossRef]

7. Li, A.; Zheng, C.; Yu, G.; Cai, J.; Li, X. Filtering and Refining: A Collaborative-Style Framework for Single-Channel Speech Enhancement. *IEEE ACM Trans. Audio Speech Lang. Process.* **2022**, *30*, 2156–2172. [CrossRef]
8. Yu, X.; Zhang, X.; Cao, Y.; Xia, M. VAEGAN: A Collaborative Filtering Framework based on Adversarial Variational Autoencoders. In Proceedings of the Twenty-Eighth International Joint Conference on Artificial Intelligence, IJCAI 2019, Macao, China, 10–16 August 2019; Kraus, S., Ed.; IJCAI.org: Occitania, France, 2019; pp. 4206–4212. [CrossRef]
9. Sohafi-Bonab, J.; Aghdam, M.H.; Majidzadeh, K. DCARS: Deep context-aware recommendation system based on session latent context. *Appl. Soft Comput.* **2023**, *143*, 110416. [CrossRef]
10. Li, B.; Li, G.; Xu, J.; Li, X.; Liu, X.; Wang, M.; Lv, J. A personalized recommendation framework based on MOOC system integrating deep learning and big data. *Comput. Electr. Eng.* **2023**, *106*, 108571. [CrossRef]
11. Xu, C.; Wang, J.; Zhu, L.; Zhang, C.; Sharif, K. PPMR: A Privacy-Preserving Online Medical Service Recommendation Scheme in eHealthcare System. *IEEE Internet Things J.* **2019**, *6*, 5665–5673. [CrossRef]
12. Lee, T.; Kim, S.; Lee, J.; Jun, C. Word2Vec-based efficient privacy-preserving shared representation learning for federated recommendation system in a cross-device setting. *Inf. Sci.* **2023**, *651*, 119728. [CrossRef]
13. Zheng, X.; Guan, M.; Jia, X.; Guo, L.; Luo, Y. A Matrix Factorization Recommendation System-Based Local Differential Privacy for Protecting Users' Sensitive Data. *IEEE Trans. Comput. Soc. Syst.* **2023**, *10*, 1189–1198. [CrossRef]
14. Zhang, C.; Xie, Y.; Bai, H.; Yu, B.; Li, W.; Gao, Y. A survey on federated learning. *Knowl.-Based Syst.* **2021**, *216*, 106775. [CrossRef]
15. Yang, Z.; Chen, M.; Wong, K.; Poor, H.V.; Cui, S. Federated Learning for 6G: Applications, Challenges, and Opportunities. *arXiv* **2021**, arXiv:2101.01338.
16. McMahan, H.B.; Moore, E.; Ramage, D.; y Arcas, B.A. Federated Learning of Deep Networks using Model Averaging. *arXiv* **2016**, arXiv:1602.05629.
17. Wu, R.; Scaglione, A.; Wai, H.; Karakoç, N.; Hreinsson, K.; Ma, W. Federated Block Coordinate Descent Scheme for Learning Global and Personalized Models. In Proceedings of the Thirty-Fifth AAAI Conference on Artificial Intelligence, AAAI 2021, Thirty-Third Conference on Innovative Applications of Artificial Intelligence, IAAI 2021, The Eleventh Symposium on Educational Advances in Artificial Intelligence, EAAI 2021, Virtual Event, 2–9 February 2021; AAAI Press: Washington, DC, USA, 2021; pp. 10355–10362. [CrossRef]
18. Xue, Y.; Niu, C.; Zheng, Z.; Tang, S.; Lyu, C.; Wu, F.; Chen, G. Toward Understanding the Influence of Individual Clients in Federated Learning. In Proceedings of the Thirty-Fifth AAAI Conference on Artificial Intelligence, AAAI 2021, Thirty-Third Conference on Innovative Applications of Artificial Intelligence, IAAI 2021, The Eleventh Symposium on Educational Advances in Artificial Intelligence, EAAI 2021, Virtual Event, 2–9 February 2021; AAAI Press: Washington, DC, USA, 2021; pp. 10560–10567. [CrossRef]
19. Xu, B.; Xia, W.; Zhao, H.; Zhu, Y.; Sun, X.; Quek, T.Q.S. Clustered Federated Learning in Internet of Things: Convergence Analysis and Resource Optimization. *IEEE Internet Things J.* **2024**, *11*, 3217–3232. [CrossRef]
20. Ang, F.; Chen, L.; Zhao, N.; Chen, Y.; Wang, W.; Yu, F.R. Robust Federated Learning with Noisy Communication. *IEEE Trans. Commun.* **2020**, *68*, 3452–3464. [CrossRef]
21. Charles, Z.; Konečný, J. Convergence and Accuracy Trade-Offs in Federated Learning and Meta-Learning. In Proceedings of the 24th International Conference on Artificial Intelligence and Statistics, AISTATS 2021, Virtual Event, 13–15 April 2021; Banerjee, A., Fukumizu, K., Eds.; PMLR: Proceedings of Machine Learning Research; Volume 130, pp. 2575–2583.
22. Zhu, C.; Xu, Z.; Chen, M.; Konečný, J.; Hard, A.; Goldstein, T. Diurnal or Nocturnal? Federated Learning of Multi-branch Networks from Periodically Shifting Distributions. In Proceedings of the Tenth International Conference on Learning Representations, ICLR 2022, Virtual Event, 25–29 April 2022; OpenReview.net: Amherst, MA, USA, 2022.
23. Wang, H.; Muñoz-González, L.; Hameed, M.Z.; Eklund, D.; Raza, S. SparSFA: Towards robust and communication-efficient peer-to-peer federated learning. *Comput. Secur.* **2023**, *129*, 103182. [CrossRef]
24. Malan, E.; Peluso, V.; Calimera, A.; Macii, E. Communication-Efficient Federated Learning with Gradual Layer Freezing. *IEEE Embed. Syst. Lett.* **2023**, *15*, 25–28. [CrossRef]
25. Vyas, J.; Das, D.; Das, S.K. Vehicular Edge Computing Based Driver Recommendation System Using Federated Learning. In Proceedings of the 17th IEEE International Conference on Mobile Ad Hoc and Sensor Systems, MASS 2020, Delhi, India, 10–13 December 2020; IEEE: Piscataway, NJ, USA, 2020; pp. 675–683. [CrossRef]
26. Yang, L.; Tan, B.; Zheng, V.W.; Chen, K.; Yang, Q. Federated Recommendation Systems. In *Federated Learning—Privacy and Incentive*; Yang, Q., Fan, L., Yu, H., Eds.; Lecture Notes in Computer Science; Springer: Cham, Switzerland, 2020; Volume 12500, pp. 225–239. [CrossRef]
27. Zhou, Y.; Liu, X.; Fu, Y.; Wu, D.; Wang, J.H.; Yu, S. Optimizing the Numbers of Queries and Replies in Convex Federated Learning with Differential Privacy. *IEEE Trans. Dependable Secur. Comput.* **2023**, *20*, 4823–4837. [CrossRef]
28. Jiang, B.; Li, J.; Wang, H.; Song, H. Privacy-Preserving Federated Learning for Industrial Edge Computing via Hybrid Differential Privacy and Adaptive Compression. *IEEE Trans. Ind. Inform.* **2023**, *19*, 1136–1144. [CrossRef]
29. Yang, X.; Huang, W.; Ye, M. Dynamic Personalized Federated Learning with Adaptive Differential Privacy. In Proceedings of the Advances in Neural Information Processing Systems 36: Annual Conference on Neural Information Processing Systems 2023, NeurIPS 2023, New Orleans, LA, USA, 10–16 December 2023.

30. Rajkumar, K.; Goswami, A.; Lakshmanan, K.; Gupta, R. Comment on "Federated Learning with Differential Privacy: Algorithms and Performance Analysis". *IEEE Trans. Inf. Forensics Secur.* **2022**, *17*, 3922–3924. [CrossRef]
31. Naseri, M.; Hayes, J.; Cristofaro, E.D. Local and Central Differential Privacy for Robustness and Privacy in Federated Learning. In Proceedings of the 29th Annual Network and Distributed System Security Symposium, NDSS 2022, San Diego, CA, USA, 24–28 April 2022; The Internet Society: Reston, VA, USA, 2022.

electronics

MDPI

Article

A Proof-of-Multiple-State Consensus Mechanism for Mobile Nodes in Internet of Vehicles

Feng Zhao [1], Ruimin Cheng [2], Chunhai Li [1,*], Zhaoyu Su [2], Guoling Liang [2] and Changsong Yang [3]

[1] Guangxi Engineering Research Center of Industrial Internet Security and Blockchain, Guilin University of Electronic Technology, Guilin 541004, China; zhaofeng@guet.edu.cn
[2] School of Information and Communication, Guilin University of Electronic Technology, Guilin 541004, China; ruimincheng@mails.guet.edu.cn (R.C.);19022201001@mails.guet.edu.cn (Z.S.); guolliang@mails.guet.edu.cn (G.L.)
[3] School of Computer Science and Information Security, Guilin University of Electronic Technology, Guilin 541004, China; csyang@guet.edu.cn
* Correspondence: chunhaili@guet.edu.cn

Abstract: Blockchain technology provides a reliable information access environment for the Internet of Vehicles, but the high latency and complex computing consensus mechanism in blockchain make it difficult to port to onboard devices. Recently, there are many methods to reduce the time cost of consensus by optimizing node grouping or reducing redundant calculations, but this would lower the security level of the blockchain. To address these issues and reduce the adverse effects of frequently changing channel quality on consensus results, a consensus mechanism based on vehicle comprehensive state factors for nodes selection (PoMS) is proposed. Firstly, the vehicle nodes utilize the machine learning model to predict local driving parameters and broadcast the predicted results to the other nodes. Secondly, each node uses interactive data to calculate the state values, and the leader comprehensively evaluates the nodes participating in the consensus and selects the nodes as relays. Finally, we also adopted a double-layer blockchain structure to accelerate the selection process of relay nodes. In order to verify the performance of the proposed consensus algorithm, we conducted tests on transmission time and communication quality. The experimental results show that compared to traditional consensus mechanisms, the algorithm proposed in this paper can reduce time overhead by an average of 12.7% and maintain a good transmission rates under a certain number of malicious nodes.

Keywords: Internet of Vehicles; blockchain; consensus mechanism; node selection

1. Introduction

The rapid development of the automotive industry and the Internet of Vehicles (IoV) has escalated concerns regarding the security of vehicle networks [1]. A primary benefit of the Internet of Vehicles (IoV) is the enhancement of traffic safety and efficiency, notably through real-time vehicle information sharing. While most vehicle information requires sharing only among nearby vehicles, certain types (e.g., announcements) demand broader dissemination. However, due to the extensive user privacy contained in these data, they are easily leaked during storage and distribution, posing significant risks to users. The presence of data security and privacy protection issues [2] presents numerous difficulties and challenges for the IoV messaging process. Given the emergence of blockchain technology, with its benefits of decentralization, immutability, and transparency [3], well-suited to the IoV complex scenarios, it can alleviate various security issues in the transmission and distribution of in-vehicle data, thereby transforming the IoV traditional centralized architecture and gaining widespread application within IoV.

In recent years, blockchain technology, particularly its consensus mechanism [4], has emerged as a significant research focus, attracting considerable scholarly interest.

Blockchain technology integrates various technologies, including P2P networks, smart contracts, consensus mechanisms, and cryptography, culminating in an innovative form of distributed ledger technology. Its decentralized, tamper-proof, traceable, and transparent characteristics afford it vast application potential in the Internet of Vehicles (IoV), particularly in addressing issues of centralization, data security, and privacy protection. Initially, blockchains employ a Proof-of-Work (PoW) mechanism, which necessitated extensive computations among nodes for transaction verification.

Despite guaranteeing network security, the mechanism's high computational resource consumption makes it difficult to implement in actual scenarios with a range of computational requirements. Later suggestions focus on the PBFT algorithm to address Byzantine fault tolerance problems and Proof-of-Stake (PoS) consensus mechanisms and their improvements [5,6]. In addition, the IoV requirement for low latency and the arithmetic bottlenecks present in vehicles limit the wider application of traditional consensus algorithms within the IoV. These traditional algorithms, despite their advancements, have limitations. First, they are designed for cryptocurrency protection and the impact of mobile nodes' dynamic characteristics is ignored in the process of consensus.

Building on the existing Proof-of-Work consensus algorithms, this paper presents an improved message transmission model for vehicular networks. The goal of the model is to ensure transmission security and stability while addressing the deterioration of communication quality brought on by fast nodes mobility in vehicular networks. It makes use of a consensus mechanism that is based on Quality of Service (PoMS). The network is initially divided into different service areas based on communication states, and nodes are first loosely clustered together. Then, using the obtained data to determine its future travel conditions, a trained machine learning model forecasts the vehicle's movement state. This method improves the efficiency and dependability of network communication by having the model determine the best transmission path. The main contributions of this article can be summarized as follows:

(1) We achieve consensus in different partitions and manage it uniformly through a two-layer chain to speed up the consensus process.
(2) We have developed a consensus on speed change factors for mobile nodes in the network so that they can adapt to dynamic networks.
(3) Based on this, we propose the PoMS consensus algorithm that takes multiple factors into account to evaluate vehicle levels and filter out better relay nodes based on this. The experiment shows that our method improves efficiency and security.

2. Related Work

In recent years, there has been an increasing integration of blockchain into the Internet of Vehicles (IoV), with the aim of considering complex vehicle scenarios and improving the provision of blockchain services in the IoV. This has led researchers to propose new consensus algorithms [7–9]. Currently, blockchain-based IoV models [10] are on the rise, leveraging decentralization, immutability, and transparency to transform traditional centralized IoV architectures. This widespread application offers significant development prospects for the IoV. Currently, significant research efforts are aimed at refining the blockchain's consensus mechanism to eliminate inefficiencies and resource waste of traditional consensus methods. Various consensus algorithms are developed that are tailored to different scenarios [11,12] and improve communication efficiency over classic consensus mechanisms.

Existing consensus mechanisms mostly refine and improve classic schemes such as Proof-of-Work (PoW) [13] and Byzantine Fault Tolerance (PBFT) [14]. The PoW algorithm requires users to perform time-consuming and complex calculations, which incurs significant costs in terms of time, equipment, and energy. The PBFT algorithm resolves node breakdown in asynchronous environments caused by malicious attacks and software errors. Current algorithms achieve a fault tolerance of $(n-1)/3$, ensuring liveliness and security. In [15], an improved DPoS algorithm is proposed that provides higher throughput and a two-layer blockchain structure for improved consensus efficiency and scalability. In addition, there are also many similar approaches to [16], which combine multiple traditional consensus mechanisms to create new consensus mechanisms. However, these classic improvement schemes tied to the static node environment have problems in systems with frequently changing node communication quality. In [17], a novel lightweight PoBT (Proof of Block and Transaction) algorithm and integration framework for the IoT blockchain is proposed, which can verify transactions and blocks with reduced computation time. Literature [18] introduces Proof of Credit (PoC), a blockchain protocol that focuses on fairness and includes a self-verification and hybrid incentive mechanism that is resistant to double-spend and self-serving mining attacks. However, the protocol oversimplifies the Proof-of-Work process to effectively select the leader nodes. Ref. [19] minimizes consensus size and network overhead by dividing nodes into communication groups and assigning node roles based on trust factors, thereby optimizing communication resources. An efficient consensus algorithm is proposed in paper [20] to reduce the communication overhead, where the leader dynamically adjusts the reputation values of nodes according to their behavior and allows high-performing nodes to transmit data efficiently. This approach significantly improves the responsiveness of the blockchain, especially in large node environments. While these consensus mechanisms optimize the dynamic attributes of the network, they primarily address the communication overhead between nodes without considering the continuous mobility of nodes. The EPoW consensus introduced in [21] shortens the waiting time for arithmetic mining by executing the algorithm regularly. It also improves consensus efficiency by managing a specific set of miners and assigning multiple accounting rights. These methods prioritize changing reputation scores and aim to limit malicious nodes within the network. However, they do not sufficiently consider the communication process between nodes.

The environments assumed by existing consensus algorithms are predominantly static and immutable. Therefore, this paper focuses on the specific requirements of IoV scenarios, especially with regard to mobile node communication. Based on various consensus schemes from previous research, we improve these models and propose a special consensus algorithm that aims to improve data quality and communication efficiency with a focus on data security during the transmission process.

3. Proposed System Model

3.1. Architecture

The mobile vehicles in the system form an in vehicle self-organizing network (VANET), which uses relays to complete message transmission. This decentralized network structure is very compatible with blockchain. Considering the dynamic characteristics of the network, communication between vehicles is achieved through the Dedicated Short Range Communication (DSRC) protocol.

This paper models the rapid mobility of numerous vehicles within the IoV scenario, with the comprehensive structure of the proposed vehicle messaging model shown in Figure 1. The model includes an edge layer with mobile vehicles and roadside units (RSUs), a blockchain layer with selected RSUs and a trusted third party (Third Party Trusted Authority (TA).

Mobile Vehicles: In this model, mobile vehicles act as primary data generators, continuously producing and transmitting significant amounts of data. Every vehicle has an on-board unit (OBU) with different computing power and storage capacity. Vehicles continuously collect data about their position, speed and direction of travel and send it to nearby vehicles and RSUs, creating the basic communication infrastructure of the IoV network. This information is not only fundamental to communication, but also serves as a crucial parameter in the consensus mechanism that assigns points to vehicles for leader node selection based on their travel status. Additionally, each vehicle is equipped with a Transient Protection Device (TPD) to store important key and identity information provided by a trusted third party.

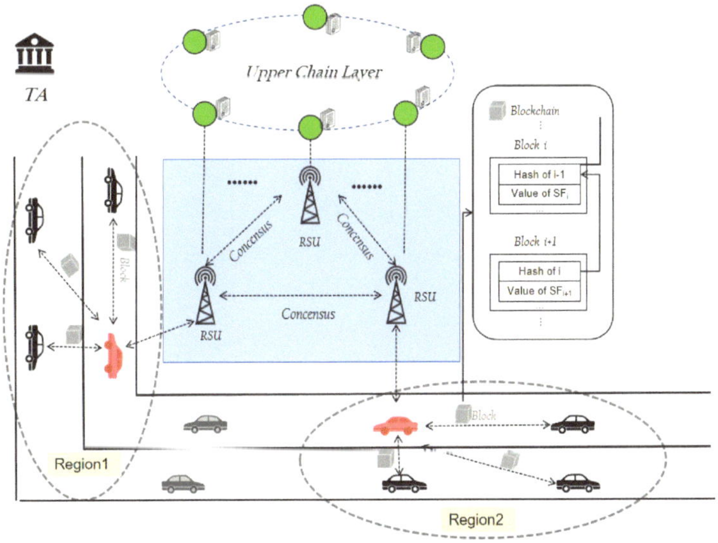

Figure 1. System Architecture.

Roadside Unit (RSU): It is arranged at a certain density on both sides of the road and maintains communication with the vehicle via the DSRC protocol commonly used in the IoV. The RSU receives and checks various information sent by the vehicle. Once validated, RSUs forward the information to the leading node, package it and upload it to the blockchain ledger. Meanwhile, RSUs communicate with each other via a wired connection.

Trusted Third Party: The Trusted Third Party (TA) is responsible for the identity and key management of the entire blockchain and is usually considered completely trustworthy and free from any malicious behavior. TA has powerful computing and storage capacities and takes over the daily work. Today's operation and maintenance of the blockchain. TA is also responsible for initializing the blockchain network, generating the system parameters, and requesting all joining vehicles to complete the registration of their identity information. Vehicles wishing to join the blockchain must first submit a registration application to TA, and only those vehicles that pass the application can join the blockchain.

Blockchain: We use a public blockchain as the decentralized underlying architecture to instantiate VANET in our scheme. The RSU validates messages based on a consensus algorithm and registered vehicles can access the blockchain via RSUS to obtain the necessary traffic flow data [22].

3.2. Implementation Process

The vehicles in the model travel on the road at different speeds depending on the predetermined density of the area. The driving process of the vehicles regularly sends their own driving data, including driving direction, driving speed, coordinate position, etc., to the RSU in the sub-region, where the RSU has larger storage space and stronger computing power of the collected vehicle data to calculate In the next action, the vehicles, which are still within the communication range of the RSU within a certain period of time, are included in the group. The schematic diagram of regional division is shown in Figure 2, where vehicles of the same color represent being within the jurisdiction of the same RSU.

In order to improve message forwarding speed, this article chooses a special grouping method based on relative position information and travel speed prediction. This method means that vehicles with similar driving status in a specific area are classified as the same group. After completing the first round of message transmission, RSU nodes collect position information and speed information for all vehicles involved in communication, and each individual RSU selects a set of vehicle nodes that meet the conditions for sending the grouping identifier in close proximity and the vehicles with the same identifier are recognized by the network as the same group in the subsequent consensus process. The execution process of the consensus algorithm in each round is shown in Figure 3.

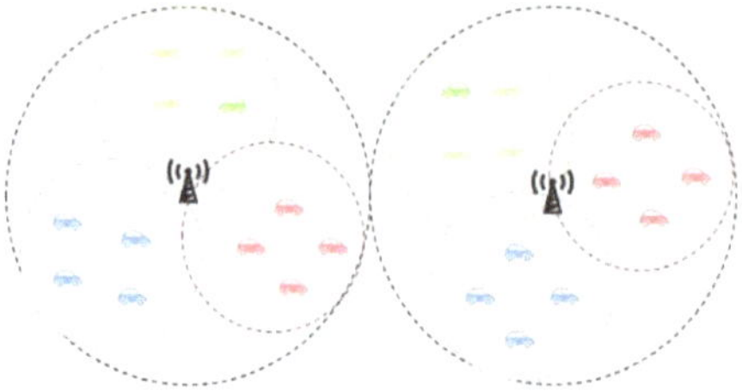

Figure 2. Schematic diagram of grouping.

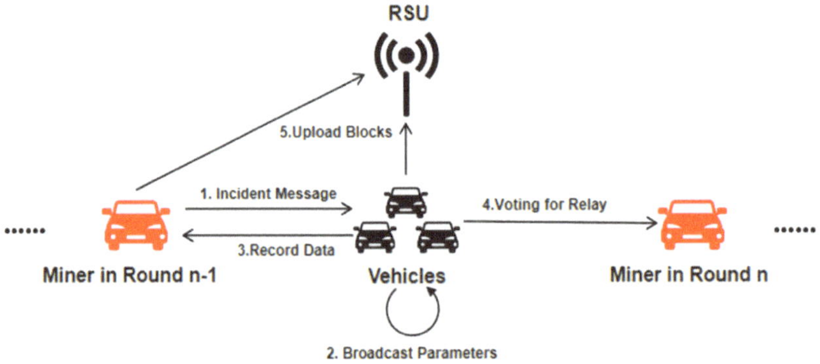

Figure 3. Consensus implementation.

After completing a certain number of rounds of consensus, the state of vehicle movement has changed significantly compared to that before consensus, and at this point the RSU needs to regroup the nodes again using the collected vehicle information. The regrouping process is similar to the initial grouping, in which the RSU removes the vehicles that have left or are about to leave a certain area from the previous group and the newly entered vehicle nodes that meet the entry criteria for the group into the Partitioned network involves participating in the subsequent consensus.

4. Consensus Mechanism Based on Integrated State

4.1. Speed Prediction Models

The vehicle speed prediction method used in this paper is based on the Long Short-Term Memory (LSTM) network model [23], which aims to predict short-term vehicle speed. The model's training data comes from the simulation environment, which includes the state data of several vehicle nodes at different points in time, such as vehicle speed, acceleration and road vehicle density information at any time. The model focuses on short-term speed predictions rather than long-term macro predictions because the simulation environment cannot fully reproduce the special factors in real-world conditions such as weather changes and holidays. This short-term prediction method can more accurately reflect the real situation in the simulation environment. Vehicle the driving speeds over a historical period are $\left[\mathrm{v}_\mathrm{i}^1, \mathrm{v}_\mathrm{i}^2, \cdots, \mathrm{v}_\mathrm{i}^\mathrm{n}\right]$, and the prediction model obtains the speed in the future Δt speed after a certain period of time, which will be the basis for subsequent state value calculations $\left[\mathrm{v}_\mathrm{i}^{1+\Delta t}, \mathrm{v}_\mathrm{i}^{1+\Delta t}, \cdots, \mathrm{v}_\mathrm{i}^{1+\Delta t}\right]$. The outputs of these models describe the possible driving state of a specific vehicle i in the future, rather than the average speed of all vehicles in the network. This is due to the relatively short monitoring time for changes in vehicle status. We are concerned about the movement mode of each vehicle node rather than the overall state changes of traffic flow. This will be an important parameter for subsequent state value calculations.

4.2. PoMS Consensus Algorithm

The flow of this consensus algorithm is as follows: Given the inefficiencies inherent in the traditional proof-of-work consensus algorithm, especially its wasteful use of system resources, this study introduces a modified proof-based consensus mechanism. This adjustment replaces the computationally intensive hash value verification with a scenario-adapted, comprehensive quality score verification process.

(1) Initialization: This study establishes a blockchain-based vehicular mobility network, described as an open, distributed peer-to-peer network in the broader vehicular network context. It denotes the total number of vehicle nodes in the network as n, where each node potentially becomes a ledger-maintaining node through competitive rotation. The total number of Roadside Unit (RSU) nodes is represented by m, where each RSU is part of a smaller network and maintains a local blockchain record.

(2) Mobility Process: Once the vehicle nodes enter the mobile stat, RSU nodes start sending messages continuously. Vehicles that receive broadcasts from RSUs respond by initiating mining activities. Using reliable on-board sensors, the vehicle collects position, speed and additional data, uses a pre-trained network model and inputs travel information to predict its state over an upcoming period, and then logs the predicted state data. The vehicle calculates its value, summarizes these findings in a block, documents essential parameters and forwards this to the mining node to complete the uplink and storage processes.

(3) Relay Nodes Selection: After receiving the position information and state prediction information of each vehicle, the RSU nodes begin to analyze all values for analysis. The time taken by each node to submit the block and the calculated value show a reverse trend, such as:

$$t_w = \frac{\tau}{SF} \tag{1}$$

where the SF represents a special value, State-Factors, which will be explained in the next section, and the parameters τ are used to ensure that the waiting time is within reasonable limits. Nodes with better channel states can transmit blocks earlier, reducing the waiting time for information transmission. At the same time, differentiate the period during which different nodes transmit blocks to prevent multiple nodes from initiating communication requests at the same time, causing transmission conflicts, and to avoid the calculations becoming untrustworthy.

(4) Messages Delivery: After the relay node is selected, the message is delivered through the chosen node, repeating the selection process throughout the delivery phase until the message count reaches the system-defined threshold. The threshold specifies both the required number of messages for delivery and the maximum hop count for message forwarding. It is determined by the road department based on the different communication requirements.

4.3. State-Factors Calculations

The SF value indicates the channel state and relative position of vehicle node i at time t, signifying its capability to relay messages. Nodes periodically send beacon messages to collect mutual position and velocity data. A relative condition value is calculated from this data, which serves as a crucial reference for the integrated quality factor. The prediction interval's time point is set with the current time denoted as t. Vehicle nodes employ a pre-trained learning model to predict future states. Each node inputs its coordinates, speed, and direction into the model, which then calculates the state information for the moment $t2$. The node forwards the result to the RSU for storage and management. The nodes forward the result to the RSU for storage and management. The RSU evaluates the status of the vehicle nodes at $t2$, regroups those within its jurisdiction, and excludes nodes out of communication range. Within each blockchain network group, nodes calculate their values and record them in blocks for transmission to the mining node.

The calculation is divided into three parts: (1) the difference between the current driving state of the vehicle and the predicted driving state; (2) the probability that the vehicle successfully sends a message to a neighboring node, the channel status; (3) the computing power of the integrated CPU which that their ability to process the messages and status data received. The calculation of these three factors is described below:

(1) $P(diff_i)$: This value indicates the probability that the message delivery at time $t2$ exceeds the range threshold, effectively preventing delivery errors due to longer distances caused by nonisotropic vehicle movements, which can lead to excessive separation of relay nodes. Assuming that the position of vehicle node i when in $t2$ is $P_i^{t2} = (X_i^{t2}, Y_i^{t2})$, for the distance difference between node i and node j after the time interval Δt is expressed as:

$$D_{i,j}^{\Delta t} = \left((X_i^{t2} - X_j^{t2})^2 + (Y_i^{t2} - Y_j^{t2})^2 \right)^{1/2} - D_{i,j}^{t1} \tag{2}$$

This study focuses on short-term forecasting, particularly on predicting vehicle movement within a few seconds. Consequently, we approximate the speed change of a single vehicle node over a short period of time as a uniform acceleration, a model that is generally consistent with the scenario. By expressing the velocity of node i at the $t2$ moment in time is denoted as v_i^{t2} and the velocity of node j is denoted as v_j^{t2}, then the vehicle's relative movement in the horizontal direction during the time interval Δt. The relative distance travelled in the horizontal direction during the time interval can be expressed as:

$$D_{ijx}^{\Delta t} = \left(\left(v_{ix}^{t2} - v_{jx}^{t2} \right) - \left(v_{ix}^{t1} - v_{jx}^{t1} \right) \right) \cdot \frac{\Delta t}{2} \tag{3}$$

The longitudinal axes are similar, so by synthesising them the relative distances between vehicle i and vehicle j can be varied as follows:

$$D_{i,j}^{\Delta t} = \sqrt{(D_{ijx}^{\Delta t})^2 + (D_{ijy}^{\Delta t})^2} \tag{4}$$

However, the relative distance does not directly reflect the probability of successful communication between vehicles, and the following function is used to reflect the relative relationship between distance and communication range:

$$P_{dis} = 1 - \frac{D_{i,j}^{\Delta t}}{R} \tag{5}$$

As the proximity between two vehicles increases, P_{dis} approaches 1, suggesting a higher likelihood of successful single communication. Conversely, a greater distance results in a negative P_{dis}, diminishing the competitiveness of the nodes that are further away.

Considering the difference in the vehicle's travel direction, we add an additional speed factor to the range factor, which ensures that the more vehicle nodes there are that maintain the same travel direction as node i, the higher the probability that the node will win the competition and become a relay node. In this article we define the speed factor as:

$$P_{velocity}^{i,j} = 1 - \alpha \frac{|v1 - v2|}{|v1| + |v2|} \tag{6}$$

where α is the weight of the adjustment factor weights, and when this value is larger, the greater the effect of the speed factor on $P(diff_i)$ produces, the greater the effect it has, and vice versa, the weaker it is. For each vehicle's communication range we define as R, so the probability that vehicle i and vehicle j are still in communication range after time period Δt

can be expressed as $P_{range}^{i,j} = \frac{\Delta D_{i,j}^{t2}}{R}$. It can be obtained that the value of $P\left(diff_i\right)$ between node i and node j at the moment $t2$ is expressed as:

$$P\left(diff_{i,j}\right) = P_{dis} \cdot P_{velocity}^{i,j} \tag{7}$$

And for a single vehicle node i, there is

$$P(diff_i) = \sum_{j=1, j \neq i}^{n_{range}} P\left(diff_{i,j}\right) \tag{8}$$

n_{range} indicates the number of communicable mobile vehicles within the management area of the RSU to which the vehicle nodes belong.

(2) $P(SINR_i)$: If node i is selected as a relay node, its channel quality at the moment $t2$ is expressed as:

$$SINR_{i,j} = \frac{\left(D_{i,j}\right)^{-\gamma}}{\sum_{k=1, k \neq i}^{n_{range}} \left(D_{j,k}\right)^{-\gamma} + P_n} \tag{9}$$

where $D_{i,j}$ is the same as above, $D_{j,k}$ denotes the distance between node j and the remaining interfering node k, while γ is the path loss exponent and P_n denotes the noise power. To ensure that the channel quality meets the message delivery requirements, we set a threshold for the SINR value. If it is higher than this threshold, it means that the message can be transmitted smoothly. That is, the term can be written as:

$$(SINR_i > \beta) = \left(\frac{\left(D_{i,j}\right)^{-\gamma}}{\sum_{k=1, k \neq i}^{n_{range}} \left(D_{j,k}\right)^{-\gamma} + P_n} \geq \beta \right) \tag{10}$$

A transformation is performed to obtain:

$$(SINR_i > \beta) = \left(D_{i,j} \leq \left(\beta \left(\sum_{k=1, k \neq i}^{n_{range}} \left(D_{j,k}\right)^{-\gamma} + P_n \right) \right)^{-\frac{1}{\gamma}} \right) \tag{11}$$

Within a packet network, every time after exchanging information about all vehicles in a group through broadcast messages, vehicle i that wants to compete for a relay node calculates its own SINR value based on different vehicle position differences and finally aggregates them. This process can be represented as follows:

$$f\left(SINR_{i,j}\right) = \begin{cases} 1, \ if \ D_{i,j} \leq \left(\beta \left(\sum_{k=1, k \neq i}^{n_{range}} \left(D_{j,k}\right)^{-\gamma} + P_n \right) \right)^{-\frac{1}{\gamma}} \\ 0, \ otherwise \end{cases} \tag{12}$$

Eventually, there is:

$$P(SINR_i) = \frac{\sum_{j=1, i \neq j}^{n_{range}} f\left(SINR_{i,j}\right)}{n_{range}} \tag{13}$$

(3) $P(Com_i)$: The value in question is dictated by the computational capability of the onboard processor, with those possessing higher arithmetic capacities enjoying a significant advantage. Given the different instruction set architectures and hardware components of CPUs, and given that a significant portion of a processor's computing capacity is dedicated to performing prediction tasks, the experiments aim to use program execution time as a metric to measure performance differences among CPUs. The main frequency of the processor, denoted by f, is a critical parameter that significantly influences its computing performance. In addition, the average number of instruction cycles is written as N_{avg} and

the number of instructions to be executed under different architectures is denoted as N_{num}, we can get the time spent by the CPU to execute the programme:

$$T_{exc} = \frac{N_{avg} \cdot N_{num}}{f} \tag{14}$$

The time taken by different vehicle nodes to run the programme is rightfully different, and nodes that can perform tasks faster will be more likely to be selected as relay nodes. In order to facilitate a subsequent more intuitive comparison of the difference in SF_i values between different nodes, this paper sets an acceptable maximum value of the running time, T_{max}, and when a node is unable to end the procedure within this time limit, it is considered that the node's computational capability does not satisfy the requirements, and it is out of the running for the miner node. Therefore, there are:

$$P(Com_i) = \frac{T_{exc}}{T_{max}} \tag{15}$$

Thus, the final SF_i value can be obtained:

$$SF_i = P(diff_i) \cdot P(SINR_i) \cdot P(Com_i) \tag{16}$$

Due to the constraints imposed on the parameters, both the first and third terms clearly fall within the range (0, 1). The second term, which represents a summation, spans the interval [0, nrange]. Consequently, the overall value range for is set to [0, nrange).

4.4. Voting Options

After calculating the value, the node initiates a local vote among the remaining nodes. Only when the number of votes inclined towards "agree" exceeds the threshold of votes, will the node be considered an honest node. Verified vehicles can package messages and send them to the miner node to participate in the next round of relay node competition, and such messages are marked as valid messages. Conversely, for vehicles below this threshold, the nodes vote "reject", meaning communication is not possible or denied. A node is considered honest and can only forward its packet to the miner node for the next relay node election if it receives a majority of "acceptance" votes, marking its messages as valid. Conversely, nodes that do not receive enough approval votes are considered malicious for that consensus round, their messages are considered invalid, and ignored by the miner nodes as harmful to the network. After enough valid messages are collected in a consensus round, miner nodes rank these messages according to their values. The node with the highest value is selected as the next relay node. If two nodes i and j have identical SF values, the miner node compares their acceptance votes. The node with more acceptance votes is considered more capable of message delivery and is therefore more suitable as a forwarding node. If the miner node fails to collect enough valid messages within the allotted time, it ends the current round of consensus and requests other nodes to begin the next round.

5. Security Analysis

5.1. Message Validation

After each message is received, it needs to be verified by the miner node [24]. The inability to verify can be classified into two cases: (a) for correct messages verified as error messages; (b) for error messages verified as correct messages. Suppose the percentage of malicious nodes among all nodes is p, and the malicious nodes always take the behaviour of initiating an error message or giving a malicious voting tendency. Thus the probability of generating an error message is p, the probability of generating a correct message is $1 - p$, the probability that a message cannot be verified in the system is denoted as:

$$F = p_m \cdot Pr(n_m \geq n_{vote}) + [1 - (1 - p_m) \cdot Pr(n_h \geq n_{vote})] \tag{17}$$

The former represents the n_m the probability that a malicious node casts enough votes for the wrong message to be authenticated as correct, and the latter denotes the probability that a miner node does not receive a sufficient number of votes such that the correct message cannot be successfully authenticated. And from Chernoff's inequality:

$$Pr(n \geq n_{vote}) \leq e^{\frac{-(n_{vote}-\mu_n)^2}{(\mu_n+n_{vote})}} \tag{18}$$

where n can denote the number of malicious or honest nodes, and μ_n denotes the expected value of the corresponding variable. It can be seen that with the same percentage of malicious nodes, due to the monotonically decreasing nature of the function, we are able to continuously reduce the probability of verification failure by increasing the voting threshold.

5.2. Attack Methods

The consensus mechanism works within a federated blockchain and requires a license from all participating nodes. In this framework, the vehicles communicate exclusively with other nodes and vehicles in the federated blockchain. Despite these precautions, potential threats [25–27] that can disrupt the blockchain network still exist. The next section explains how the PoMS algorithm counteracts such attacks.

Double Spending Attack: The double spending attack is a widespread form of attack in blockchain technology. The PoMS consensus mechanism verifies every transaction message. For a double-spending attack to be successful, the initiator of the fraudulent message must be verified as legitimate, which means that the initiator has a number of votes that exceeds the threshold set by the system, as follows. By adjusting the value threshold for successful message validation, we can change the difficulty of successful message validation, challenging attackers who want to perform a double-spending attack. At the same time, manipulating a malicious node to obtain voting rights is not possible because the value calculation relies on predicting relative speed and position. Given the frequent changes in a vehicle's motion state within a consensus round, it is difficult to ensure that the state factor of a malicious node exceeds the state of normal nodes, so the algorithm can effectively prevent double-spending attacks.

False message attack: Malicious nodes can significantly disrupt network communications by sending false messages, including false status factors or numerous invalid message frames. The algorithm presented here encodes the sender's identity in each broadcast message frame along with a unique sequence number to identify the message, allowing RSUs to easily locate the sender vehicle. Penalties are imposed on malicious activities by reducing the network weight of the node, thereby curbing further adverse actions.

Malicious rating attack: Malicious nodes can negatively rate other nodes to reduce their weight and increase their chances of becoming a miner node. However, the consensus algorithm presented in this article includes a voting mechanism. The presence of sufficient honest nodes participating in the voting ensures the integrity of the algorithm and renders the voting of a single malicious node ineffective in changing the outcome.

Sybil attack: A hex attack is an attack in which an attacker using multiple virtual identities sends false messages in the system, compromising the security of the system. However, no matter how the malicious nodes forge the identity information and message IDs, the status factor of the message sender is calculated in the same way, and a large number of similar SF values can be easily detected by the RSU and then recorded, and the conflict mechanism is triggered, when the miner node compares the received values. When the miner nodes compare the received values, the conflict mechanism is triggered. If the relay node cannot be selected after frequent triggering of this mechanism, the consensus in this round will be reset. This effectively prevents switching.

6. Simulation Results

The simulation experiments in this paper are conducted based on the OMNET platform, incorporating the urban traffic simulation software SUMO (https://sumo.dlr.de/docs/index.html (accessed on 16 April 2024)) to complete the visualisation function of the network, to simulate the process of message passing in a complex scenario of multi-vehicle movement at a certain speed, and to analyse the performance of the proposed blockchain and PoMS consensus.

The vehicle mobility model used in this simulation is the Freeway model proposed in [28], where the vehicle is limited to the driving road and the vehicle speed relationship can be expressed as:

$$v_i(t+1) = v_i(t) + random(\,) * a_i(t) \tag{19}$$

where $a_i(t)$ represents the acceleration constant of vehicle i at time t, which is consistent with our analysis above. In our initial setup, the vehicle sends message packets every 0.1 s, and a total of approximately 2000–4000 message data will be sent during the simulation duration. Each message contains a data volume of 512 KB. For vehicle nodes that frequently send information, the simulation uses the MAC protocol to control the forwarding of message packets at the Data Link Layer, which prevents message conflicts between vehicles.

In the network simulation environment, the value of the neighbourhood node threshold nrange of the vehicles is kept below 40 in the experiments and the density of the vehicles within the whole map is kept at 100 nodes/km^2, which is set according to the derivation in the literature [29] to ensure that the vehicles can remain free to drive during the simulation without being blocked due to the over-dense traffic. The results obtained are the average of 100 simulation runs.

Figure 4 shows the probability that vehicle-generated message packets successfully reach their destination at different average movement speeds. The results show that the success rate of data transmission continues to decrease as vehicle speed increases, especially in high-speed scenarios where transmission becomes significantly more difficult. The main reason is that a vehicle traveling at high speed may leave the reachable area of the message before communication is established, resulting in packet loss. For this situation, the relative speed factor is defined in this document. Vehicles traveling at high speeds in the opposite direction receive lower campaign weights to reduce the likelihood of communication equipment failure. In low-speed scenarios, the consensus mechanism proposed in this study performs slightly better than other approaches. Especially in the high-speed scenario, the relay nodes using the PoMS algorithm perform better than PoET in literature [27] and TIA in literature [30], although the packet loss rate still inevitably increases. This is attributed to the fact that the algorithm takes into account the speed fluctuations and effectively avoids the problem that the distance between nodes exceeds the communication range due to the speed difference, thereby performing well in terms of transmission efficiency.

Figure 5 shows the effect of vehicle speed on node consensus delay. Higher speed increases the difficulty of selecting the relay node, which in turn increases the time required for the consensus process. With the same number of nodes, the PoMS algorithm is able to complete the consensus process in less time and with higher quality at different average speeds. This is due to the algorithm's prediction of speed fluctuations, which effectively resists the effects of driving state changes. The effect of speed fluctuations of mobile nodes is not considered in any of the schemes [27,30], where the consensus delay increases rapidly with higher node mobility. On the other hand, in the literature [29], a probabilistic model is used in the PoQF to simulate the speed change while combining the vehicle location information for consensus between nodes, which effectively reduces the consensus time of the vehicle in the mobile state, but the algorithm's effectiveness decreases, when the speed reaches a higher threshold. The algorithm proposed in this article takes the speed factor into account. The algorithm proposed in this article attenuates the impact of relative speed changes on consensus by taking the speed factor into account, ensuring that the future driving speeds predicted by the model are more accurate than the probabilistic predictions.

This allows PoMS to filter out better relay nodes within a fixed communication distance to ensure a more stable and reliable connection. At high driving speeds, the consensus time of PoMS is reduced by an average of 13.3% compared to the method in literature [26].

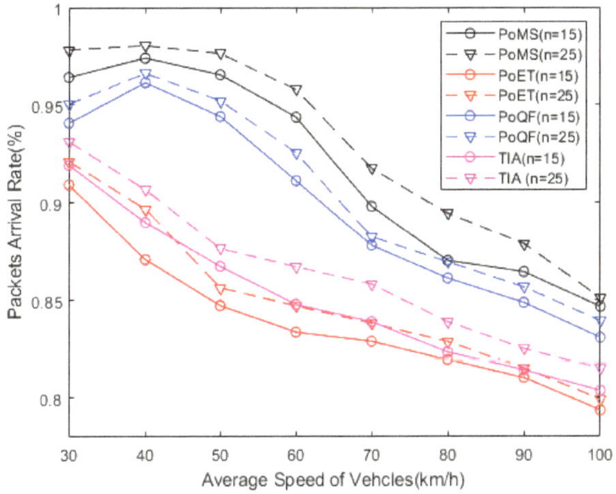

Figure 4. Success rate of message transmission at different speeds.

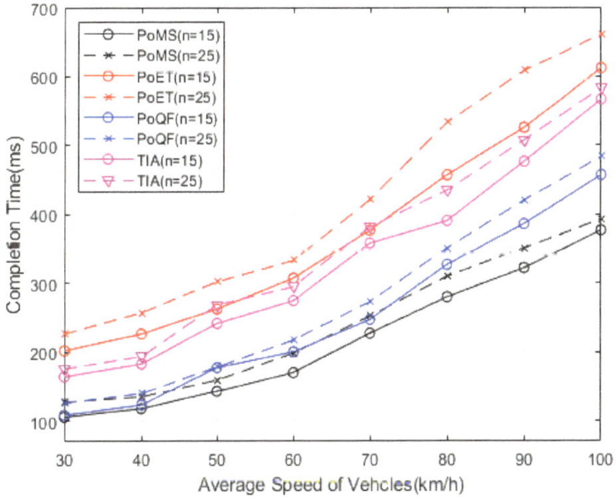

Figure 5. Consensus time at different speeds.

Figure 6 illustrates the variation in the time required for the vehicle to complete consensus for different probabilities of malicious node generation. Malicious nodes disrupt the network by generating useless packets with no information load, consuming resources, or interrupting message transmission. Therefore, the question of how to effectively identify malicious nodes as relay nodes and reduce their probability has become an important research topic. The PoMS algorithm proposed in this study is able to verify all node behaviors in the next consensus round by recording node behaviors and reporting them back to the blockchain, thereby reducing the weight of malicious nodes during the selection process. As the probability of malicious nodes increases, the increase of invalid messages in the network has a significant impact on the speed of consensus execution. In networks with less malicious nodes, the time cost in [27] is mainly the baseline waiting time, while [29] and PoMS perform similarly; in networks containing more malicious nodes, [30] it spends more rounds to check credible nodes for the election period and the waiting time increases; The PoQF determines the normality of behavior based on the node's votes. The more malicious nodes there are, the longer it takes to get enough votes, the larger the number of malicious nodes, which increases the time consumption. and the PoMS consensus shows more efficient resistance by assigning weights based on the historical behavior of nodes. As the number of malicious nodes increases, RSU nodes can collect node behavior information and report back to miner nodes more quickly, thereby improving the anti-interference ability of the network. In a high probability malicious node environment, the consensus time required by PoMS is reduced by 9.8% on average.

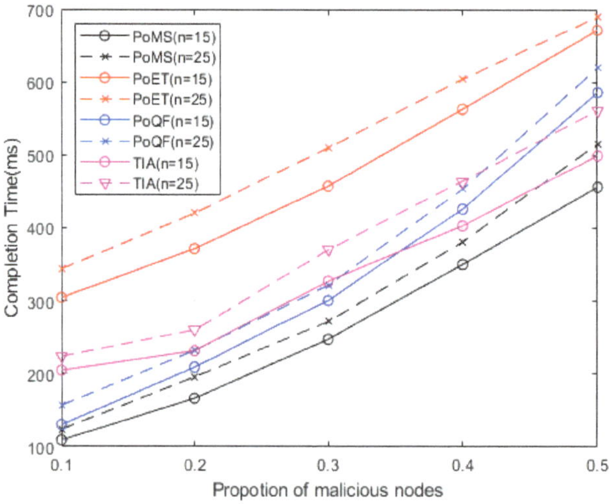

Figure 6. Consensus time for different number of malicious nodes.

Figure 7 shows the resilience of PoMS to different proportions of malicious nodes in the network. The upper blockchain of the algorithm records the behavior of vehicles in the system and dynamically adjusts the weights of nodes in the consensus process according to their performance to resist the impact of malicious nodes on the system. As the proportion of malicious nodes increases, more invalid blocks are generated in the network and the validity of miner nodes' collected values and the number of votes decrease, resulting in slower blockout. However, it can still be seen that the throughput of the blockchain proposed in this paper decreases more slowly, and in the presence of malicious nodes, PoMS consensus is still the more powerful algorithm, maintaining a more efficient blockout efficiency in all cases.

Figure 8 shows the average time spent for each additional hop of a message in the network. The number of message hops in PoMS reaches the specified threshold. The number of message hops in PoMS reaches the set threshold and it is proven that the message has been successfully transmitted to the destination and the entire network establishes a communication link. Malicious nodes increase the time it takes for miner nodes to collect enough blocks, which leads to an increase in the selection time of each relay node, thus affecting the time to complete the final round of consensus. The PoMS algorithm has a relative speed and a relative distance The calculation in the PoMS algorithm causes the miner nodes to select more distant vehicles as relay nodes as much as possible and to connect within the communication range in fewer hops during the transmission process final destination, effectively reducing the average time spent per hop.

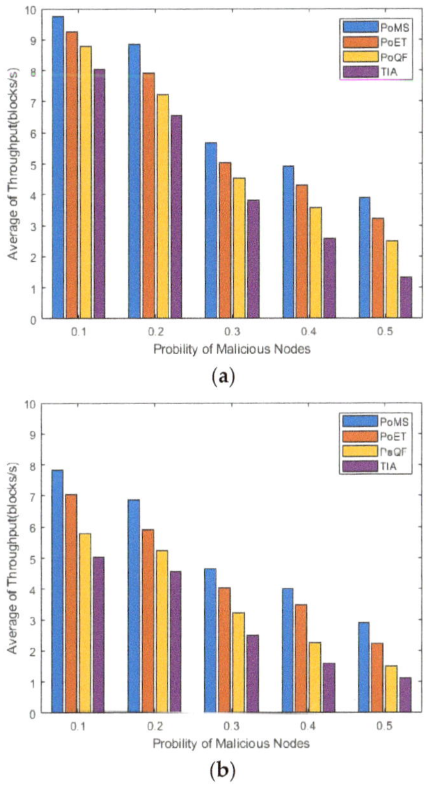

Figure 7. Variation of throughput with different occupancy of malicious nodes: n = 15 in (**a**) and n = 25 in (**b**).

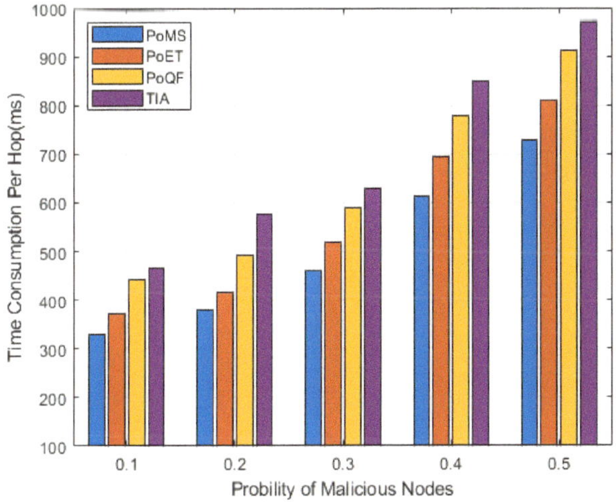

Figure 8. Single hop time with different occupancy of malicious nodes.

While Figure 9 shows the effect of vehicle speed on the time per hop. the PoET consensus time overhead has nothing to do with the vehicle speed itself, and the reason for its time increase lies more in the increased difficulty of establishing communication connections at high speeds; SF_i Compared with [29], the consensus proposed in this paper increases the weight of the speed parameter in the state factor, and distinguishes between same-direction and opposite-direction vehicles. $SF_i > SF_j$, whereupon the miner nodes are able to complete the construction of forward transmission links more easily, reducing the time spent on each message hop.

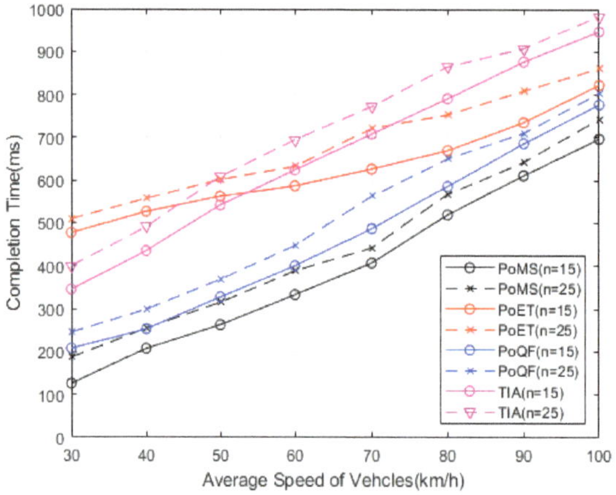

Figure 9. Effect of vehicle speed on single hop time.

Figure 10 shows the ability of other normal nodes to successfully participate in consensus when there are different percentages of malicious nodes in the network. A specific reputation mechanism in the literature [30] ensures that honest nodes can be effectively verified to participate in the consensus when malicious nodes exist in the system; The algorithm proposed in this article is able to receive fewer blocks of valid votes as the number of malicious nodes increases, and the number of nodes participating in the consensus gradually decreases. However, with the function of RSU to record the malicious behavior of nodes, the algorithm can still allow the remaining nodes to successfully complete consensus if half of the nodes are malicious nodes and the network is able to resist the attack of malicious nodes.

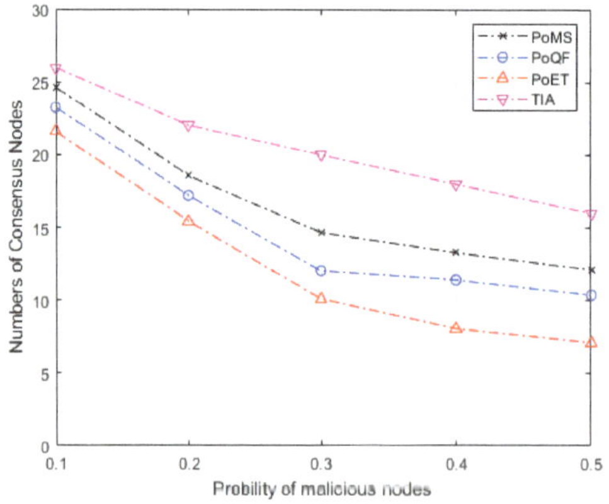

Figure 10. Number of nodes involved in mining.

In summary, the experimental tests conducted in this article demonstrate that the proposed consensus algorithm has less time overhead and better transmission rate compared to the selected consensus. This is due to the algorithm optimizing the computational difficulty required for nodes to obtain accounting rights, and dynamically adjusting the weights of different nodes based on multiple state factors ($P(diff_i)$, $P(SINR_i)$ and $P(Com_i)$). Nodes with excellent communication conditions in the network are more likely to become relays, and the voting verification mechanism of nodes limits the harm that malicious nodes can cause to system security.

7. Conclusions

This paper analyzes the current research landscape on blockchain technology in the Internet of Vehicles (IoV) and presents a blockchain solution that uses the PoMS consensus algorithm. This solution is designed to optimize the selection of relay nodes for message dissemination within the IoV. Using a machine learning model, we predict the upcoming driving states of mobile vehicles and, based on these predictions, calculate the state values of all nodes participating in the consensus. In addition to evaluating node performance, the algorithm takes into account vehicles' tuning tendencies to strategically select high-quality relay nodes to improve wireless communication between vehicles. We evaluate the theoretical performance of the proposed consensus algorithm by analyzing transmission reception rate, delay, throughput and security. Simulation results show that our consensus algorithm has significantly lower packet loss rates and consensus delays compared to similar current proposals for vehicular networks in high-speed scenarios, highlighting its effectiveness in rapidly changing and complex environments.

Future research directions include improving vehicle node behavior evaluation by integrating more specific indicators into consensus selection processes that go beyond historical records, or using methods similar to those in [31] to improve vehicle speed prediction models with other factors to improve prediction stability and accuracy, while enhancing system safety to best adapt to driving conditions.

Author Contributions: Conceptualization, R.C. and G.L.; Data curation, R.C. and G.L.; Formal analysis, R.C. and Z.S.; Funding acquisition, F.Z., C.L. and C.Y.; Investigation, R.C., F.Z., Z.S., G.L. and C.Y.; Methodology, R.C.; Project administration, F.Z., C.L. and C.Y.; Resources, F.Z. and C.L.; Software, R.C.; Supervision, F.Z., C.L. and C.Y.; Validation, R.C., C.L. and C.Y.; Visualization, R.C.; Writing-original draft, R.C.; Writing-review & editing, R.C., C.L. and C.Y. All authors have read and agreed to the published version of the manuscript.

Funding: This work was supported by grants from the Guangxi Natural Science Foundation (2023GXNSFAA026294) and the National Natural Science Foundation of China (62362013).

Data Availability Statement: Data are contained within the article.

Conflicts of Interest: The authors declare no conflicts of interest.

References

1. Liu, Y.; Li, Y.; Chen, S. A survey of Internet of vehicles/vehicles to everything security based on Blockchain. *Sci. Sin. Inform.* **2023**, *53*, 841. (In Chinese) [CrossRef]
2. Islam, M.R.; Rashid, M.M. A Survey on Blockchain Security and Its Impact Analysis. In Proceedings of the 2023 9th International Conference on Computer and Communication Engineering (ICCCE), Kuala Lumpur, Malaysia, 15–16 August 2023; pp. 317–321.
3. Zhang, C.; Zhao, M.; Zhu, L.; Zhang, W.; Wu, T.; Ni, J. FRUIT: A Blockchain-Based Efficient and Privacy-Preserving Quality-Aware Incentive Scheme. *IEEE J. Sel. Areas Commun.* **2022**, *40*, 3343–3357. [CrossRef]
4. Wen, X.; Guan, Z.; Li, D.; Lyu, H.; Li, H. A Blockchain-Based Framework for Information Management in Internet of Vehicles. In Proceedings of the 2021 8th IEEE International Conference on Cyber Security and Cloud Computing (CSCloud)/2021 7th IEEE International Conference on Edge Computing and Scalable Cloud (EdgeCom), Washington, DC, USA, 26–28 June 2021; pp. 18–23.
5. Badertscher, C.; Gaži, P.; Kiayias, A.; Russell, A.; Zikas, V. Ouroboros Genesis: Composable Proof-of-Stake Blockchains with Dynamic Availability. In Proceedings of the 2018 ACM SIGSAC Conference on Computer and Communications Security, Toronto, ON, Canada, 15–19 October 2018; pp. 913–930.
6. Tong, W.; Dong, X.; Zheng, J. Trust-PBFT: A PeerTrust-Based Practical Byzantine Consensus Algorithm. In Proceedings of the 2019 International Conference on Networking and Network Applications (NaNA), Daegu, Republic of Korea, 10–13 October 2019; pp. 344–349.

7. Ur Rehman, M.H.; Salah, K.; Damiani, E.; Svetinovic, D. Towards Blockchain-Based Reputation-Aware Federated Learning. In Proceedings of the IEEE Conference on Computer Communications Workshops (INFOCOM WKSHPS), Virtual, 6–9 July 2020; pp. 183–188.
8. Xu, M.; Zou, Z.; Cheng, Y.; Hu, Q.; Yu, D.; Cheng, X. SPDL: A Blockchain-Enabled Secure and Privacy-Preserving Decentralized Learning System. *IEEE Trans. Comput.* **2023**, *72*, 548–558. [CrossRef]
9. Li, W.; Zhao, Z.; Ma, P.; Xie, Z.; Palade, V.; Liu, H. Graphical Consensus-Based Sharding for Efficient and Secure Sharings in Blockchain-Enabled Internet of Vehicles. *IEEE Trans. Veh. Technol.* **2024**, *73*, 1991–2002. [CrossRef]
10. Du, J.; Cheng, W.; Lu, G.; Cao, H.; Chu, X.; Zhang, Z.; Wang, J. Resource Pricing and Allocation in MEC Enabled Blockchain Systems: An A3C Deep Reinforcement Learning Approach. *IEEE Trans. Netw. Sci. Eng.* **2022**, *9*, 33–44. [CrossRef]
11. Liu, L.; Feng, J.; Mu, X.; Pei, Q.; Lan, D.; Xiao, M. Asynchronous Deep Reinforcement Learning for Collaborative Task Computing and On-Demand Resource Allocation in Vehicular Edge Computing. *IEEE Trans. Intell. Transp. Syst.* **2023**, *24*, 15513–15526. [CrossRef]
12. Zhang, J.; Liu, Y.; Qin, X.; Xu, X.; Zhang, P. Adaptive Resource Allocation for Blockchain-Based Federated Learning in Internet of Things. *IEEE Internet Things J.* **2023**, *10*, 10621–10635. [CrossRef]
13. Ul Abadin, Z.; Syed, Z. A Pattern for Proof of Work Consensus Algorithm in Blockchain. In Proceedings of the 26th European Conference on Pattern Languages of Programs, Graz, Austria, 7–11 July 2021; pp. 1–6.
14. Xu, H.; Yu, L.; Liu, Z.; Liu, Z.; Gu, D. Dynamic Practical Byzantine Fault Tolerance. In Proceedings of the IEEE Conference on Communications and Network Security (CNS), Beijing, China, 30 May–1 June 2018; pp. 1–8.
15. Bachani, V.; Bhattacharjya, A. Preferential Delegated Proof of Stake (PDPoS)—Modified DPoS with Two Layers towards Scalability and Higher TPS. *Symmetry* **2022**, *15*, 4. [CrossRef]
16. Fitzi, M.; Wang, X.; Kannan, S.; Kiayias, A.; Leonardos, N.; Viswanath, P.; Wang, G. Minotaur: Multi-Resource Blockchain Consensus. In Proceedings of the 2022 ACM SIGSAC Conference on Computer and Communications Security, Los Angeles, CA, USA, 7–11 November 2022; pp. 1095–1108.
17. Biswas, S.; Sharif, K.; Li, F.; Maharjan, S.; Mohanty, S.; Wang, Y. PoBT: A Lightweight Consensus Algorithm for Scalable IoT Business Blockchain. *IEEE Internet Things J.* **2020**, *7*, 2343–2355. [CrossRef]
18. Han, X.; Yuan, Y.; Wang, F.Y. A Fair Blockchain Based on Proof of Credit. *IEEE Trans. Comput. Soc. Syst.* **2019**, *6*, 922–931. [CrossRef]
19. Yu, J.; Shen, T.; Bai, F.; Yu, Z.; Luo, J. A Blockchain Communication Resource Optimisation Consensus Method. In Proceedings of the 2022 4th Blockchain and Internet of Things Conference, Tokyo, Japan, 8–10 July 2022; pp. 107–114.
20. Chen, C.; Liu, M.; Mo, P.; Yuan, C.; Dai, P. LBLCO: A Lightweight Blockchain with Low Communication Overhead for Internet of Things. In Proceedings of the 2022 4th Blockchain and Internet of Things Conference, Tokyo, Japan, 8–10 July 2022; pp. 92–99.
21. 21. Du, G; Cao, Y.; Li, J.; Yan, Z.; Chen, X.; Li, Y.; Chen, J. A Blockchain-Based Trust-Value Management Approach for Secure Information Sharing in Internet of Vehicles. *IEEE Internet Things J.* **2024**, *11*, 333–344. [CrossRef]
22. Zhang, C.; Luo, X.; Liang, J.; Liu, X.; Zhu, L.; Guo, S. POTA: Privacy-Preserving Online Multi-Task Assignment with Path Planning. *IEEE Trans. Mob. Comput.* **2024**, *23*, 5999–6011. [CrossRef]
23. Cao, M.; Li, V.O.K.; Chan, V.W.S. A CNN-LSTM Model for Traffic Speed Prediction. In Proceedings of the IEEE 91st Vehicular Technology Conference (VTC2020-Spring), Antwerp, Belgium, 25–28 May 2020; pp. 1–5.
24. Zhang, C.; Zhao, M.; Liang, J.; Fan, Q.; Zhu, L.; Guo, S. NANO: Cryptographic Enforcement of Readability and Editability Governance in Blockchain Databases. *IEEE Trans. Dependable Secur. Comput.* **2023**. *early access*. [CrossRef]
25. Chao, D.; Xu, D.; Gao, F.; Zhang, C.; Zhang, W.; Zhu, L. A Systematic Survey On Security in Anonymity Networks: Vulnerabilities, Attacks, Defenses, and Formalization. *IEEE Commun. Surv. Tutor.* **2021**. *early access*. [CrossRef]
26. Yuan, Y.; Wang, B.; Zhang, C.; Xiong, Z.; Li, C.; Zhu, L. Towards Efficient and Robust Federated Unlearning in IoT Networks. *IEEE Internet Things J.* **2024**, accepted. [CrossRef]
27. Liu, Y.; Ma, Y.; Tia, D.; Li, G. Research on consensus optimization of trusted incentive algorithm for blockchain mobile nodes. *Sichuan Univ. Nat. Sci. Ed.* **2022**, *59*, 062004.
28. Bai, F.; Sadagopan, N.; Helmy, A. IMPORTANT: A framework to systematically analyze the impact of mobility on performance of routing protocols for ad hoc networks. In Proceedings of the IEEE INFOCOM—Twenty-Second Annual Joint Conference of the IEEE Computer and Communications Societies, San Francisco, CA, USA, 30 March–3 April 2023; pp. 825–835.
29. Salimitari, M.; Joneidi, M.; Fallah, Y. BATS: A Blockchain-based Authentication and Trust Management System in Vehicular Networks. In Proceedings of the IEEE International Conference on Blockchain (Blockchain), Melbourne, Australia, 6–8 December 2021; pp. 333–340.
30. Ayaz, F.; Sheng, Z.; Tian, D.; Guan, Y. A Proof-of-Quality-Factor (PoQF)-Based Blockchain and Edge Computing for Vehicular Message Dissemination. *IEEE Internet Things J.* **2021**, *8*, 2468–2482. [CrossRef]
31. Zhang, C.; Hu, C.; Wu, T.; Zhu, L.; Liu, X. Achieving Efficient and Privacy-Preserving Neural Network Training and Prediction in Cloud Environments. *IEEE Trans. Dependable Secur. Comput.* **2023**, *20*, 4245–4257. [CrossRef]

electronics MDPI

Article

A Generation of Enhanced Data by Variational Autoencoders and Diffusion Modeling

Young-Jun Kim [1] and Seok-Pil Lee [2,*]

1 Department of Computer Science, Graduate School, SangMyung University, Seoul 03016, Republic of Korea; 202231040@sangmyung.kr
2 Department of Intelligent IoT, SangMyung University, Seoul 03016, Republic of Korea
* Correspondence: esprit@smu.ac.kr

Abstract: In the domain of emotion recognition in audio signals, the clarity and precision of emotion delivery are of paramount importance. This study aims to augment and enhance the emotional clarity of waveforms (wav) using a technique called stable diffusion. Datasets from EmoDB and RAVDESS, two well-known repositories of emotional audio clips, were utilized as the main sources for all experiments. We used the ResNet-based emotion recognition model to determine the emotion recognition of the augmented waveforms after emotion embedding and enhancement, and compared the enhanced data before and after the enhancement. The results showed that applying a mel-spectrogram-based diffusion model to the existing waveforms enlarges the salience of the embedded emotions, resulting in better identification. This augmentation has significant potential to advance the field of emotion recognition and synthesis, paving the way for improved applications in these areas.

Keywords: deep learning; generative adversarial networks; data augmentation; speech emotion recognition; speech emotion synthesis; diffusion; speech emotion recognition

1. Introduction

Accurate recognition of emotions from audio signals has long been a topic of intense research. Scholars have explored ways to capture and analyze the subtle nuances and intensity of emotions in audio signals. Previous work has utilized various feature extraction techniques and machine learning models to classify and predict emotions from audio signals. Also, in the area of emotion synthesis, various technical approaches have been proposed to generate speech recordings with natural emotions [1–6].

At the core of these studies is the need for high-quality data. In AI research, good quality data is necessary to train a model that performs well. In recent years, as the level of artificial intelligence research has been increasingly advanced, the need to build high-quality data has become increasingly necessary and the process has become increasingly difficult. In addition, in recent deep learning research, generative models are in the spotlight, and the quality of the generated results depends on the data used, so the importance of data is becoming more important. In recent generative model research, the focus has been on diffusion. Generative models such as conventional synthetic models or GANs have problems such as too much computation, long training time and cost, and poor accuracy in the inference process. Therefore, applying diffusion, which has been actively utilized in the image domain, to audio data is expected to facilitate the development of emotion recognition and synthesis by obtaining high-quality data [7].

In this paper, we applied the diffusion technique to enhance the emotion clarity of audio clips by utilizing the mel-spectrogram, a unique feature of audio [8]. The process of emotion synthesis using diffusion is divided into emotion embedding, utterance-style embedding, and the diffusion process. Emotion embedding is used to extract emotion information, utterance-style embedding is used to identify the features of emotion-specific mel-spectrogram images, and then diffusion is used to generate mel-spectrograms that meet the user's conditional input. The augmented emotional utterance data obtained through this process was evaluated using a residual network (ResNet)-based emotion classification model. The evaluation showed that the emotion recognition rate was higher than the existing dataset, which means that the augmented dataset contains clearer emotions than the existing emotion dataset, confirming the advantages of augmented emotional utterance data in emotion research.

The organization of this paper is as follows. Section 2 describes the background of the techniques utilized in the research. We overview and summarize diffusion, mel-spectrograms, Convolutional Neural Networks (CNNs), and the Emotional Speech Database. Section 3 describes related research. Starting with the work that precedes this thesis, synthesizing emotional speech data using GANs, we describe and review the work on synthesizing emotional speech data using diffusion models. In Section 4, we propose a diffusion-based sentiment synthesis model, which is the method of sentiment utterance data synthesis proposed in this paper, followed by the experimental design and experimental results in Section 5, and concluding remarks in Section 6.

This paper aims to respond to the need for high-quality emotion data and to explore quality data augmentation methods in the field of audio emotion recognition and synthesis by utilizing diffusion models. We demonstrate the improvement of emotion clarity through mel-spectrograms and diffusion techniques and propose a novel approach to improve the accuracy of emotion recognition. This represents a technological advance in emotion research and is expected to have a good impact on the future development of emotion recognition and synthesis technology.

2. Related Work

Research on the augmentation and generation of emotional utterance data has been continuously evolving from the past to the present, and various approaches have been tried in this field, including emotion data augmentation using GANs, data generation using diffusion models, and emotion synthesis models using existing neural networks. In particular, recent research has focused on augmentation using GANs and data generation using diffusion models.

First, in [9], DCGAN among GANs was used to augment data for each emotion using mel-spectrograms. By comparing the emotion recognition rate of EmoDB and RAVDESS datasets used in the experiment, this study showed that data augmentation using DCGAN contributes to increasing the emotion recognition rate.

Next, studies using diffusion models, such as papers [10–13], proposed to augment emotional utterance data by using mel-spectrograms of spoken utterances as input data for diffusion models.

Among the studies using diffusion, paper [10] used a refinement process of injecting and extracting Gaussian noise for learning sentiment data, and introduced a method of receiving conditional input from users by utilizing U-Net, a basic type of BERT model and diffusion model.

Next, paper [11] proposed the design of Grad-TTS [14] using a sentiment synthesis method based on stochastic differential equation (SDE) [15] formulation and de-noised diffusion probability model (DDPM) [16]. This study directly injected sentiment data into the learning process, introduced SER to encode sentiment information, utilized text as conditional input from the user, and used the wav2vec 2.0 model [17] to capture speaker embeddings. The speaker embeddings and emotion information were used to augment the new dataset by de-noising the mel-spectrograms. This work differs from paper [15] in that it achieves emotion synthesis using emotion embeddings rather than simply using emotion data for training, and shows that emotion embedding techniques improve the performance of emotion data augmentation, increasing the depth of emotion information.

Paper [12] had the structure of text encoder–emotion embedding–diffusion decoder, and used adversarial learning to separate speaker features, while emotion embedding used orthogonal projection, considering that speaker separation may weaken emotion expressiveness. Finally, diffusion decoders used emotion-related distributions to recover the mel-spectrogram.

Finally, ref. [13] had a phoneme encoder, speaker encoder, and emotion encoder similar to [18], and used the mel-spectrograms of emotion data for training without further adjustment, but differed in that it applied the information from the resulting emotion embeddings for inference.

In this paper, we propose a model that contains sufficient emotion information and generates augmented datasets of much higher quality than existing emotion datasets for superior performance in the synthesis of emotional utterance data by referring to emotion embedding techniques in related research, as well as techniques such as utterance encoders and conditional inputs.

3. Background

3.1. Diffusion

Diffusion models, as referenced in [16], are a form of latent variable models characterized by the equation $p_\theta(x_0) = \int p_\theta(x_0 : T)\, dx_1 : T$. In this equation, $x_1, \cdots, x_T$ are latent variables having the same dimensionality as the observed data x_0, which is drawn from the distribution $q(x_0)$. The combined distribution $p_\theta(x_0 : \mathrm{T})$ is recognized as the reverse process and is characterized by a Markov chain using learned Gaussian transitions, originating from the distribution $p(x_\mathrm{T}) = \mathcal{N}(x_\mathrm{T}; 0, \mathrm{I})$.

The cornerstone idea of the diffusion model emanates from the diffusion process, where Gaussian noise is sequentially added to the original image, converting it into pure random noise. This diffusion process essentially has the structure $q(x_\mathrm{T}|x_{\mathrm{T}-1})$, as expressed in Equation (1), and it involves the continuous application of a Gaussian Markov chain to the original image x_0. After multiple iterations, x_T adheres to a complete random Gaussian distribution.

$$q(x_{1:T}|x_0) = \prod_{t=1}^{T} q(x_t|x_{t-1}), \quad q(x_t|x_{t-1}) = \mathcal{N}(x_t; \sqrt{1-\beta_t}x_{t-1}, \beta_t \mathrm{I}) \tag{1}$$

Subsequently, an essential aspect is learning the inverse transformation of Equation (1), termed the inverse process. The inverse process begins when x_T follows a thorough Gaussian distribution and seeks to convert it back to the original x_0. This inverse process is defined by the parameters of the Gaussian Markov chain, μ_θ and Σ_θ, and is represented as Equation (2).

$$\begin{aligned} p_\theta(x_{0:T}) &:= p(x_T) \prod_{t=1}^{T} p_\theta(x_{t-1}|x_t), \\ & p_\theta(x_{t-1}|x_t) := \mathcal{N}(x_{t-1}; \mu_\theta(x_t, t), \Sigma_\theta(x_t, t)) \end{aligned} \tag{2}$$

By optimizing the diffusion process and the inverse process, the training objective, in terms of the ELBO, is given by Equation (3).

$$\mathbb{E}_q \left[\underbrace{D_{KL}(q(x_T|x_0)||p(x_T))}_{L_t} + \underbrace{\sum_{t>1} D_{KL}(q(x_{t-1}|x_t, x_0)||p_\theta(x_{t-1}|x_t))}_{L_{1:T-1}} - \underbrace{log p_\theta(x_0|x_1)}_{L_0} \right] \tag{3}$$

In Equation (3), L_t signifies the forward process, while $L_{1:T-1}$ pertains to the reverse process. The critical learning parameter is denoted by p_θ. As L_t lacks trainable parameters, it can be regarded as a constant during the learning phase. Consequently, the essence is optimizing the $L_{1:T-1}$ segment. The optimization results are represented by Equation (4).

$$p_\theta(x_{t-1}|x_t) = \mathcal{N}(x_{t-1}; \mu_\theta(x_t, t), \textstyle\sum_\theta(x_t, t)), \ (t = 1 \sim T-1) \tag{4}$$

Therefore, this paper utilized the diffusion and backward process of the diffusion model to generate mel-spectrograms using de-noising techniques, and combined with techniques such as emotion embedding, text embedding, feature extraction, encoder, and decoder to generate emotional speech data in the form of mel-spectrograms with improved emotion.

3.2. Mel-Spectrograms

A mel-spectrogram is a visual representation of the spectrum of sound that utilizes the mel frequency scale to show one of the salient features of speech and voice. The mel frequency scale is often used in speech and audio processing because it is intentionally designed to reflect the way the human ear is sensitive to certain frequencies. Whereas standard spectrograms operate on a logarithmic frequency scale, mel-spectrograms are constructed using a mel frequency scale. This design choice allows it to more closely match human auditory characteristics, focusing specifically on the frequencies that the human ear perceives most distinctly.

To obtain a mel-spectrogram, speech utterances and speech are divided into short frames of uniform length. To perform spectral analysis on each frame, it must be transformed from the time domain to the frequency domain. This transformation step uses techniques such as the Fast Fourier Transform (FFT) and the Short Time Fourier Transform (STFT). The transformation step uses a Hamming window to reduce frequency leakage, which occurs when a signal is truncated to a certain length and the periods of the signal are not exactly aligned, and edge effects, which are distortions of the signal at the beginning and end of the signal in the time domain. After this transformation, the derived spectrum is interfaced with a bank of mel filters to extract the energy associated with each frequency bank on the mel scale. The mel-spectrogram effectively encapsulates relevant information about speech by representing three-dimensional data of time, frequency, and amplitude as a two-dimensional image [19].

Therefore, in this study, we use mel-spectrograms as input data to augment speech data through the diffusion process. Furthermore, the reason why we do not use features other than mel-spectrograms in this study is that if we use features such as MFCC or chroma in the diffusion model, we are trying to generate the value of the feature rather than the speech information itself, and we use mel-spectrograms because the diffusion model originated in the image domain and we want to extend it to the speech domain. In addition, by evaluating the enhanced emotional speech data by using it as input to the emotion evaluation model, we can comprehensively analyze the trajectories of complex speech features and emotional nuances [20].

3.3. Convolutional Neural Networks

Convolutional Neural Networks (CNNs) originated from the necessity of deep learning models that accommodate local features within image patterns, adeptly capturing their spatial structures. CNNs have been predominantly employed in various computer vision tasks, including image classification, object detection, medical image analysis, and face recognition. Due to their remarkable performance in learning based on spatial structures, patterns, and features of images, their usage has extended beyond vision tasks to various signal data, encompassing audio and sensors [21].

A CNN processes input images through several layers, such as convolutional layers, pooling layers, and fully connected layers, to distill information. The convolutional layers are primarily utilized to detect features from the input data, while pooling layers serve the purpose of reducing the data's dimensionality.

In this study, we investigate the change in emotion recognition rate of emotional audio data enhanced by a diffusion model. The diffusion model is used for feature extraction, pattern-based learning, feature map generation, etc.

3.4. Emotional Speech Database

The main objective of this thesis is to identify clearer emotional distinctions through the enhancement of emotional speech data, where the chosen database plays a pivotal role. Two databases were used in this thesis: EmoDB and RAVDESS.

EmoDB, originating from the Technical University of Berlin, consists of data sampled at 16 kHz. It contains emotions such as neutral, happy, sad, angry, fear, and disgust. There are 10 speakers in the database, five male and five female. The recordings consist of different emotional states conveyed through German sentences and are characterized by the fact that the speakers were genuinely experiencing the emotions they described during the recording.

RAVDESS, on the other hand, is a product of the University of Toronto that records data sampled at 48 kHz in English [18]. While RAVDESS provides a wider spectrum of emotions, including neutral, calm, happy, sad, angry, surprised, fearful, and disgust, we specifically used neutral, happy, sad, angry, surprised, fear, and disgust in this paper to maintain consistency with EmoDB. The database contains recordings from 24 speakers, 12 male and 12 female. A unique feature of RAVDESS is that the speakers expressed emotions with two different intensities, and all recordings were made under controlled conditions using the same sentences.

A high-quality database is indispensable for sentiment-based analysis. In this paper, we utilized both EmoDB and RAVDESS. Due to the difference in sampling rate of the two, we resampled all data to 22,025 Hz for uniformity.

Table 1 shows the number of datasets per emotion.

Table 1. The count of datasets per emotion.

Emotions	EmoDB	RAVDESS
Neutrality	79	96
Angry	127	192
Sadness	62	192
Fear	69	192
Happy	71	192
Disgust	46	192
Total	454	1056

4. Proposed Method

4.1. Data Preprocessing

In this paper, we used the EmoDB and RAVDESS datasets. For our experiments, nested emotions such as happiness, anger, sadness, fear, neutrality, and disgust were used from both the EmoDB and RAVDESS datasets. EmoDB has a sampling rate of 16 kHz and RAVDESS has a sampling rate of 48 kHz, so both datasets were resampled to 22,025 Hz.

To ensure consistent conditions across the datasets, we adjusted the length of the emotion speech samples by padding shorter samples to match the length of the longest sample, so that all data was 10 s long, and we grouped and reorganized the datasets according to each emotion.

Table 2 shows the emotion data information.

Table 2. Emotion data information.

Emotions	Number of Experimenters	Data Time Length	Sampling Rate
EmoDB	5 males, 5 females	10 s	22,025 Hz
RAVDESS	12 males, 12 females	10 s	22,025 Hz

In this paper, we also considered the utilization of diffusion by treating speech like an image [22]. Therefore, all the speech data were converted into mel-spectrograms using

Python's librosa library. The reason why we do not detect utterance segments in this process is that we use mel-spectrograms like images, where noise is injected during the diffusion and inversion process and subsequently removed. This way, the firing part of the image is reconstructed according to the features of the original data, while the padded part, which has no mel-spectrogram image, is not reconstructed. This approach justified bypassing the firing part. To avoid the loss of temporal information in the data, we did not use the Fast Fourier Transform (FFT), but rather the Short Time Fourier Transform (STFT) during the conversion. As a result, the emotional speech was converted into a mel-spectrogram using the STFT, and after several iterations of parameter tuning, considering the overall length and sampling rate of the WAV file, we chose a hop length of 256 and a window size of 1024 for the STFT [23]. The converted mel-spectrograms were then subjected to Z-score normalization for standardization [24].

4.2. Speech Emotion Recognition (SER)

In this study, we used speech emotion recognition in two steps [25]. First, emotion embeddings were utilized to generate emotion information for typical utterances. Mel-spectrograms containing emotion information were used as input data, and the minibatch technique was used to reduce the amount of computation during the training process. The model was constructed using Pytorch, based on Python, and the model was implemented using the ResNet-50 model, based on CNN specialized in feature extraction and classification. The labels mapped to the data were created by integer encoding of sentiment information followed by one-hot encoding. The training data and validation data were divided 8:2 for training, Adam was used as the optimization function, the learning rate was set to 1×10^{-4}, the CrossEntropyLoss function was used as the loss function, and the Epoch was set to 800 [26,27]. After training, we measured performance based on accuracy and F1 score for each label prediction and used an emotion classification model with a classification performance of 98.31% and an F1 score of 0.9831. We used the trained model in inference mode, where the output is an embedding vector containing emotion information rather than classification results, and then combined it with the utterance-style vector to perform emotion embedding.

Table 3 shows the parameters of the emotion recognition model for emotion embedding, and Figure 1 shows the confusion matrix of the spoken emotion recognition model.

Table 3. Experiment settings of emotion recognition models for emotion embedding.

Experiment Settings	Value
Label	Anger, Sadness, Happiness, Neutral, Fear, Disgust
Optimizer	Adam
Learning rate	1×10^{-4}
Loss function	CrossEntropyLoss
Epoch	800

We used the generated mel-spectrograms to validate the emotion feature enrichment. We compared the input EmoDB and RAVDESS data with the generated data based on the accuracy of the confusion matrix [28].

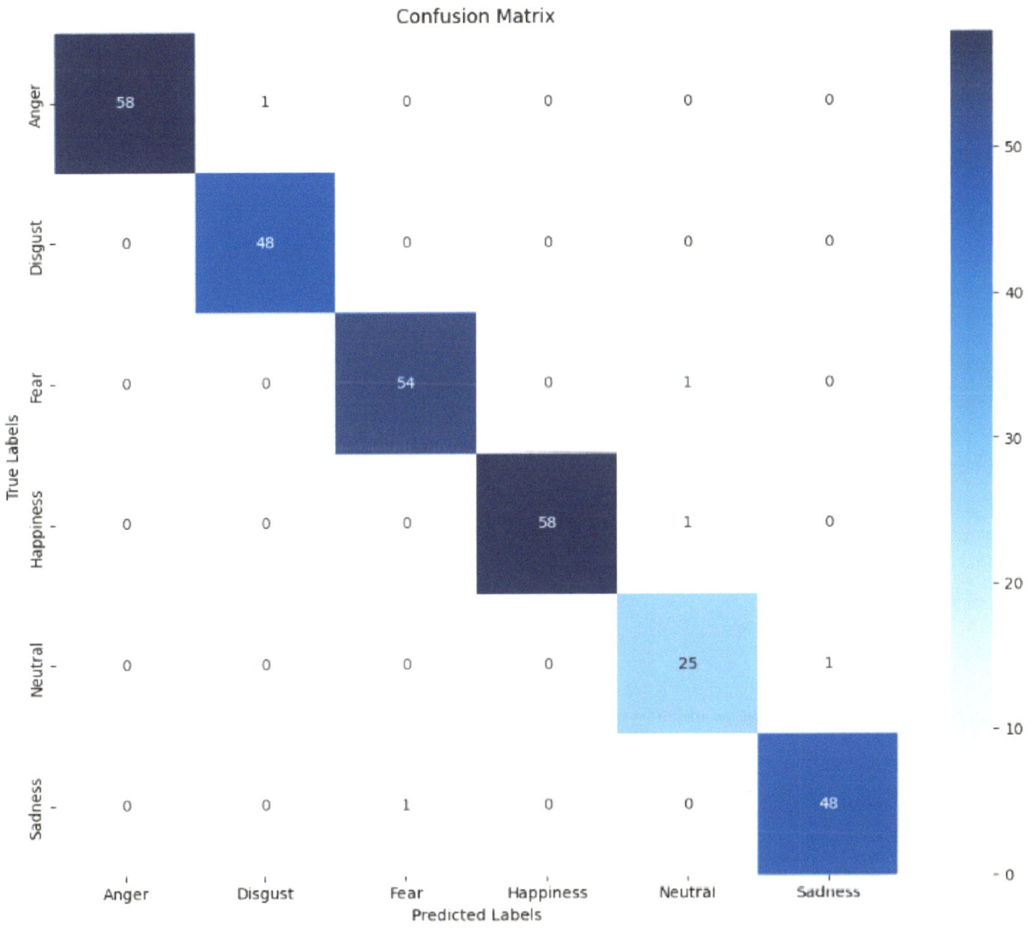

Figure 1. Confusion matrix for our proposed emotion recognition model.

4.3. Diffusion Models with Mel-Spectrograms

In this paper, we utilized a diffusion model to improve the quality of emotional speech data. The diffusion model is a generative AI model that generates data based on the user's conditional input, input data, and trained data. The generation process is the process of injecting and extracting noise and producing the results requested by the user. It is mainly used in video, and we used mel-spectrograms to generate speech via a diffusion model in terms of signals like video [14].

First, we embedded the utterance. Speech embedding refits data that are not sampled at 22,025 Hz, normalizes the wav, locates the start of the speech, and includes information about the start and end of the speech. It creates a mel-spectrogram for the input wav and normalizes it to prepare the mel-spectrogram for use as input data. The model also uses the mel-spectrogram obtained from the original emotional speech as one of the input data items, the emotion vector.

To solve the memory problem in training the model, we used mel-spectrogram resizing and a batch-based training process. The model is built on Python-based Pytorch and uses a CNN and attention-based encoder to extract features from the input mel-spectrograms. During this process, the utterance style of the mel-spectrogram was extracted, and the attention layer was used in each ResNet block to further focus on the noteworthy features.

The second half of the diffusion model, the decoder, was then trained. The decoder used trigonometric and sequential functions to account for temporal information about the data, and the ResNet-based model structure was used to learn based on the features of the data. When using ResNet, we added temporal embeddings and emotion embeddings to focus on information about utterance and emotion and used a linear attention mechanism to focus more on information such as emotion, time, and intonation [29].

Table 4 shows the overall model design structure of the diffusion model for emotional speech generation.

Table 4. Diffusion model architecture for emotional speech generation.

	Block (Layers)	Input Dimension	Stride	Output Dimension
Diffusion	Initial input	(32, 80, 861)	-	(32, 256, 861)
	ResNet block	(32, 256, 861)	1	(32, 256, 861)
	Downsample	(32, 256, 861)	2	(32, 512, 430)
	ResNet block	(32, 512, 430)	1	(32, 1024, 215)
	Upsample	(32, 1024, 215)	2	(32, 512, 430)
	ResNet block	(32, 512, 430)	1	(32, 256, 861)
	Final Conv2d	(32, 256, 861)	1	(32, 1, 861)

The structure of the emotional speech generation model implemented in this paper is shown in Figure 2 below.

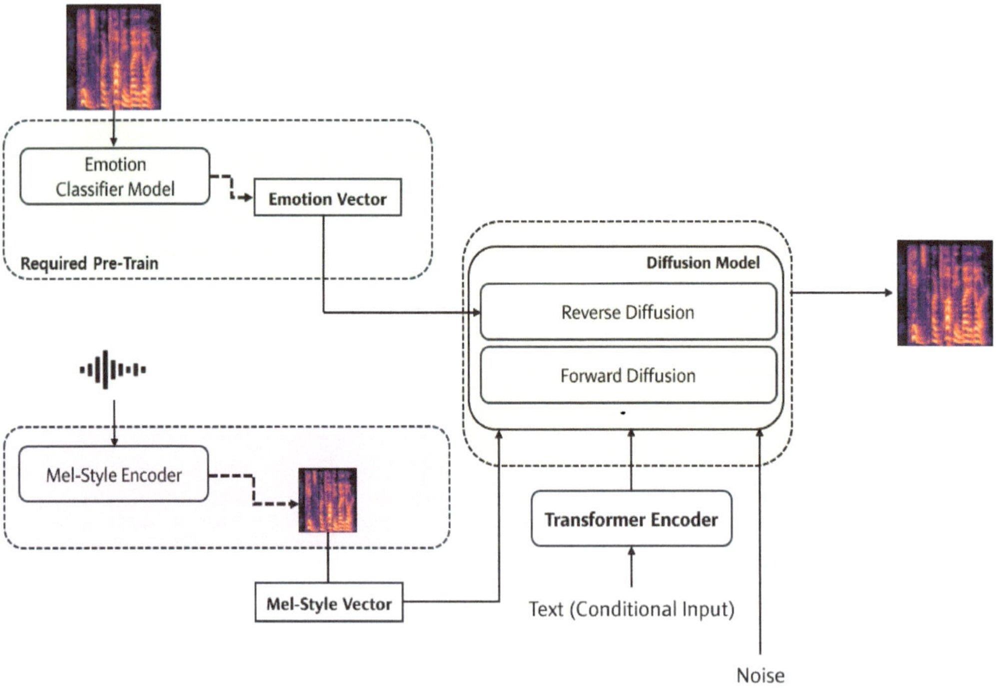

Figure 2. Diffusion model structure for emotional speech generation.

The proposed method in this paper focuses on the augmented data containing more emotions, which is an important point in related works. It can be seen that the proposed method focuses more on the augmentation of the emotional utterance dataset than the emotional speech utterance, and we note that it is very difficult to obtain good quality data in this process, because of limitations in the emotional utterance dataset for emotion-related learning of artificial intelligence. From this perspective, the authors believe it will be helpful for future emotion-related research if the dataset is augmented with more emotions.

The diffusion model-based emotion synthesis model proposed in this paper is divided into two styles [25].

The first is the emotion embedding module. The emotion embedding module requires a pre-trained emotion recognition model as mentioned above and extracts the emotion vector inferred from the emotion recognition model. It is confirmed that if the diffusion model is used without emotion embedding or in the learning process, as in [10,13], relatively little consideration is given to emotions when data augmentation is performed. Therefore, in [11,12], emotion embedding is used to extract emotion information from the emotion data to be used as training data, and then emotion embedding is performed in the learning process, such as emotion labels.

The second module is the mel-style embedding module, which focuses on utterance information. It utilizes the mel-spectrogram as training data to extract utterance information by emotion. In this paper, we consider using mel-spectrograms as images and use the mel-style embedding module to learn the progression structure, shape, and features of mel-spectrograms. In this way, emotion information can be embedded in the style of each emotion-specific mel-spectrogram to augment new emotional utterance data using a diffusion model, and it is expected that more emotion data will be augmented.

Since this paper focuses on augmenting emotional utterance data with more emotions, we evaluated the recognition rate of each emotion with an emotion recognition model, and since we use mel-spectrograms to do this, we stopped the augmentation step using the diffusion model at the mel-spectrogram.

The proposed method in this paper simplifies the emotion synthesis method into three steps: emotion, utterance information, and generation and purification, which enables the augmentation of emotional utterance data with a small amount of computing power and computation. In addition, it has the advantage of freely obtaining mel-spectrograms that can be utilized as speech features by adding conditional inputs from users to the trained model without having to spend a lot of time and money on data collection.

5. Experiment

5.1. Experimental Design

In this paper, we compare the ground-truth and prediction values of the original data and the generated data using an emotion recognition model to see if the generated data contain improved emotion information.

In addition, there are many considerations for performance improvement such as time complexity, computational cost, and data collection cost, but this paper focuses on the improvement of the generated emotional speech data, so the experiments are focused on how well the emotions are classified.

Each item of generated emotion speech data was given a percentage score for each emotion, considering the balance of the data distribution, and the comparison was performed on EmoDB and RAVDESS, which were used to train the existing emotion embedding and diffusion models for emotion speech generation.

5.2. Synthetic Emotion Speech Data

An example of the mel-spectrogram data generated by the proposed diffusion process is shown in Figure 3, which shows (a) the original mel-spectrogram of the anger emotion speech data and (b) the improved mel-spectrogram of anger emotion using the emotion speech generation diffusion model.

The mel-spectrogram image has temporal information on the x-axis and frequency information on the y-axis. As you can see from the color map information in the mel - spectrogram shown in Figure 3, it closely depicts the original tempo information, amplitude, and emphasis of the utterance. You can also see that the parts of the audio that were padded to match the length of the audio were similarly padded during the WAV generation process.

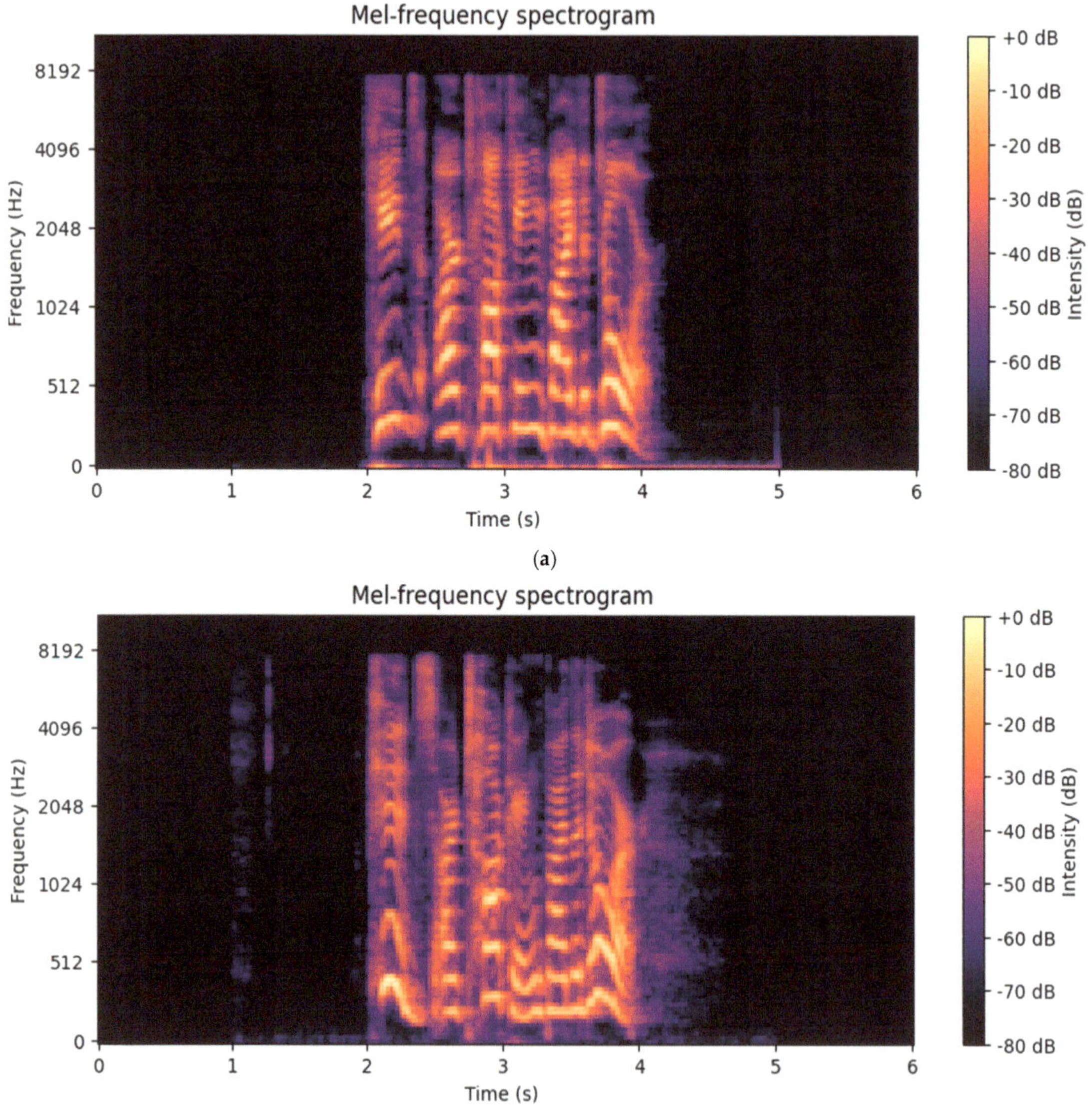

Figure 3. Mel-spectrograms improved with diffusion models. (**a**) Original mel-spectrogram of angry emotion speech data, (**b**) improved mel-spectrogram of angry emotion with diffusion model.

If you look at Figure 3a,b, you can see that the emotional features are captured and closely mimicked by the duration of the utterance, and the similarity of the frequency flow is very close. We can also see that the high intensity of the frequencies from the emotion of anger is also a good reflection of the characteristics of the existing emotion.

5.3. Result

The reason we used an emotion recognition model for our experiment was to see if the enhanced emotional speech data has clearer emotional attributes. Therefore, we compared the original and the generated emotional speech data. In general, weighted and unweighted accuracy are used in emotion recognition. Weighted accuracy evaluates performance by considering the distribution of each class in the dataset, while unweighted accuracy calculates the overall accuracy by giving equal importance to all classes. Therefore, we used both metrics to gain insight into the overall performance of the model and its performance on individual classes [30].

To compare the UA and WA of the generated data with the original data, we ran experiments using the EmoDB and RAVDESS datasets as shown in Table 5. For EmoDB, the recorded WA was 82.1% and the UA was 81.7% when tested with the original data only. When we also used the generated data for testing, the WA increased to 94.3% and the UA to 91.6%, an improvement of about 10–12%. Similarly, for RAVDESS, using only the original dataset, the WA was 67.7% and the UA was 65.1%. However, using the data generated for the experiment, the WA increased to 77.8% and the UA to 79.7%, a noticeable increase [14].

Table 5. Contrast of WA and UA between original data and generated data.

Dataset	WA	UA
EmoDB	82.1%	81.7%
Generated data	94.3%	91.6%
RAVDESS	67.7%	65.1%
Generated data	77.8%	79.7%

The above results show that data generation using latent diffusion yields meaningful results. To further measure the prediction accuracy for individual emotions, we also performed per-emotion accuracy measurements. The following table (Tables 6–9) shows the per-emotion accuracy results for our dataset [9].

Table 6. Confusion matrix for the RAVDESS dataset.

		Predict					
		Neutrality	**Happiness**	**Sadness**	**Anger**	**Fear**	**Disgust**
True	**Neutrality**	82.1%	7%%	4.7%	3.5%	3.3%	2.1%
	Happiness	9.8%	72.4%	0%	8.8%	0.3%	0.3%
	Sadness	1.1%	0.4%	87.2%	0.4%	9.2%	7.9%
	Anger	0.3%	8.1%	1.7%	81.9%	5.4%	10%
	Fear	4.2%	8.6%	5.6%	3.6%	77.5%	5%
	Disgust	2.5%	3.5%	0.8%	1.8%	4.3%	74.7%

Table 7. Confusion matrix for the RAVDESS dataset and generated dataset.

		Predict					
		Neutrality	**Happiness**	**Sadness**	**Anger**	**Fear**	**Disgust**
True	**Neutrality**	86.6%	0.8%	2.4%	0%	0.5%	1.2%
	Happiness	4.4%	83.4%	0.7%	5.1%	0.3%	0%
	Sadness	1.0%	0.4%	88.9%	0.1%	8.7%	4.2%
	Anger	0.3%	7.2%	0.8%	84.1%	6.7%	7.5%
	Fear	3.1%	3%	3.4%	4.3%	79.2%	2.8%
	Disgust	0.7%	3.5%	0.4%	3.7%	3.6%	81.7%

Table 8. Confusion matrix for the EmoDB dataset.

		Predict					
		Neutrality	Happiness	Sadness	Anger	Fear	Disgust
True	Neutrality	96.9%	8.4%	5.6%	2.5%	0%	0%
	Happiness	0.4%	78.8%	2.1%	4%	3.1%	0%
	Sadness	1.1%	0.8%	91.4%	0%	8.5%	0.4%
	Anger	0.2%	4.3%	0%	95.1%	0%	0%
	Fear	0%	0%	8.7%	0.1%	84.2%	0.3%
	Disgust	0%	0%	4.3%	0%	6.6%	74.9%

Table 9. Confusion matrix for the EmoDB dataset and generated dataset.

		Predict					
		Neutrality	Happiness	Sadness	Anger	Fear	Disgust
True	Neutrality	100%	0%	2.9%	0%	0%	0%
	Happiness	0%	87.3%	0%	4.5%	0%	0%
	Sadness	0%	0%	95.6%	0.1%	0%	0%
	Anger	0%	2.5%	0%	95.1%	0%	0%
	Fear	0%	0%	3.6%	0%	92.5%	2.4%
	Disgust	0%	0%	0%	1.4%	4.1%	86.6%

The above experimental results show that, overall, the classification accuracy of the generated emotion speech data is higher than that of the EmoDB and RAVDESS datasets, but when looking at the emotions of anger and fear, the number of misclassifications of anger as fear in RAVDESS increased by 1.3%, and the number of misclassifications of happiness as anger in EmoDB increased by 0.5%. Therefore, although improvements were made for each emotion, it was confirmed that there are generated data where the boundaries between specific emotions are blurred.

In [9], data augmentation and dataset construction using DCGAN were performed using EmoDB and RAVDESS in the same way as this paper, and it can be seen from the results of the augmented dataset that the emotion recognition model was used to complete data augmentation with a higher emotion recognition rate than the existing emotion datasets, EmoDB and RAVDESS.

This paper augments the data compared to [9], but the experimental design and process are different, so we checked the emotion recognition rate of the proposed diffusion model compared to the results of existing studies.

The following tables (Tables 10 and 11) compare the difference between the emotion recognition accuracy results (the match between the ground-truth and the predicted emotion) of this paper and paper [9] for each emotion with the results of the datasets generated based on the RAVDESS and EmoDB datasets.

Table 10. Comparing the accuracy of emotion recognition methods using EmoDB-based augmented datasets.

Differences in Recognition Accuracy		Proposed Method					
		Neutrality	Happiness	Sadness	Anger	Fear	Disgust
Baek, Ji-Young et al. [9]	Neutrality	0%p	0%p	2.9%p	0%p	0%p	0%p
	Happiness	0%p	5.5%p	0%p	−13.7%p	0%p	0%p
	Sadness	0%p	0%p	6.7%p	0.1%p	−11.1%p	0%p
	Anger	0%p	−2.8%p	0%p	0.4%p	0%p	0%p
	Fear	0%p	0%p	−5.4%p	0%p	1.6%p	2.4%p
	Disgust	0%p	0%p	−14.3%p	1.4%p	4.1%p	0.9%p

Table 11. Comparing the accuracy of emotion recognition methods using RAVDESS-based augmented datasets.

Differences in Recognition Accuracy		Proposed Method					
		Neutrality	**Happiness**	**Sadness**	**Anger**	**Fear**	**Disgust**
Baek, Ji-Young et al. [9]	**Neutrality**	15.2%p	0.8%p	−14.8%p	−7.1%p	−6.6%p	−13.1%p
	Happiness	−2.5%p	31.7%p	−16.5%p	−5.2%p	−6.6%p	−6.9%p
	Sadness	−2.4%p	−3%p	6.1%p	0.1%p	1.8%p	0.8%p
	Anger	0.3%p	−3.1%p	0.8%p	1.3%p	−0.2%p	0.6%p
	Fear	−3.8%p	3.1%p	−13.8%p	0.9%p	13.7%p	−4.1%p
	Disgust	0.7%p	−3.4%p	−13.4%p	3.7%p	3.6%p	2.4%p

Tables 10 and 11 compare the emotion recognition accuracy of the proposed method in this paper with the results of paper [9]. This is a comparative analysis of how much higher or lower the emotion recognition performance of the proposed method is compared to paper [9].

The results show that for the same emotion, the proposed method is more accurate than the original study [9]. The proposed method and paper [9] have the same dataset augmented with a generative model, but paper [9] only imitates the original correct answer data and does not generate it perfectly. However, the proposed method differs from paper [9] in that the diffusion model trained with emotion and speech information generates a new mel-spectrogram in response to the user's conditional input.

Also, the accuracy of misclassification in the proposed method is high in some cases, such as nervous–angry, which is one of the points to be improved in future research, but since the purpose of this paper is to augment good emotion data, we focused on accurate emotion classification, and the comparison shows that the proposed method performs better in augmenting and generating emotion data.

Finally, the learning completeness of a classification model is evaluated by precision, recall, F1 score, etc. Therefore, we objectively checked the degree of emotion improvement of the generated data through the classification model evaluation metrics. The evaluation was conducted on the emotion labels of the existing dataset and the generated dataset, and the amount of data in EmoDB and RAVDESS was adjusted appropriately [31].

Table 12 shows the classification model evaluation metrics between the generated dataset and the existing dataset.

Table 12. Emotion classification model evaluation metrics.

	EmoDB, Generated Data	**RAVDESS, Generated Data**
Accuracy	0.9831	0.8436
Precision	0.9834	0.8511
Recall	0.9831	0.8436
F1 score	0.9831	0.8437

6. Conclusions

In this study, we generated emotional speech data using diffusion models, which have recently gained attention, and conducted experiments to verify whether the generated data represent distinct emotions. RAVDESS and EmoDB datasets were used for the experiments. We extracted mel-spectrogram features from the emotional speech data and used them as input data for the diffusion model and implemented an encoder to convert the data into training data, including mel-spectrogram feature extraction and normalization, a diffusion model, and an emotion recognition model to evaluate the generated data and embed emotions in the data.

The diffusion model is a model that is currently prominent in the image field, which injects and extracts noise to generate data that the user wants. Therefore, in this paper, in addition to mel-spectrogram data with emotion embedding through the encoder, we used text containing the user's requirements as a conditional input to the model to generate the desired data.

To evaluate the quality of the generated data, we judged the degree of emotion enhancement with the ResNet-based model used in the emotion embedding process. We compared the recognition accuracy for each emotion with WA and UA to see if the emotion attributes of the generated data became clearer, which can be helpful for emotion recognition and synthesis. We also checked the prediction accuracy of the generated data by label with the confusion matrix, and checked whether the emotion classification of the generated data was correct in terms of recall, precision, and F1 score, which are classification model evaluation metrics.

As AI advances, the most important issue is data-related. In order to create a well-performing AI model, you need to have good quality data. It is very difficult to collect good quality data, but this paper confirmed that the diffusion model is an effective method for building a high-performance model by generating data that is improved from the existing data. In future research, along with the improvement of the diffusion model, we will explore ways to improve the regions where the boundaries are blurred in certain emotions by utilizing more datasets, and explore more emotions and situations, and apply and test it in real-world applications to increase the naturalness of the generated data and the accuracy of emotion expression.

This research shows that voice data generation technology that can accurately express emotions can make human–machine interaction more natural and humanized. This can lead to applications in various industries such as education, entertainment, and virtual reality, as well as the development of emotional AI, and will inspire new forms of communication and content creation. Therefore, this paper makes an important contribution to the field of emotional speech data generation using diffusion models and is expected to further promote research and development in this field.

Author Contributions: Conceptualization, Y.-J.K. and S.-P.L.; methodology, Y.-J.K.; investigation, Y.-J.K.; writing—original draft preparation, Y.-J.K.; writing—review and editing, S.-P.L.; project administration, S.-P.L. All authors have read and agreed to the published version of the manuscript.

Funding: This work was supported by the 2024 Research Grant from SangMyung University (2024-A001-0123).

Data Availability Statement: Experiments used publicly available datasets.

Conflicts of Interest: The authors declare no conflicts of interest.

Abbreviations

The following abbreviations are used in this manuscript:

CNN	Convolutional Neural Network
ResNet	Residual Network
FFT	Fast Fourier Transform
SDE	Stochastic Differential Equation
DM	Diffusion Model
DDPM	Denoised Diffusion Probability Model
STFT	Short Time Fourier Transform
WA	Weighted accuracy
UA	Unweighted accuracy

References

1. Swain, M.; Routray, A.; Kabisatpathy, P. Databased, features and classifiers for speech emotion recognition: A review. *Int. J. Speech Technol.* **2018**, *21*, 93–120. [CrossRef]
2. Lalitha, S.; Madhavan, A.; Bhushan, B.; Saketh, S. Speech emotion recognition. In Proceedings of the 2014 International Conference on Advances in Electronics Computers and Communications, Bangalore, India, 10–11 October 2014; pp. 1–4.

3. Akcay, M.B.; Oguz, K. Speech emotion recognition: Emotional models, databases, features, preprocessing methods, supporting modalities, and classifiers. *Speech Commun.* **2020**, *116*, 56–76. [CrossRef]
4. Koduru, A.; Valiveti, H.B.; Budati, A.K. Feature extraction algorithms to improve the speech emotion recognition rate. *Int. J. Speech Technol.* **2020**, *23*, 45–55. [CrossRef]
5. Liu, Z.T.; Xie, Q.; Wu, X.; Cao, W.H.; Mei, Y.; Mao, J.W. Speech emotion recognition based on an improved brain emotion learning model. *Neurocomputing* **2018**, *309*, 145–156. [CrossRef]
6. Abdilmohsin, H.A.; Wahab, H.B.A.; Hossen, A.M.J.A. A new proposed statistical feature extraction method in speech emotion recognition. *Comput. Electr. Eng.* **2021**, *93*, 107–172. [CrossRef]
7. Saharia, C.; Chan, W.; Chang, H.; Lee, C.; Ho, J.; Salimans, T.; Fleet, D.; Norouzi, M. Palette: Image-to-image diffusion models. In *ACM SIGGRAPH 2022 Conference Proceedings*; Association for Computing Machinery: New York, NY, USA, 2022.
8. Hwang, Y.; Cho, H.; Yang, H.; Won, D.O.; Oh, I.; Lee, S.W. Mel-spectrogram augmentation for sequence to sequence voice conversion. *arXiv* **2020**, arXiv:2001.01401.
9. Baek, J.Y.; Lee, S.P. Enhanced Speech Emotion Recognition Using DCGAN-Based Data Augmentation. *Electronics* **2023**, *12*, 3966. [CrossRef]
10. Malik, I.; Latif, S.; Jurdak, R.; Schuller, B. A preliminary study on augmenting speech emotion recognition using a diffusion model. *arXiv* **2023**, arXiv:2305.11413.
11. Tang, H.; Zhang, X.; Wang, J.; Cheng, N.; Xiao, J. Emomix: Emotion mixing via diffusion models for emotional speech synthesis. *arXiv* **2023**, arXiv:2306.00648.
12. Li, T.; Hu, C.; Cong, J.; Zhu, X.; Li, J.; Tian, Q.; Wang, Y.; Xie, L. DiCLET-TTS: Diffusion model based cross-lingual emotion transfer for text-to-speech—A study between English and Mandarin. *IEEE/ACM Trans. Audio Speech Lang. Process.* **2023**, *31*, 3418–3430. [CrossRef]
13. Prabhu, N.R.; Lay, B.; Welker, S.; Lehmann-Willenbrock, N.; Gerkmann, T. EMOCONV-DIFF: Diffusion-based Speech Emotion Conversion for Non-parallel and In-the-wild Data. *arXiv* **2023**, arXiv:2309.07828.
14. Popov, V.; Vovk, I.; Gogoryan, V.; Sadekova, T.; Kudinov, M. Grad-tts: A diffusion probabilistic model for text-to-speech. In Proceedings of the International Conference on Machine Learning, PMLR, Virtual, 13 December 2021; pp. 8599–8608.
15. Song, Y.; Sohl-Dickstein, J.; Kingma, D.P.; Kumar, A.; Ermon, S.; Poole, B. Score-based generative modeling through stochastic differential equations. In Proceedings of the International Conference on Learning Representations, Vienna, Austria, 4 May 2021.
16. Jonathan, H.; Jain, A.; Abbeel, P. Denoising diffusion probabilistic models. *Adv. Neural Inf. Process. Syst.* **2020**, *33*, 6840–6851.
17. Baevski, A.; Zhou, Y.; Mohamed, A.; Auli, M. wav2vec 2.0: A framework for self-supervised learning of speech representations. *Adv. Neural Inf. Process. Syst.* **2020**, *33*, 12449–12460.
18. Livingstone, S.R.; Russo, F.A. The Ryerson Audio-Visual Database of Emotional Speech and Song (RAVDESS): A dynamic, multimodal set of facial and vocal expressions in North American English. *PLoS ONE* **2018**, *13*, e0196391. [CrossRef] [PubMed]
19. Logan, B. Mel frequency cepstral coefficients for music modeling. In Proceedings of the 1st International Symposium on Music Information Retrieval (ISMIR 2000), Plymouth, MA, USA, 23–25 October 2000; Volume 270.
20. Yenigalla, P.; Kumar, A.; Tripathi, S.; Singh, C.; Kar, S.; Vepa, J. Speech Emotion Recognition Using Spectrogram & Phoneme Embedding. In Proceedings of the Interspeech 2018, Hyderabad, India, 2–6 September 2018; Volume 2018.
21. Jogin, M.; Madhulika, M.S.; Divya, G.D.; Meghana, R.K.; Apoorva, S. Feature extraction using convolution neural networks (CNN) and deep learning. In Proceedings of the 2018 3rd IEEE International Conference on Recent Trends in Electronics, Information & Communication Technology (RTEICT), Bangalorem, India, 18–19 May 2018; IEEE: New York, NY, USA, 2018.
22. Lu, Y.J.; Wang, Z.Q.; Watanabe, S.; Richard, A.; Yu, C.; Tsao, Y. Conditional diffusion probabilistic model for speech enhancement. In Proceedings of the ICASSP 2022-2022 IEEE International Conference on Acoustics, Speech and Signal Processing (ICASSP), Virtual, 7–13 May 2022; IEEE: New York, NY, USA, 2022.
23. Griffin, D.; Lim, J. Signal estimation from modified short-time Fourier transform. *IEEE Trans. Acoust. Speech Signal Process.* **1984**, *32*, 236–243. [CrossRef]
24. Patro, S.G.K.; Sahu, K.K. Normalization: A preprocessing stage. *arXiv* **2015**, arXiv:1503.06462. [CrossRef]
25. Kang, M.; Han, W.; Hwang, S.J.; Yang, E. ZET-Speech: Zero-shot adaptive Emotion-controllable Text-to-Speech Synthesis with Diffusion and Style-based Models. *arXiv* **2023**, arXiv:2305.13831.
26. Zhang, Z.; Sabuncu, M. Generalized cross entropy loss for training deep neural networks with noisy labels. In Proceedings of the Advances in Neural Information Processing Systems, Montréal, QC, Canada, 3–8 December 2018; Volume 31.
27. Kingma, D.P.; Ba, J. Adam: A method for stochastic optimization. *arXiv* **2014**, arXiv:1412.6980.
28. Luque, A.; Carrasco, A.; Martín, A.; de Las Heras, A. The impact of class imbalance in classification performance metrics based on the binary confusion matrix. *Pattern Recognit.* **2019**, *91*, 216–231. [CrossRef]
29. Popov, V.; Vovk, I.; Gogoryan, V.; Sadekova, T.; Kudinov, M.; Wei, J. Diffusion-based voice conversion with fast maximum likelihood sampling scheme. *arXiv* **2021**, arXiv:2109.13821.

30. Parry, J.; Palaz, D.; Clarke, G.; Lecomte, P.; Mead, R.; Berger, M.; Hofer, G. Analysis of Deep Learning Architectures for Cross-Corpus Speech Emotion Recognition. In Proceedings of the Interspeech 2019, Graz, Austria, 15–19 September 2019.
31. Axman, D.; Yacouby, R. Probabilistic extension of precision, recall, and F1 score for more thorough evaluation of classification models. In *Proceedings of the First Workshop on Evaluation and Comparison of NLP Systems*; Association for Computational Linguistics: Toronto, ON, Canada, 2020.

electronics

MDPI

Article

A Swell Neural Network Algorithm for Solving Time-Varying Path Query Problems with Privacy Protection

Man Zhao

School of Electrical and Electronic Engineering, North China Electric Power University, Beijing 102206, China; 50301363@ncepu.edu.cn

Abstract: In this paper, a swell neural network (SNN) algorithm was proposed for solving time-varying path query (TVPQ) problems with privacy protection with the following goals: (i) querying the K-nearest paths with time limitations in a time-varying scenario, and (ii) protecting private information from neighborhood attacks. The proposed SNN is a network in which the optimal paths can be calculated at the same time with no need for training. For TVPQ, a node is considered a neuron, and time-varying means that an edge has different costs in different time windows. For SNN, the query paths are swell sets from the start to the target within an upper limit. An encrypted index is designed for privacy protection. The evaluation of the efficiency and accuracy of the SNN was carried out based on New York road instances.

Keywords: time-varying path query (TVPQ); swell neural network (SNN); privacy protection; encrypted index

1. Introduction

Path query problems with privacy protection have attracted attention in many fields, such as industry [1,2], management science [3], computer science [4], and transportation [5]. Path query problems with privacy protection were first proposed in 2011 by Cao [4], who proposed utilizing the principle of filtering and verification to keep cloud data secure. Shang H [6], Gouda K [7], and Lin W [8] carried out further research based on this idea. Meng X studied the problem of graph encryption and proposed an approximate shortest distance query method (GRECS) for encrypted graphs [9]. A CryptGraph scheme has been designed, with which graph analysis can be performed on encrypted graphs, and the privacy of users' graph data and analysis results can be protected [10]. However, these studies lack consideration of time variation.

There is a suite of studies addressing the time-varying path query problem. The shortest path algorithm through a time-varying network was first proposed in 1966 by Cooke and Halsey [11]. Such path query methods for dynamic graphs are valuable references. Frigioni D proposed the global dynamic algorithm FMN to solve the single-source shortest path problem for dynamic graphs [12]. Additionally, SWSF-FP was proposed by Ramalingam G [13]. A global dynamic algorithm for computing the shortest paths between all pairs of vertices in a dynamic graph was also proposed [14]. An improved algorithm was proposed to maintain the shortest paths between all pairs of vertices in a dynamic graph [15]. In addition, Liu C [16], Ghosh E [17], Sun F [18], and Wu B [19] described their research on this topic. However, these works neglect privacy protection.

To our knowledge, current algorithmic models either ignore the effect of the time factor or the need for privacy protection. There are still unresolved TVPQ problems regarding privacy protection, despite the urgent need for solutions in applications such as mapping services [20]. Different departure times and expected arrival times lead to changes in planned routes. Users expect to obtain the top recommended routes under the current time constraints. Pioneering works by Huang W [3,21,22], Zhang C [23], and Shen M [24] provided schemes for reference. Huang W's work lacks a design for multiple paths, and accuracy cannot be fully guaranteed in Shen M's work. Current algorithms have limitations in terms of multipath requirements and accuracy guarantees.

In this paper, an SNN algorithm was proposed to solve TVPQ problems with privacy protection. An SNN is a network in which the optimal paths can be calculated at the same time and there is no need for training. For TVPQ, nodes are considered neurons, and time-varying means that an edge has different costs in different time windows. The core of the SNN is that the query paths are swell sets from the start node to the target node, and their arrival times are less than the upper limit.

The main contributions of this paper are as follows:

1. The SNN algorithm can help to find multiple paths at once, including the shortest paths. This is difficult to achieve with other algorithms under time-varying conditions.
2. For privacy protection, a scheme was designed with an encrypted index that effectively prevents the leakage of user information.
3. Theoretical analyses and contrasting experimental results prove the efficiency, security, and accuracy of the algorithm.

The remainder of this paper is organized as follows. Section 2 introduces prerequisites, Section 3 presents the SNN algorithm, Section 4 reports the experimental results, and concluding statements are presented in Section 5.

2. Preliminaries

This section introduces several prerequisites that will be used throughout this paper.

2.1. Definition of Time-Varying Path Query

Definition 1 (Time-Varying Network). *A time-varying network graph is defined as $G = (N, E)$, where N represents the set of nodes and E denotes the set of network edges. $E_{ij} \in E$ stands for the edge from node i to node j, and it is associated with different time weights c^r_{ij} for different time windows D^r_{ij}.*

Definition 2 (Path of a Time-Varying Network). *A path P_{1k} on a time-varying network is defined as a sequence of nodes $< n_1, \ldots, n_i, \ldots, n_k >$, where n_1 is the start node, n_k is the target node, n_i is the ith node in the path, and T_e is the arrival time at n_k. A route based on P_{1k} is a sequence of nodes $< n_1, \ldots, n_i, \ldots, n_k >$ [25].*

According to the definition of the path of a time-varying network, the arrival time is $Te = Ts + \sum_{i=1}^{k} c_{n_i, n_{i+1}}$ for a path $P_{1k} =< n_1, \ldots, \mathrm{n_i}, \ldots, n_k >$.

2.2. Model of a Time-Varying Network Query

Given a directed graph $G = (N, E)$, a start node $n_s \in N$, a target node $n_t \in N$, a start time T_s, an upper limit of the arrival time T_u, and the number f of paths to query for, a time-varying network query finds the set of paths $(p1_{st},\ p2_{st}, \ldots\ldots)$ such that the arrival time is less than T_u.

For node i, the successor set can be defined as $S_i = \{sd_j | n_j \in N\}$, where the length of d_i represents the number of swells from node i to other nodes.

$$sd_i = \begin{cases} [], d_i = 0 \\ [[t_1, t_2]], d_i = 1 \\ [[t_1, t_2], \ldots, [t_k, t_{k+1}]], d_i = k \end{cases}$$

For node j, the predecessor set can be defined as $F_j = \{fd_i | n_i \in N\}$, where the length of e_j represents the number of swells from other nodes to j.

$$fd_i = \begin{cases} [], e_j = 0 \\ [[t_1, t_2]], e_j = 1 \\ [[t_1, t_2], \ldots, [t_k, t_{k+1}]], ej = k \end{cases}$$

Clearly, if there is one swell from n_i to n_j, at t_1 to t_2 both sd_j and fd_i above contain $[t_1, t_2]$. The predecessor set of n_t collects the swells leading to n_t with the arrival times. Based on the above two features, paths can be obtained by tracing the predecessor sets of n_t iteratively.

For privacy protection, three algorithms were used: RSA, AES, and ORE.

In RSA, the encryption keys are public, while the decryption keys are not, so only the person with the correct decryption key can decipher an encrypted message. This avoids the need for a "courier" to deliver keys to recipients through another secure channel before transmitting the originally intended message [26,27].

AES is a substitution-permutation network block cipher based on the design principles of Ron Rivest, Adi Shamir, and Leonard Adleman's earlier Data Encryption Standard (DES). It uses a variable-length key from 128 bits to 256 bits and operates on fixed-size blocks of 128 bits. Both parties must agree on the key in advance to ensure that the key information cannot be obtained by a third party [27,28].

An order-revealing encryption (ORE) scheme is a tuple of three algorithms Π = (ORE.Setup, ORE.Encrypt, ORE.Compare) defined over a well-ordered domain D with the following properties:

ORE.Setup(1^λ)→sk: On inputting a security parameter λ, the setup algorithm outputs a secret key sk.

ORE.Encrypt(sk, m)→ct: On inputting a secret key sk and a message $m \in D$, the encryption algorithm outputs a ciphertext ct.

ORE.Compare($ct1$, $ct2$)→b: On inputting two ciphertexts $ct1$, $ct2$, the compare algorithm outputs a bit $b \in \{0, 1\}$.

An ORE scheme over a well-ordered domain D is correct if for $sk \leftarrow ORE.Setup(1^\lambda)$ and all messages $m1,\ m2 \in D$ [29–31]:

$$Pr[ORE.Compare(ct1,\ ct2) = 1(m1 < m2)] = 1 - negl(\lambda)$$

Definition 3 (Encrypted Index). *An encrypted index consists of two parts, as follows:*

- T_e *encrypted with the ORE key*
- P_{st} *encrypted with the public secret key of RSA-1.*

Definition 4 (Encrypted Query). *An encrypted message for a query consists of three parts, as follows:*

- (s, t, T_s) *encrypted with the AES key*
- T_u *encrypted with the ORE key and the AES key*
- f *is the plaintext representing the number of paths queried.*

3. Construction of the SNN

This section presents the SNN algorithm and its complexity and security analyses.

3.1. Design of the SNN Algorithm

The SNN is a swell neural network without any training. To formalize the SNN, each node is viewed as a neuron and the graph composed of nodes and the edges connecting them is viewed as a neural network.

Figure 1 illustrates a general neuron structure for an SNN. As shown in Figure 1, there are four parts in each loop: the input, the neuron state, the neuron feedback, and the output. The main functions of these four parts are as follows: the input swell coming from its predecessor nodes over time, the neuron state that determines whether to spread, the feedback that updates the neuron state, and the output swells that spread to the successor nodes.

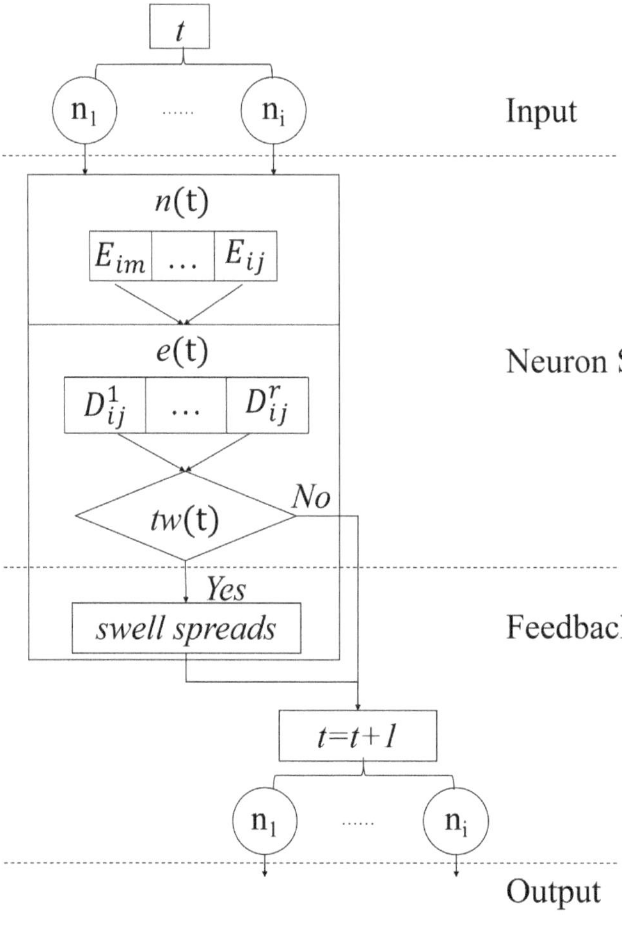

Figure 1. A general neuron structure of SNN.

1. Input: The input swells come from the predecessor nodes.
2. Neuron state: The neuron state consists of three parts: nodes, edges, and time windows. The functions *n(t)*, *e(t)* and *tw(t)* represent the processing of the node, edge, and time window, respectively, and *t* represents the current time. For n_i, the successor set can be defined as $S_i = \{sdj|nj \in N\}$, where the length of d_i represents the number of swells from n_i to n_j.

$$sd_i = \begin{cases} [], d_i = 0 \\ [[t_1, t_2]], d_i = 1 \\ [[t_1, t_2], \ldots, [t_k, t_{k+1}]], d_i = k \end{cases}$$

The predecessor set can be defined similarly. For edge E_{ij}, the time set collects the arrival times of n_i for which no swell is currently formed.

$$P_{ij} = \begin{cases} [], no \\ [t_1, t_2 \ldots], yes \end{cases}$$

For time window D^r_{ij}, v^r_{ij} represents the set of key-value pairs for arrival and available times when no swell is formed.

$$v^r_{ij} = \begin{cases} [], no \\ [t_1, t_2 \ldots], yes \end{cases}$$

3. Feedback: The swells spread along the edge in the time window for which the available time c_k satisfies the cost c^r_{ij}, and c_k is computed as follows:

$$c_k = \begin{cases} t - t_k, if\ l^r_{ij} <= t_k < u^r_{ij} \\ t - l^r_{ij}, if\ t_k < l^r_{ij} \end{cases}$$

4. Output: The output swells continue to spread to the successor nodes.

The overall algorithm, referred to as Algorithm 1, serves as the foundation for the SNN. The partitioning algorithms of the SNN algorithm are introduced as follows. To find the shortest paths, the SNN algorithm works as follows:

- Initialize the graph as Algorithm 2.
- Activate the start node directly as Algorithm 3.
- Iterate over the successor edges of the start node as Algorithm 4 to spread ripples.
- Iterate over all nodes over time to activate the nodes as Algorithm 4 until the target node is activated. The path can be obtained if the current time is within the maximum time range. Otherwise, no path meets the requirements.

Algorithm 1 Encrypted Index Construction (EIC)

```
Input: G, s, t, T_s, T_u, f
Output: P_st, T_e
Initialize G as Algorithm 2.
T_e = T_s
Initialize n_s as Algorithm 3.
while l_st < f and T_e <= T_u do
    T_e = T_e + 1
    for n_i ∈ G do
        Try to activate n_i as Algorithm 4.
    if F_t has been changed do
        p_st >> P_st as Algorithm 5.
    end if
end while
Encrypt each path with K_ORE and Pk_RSA2.
```

First, initialize the graph as shown in Algorithm 2. A directed graph is constructed. Each node is initialized with an empty father set and son set for collecting predecessors and successors. For the edges, a time set is initialized for the arrival times of the predecessors, and time windows with boundaries, costs, and the set of key-value pairs for arrival and available times are initialized.

The start node is initialized according to Algorithm 3. The algorithm iterates over the predecessor edges of the start node n_s and adds the start time T_s to its time set and time window set.

Algorithm 2 Graph Initialization (GI)

```
Input: G
Output: G
for E_ij ∈ G do
      F_i = None
   S_i = None
   F_j = None
   S_j = None
      c_ij = None
      for D^r_ij ∈ D_ij do
         v^r_ij = None
end for
end for
return G
```

Algorithm 3 Start Node Initialization (SI)

```
Input: G, n_s, T_s
Output: G
for E_si ∈ E^S_s do
      T_s >> E_sj
      for D^r_si ∈ D_si do
            (T_s, 0) >> v^r_ij.
      end for
end for
```

To activate the nodes over time, if the input node is a start node or its father set is not empty, then the algorithm iterates over the successor edges of the input node to spread swells, as Algorithm 4.

Algorithm 4 Node Activation (NA)

```
Input: G, n_i, n_s
Output: G
if n_i = n_s or F_i ≠ None:
      for E_ij ∈ E^S_i do
            Spread as Algorithm 6
      end for
end if
```

New paths are added to paths according to Algorithm 5. The function AP is executed iteratively until f paths are found that meet the requirements.

The swells spread along the edge as shown in Algorithm 6. Whether the swells spread is dependent on the determination of the time window over time. The swells are retained, process records are deleted, and the network prepares for the next iteration, as shown in Algorithm 3, after the swells spread.

Determine each time window of the edges over time, as shown in Algorithm 7. The swells spread along the edge in the time window for which the available time satisfies the cost.

Algorithm 5 Add Paths (AP)

Input: G, n_i, p_{jt}, n_s, f
Output: P_{st}
if $l_{st} < f$ do
    $p_{it} = [i] + p_{jt}$
    if $n_i = n_s$
        $p_{st} >> P_{st}$
        if $l_{st} = f$ do
            break
        end if
    end if
    else
    for $j \in F_i$ do
        AP(Algorithm 5)
    end for
end if

Algorithm 6 Swell Spreading (SS)

Input: $G,\ E_{ij},\ T\ (current\ time)$
Output: G
$de_{ij} = None//$Initialize the set of arrival times to be deleted from E_{ij}
for $D^r_{ij} \in D_{ij}$
    key = Perform time window determination as Algorithm 7
    if $key \neq None$ do
        $key >> de_{ij}$
    end if
end for
for $de \in de_{ij}$:
    Delete de from c_{ij}
    Delete (de,*) from v^r_{ij}
    $(i\ , [time, T]) >> F_j,\ (j\ , [time, T]) >> S_i$ and $(T,\ 0) >> v^r_{ij}$ as Algorithm 3
end for

Algorithm 7 Time Window Determination (TD)

Input: $G, D^r_{ij}, T(currenttime)$.
Output: G
$de = None//$ Initialize the arrival time to be deleted from E_{ij}
for $key \in v^r_{ij}$ (the key-value pair set of D^r_{ij})
    if $l^r_{ij} <= key < u^r_{ij}$ do
        $v^r_{ij}[key] = T - key$
    else if $key < l^r_{ij}$ do
        $v^r_{ij}[key] = T - l^r_{ij}$
    end if
    if $v^r_{ij}[key] = c^r_{ij}$ do
        $de = key$
    end if
end for
return de

3.2. An Example of the SNN Algorithm

To illustrate the SNN algorithm, let us consider the example shown in Figure 2 and Table 1. There are three nodes and three edges in the time-varying network, where A is the start node, C is the target node, the start time is 0, the upper limit of the arrival time is 5, and the number f of paths to query is 2. For each edge, there are two time windows.

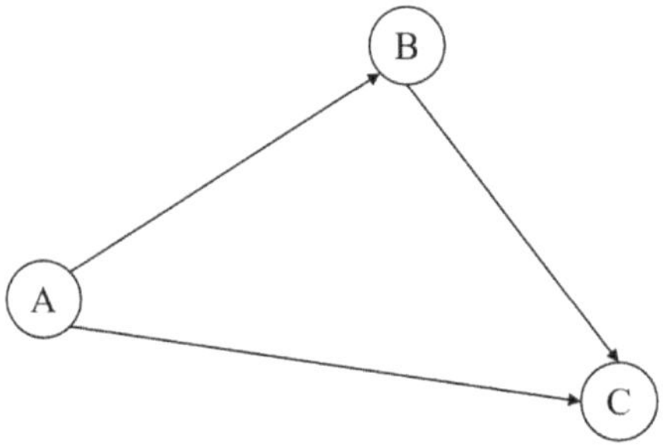

Figure 2. An example of a time-varying neural network.

Table 1. Description of the example.

Node	Edge	Time Window	Cost
A	AB	$[0, 3)$	1
		$[3, +\infty)$	2
	AC	$[0, 2)$	2
		$[3, +\infty)$	4
B	BC	$[0, 3)$	2
		$[3, +\infty)$	3

Table 2 illustrates the detailed steps of the running algorithm on the SNN. It is evident that the paths are <A, C> and <A, B, C>. At moment 0, only n_A is reached and the swell has not spread to the next node. At moment 1, a swell spread to n_B, which is a child of n_A. At moment 2, a swell reaches C and a path from A to C is found as [A, C] in time 2. At moment 3, the swell that spread to n_B at moment 1 arrived at n_C, and the second path from A to C is found as [A, B, C], in time 3.

Furthermore, to ensure the data security of the cloud and users, four sets of keys for three encryption algorithms were configured. Initially, the cloud server holds the private key of RSA1. A user is authorized if he or she has obtained the private secret key of RSA1 and the public secret key of RSA2. The user constructs the encrypted index, as demonstrated in definition 3 for the graph, and outsources indexes to the cloud server.

The system interaction is as follows:

1. The user, say Bob, generates a unique secret key for AES K_{AES}, distinguished from those of other users to prevent leakage from others.
2. Bob→Cloud: Send K_{AES}, which is encrypted by Pk_{RSA2}
3. Bob→Cloud: Encrypt $(A, C, 0, 5, 2)$ as an encrypted query according to Definition 4, encrypt $(A, C, 0)$ with the AES key K_{AES} and encrypt 5 with the ORE key K_{ORE} and the AES key K_{AES}.
4. Cloud: Decrypt the query with K_{AES}, use $(A, C, 0)$ to find f matching encrypted indices, and compare the second part of the encrypted index with 5. If the former is not greater, the item meets the query.
5. Cloud→Bob: Query the result encrypted with K_{AES}.
6. Bob: Decrypt the information with K_{AES} and then with Sk_{RSA1} to obtain the query result $< A, C >: 1, < A, B, C >: 3$.

Table 2. Steps of SNN as an example.

node	n_A				n_B		n_C
edge	E_{AB}		E_{AC}		E_{BC}		-
Time window	D_{AB}^1	D_{AB}^2	D_{AC}^1	D_{AC}^2	D_{BC}^1	D_{BC}^2	-
(a) Running SI ($t = 0$)							
S_i	None				None		None
F_i	None				None		None
P_{ij}	[0]		[0]		None		-
v_{ij}^r	$\{0:0\}$	$\{0:0\}$	$\{0:0\}$	$\{0:0\}$	None	None	-
(b) Running NA ($t = 1$)							
S_i	$\{B:[[0,1]]\}$				None		None
F_i	None				$\{A:[[0,1]]\}$		None
P_{ij}	None		[0]		[1]		-
v_{ij}^r	None	None	$\{0:1\}$	$\{0:-2\}$	$\{1:0\}$	$\{1:0\}$	-
(c) Running NA ($t = 2$)							
S_i	$\{B:[[0,1]], C:[[0,2]]\}$				None		None
F_i	None				$\{A:[[0,1]]\}$		$\{A:[[0,2]]\}$
P_{ij}	None		None		[1]		-
v_{ij}^r	None	None	None	None	$\{1:1\}$	$\{1:-1\}$	-
(d) Running AP							
paths	$[[A,C,2]]$						
(e) Running NA ($t = 3$)							
S_i	$\{B:[[0,1]], C:[[0,2]]\}$				$\{C:[[1,3]]\}$		None
F_i	None				$\{A:[[0,1]]\}$		$\left\{\begin{array}{l} A:[[0,2]] \\ B:[[1,3]] \end{array}\right\}$
P_{ij}	[0]		[0]		None		-
v_{ij}^r	$\{0:0\}$	$\{0:0\}$	$\{0:0\}$	$\{0:0\}$	None	None	-
(f) Running AP							
paths	$[[A,C,2],[A,B,C,3]]$						

3.3. Complexity

Theorem 1 (Time Complexity of the SNN). *A directed graph G with n nodes and m edges is given, where each edge has an average of k time windows. The SNN algorithm finds the result in* $O(n^2 \times k \times m \times f)$ *time for f paths.*

Proof of Theorem 1 . The complexity of Algorithm 1 needs to be combined with the complexity of graph initialization, start node initialization, node activation, and path addition, i.e., Algorithms 2–7.

(1) Algorithm 2 focuses on traversing the edges to initialize the time windows on each edge. The complexity of graph initialization is $O(m \times k)$.

(2) Algorithm 3 involves traversing the time windows of the successor edge set of n_i. The time complexity is approximately $O(m \times k)$.

(3) Algorithm 4 involves judgement. When the judgement condition is true, the time complexity is $O(m \times k \times n)$, after considering Algorithm 6.

(4) Algorithm 5 is an iteration related to the number of nodes and edges. The time complexity is $O(m \times n)$.

(5) Algorithm 6 includes two side-by-side cyclic operations, one related to the number of time windows of the edges, and the other is the removal operation in the process processing which makes a call to Algorithm 3. The time complexity of Algorithm 6 is approximately $O(m \times k)$.

(6) The complexity of Algorithm 7 is $O(1)$ obviously.

Combining the calls of Algorithm 1 to other algorithms and the call relationships between the algorithms, the time complexity of the SNN can be calculated using the following expression:

$$O(n^2 \times k \times m \times f)$$

Theorem 1 is proven. □

3.4. Security

The design of the encrypted index incorporates three different cryptography techniques: RSA, AES, and ORE. Each of these three algorithms plays an important role in the field of cryptography, and together they provide a multi-layered security.

Assuming that the cloud provider is secure and trustworthy, i.e., it does not tamper with the data and returns the query results truthfully, it is assumed that the key distribution process is secure.

The security of RSA depends on the key length and the complexity of the factorization algorithm. As the computational power increases, the key length of RSA increases to maintain its security. Although quantum computing may pose a threat to the security of RSA, RSA keys of a sufficient length are still secure for the time being. RSA is used to make real data transparent to the cloud provider and to protect the user's independent secret key [26,27].

The design of AES consists of a multi-round encryption process, with each round including operations such as byte substitution, row shifting, column mixing, and round key addition. The security of AES has been extensively researched and empirically verified, and to date, no effective attack method has been found that can break AES-256 in a practicable amount of time. AES is used to prevent information leakage between users. Even if a user has access to another user's information, the data cannot be deciphered without the user's secret key [27,28].

ORE is designed to prevent the inference of sensitive information through sequential relationships, thus providing greater security than traditional OPE. ORE is secure, in that it hides the sequential information of the data, making it impossible to infer anything about the original data even when the encrypted data is sorted or a range query is performed. ORE is for path filtering in the cloud [29–31].

4. Experiments

This section presents the evaluation of the SNN algorithm through experiments on New York road instances.

To illustrate the efficiency and accuracy of the SNN algorithm, four random network topologies with 50 nodes, 100 nodes, 500 nodes, and 1000 nodes were considered. The time limits for the above topologies are 50, 200, 500, and 1000, respectively. All the algorithms in our experiment are implemented in Python. The experiments are conducted using a desktop PC sourced from Dell, headquartered in Round Rock, Texas, USA. The PC is equipped with an 11th Gen Intel(R) Core (TM) i7-11390H processor at 3.40 GHz and 16 GB of RAM.

The datasets used in our experiments are listed in Table 3.

Table 3. Datasets for Experiments.

Dataset	Nodes	Edges	Time Windows	T_u	Storage
Dataset 1	50	115	230	50	4 KB
Dataset 2	100	230	460	200	7 KB
Dataset 3	500	1244	2488	500	44 KB
Dataset 4	1000	2493	4986	1000	92 KB

Table 4 shows the query time statistics of existing algorithms before as Dijkstra [32], PCNN [33], and TDNN without the time-varying [25]. These algorithms have the same accuracy, i.e., they all find the shortest paths. The optimal algorithm TDNN was selected for comparison experiments with SNN.

Table 4. Comparison of existing algorithms.

Dataset	Dijkstra	PCNN	TDNN
Dataset 1	0.001	0.001	0.001
Dataset 2	0.004	0.003	0.003
Dataset 3	0.10	0.08	0.08
Dataset 4	0.26	0.31	0.24

Table 5 shows the efficiency comparison of TDNN and SNN with time-varying factors. As the size of datasets grows, both algorithms show a substantial increase in the time required. However, the TDNN algorithm takes significantly longer than SNN, and the time difference between the two algorithms is becoming greater. The SNN algorithm has better efficiency than TDNN with time-varying factors, and it can find multiple paths at once and contains the shortest path, which indicates that the accuracy of SNN is significantly better than that of others (e.g., TDNN).

Table 5. Efficiency Comparison of SNN, TDNN, Connor.

Dataset	SNN	TDNN	Connor
Dataset 1	0.03	0.08	0.05
Dataset 2	0.12	0.53	0.1
Dataset 3	3.13	64.10	0.8
Dataset 4	18.72	225.75	8.9

Accuracy comparison of SNN, TDNN, and Connor is presented in the form of line chart in Figure 3. In addition, the SNN is significantly less efficient compared to the Connor. However, the Connor framework has the obvious limitation that it sacrifices accuracy [24]. This is less applicable in multiple scenarios such as map services. This leads to its low applicability in scenarios where accuracy is required.

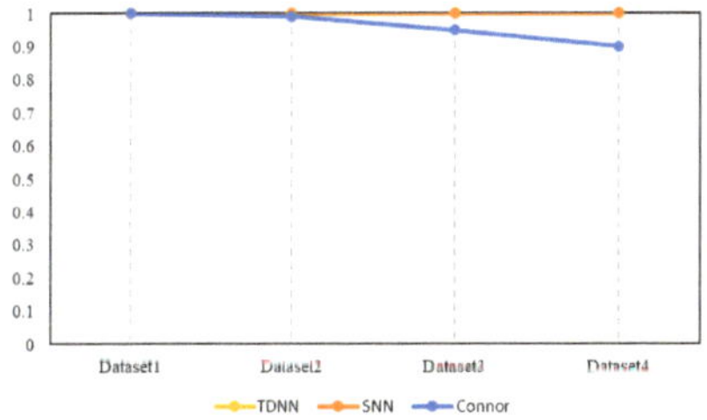

Figure 3. Accuracy Comparison of SNN, TDNN, and Connor.

Tables 6 and 7 show the time statistics for different numbers of edges, nodes, time windows and T_u, which are presented in the form of a line chart in Figure 4. For practical reasons, the number of time windows will not change exponentially. It can be easily seen that the time consumption of SNN is positively correlated with the number of nodes, edges, time windows, and the upper limit of time.

In summary, the SNN algorithm shows more comprehensive advantages in terms of efficiency, accuracy, etc. The SNN algorithm is of great significance for solving time-varying path query problems with privacy protection.

However, the efficiency decreases significantly as the scale of the graph increases according to the experimental results. To adapt to more demand scenarios, such as large-scale graph applications, the hardware configuration can be improved or more research on optimization and iteration needs to be performed.

Table 6. SNN experimental results (k = 2).

Dataset	T_u = 50 s	T_u = 200s	T_u = 500 s	T_u = 1000 s
Dataset 1	0.04	0.04	0.03	0.03
Dataset 2	0.04	0.17	0.16	0.16
Dataset 3	0.06	0.60	4.36	4.10
Dataset 4	0.08	0.88	5.34	26.41

Table 7. SNN experimental results (k = 4).

Dataset	T_u = 50 s	T_u = 200 s	T_u = 200 s	T_u = 200 s
Dataset 1	0.04	0.04	0.04	0.04
Dataset 2	0.05	0.18	0.15	0.15
Dataset 3	0.07	0.4	3.16	3.32
Dataset 4	0.10	0.62	4.86	29.18

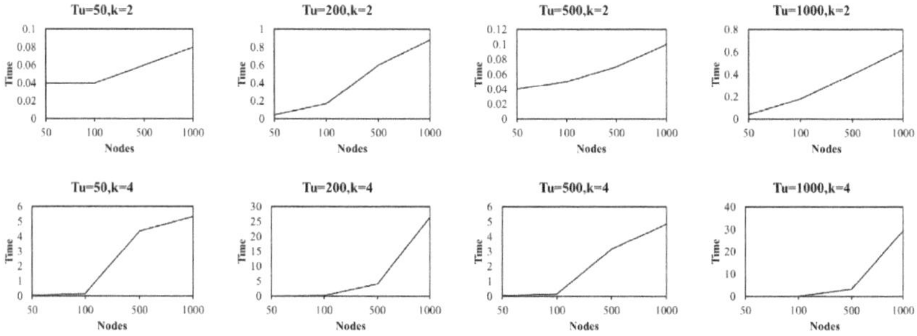

Figure 4. Comprehensive comparison of SNN experimental results.

5. Conclusions

In this paper, the SNN algorithm was proposed for solving TVPQ problems with privacy protection. This approach is highly important for road planning, network routing, project scheduling, and other issues in data outsourcing scenarios. The most prominent advantage is that it can find multiple paths at once, including the shortest paths, which other algorithms cannot find. Additionally, an encrypted index for privacy protection has been designed. Experiments with New York road instances demonstrated the efficiency and accuracy of the SNN algorithm.

In future work, further studies of path planning algorithms with privacy protection can be conducted, such as optimization algorithms for large-scale encrypted graphs.

Funding: This research received no external funding.

Data Availability Statement: Publicly available datasets were analyzed in this study. This data can be found here: https://www.diag.uniroma1.it/challenge9/download.shtml (accessed on 15 September 2022).

Conflicts of Interest: The author declares no conflicts of interest. The funders had no role in the design of the study; in the collection, analyses, or interpretation of data; in the writing of the manuscript; or in the decision to publish the results.

Abbreviations

The following abbreviations are used in this manuscript:

Symbols	Explanation
G	The graph
n_s	The start node
n_t	The target node
T_s	The departure time
T_e	The arrival time
Sk_{RSA1}	The private key of RSA-1
Pk_{RSA1}	The public key of RSA-1
Sk_{RSA2}	The private key of RSA-2
Pk_{RSA2}	The public key of RSA-2
K_{AES}	The key of AES
K_{ORE}	The key of ORE
T_u	The upper limit of the arrival time
p_{st}	One path from n_s to n_t
P_{st}	The paths set from n_s to n_t
l_{st}	The length of P_{st}
E_{ij}	The edge from n_i to n_j
D_{ij}	The time window of the edge from n_i to n_j
D_{ij}^r	The rth time window of the edge from n_i to n_j
l_{ij}^r	The lower boundary of D_{ij}^r
u_{ij}^r	The upper boundary of D_{ij}^r
c_{ij}	The cost of E_{ij}
c_{ij}^r	The cost of D_{ij}^r
v_{ij}^r	The cost of D_{ij}^r in real time
N_{ij}^P	The predecessor n_i of n_j
N_{ij}^S	The successor n_j of node i
E_i^P	The predecessor edge set of n_i
E_i^S	The successor edge set of n_i
N_s	The number of nodes
f	The number of paths queried
k	The number of time windows of each edge
F_i	The father set of n_i
P_{ij}	The arrival time set of n_j with that swell has not spread to next node currently
S_i	The son set of n_i

References

1. References Ge, X.; Yu, J.; Zhang, H.; Bai, J.; Fan, J.; Xiong, N.N. SPPS: A search pattern privacy system for approximate shortest distance query of encrypted graphs in iiot. *IEEE Trans. Syst. Man Cybern. Syst.* **2022**, *52*, 136–150.
2. Zhou, Y.; Lu, Y.; Lv, L. Grid-based non-uniform probabilistic roadmap-based agv path planning in narrow passages and complex environments. *Electronics* **2024**, *13*, 225–240. [CrossRef]
3. Huang, W.; Gao, L. A time wave neural network framework for solving time-dependent project scheduling problems. *IEEE Trans. Neural Netw. Learn. Syst.* **2020**, *31*, 274–283. [CrossRef] [PubMed]
4. Cao, N.; Yang, Z.; Wang, C.; Ren, K.; Lou, W. Privacy-preserving query over encrypted graph-structured data in cloud computing. In Proceedings of the 2011 31st International Conference on Distributed Computing Systems, Minneapolis, MN, USA, 20–24 June 2011; pp. 105–117.
5. Memon, I.; Arain, Q.A. Dynamic path privacy protection framework for continuous query service over road networks. *World Wide Web* **2017**, *20*, 639–672. [CrossRef]
6. Shang, H.; Zhang, Y.; Lin, X.; Yu, J.X. Taming verification hardness: An efficient algorithm for testing subgraph isomorphism. *Proc. Vldb Endow.* **2008**, *1*, 364–375. [CrossRef]
7. Gouda, K.; Hassaan, M. Compressed feature-based filtering and verification approach for subgraph search. In Proceedings of the EDBT'13: Proceedings of the 16th International Conference on Extending Database Technology, Genoa, Italy, 18–22 March 2013; pp. 201–213.
8. Lin, W.; Xiao, X.; Cheng, J.; Bhowmick, S.S. Efficient algorithms for generalized subgraph query processing. In Proceedings of the CIKM'12: Proceedings of the 21st ACM international conference on Information and knowledge management, Maui, HI, USA, 29 October–2 November 2012; Association for Computing Machinery: New York, NY, USA, 2012; pp. 325–352.

9. Meng, X.; Kamara, S.; Nissim, K.; Kollios, G.N. GRECS: Graph encryption for approximate shortest distance queries. In Proceedings of the CCS'15: Proceedings of the 22nd ACM SIGSAC Conference on Computer and Communications Security, Denver, CO, USA, 12–16 October 2015; Association for Computing Machinery: New York, NY, USA, 2015; pp. 25–42.
10. Xie, P.; Xing, E. CryptGraph: Privacy Preserving Graph Analytics on Encrypted Graph. *arXiv* **2014**, arXiv:1409.5021.
11. Cooke, K.L.; Halsey, E. The shortest route through a network with time-dependent internodal transit times. *J. Math. Anal. Appl.* **1966**, *14*, 493–498. [CrossRef]
12. Frigioni, D.; Marchetti-Spaccamela, A.; Nanni, U. Fully dynamic output bounded single source shortest path problem. In Proceedings of the SODA'96: Proceedings of the Seventh Annual ACM-SIAM Symposium on Discrete Algorithms, Atlanta, GA, USA, 28–30 January 1996; pp. 212–221.
13. Ramalingam, G.; Reps, T. An incremental algorithm for a generalization of the shortest-path problem. *J. Algorithms* **1996**, *21*, 267–305. [CrossRef]
14. King, V. Fully dynamic algorithms for maintaining all-pairs shortest paths and transitive closure in digraphs. In Proceedings of the 40th Annual Symposium on Foundations of Computer Science, New York, NY, USA, 17–19 October 1999; pp. 81–89.
15. Demetrescu, C.; Italiano, G. A new approach to dynamic all pairs shortest paths. *J. ACM* **2004**, *51*, 968–992. [CrossRef]
16. Liu, C.; Zhu, L.; He, X.; Chen, J. Enabling privacy-preserving shortest distance queries on encrypted graph data. *IEEE Trans. Dependable Secur. Comput.* **2021**, *18*, 192–204. [CrossRef]
17. Ghosh, E.; Kamara, S.; Tamassia, R. Efficient graph encryption scheme for shortest path queries. In Proceedings of the ASIA CCS'21: ACM Asia Conference on Computer and Communications Security, Hong Kong, China, 7–11 June 2021; pp. 31–43.
18. Sun, F.; Yu, J.; Ge, X.; Yang, M.; Kong, F. Constrained top-k nearest fuzzy keyword queries on encrypted graph in road network. *Comput. Secur.* **2021**, *111*, 430–442. [CrossRef]
19. Wu, B.; Chen, X.; Wu, Z.; Zhao, Z.; Mei, Z.; Zhang, C. Privacy-guarding optimal route finding with support for semantic search on encrypted graph in cloud computing scenario. *Wirel. Commun. Mob. Comput.* **2021**, *2021*, 6617959. [CrossRef]
20. Zhang, D.; Liu, Y.; Liu, A.; Mao, X.; Li, Q. Efficient path query processing through cloud-based mapping services. *IEEE Access* **2017**, *5*, 12963–12973. [CrossRef]
21. Huang, W.; Sun, M.; Zhu, L.; Oh, S.; Pedrycz, W. Deep fuzzy min-max neural network: Analysis and design. *IEEE Trans. Neural Netw. Learn. Syst.* **2022**. [CrossRef]
22. Huang, W.; Wang, Y.; Zhu, L. A time impulse neural network framework for solving the minimum path pair problems of the time-varying network. *IEEE Trans. Knowl. Data Eng.* **2023**, *35*, 7681–7692. [CrossRef]
23. Zhang, C.; Luo, X.; Liang, J.; Liu, X.; Zhu, L.; Guo, S. POTA: Privacy-preserving online multi-task assignment with path planning. *IEEE Trans. Mob. Comput.* **2023**, *4*, 1–13. [CrossRef]
24. Shen, M.; Ma, B.; Zhu, L.; Mijumbi, R.; Du, X.; Hu, J. Cloud-based approximate constrained shortest distance queries over encrypted graphs with privacy protection. *IEEE Trans. Inf. Forensics Secur.* **2018**, *13*, 940–953. [CrossRef]
25. Huang, W.; Wang, J.; Wang, W. A time-delay neural network for solving time-dependent shortest path problem. *Neural Netw.* **2017**, *90*, 21–28. [CrossRef]
26. Tahat, N.; Tahat, A.A.; Abu-Dalu, M. A new RSA public key encryption scheme with chaotic maps. *Int. J. Electr. Comput. Eng.* **2020**, *10*, 1430–1437. [CrossRef]
27. Huang, X.; Wang, W. A novel and efficient design for an rsa cryptosystem with a very large key size. *IEEE Trans. Circuits Syst.* **2015**, *62*, 972–976. [CrossRef]
28. Masoumi, M. Novel hybrid cmos/memristor implementation of the aes algorithm robust against differential power analysis attack. *IEEE Trans. Circuits Syst.* **2020**, *67*, 1314–1318. [CrossRef]
29. Peyrin, T. *Practical Order-Revealing Encryption with Limited Leakage*; Springer: Berlin/Heidelberg, Germany, 2016; Volume 9783, pp. 474–493.
30. Zhang, C.; Zhao, M.; Liang, J.; Fan, Q.; Zhu, L.; Guo, S. NANO: Cryptographic enforcement of readability and editability governance in blockchain databases. *IEEE Trans. Dependable Secur. Comput.* **2023**, *4*, 1–14. [CrossRef]
31. Hu, C.; Zhang, C.; Lei, D.; Wu, T.; Liu, X.; Zhu, L. Achieving privacy-preserving and verifiable support vector machine training in the cloud. *IEEE Trans. Inf. Forensics Secur.* **2023**, *18*, 3476–3491. [CrossRef]
32. Zhu, D.; Sun, J. A new algorithm based on dijkstra for vehicle path planning considering intersection attribute. *IEEE Access* **2021**, *9*, 19761–19775. [CrossRef]
33. Sang, Y.; Lv, J.; Qu, H.; Yi, Z. Shortest path computation using pulse-coupled neural networks with restricted autowave. *Knowl.-Based Syst.* **2016**, *114*, 1–11. [CrossRef]

electronics

MDPI

Article

Multisource Sparse Inversion Localization with Long-Distance Mobile Sensors

Jinyang Ren [1], Peihan Qi [1], Chenxi Li [1,*], Panpan Zhu [1] and Zan Li [2]

[1] State Key Laboratory of Integrated Service Networks, Xidian University, Xi'an 710071, China
[2] School of Telecommunications Engineering, Xidian University, Xi'an 710071, China
* Correspondence: chenxili@xidian.edu.cn

Abstract: To address the threat posed by unknown signal sources within Mobile Crowd Sensing (MCS) systems to system stability and to realize effective localization of unknown sources in long-distance scenarios, this paper proposes a unilateral branch ratio decision algorithm (UBRD). This approach addresses the inadequacies of traditional sparse localization algorithms in long-distance positioning by introducing a time–frequency domain composite block sparse localization model. Given the complexity of localizing unknown sources, a unilateral branch ratio decision scheme is devised. This scheme derives decision thresholds through the statistical characteristics of branch residual ratios, enabling adaptive control over iterative processes and facilitating multisource localization under conditions of remote blind sparsity. Simulation results indicate that the proposed model and algorithm, compared to classic sparse localization schemes, are more suitable for long-distance localization scenarios, demonstrating robust performance in complex situations like blind sparsity, thereby offering broader scenario adaptability.

Keywords: mobile sensors; compressive sensing; block sparsity; blind sparsity; passive localization

1. Introduction

With the advancement of digital technologies such as smartphones, Mobile Crowd Sensing (MCS) technologies [1–3] and wireless sensor network positioning [4] are increasingly applied in fields like communications and the Internet of Things (IoT) [5–7]. Traditional positioning techniques often rely on static wireless sensor networks (WSNs) [8], which are costly to construct and lack mobility. In contrast, positioning technologies based on MCS [9] offer the advantages of low cost and broad applicability, possessing significant appeal and competitive advantages.

Positioning technologies based on MCS can be categorized into two main types: range-based and range-free positioning [10]. Range-free positioning algorithms [11–13] do not require the measurement of distances, signal strengths, or angle information between terminals within the environment as model inputs. Classical algorithms include the centroid algorithm, channel-aware positioning, Distance Vector-Hop (DV-Hop) algorithm [14], and convex programming, among others. On the other hand, range-based positioning algorithms conduct raw signal collection through MCS, extracting feature information parameters to construct mathematical equations for solving the target's location. Classical algorithms in this category include techniques based on received signal strength (RSS), Angle of Arrival (AoA), Time of Arrival (ToA), and Time Difference of Arrival (TDoA) [15–18].

However, the aforementioned methods all possess certain limitations. While range-free positioning techniques have lower hardware requirements, they suffer from poor positioning accuracy. Conversely, range-based positioning techniques offer higher accuracy, but technologies such as TDoA and ToA have higher hardware demands and are not well-suited for MCS scenarios. Moreover, in MCS environments, the application of multiple access technologies [19] introduces scenarios with multiple coexisting and co-frequency signal sources. Existing technologies have conducted specific research [20,21] on positioning in multisource environments, but most struggle to accurately locate signal sources in such complex scenarios.

In recent years, with the advent of compressive sensing theory [22], research [23] has introduced a multisource positioning technique based on compressive sensing, providing a novel research paradigm for multi-target positioning [24]. This positioning technology relies solely on the sparsity of received signal strengths and receiver location information to locate multiple signal sources, enabling the positioning of several simultaneous co-frequency signal sources. One study [25] has rigorously demonstrated the efficacy of the sparse optimization problem formulation for positioning and proven that the sensing matrix satisfies the Restricted Isometry Property (RIP).

Existing sparse positioning techniques still have limitations; traditional sparse positioning methods based on MCS can only position signal sources within the coverage area of MCS devices [26], and they are incapable of performing long-distance sparse positioning on signal sources outside the coverage area. Additionally, most current compressive sensing techniques require a known sparsity level [27] as a prior condition for iterative process control, which is challenging to obtain in practical MCS scenarios as the exact number of signal sources is often unknown.

With further research into compressive sensing technologies, such as block sparsity [28,29], scholars have proposed and validated their RIPs. However, in the field of sparse positioning, there has yet to be research specifically addressing positioning problems based on block sparsity, indicating room for further exploration in sparse positioning.

In view of the current research deficiencies, this paper proposes a block sparsity system model constructed based on time-domain and energy-domain for addressing the problem of long-distance sparse positioning in MCS scenarios. Furthermore, it introduces a unilateral branch ratio decision (UBRD) algorithm based on the block sparsity system model to achieve blind sparsity adaptive iterative control.

The research work in this paper is as follows:

1. Based on the MCS context, this study implements long-distance sparse positioning by constructing and solving a block sparsity model synthesized from time and energy domains. Compared to the aforementioned sparse inversion positioning algorithms, the block sparsity-based positioning algorithm can achieve simultaneous co-frequency multisource positioning within the periphery of the sensor network.
2. Within the framework of sparse positioning, this study introduces an adaptive iterative recovery by unilateral detection of branch residuals during the iteration process and provides expressions for false alarm probability and decision thresholds. Compared to traditional compressive sensing algorithms, the UBRD algorithm can adaptively control the iterative process under blind sparsity conditions.
3. Simulation results for different algorithms under various scenarios indicate that the block sparsity-based sparse positioning technology can achieve long-distance simultaneous co-frequency multisource positioning and has broader scenario adaptability. Under conditions of unknown sparsity, the UBRD algorithm demonstrates superior performance compared to algorithms that make decisions based on energy thresholds.

2. MCS Positioning and Problem Description

To facilitate the subsequent elaboration of the proposed unilateral branch ratio decision (UBRD) algorithm in later sections, we first revisit the traditional framework of MCS sparse positioning. Subsequently, we discuss the issues associated with long-distance positioning within this framework and introduce the block sparsity positioning model. Building on this model, we then present the iterative control problem inherent in the process.

2.1. MCS Sparse Localization Framework and Issues

In the context of MCS scenarios, multisource sparse localization is depicted in the lower half of Figure 1, where the source of the signal is positioned within the enveloping range of sensors. Under the conventional framework for sparse localization, the sensor coverage space is subjected to grid partitioning. This approach utilizes the grid positions as approximations for estimating the target location. Assume that in this scenario, there are K signal sources and M mobile devices, with the position of the ith mobile device denoted as $m_i = [x_{m_i}, y_{m_i}]$. The space is divided into N grids, with the position of the jth grid represented as $n_j = [x_{n_j}, y_{n_j}]$.

The scenario of multisource perception based on ubiquitous passive radar is depicted in Figure 1. It consists of M passive radars and K radiating sources.

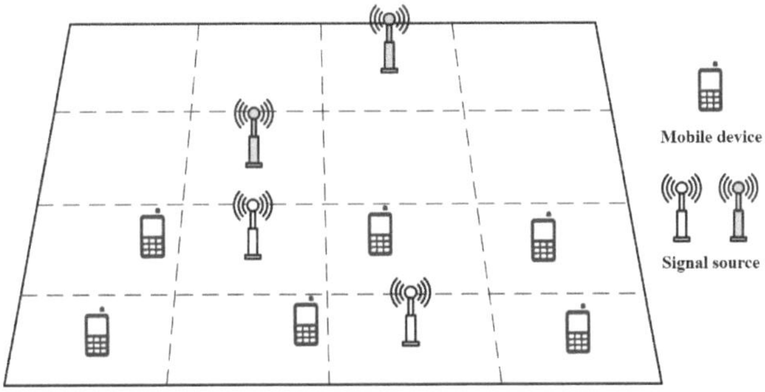

Figure 1. MCS sparse localization scene.

In the MCS localization scenario, within the same frequency f, the number of signal sources is limited. The number of grid units and signal sources satisfy the condition $N \gg K$. Hence, the positions of the signal sources exhibit sparsity in the spatial domain. According to compressive sensing theory, a sparse model can be constructed to solve the multisource localization problem. The model is formulated as follows:

Without loss of generality, consider the scene area uniformly discretized into N square grids. Among them, M passive radars are randomly distributed in the scene, and K signal sources are randomly distributed within the grids. Since $N \gg K$, the positional information of signal sources exhibits sparsity within the target scene.

$$\mathbf{y} = \mathbf{A}\mathbf{x} + \mathbf{n}, \tag{1}$$

where $\mathbf{y}$ represents the received signal vector. $\mathbf{A}$ is an $M * N$ dimensional sensing matrix, $\mathbf{x}$ is the sparse vector of signal sources, and $\mathbf{n}$ denotes Gaussian noise within the scene. The detailed meanings of the aforementioned parameters are as follows:

(1) Received Signal Vector $\mathbf{y}$

$\mathbf{y} = [y_1, y_2, \ldots, y_M]^T$ represents the received signal vector composed of the received signal strength (RSS) from M mobile devices, where each element y_i signifies the received signal strength value P_i of the ith mobile device at frequency f. P_i denotes the sum of energy from all signal sources attenuated and reaching mobile device i.

(2) Signal Source Sparse Vector $\mathbf{x}$

$\mathbf{x} = [x_1, x_2, \ldots, x_N]^T$ represents the sparse vector of signal sources at frequency f within the scene, where each element x_j signifies the signal source energy intensity within the jth grid region. The majority of elements in $\mathbf{x}$ possess a value of 0, rendering $\mathbf{x}$ a sparse vector.

(3) Sensing Matrix $\mathbf{A}$

Given that P_i represents the summation of energy attenuated from $\mathbf{x}$ reaching the ith location, namely:

$$P_i = \sum_{j=1}^{N} E_{ij} x_j, \tag{2}$$

where E_{ij} denotes the energy attenuation coefficient, representing the energy intensity loss between the ith mobile device location and the jth grid location. E_{ij} is obtained through the free-space loss formula, F_{ij}, with the specific formula outlined as follows:

$$F_{ij} = 20\log(4\pi/c) + 20\log(d_{ij}) + 20\log(f) - G_r - G_t, \tag{3}$$

where c represents the speed of light, $d_{ij} = \sqrt{\left(x_{m_i} - x_{n_j}\right)^2 + \left(y_{m_i} - y_{n_j}\right)^2}$ signifies the distance between the ith mobile device location and the jth grid location, and G_t and G_r denote the antenna gains of the signal source and the mobile device, respectively. The energy attenuation coefficient $E_{ij} = 10^{\left(F_{ij}/20\right)}$ can be obtained based on Equation (3).

The sensing matrix $\mathbf{A}$ is composed of energy attenuation coefficients E_{ij}, and $\mathbf{A}$ is specifically represented as follows:

$$\mathbf{A} = \begin{bmatrix} \mathbf{A}_1 \\ \mathbf{A}_2 \\ \vdots \\ \mathbf{A}_N \end{bmatrix}^T = \begin{bmatrix} E_{11} & E_{12} & \cdots & E_{1N} \\ E_{21} & E_{22} & \cdots & E_{2N} \\ \vdots & \vdots & \ddots & \vdots \\ E_{M1} & E_{M2} & \cdots & E_{MN} \end{bmatrix}. \tag{4}$$

Combining the aforementioned derivations, the localization problem based on MCS can be equivalently formulated as solving $\mathbf{y} = \mathbf{Ax} + \mathbf{n}$. Due to sparsity, this equation can be solved using compressive sensing algorithms. In the classic MCS-based localization scenario, the Orthogonal Matching Pursuit (OMP) algorithm can be employed to solve the sparse equation. The algorithmic procedure for the OMP is illustrated in Algorithm 1.

Algorithm 1 The OMP Algorithm

Input: mobile device reception vector $\mathbf{y}$; sensor matrix $\mathbf{A}$.
Initialize: number of iterations $\tau = 0$; residual vector $\mathbf{r^0} = \mathbf{y}$; support set $Supp^0 = \varnothing$; sensing matrix reconstruction $\hat{\mathbf{A}} = \varnothing$; reconstruction of signal source vectors $\mathbf{x^0} = \varnothing$; sparsity K.
while $\tau < K$
1: $\tau = \tau + 1$.
2: $B^\tau = \arg\max_{j \notin Supp^{\tau-1}} \left|\langle \mathbf{r}^{\tau-1}, \mathbf{A}_j \rangle\right|$.
3: $Supp^\tau = Supp^{\tau-1} \cup B^\tau$.
4: $\hat{\mathbf{A}}^\tau = \left[\hat{\mathbf{A}}^{\tau-1}, \mathbf{A}_{B^\tau}\right]$.
5: $\mathbf{x}^\tau = \arg\min_{\mathbf{x}^\tau} \left\|\mathbf{y} - \hat{\mathbf{A}}^\tau \mathbf{x}^\tau\right\|_2^2$.
6: $\mathbf{r}^\tau = \mathbf{y} - \hat{\mathbf{A}}^\tau \mathbf{x}^\tau$.
Output: location information support set $Supp$.

Following the aforementioned steps, the positional support set $Supp$ can be acquired to enable multisource localization. However, this method is applicable exclusively to scenarios where the signal source is surrounded by sensors, as depicted in the traditional framework. In instances where the signal source, exemplified by the red signal sources in Figure 1, is located outside the sensor envelopment range, this methodology proves to be inapplicable. The results of employing this method for locating signal sources situated outside the sensor envelopment range are presented in subsequent chapters.

2.2. The Block Sparse Long-Range Localization Model and Its Associated Issues

The block sparse long-range localization model is akin to the classical sparse localization model in its approach. This model involves gridding the target space and approximating the target's position using grid locations. In this scenario, there are K signal sources and M mobile devices, where the position of the ith mobile device is denoted as $m_i = [x_{m_i}, y_{m_i}]$, and the number of grids in the signal source area is N, with the jth grid position represented as $n_j = [x_{n_j}, y_{n_j}]$. Unlike the classical sparse localization model, this model integrates temporal and energy domains, where both the measured signal and sparse signal sources are in the frequency domain. The specific formulation of the block sparse long-range localization model is as follows:

$$\mathbf{Y} = \mathbf{A}\mathbf{X} + \mathbf{N}, \tag{5}$$

where $\mathbf{Y}$ represents the received signal vector. $\mathbf{A}$ stands for the sensing matrix, $\mathbf{X}$ denotes the signal source block sparse vector, and $\mathbf{N}$ represents the Gaussian noise within the scene. In this scenario, the mobile devices receive not just simple power intensities but rather discrete signals of length L. The detailed interpretations of the aforementioned parameters are as follows:

(1) The received signal vector $\mathbf{Y}$

$\mathbf{Y}$ represents the signals received from a collective set of M mobile devices, with each individual mobile device capturing a discrete signal block of length L. The received signal vector $\mathbf{Y}$ is characterized by a total length of L_M, precisely$L_M = M * L$. The specific representation of vector $\mathbf{Y}$ is detailed as follows:

$$\mathbf{Y} = \left[\underbrace{Y_0, \cdots, Y_{L-1}}_{\mathbf{Y}_1^T}, \underbrace{Y_L, \cdots, Y_{2L-1}}_{\mathbf{Y}_2^T}, \cdots, \underbrace{Y_{L_M-L-1}, \cdots, Y_{L_M-1}}_{\mathbf{Y}_M^T} \right]^T, \tag{6}$$

where $\mathbf{Y}_i^T$ represents the frequency-domain received signal of the ith mobile device. This received signal is the superposition of frequency-domain transformations at the mobile device location, resulting from all signal source signals after energy attenuation and time delay.

(2) The signal source block sparse vector $\mathbf{X}$

$\mathbf{X}$ represents the output vector of signal sources within N grids, where each signal source emits a frequency-domain discrete signal block of length L. $\mathbf{X}$ is characterized by a total length of L_N, precisely$L_N = N * L$. The specific representation of vector $\mathbf{X}$ is detailed as follows:

$$\mathbf{X} = \left[\underbrace{X_0, \cdots, X_{L-1}}_{\mathbf{X}_1^T}, \underbrace{X_L, \cdots, X_{2L-1}}_{\mathbf{X}_2^T}, \cdots, \underbrace{X_{L_N-L-1}, \cdots, X_{L_N-1}}_{\mathbf{X}_N^T} \right]^T, \tag{7}$$

where $\mathbf{X}_j^T$ represents the frequency-domain output vector of the jth signal source within the scene's grid. In most grids, there are no signal sources present, thus the value for the corresponding block is 0, rendering $\mathbf{X}_j^T$ as a block sparse vector.

(3) Sensing Matrix $\mathbf{A}$

The signal travels a certain distance to reach the mobile device, experiencing energy attenuation during propagation. Additionally, due to varying positions of different signal sources concerning the mobile device, there are differences in signal transmission distances. This results in the same signal reaching different mobile devices at different times. Based on the properties of Discrete Fourier Transform, the formula representing the frequency-domain signal received by the specific ith mobile device at the jth grid location is as follows:

$$\begin{pmatrix} Y_{(i-1)L-1} \\ Y_{(i-1)L} \\ \vdots \\ Y_{iL-1} \end{pmatrix} = \begin{pmatrix} A_{ij0} & 0 & \cdots & 0 \\ 0 & A_{ij1} & \cdots & 0 \\ \vdots & \vdots & \ddots & \vdots \\ 0 & 0 & \cdots 0 & A_{ijL-1} \end{pmatrix} \begin{pmatrix} X_{(j-1)L-1} \\ X_{(j-1)L} \\ \vdots \\ X_{jL-1} \end{pmatrix}. \quad (8)$$

Equation (8) can be abbreviated as $\mathbf{Y}_{ij} = \mathbf{A}_{ij}\mathbf{X}_j$, where $\mathbf{Y}_{ij}$ represents the frequency-domain signal obtained by the ith mobile device from the jth grid, $\mathbf{X}_j$ signifies the frequency-domain output vector of the signal source within the jth grid in the scenario, and $\mathbf{A}_{ij}$ denotes the sensing matrix between the two nodes. The specific construction of the aforementioned formula is detailed below.

$$\mathbf{x}\left[t - t_{ij}\right] \leftrightarrow \mathbf{X}[l]e^{-j2\pi l t_{ij}/L}. \quad (9)$$

From Equation (3), the energy attenuation coefficient E_{ij} between nodes i and j can be derived. Combining this with Equation (9), the calculation of the element A_{ijl} in matrix $\mathbf{A}_{ij}$ is computed as follows:

$$\mathrm{A}_{ijl} = E_{ij} * e^{-j2\pi l t_{ij}/L}. \quad (10)$$

In the long-distance localization model based on MCS, the ith mobile device is required to receive signals from all signal sources within the scene. The frequency-domain received signal for the ith node is expressed as follows:

$$\mathbf{Y}_i = \sum_{j=1}^{N} \mathbf{Y}_{ij} = \sum_{j=1}^{N} \mathbf{A}_{ij}\mathbf{X}_j. \quad (11)$$

Expanding Equation (11) to encompass all mobile devices, we can derive the sensing matrix $\mathbf{A}$ as follows:

$$\mathbf{A} = \begin{bmatrix} \mathbf{A}_1 \\ \mathbf{A}_2 \\ \vdots \\ \mathbf{A}_N \end{bmatrix}^T = \begin{bmatrix} \mathbf{A}_{11} & \mathbf{A}_{12} & \cdots & \mathbf{A}_{1N} \\ \mathbf{A}_{21} & \mathbf{A}_{22} & \cdots & \mathbf{A}_{2N} \\ \vdots & \vdots & \ddots & \vdots \\ \mathbf{A}_{M1} & \mathbf{A}_{M2} & \cdots & \mathbf{A}_{MN} \end{bmatrix}. \quad (12)$$

Taking into account the derivations presented above, we can formulate the long-range block sparse localization model under the MCS framework as follows:

$$\begin{bmatrix} \mathbf{Y}_1 \\ \mathbf{Y}_2 \\ \vdots \\ \mathbf{Y}_M \end{bmatrix} = \begin{bmatrix} \mathbf{A}_{11} & \mathbf{A}_{12} & \cdots & \mathbf{A}_{1N} \\ \mathbf{A}_{21} & \mathbf{A}_{22} & \cdots & \mathbf{A}_{2N} \\ \vdots & \vdots & \ddots & \vdots \\ \mathbf{A}_{M1} & \mathbf{A}_{M2} & \cdots & \mathbf{A}_{MN} \end{bmatrix} \begin{bmatrix} \mathbf{X}_1 \\ \mathbf{X}_2 \\ \vdots \\ \mathbf{X}_N \end{bmatrix} + \begin{bmatrix} \mathbf{N}_1 \\ \mathbf{N}_2 \\ \vdots \\ \mathbf{N}_N \end{bmatrix}, \quad (13)$$

where $\mathbf{Y} = [\mathbf{Y}_1, \mathbf{Y}_2, \ldots, \mathbf{Y}_M]^T$ represents the combined vector of frequency-domain signals received by M mobile devices over a specified time period. $\mathbf{X} = [\mathbf{X}_1, \mathbf{X}_2, \ldots, \mathbf{X}_N]^T$ corresponds to the vector of block coefficient signals for N grid regions. The sensing matrix $\mathbf{A}$ is formed by the signal transformation coefficients between the grid locations within the scene and the mobile devices, thereby constituting an overcomplete dictionary.

Similar to the OMP algorithm, the presented model can be solved using greedy algorithms such as BOMP. The detailed steps of the BOMP algorithm are outlined in Algorithm 2, as shown below.

Algorithm 2 The BOMP Algorithm

Input: mobile device reception vector $\mathbf{Y}$; sensor matrix $\mathbf{A}$.
Initialize: number of iterations $\tau = 0$; residual vector $\mathbf{Y}^0 = \mathbf{Y}$; support set $Supp^0 = \varnothing$; sensing matrix reconstruction $\hat{\mathbf{A}} = \varnothing$; reconstruction of signal source vectors $\mathbf{X}^0 = \varnothing$; sparsity K.
while $\tau < K$
1: $\tau = \tau + 1$.
2: $B^\tau = \underset{j \notin Supp^{\tau-1}}{\arg\max} \left\| \mathbf{A}_j{}^T \mathbf{Y}^{\tau-1} \right\|_2$.
3: $Supp^\tau = Supp^{\tau-1} \cup B^\tau$.
4: $\hat{\mathbf{A}}^\tau = \left[\hat{\mathbf{A}}^{\tau-1}, \mathbf{A}_{B^\tau}\right]$.
5: $\mathbf{X}^\tau = \arg\min_{\mathbf{X}^\tau} \left\| \mathbf{Y} - \hat{\mathbf{A}}^\tau \mathbf{X}^\tau \right\|_2^2$.
6: $\mathbf{Y}^\tau = \mathbf{Y} - \hat{\mathbf{A}}^\tau \mathbf{X}^\tau$.
Output: location information support set $Supp$.

Similar to traditional sparse algorithms, block sparse models are typically reconstructed using greedy algorithms through iterative processes. However, akin to the challenges faced by conventional sparse algorithms, many existing block sparse algorithms suffer from practical limitations in controlling the iterative process. Classical sparse algorithms utilize sparsity control in the iterative process, which exhibits favorable performance but necessitates knowledge of the number of signal sources within the scene as the sparsity parameter. Nevertheless, in practical localization scenarios, estimating the number of signal sources is often challenging.

Taking the Threshold-Based Orthogonal Matching Pursuit (TBOMP) algorithm as an example, some improved algorithms employ predetermined residual thresholds for iterative control. Such methods do not require prior knowledge of sparsity but do necessitate information about background noise. The algorithm is outlined in Algorithm 3.

Algorithm 3 The TBOMP Algorithm

Input: mobile device reception vector $\mathbf{Y}$; sensor matrix $\mathbf{A}$.
Initialize: number of iterations $\tau = 0$; residual vector $\mathbf{Y}^0 = \mathbf{Y}$; support set $Supp^0 = \varnothing$; sensing matrix reconstruction $\hat{\mathbf{A}} = \varnothing$; reconstruction of signal source vectors $\mathbf{X}^0 = \varnothing$; preset threshold ε.
while $\text{norm}(\mathbf{Y}^\tau) > \varepsilon$
1: $\tau = \tau + 1$.
2: $B^\tau = \underset{j \notin Supp^{\tau-1}}{\arg\max} \left\| \mathbf{A}_j{}^T \mathbf{Y}^{\tau-1} \right\|_2$.
3: $Supp^\tau = Supp^{\tau-1} \cup B^\tau$.
4: $\hat{\mathbf{A}}^\tau = \left[\hat{\mathbf{A}}^{\tau-1}, \mathbf{A}_{B^\tau}\right]$.
5: $\mathbf{X}^\tau = \arg\min_{\mathbf{X}^\tau} \left\| \mathbf{Y} - \hat{\mathbf{A}}^\tau \mathbf{X}^\tau \right\|_2^2$.
6: $\mathbf{Y}^\tau = \mathbf{Y} - \hat{\mathbf{A}}^\tau \mathbf{X}^\tau$.
Output: location information support set $Supp$.

Due to the variability inherent in MCS scenarios, it is challenging for the TBOMP algorithm to achieve adaptive and effective iterative control. To address the aforementioned issues, this paper proposes a unilateral branch ratio decision (UBRD) algorithm. The UBRD algorithm employs a false alarm method to make decisions based on the branch residual ratio, thus achieving iterative control. For the sake of subsequent computations, the false alarm probability is defined as follows:

$$P_{fa} = \Pr\{Supp \neq \mathbf{S}\}, \tag{14}$$

where $Supp$ denotes the computed position support set, and $\mathbf{S}$ signifies the actual position support set, both representing the indices of signal source locations within N grid regions.The false alarm probability P_{fa} signifies the probability of a mismatch between the inferred position support set and the actual position support set, which can be further divided into the probability of under-recovery and the probability of over-recovery.

Following the definition of the false alarm probability, the UBRD module is designed based on this probability. Within the iterative process of determining the position support set, this module achieves iterative control by examining whether the residual vector retains signal source components. In each iteration, it assesses the residual ratios among different branches to ascertain whether the iterative process has acquired a complete support set. This process can be summarized as a set of binary hypothesis testing problems:

$$\mathbf{Y}^{\tau} = \begin{cases} \mathbf{A}^{\tau}\mathbf{N}, & G_{0,\tau} \\ \mathbf{A}^{\tau}(\mathbf{X}+\mathbf{N}), & G_{1,\tau}, \end{cases} \tag{15}$$

where $\mathbf{Y}^{\tau}$ represents the residual vector, which corresponds to the residuals of mobile sensing nodes in the τth iteration process. $\mathbf{A}^{\tau}$ denotes the sensing matrix in the τth iteration, and the specific expressions for these two parameters are provided in the subsequent algorithm section. $\mathbf{X}$ represents the block sparse signal sources within the target area, and $\mathbf{N}$ signifies Gaussian white noise within the scene. $G_{0,\tau}$ represents the hypothesis in the τth iteration where the residual only contains noise components, indicating that the position information support set has been completely acquired and the iterative process should be terminated. $G_{1,\tau}$ represents the hypothesis in the τth iteration where the residual contains signal components, suggesting that the position information support set has not been fully acquired and the iterative process should continue.

3. Algorithm Design

In this section, we introduce the unilateral branch ratio decision (UBRD) algorithm based on the long-range localization model established in the previous section. We calculate the residual for each branch and investigate its statistical characteristics. Subsequently, we derive the expressions for false alarm probability and decision threshold.

3.1. Algorithm Steps

As illustrated in Figure 2, this paper introduces the UBRD algorithm. Similar to the traditional sparse localization algorithms mentioned in the previous section, this algorithm is a greedy algorithm. It comprises four main steps:

1. Most Relevant Block Selection: In the first step, the algorithm calculates the index of the most relevant block by comparing the sensing matrix with the received signal vector.
2. Support Set Update: In the second step, the algorithm updates the position support set based on the index of the most relevant block, and consequently updates the sensing matrix.
3. Residual Update: The third step involves updating the residual vector using the sensing matrix obtained in the previous step.
4. UBRD Module: In the fourth step, the UBRD module adaptively controls the iterative process by adjusting the residual detection threshold based on a predefined false alarm probability.

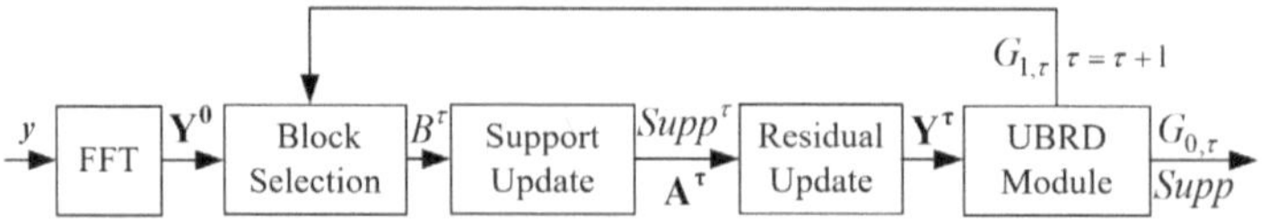

Figure 2. Flowchart of the UBRD algorithm.

The detailed steps of the UBRD algorithm proposed in this paper are presented in Algorithm 4.

Algorithm 4 The UBRD Algorithm

Input: mobile device reception vector $\mathbf{Y}$; sensor matrix $\mathbf{A}$; false alarm rate of residual detection P_{fa}.
Initialize: number of iterations $\tau = 0$; residual vector $\mathbf{Y^0} = \mathbf{Y}$; support set $Supp^0 = \varnothing$; sensing matrix reconstruction $\hat{\mathbf{A}} = \varnothing$; reconstruction of signal source vectors $\mathbf{X^0} = \varnothing$.
Repeat:

$\tau = \tau + 1$.

$B^\tau = \underset{j \notin Supp^{\tau-1}}{\arg\max} \left\| \mathbf{A}_j{}^T \mathbf{Y}^{\tau-1} \right\|_2 \Big/ \left\| \mathbf{A}_j{}^T \mathbf{A}_j \right\|_2$.

$Supp^\tau = Supp^{\tau-1} \cup B^\tau$; $\hat{\mathbf{A}}^\tau = \left[\hat{\mathbf{A}}^{\tau-1}, \mathbf{A}_{B^\tau}\right]$.

$\mathbf{X}^\tau = \mathbf{A}^\dagger \mathbf{Y}^0$; $\mathbf{A}^\dagger = \left((\hat{\mathbf{A}}^\tau)^T \hat{\mathbf{A}}^\tau \right)^{-1} (\hat{\mathbf{A}}^\tau)^T$

$\mathbf{Y}^\tau = \mathbf{W}^\tau \mathbf{R}^\tau$; $\mathbf{R}^\tau = \mathbf{Y}^0 - \hat{\mathbf{A}}^\tau \mathbf{X}^\tau$; $\mathbf{W}^\tau = \mathrm{diag}(W_1^\tau, \ldots, W_{il}^\tau, \ldots, W_{L_M}^\tau)$;
$W_{il}^\tau = 1 \Big/ \sqrt{\sum_{jl=1}^{L_N} \left| H_{iljl}^\tau \right|^2}$; $\mathbf{H}^\tau = (\mathbf{E} - \hat{\mathbf{A}}^\tau \mathbf{A}^\dagger)\mathbf{A}$.

$\gamma_i^\tau = Z_i^\tau / Z_{i+1}^\tau$; $Z_i^\tau = \frac{1}{L} \sum_{l=0}^{L-1} \left| \mathbf{Y}_{il}^\tau \right|^2$; $Z_{M+1}^\tau = Z_1^\tau$.

$\delta_i^{\tau,f} = \varphi\left(\mathbf{A}^\tau, P_{fa}, L\right)$; $\mathbf{A}^\tau = \mathbf{W}^\tau \mathbf{H}^\tau$.

if $\gamma_i^\tau \le \delta_i^{\tau,f}$ **then**
    The situation is $G_{0,\tau}$; $Supp = Supp^\tau$;
end if

Until: stopping criterion $G_{0,\tau}$ is met.
Output: location information support set $Supp$.

In the procedural steps of the UBRD algorithm, the first stage involves locating the index of the most matching position for the current residual. This is initiated by projecting the residual vector in $\mathbf{Y}^{\tau-1}$ onto each column block of the sensing matrix $\mathbf{A}$ and computing the Euclidean norm for each block's outcome. These values are then normalized and the maximum value is selected to identify the block most correlated with the current residual. The second stage updates the support set of positions, refining the current position support set according to the most matching position index and subsequently updating the intermediary projection matrix. The third stage entails updating the residual, where the intermediate projection matrix and the received signal are utilized to compute the reconstructed source signal, from which the original residual $\mathbf{R}^\tau$ is derived. This original residual is then normalized to obtain the residual $\mathbf{Y}^{\tau-1}$. The fourth stage involves calculating the branch residual ratio by first determining the residual energy of each branch and then computing the ratio between adjacent branches. The fifth stage focuses on computing the decision threshold, which is derived using an equivalent matrix, the false alarm probability, and the length of the signal sequence, with the detailed process outlined in the subsequent subsection. The sixth and final stage is the iterative stopping decision, where the branch residual ratio is compared with the decision threshold. If the branch residual ratio is less than or equal to the decision threshold, it is inferred that the residual contains only ambient noise, the support set is deemed complete, and the iteration ceases.

3.2. Threshold Calculation for Decision

In the aforementioned UBRD algorithm, the iteration process is controlled via a decision threshold. This decision threshold is calculated based on parameters such as the false alarm probability. The process can be represented as follows:

$$P_{fi}^\tau = \Pr\left\{ \gamma_i^\tau \le \delta_i^{\tau,f} | G_{0,\tau} \right\}. \quad (16)$$

From Equation (16), it can be derived that the overall detection false alarm probability is represented as follows:

$$P_{fa}^{\tau} = 1 - \prod_{i=1}^{M} \left(1 - P_{fi}^{\tau}\right). \tag{17}$$

Within this context, the false alarm probability for each branch is determined through analytical computation based on the assumption of a $G_{0,\tau}$ scenario.

Derived from Equation (15), it is evident that under the $G_{0,\tau}$-scenario assumption, all position support sets have been fully acquired, leaving the residual vector $\mathbf{Y}^{\tau}$ devoid of any remaining source signal, composed only of the DFT of Gaussian white noise. Given the linear characteristic of the DFT operation, it is understood that $\mathbf{N}$ is Gaussian white noise and $\mathbf{Y}^{\tau}$ is thus composed of Gaussian white noise. Within the $G_{0,\tau}$-scenario, the residual vector $\mathbf{Y}^{\tau}$ is calculated through the interplay of Gaussian white noise and the equivalent sensing matrix $\mathbf{A}^{\tau} = \mathbf{W}^{\tau}\mathbf{H}^{\tau}$. According to the associative and distributive laws of matrices, it is established that matrices $\mathbf{A}^{\tau}$ and $\mathbf{A}$ equivalently influence the statistical properties of the residual vector [27].

From Algorithm 4, it is discernible that the residual energy of each branch is given as $Z_i^{\tau} = \frac{1}{L}\sum_{l=0}^{L-1} |\mathbf{Y}_{il}^{\tau}|^2$. As derived from Equation (15), under the $G_{0,\tau}$-scenario, the elements within the residual vector $\mathbf{Y}_{il}^{\tau}$ are equivalently represented as follows:

$$\mathbf{Y}_{il}^{\tau} = \sum\nolimits_{j=1}^{N} \mathbf{A}_{ijl}^{\tau} \mathbf{N}_{jl}. \tag{18}$$

Given that $\mathbf{N}$ is Gaussian white noise, it is known that the mean of both the real and imaginary parts of $\mathbf{N}$ is 0; the variance of both the real and imaginary parts of $\mathbf{N}$ is $LN\sigma^2/2$; and the covariance between the real and imaginary parts of $\mathbf{N}$ is 0. Consequently, the mean and variance of $\Re(\mathbf{Y}_{il}^{\tau})$ and $\Im(\mathbf{Y}_{il}^{\tau})$ can be calculated as follows:

$$E(\Re(\mathbf{Y}_{il}^{\tau})) = E(\Im(\mathbf{Y}_{il}^{\tau})) = 0, \tag{19a}$$

$$D(\Re(\mathbf{Y}_{il}^{\tau})) = D(\Im(\mathbf{Y}_{il}^{\tau})) = LN\sigma_w^2 \big/ 2, \tag{19b}$$

where $i = 1, 2, \ldots, M$ and $l = 0, 1, \ldots, L-1$. Consequently, the covariance of $\Re(\mathbf{Y}_{il}^{\tau})$ and $\Im(\mathbf{Y}_{il}^{\tau})$ can be calculated as follows:

$$\begin{aligned}
&\mathrm{Cov}[\Re(\mathbf{Y}_{il}^{\tau}), \Im(\mathbf{Y}_{il}^{\tau})] \\
&= E[\Re(\mathbf{Y}_{il}^{\tau})\Im(\mathbf{Y}_{il}^{\tau})] - E[\Re(\mathbf{Y}_{il}^{\tau})]E[\Im(\mathbf{Y}_{il}^{\tau})] \\
&= E\left\{\left[\sum_{j=1}^{N}\left(\Re\left(\mathbf{A}_{ijl}^{\tau}\right)\Re\left(\mathbf{N}_{jl}\right) - \Im\left(\mathbf{A}_{ijl}^{\tau}\right)\Im\left(\mathbf{N}_{jl}\right)\right)\right]\right. \\
&\times \left.\left[\sum_{j=1}^{N}\left(\Re\left(\mathbf{A}_{ijl}^{\tau}\right)\Im\left(\mathbf{N}_{jl}\right) + \Im\left(\mathbf{A}_{ijl}^{\tau}\right)\Re\left(\mathbf{N}_{jl}\right)\right)\right]\right\} \\
&= 0
\end{aligned} \tag{20}$$

From Equation (20), it can be derived that the mean and variance of $|\mathbf{Y}_{il}^{\tau}|^2$ are as follows:

$$E\left[|\mathbf{Y}_{il}^{\tau}|^2\right] = LN\sigma_w^2, \tag{21a}$$

$$D\left[|\mathbf{Y}_{il}^{\tau}|^2\right] = L^2N^2\sigma_w^4. \tag{21b}$$

According to the Central Limit Theorem, when there is a sufficiently large number of signal samples, the branch residual energy approximately follows a Gaussian distribution. Consequently, under the $G_{0,\tau}$-scenario, the mean and variance of Z_i^{τ} are as follows:

$$E[Z_i^{\tau}|G_{0,\tau}] = \frac{1}{L}\sum_{l=0}^{L-1} E\left[|\mathbf{Y}_{il}^{\tau}|^2\right] = LN\sigma_w^2, \tag{22a}$$

$$D[Z_i^\tau|G_{0,\tau}] = \frac{1}{L}\sum_{l=0}^{L-1} D\left[|\mathbf{Y}_{il}^\tau|^2\right] = L^2N^2\sigma_w^4. \tag{22b}$$

Based on the aforementioned formulation, the covariance of the energy across different branches can be calculated.

The covariance between different branches $\left|\mathbf{Y}_{pe}^\tau\right|^2$ and $\left|\mathbf{Y}_{qt}^\tau\right|^2$ is expressed as follows:

$$\mathrm{Cov}\left[\left|\mathbf{Y}_{pe}^\tau\right|^2, \left|\mathbf{Y}_{qt}^\tau\right|^2\right] = \begin{cases} 0, & p = i, q = i, e \neq t \\ \frac{L^2N^2\sigma_w^4}{2}\sum_{n=0}^{3}\left(\rho_i^{\tau,n}\right)^2, & p = i, q = i+1, e = t, \\ 0, & p = i, q = i+1, e \neq t \end{cases} \tag{23}$$

where $i = 1, 2, \ldots, M; e, t = 0, 1, \ldots, L-1$, $\rho_i^{\tau,n}$ denotes the correlation coefficient, which is expressed by the following formula:

$$\rho_i^{\tau,0} = \sum_{j=1}^{N}\left[\Re\left(\mathbf{A}_{ij}^\tau\right)\Im\left(\mathbf{A}_{i+1,j}^\tau\right) - \Re\left(\mathbf{A}_{i+1,j}^\tau\right)\Im\left(\mathbf{A}_{ij}^\tau\right)\right], \tag{24a}$$

$$\rho_i^{\tau,1} = \sum_{j=1}^{N}\left[\Im\left(\mathbf{A}_{ij}^\tau\right)\Re\left(\mathbf{A}_{i+1,j}^\tau\right) - \Re\left(\mathbf{A}_{i+1,j}^\tau\right)\Im\left(\mathbf{A}_{ij}^\tau\right)\right], \tag{24b}$$

$$\rho_i^{\tau,2} = \sum_{j=1}^{N}\left[\Re\left(\mathbf{A}_{ij}^\tau\right)\Re\left(\mathbf{A}_{i+1,j}^\tau\right) + \Im\left(\mathbf{A}_{i+1,j}^\tau\right)\Im\left(\mathbf{A}_{ij}^\tau\right)\right], \tag{24c}$$

$$\rho_i^{\tau,3} = \sum_{j=1}^{N}\left[\Re\left(\mathbf{A}_{ij}^\tau\right)\Re\left(\mathbf{A}_{i+1,j}^\tau\right) + \Im\left(\mathbf{A}_{i+1,j}^\tau\right)\Im\left(\mathbf{A}_{ij}^\tau\right)\right]. \tag{24d}$$

Derived from Equation (24), the correlation coefficient between adjacent branches Z_i^τ and Z_{i+1}^τ can be obtained as follows:

$$\rho_i^\tau = \frac{\mathrm{Cov}\left[Z_i^\tau, Z_{i+1}^\tau\right]}{\sqrt{D\left[Z_i^\tau|G_{0,\tau}\right]D\left[Z_{i+1}^\tau\middle|G_{0,\tau}\right]}} = \frac{\left(\rho_i^{\tau,0}\right)^2 + \left(\rho_i^{\tau,1}\right)^2 + \left(\rho_i^{\tau,2}\right)^2 + \left(\rho_i^{\tau,3}\right)^2}{2}. \tag{25}$$

Thus, the calculation of the covariance of the residual energy across different branches is as follows:

$$\begin{aligned} \mathrm{Cov}\left[Z_i^\tau, Z_{i+1}^\tau\right] &= \mathrm{Cov}\left[\frac{1}{L}\sum_{l=0}^{L-1}|\mathbf{Y}_{il}^\tau|^2, \frac{1}{L}\sum_{l=0}^{L-1}\left|\mathbf{Y}_{i+1,l}^\tau\right|^2\right] \\ &= \frac{1}{L^2}\sum_{l=0}^{L-1}\mathrm{Cov}\left[|\mathbf{Y}_{il}^\tau|^2, \left|\mathbf{Y}_{i+1,l}^\tau\right|^2\right] \\ &= L^2N^2\sigma_w^4\rho_i^\tau \end{aligned} \tag{26}$$

Based on the aforementioned derivations, given that the branch residual ratio γ_i^τ is the ratio of two Gaussian variables, the following theorem can be stated:

Theorem 1. *Under the assumption of $G_{0,\tau}$, the false alarm probability P_{fa}^τ can be computed based on the decision threshold $\delta_i^{\tau,f}$ through the Gaussian cumulative distribution function (CDF).*

The properties of the Gaussian cumulative distribution function are as follows:

Property 1. *The cumulative distribution function for the ratio $R = I_1/I_2$ of two Gaussian variables is given as follows [30]:*

$$F_R(r) = \Pr(R < r) = \Phi\left(\frac{r\mu_2 - \mu_1}{\sqrt{\sigma_1^2 - 2r\rho\sigma_1\sigma_2 + r^2\sigma_2^2}}\right), \tag{27}$$

where ρ is the correlation coefficient between I_1 and I_2. The Gaussian cumulative distribution function is $\Phi(x) = \frac{1}{\sqrt{2\pi}}\int_{-\infty}^{x} e^{-\frac{\xi^2}{2}} d\xi$; μ_1, μ_2 are the mean of I_1 and I_2; and σ_1^2, σ_2^2 are the variance of I_1 and I_2.

Based on the aforementioned derivations, the false alarm probability P_{fa}^{τ} can be expressed by the following formula:

$$P_{fa}^{\tau} = \Pr\left(\frac{Z_i^{\tau}}{Z_{i+1}^{\tau}} \leq \delta_i^{\tau,f} \middle| G_{0,\tau}\right) = \Phi\left(\frac{\sqrt{L}\delta_i^{\tau,f} - \sqrt{L}}{\sqrt{1 - 2\delta_i^{\tau,f}\rho_i^{\tau} + \left(\delta_i^{\tau,f}\right)^2}}\right). \tag{28}$$

Under the rational assumption that all branch detections have the same false alarm probability, Equation (17) can equivalently be represented as follows:

$$P_{fa}^{\tau} = 1 - \left(1 - P_{fi}^{\tau}\right)^M. \tag{29}$$

Based on the above derivations, the decision threshold can be inversely calculated as follows:

$$\delta_i^{\tau,f} = \frac{L - \rho_i^{\tau}\left[\Phi^{-1}\left(1 - P_{fi}^{\tau}\right)\right]^2 + \Phi^{-1}\left(1 - P_{fi}^{\tau}\right)\sqrt{\left(\left(\rho_i^{\tau}\right)^2 - 1\right)\left[\Phi^{-1}\left(1 - P_{fi}^{\tau}\right)\right]^2 + 2L\left(\rho_i^{\tau} - 1\right)}}{L - \left[\Phi^{-1}\left(1 - P_{fi}^{\tau}\right)\right]^2}. \tag{30}$$

Through the UBRD algorithm and the aforementioned formulas, it is known that the decision threshold $\delta_i^{\tau,f} = \varphi\left(\mathbf{A}^{\tau}, P_{fa}, L\right)$ can control the iterative process without the need for known sparsity and noise information.

4. Performance Simulation and Analysis

To validate the performance of this algorithm in long-range, multisource localization scenarios, this section initially defines the simulation scenario settings and verifies the impact of long-range conditions on the localization capabilities of various algorithms. A comparison is made between multiple classic sparse optimization algorithms and block sparse localization algorithms. Furthermore, an assessment of the performance of the UBRD algorithm and the BOMP algorithm in different scenarios is conducted.

4.1. Simulation Scenario Setting

The MCS and target signal source regions are both set as 1 km by 1 km square areas. The target signal source region is divided into a 10 by 10 grid, with K signal sources randomly distributed within the 100 grids. It is assumed that the signal sources are omnidirectional, radiating a power of $P = 10$ dB. M mobile devices are randomly distributed within the sensing area and simultaneously sample the signals at a frequency of $f = 500$ MHz, with a total of $L = 20$ sampling points. The noise is set to be Gaussian white noise, with a false alarm probability $P_{fa}^{\tau} = 0.04$. To effectively validate the algorithm's localization performance and mitigate the impact of randomness, the mean of 1000 simulation runs is taken as the experimental result, with signal sources and mobile devices redistributed in each experiment.

4.2. Simulation Result

Assuming a scenario with two signal sources and thirty mobile devices, Figure 3 shows the residual projection results of a classical sparse optimization algorithm, where the signal sources are encompassed within the mobile devices' range. This is based on a compressed sensing algorithm that facilitates the estimation of the signal sources' positions by acquiring the most compatible atoms. However, in this scenario, the signal sources are situated within the mobile devices' surrounding area. In practical localization scenarios, signal sources are often positioned outside the mobile devices' envelopment, necessitating the devices to locate distant signal sources.

Figure 4 shows the residual projection results of a classical sparse optimization algorithm when the signal source is located outside the envelopment of mobile devices. In scenarios involving long-distance localization, the residual projection fails to accurately highlight the target location information. This limitation arises because the signal source in this scenario is positioned behind the mobile devices, leading to the concentration of the peak regions of the residual projection near the edge closest to the mobile devices' direction. Consequently, traditional sparse localization methods are ineffective for long-distance localization.

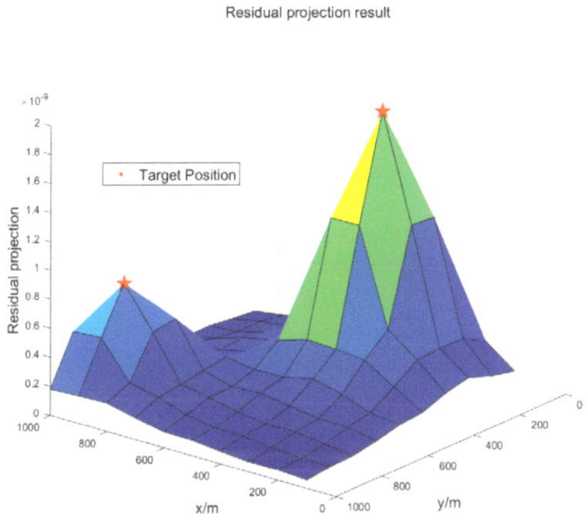

Figure 3. The residual projection result of signal sources within the vicinity surrounded by mobile devices.

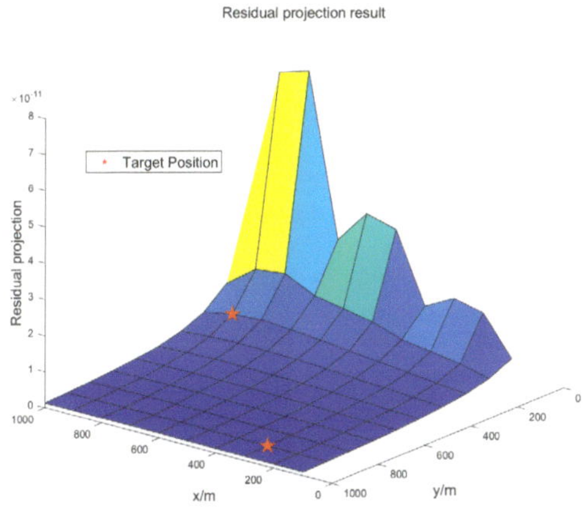

Figure 4. The residual projection result of the signal source situated outside the enclosure formed by mobile devices.

As depicted in Figure 5, the residual projection results in long-distance localization scenarios indicate that, under the block sparse model, the residual projection is globally influenced by the long-distance context, with projections near the direction of mobile devices being generally elevated. However, with the incorporation of the time-delay element in the model, it is evident from the residual projections that the block sparse model is capable of facilitating the localization of signal sources situated outside the envelopment of mobile devices.

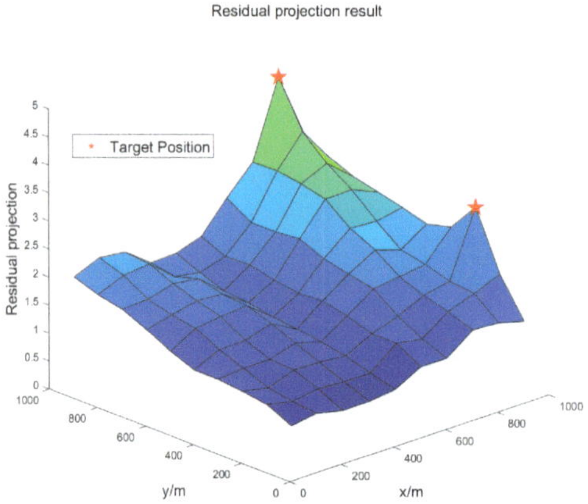

Figure 5. Residual projection result for block sparse localization in long-range localization scenarios.

To assess the impact of the mobile devices' coverage status of the signal source on localization performance, it is assumed that the two regions gradually separate from an overlapping state, with the signal source region shifting to one side by a distance of $D = 6$ km. The MCS and target signal source regions are both set as 4 km by 4 km square areas. Figure 6 shows the impact of mobile device coverage of signal sources on localization performance. As the signal source region progressively shifts to one side, the mobile devices transition from encompassing the signal sources to being situated on one side of them. The scenario is set with $K = 3$ signal sources and $M = 40$ mobile devices, with an SNR of 15dB. In this simulation, the impact on traditional sparse localization algorithms and block sparse localization algorithms is compared. Traditional sparse localization algorithms employ Orthogonal Matching Pursuit (OMP), Subspace Pursuit (SP), and Sparsity Adaptive Matching Pursuit (SAMP) algorithms. The OMP algorithm is a classical compressed sensing algorithm. The SP and SAMP algorithms, which introduce a subspace mechanism, exhibit a certain improvement in positioning performance over the OMP algorithm. As the distance of the signal source region's shift increases, the accuracy of localization gradually decreases, dropping to zero when the two regions are completely separated. Block sparse localization algorithms employ the BOMP and UBRD methods. Even when the two regions are completely separated, block sparse algorithms experience a reduction in localization precision but still maintain a high probability of accurate localization.

Figure 7 shows the performance of different block sparse algorithms under various scenarios. In this simulation, the number of signal sources and mobile devices is the same as in the previous example, with the SNR ranging from -15 dB to 15 dB. Two scenarios are presented in the simulation: source encirclement, where the mobile devices encompass the signal sources, and source isolation, where the signal sources are outside the mobile device enclosure. The threshold for the TBOMP algorithm is set at $\varepsilon = 2.5 \times 10^{-4}$, while the false alarm probability for the UBRD algorithm is set at $P_{fa}^{\tau} = 0.04$. As shown, the localization performance of block sparse algorithms in the source isolation scenario is slightly reduced compared to the source encirclement scenario, yet still achieves an accuracy rate of over 0.95. Due to the known sparsity, the BOMP algorithm exhibits the highest accuracy, although sparsity is difficult to predetermine in real-world scenarios.

The UBRD algorithm maintains commendable localization precision even in low-SNR conditions with unknown sparsity.

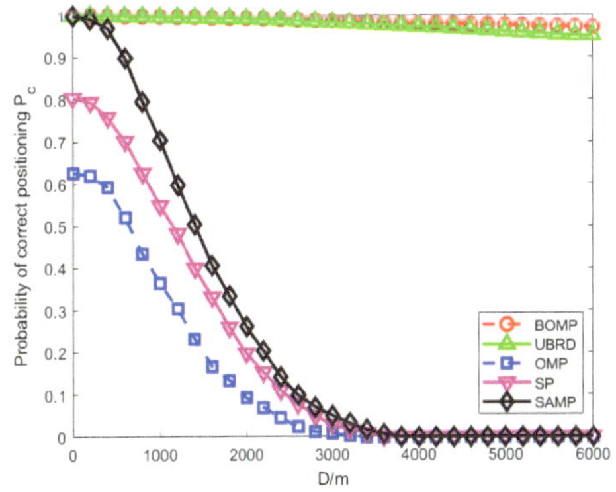

Figure 6. The impact of mobile device coverage of signal sources on localization performance.

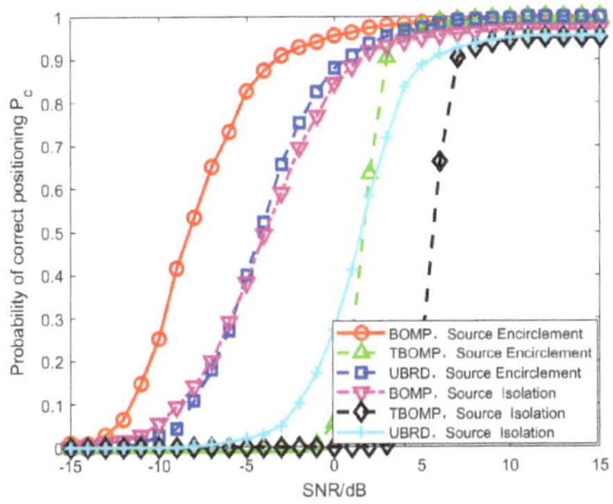

Figure 7. The performance of different block sparse algorithms in various scenarios.

In practical scenarios, off-grid issues frequently arise, which can be equivalently characterized as situations involving a reduction in the number of sensors. Figure 8 shows the impact of the number of mobile devices on localization performance, set in a scenario with an SNR of 15 and $K = 3$ signal sources. As demonstrated in the figure, an increase in the number of mobile devices results in higher localization accuracy.

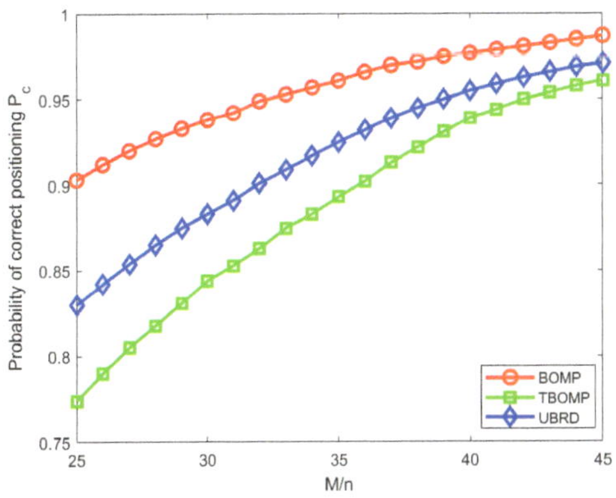

Figure 8. The impact of the number of mobile devices on localization performance.

Figure 9 shows the impact of different scenarios on localization performance. In Figure 9a, the sensor node area is offset from the signal source area by D = 7000 m, and in Figure 9b, the offset is set to D = 8000 m. From the signal-to-noise ratio and positioning accuracy curves, it can be inferred that even in long-distance positioning scenarios at greater distances, the UBRD algorithm achieves commendable localization results, demonstrating robust adaptability to different environments. Figure 9c and Figure 9d, respectively, showcase the signal-to-noise ratio and positioning accuracy graphs for areas of size 500 m by 500 m and 2 km by 2 km. These figures illustrate that the UBRD algorithm maintains high positioning accuracy across different area sizes, verifying the algorithm's precision in localization. In Figure 9e,f, the signal source frequencies are set to f = 100 MHz and f = 800 MHz, respectively. The results illustrate that the algorithm is capable of achieving commendable localization performance across a wide range of frequencies.

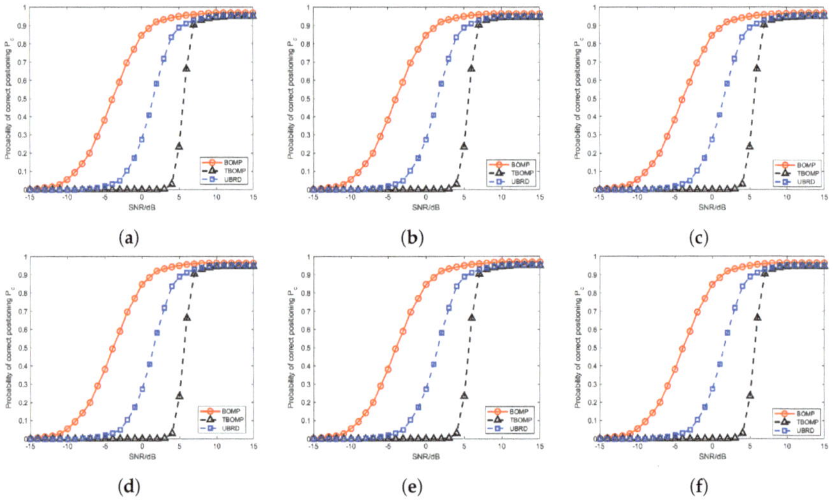

Figure 9. Impact of different scenarios on localization performance. (**a**) SNR and positioning accuracy graph at D = 7000 m. (**b**) SNR and positioning accuracy graph at D = 8000 m. (**c**) SNR and positioning accuracy graph in a 500 m × 500 m area. (**d**) SNR and positioning accuracy graph in a 2 km × 2 km area. (**e**) SNR and positioning accuracy graph at f = 100MHz. (**f**) SNR and positioning accuracy graph at f = 800 MHz.

Figure 10 shows the localization accuracy across different algorithmic parameters, setting the threshold of the TBOMP algorithm at $\varepsilon = 2.5 \times 10^{-4}$ and $\varepsilon = 3 \times 10^{-4}$, and the false alarm probability of the UBRD algorithm at $P^{\tau}_{fa} = 0.04$ and $P^{\tau}_{fa} = 0.05$. The simulation results reveal that an increased threshold setting for the TBOMP algorithm improves localization accuracy under conditions of low SNR, yet diminishes accuracy under high SNR conditions. Similarly, setting a higher false alarm probability for the UBRD algorithm enhances localization accuracy under low SNR conditions, but reduces precision under high SNR conditions.

Figure 11 shows the accuracy of positioning in scenarios where the strength of the signal source is inconsistent. From Figure 11, the strength of the signal source, denoted as P, was configured to randomly fluctuate between 10 dB and 20 dB. The results from the simulation indicate that discrepancies in signal source strength lead to a decrease in positioning precision. However, accurate positioning can be achieved under conditions of higher signal-to-noise ratios.

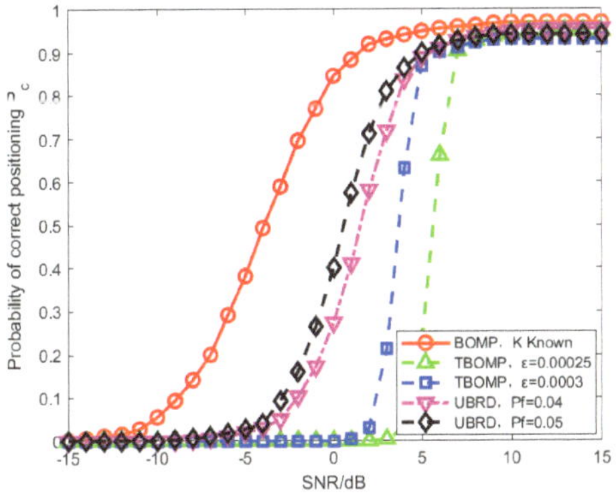

Figure 10. Localization accuracy under different algorithmic parameters.

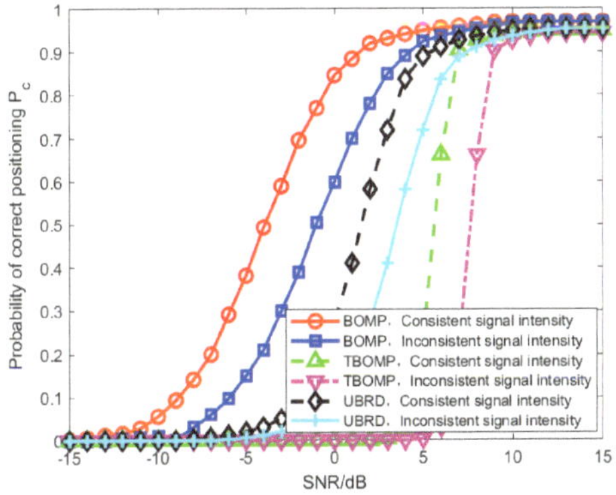

Figure 11. Localization accuracy in scenarios with inconsistent signal source intensity.

5. Conclusions

This paper introduces a proposed unilateral branch ratio decision (UBRD) algorithm. The UBRD algorithm, grounded in block sparsity concepts, facilitates signal source localization. Leveraging a time–frequency domain composite block sparse model proposed in this study, the UBRD algorithm surpasses traditional sparse localization methods in achieving localization functionality in scenarios such as long-distance environments. By statistically deriving the branch residual ratio, an adaptive decision threshold for controlling the iterative process is obtained. Simulation results indicate that the UBRD algorithm, even in long-distance scenarios without prior information, attains a higher probability of accurate localization, demonstrating its broader adaptability across various contexts.

Author Contributions: Conceptualization, C.L. and Z.L.; Methodology, J.R. and P.Q.; Validation, J.R.; Writing—original draft, J.R.; Writing—review & editing, J.R. and P.Z. All authors have read and agreed to the published version of the manuscript.

Funding: This research was funded by the National basic scientific research of China under Grants JCKY2023110C099, and the National Natural Science Foundation of China under Grants 62171334.

Data Availability Statement: Data are contained within the article.

Conflicts of Interest: The authors declare no conflicts of interest.

References

1. Capponi, A.; Fiandrino, C.; Kantarci, B.; Foschini, L.; Kliazovich, D.; Bouvry, P. A survey on mobile crowdsensing systems: Challenges, solutions, and opportunities. *IEEE Commun. Surv. Tutor.* **2019**, *21*, 2419–2465. [CrossRef] [CrossRef]
2. Zhang, C.; Zhu, L.; Xu, C.; Liu, X.; Sharif, K. Reliable and privacy-preserving truth discovery for mobile crowdsensing systems. *IEEE Trans. Dependable Secur. Comput.* **2019**, *3*, 1245–1260. [CrossRef] [CrossRef]
3. Zhang, C.; Zhao, M.; Zhu, L.; Wu, T.; Liu, X. Enabling efficient and strong privacy-preserving truth discovery in mobile crowdsensing. *IEEE Trans. Dependable Secur. Comput.* **2022**, *17*, 3569–3581. [CrossRef] [CrossRef]
4. Friedlander, B. A passive localization algorithm and its accuracy analysis. *IEEE J. Ocean. Eng.* **1987**, *1*, 234–245. [CrossRef] [CrossRef]
5. Zhang, W.; Yang, D.; Wu, W.; Peng, H.; Zhang, N.; Zhang, H.; Shen, X. Optimizing federated learning in distributed industrial IoT: A multi-agent approach. *IEEE J. Sel. Areas Commun.* **2021**, *12*, 3688–3703. [CrossRef] [CrossRef]
6. Abualsaud, K.; Elfouly, T.M.; Khattab, T.; Yaacoub, E.; Ismail, L.S.; Ahmed, M.H.; Guizani, M. A survey on mobile crowd-sensing and its applications in the IoT era. *IEEE Access* **2018**, *7*, 3855–3881. [CrossRef] [CrossRef]
7. Fawad, M.; Khan, M.Z.; Ullah, K.; Alasmary, H.; Shehzad, D.; Khan, B. Enhancing Localization Efficiency and Accuracy in Wireless Sensor Networks. *Sensors* **2023**, *5*, 2796. [CrossRef] [CrossRef] [PubMed]
8. Viani, F.; Rocca, P.; Benedetti, M.; Oliveri, G.; Massa, A. Electromagnetic passive localization and tracking of moving targets in a WSN-infrastructured environment. *Inverse Probl.* **2010**, *7*, 074003. [CrossRef] [CrossRef]
9. Guo, W.; Zhu, W.; Yu, Z.; Wang, J.; Guo, B. A survey of task allocation: Contrastive perspectives from wireless sensor networks and mobile crowdsensing. *IEEE Access* **2019**, *7*, 78406–78420. [CrossRef] [CrossRef]
10. Amundson, I.; Koutsoukos, X.D. A survey on localization for mobile wireless sensor networks. In *International Workshop on Mobile Entity Localization and Tracking in GPS-Less Environments*; Springer: Berlin/Heidelberg, Germany, 2009; pp. 235–254. [CrossRef]
11. Niculescu, D.; Nath, B. Ad hoc positioning system (APS). In *GLOBECOM'01. IEEE Global Telecommunications Conference (Cat. No. 01CH37270)*; IEEE: Washington, DC, USA, 2001; Volume 5, pp. 2926–2931. [CrossRef]
12. Patwari, N.; Hero, A.O.; Perkins, M.; Correal, N.S.; O'dea, R.J. Relative location estimation in wireless sensor networks. *IEEE Trans. Signal. Proces.* **2003**, *8*, 2137–2148. [CrossRef] [CrossRef]
13. Vossiek, M.; Wiebking, L.; Gulden, P.; Wieghardt, J.; Hoffmann, C.; Heide, P. Wireless local positioning. *IEEE Microw. Mag.* **2003**, *4*, 77–86. [CrossRef] [CrossRef]
14. Gui, L.; Val, T.; Wei, A.; Dalce, R. Improvement of range-free localization technology by a novel DV-hop protocol in wireless sensor networks. *Ad Hoc Netw.* **2015**, *24*, 55–73. [CrossRef] [CrossRef]
15. Tomic, S.; Beko, M.; Dinis, R. RSS-based localization in wireless sensor networks using convex relaxation: Noncooperative and cooperative schemes. *IEEE Trans. Veh. Technol.* **2014**, *5*, 2037–2050. [CrossRef] [CrossRef]
16. Wang, Y.; Ho, K.C. An asymptotically efficient estimator in closed-form for 3-D AOA localization using a sensor network. *IEEE Trans. Wirel. Commun.* **2015**, *12*, 6524–6535. [CrossRef] [CrossRef]
17. Pak, J.M.; Ahn, C.K.; Shi, P.; Shmaliy, Y.S.; Lim, M.T. Distributed hybrid particle/FIR filtering for mitigating NLOS effects in TOA-based localization using wireless sensor networks. *IEEE Trans. Ind. Electron.* **2016**, *6*, 5182–5191. [CrossRef]
18. Gholami, M.R.; Gezici, S.; Strom, E.G. TDOA based positioning in the presence of unknown clock skew. *IEEE Trans. Commun.* **2013**, *6*, 2522–2534. [CrossRef] [CrossRef]
19. Dai, L.; Wang, B.; Yuan, Y.; Han, S.; Chih-Lin, I.; Wang, Z. Non-orthogonal multiple access for 5G: Solutions, challenges, opportunities, and future research trends. *IEEE Commun. Mag.* **2015**, *9*, 74–81. [CrossRef] [CrossRef]
20. Moreno-Salinas, D.; Pascoal, A.M.; Aranda, J. Optimal sensor placement for multiple target positioning with range-only measurements in two-dimensional scenarios. *Sensors* **2013**, *8*, 10674–10710. [CrossRef] [CrossRef] [PubMed]
21. Xu, S.; Wu, L.; Doğançay, K.; Alaee-Kerahroodi, M. A hybrid approach to optimal TOA-sensor placement with fixed shared sensors for simultaneous multi-target localization. *IEEE Trans. Signal Process.* **2022**, *70*, 1197–1212. [CrossRef] [CrossRef]
22. Candès, E.J.; Wakin, M.B. An introduction to compressive sampling. *IEEE Signal. Process. Mag.* **2008**, *2*, 21–30. [CrossRef] [CrossRef]
23. Cevher, V.; Duarte, M.F.; Baraniuk, R.G. Distributed target localization via spatial sparsity. In Proceedings of the 2008 16th European Signal Processing Conference, Lausanne, Switzerland, 25–29 August 2008; IEEE: Washington, DC, USA, 2008; pp. 1–5. [CrossRef]
24. Feng, C.; Valaee, S.; Tan, Z. Multiple target localization using compressive sensing. In Proceedings of the GLOBECOM 2009–2009 IEEE Global Telecommunications Conference, Honolulu, HI, USA, 4 March 2010; IEEE: Washington, DC, USA, 2009; pp. 1–6. [CrossRef]
25. Zhang, B.; Cheng, X.; Zhang, N.; Cui, Y.; Li, Y.; Liang, Q. Sparse target counting and localization in sensor networks based on compressive sensing. In Proceedings of the 2011 Proceedings IEEE INFOCOM, Shanghai, China, 10–15 April 2011; IEEE: Washington, DC, USA, 2011; pp. 2255–2263. [CrossRef]
26. Feng, C.; Au, W.S.A.; Valaee, S.; Tan, Z. Received-signal-strength-based indoor positioning using compressive sensing. *IEEE Trans. Mob. Comput.* **2011**, *12*, 1983–1993. [CrossRef] [CrossRef]
27. Qi, P.; Li, Z.; Li, H.; Xiong, T. Blind sub-Nyquist spectrum sensing with modulated wideband converter. *IEEE Trans. Veh. Technol.* **2018**, *5*, 4278–4288. [CrossRef] [CrossRef]
28. Baraniuk, R.G.; Cevher, V.; Duarte, M.F.; Hegde, C. Model-based compressive sensing. *IEEE Trans. Inf. Theory* **2010**, *4*, 1982–2001. [CrossRef] [CrossRef]

29. Zhang, X.; Xu, W.; Cui, Y.; Lu, L.; Lin, J. On recovery of block sparse signals via block compressive sampling matching pursuit. *IEEE Access* **2019**, *7*, 175554–175563. [CrossRef] [CrossRef]
30. Hinkley, D.V. On the ratio of two correlated normal random variables. *Biometrika* **1969**, *3*, 635–639. [CrossRef] [CrossRef]

electronics

Article

Efficient Electronic Voting System Based on Homomorphic Encryption

Yu Zhan [1], Wei Zhao [2,*], Chaoxi Zhu [2], Zhen Zhao [1], Ning Yang [1] and Baocang Wang [1]

[1] The State Key Laboratory of Integrated Service Networks, Xidian University, Xi'an 710071, China; zhanyu@xidian.edu.cn (Y.Z.)
[2] The Science and Technology on Communication Security Laboratory, Chengdu 610041, China
* Correspondence: zhaowei9801@163.com

Abstract: In the last decade, E-voting has received great attention due to its advantages in efficiency and accuracy. Fan et al. presented a novel E-voting system named HSE-Voting by utilizing homomorphic signcryption. The HSE-Voting system was claimed to gain a provable security goal under the standard proof. In this paper, we illustrate that their scheme may suffer from some potential security issues. On the one hand, the voting information could be recovered by the authentication center (AC). On the other hand, any malicious voter could disrupt the voting system undetected by locally modifying his ballot. In order to increase the resilience of the voting system to risks, an improvement of the HSE-Voting system is developed. Our improved system fixes the above security weaknesses but increases the computation cost on the AC side by a small amount. In addition, the proposed scheme satisfies voter anonymity, ballot privacy, and verifiability of election results.

Keywords: e-voting; homomorphic encryption; privacy-preserving; efficiency

1. Introduction

E-voting refers to voting that allows voters to cast their votes through the internet. Compared with traditional elections, E-voting not only saves a lot of ballot printing, transportation, and manual counting costs but also improves voting efficiency and convenience. For example, the 2020 US presidential election coincides with the national public health security problem. If the traditional voting method is adopted, it will inevitably cause a large number of people to gather, while electronic voting can solve this problem well. Many countries, including India and Brazil, have used electronic voting technology in many different electoral fields [1].

In 2020, Fan et al. [2] proposed a homomorphic signcryption scheme to construct an E-voting system named HSE-Voting in order to improve the efficiency of E-voting. Due to the integrated design of signcryption, its efficiency has been greatly optimized compared with Yang et al.'s system [3] on the agency side. Furthermore, it gives a comparative security analysis. However, there are some security issues in Fan et al.'s system, such as voter privacy being leaked, and the E-voting system may not properly being completed.

In this paper, we propose two cryptanalytic attacks on Fan et al.'s system [2]. In the first attack algorithm, we show that an honest-but-curious authentication center (AC) can recover the voter's voting information from the corresponding ballot. In the second attack algorithm, we reveal that malicious voters can disrupt the election process by sending special incorrect ballots. Moreover, in order to enhance the security of the HSE-Voting system, we propose an improved HSE-Voting system by combining the signature and the proof of partial-knowledge protocol (PPK). While avoiding the above security risks, our system also reduces the computation cost on the agency-side compared to the existing work.

1.1. Related Work

Electronic voting [4–6] has been one of the key areas of focus for researchers. Over the past decade, many E-voting schemes have been proposed [7–10]. Most efficient E-voting protocols can be categorized by their approaches into the following types: blind signature [11–13], mix-nets [14], and homomorphic encryption [3,11,12,14–17]. In this subsection, we focus on the homomorphic encryption-based E-voting system.

Homomorphic encryption has been utilized in E-voting systems. The benefit of its homomorphic property is that ballots can be tallied without accessing the content of any ballot [18]. The ElGamal scheme [19] is one of the most widely used homomorphic encryption schemes in electronic voting. For instance, Refs. [3,11,12,14–16] exploit ElGamal to encrypt the ballots, thereby constructing an E-voting system with some existing cryptography tools, such as the proof of zero-knowledge [20] and the proof of partial knowledge [21].

In [14], Adida proposed a web-based E-voting system named Helios, which achieved open-audit voting using ElGamal encryption. Helios has strong security. Assuming that there are enough auditors, even if all the authorities collaborate to corrupt the system, there is a high probability of being exposed. Nevertheless, the security of Helios is closely related to the shuffling mechanism. It follows that if the Helios server is corrupted, then the submitted votes may be shuffled incorrectly, or the encrypted votes may be decrypted incorrectly. Furthermore, the performance results reported in [14] demonstrate that there is a large time overhead in the actual application. In an election with only two options in each vote and 500 voters, the Helios program takes more than 8 h.

In [12], the Helios system made several dramatic improvements to form the Helios 2.0 program, which was applied to support a real-world election. Specifically, Helios 2.0 updated the open audit mechanism. However, the key generation and decryption codes of Helios 2.0 are required to be completed by several trusted election committees. In fact, it is difficult to guarantee that the trustees are trusted in real environments. In addition, Helios 2.0 does not optimize its efficiency.

In [3], Yang et al. proposed a ranked choice E-voting system based on homomorphic encryption. Compared with the similar previous work, this system greatly improves the computation efficiency on the voter side. However, in this system, signature and encryption exist independently; the computation cost of the election agency increases rapidly as the number of voters grows. In addition, it also lacks the standardized proof of security.

Yuan et al. proposed an E-Voting scheme [7] based on Paillier homomorphic encryption and decentralization. The scheme utilizes signatures and double-encrypted technologies to secure the ballot information during transmission. In addition, the decentralization character avoids the risks associated with the corruption of a single institution and increases the openness and transparency of the system.

Qu et al. proposed an electronic voting protocol [8] based on the homomorphic signcryption. This protocol utilizes blockchain to make the election procedure public. Benefiting from the decentralized nature of blockchain, their protocol eliminates the requirement for trusted institutions.

In addition, Sheela et al. [9] and Saproo et al. [10] developed E-voting software based on homomorphic encryption, which further promotes the application of E-voting technology in practice.

E-voting represents a complex practical application scenario that necessitates the comprehensive consideration of multiple factors. Beyond safeguarding the privacy of voters' ballot information as a fundamental requirement, it is imperative to ensure eligibility, accuracy, non-repeatability, reliability, verifiability and so on. Consequently, existing schemes enrich the functionality of the voting system to align with practical demands. On the other hand, there is a need to strike a balance between functionality and efficiency to ensure the practicality of the voting system.

1.2. Organization

Sections 2 and 3 describe cryptographic tools and Fan et al.'s HSE-Voting system, respectively. Section 4 presents the cryptanalytic algorithm, and Section 5 proposes our improved HSE-Voting system. Section 6 provides the characteristic analysis of our system. The performance analysis is shown in Section 7. Section 8 concludes this paper.

2. Preliminaries

In this section, we introduce the notations and the basics of cryptography used in this paper. In the content described, the Diffie–Hellman problem is the intractability problem on which the security of the improvement scheme is based. We use the ElGamal scheme to protect ballot privacy and use its additive homomorphism to count ballot information. The proof of partial knowledge and proof of zero-knowledge (PZK) are adopted to provide the verifiability of election results. These concepts are important in enhancing the security of the HSE-Voting system.

2.1. Diffie–Hellman Problem

The Diffie–Hellman problem is a difficult problem of cryptography proposed by Whitfield Diffie and Martin Hellman in [22].

Definition 1 (Computational Diffie–Hellman Assumption, CDH). *Considering $\mathbb{G}$ is a cyclic group of order q, g is a generator of $\mathbb{G}$ and two elements $a, b \leftarrow \mathbb{Z}_q$. Given g^a and g^b, it is computationally intractable to compute the value g^{ab}.*

Definition 2 (Decisional Diffie–Hellman Assumption, DDH). *Considering $\mathbb{G}$ is a cyclic group of order q, g is a generator of $\mathbb{G}$, three elements $a, b, c \leftarrow \mathbb{Z}_q$. The DDH tuple $D = \left(g, g^a, g^b, g^{ab}\right)$ and random tuple $R = \left(g, g^a, g^b, g^c\right)$ are computationally indistinguishable.*

2.2. Elgamal Cryptography

ElGamal cryptography [19] is a well-known homomorphic encryption scheme. We select a safe-prime p of the form $p = 2q + 1$, where q is also a prime. In the remainder of this paper, we consider $\mathbb{G}$ is a cyclic group of quadratic residues modulo p. The ElGamal scheme consists of the following three algorithms.

KeyGen: Let g be a generator of $\mathbb{G}$. Randomly choose $x \leftarrow \mathbb{Z}_q$, then compute $y = g^x$. Output the key pair (SK, PK) as follows.

$$(SK, PK) = (x, y).$$

Enc: Given a message $m \in \mathbb{Z}_q$, randomly choose element $r \leftarrow \mathbb{Z}_q$, and encrypt m as follows.

$$\mathrm{Enc}(m) = c = (c_0, c_1) = (g^r, g^m y^r).$$

Dec: Given the ciphertext c, decrypt the ciphertext as follows.

$$\mathrm{Dec}(c) = c_1 / c_0^x = g^m,$$

where m can be revealed by computing a discrete algorithm.

Homomorphism: We show that the multiplication of $\mathrm{Enc}(m_1)$ and $\mathrm{Enc}(m_2)$ is a ciphertext corresponding to $m_1 + m_2$. Note that

$$\begin{aligned} \mathrm{Enc}(m_1) \cdot \mathrm{Enc}(m_2) &= (g^{r_1}, g^{m_1} y^{r_1}) \cdot (g^{r_2}, g^{m_2} y^{r_2}) \\ &= \left(g^{r_1+r_2}, g^{m_1+m_2} y^{r_1+r_2}\right) \\ &= \mathrm{Enc}(m_1 + m_2). \end{aligned}$$

2.3. Proof of Partial Knowledge

In an ElGamal cryptography system, there is a cyclic group of quadratic residues $\mathbb{G}$ of order q with a generator g, the public key $y = g^x$, and the secret key is x. Randomly select two plaintexts $m_1, m_2 \in \mathbb{Z}_q$, compute $\mathrm{Enc}(m_1) = (c_0, c_1) = (g^r, g^{m_1}y^r)$. Then, we describe the process of proof of partial knowledge based on the ElGamal scheme [21], in which the prover P can prove to the verifier V that the provided ciphertext is one of $\mathrm{Enc}(m_1)$ and $\mathrm{Enc}(m_2)$, but the verifier V cannot determine which plaintext corresponds to the ciphertext.

Firstly, the prover P generates the PPK parameters PPK as Algorithm 1.

Algorithm 1 Generating the PPK verification parameters

Input: c_0, c_1, m_1, m_2, y
Output: $PPK = (c_0, c_1, T_0, T_1, T_2, v_1, v_2, s_1, s_2)$
1: **Prover** P:
2: Generate $e, v_2 \leftarrow \mathbb{Z}_q$.
3: Compute $s_2 = r \cdot v_2 + e \bmod q$.
4: Compute $T_0 = g^e$.
5: Compute $T_1 = y^e$.
6: Compute $T_2 = (g^{m_2 v_2} y^{s_2}) / c_1^{v_2}$.
7: Compute $v = \mathrm{hash}(T_0 || T_1 || T_2 || c_0 || c_1)$.
8: Compute $v_1 = v_2 \oplus v$.
9: Compute $s_1 = r \cdot v_1 + e \bmod q$.
10: $PPK = (c_0, c_1, T_0, T_1, T_2, v_1, v_2, s_1, s_2)$
11: **return** PPK

Then, the prover P sends PPK to the verifier V. After that, the verifier V verifies the correctness of the PPK parameters as Algorithm 2.

If Algorithm 2 outputs true, verifier V believes that the ciphertext is either $\mathrm{Enc}(m_1)$ or $\mathrm{Enc}(m_2)$, but the exact value of the plaintext cannot be determined. If the m_2 is chosen to be encrypted, let step 6 in Algorithm 1 be $T_2 = (g^{m_1 v_2} y^{s_2} / c_1^{v_2})$, and set $m_1 = m_2, m_2 = m_1$ for Algorithm 2. More details can be seen in [21].

Algorithm 2 Verifying the PPK parameters

Input: PPK, m_1, m_2
Output: true or false
1: **Verifier** V:
2: Verify $v_1 \oplus v_2 = \mathrm{hash}(T_0 || T_1 || T_2 || c_0 || c_1)$.
3: Verify $g^{s_1} = T_0 \cdot c_0^{v_1}$.
4: Verify $g^{s_2} = T_0 \cdot c_0^{v_2}$.
5: Verify $y^{s_1} = T_1 \cdot (c_1 / g^{m_1})^{v_1}$.
6: Verify $y^{s_2} = T_2 \cdot (c_1 / g^{m_2})^{v_2}$.
7: If all equations hold, return true, otherwise, return false.

2.4. Proof of Zero-Knowledge

This subsection introduces the preliminary knowledge related to proof of zero-knowledge [20]. As in the previous subsection, this part is still based on the ElGamal cryptography system definition. The process of PZK [20] is described as follows in which the prover P can prove to the verifier V that the return value t and the prover's public key $h = g^x$ have the same exponentiation, i.e., x. However, the verifier V cannot obtain any information about the prover's secret key $sk = x$.

Firstly, the verifier V generates and discloses a random parameter $a \leftarrow \mathbb{Z}_q$. Then, the prover P generates the PZK parameters as Algorithm 3.

Algorithm 3 Generating the verification parameters

Input: a, h, x
Output: $PZK = (t, s, v, T_0, T_1)$
1: **Prover** P:
2: Generate $e \leftarrow \mathbb{Z}_q$.
3: Compute $t = a^x$.
4: Compute $T_0 = g^e$.
5: Compute $T_1 = a^e$.
6: Compute $v = \text{hash}(t||a||T_0||T_1)$.
7: Compute $s = x \cdot v + e \bmod q$.
8: $PZK = (t, s, v, T_0, T_1)$
9: **return** PZK

After that, the prover P sends PZK parameters PZK to the verifier V. Then, the verifier V verifies the correctness of the PZK protocol with the parameters.

If Algorithm 4 outputs true, the verifier V trusts the statement of the prover P.

Algorithm 4 Verifying the PZK parameters

Input: a, PZK
Output: true or false
1: **Verifier** V:
2: Verify $v = \text{hash}(t||a||T_0||T_1)$.
3: Verify $g^s = T_0 \cdot h^v$.
4: Verify $a^s = T_1 \cdot t^v$.
5: If all equations hold, return true; otherwise, return false.

3. HSE-Voting System Overview

In this section, we briefly introduce the entities and election processes included in the HSE-Voting system [2].

3.1. Entities in the HSE-Voting System

Here, we list all entities involved in the HSE-Voting system.

1. Voters: People who are authorized to vote.
2. Authentication Center: AC takes responsibility for verifying the identification of voters, tallying and other related work in an election. Especially, AC is honest-but-curious.
3. Bulletin Board (B Board): An insert-only bulletin board, which displays all information about the election.
4. Auditors: Auditors are responsible for supervising the voting process and verifying the election result. Furthermore, the auditors are credible.

3.2. Initialization and Registration

In the initialization phase, AC applies the safe parameter λ to generate the parameters $params = (\mathbb{G}, g, q)$ and a key pair (SK, PK), where $SK = (x_0, x_1, x_2) \leftarrow \mathbb{Z}_q^3$, $PK = (y_0, y_1, y_2) = (g^{x_0}, g^{x_1}, g^{x_2})$, then publishes $params$ and PK on the B Board.

In order to register with the HSE-Voting system, every voter has to provide valid identification. Once a voter's identity has been verified, AC sends a random ID number to them through a secure channel. In the subsequent election process, the HSE-Voting system requires voters to identify themselves using an ID number. Obviously, AC can easily determine the voter identity corresponding to the allocated ID number.

3.3. Ballot Generation

The voter V_i generates plaintext votes $b_{i,j} \in \{0, 1\}$ for each candidate, where $i \in \{1, \ldots, N_v\}$, $j \in \{1, \ldots, N_c\}$ (1 means support the candidate, 0 means do not support the candidate). The voter V_i computes the signcryption of plaintext vote $b_{i,j}$, the corresponding PPK parameters PPK_i and their public key pk_i as Algorithm 5, and sends c_i, PPK_i, ID_i as well as pk_i to AC.

Algorithm 5 Computing Signcrypt and PPK

Input: $b_{i,1}, \ldots, b_{i,N_c}, PK, params,$
Output: V_i's signcryption ballots: $c_i = (c_{i,1}, \ldots, c_{i,N_c})$
Corresponding PPK: $PPK_i = (PPK_{i,1}, \ldots, PPK_{i,N_c})$

Set $sk_i = w_i \leftarrow \mathbb{Z}_q$, $pk_i = g^{w_i}$.
while $j = 1, \ldots, N_c$ **do**
  Signcrypt:
  Set $r_{i,j} \leftarrow \mathbb{Z}_q$.
  Compute: $c_{i,j} = (c_{i,j,0}, c_{i,j,1}, c_{i,j,2})$
  $= \left(g^{r_{i,j}}, g^{b_{i,j}} {y_0}^{r_i}, {y_1}^{w_i} y_1^{b_{i,j}} {y_2}^{r_i}\right)$
  PPK:
  Set $t^{i,j}, {a_1}^{i,j}, {d_1}^{i,j} \leftarrow \mathbb{Z}_q$.
  Set $b'_{i,j} \in \{0,1\}$ and $b'_{i,j} \neq b^{i,j}$.
  Compute ${P_0}^{i,j} = g^{t^{i,j}}$.
  Compute ${P_1}^{i,j} = {y_0}^{t^{i,j}}$.
  Compute ${P_2}^{i,j} = g^{b'_{i,j} \cdot {a_1}^{i,j}} \cdot {y_0}^{{d_1}^{i,j}} / {c_{i,j,1}}^{{a_1}^{i,j}}$.
  Set $P^{i,j} = \left({P_0}^{i,j}, {P_1}^{i,j}, {P_2}^{i,j}\right)$.
  Compute $a^{i,j} = \text{hash}\left(c_{i,j,0} || c_{i,j,1} || {P_0}^{i,j} || {P_1}^{i,j} || {P_2}^{i,j}\right)$.
  Compute ${a_0}^{i,j} = {a_1}^{i,j} \oplus a^{i,j}$.
  Compute $d_0^{i,j} = r_{i,j} \cdot {a_0}^{i,j} + t^{i,j}$.
  Set $PPK_{i,j} = \left(c_{i,j}, P^{i,j}, {a_0}^{i,j}, {a_1}^{i,j}, {d_0}^{i,j}, {d_1}^{i,j}\right)$.
end while
Set $PPK_i = (PPK_{i,1}, \ldots, PPK_{i,N_c})$.
Set $c_i = (c_{i,1}, \ldots, c_{i,N_c})$.
return c_i and PPK_i

3.4. Vote Tallying

AC performs the verifications as follows.

1. Verifying the legitimacy of each ID_i.
2. Verifying the eligibility of each ballot c_i through PPK_i.

AC tallies all eligibility ballots (i.e., $flag_i = 1$) as follows.

$$C_j = (C_{j,0}, C_{j,1}, C_{j,2}) = \left(\prod_{i=1}^{N_v} c_{i,j,0}, \prod_{i=1}^{N_v} c_{i,j,1}, \prod_{i=1}^{N_v} c_{i,j,2}\right).$$

Then, AC decrypts the tallied ballot and computes the voters' joint public key as follows.

$$b_j = \log_g \frac{C_{j,1}}{C_{j,0}^{x_0}}, \quad pk = \prod_{i=1}^{N_v} pk_i.$$

After that, AC verifies whether the following equation holds.

$$C_{j,2} = pk^{x_1} y_1^{b_j} C_{j,0}^{x_2}.$$

If the above equation holds, AC publishes the election results $B = (b_1, \ldots, b_{N_c})$, where b_j is the total number of votes received by the j-candidate.

3.5. Vote Audit

The auditor firstly asks the AC for secret key x_0 and then verifies

1. $g^{x_0} = y_0$,
2. $C_{j,1} = C_{j,0}{}^{x_0} \cdot g^{b_j}, j \in \{1, \ldots, N_c\}$.

If both equations hold, the auditor believes that the election result is fair, impartial, and credible.

4. Cryptanalysis of the HSE-Voting System

In this section, we describe our attack algorithms about recovering electoral preference from the ballot and sabotaging the election with the wrong signcryption in detail.

4.1. Recovering Electoral Preference from the Ballot

Theorem 1. In the HSE-Voting system, the AC can recover every voter's electoral preference from his ballot.

Proof. As shown in the Section 3.1, the AC generates (PK, SK), and the voters send their ballots to the AC. Through the components of the ballots, the AC can resume the electoral preference in two ways. The first method is as follows.

1. The AC computes $CT_{i,j} = pk_i^{x_1} c_{i,j,0}^{x_2} = y_1^{\omega_i} y_2^{r_{i,j}}$.
2. With the voter's ballot $c_{i,j} = (c_{i,j,0}, c_{i,j,1}, c_{i,j,2})$, the AC computes $CT'_{i,j} = c_{i,j,2}/CT_{i,j} = y_1^{b_{i,j}}$.
3. If $CT'_{i,j} = 1$, the plaintext vote is 0; otherwise, the plaintext vote is 1.

In the second method, since all ballots are posted on the B Board, the adversary can obtain the signcryption and corresponding PPK of the voter V_i. According to the generation method of $PPK_{i,j}$, the parameters $a_1{}^{i,j}$ and $d_1{}^{i,j}$ are two random elements in $\mathbb{Z}_q$. Therefore, the probability of the following equation is $\frac{1}{q}$.

$$g^{d_1{}^{i,j}} = P_0{}^{i,j} \cdot c_{i,j,0}{}^{a_1^{i,j}}.$$

According to the verification equations in Algorithm 6, there is

$$g^{d_0{}^{i,j}} = P_0{}^{i,j} \cdot c_{i,j,0}{}^{a_0^{i,j}}.$$

As a consequence, the adversary can easily distinguish between $d_0{}^{i,j}$ and $d_1{}^{i,j}$. Obviously, the vote $b_{i,j}$ satisfies the following equation.

$$y_0^{d_0{}^{i,j}} = P_1{}^{i,j} \cdot (c_{i,j,1}/g^{b_{i,j}})^{a_0^{i,j}}.$$

Because of $b_{i,j} \in \{0, 1\}$, we can retrieve the voting preference easily.

As voters register with the AC, the AC can confirm the real identity of the voter by ID_i. In summary, the AC can recover every voter's electoral preference from his ballot. The reason for this security risk is that the AC has all the private keys $SK = (x_0, x_1, x_2)$. One potential solution is to encrypt the ballot using a collaborative public key approach, thereby circumventing the issue where the AC could decrypt a single ballot. □

Algorithm 6 Verifying PPK

Input: $c_1, \ldots, c_{N_v}, PPK_1, \ldots, PPK_{N_v}, PK, params$
Output: $flag_i = 0$ or 1

Set $flag_i = 1$.
while $j = 1, \ldots, N_c$ **do**
  if ${a_0}^{i,j} \oplus {a_1}^{i,j} \neq \text{hash}\left(c_{i,j,0}||c_{i,j,1}||{P_0}^{i,j}||{P_1}^{i,j}||{P_2}^{i,j}\right)$ **then**
    Set $flag_i = flag_i \times 0$.
  end if
  if $g^{{d_0}^{i,j}} \neq {P_0}^{i,j} \cdot {c_{i,j,0}}^{a_0^{i,j}}$ **then**
    Set $flag_i = flag_i \times 0$.
  end if
  if $y_0^{{d_0}^{i,j}} \neq {P_1}^{i,j} \cdot (c_{i,j,1}/g^{m_0})^{a_0^{i,j}}$ **then**
    Set $flag_i = flag_i \times 0$.
  end if
  if $y_0^{{d_1}^{i,j}} \neq {P_2}^{i,j} \cdot (c_{i,j,1}/g^{m_1})^{a_1^{i,j}}$ **then**
    Set $flag_i = flag_i \times 0$.
  end if
end while
return $flag_i$

4.2. Sabotaging the Election with the Wrong Signcryption

Theorem 2. *Malicious voters can disrupt the election process by sending the wrong signcryption.*

Proof. In the phase of ballot generation, the adversary can choose a random element $R \leftarrow \mathbb{Z}_q$ and generate a partially incorrect signcryption for ballot $b_{i,j}$.

$$c'_{i,j} = (c'_{i,j,0}, c'_{i,j,1}, c'_{i,j,2}) = \left(g^{r_i}, g^{b_{i,j}}{y_0}^{r_i}, R\right).$$

After that, the adversary generates a $PPK'_{i,j}$ corresponding to $c'_{i,j}$ and sends the signcryption $c'_{i,j}$, the PPK parameters $PPK'_{i,j}$, the identity number ID_i, and pk_i to the AC. According to the validation rules in the phase of vote tallying, the adversary's identity number ID_i is legitimate, and the verification of PPK'_i does not involve R. Therefore, the erroneous ballot can pass the verification.

Therefore, the tallied ballot is

$$\begin{aligned} C'_j &= \left(C'_{j,0}, C'_{j,1}, C'_{j,2}\right) \\ &= \left(\prod_{t=1}^{N_v} c'_{t,j,0}, \prod_{t=1}^{N_v} c'_{t,j,1}, R \cdot \prod_{t=1}^{i-1} c'_{t,j,2} \cdot \prod_{t=i+1}^{N_v} c'_{t,j,2}\right). \end{aligned}$$

The AC computes the voters' joint public key and the election result as follows.

$$pk = \prod_{i=1}^{N_v} pk_i, \; b'_j = \log_g \frac{C'_{j,1}}{C'^{x_0}_{j,0}}.$$

At this point, it is clear that the following inequality holds.

$$C'_{j,2} \neq pk^{x_1} y_1^{b'_j} C'^{x_2}_{j,0}.$$

In this case, even if the election process is restarted, the adversary can still cause the election process to fail in the same way. This means that the adversary can achieve the purpose of disrupting the election process through the above steps. This occurred because the voting system was unable to precisely identify the questionable ballots, necessitating a re-initiation of the election. Furthermore, the verification procedure omits the involvement of the third component from the ciphertext. To address this limitation, it would be advisable to enhance the system's verifiability. □

5. Improved HSE-Voting System

This section describes the details of our improved HSE-Voting system, which applies the same entities as in [2] but makes some minor changes to their specific functions. While retaining the advantages of the HSE-Voting system, we solve the security problem described in Section 4.

5.1. Entities of Our System

In our system, we modify the functions of entities AC and auditor as follows and leave the definitions of the other unchanged entities.

1. Authentication Center: As a voting institution, the AC is still responsible for verifying the identification of voters, tallying, and other related work. However, voters no longer only use the AC's public key to encrypt their ballots. Similarly, we assume that the AC is honest-but-curious.
2. Auditor: As a voting institution, the auditor is added with a new function to generate a part of the election public key. In our system, the auditor is no longer credible.

5.2. Initialization of Election

At the beginning of an election, the AC generates the election public parameters *params* and its public key PK_a. Then, the AC posts the *params* and PK_a on the B Board. Then, the auditor creates its own key pair (PK_r, SK_r) and uploads its public key on the B Board.

1. The AC generates public *params* $(\mathbb{G}, g, q)$.
2. The AC uses *params* to generate its key pair (PK_a, SK_a), where $SK_a = (x_0, x_1) \leftarrow \mathbb{Z}_q$, $PK_a = (y_0, y_1) = (g^{x_0}, g^{x_1})$.
3. The auditor generates its own key pair, where $SK_r = x_2 \leftarrow \mathbb{Z}_q$, $PK_r = y_2 = g^{x_2}$.
4. The AC and auditor calculate the joint public key $PK = y = y_0^{x_2} = y_2^{x_0} = g^{x_0 x_2}$ and make it public.

5.3. Registration of Voters

In the registration phase, each voter V_i should generate an ElGamal key pair $(pk_{v_i}, sk_{v_i}) = (g^{w_i}, w_i)$. Then, every voter provides the AC with his real valid identification (e.g., identification card) and public key pk_{v_i}. Once a voter's identity has been verified, its corresponding voter public key will be added to the registration list, which will be posted on the B Board.

5.4. Generate Ballot

The voter V_i generates the binary plaintext votes $b_i = (b_{i,1}, \ldots, b_{i,N_c})$ (where $b_{i,j} = 0$ or 1) for all candidates. Then, V_i computes his own encrypted vote as Algorithm 7.

Algorithm 7 Generating an encrypted vote

Input: $b_{i,1}, \ldots, b_{i,N_c}, PK, params$
Output: $c_i = (c_{i,1}, c_{i,2}, \ldots, c_{i,N_c})$
1: **while** $j = 1, \ldots, N_c$ **do**
2: Set $r_{i,j} \leftarrow \mathbb{Z}_q$.
3: Compute $c_{i,j} = (c_{i,j,0}, c_{i,j,1}) = \left(g^{r_{i,j}}, g^{b_{i,j}} y^{r_{i,j}}\right)$.
4: **end while**
5: Set $c_i = (c_{i,1}, c_{i,2}, \ldots, c_{i,N_c})$.
6: **return** c_i

After obtaining the encrypted vote c_i, V_i generates the PPK parameters PPK_i corresponding to the c_i using his secret key sk_{v_i}, the random parameters $r_1, \ldots r_{N_c}$, the AC's public key PK_a, and the auditor's public key PK_r. The details are described in Algorithm 8.

Algorithm 8 Generating a PPK of an encrypted vote

Input: $b_{i,1}, \ldots, b_{i,N_c}, r_{i,1}, \ldots, r_{i,N_c}, c_i, PK_a, PK_r, PK, sk_{v_i}, params$
Output: $PPK_i = (PPK_{i,1}, PPK_{i,2}, \ldots, PPK_{i,N_c})$

Set $sig_i = y_1^{\omega_i}$
while $j = 1, \ldots, N_c$ **do**
  Set $a_{i,j} \leftarrow \{0,1\}$ and $a_{i,j} \neq b_{i,j}$.
  Set $e_{i,j}, u_{i,j,2} \leftarrow \mathbb{Z}_q$.
  Compute $l_{i,j,2} = r_{i,j} \cdot u_{i,j,2} + e_{i,j} \bmod q$.
  Compute $T_{i,j,0} = g^{e_{i,j}}$.
  Compute $L_{i,j,1} = y^{e_{i,j}}$.
  Compute $L_{i,j,2} = \left[g^{a_{i,j} u_{i,j,2}} y^{l_{i,j,2}}\right] / (c_{i,j,1})^{u_{i,j,2}}$.
  if $b_{i,j} = 0$ **then**
    Set $(T_{i,j,1}, T_{i,j,2}) = (L_{i,j,1}, L_{i,j,2})$.
  else
    Set $(T_{i,j,1}, T_{i,j,2}) = (L_{i,j,2}, L_{i,j,1})$.
  end if
  Compute $u_{i,j} = \text{hash}(T_{i,j,0} || T_{i,j,1} || T_{i,j,2} || c_{i,j,0} || c_{i,j,1})$.
  Compute $u_{i,j,1} = u_{i,j,2} \oplus u_{i,j}$.
  Compute $l_{i,j,1} = r_{i,j} \cdot u_{i,j,1} + e_{i,j} \bmod q$.
  if $b_{i,j} = 0$ **then**
    Set $(s_{i,j,1}, s_{i,j,2}) = (l_{i,j,1}, l_{i,j,2})$.
    Set $(v_{i,j,1}, v_{i,j,2}) = (u_{i,j,1}, u_{i,j,2})$.
  else
    Set $(s_{i,j,1}, s_{i,j,2}) = (l_{i,j,2}, l_{i,j,1})$.
    Set $(v_{i,j,1}, v_{i,j,2}) = (u_{i,j,2}, u_{i,j,1})$.
  end if
  Compute $V_{i,j,1} = v_{i,j,1} \oplus sig_i$.
  Compute $V_{i,j,2} = v_{i,j,2} \oplus sig_i$.
  Set $PPK_{i,j} = (T_{i,j,0}, T_{i,j,1}, T_{i,j,2}, V_{i,j,1}, V_{i,j,2}, s_{i,j,1}, s_{i,j,2})$.
end while
Set $PPK_i = (PPK_{i,1}, PPK_{i,2}, \ldots, PPK_{i,N_c})$.
return PPK_i

The voter V_i posts c_i, PPK_i, and pk_{v_i} on the B Board as their ballot.

5.5. Verifications of Each Submission

As shown in the previous subsection, the contents of all ballots are posted on the B Board, including the encrypted votes, the PPK parameters, and the public key of voters. However, in order to avoid tallying any illegal ballots to the final result, the verification of each submission is an essential and crucial part of the election process. It contains the following three verification steps.

1. Verifying whether the sender is authorized: in order to prevent unauthorized people from illegally voting, each voter is required to send a ballot with their public key pk_{v_i}. The pk_{v_i} of each authorized voter is added to the registration list once they successfully register, and the AC posts a registration list on the B Board. Thus, anyone can verify whether a subsequent submission is sent by an authorized voter or not. For example, if pk_{v_i} belongs to the registration list, the sender is an authorized person. Otherwise, the submission will be discarded.
2. Verifying whether the public key has not been accepted: in order to prevent unauthorized people from using authorized voters' information posted on the B Board

and prevent authorized voters from repeating voting, the AC is required to check whether it has accepted another submission that contains the same public key. If not, this submission is legal. Otherwise, the submission will be discarded.

3. Verifying the eligibility of the encrypted ballot: our system stipulates that each vote of a valid submitted encrypted ballot must be either Enc(1) or Enc(0). The proof of each voter's submission is based on the well-known PPK protocol [21]. Specific details are described in Algorithm 9.

Algorithm 9 Verifying the eligibility of encrypted ballot c_i

Input: $c_i, PPK_i, PK_a, SK_a, PK_r, pk_{v_i}, params$
Output: $Flag_{v_i}$=1 (means true) or 0 (means false).
Set $Flag_{v_i} = 1, m_0 = 0, m_1 = 1, sig_i = pk_{v_i}^{x_1}$.
Compute $v_{i,j,1} = V_{i,j,1} \oplus pk_{v_i}^{x_1}$.
Compute $v_{i,j,2} = V_{i,j,1} \oplus pk_{v_i}^{x_1}$.
while $j = 1, \ldots, N_c$ **do**
  if $v_{i,j,1} \oplus v_{i,j,2} \neq \text{hash}(T_{i,j,0}||T_{i,j,1}||T_{i,j,2}||c_{i,j,0}||c_{i,j,1})$ **then**
    Set $flag_{v_{i,1}} = flag_{v_i} \times 0$.
  end if
  if $g^{s_{i,j,1}} \neq T_{i,j,0} \cdot C_{i,j,0}^{v_{i,j,1}}$ **then**
    Set $flag_{v_{i,1}} = flag_{v_i} \times 0$.
  end if
  if $g^{s_{i,j,2}} \neq T_{i,j,0} \cdot C_{i,j,0}^{v_{i,j,2}}$ **then**
    Set $flag_{v_{i,1}} = flag_{v_i} \times 0$.
  end if
  if $y^{s_{i,j,1}} \neq T_{i,j,1} \cdot (C_{i,j,1}/g^{m_0})^{v_{i,j,1}}$ **then**
    Set $flag_{v_{i,1}} = flag_{v_i} \times 0$.
  end if
  if $y^{s_{i,j,2}} \neq T_{i,j,2} \cdot (C_{i,j,1}/g^{m_1})^{v_{i,j,2}}$ **then**
    Set $flag_{v_{i,1}} = flag_{v_i} \times 0$.
  end if
end while
return $Flag_{v_i}$

If $Flag_{v_i} = 1$, the ballot meets the eligibility criteria. Otherwise, the submission is discarded. The submissions that pass all the verification processes will be posted on the B Board. Then, the AC accepts these ballots as valid ballots.

5.6. Tallying All Valid Ballots and Decryption

After the voting process, the AC counts all valid ballots $c_1, \ldots, c_{N_v}$, which is described in Algorithm 10.

Algorithm 10 Tallying all valid ballots

Input: $c_1, \ldots, c_{N_v}, params$
Output: $TC = (TC_1, TC_2, \ldots, TC_{N_c})$
while $j = 1, \ldots, N_c$ **do**
  Compute $TC_{j,0} = \prod_{i=1}^{N_v} c_{i,j,0}$.
  Compute $TC_{j,1} = \prod_{i=1}^{N_v} c_{i,j,1}$.
  Set $TC_j = (TC_{j,0}, TC_{j,1})$
end while
Set $TC = (TC_1, TC_2, \ldots, TC_{N_c})$.
return TC

Then, the AC announces the valid ballot-ciphertext TC and the secret key x_1 on the B Board. After that, every entity can verify the legitimacy of each ballot.

Afterward, the auditor generates the intermediate parameter *key* and its corresponding PZK parameters *PZK* as Algorithm 11.

Algorithm 11 Generating intermediate parameter and PZK

Input: $TC, sk_r, params$
Output: Intermediate parameter: $key = (key_1, \ldots, key_{N_c})$
PZK of *key*: $PZK = (PZK_1, \ldots, PZK_{N_c})$
while $j = 1, \ldots, N_c$ **do**
    Compute $key_j = TC_{j,0}^{x_2}$.
    Set $ez_j \leftarrow \mathbb{Z}_q$.
    Compute $TZ_{j,0} = g^{ez_j}$.
    Compute $TZ_{j,1} = TC_{j,0}^{ez_j}$.
    Compute $vz_j = \text{hash}(TZ_{j,0}||TZ_{j,1}||TC_{j,0})$.
    Compute $sz_j = x_2 \cdot vz_j + ez_j \bmod q$.
    Set $PZK_j = (TZ_{j,0}, TZ_{j,1}, vz_j, sz_j)$.
end while
Set $key = (key_1, \ldots, key_{N_c})$.
Set $PZK = (PZK_1, \ldots, PZK_{N_c})$.
return *key* and *PZK*

AC verifies the correctness of intermediate parameter *key* through the PZK parameters *PZK* as Algorithm 12.

Algorithm 12 Verifying the *PZK* of *TC*

Input: $key, TC, PK_r, PZK, params$
Output: $FlagZ = 1$ (means true) or 0 (means false)
Set $FlagZ = 1$.
while $j = 1, \ldots, N_c$ **do**
    if $vz_j \neq \text{hash}(TZ_{j,0}||TZ_{j,1}||TC_{j,1})$ **then**
        Set $FlagZ = FlagZ_j \times 0$.
    end if
    if $g^{sz_j} \neq TZ_{j,0} \cdot {y_2}^{vz_j}$ **then**
        Set $FlagZ = FlagZ_j \times 0$.
    end if
    if $TC_{j,0}^{sz_j} \neq TZ_{j,1} \cdot {key_j}^{vz_j}$ **then**
        Set $FlagZ = FlagZ_j \times 0$.
    end if
end while
return *FlagZ*

After that, AC decrypts the valid ballot-ciphertext *TC* using its secret key SK_a and intermediate parameter *key* as Algorithm 13. Finally, the AC publishes the election results on the B Board.

Algorithm 13 Decrypting the valid ballot-ciphertext

Input: $TC, SK_a, key, params$
Output: Final result: $B = (B_1, B_2, \ldots, B_{N_c})$
while $j = 1, \ldots, N_c$ **do**
    Compute $b_j = \log_g(TC_{j,1}/key_j^{x_0})$.
end while
Set $B = (B_1, B_2, \ldots, B_{N_c})$
return *B*

5.7. Results Auditing

During the results auditing phase, the auditor (or any voter) verifies the correctness of the final result as follows.

1. The AC computes and publishes $TC_{j,0}^{x_0}$ and its corresponding PZK parameters.
2. The auditor verifies the PZK parameters (the details are omitted here since the procedure is similar to Algorithm 12) and verifies the following equation.
$$TC_{j,1} = (TC_{j,0}^{x_0})^{x_2} \cdot g^{b_j}.$$

If the verifications pass, the election result is believed to be credible. The auditor accepts the result and posts it on the B Board.

6. Characteristic Analysis

This section is devoted to giving a detailed security analysis of our improved HSE-Voting system, including the privacy of voters, the correctness of the final election result, and the voting verifiability.

6.1. Privacy of Voters

It is very necessary to protect the voters' voting preferences. We argue for voter privacy from the following two points: (i) any probabilistic polynomial time adversary cannot distinguish whether a ballot is encrypted by 0 or 1 based on the information on the B Board; (ii) when using the PPK protocol, voters' voting preferences of ballots will not be revealed during ballot verification.

Theorem 3. *If the ElGamal cryptosystem is semantically secure, any probabilistic polynomial time adversary cannot obtain the voters' voting preferences from the B Board.*

Proof. Every cast ballot has been encrypted using the ElGamal cryptosystem (cf. Section 2.2) before submitting. ElGamal has homomorphic properties and semantic security. Thus, in our system, there is no probabilistic polynomial time adversary that can distinguish whether a ballot-ciphertext is Enc(0) or Enc(1) from the information published on the B Board. As mentioned above, the voting preferences of ballots remain secure. □

Theorem 4. *When using the PPK protocol and PZK protocol, the voting preferences and the information of the auditor's secret key will not be revealed during verification.*

Proof. The PPK parameters $PPK_{i,j}$ are generated by using the PPK protocol, which consists of $T_{i,j,0}$, $T_{i,j,1}$, $T_{i,j,2}$, $V_{i,j,1}$, $V_{i,j,2}$, $s_{i,j,1}$, and $s_{i,j,2}$, where $v_{i,j,2}$ and $s_{i,j,1}$ are random integers, $T_{i,j,0}$, $T_{i,j,1}$, $T_{i,j,2}$, $v_{i,j,1}$ are computed by using random numbers $v_{i,j,2}$, $s_{i,j,2}$, $e_{i,j}$, and $V_{i,j,1}$, $V_{i,j,2}$ are computes by $sig_{i,j}$, $v_{i,j,1}$, as well as $v_{i,j,2}$. The parameter $sig_{i,j}$ is the Diffie–Hellman signature between the AC and the voter V_i. The PPK protocol is given in [21], which shows the details of proof that PPK will not reveal the original message. By using the PPK protocol, the verifier can verify all the elements without decryption. The verifier could only know whether an element is encrypted by 0 or 1, but cannot determine the exact value of plaintext.

The PZK parameters PZK_j are computed by the PZK protocol, which consists of $TZ_{j,0}$, $TZ_{j,1}$, vz_j, and sz_j, where vz_j is a random number, $TZ_{j,0}$, $TZ_{j,1}$ are computed by random number $e_{i,j}$, and sz_j is computed by random numbers $e_{i,j}$ as well as vz_j. The PZK protocol is given in [20], which shows the PZK protocol has zero-knowledge and will not reveal any additional information.

Based on the security of the PPK and PZK protocols, the relevant parameters are not considered to readily reveal private information about voters' electoral preferences. □

6.2. Correctness of the Election Result

In this subsection, we analyze the correctness of the election results from two aspects: the correctness of ballot delivery and the correctness of ballot integration and decryption.

Theorem 5. *Only authorized voters can vote, and no one can vote repeatedly.*

Proof. Suppose an unauthorized adversary attempts to use the i-th voter's public key pk_{v_i} to participate in the election. For the PPK parameter $V_{i,j,1} = v_{i,j,1} \oplus y_1^{\omega_i}$ in $PPK_{i,j}$, due to Definition 1, the difficulty of the CDH problem shows the probability of the adversary successfully forging $y_1^{\omega_i} = g^{\omega_i \cdot x_1}$ when they only know g, g^{ω_i} and g^{x_1} is negligible. Therefore, the probability of the adversary successfully forging a valid PPK parameter $V'_{i,j,1}$ that satisfies $V'_{i,j,1} = v_{i,j,1} \oplus y_1^{\omega_i}$ is negligible. In addition, our system ensures that each voter can vote only once by verifying whether their public key is included in other accepted ballots. □

Theorem 6. *The election process during ballot tallying and valid ballot-ciphertext decrypting is correct.*

Proof. In Section 2.2, we introduced the additive homomorphism of the ElGamal scheme. Therefore, the AC can count all the ballots on the B Board according to the correct steps.

$$TC_{j,0} = \prod_{i=1}^{N_v} C_{i,j,0} = \prod_{i=1}^{N_v} g^{r_{i,j}} = g^{\sum_{i=1}^{N_v} r_{i,j}},$$

$$TC_{j,1} = \prod_{i=1}^{N_v} C_{i,j,1} = \prod_{i=1}^{N_v} g^{b_{i,j}} y^{r_{i,j}} = g^{\sum_{i=1}^{N_v} b_{i,j}} g^{x_0 x_2 \sum_{i=1}^{N_v} r_{i,j}}.$$

Then, the AC uploads all accepted ballots to the B Board. At this time, everyone can check if their ballot is lost. In the end, the AC and auditors jointly decrypt valid ballot-ciphertext to obtain the election result.

Auditors compute

$$key_j = TC_{j,0}^{x_2} = g^{x_2 \sum_{i=1}^{N_v} r_{i,j}}.$$

Then, the AC computes

$$\log_g(TC_{j,1}/key_j^{x_0}) = \log_g(g^{\sum_{i=1}^{N_v} b_{i,j}} y^{\sum_{i=1}^{N_v} r_{i,j}} / (g^{x_2 \sum_{i=1}^{N_v} r_{i,j}})^{x_0}) = \log_g(g^{\sum_{i=1}^{N_v} b_{i,j}}) = \sum_{i=1}^{N_v} b_{i,j} = b_j.$$

Since $b_{i,j} \in \{0,1\}$, $b_j = \sum_{i=1}^{N_v} b_{i,j} \leq N_v$ is small in practice. It is feasible to compute the discrete logarithm $\log_g(g^{b_j})$. Therefore, the election process of ballot tallying and valid ballot-ciphertext decryption is correct. □

Theorem 7. *The AC can check PPK and PZK in order to ensure the legality of the contents.*

Proof. According to the properties of PPK outlined in Section 2.3, the AC can utilize the voter's public key pk_{v_i} to ascertain whether the plaintext corresponding to an encrypted ballot represents 0 or 1, thereby confirming the legitimacy and validity of this ballot. Similarly, in accordance with the PZK properties delineated in Section 2.4, the AC can confirm that the auditor has provided the correct decryption information *key*, thus ensuring the accurate decryption of the election results. □

6.3. Voting Verifiability

In this section, we divide the verifiability requirements into two parts: universal verifiability and individual verifiability.

Universal verifiability: the B Board in our E-voting system is public, so everyone can check the accepted ballots and the election result on the B Board. In addition, since all accepted ballots are disclosed, voters can check the correctness of their ballots and prevent their ballots from being forged or tampered with.

Individual verifiability: the auditor (as well as each voter) can verify the final result of the election. The legality of verification is proved in Theorem 8.

Theorem 8. *The auditor (or each voter) can correctly verify the final election result.*

Proof. The auditor first verifies the PZK to prove that the correctness of $TC_{j,0}^{x_0}$. Then, he checks the correctness of the final election result by verifying the equation. The correctness of the verification equation is as follows.

$$(TC_{j,0}^{x_0})^{x_2} \cdot g^{\sum_{i=1}^{N_v} b_{i,j}} = g^{x_0 x_2 \sum_{i=1}^{N_v} r_{i,j}} \cdot g^{\sum_{i=1}^{N_v} b_{i,j}} = TC_{j,1}.$$

□

6.4. Comparison of Characteristics with Related Work

In order to provide a clearer indication of the contribution of the proposed scheme, we compared the characteristics of the proposed scheme with related work, and the results are shown in Table 1. In Yuan et al.'s scheme [7], the RSA signature scheme is employed to guarantee the integrity of ballots. However, there is no consideration of validating the legality of the ballot, i.e., the ciphertext is $Enc(0)$ or $Enc(1)$. In Qu et al.'s scheme [8], the smart contract with the decryption key is able to decrypt the ciphertext of each ballot and verify its legality. Therefore, this scheme lacks the public verifiability. In Fan et al.'s HSE-Voting system [2], only the trusted auditor can verify the election results.

Table 1. Characteristic comparison.

System	Eligibility	Uniqueness	Single Ballot Privacy	Public Verification of Ballot Legality	Public Verification of Electoral Correctness
Yuan et al.'s system [7]	✓	✓	✓	×	✓
Qu et al.'s system [8]	✓	✓	×	×	×
Yang et al.'s system [3]	✓	✓	✓	✓	✓
HSE-Voting system [2]	✓	✓	×	✓	×
Our system	✓	✓	✓	✓	✓

The symbol ✓ represents that the characteristic is supported by the system and the symbol × indicates that it is not supported.

7. Performance Analysis

This section presents the performance analysis of our improved HSE-Voting system. We use $cost_t$ to denote the computation time of one exponentiation. Meanwhile, we separately analyze the computation cost on the voter side and the AC side. Due to the small computation cost and little use of the auditor side, no detailed analysis is performed here. Furthermore, the comparison of our improved HSE-Voting system with the HSE-Voting system [2] and Yang et al.'s system [3] is given below.

7.1. Performance of the Voter Side

On the voter side, every voter should generate their ballot and submit it to AC. According to Section 5.4, the total computation cost for a voter can be present as the sum of the time of computing the encrypted vote c_i and the corresponding PPKs, which can be expressed as follows.

$$2 \times cost_t \times N_c + 5 \times cost_t \times N_c + cost_t.$$

See Table 2 for a detailed comparison.

Table 2. Performance comparison.

System	Computational Cost of Voter	Computational Cost of AC
Yang et al.'s system [3]	$7 \times cost_t \times N_c + 3 \times cost_t$	$8 \times cost_t \times N_c \times N_v + 6 \times cost_t \times N_v + cost_t \times N_c$
HSE-Voting system [2]	$9 \times cost_t \times N_c$	$6 \times cost_t \times N_c \times N_v + 4 \times cost_t$
Our system	$7 \times cost_t \times N_c + cost_t$	$8 \times cost_t \times N_c \times N_v + 5 \times cost_t \times N_c + N_v \times cost_t$

7.2. Performance of the AC Side

The performance of the AC side can be summarized in three parts: verifying the *PPK*s of ballots, checking the *PZK*s of intermediate parameters, and decrypting the valid ballot-ciphertext. The total computation time of the AC side is as follows; see Table 2 for a detailed comparison.

$$8 \times cost_t \times N_c \times N_v + cost_t \times N_v + 4 \times cost_t \times N_c + cost_t \times N_c.$$

7.3. Experimental Simulation

In this subsection, all tests were performed on a laptop with the following specifications: 2.4 GHz quad-core Intel Core i7 with 16 GB of 1600 MHz DDR3L onboard memory. We used a high-performance implementation from libgmp via the gmpy2 Python module (https://gmpy2.readthedocs.io/en/latest/ (accessed on 4 January 2024)).

As depicted in Figure 1 and based on our experimental findings, it appears that our scheme may exhibit some efficiency benefits over the HSE-Voting system [2] in ballot casting, while the computational overhead seems to align closely with that of Yang et al.'s scheme [3].

As shown in Figure 2, the computational overhead for the AC side in our enhanced scheme is slightly higher than that of the HSE-Voting system [2]. This increase can be attributed to the integration of additional computational components aimed at bolstering security. In addition, the computational overhead of our AC side is slightly smaller than Yang et al.'s scheme [3], which is one of the design goals of the HSE system.

Combining the comparison results of characteristics and efficiency, the contribution of our scheme is to support the public verification of the ballot legality as well as the validity of election results, and the overall efficiency is slightly higher than Yang et al.'s scheme [3].

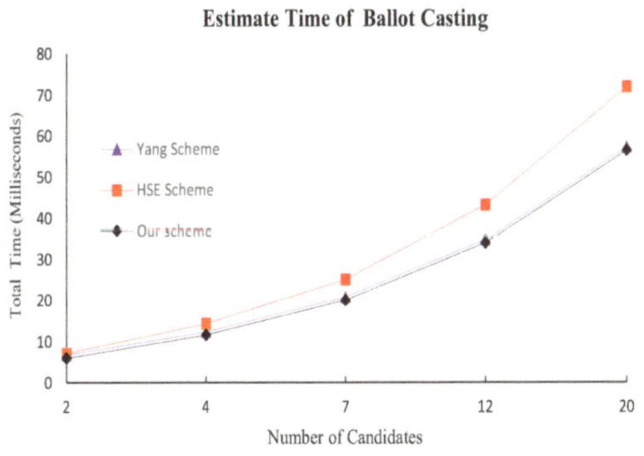

Figure 1. Estimate total time comparison for a voter of the three systems.

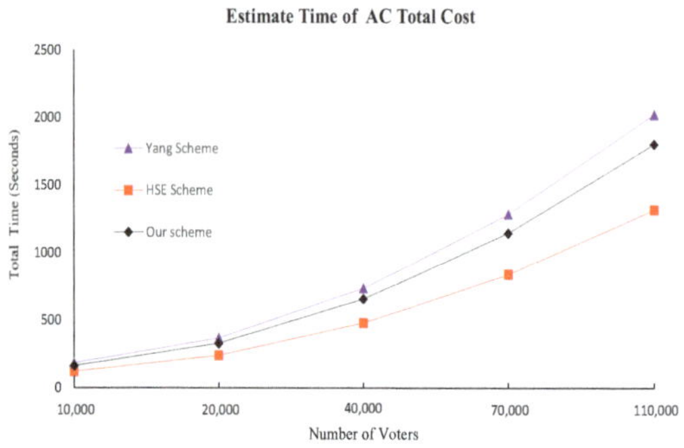

Figure 2. Estimate total time comparison for AC of 5 candidates.

8. Conclusions

In this paper, we indicated two potential security threats to the HSE-Voting system and proposed a security-enhanced system based on Fan et al.'s scheme. Firstly, we pointed out that the content of each voter's ballot could be obtained by the AC. Then, we discovered that malicious voters could create illegitimate ballots to disrupt the election process without being detected. Further, we proposed an improved scheme to avoid the above security risks. In addition, we showed a detailed analysis and demonstration of the characteristics of the improved HSE-Voting system. Comparison results of theoretical analyses and experimental tests suggest that our proposed scheme might offer some insights or benefits when compared to related schemes.

Author Contributions: Conceptualization, Y.Z. and N.Y.; methodology, Y.Z., Z.Z. and N.Y.; validation, C.Z. and W.Z.; writing—original draft preparation, Y.Z. and N.Y.; supervision, W.Z. and B.W. All authors have read and agreed to the published version of the manuscript.

Funding: This research was funded by the National Key R&D Program of China No. 2023YFB3106100, the National Natural Science Foundation of China under Grant 62202363, 62272362, U19B2021,62102299, and the Youth Innovation Team of Shaanxi Universities, Science and Technology on Communication Security Laboratory Foundation (61421030202012103), the Henan Key Laboratory of Network Cryptography Technology under No. LNCT2022-A05.

Data Availability Statement: The data can be shared up on request.

Conflicts of Interest: The authors declare no conflicts of interest.

Notations

Notations used in the rest of this paper:

$\mathbb{Z}$	The integer ring
$\mathbb{Z}_q$	$\mathbb{Z}_q = \{0, 1, 2, \ldots, q-1\}$
$\leftarrow$	Uniform and random select
hash$(\cdot)$	Hash function
$\oplus$	XOR
PPK	The parameters of proof of partial knowledge
PZK	The parameters of proof of zero-knowledge
N_v	The number of voters
V_i	i-th Voter, where $i \in \{1, 2, \ldots, N_v\}$
N_c	The number of candidates
Can_j	j-th candidate, where $j \in \{1, 2, \ldots, N_c\}$
$b_{i,j}$	The ballot belonging to V_i for Can_j
b_i	The ballot belonging to V_i
sig_i	The Diffie–Hellman signature
PK	The public key

SK	The secret key
pk_{v_i}	The public key of V_i
sk_{v_i}	The secret key of V_i
$c_{i,j}$	A ballot-ciphertext of $b_{i,j}$
c_i	A ballot-ciphertext of b_i
TC_j	A valid ballot-ciphertext of b_j
key	Intermediate parameter for TC
B	The final result of election

References

1. Scott, P. US Election 2016: Voter turnout fell to 58 per cent this year, estimates show. *Telegraph* **2016**, *14*. Available online: https://www.telegraph.co.uk/news/2016/11/14/us-election-2016-voter-turnout-fell-to-58-per-cent-this-year-est/ (accessed on 4 January 2024).
2. Fan, X.; Wu, T.; Zheng, Q.; Chen, Y.; Alam, M.; Xiao, X. HSE-Voting: A secure high-efficiency electronic voting scheme based on homomorphic signcryption. *Future Gener. Comput. Syst.* **2020**, *111*, 754–762. [CrossRef]
3. Yang, X.; Yi, X.; Nepal, S.; Kelarev, A.; Han, F. A secure verifiable ranked choice online voting system based on homomorphic encryption. *IEEE Access* **2018**, *6*, 20506–20519. [CrossRef]
4. Saracevic, M.; Selimi, A. Convex polygon triangulation based on planted trivalent binary tree and ballot problem. *Turk. J. Electr. Eng. Comput. Sci.* **2019**, *27*, 346–361. [CrossRef]
5. Fujioka, A.; Okamoto, T.; Ohta, K. A Practical Secret Voting Scheme for Large Scale Elections. In *Advances in Cryptology—AUSCRYPT'92*; Springer: Berlin/Heidelberg, Germany, 1992; Volume 718, pp. 244–251.
6. Shahzad, B.; Crowcroft, J. Trustworthy Electronic Voting Using Adjusted Blockchain Technology. *IEEE Access* **2019**, *7*, 24477–24488. [CrossRef]
7. Yuan, K.; Sang, P.; Zhang, S.; Chen, X.; Yang, W.; Jia, C. An electronic voting scheme based on homomorphic encryption and decentralization. *PeerJ Comput. Sci.* **2023**, *9*, e1649. [CrossRef] [PubMed]
8. Qu, W.; Wu, L.; Wang, W.; Liu, Z.; Wang, H. A electronic voting protocol based on blockchain and homomorphic signcryption. *Concurr. Comput. Pract. Exp.* **2022**, *34*, e5817. [CrossRef]
9. Sheela, A.S.; Franklin, R.G. E-Voting System Using Homomorphic Encryption Technique. *J. Phys. Conf. Ser.* **2021**, *1770*, 012011. [CrossRef]
10. Saproo, S.; Warke, V.; Pote, S.; Dhumal, R. Online voting system using homomorphic encryption. In Proceedings of the ITM Web of Conferences, Navi Mumbai, India, 27–28 June 2020; EDP Sciences: Les Ulis, France, 2020; Volume 32, p. 03023.
11. Kiayias, A.; Zacharias, T.; Zhang, B. An Efficient E2E Verifiable E-voting System without Setup Assumptions. *IEEE Secur. Priv.* **2017**, *15*, 14–23. [CrossRef]
12. de Marneffe, O.; Pereira, O.; Quisquater, J. Electing a University President Using Open-Audit Voting: Analysis of Real-World Use of Helios. In Proceedings of the 2009 Electronic Voting Technology Workshop/Workshop on Trustworthy Elections, EVT/WOTE'09, Montreal, QC, Canada, 10–11 August 2009; Jefferson, D., Hall, J.L., Moran, T., Eds.; USENIX Association: Berkeley, CA, USA, 2009.
13. Kumar, M.; Katti, C.P.; Saxena, P.C. A Secure Anonymous E-Voting System Using Identity-Based Blind Signature Scheme. In Proceedings of the Information Systems Security—13th International Conference, ICISS 2017, Mumbai, India, 16–20 December 2017; Lecture Notes in Computer Science; Springer: Cham, Switzerland, 2017; Volume 10717, pp. 29–49. [CrossRef]
14. Adida, B. Helios: Web-based Open-Audit Voting. In Proceedings of the 17th USENIX Security Symposium, San Jose, CA, USA, 28 July–1 August 2008; van Oorschot, P.C., Ed.; USENIX Association: Berkeley, CA, USA, 2008; pp. 335–348.
15. Mateu, V.; Miret, J.M.; Sebé, F. A hybrid approach to vector-based homomorphic tallying remote voting. *Int. J. Inf. Sec.* **2016**, *15*, 211–221. [CrossRef]
16. Huszti, A. A homomorphic encryption-based secure electronic voting scheme. *Publ. Math. Debr.* **2011**, *79*, 479–496. [CrossRef]
17. Hirt, M.; Sako, K. Efficient Receipt-Free Voting Based on Homomorphic Encryption. In Proceedings of the Advances in Cryptology—EUROCRYPT 2000, Bruges, Belgium, 14–18 May 2000; Springer: Berlin/Heidelberg, Germany, 2000; Volume 1807, pp. 539–556.
18. Yi, X.; Paulet, R.; Bertino, E. *Homomorphic Encryption and Applications*; Springer Briefs in Computer Science; Springer: Cham, Switzerland, 2014. [CrossRef]
19. ElGamal, T. A Public Key Cryptosystem and a Signature Scheme Based on Discrete Logarithms. In *Advances in Cryptology, Proceedings of the CRYPTO'84, Santa Barbara, CA, USA, 19–22 August 1984*; Lecture Notes in Computer Science; Blakley, G.R., Chaum, D., Eds.; Springer: Berlin/Heidelberg, Germany, 1984; Volume 196, pp. 10–18. [CrossRef]
20. Chaum, D.; Pedersen, T.P. Wallet Databases with Observers. In *Advances in Cryptology, Proceedings of the CRYPTO'92, 12th Annual International Cryptology Conference, Santa Barbara, CA, USA, 16–20 August 1992*; Lecture Notes in Computer Science; Brickell, E.F., Ed.; Springer: Berlin/Heidelberg, Germany, 1992; Volume 740, pp. 89–105. [CrossRef]

21. Cramer, R.; Damgård, I.; Schoenmakers, B. Proofs of Partial Knowledge and Simplified Design of Witness Hiding Protocols. In *Advances in Cryptology, Proceedings of the CRYPTO'94, 14th Annual International Cryptology Conference, Santa Barbara, CA, USA, 21–25 August 1994*; Lecture Notes in Computer Science; Desmedt, Y., Ed.; Springer: Berlin/Heidelberg, Germany, 1994; Volume 839, pp. 174–187. [CrossRef]
22. Diffie, W.; Hellman, M.E. New directions in cryptography. *IEEE Trans. Inf. Theory* **1976**, *22*, 644–654. [CrossRef]

electronics

Article

A Privacy-Preserving Testing Framework for Copyright Protection of Deep Learning Models

Dongying Wei [1], Dan Wang [2,*], Zhiheng Wang [1] and Yingyi Ma [1]

[1] School of Geology and Geomatics, Tianjin Chengjian University, Tianjin 300392, China; weidongying@tcu.edu.cn (D.W.); wangzhiheng@tcu.edu.cn (Z.W.); mayy@tcu.edu.cn (Y.M.)
[2] College of Artificial Intelligence, Tianjin University of Science and Technology, Tianjin 300453, China
* Correspondence: wanghzc@tust.edu.cn

Abstract: Deep learning is widely utilized to acquire predictive models for mobile crowdsensing systems (MCSs). These models significantly improve the availability and performance of MCSs in real-world scenarios. However, training these models requires substantial data resources, rendering them valuable to their owners. Numerous protection schemes have been proposed to mitigate potential economic loss arising from legal issues pertaining to model copyright. Although capable of providing copyright verification, these schemes either compromise the model utility or prove ineffective against adversarial attacks. Additionally, the privacy concern surrounding copyright verification is noteworthy, given the increasing privacy concerns among model owners. This paper introduces a privacy-preserving testing framework for copyright protection (PTFCP) comprising multiple protocols. Our protocols adhere to the two-cloud server model, where the owner and the suspect transmit their model output to non-colluding servers for evaluating model similarity through the public-key cryptosystem with distributed decryption (PCDD) and garbled circuits. Additionally, we have developed novel techniques to enable secure differentiation for absolute values. Our experiments in real-world datasets demonstrate that our protocols in the PTFCP successfully operate under numerous copyright violation scenarios, such as finetuning, pruning, and extraction.

Keywords: mobile crowdsensing; deep learning model copyright protection; privacy preservation

1. Introduction

Deep learning, as a promising and practical technology, has been extensively adopted to enhance the performance of mobile crowdsensing systems (MCSs) [1–4]. For instance, in [5], the authors utilize deep neural networks (DNNs) and employ graph convolutional reinforcement learning to achieve Aoi-minimal UAV crowdsensing. Similarly, in [6], the DNN is utilized to implement a heterogeneous task allocation in MCSs, employing a modified approximate policy approach. Furthermore, in [7], Xu et al. combine the concepts of the graph attention network and deep reinforcement learning to propose an intelligent task allocation scheme for MCSs. It is evident that well-trained DNN models can significantly enhance the performance of MCSs.

However, as the model complexity, data volume, and number of tasks grow, the cost of training an applicable model, particularly for deep neural networks (DNNs), also increases. For instance, training a model with 1.5 billion parameters, such as the BERT model on Wikipedia, can cost nearly $1.6 million. Therefore, safeguarding the trained models from duplication, theft, or unauthorized reproduction by adversaries is necessary and crucial [8,9].

It is worth noting that, to enhance the provision of machine learning as a service (MLaaS), certain organizations or companies opt to offer open-source toolkits, remote services, or cloud platforms to the public. However, despite its potential for commercial profit, this approach exposes the trained DNN models (which are often trained at considerable cost) to the public, enabling adversaries to steal the models discreetly and conveniently. These potential risks can lead to substantial economic losses [10–12] and even involve legal issues [13–16] related to copyright infringement for the model owners. Researchers have already highlighted that adversaries can stealthily and efficiently steal DNN models [17,18]. In cases where the adversary possesses greater knowledge about the model or when the model parameters are publicly available, two commonly employed white-box attacks are unauthorized finetuning and pruning [19]. Furthermore, recent studies have shown that even under a black-box attack scenario [17,20], the core functionalities of a DNN model can still be extracted. Despite the adversary's limited access to the exposed API, they can employ advanced model extraction approaches to reconstruct the underlying core functionality of the model. In conclusion, there has been a rapid growth in the threat to the copyright of DNN models, highlighting the urgent need for effective and practical countermeasures.

In recent years, numerous schemes have been proposed to protect model copyrights. DNN watermarking is a commonly employed scheme among these, known for its effectiveness in practical scenarios [21,22]. It utilizes the over-parameterization properties of DNNs to secretly embed a designed watermark (e.g., a signature or logo representing ownership information) into the model. Verifying the ownership of a suspected model can be easily accomplished by extracting potential embedded watermarks from the model [23]. Consequently, DNN watermarking is considered a promising technique with significant advantages. However, these schemes still have some crucial drawbacks [24]. Notably, the essential attribute of these schemes is their invasive nature, where the model content or training process is modified after watermark embedding. Recent studies have shown that such modifications can severely compromise the utility of DNN models or introduce additional vulnerabilities [25,26].

To overcome the limitations of invasive techniques such as watermarking, researchers have proposed DNN fingerprinting, which has garnered significant attention [27,28]. Fingerprinting is rooted in the uniqueness of a DNN model, which embodies its distinct characteristics. Specifically, a distinctive fingerprint is extracted from the owner model, serving as an identifier to differentiate it from other models. If the extracted fingerprint from a suspect model matches that of the owner model, the model owner can assert ownership based on this result. However, in real-world scenarios, relying solely on the fingerprint as a feature or metric for justifying model ownership is insufficiently persuasive. Nonetheless, DNN fingerprinting is also vulnerable to state-of-the-art model stealing attacks. In conclusion, the distinctive characteristics of a DNN model may be compromised or unavailable in various situations.

To address the limitations of DNN fingerprinting, researchers have turned their attention to assessing the similarity between distinct models [29–31]. Traditional approaches employ direct calculations, such as the Euclidean distance [29], Kullback–Leibler divergence, or Jensen–Shannon divergence [31], to measure the dissimilarity between the contents of distinct models in parameter space or output space. This methodology is based on the premise that the similarity between two different models stems from the resemblance of their internal contents. However, this simplistic approach lacks persuasiveness and practicality. For example, computing the Euclidean distance in the parameter space of DNN models can result in significant computational expenses [32]. If these costs are deemed acceptable, copyright verification becomes unnecessary. Moreover, there is a possibility that the two models exhibit substantial differences [33] in parameter space despite sharing the same training dataset and initialization due to potential bugs in floating-point operations or stochasticity in the training process.

To enhance the assessment of similarity between distinct models, Chen et al. [30] introduced a testing framework called DeepJudge. In their study, they evaluate the similarity of two distinct models using six metrics across three levels, which are based on the generated test cases. Their experiments provide evidence of DeepJudge's effectiveness. Despite the promise of DeepJudge compared to traditional approaches, it assumes that the model owner grants unrestricted access to the architecture, parameters, and datasets, including training details in some cases. However, in real-world scenarios, ownership verification is typically conducted by a third party, and the model owner is reluctant to provide such access due to concerns about model privacy. Consequently, there is an urgent need for a method that can measure model similarity while maintaining model privacy. However, to the best of our knowledge, this problem has been largely overlooked.

This paper focuses on evaluating the similarity between two distinct models in a privacy-preserving manner using cryptographic techniques. We propose a set of protocols based on the two-cloud model for conducting privacy-preserving model similarity evaluation. In these protocols, the model owner (referred to hereafter as the "victim") and the party holding a suspect model (referred to hereafter as the "suspect") transmit encrypted data to the cloud server. During the computation phase, the two non-colluding servers can evaluate the similarity using different metrics without accessing any sensitive information about the model data. Subsequently, the encrypted evaluation result is returned to the victim for further estimation purposes. In real-world scenarios, when two AI companies or organizations face a copyright infringement conflict, the details of their respective models are confidential due to commercial competition. Therefore, adopting these protocols encourages the entities to pursue judgment by the authorized third party while alleviating concerns about unintentional leakage of confidential model information.

In summary, our main contributions are:

- We address a realistic and often overlooked problem: preserving privacy in model copyright verification. To the best of our knowledge, this paper is the first to discuss privacy preservation in this context.
- We propose a set of protocols based on the two-cloud model that enables the evaluation of similarity between distinct models while safeguarding model privacy. Our protocols encompass multiple metrics at various levels, providing a comprehensive evaluation of model similarity.
- Through extensive experiments conducted on various real-world DNN models and datasets, we demonstrate the effectiveness of our protocols.

The structure of this paper is as follows: Section 2 provides an introduction to the system and the threat model. Section 3 presents the preliminaries, while Section 4 describes the details of the proposed protocols. In Section 5, we discuss the experimental results to demonstrate the effectiveness of the proposed protocols. Section 6 highlights relevant works on model copyright. Finally, we conclude our work in Section 7. The detailed roadmap is illustrated in Figure 1.

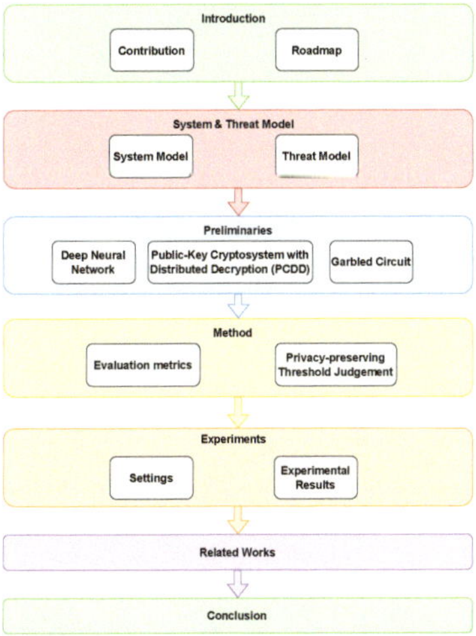

Figure 1. The roadmap of this paper.

2. System and Threat Model

2.1. System Model

As illustrated in Figure 2, our PTFCP consists of three main entities: the model owner, suspect, and cloud servers.

- The model owner, referred to as the victim, possesses a model (referred to as the victim model for simplicity) that has been trained using private and valuable resources. In order to ascertain whether the suspect model is an illicit copy of the victim's model, the victim utilizes its test cases to generate the outputs from its own model. Subsequently, these outputs are encrypted and utilized as inputs for the protocols within our PTFCP.
- The suspect possesses a model that potentially infringes upon the copyright of the victim's model. To determine the occurrence of infringement, the suspect follows the subsequent steps. Initially, it employs the test cases of the victim to obtain outputs using its own model. Subsequently, these outputs are encrypted and utilized as inputs for the judgment protocols.
- Initially, the cloud servers receive the encrypted outputs from both the victim and the suspect based on the determined public key pk. Subsequently, these two servers, denoted as S_1 and S_2 respectively, collaboratively execute the protocols within our PTFCP to acquire the encrypted judgment results.

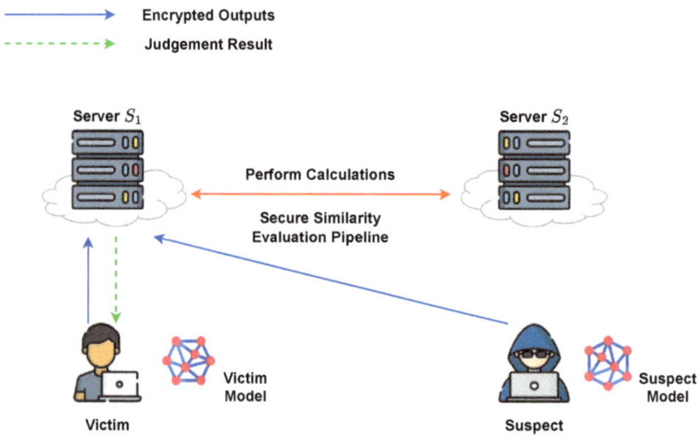

Figure 2. The system model.

2.2. Threat Model

This section focuses on a typical attack–defense scenario in which the victim endeavors to safeguard the copyright of its model and identify potential instances of infringement. Conversely, the suspect's objective is to illicitly acquire either the functionality or the complete information of the victim model. Moreover, the suspect employs various techniques to obfuscate the stolen model and avoid its detection as an unauthorized replica. Furthermore, in consideration of data privacy requirements such as model parameter privacy and architecture privacy, privacy-preserving measures are also taken into account within the threat model.

2.2.1. Model Copyright

We summarize three major threats to the copyright of models based on state-of-the-art model stealing attacks.

1. Finetuning In this scenario, it is assumed that the suspect possesses complete knowledge of both the model parameters and architecture, along with an additional dataset for finetuning the target model. For example, even if certain model owners have open-sourced their trained models solely for academic or open-source purposes, the

suspect can still exploit finetuning techniques in a malicious manner to construct their own model for commercial gain.

2. Pruning In this scenario, it is also assumed that the suspect has acquired complete information regarding the parameters and architecture of the victim model. In order to perform model pruning, the suspect initially employs various pruning techniques to reduce the size of the victim model. Subsequently, the suspect employs its auxiliary dataset to conduct finetuning on the pruned model obtained in the previous step.
3. Model Extraction In this scenario, the suspect has restricted access and can only retrieve the prediction results, such as probability vectors, from the victim model by utilizing the exposed API. Occasionally, the suspect may possess information regarding the architecture of the victim model, while the model parameters of the victim model remain inaccessible. The primary objective of the suspect is to accurately replicate the core functionality of the victim model by leveraging the exposed API. Based on recent proposed works, the suspect can initially utilize selected samples to query the exposed API and generate a labeled dataset. Subsequently, using the labeled dataset, the suspect trains an alternative model capable of replicating the functionality of the victim model. The selected samples can be sourced either from the suspect's auxiliary dataset or generated using advanced techniques.

2.2.2. Data Privacy

In our PTFCP, it is assumed that the victim, suspect, and two cloud servers are all characterized as honest-but-curious. This implies that they will faithfully execute the steps outlined in the protocols during the similarity evaluation process. Nevertheless, they may possess an interest in the information pertaining to other entities and have the capability to compromise data privacy through the utilization of their knowledge. Additionally, it is assumed that the two cloud servers are non-colluding, a common and reasonable assumption in numerous application scenarios [34–37]. Furthermore, it is further assumed that neither the owner nor the suspect will engage in collusion with the cloud servers.

3. Preliminaries

3.1. Deep Neural Network

Deep Neural Networks (DNNs) serve as a fundamental technology in the domain of deep learning, enabling the learning of intricate relationships between input and output in high-dimensional spaces. Consequently, DNNs have found applications in diverse fields such as voice recognition, image classification, and natural language processing. In general, a canonical neural network comprises three essential components: an input layer, an output layer, and at least one hidden layer. Figure 3 illustrates a representative example of a fully connected DNN.

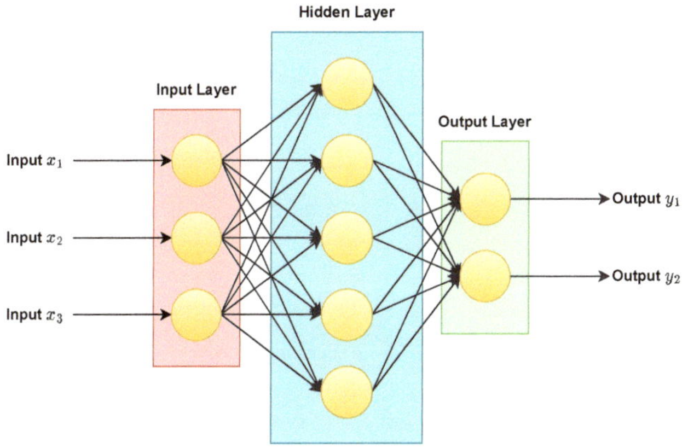

Figure 3. An example of DNN.

Without loss of generality, our primary focus here is on the DNN classifier. The DNN classifier possesses a decision function that maps an input to its corresponding label. The classifier consists of L layers: $f^1, f^2, \cdots, f^{L-1}, f^L$. Here, f^1 represents the input layer, f^L is the output layer that generates the probability vector, and $f^2, \cdots, f^{L-1}$ refer to the hidden layers. The total number of classes is denoted as C. Each layer f^l consists of a set of neurons: $n_1^l, n_2^l, \cdots, n_{N_l}^l$, with N_l representing the number of neurons in that layer. The output of the neuron n_i^l, given a specific input x, is denoted as $\varphi_i^l(x)$. Consequently, the output vector for layer f^l $(2 \leq l \leq L)$ can be defined as $f^l(x) = < \varphi_1^l(x), \varphi_2^l(x), \cdots, \varphi_{N_l}^l(x) >$. The prediction result can be obtained by evaluating $\arg\max f^L(x)$.

3.2. *Secure Computation*

3.2.1. Public-Key Cryptosystem with Distributed Decryption (PCDD)

The two-trapdoor public-key cryptosystem was first proposed by Bresson et al. [38]. In addition to the ordinary private key (also known as the weak key) *sk*, the cryptosystem employs a strong private key *SK* that can decrypt the encrypted data under different public keys. To reduce the risk of strong private key leakage, Liu et al. [39] adapted the cryptosystem by splitting the strong key into two shares, enabling distributed decryption. PCDD is defined as follows:

KeyGen: Let $N = pq$ and $\lambda = \text{lcm}(p-1, q-1)/2$, where p and q are large prime numbers, $L(p) = L(q) = k$. Define a function $L(x) = (x-1)/N$, and pick an element g from the multiplicative group $\mathbb{Z}_{N^2}^*$, whose order is $(p-1)(q-1)/2$. Then, randomly select θ_i from the interval $[1, N/4]$ and compute $h_i = g^{\theta_i} \mod N^2$ for party i. The public key is $pk_i = (N, g, h_i)$, and the corresponding weak private key is $sk_i = \theta_i$. The strong private key is $SK = \lambda$.

Encryption: Given the public key pk_i, one can encrypt a message $m \in \mathbf{Z}_N$ by randomly choosing $r \in [1, N/4]$ and computing $Enc_{pk_i}[m] = \{T_{i,1}, T_{i,2}\}$, where $T_{i,1} = g^{r\theta_i}(1 + mN) mod N^2$ and $T_{i,2} = g^r mod N^2$.

Decryption with weak private key: One can decrypt the ciphertext $Enc_{pk_i}[m]$ with the weak private key $sk_i = \theta_i$ by computing

$$m = D_{sk_i}(Enc_{pk_i}[m]) = L((T_{i,1} \cdot (T_{i,2}^{\theta_i})^{-1}) mod N^2). \tag{1}$$

Decryption with strong private key: Any ciphertext $Enc_{pk_i}[m]$ can be decrypted using the decryption algorithm $D_{SK}(\cdot)$ with the strong private key $SK = \lambda$ by first calculating:

$$T_{i,1}^{\lambda} mod N^2 = g^{\lambda\theta_i r} \cdot (1 + mN\lambda) mod N^2 = 1 + mN\lambda. \tag{2}$$

Then, m can be recovered as:

$$m = L(T_{i,1}^{\lambda} mod N^2) \cdot \lambda^{-1} mod N. \tag{3}$$

Strong private key splitting: The strong private key $SK = \lambda$ can be randomly split into two parts. The partial string private keys $SK^{(j)} = \lambda_j (j = 1, 2)$, s.t., $\lambda_1 + \lambda_2 \equiv 0 mod \lambda$ and $\lambda_1 + \lambda_2 \equiv 1 mod N^2$ hold at the same time.

Partial decryption with partial strong private key: The algorithm $D_{SK^{(j)}}^{+}(\cdot)$ takes as input $T_{i,1}$ and a partial strong private key $SK^{(j)} = \lambda_j$ and then outputs the partially decrypted ciphertext

$$CT_{i,j} = (T_{i,1})^{\lambda_j} = g^{\lambda_j \theta_i r} \cdot (1 + mN\lambda_j) mod N^2. \tag{4}$$

Decryption with partially decrypted ciphertext: The algorithm $D^{-}(\cdot)$ takes as input $CT_{i,1}$ and $CT_{i,2}$ and then computes

$$m = L(CT_{i,1} \cdot CT_{i,2}). \tag{5}$$

Ciphertext Refresh: This algorithm can refresh the ciphertext $Enc_{pk_i}[m]$ to obtain $Enc'_{pk_i}[m] = \{T'_{i,1}, T'_{i,2}\}$ without changing the original message m as follows. Choose a random number $r' \in \mathbf{Z}_N$ and then compute

$$T'_{i,1} = T_{i,1} \cdot h_i^{r'} modN^2, T'_{i,2} = T_{i,2} \cdot g^{r'} modN^2. \tag{6}$$

Note that the numbers involved in the PCDD can be integers, meaning that m can take positive, negative, or zero values. However, the sign bit is lost in a modular operation. The method for handling this issue can be found in [39]. Additionally, the PCDD cryptosystem exhibits homomorphic additivity as follows:

$$\begin{aligned} D_{sk_i}(Enc_{pk_i}[x+y]) &= D_{sk_i}(Enc_{pk_i}[x] \cdot Enc_{pk_i}[y] modN^2). \\ D_{sk_i}(Enc_{pk_i}[a \cdot x]) &= D_{sk_i}((Enc_{pk_i}[x])^a modN^2). \end{aligned} \tag{7}$$

3.2.2. Garbled Circuit

Garbled circuits (GCs) were initially introduced by Yao [40] as a means to facilitate secure two-party computation. Broadly speaking, a canonical garbling scheme consists of three main components: a garbling algorithm, a function f, and a decoding table Tab_{Dec}. A randomly chosen seed σ is used in the algorithm, while the function f is employed to generate the garbled circuit F. Specifically, for a given input x, the encoding algorithm generates the garbled representation $\hat{x}$ using x and the random seed σ. Subsequently, the garbled output $\hat{z}$ is obtained through the evaluation algorithm by utilizing $\hat{x}$ and the garbled circuit F. Finally, by utilizing Tab_{Dec} and the garbled output $\hat{z}$, the decoding algorithm yields the result $f(x)$.

4. Method

4.1. Evaluation Metrics

In order to assess the similarity between two distinct models more rigorously, we have identified metrics in the white-box setting and the black-box setting, drawing from [27,30,41]. The details of these metrics are presented in Table 1.

Table 1. Distance metrics in different settings.

Settings	Distance Metric
White-Box	Neuron Outputs Layer Outputs
Black-Box	Model Robustness

4.1.1. Neuron Perspective

We begin by evaluating the similarity of two distinct models from a fine-grained perspective. Based on the mathematical attributes, each neuron in a deep learning model consistently adheres to its respective statistical distribution. Consequently, when two models differ, their neuron outputs should exhibit variations as well [42]. Building upon this observation, we focus on the values of neuron outputs to assess the similarity between $Model_{Vic}$ and $Model_{Sus}$, utilizing the NOD metric, which is defined at the neuron level.

Neuron Outputs Distance (NOD)

For a specific neuron, we denote n_i^l as the i-th neuron in the l-th layer of a given DNN. We represent the neuron output functions for $Model_{Vic}$ and $Model_{Sus}$ as φ_i^l and $\hat{\varphi}_i^l$, respectively. The NOD metric calculates the average difference of neuron outputs across a predefined set $T_x = x_1, x_2, \cdots$ containing test samples:

$$NOD(T_x, \varphi_i^l, \hat{\varphi}_i^l) = \frac{\sum_{x_t \in T_x} |\varphi_i^l(x_t) - \hat{\varphi}_i^l(x_t)|}{|T_x|}. \tag{8}$$

4.1.2. Layer Perspective

In addition to the neuron perspective, we also examine layer-level metrics that take into account the output status of entire layers in a DNN model [41]. It is evident that the metrics from the layer-level perspective provide a more comprehensive assessment of the similarity between $Model_{Vic}$ and $Model_{Sus}$ based on the differences in intermediate layer output status.

Layer Outputs Distance (LOD)

For a given DNN, let us consider layer l. Let f^l and $\hat{f}^l$ represent the output functions of layer l for $Model_{Vic}$ and $Model_{Sus}$, respectively. The LOD formula is used to assess the distance between the l-th layer of $Model_{Vic}$ and $Model_{Sus}$ and is given as:

$$LOD(T_x, f^l, \hat{f}^l) = \frac{\sum_{x\in T_x} ||f^l(x_t) - \hat{f}^l(x_t)||_p}{|T_x|}, \tag{9}$$

where $||\cdot||_p$ represents the L_p-norm, and we take $p = 1$ in our scheme.

4.1.3. Attribute Perspective

Model Robustness Distance (MRD)

In recent years, several characteristics have been proposed based on model properties to measure the similarity between different models. For example, some studies define the adversarial robustness property [27,28] as a characteristic, while others focus on the fairness property [43]. In our approach, we employ the initial characteristic and introduce the *Model Robustness Distance (MRD)* to assess the similarity in adversarial robustness between two different models using a provided set of test samples. Since a model's robustness is closely tied to its learned decision boundary during the optimization process, it can serve as a practical indicator to evaluate the similarity between two models.

Without loss of generality, we denote the function of the victim model $Model_{Vic}$ as f. Given an input x_t and its corresponding label y_t, a canonical adversarial sample can be generated by iteratively adding noise to x_t in order to maximize the classification error of the function f. This type of attack is commonly referred to as an adversarial attack, and, if the final adversarial sample $x_t^{'}$ satisfies $f(x_t^{'}) \neq y_t$, it indicates the success of the adversarial attack. To generate effective adversarial examples, one can utilize various existing methods, such as FGSM or PGD. In this case, given a set of test samples, the adversarial counterparts can be generated as $T_{adv} = x_1^{'}, x_2^{'}, \cdots$, where $x_t^{'}$ represents the adversarial version of the sample $x_t^{'}$. We can define the characteristic of model robustness, denoted as MR, as follows:

$$MR(T_{adv}, f) = \frac{\sum_{t=1}^{|T_{adv}|}(f(x_t^{'}) = y_t)}{|T_{adv}|}. \tag{10}$$

Next, we assume $\hat{f}$ represents the suspect model $Model_{Sus}$, as mentioned earlier. Based on the aforementioned context, we can define the Model Robustness Distance (MRD) between $Model_{Vic}$ and $Model_{Sus}$ as follows:

$$MRD(T_{adv}, f, \hat{f}) = |MR(T_{adv}, f) - MR(T_{adv}, \hat{f})|. \tag{11}$$

As observed, the MRD solely relies on the output labels from the model without requiring any additional knowledge or information.

4.2. *Privacy-Preserving Threshold Judgement*

This part presents our protocols for the privacy-preserving evaluation of model similarity using the aforementioned metrics. Firstly, we describe two auxiliary protocols for comparison and absolute value difference in Section 4.2.1, which rely solely on the PCDD and garbled circuits. Subsequently, we delve into the secure evaluation of similarity by employing model robustness in Section 4.2.2. Furthermore, we extend our techniques to facilitate secure evaluation at the neuron and layer levels, as discussed in Sections 4.2.3 and 4.2.4.

4.2.1. Auxiliary Privacy-Preserving Protocols

Prior to illustrating our proposed protocols, we will first discuss two critical operations that play an indispensable role in these protocols. We will then design the corresponding auxiliary privacy-preserving protocols for each operation. The first operation is comparison, while the second operation involves calculating the absolute value difference.

Given the significance of comparison in our proposed protocols, it is crucial to establish an efficient and privacy-preserving comparison protocol as the foundation for our work. Since we have already assumed that the two cloud servers S_1 and S_2 are non-colluding, we can employ various cryptographic techniques, such as garbled circuits and pure homomorphic encryption (HE), to compare two encrypted values on the server. Regarding HE-based schemes [44,45], it is stated in [46] that evaluating a specific function requires homomorphic operations and bit-wise encryption. However, these processes can result in significant time consumption and impose a high bandwidth burden, rendering them impractical in real-world scenarios. An alternative solution is to utilize garbled circuits, which allow for offline transfer of computationally expensive operations such as oblivious transfer or circuit generation. However, as Evans et al. [47] mentioned, a hybrid scheme that combines both garbled circuits and HE appears more promising in practical scenarios.

Thus, taking into account the aforementioned contexts, we implement the privacy-preserving comparison protocol for our proposed protocols using garbled circuits with the combination of the PCDD. The circuit's structure is depicted in Figure 4. The circuit consists of two types of circuits: SUB, which is used for bit-wise subtraction, and CMP, which facilitates bit-wise comparison [48].

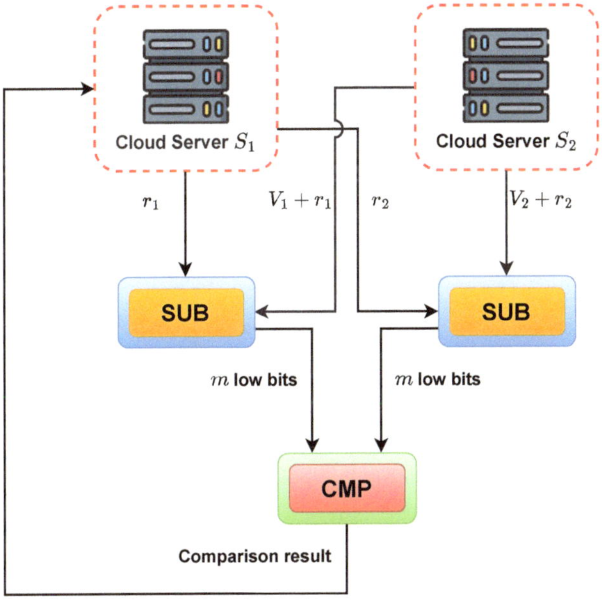

Figure 4. The garbled circuit for privacy-preserving comparison.

Specifically, cloud server S_1 possesses two encrypted values $Enc_{pk}[V_1], Enc_{pk}[V_2]$ that are awaiting comparison. Without loss of generality, we assume that all values, namely V_1 and V_2, have a length of at most s bits. Server S_1 applies masking to the encrypted value $Enc_{pk}[V_i]$, $i \in 1,2$ by utilizing a randomly chosen k-bit ($k < s$) number r_i, $i \in 1,2$

through the additive homomorphic property. The masking operation, as described in [47], ensures a statistical hiding security level of approximately 2^{s-k} for V_i. Subsequently, server S_1 computes the partial decryption of $Enc_{pk}[V_1 + r1]$ and $Enc_{pk}[V_2 + r_2]$ using the corresponding partial strong private keys. The information transmitted to cloud server S_2 comprises a set comprising $Enc_{pk}[V_1 + r_1]$, $Enc_{pk}[V_2 + r_2]$ and their corresponding partial descriptions. Upon receiving these data, server S_2 retrieves the plaintext values $V_1 + r_1$ and $V_2 + r_2$ using its corresponding partial strong private key. Now, in regard to the garbled circuit, server S_1 receives r_1 and r_2 as inputs, while server S_2 receives $V_1 + r_1$ and $V_2 + r_2$ as inputs. Upon completion of the circuit evaluation, the output bit b_{comp} signifies the result of the comparison. If $b_{comp} = 1$, it implies that $V_1 > V_2$, while $b_{comp} = 0$ indicates otherwise. It is worth noting that due to the utilization of the free-XOR technique [49], the cost of XOR gates can be disregarded when considering the overall cost of the circuit evaluation. The details of this protocol are illustrated in Algorithm 1.

Subsequently, utilizing the privacy-preserving comparison protocol described above, it is possible to design a privacy-preserving protocol for calculating the absolute value difference. In particular, without loss of generality, we assume that cloud server S_1 possesses two encrypted values, $Enc_{pk}[V_1]$ and $Enc_{pk}[V_2]$, which are intended for calculating the absolute value difference. Initially, it collaborates with server S_2 to compare $Enc_{pk}[V_1]$ and $Enc_{pk}[V_2]$ using the privacy-preserving comparison protocol. Upon receiving the comparison result, server S_1 employs the additively homomorphic property to compute the absolute value within the ciphertext domain. Specifically, if $V_1 > V_2$, the encrypted absolute value $Enc_{pk}[abs]$ can be calculated as $Enc_{pk}[abs] = Enc_{pk}[V_1 - V_2] = Enc_{pk}[V_1] \cdot (Enc_{pk}[V_2])^{-1}$. In the alternate case, simply interchange the order of V_1 and V_2 while leaving the remaining parts unchanged. The detailed process for this protocol is presented in Algorithm 2.

Algorithm 1 SecureCMP(V_1, V_2)

1: S_1 chooses two k-bit random number r_1, r_2, where $k < s$;
2: S_1 utilizes the additively homomorphic attribute of the PCDD to obtain $Enc_{pk}[V_1 + r_1]$ and $Enc_{pk}[V_2 + r_2]$;
3: S_1 computes the partial decryption for $Enc_{pk}[V_1 + r_1]$ and $Enc_{pk}[V_2 + r_2]$, respectively;
4: S_1 sends $Enc_{pk}[V_1 + r_1]$, $Enc_{pk}[V_2 + r_2]$ and the corresponding partial decryptions to the cloud server S_2;
5: S_2 decrypts the ciphertext and recovers $V_1 + r_1, V_2 + r_2$;
6: S_1 provides r_1, r_2 as the inputs for the garbled circuit, while $V_1 + r_1, V_2 + r_2$ are the inputs from S_2;
7: S_1 receives the comparison result.

Algorithm 2 SecureABSD(V_1, V_2)

1: S_1 compares $Enc_{pk}[V_1]$ and $Enc_{pk}[V_2]$ with the use of Algorithm 1.
2: **if** $V_1 > V_2$ **then**
3: S_1 computes $Enc_{pk}[abs] = Enc_{pk}[V_1] \cdot (Enc_{pk}[V_2])^{-1}$
4: **else**
5: S_1 computes $Enc_{pk}[abs] = Enc_{pk}[V_2] \cdot (Enc_{pk}[V_1])^{-1}$
6: **end if**

4.2.2. Similarity Evaluating Protocol for Robustness

In this part, we present a protocol to facilitate the privacy-preserving evaluation of model similarity using model robustness. It should be noted that calculating the Model Robustness Distance for similarity evaluation involves using Equation (11), which necessitates the computation of absolute value difference. Consequently, we employ the auxiliary protocol introduced in Section 4.2.1 to perform the evaluation while preserving privacy. Initially, both the victim and the suspect encrypt their respective model robustness values and transmit them to the cloud server S_1 using the public key pk. Subsequently, the two cloud servers collaborate to finalize the similarity evaluation and relay the outcome to the victim. Specifically, the protocol operates as follows:

1. Both victim and suspect leverage the set of adversarial samples T_{adv} to obtain their corresponding model robustness MR according to Equation (10).
2. Then, the victim encrypted the threshold $\delta \cdot T$ and its model robustness value $MR(T_{adv}, f)$ as $Enc_{pk}[\delta \cdot T]$ and $Enc_{pk}[MR(T_{adv}, f)]$ by using the public key pk. The suspect also operates a similar process to obtain $Enc_{pk}[MR(T_{adv}, \hat{f})]$.
3. The victim and the suspect send their encrypted value to the cloud server S_1. After that, S_1 cooperates with the cloud server S_2 with the use of Algorithm 2 to obtain the encrypted MRD result $Enc_{pk}[MRD(T_{adv}, f, \hat{f})]$.
4. S_1 utilizes Algorithm 1 to judge whether the MRD result has reached the threshold from the victim with the cooperation of S_2.
5. Once the comparison result is obtained by S_1, it will be encrypted and returned to the victim.

The details of this protocol are outlined in Algorithm 3. This indicates that data privacy is effectively safeguarded against potential breaches.

Algorithm 3 SecureMRD($T_{adv}, f, \hat{f}, \delta$)

1: The victim computes $MR(T_{adv}, f)$, and the suspect computes $MR(T_{adv}, \hat{f})$ according to Equation (10).
2: The victim uses the PCDD to obtain $Enc_{pk}[MR(T_{adv}, f)]$ and $Enc_{pk}[\delta \cdot T]$. Then, the suspect obtains $Enc_{pk}[MR(T_{adv}, \hat{f})]$.
3: The victim sends $Enc_{pk}[MR(T_{adv}, f)]$ and $Enc_{pk}[\delta \cdot T]$ to the cloud server S_1.
4: The suspect sends $Enc_{pk}[MR(T_{adv}, \hat{f})]$ to S_1.
5: S_1 computes $Enc_{pk}[MRD(T_{adv}, f, \hat{f})]$ with the cooperation of the cloud server S_2 according to Equation (11) and Algorithm 2.
6: S_1 compares $Enc_{pk}[MRD(T_{adv}, f, \hat{f})]$ and $Enc_{pk}[\delta \cdot T]$ according to Algorithm 1.
7: S_1 returns the comparison result.

4.2.3. Similarity Evaluating Protocol for Neuron Distance

This part focuses on the privacy-preserving evaluation of model similarity at the neuron level. In addition to the concerns discussed in Section 4.2.2, there is another challenge of performing a privacy-preserving summation as indicated in Equation (8). Therefore, we exploit the additively holomorphic characteristics of the PCDD to aggregate the absolute differentiation values within the ciphertext domain as follows:

1. Based on the determined set of test samples T_x, the victim calculates the output result for each neuron and encrypts them as $\{Enc_{pk}[\varphi_i^l(x_1)], Enc_{pk}[\varphi_i^l(x_2)], \cdots, Enc_{pk}[\varphi_i^l(x_T)]\}$. Similarly, the suspect also obtains the encrypted set $\{Enc_{pk}[\hat{\varphi}_i^l(x_1)], Enc_{pk}[\hat{\varphi}_i^l(x_2)], \cdots, Enc_{pk}[\hat{\varphi}_i^l(x_T)]\}$.
2. Then, the victim sends the encrypted output values and the encrypted threshold $Enc_{pk}[\delta \cdot T]$ to the cloud server S_1, while the suspect also sends the encrypted output values to S_1.
3. S_1 cooperates with the cloud server S_2 to calculate the absolute value difference for each neuron output between the victim and the suspect (e.g., $Enc_{pk}[absD_t] = Enc_{pk}[|\varphi_i^l(x_t) - \hat{\varphi}_i^l(x_t)|]$), respectively.
4. After that, S_1 adopts the additively homomorphic property to sum up the absolute difference values in the ciphertext domain as $Enc_{pk}[absD] = Enc_{pk}[\sum_{t=1}^{T} absD_t] = \prod_{t=1}^{T} Enc_{pk}[absD_t]$.
5. S_1 compares $Enc_{pk}[absD]$ and $Enc_{pk}[\delta \cdot T]$ with the use of Algorithm 1. Once the comparison result is obtained, it will be encrypted and returned to the victim.

The details of the NOD protocol are presented in Algorithm 4.

Algorithm 4 SecureNOD(T_x, φ_i^l, $\hat{\varphi}_i^l$, δ)

for $x_t \in T_x$ **do**
  The victim computes $\varphi_i^l(x_t)$, and the suspect computes $\hat{\varphi}_i^l(x_t)$.
  The victim uses the PCDD to obtain $Enc_{pk}[\varphi_i^l(x_t)]$ and $Enc_{pk}[\delta \cdot T]$. Then, the suspect obtains $Enc_{pk}[\hat{\varphi}_i^l(x_t)]$.
  The victim sends $Enc_{pk}[\varphi_i^l(x_t)]$ and $Enc_{pk}[\delta \cdot T]$ to the cloud server S_1.
  The suspect sends $Enc_{pk}[\hat{\varphi}_i^l(x_t)]$ to S_1.
  S_1 computes $Enc_{pk}[absD_t] = Enc_{pk}[|\varphi_i^l(x_t) - \hat{\varphi}_i^l(x_t)|]$ according to Algorithm 2.
end for
S_1 computes $Enc_{pk}[absD] = \prod_{t=1}^{T} Enc_{pk}[absD_t]$.
S_1 compares $Enc_{pk}[absD]$ and $Enc_{pk}[\delta \cdot T]$ according to Algorithm 1.
S_1 returns the comparison result.

4.2.4. Similarity Evaluating Protocol for Layer Distance

In this section, we introduce privacy-preserving protocols that facilitate model similarity evaluation at the layer level. Algorithm 5 is devised specifically for LOD, as specified in Equation (9).

Concretely, the protocol performs as follows:

1. First, for each sample in the test set T_x, the victim and the suspect obtain the output of layer l as $f^l(x_t)$ and $\hat{f}^l(x_t)$, respectively. After that, these values will be encrypted and sent to the cloud server S_1. The encrypted threshold $Enc_{pk}[\delta \cdot T]$ is also sent to S_1 by the victim.
2. Then, by utilizing Algorithm 2, S_1 cooperates with the cloud server S_2 to calculate the absolute difference value of $f^l(x_t)$ and $\hat{f}^l(x_t)$ in the ciphertext domain. The result is defined as $Enc_{pk}[absLOD_t]$.
3. Next, S_1 adopts the additively homomorphic property for summing up the absolute difference as $Enc_{pk}[absLOD] = Enc_{pk}[\sum_{t=1}^{T} absLOD_t] = \prod_{t=1}^{T} Enc_{pk}[absLOD_t]$.
4. Finally, S_1 compares $Enc_{pk}[absLOD]$ and $Enc_{pk}[\delta \cdot T]$ with the use of Algorithm 1. Once the comparison result is obtained, it will be encrypted and returned to the victim.

Algorithm 5 SecureLOD(T_x, f^l, $\hat{f}^l$, δ)

for $x_t \in T_x$ **do**
  The victim computes $f^l(x_t)$, and the suspect computes $\hat{f}^l(x_t)$.
  The victim uses the PCDD to obtain $Enc_{pk}[f^l(x_t)]$ and $Enc_{pk}[\delta \cdot T]$. Then, the suspect obtains $Enc_{pk}[\hat{f}^l(x_t)]$.
  The victim sends $Enc_{pk}[f^l(x_t)]$ and $Enc_{pk}[\delta \cdot T]$ to the cloud server S_1.
  The suspect sends $Enc_{pk}[\hat{f}^l(x_t)]$ to S_1.
  S_1 computes $Enc_{pk}[absL_t] = Enc_{pk}[|f^l(x_t) - \hat{f}^l(x_t)|]$ according to Algorithm 2.
end for
S_1 computes $Enc_{pk}[absL] = \prod_{t=1}^{T} Enc_{pk}[absL_t]$.
S_1 compares $Enc_{pk}[absL]$ and $Enc_{pk}[\delta \cdot T]$ according to Algorithm 1.
S_1 returns the comparison result.

5. Experiments

We have implemented a testing framework that ensures privacy preservation using our protocols, and, in this section, we present the experimental results.

5.1. Settings

The system is implemented using the Python, Java, and C programming languages. The core components of the machine learning algorithm and models are implemented in PyTorch, while the additively homomorphic cryptosystem is implemented in Java using the JPBC library. For enhanced performance, we utilize Obliv-C, a C-based framework that incorporates GC implementations with optimization techniques, to construct the garbled circuit (GC) of the framework. The framework is designed to run on the Ubuntu 20.04 LTS operating system, utilizing Python 3.9.12, Java 11, and GCC compiler version 4.8.5. Furthermore, the platform server hosting the framework is equipped with four Nvidia RTX 3090 GPUs and 256 GB of RAM.

Datasets and Model

In our experimental setup, we utilize four real-world datasets: MNIST, CIFAR-10, SVHN, and ImageNet. Subsequently, we consider three commonly used models (LeNet, ResNet, and VGG) in our experimental settings. The details of the models and datasets can be seen in Table 2. We divide each training dataset into two parts, with the first part being used for training the victim model. The samples are divided with a ratio of 50%.

Table 2. Models and datasets in experiments.

Dataset	Size	Model	Parameters	Accuracy
MNIST	60,000	LeNet	107.8 K	97.7%
CIFAR-10	60,000	ResNet	274.4 K	85.2%
SVHN	630,420	ResNet	274.4 K	83.9%
ImageNet	14,197,122	VGG	33.65 M	76.3%

In order to assess the effectiveness of our proposed protocols, we define two categories of models: Questionable Models and Normal Models. The Questionable Models are derived from the victim model through model-stealing techniques such as finetuning, pruning, and extraction. These models are classified as questionable since they infringe upon the victim's copyright, and the PTFCP aims to provide evidential support to assist the victim in asserting their copyright. On the other hand, the Normal Models, while sharing the same architecture as the victim model, are trained using either the second part of the divided dataset independently or the first part with a differing random initialization. Thus, these models serve as the control group to illustrate that the proposed protocols in our PTFCP do not assert ownership over unrelated models. It is important to note that these models are trained using the same settings. Specifically, "Norm-I" refers to models trained with a distinct dataset (the second part), whereas "Norm-II" denotes models trained with varying random initialization. In our experiments, we employ two classical techniques [50,51] to generate adversarial samples.

5.2. Experimental Results

5.2.1. Model Finetuning

Model finetuning, the most commonly employed method in DNN model stealing, has been extensively investigated in numerous studies [30,52,53]. In this section, we evaluate the effectiveness of our PTFCP in defending against model finetuning. Specifically, we consider two common model finetuning techniques for a specified victim model and a small dataset drawn from the same distribution. The first technique, referred to as finetuning the last layer (FineTuning-I), involves freezing all layers except the last one and updating only the parameters of the last layer. The second technique, known as finetuning all layers (FineTuning-II), directly updates all parameters of the model.

To assess the performance of the PTFCP more effectively, we conducted separate experiments under both white-box and black-box settings. The experimental results are presented in Figure 5. In the white-box settings, we can access all intermediate outputs from the layers of both the victim model and the suspect model in a privacy-preserving manner. Specifically, we utilize two protocols from the PTFCP that operate within the white-box settings: SecureNOD and Secure LOD. It is worth noting that we conducted over 1000 random repetitions of the experiments to obtain more precise estimation accuracy results. As shown in Figure 5a, the majority of estimation accuracy results for the finetuned models exceed 70%. Notably, for the MNIST and CIFAR-10 datasets, the results approach nearly 80%. Furthermore, the performance on normal models (Norm-I and Norm-II) demonstrates the PTFCP's ability to effectively distinguish between stolen models and other normal models.

In the black-box setting, we can only access the output probabilities of the models while preserving privacy. Specifically, we employ the protocol from PTFCP that operates within the black-box settings: SecureMRD. The effectiveness of the black-box protocol in defending against the finetuning attack is illustrated in Figure 5b. Overall, the experimental results demonstrate that PTFCP remains practical in the black-box setting, enabling privacy-preserving model copyright auditing. It is worth noting that the evaluation accuracy results in the white-box setting surpassing those in the black-box setting. This is logical since the protocols in the white-box setting have access to more information, allowing for more accurate decision making.

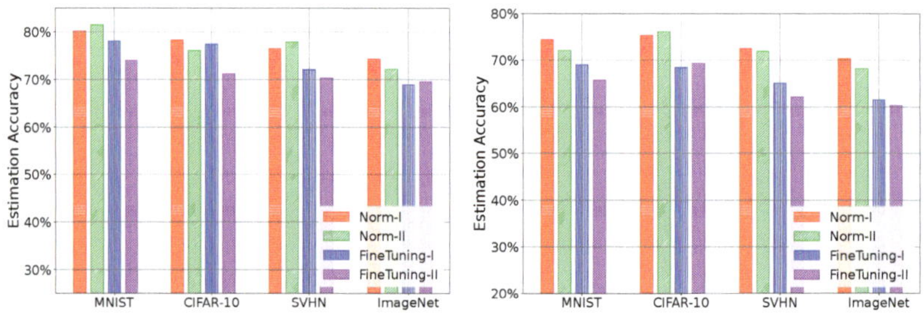

(**a**) (**b**)

Figure 5. The performance of PTPFC in defending against model finetuning. (**a**) is the evaluation in the white-box setting, while (**b**) is the one in the black-box setting.

5.2.2. Model Pruning

In addition to the model finetuning method, model pruning is another commonly employed technique for stealing valuable DNN models. In this section, we evaluate the effectiveness of PTFCP in defending against model pruning. Utilizing the same configuration for the victim model and datasets, we focus on two distinct types of model pruning attacks, distinguished primarily by the percentage parameter r. In these attacks, the attacker prunes the parameters with the lowest absolute values, based on a percentage ratio of r. To preserve utility, the attacker also conducts finetuning on the pruned model. We conduct experiments using both a low ratio ($r = 25\%$, Pruning-I) and a high ratio ($r = 75\%$, Pruning-II). It should be noted that canonical data augmentation techniques are also employed to enhance the effectiveness of the model pruning attack.

Similar to the finetuning attack, we conducted separate evaluations of the PTFCP in both the white-box and black-box settings. The corresponding experimental results are depicted in Figure 5. The evaluation results in Figure 6a indicate that the majority of the evaluations exceed 70%. Moreover, for the MNIST and CIFAR-10 datasets, the evaluations can reach up to 75%. In the black-box setting (as depicted in Figure 6b), while the evaluation results are slightly lower than those in the white-box setting due to the absence of certain intermediate knowledge, the results demonstrate that the PTFCP can detect stolen models obtained through model pruning attacks. In conclusion, these results demonstrate that the PTFCP is effective in defending against model pruning attacks as well.

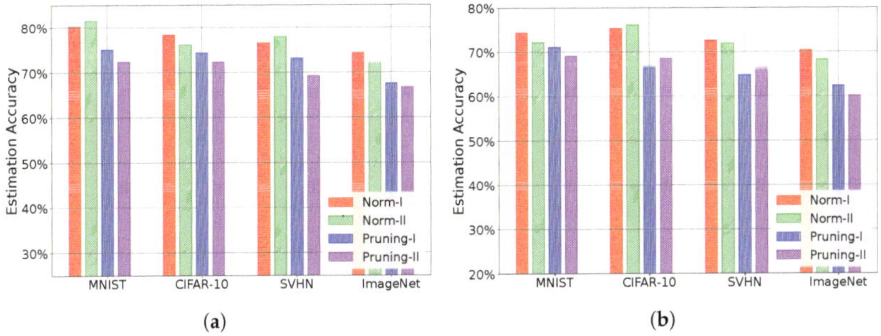

Figure 6. The performance of PTPFC in defending against model pruning. (**a**) is the evaluation in the white-box setting, while (**b**) is the one in the black-box setting.

5.2.3. Model Extraction

Among the model finetuning, model pruning, and model extraction attacks, the model extraction attack is considered the most significant threat to DNN model copyright protection. Studies have revealed that conventional DNN watermarking methods are ineffective in establishing ownership claims for DNN models when confronted with the model extraction attack [30]. One possible explanation is that watermarks are intended to be inconspicuous elements of learning tasks and do not specifically address the model extraction attack. Consequently, attackers can readily exploit model extraction attacks to remove the watermarks from DNN models. In this section, we evaluate the effectiveness of the PTFCP in defending against the model extraction attack. Specifically, we consider two well-known model extraction attacks from recent state-of-the-art studies. The first attack is called Jacobian-based augmentation (JBA) [54], which involves sampling a set of seeds based on the test dataset and utilizing the Jacobian-based data augmentation technique to generate additional data samples from these seeds. The second attack is known as Knockoff Nets (KnockOff) [55], which employs an auxiliary dataset that shares similar characteristics with the original training dataset used for the victim model.

Figure 7 illustrates the experimental results of the PTFCP in defending against the model extraction attack in both the white-box and black-box settings. Despite a decline in performance compared to the model finetuning and pruning scenarios, the evaluation accuracy in the white-box setting remains above 60%. In the black-box setting, it is expected that the results would be inferior to those in the white-box setting due to the absence of intermediate knowledge from the models. Nevertheless, the majority of the results still reach nearly 60%. Additionally, as indicated in various studies on model extraction [54–56], model extraction attacks are not consistently successful. While it may be challenging to accurately identify poorly performing extracted models, their subpar performance may not pose significant threats to model copyright. Furthermore, it can be observed that as the model extraction attack achieves better performance, the extracted model becomes more similar to the victim model. Thus, the PTFCP presents an effective countermeasure against the primary objective of achieving perfect parameter or functionality matching in model extraction attacks.

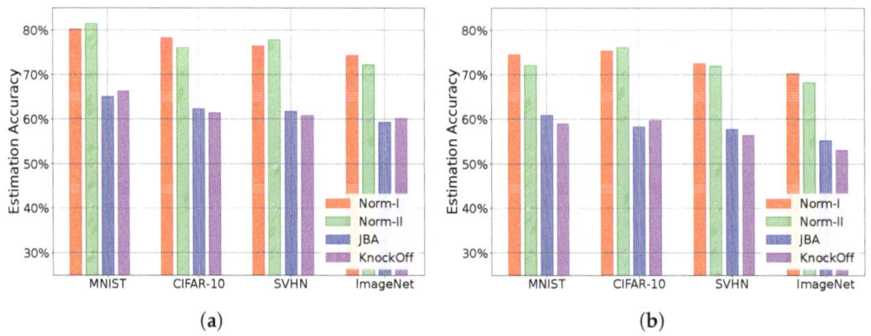

Figure 7. The performance of PTPFC in defending against model extraction. (**a**) is the evaluation in the white-box setting, while (**b**) is the one in the black-box setting.

6. Related Works

6.1. DNN Watermarking

Numerous watermarking technology solutions have been proposed to safeguard the copyright of DNN models. Similar to the techniques utilized in the traditional multimedia domain, existing DNN watermarking approaches comprise two primary steps. The initial step involves embedding, whereas the subsequent step entails verification. In the embedding step, the designated watermark, owned by the creator, is incorporated into the model during the training process. Regarding the verification step, DNN watermarking approaches can be primarily classified into two categories: white-box and black-box. Categorization is based on the level of knowledge accessible during the verification step.

In white-box watermarking, the availability of model information allows for the embedding of a pre-determined signature into the model's parameter spaces using various methods, such as regularization terms. Thus, if the extracted watermark from a suspect model closely matches the owner's signature, the copyright of that model can be readily justified. In contrast, black-box watermarking employs backdoor attack techniques due to the absence of model information. Specifically, the model owner trains the model with a trigger set to compel the model to categorize certain samples into a specific hidden class, acting as a backdoor. The watermark is also injected into the model upon completion of the training procedure. Thus, to verify the copyright of a suspect model, the owner simply needs to query the suspect model using samples from the trigger set and examine whether the predicted result corresponds to the predetermined hidden class.

Despite its effectiveness and simplicity, watermarking inevitably possesses significant drawbacks. In addition to its invasive nature, which interferes with the training process, the performance of watermarking is heavily reliant on the model's ability to memorize. Essentially, watermarking aims to maximize the model's retention of the watermark content, and the degree of memorization determines the robustness of the watermark against attacks. As indicated in numerous studies, watermarking proves effective in countering finetuning and pruning attacks but is susceptible to various model extraction attacks. One critical factor is that model extraction attacks aim to pilfer the model's functionality rather than its entire contents, whereas most watermarks are often task-irrelevant. Despite the aforementioned disadvantages of watermarking, it remains the sole method for owners to embed their signature into their models, surpassing the capabilities of other techniques.

6.2. DNN Fingerprinting

In recent years, numerous researchers have focused on DNN fingerprinting techniques as an alternative method for verifying ownership. Similar to DNN watermarking, DNN fingerprinting involves two steps: fingerprint extraction and fingerprint verification. Importantly, fingerprinting is considered non-invasive, distinguishing it from watermarking schemes. Unlike watermarking, where intervention in the model training process is required to embed a watermark, fingerprinting techniques directly extract a distinctive feature or attribute from the model to act as a fingerprint. If the fingerprint of a suspect model matches that of the owner's model, the owner can assert ownership of the suspect model.

For example, in [28], the authors introduced IPGuard, a fingerprinting scheme. IPGuard characterizes the fingerprint by utilizing data points located near the classification boundary to capture the model's boundary property. If a suspect model produces identical predictions for a majority of these points, IPGuard identifies it as an unauthorized copy of the owner's victim model. Additionally, in [27], a Conferrable Ensemble Method (CEM) is introduced to capture the overlap between the decision boundary or adversarial subspaces of the victim model and those of the suspect model. Specifically, this CEM generates conferrable adversarial examples, which are a specific type of transferable examples, to facilitate characterization. In [27], the authors demonstrate the robustness of a CEM against common DNN removal attacks, such as finetuning, pruning, and extraction attacks. However, it is incapable of addressing certain adapted attacks, including adversarial learning.

In conclusion, as evidenced, the majority of fingerprinting schemes concentrate on establishing the "uniqueness" of a particular model. However, in practical scenarios, relying solely on or being limited to a specific metric is not practical. Consequently, relying solely on fingerprinting is insufficient to provide convincing evidence or support for verifying model ownership. A potentially promising approach to address this challenge is to combine various existing methods to create a comprehensive mechanism.

6.3. Model Similarity Evaluation

The evaluation of model similarity has emerged as a crucial metric used to assess performance in diverse scenarios, including Machine Unlearning [32] and model copyright protection [30]. Consequently, numerous researchers have dedicated their efforts to this area and proposed a range of schemes.

Wu et al. [29] utilized the Euclidean distance as a measure of similarity between two distinct DNN models in the context of machine unlearning, based on the intuition that the parameter distance reflects their similarity. However, experiments conducted on ResNet by the authors of [33] revealed that relying solely on the l_2-Norm to evaluate DNN model similarity is insufficiently accurate and practical. Specifically, various complex factors such as learning rate and floating-point operations can result in significantly different model parameter outcomes, even when the training datasets and initialization are identical. Additionally, for large DNN models with a substantial number of parameters, the computational costs become impractical in real-world applications [32].

To address the mentioned limitations, Golarkar et al. [31] employ the extensively used the Jensen–Shannon divergence, based on the Kullback–Leibler divergence, to assess the distance between two distinct DNN models in the parameter space. Similarly, in [57], the authors utilize the Jensen–Shannon divergence to quantify the distance between probability distributions of two different DNN models. Another notable metric, known as activation distance, is employed in certain studies [57,58]. It represents the average l_2-Norm distance between probability distributions of two distinct models. Furthermore, to provide a comprehensive evaluation at a broader level, model similarity measurement employs layer-wise distance [41]. This approach computes the distance between two models considering their parameters or the output of each layer.

Recently, Chen et al. [30] introduced a framework known as DeepJudge. DeepJudge combines multiple metrics to provide a comprehensive evaluation of the similarity between two distinct DNN models. Specifically, the framework categorizes six distinct metrics into three main categories. When assessing the similarity between two different DNN models, DeepJudge initially calculates the distance value for each respective metric separately. Subsequently, it determines whether the suspect model exhibits sufficient similarity to the victim model within the specified metric, based on a predetermined threshold. Finally, a straightforward majority voting scheme is employed to determine whether the suspect model constitutes an illicit copy of the victim model. However, this necessitates the victim granting DeepJudge full access to their DNN model, including model parameters and architecture. Consequently, this approach is impractical in real-world scenarios where concerns about model data privacy have already arisen, as some model owners may be unwilling to provide DeepJudge with such privileges due to the potential risk of private model information leakage.

7. Conclusions

This work presents our PTFCP, a privacy-preserving testing framework designed to protect the copyright of deep learning models in mobile crowdsensing scenarios. Our PTFCP consists of multiple protocols that assess the similarities between two distinct models while maintaining privacy. In contrast to existing schemes, the PTFCP ensures that model utility remains intact throughout the training process while providing defense against various attacks in a privacy-preserving manner. Extensive experiments using real-world datasets were conducted to demonstrate the effective performance of the PTFCP.

Author Contributions: Methodology, D.W. (Dongying Wei); Formal analysis, Z.W.; Investigation, D.W. (Dan Wang); Writing—original draft, Y.M. All authors have read and agreed to the published version of the manuscript.

Funding: This work is supported by the Key Experimental Fund Project for Complex Electronic System Simulation (DXZT-JC-ZZ-2020-013), and the Open Fund of Engineering Research Centre of the Ministry of Education for Intelligent Computing of Complex Energy Systems (ESIC202102).

Data Availability Statement: All data underlying the results are available as part of the article and no additional source data are required.

Conflicts of Interest: The authors declare no conflict of interest.

Abbreviations

The following notations and abbreviations are used in this manuscript:

Notations	Definitions
f^i	The layer i in the DNN
n_i^l	The i-th neuron in the layer l
$\varphi_i^l(x)$	The output of the neuron n_i^l for the given input x
lcm	Least common multiple
SK	The strong private key
sk	The ordinary private key
pk	The public key
$Enc_{pk}[m]$	The ciphertext of message m encrypted by pk
T_x	The test case set
T_{adv}	The test case set of adversarial samples
δ	The threshold of the similarity
Abbreviations	Definitions
MCS	mobile crowdsensing systems
PTFCP	privacy-preserving testing framework for copyright protection
PCDD	public-key cryptosystem with distributed decryption
DNN	deep neural network
GC	garbled circuits
NOD	neuron outputs distance
LOD	layer outputs distance
MRD	model robustness distance

References

1. Xiao, L.; Jiang, D.; Xu, D.; Su, W.; An, N.; Wang, D. Secure mobile crowdsensing based on deep learning. *China Commun.* **2018**, *15*, 1–11. [CrossRef]

2. Liu, C.H.; Chen, Z.; Zhan, Y. Energy-efficient distributed mobile crowd sensing: A deep learning approach. *IEEE J. Sel. Areas Commun.* **2019**, *37*, 1262–1276. [CrossRef]
3. Tao, X.; Hafid, A.S. DeepSensing: A novel mobile crowdsensing framework with double deep Q-network and prioritized experience replay. *IEEE Internet Things J.* **2020**, *7*, 11547–11558. [CrossRef]
4. Zhang, C.; Luo, X.; Liang, J.; Liu, X.; Zhu, L.; Guo, S. POTA: Privacy-Preserving Online Multi-Task Assignment with Path Planning. *IEEE Trans. Mob. Comput.* **2023**, 1–13. [CrossRef]
5. Dai, Z.; Liu, C.H.; Ye, Y.; Han, R.; Yuan, Y.; Wang, G.; Tang, J. Aoi-minimal uav crowdsensing by model-based graph convolutional reinforcement learning. In Proceedings of the IEEE INFOCOM 2022-IEEE Conference on Computer Communications, Virtual Conference, 2–5 May 2022; IEEE: Piscataway, NJ, USA; pp. 1029–1038.
6. Vahedi, Z.; Mahdavi Chabok, S.J.; Veisi, G. Heterogeneous task allocation in mobile crowd sensing using a modified approximate policy approach. *Int. J. Nonlinear Anal. Appl.* **2023**. [CrossRef]
7. Xu, C.; Song, W. Intelligent Task Allocation for Mobile Crowdsensing With Graph Attention Network and Deep Reinforcement Learning. *IEEE Trans. Netw. Sci. Eng.* **2023**, *10*, 1032–1048. [CrossRef]
8. Ren, H.; Xu, G.; Qi, H.; Zhang, T. PriFR: Privacy-preserving Large-scale File Retrieval System via Blockchain for Encrypted Cloud Data. In Proceedings of the 2023 IEEE 9th Intl Conference on Big Data Security on Cloud (BigDataSecurity), IEEE Intl Conference on High Performance and Smart Computing, (HPSC) and IEEE Intl Conference on Intelligent Data and Security (IDS), New York, NY, USA, 6–8 May 2023; pp. 16–23. [CrossRef]
9. Ren, H.; Li, H.; Liu, D.; Xu, G.; Cheng, N.; Shen, X. Privacy-Preserving Efficient Verifiable Deep Packet Inspection for Cloud-Assisted Middlebox. *IEEE Trans. Cloud Comput.* **2022**, *10*, 1052–1064. [CrossRef]
10. Huang, C.; Wang, W.; Liu, D.; Lu, R.; Shen, X. Blockchain-assisted personalized car insurance with privacy preservation and fraud resistance. *IEEE Trans. Veh. Technol.* **2022**, *72*, 3777–3792. [CrossRef]
11. Zhang, C.; Hu, C.; Wu, T.; Zhu, L.; Liu, X. Achieving Efficient and Privacy-Preserving Neural Network Training and Prediction in Cloud Environments. *IEEE Trans. Dependable Secur. Comput.* **2023**, *20*, 4245–4257. [CrossRef]
12. Liang, H.; Li, Y.; Zhang, C.; Liu, X.; Zhu, L. EGIA: An External Gradient Inversion Attack in Federated Learning. *IEEE Trans. Inf. Forensics Secur.* **2023**, *18*, 4984–4995. [CrossRef]
13. Ren, H.; Li, H.; Liu, D.; Xu, G.; Shen, X.S. Enabling Secure and Versatile Packet Inspection with Probable Cause Privacy for Outsourced Middlebox. *IEEE Trans. Cloud Comput.* **2022**, *10*, 2580–2594. [CrossRef]
14. Hu, C.; Zhang, C.; Lei, D.; Wu, T.; Liu, X.; Zhu, L. Achieving Privacy-Preserving and Verifiable Support Vector Machine Training in the Cloud. *IEEE Trans. Inf. Forensics Secur.* **2023**, *18*, 3476–4291. [CrossRef]
15. Huang, C.; Liu, D.; Yang, A.; Lu, R.; Shen, X. Multi-client secure and efficient dpf-based keyword search for cloud storage. *IEEE Trans. Dependable Secur. Comput.* **2023**, *early access*.
16. Zhang, C.; Zhao, M.; Liang, J.; Fan, Q.; Zhu, L.; Guo, S. NANO: Cryptographic Enforcement of Readability and Editability Governance in Blockchain Database. *IEEE Trans. Dependable Secur. Comput.* **2023**, 1–14. [CrossRef]
17. Zhu, Y.; Cheng, Y.; Zhou, H.; Lu, Y. Hermes attack: Steal {DNN} models with lossless inference accuracy. In Proceedings of the 30th USENIX Security Symposium (USENIX Security 21), Virtual Event, 11–13 August 2021.
18. Rakin, A.S.; Chowdhuryy, M.H.I.; Yao, F.; Fan, D. Deepsteal: Advanced model extractions leveraging efficient weight stealing in memories. In Proceedings of the IEEE Symposium on Security and Privacy (SP), San Francisco, CA, USA, 23–26 May 2022; IEEE: Piscataway, NJ, USA, 2022; pp. 1157–1174.
19. Wang, R.; Ren, J.; Li, B.; She, T.; Lin, C.; Fang, L.; Chen, J.; Shen, C.; Wang, L. Free Fine-tuning: A Plug-and-Play Watermarking Scheme for Deep Neural Networks. *arXiv* **2022**, arXiv:2210.07809.
20. Correia-Silva, J.R.; Berriel, R.F.; Badue, C.; De Souza, A.F.; Oliveira-Santos, T. Copycat CNN: Are random non-Labeled data enough to steal knowledge from black-box models? *Pattern Recognit.* **2021**, *113*, 107830. [CrossRef]
21. Yang, P.; Lao, Y.; Li, P. Robust watermarking for deep neural networks via bi-level optimization. In Proceedings of the IEEE/CVF International Conference on Computer Vision, Virtual Conference, 11–17 October 2021; pp. 14841–14850.
22. Jia, J.; Wu, Y.; Li, A.; Ma, S.; Liu, Y. Subnetwork-Lossless Robust Watermarking for Hostile Theft Attacks in Deep Transfer Learning Models. *IEEE Trans. Dependable Secur. Comput.* **2022**, *early access*.
23. Li, Y.; Wang, H.; Barni, M. A survey of deep neural network watermarking techniques. *Neurocomputing* **2021**, *461*, 171–193. [CrossRef]
24. Barni, M.; Pérez-González, F.; Tondi, B. DNN watermarking: Four challenges and a funeral. In Proceedings of the 2021 ACM Workshop on Information Hiding and Multimedia Security, Virtual Event, 22–25 June 2021; pp. 189–196.
25. Wang, R.; Li, H.; Mu, L.; Ren, J.; Guo, S.; Liu, L.; Fang, L.; Chen, J.; Wang, L. Rethinking the Vulnerability of DNN Watermarking: Are Watermarks Robust against Naturalness-aware Perturbations? In Proceedings of the 30th ACM International Conference on Multimedia, Lisboa, Portugal, 10–14 October 2022; pp. 1808–1818.
26. Wang, Y.; Li, W.; Sarkar, E.; Shafique, M.; Maniatakos, M.; Jabari, S.E. PiDAn: A Coherence Optimization Approach for Backdoor Attack Detection and Mitigation in Deep Neural Networks. *arXiv* **2022**, arXiv:2203.09289.
27. Lukas, N.; Zhang, Y.; Kerschbaum, F. Deep neural network fingerprinting by conferrable adversarial examples. *arXiv* **2019**, arXiv:1912.00888.

28. Cao, X.; Jia, J.; Gong, N.Z. IPGuard: Protecting intellectual property of deep neural networks via fingerprinting the classification boundary. In Proceedings of the 2021 ACM Asia Conference on Computer and Communications Security, Virtual Event, 7–11 June 2021; pp. 14–25.
29. Wu, Y.; Dobriban, E.; Davidson, S. Deltagrad: Rapid retraining of machine learning models. In Proceedings of the International Conference on Machine Learning, PMLR, Online, 3–18 July 2020; pp. 10355–10366.
30. Chen, J.; Wang, J.; Peng, T.; Sun, Y.; Cheng, P.; Ji, S.; Ma, X.; Li, B.; Song, D. Copy, right? A testing framework for copyright protection of deep learning models. In Proceedings of the 2022 IEEE Symposium on Security and Privacy (SP), San Francisco, CA, USA, 23–26 May 2022; IEEE: Piscataway, NJ, USA, 2022; pp. 824–841.
31. Golatkar, A.; Achille, A.; Soatto, S. Forgetting outside the box: Scrubbing deep networks of information accessible from input-output observations. In Proceedings of the European Conference on Computer Vision, Glasgow, UK, 23–28 August 2020; Springer: Berlin/Heidelberg, Germany, 2020; pp. 383–398.
32. Nguyen, T.T.; Huynh, T.T.; Nguyen, P.L.; Liew, A.W.C.; Yin, H.; Nguyen, Q.V.H. A survey of machine unlearning. *arXiv* **2022**, arXiv:2209.02299.
33. Jia, H.; Yaghini, M.; Choquette-Choo, C.A.; Dullerud, N.; Thudi, A.; Chandrasekaran, V.; Papernot, N. Proof-of-learning: Definitions and practice. In Proceedings of the 2021 IEEE Symposium on Security and Privacy (SP), San Francisco, CA, USA, 24–27 May 2021; IEEE: Piscataway, NJ, USA, 2021; pp. 1039–1056.
34. Xu, G.; Li, H.; Liu, S.; Yang, K.; Lin, X. Verifynet: Secure and verifiable federated learning. *IEEE Trans. Inf. Forensics Secur.* **2019**, *15*, 911–926. [CrossRef]
35. Xu, G.; Li, H.; Zhang, Y.; Xu, S.; Ning, J.; Deng, R.H. Privacy-preserving federated deep learning with irregular users. *IEEE Trans. Dependable Secur. Comput.* **2020**, *19*, 1364–1381. [CrossRef]
36. Yu, H.; Jia, X.; Zhang, H.; Yu, X.; Shu, J. PSRide: Privacy-preserving shared ride matching for online ride hailing systems. *IEEE Trans. Dependable Secur. Comput.* **2019**, *18*, 1425–1440. [CrossRef]
37. Guan, Y.; Lu, R.; Zheng, Y.; Zhang, S.; Shao, J.; Wei, G. Achieving Efficient and Privacy-Preserving (,)-Core Query over Bipartite Graphs in Cloud. *IEEE Trans. Dependable Secur. Comput.* **2022**, *20*, 1979–1993. [CrossRef]
38. Bresson, E.; Catalano, D.; Pointcheval, D. A simple public-key cryptosystem with a double trapdoor decryption mechanism and its applications. In Proceedings of the International Conference on the Theory and Application of Cryptology and Information Security, Taipei, Taiwan, 30 November–4 December 2003; Springer: Berlin/Heidelberg, Germany, 2003; pp. 37–54.
39. Liu, X.; Qin, B.; Deng, R.H.; Lu, R.; Ma, J. A privacy-preserving outsourced functional computation framework across large-scale multiple encrypted domains. *IEEE Trans. Comput.* **2016**, *65*, 3567–3579. [CrossRef]
40. Yao, A.C.C. How to generate and exchange secrets. In Proceedings of the 27th Annual Symposium on Foundations of Computer Science (SFCS 1986), Washington, DC, USA, 27–29 October 1986; IEEE: Piscataway, NJ, USA, 1986; pp. 162–167.
41. Tarun, A.K.; Chundawat, V.S.; Mandal, M.; Kankanhalli, M. Fast yet effective machine unlearning. *arXiv* **2021**, arXiv:2111.08947.
42. Cao, Y.; Yang, J. Towards making systems forget with machine unlearning. In Proceedings of the 2015 IEEE Symposium on Security and Privacy, San Jose, CA, USA, 17–21 May 2015; IEEE: Piscataway, NJ, USA, 2015; pp. 463–480.
43. Mehrabi, N.; Morstatter, F.; Saxena, N.; Lerman, K.; Galstyan, A. A survey on bias and fairness in machine learning. *ACM Comput. Surv. (CSUR)* **2021**, *54*, 1–35. [CrossRef]
44. Bost, R.; Popa, R.A.; Tu, S.; Goldwasser, S. Machine learning classification over encrypted data. *Cryptol. ePrint Arch.* **2014**. [CrossRef]
45. Damgard, I.; Geisler, M.; Kroigard, M. A correction to 'efficient and secure comparison for on-line auctions'. *Int. J. Appl. Cryptogr.* **2009**, *1*, 323–324. [CrossRef]
46. Damgard, I.; Geisler, M.; Kroigard, M. Homomorphic encryption and secure comparison. *Int. J. Appl. Cryptogr.* **2008**, *1*, 22–31. [CrossRef]
47. Evans, D.; Huang, Y.; Katz, J.; Malka, L. Efficient privacy-preserving biometric identification. In Proceedings of the 17th conference Network and Distributed System Security Symposium, NDSS, San Diego, CA, USA, 6–9 February 2011; Volume 68, pp. 90–98.
48. Kolesnikov, V.; Sadeghi, A.R.; Schneider, T. Improved garbled circuit building blocks and applications to auctions and computing minima. In Proceedings of the International Conference on Cryptology and Network Security, Kanazawa, Japan, 12–14 December 2009; Springer: Berlin/Heidelberg, Germany, 2009; pp. 1–20.
49. Kolesnikov, V.; Schneider, T. Improved garbled circuit: Free XOR gates and applications. In *Proceedings of the International Colloquium on Automata, Languages, and Programming*; Springer: Berlin/Heidelberg, Germany, 2008; pp. 486–498.
50. Carlini, N.; Wagner, D. Towards evaluating the robustness of neural networks. In Proceedings of the 2017 IEEE Symposium on Security and Privacy (SP), San Jose, CA, USA, 22–26 May 2017; IEEE: Piscataway, NJ, USA, 2017; pp. 39–57.
51. Madry, A.; Makelov, A.; Schmidt, L.; Tsipras, D.; Vladu, A. Towards deep learning models resistant to adversarial attacks. *arXiv* **2017**, arXiv:1706.06083.
52. Adi, Y.; Baum, C.; Cisse, M.; Pinkas, B.; Keshet, J. Turning your weakness into a strength: Watermarking deep neural networks by backdooring. In Proceedings of the 27th USENIX Security Symposium (USENIX Security 18), Baltimore, MD, USA, 15–17 August 2018; pp. 1615–1631.
53. Uchida, Y.; Nagai, Y.; Sakazawa, S.; Satoh, S. Embedding watermarks into deep neural networks. In Proceedings of the 2017 ACM on International Conference on Multimedia Retrieval, Bucharest, Romania, 6–9 June 2017; pp. 269–277.

54. Papernot, N.; McDaniel, P.; Goodfellow, I.; Jha, S.; Celik, Z.B.; Swami, A. Practical black-box attacks against machine learning. In Proceedings of the 2017 ACM on Asia Conference on Computer and Communications Security, Abu Dhabi, United Arab Emirates, 2–6 April 2017; pp. 506–519.
55. Orekondy, T.; Schiele, B.; Fritz, M. Knockoff nets: Stealing functionality of black-box models. In Proceedings of the IEEE/CVF Conference on Computer Vision and Pattern Recognition, Long Beach, CA, USA, 15–20 June 2019; pp. 4954–4963.
56. Yuan, X.; Ding, L.; Zhang, L.; Li, X.; Wu, D.O. Es attack: Model stealing against deep neural networks without data hurdles. *IEEE Trans. Emerg. Top. Comput. Intell.* **2022**, *6*, 1258–1270. [CrossRef]
57. Chundawat, V.S.; Tarun, A.K.; Mandal, M.; Kankanhalli, M. Can Bad Teaching Induce Forgetting? Unlearning in Deep Networks using an Incompetent Teacher. *arXiv* **2022**, arXiv:2205.08096.
58. Golatkar, A.; Achille, A.; Ravichandran, A.; Polito, M.; Soatto, S. Mixed-privacy forgetting in deep networks. In Proceedings of the IEEE/CVF Conference on Computer Vision and Pattern Recognition, Virtual Conference, 19–25 June 2021; pp. 792–801.

electronics

Article

MLPPF: Multi-Label Prediction of piRNA Functions Based on Pretrained k-mer, Positional Embedding and an Improved TextRNN Model

Yajun Liu [1,*], Ru Li [1], Yang Lu [1], Aimin Li [1], Zhirui Wang [2] and Wei Li [1]

[1] Shaanxi Key Laboratory for Network Computing and Security Technology, School of Computer Science and Engineering, Xi'an University of Technology, Xi'an 710048, China
[2] College of Life Sciences, Northwest A&F University, Yangling 712100, China
* Correspondence: liuyajun@xaut.edu.cn

Abstract: PIWI-interacting RNAs (piRNAs) are a kind of important small non-coding RNAs and play a vital role in maintaining the stability of genome. Previous studies have revealed that piRNAs not only silence transposons, but also mediate the degradation of a large number of mRNAs and lncRNAs. Existing computational models only focus on mRNA-related piRNAs and rarely concentrate on lncRNA-related piRNAs. In this study, we propose a novel method, MLPPF, which is designed for multi-label prediction of piRNA functions based on pretrained k-mer, positional embedding and an improved TextRNN model. First, a benchmark dataset, which contains two types of functional labels, namely mRNA-related and lncRNA-related piRNAs, was constructed by processing piRNA-function-annotated data and sequence data. Moreover, pretrained k-mer embedding fused with positional embedding was applied to get the sequence representation with biological significance. Finally, an improved textRNN model with Bi-GRU and an attention mechanism was employed for implementing the piRNA functional label prediction task. Experiments substantiate that our model can effectively identify the piRNA functional labels, reveal the key factors of its subsequences and be helpful for in-depth investigations into piRNA functions.

Keywords: piRNA functional label predictor; k-mer positional embedding; multi-label classification

1. Introduction

Genetic factors have important biological functions and are closely related to diseases. Identifying the biological functions of genetic factors is useful in analyzing the complex mechanisms of diseases and helpful in disease prevention, diagnosis, and treatment. piRNAs are a kind of small non-coding RNA (sncRNA) discovered in 2006 that bind to the PIWI subfamily of the Argonaute protein. They are slightly longer than miRNAs by approximately 24–32 nucleotides. They lack clear secondary structures but have two sequence preferences (the 5′ end uridine or 10th adenosine) [1,2].

Based on their origins, piRNAs are divided into three categories: piRNAs derived from inter-gene regions, piRNAs derived from mRNA, and piRNAs derived from lncRNA. Given their different origins, piRNAs have a variety of functions. Early studies found that piRNAs can recognize and silence transposons, thereby maintaining the stability of the genome structure [3]. As early as 2014, Gou et al. [4] found that piRNAs guided the large-scale elimination of mRNAs at the later stage of spermatogenesis in mice; that was the first research to demonstrate that piRNAs regulate mRNAs. In 2015, Watanabe et al. [5] discovered that piRNAs from transposons and pseudogenes mediate the degradation of large amounts of mRNA and lncRNA in mice. In 2019, Dai et al. [6] revealed that piRNAs are widely involved in mRNA translational activation in sperm cells and conducted in-depth and systematic research on the molecular mechanisms of positive piRNA regulation in target gene translation. Recent research on a *C. elegans* model showed that the regulatory range of piRNAs involves almost all mRNAs in germ cells [7]. In summary, these breakthrough studies suggest that piRNA functions are important and diverse and that they mediate a highly complex RNA regulatory network.

Identifying piRNA functions is a fundamental and challenging problem. There are currently two existing recognition methods: biological experimental methods and computational methods. Many biological experimental techniques can be used to recognize piRNA functions, such as immunoprecipitation. However, experiments identifying piRNA functions are time-consuming, expensive, have only a minor flux, and require professional operators. With the establishment of piRNA-specific databases and the accumulation of piRNA-related functional data, it is possible to predict piRNA functional labels via computational methods [8].

Much research has been conducted in identifying the functional labels of miRNAs and lncRNAs, but prediction algorithm research on piRNA functional labels is still in its infancy. The current study focuses on mRNA-related piRNA using a miRNA-like mechanism [4,9,10], and lncRNA-related piRNA is disregarded. In 2017, Liu et al. [11] proposed 2L-piRNA, the first piRNA function predictor. By extracting features such as pseudo-nucleotide components (PseKNC) and using SVM classifiers, the authors built a two-layer ensemble classifier. The first layer is used to identify whether a query RNA molecule is piRNA or non-piRNA with 86.1% accuracy. The second layer identifies whether a piRNA is involved in mRNA deadenylation with 77.6% accuracy. In 2018, Li et al. [12] presented a 2L-piRNAPred algorithm based on features including nucleotide composition, positional specificity, physicochemical properties, and an F-value feature selection algorithm, achieving accuracies of 89% (first layer) and 84% (second layer). In 2019, Khan et al. proposed the first computational tool based on deep learning, 2L-piRNADNN [13]. This method constructs a deep neural network based on feature vectors containing dinucleotide autocovariance and physicochemical properties, with accuracies of 91.81% (first layer) and 84.52% (second layer). In 2020, Zuo et al. [14] proposed 2lpiRNAred using a sparse representation classifier (SRC) and a support vector machine with a radial basis function using Markov distance (SVMMDRBF). This study also proposed a new feature selection algorithm based on Luca fuzzy entropy and Gaussian membership function (LFE-GM), with accuracies of 88.72% (first layer) and 79.97% (second layer). Meanwhile, Khan et al. [15] proposed a 2L-PseKNC algorithm based on PseKNC and deep neural networks. This algorithm uses principal component analysis (PCA) to select features and can achieve accuracies of 94.73% (first layer) and 85.21% (second layer). In summary, such studies only focus on mRNA-related piRNA recognition and their performance still needs to be improved.

In addition to the above studies, only a few prediction tools for piRNA target loci are available. Gou et al. [4] were the first to identify the potential targeting sites of piRNAs within the three prime untranslated regions ($3'$ UTRs) of MIWI-associated mRNAs. In that study, miRanda [16], a miRNA target prediction tool, was used. Based on the experimental data of Gou et al. [17], pirnaPre was the first tool designed for piRNA target locus identification. It used mouse data and selected a combination of MIWI CLIP-seq-derived features and position-derived features to train an SVM classifier. A training area under the curve (AUC) of 0.87 was achieved, and 3781 mRNAs from 2587 protein-coding genes were predicted as potential piRNA targets. pirScan [18,19] is another tool for predicting piRNA target sites based on established targeting rules from *C. elegans* and *C. briggsae* data. Yang et al. [20] developed the first deep learning method based on multi-head attention, identifying piRNA targeting sites on *C. elegans* mRNAs and obtaining an AUC of 93.3% using an independent test set. However, these methods used experimentally validated data from specific species and cannot currently be extended to other organisms.

Recent studies have demonstrated that a piRNA can perform different functions in different times and spaces and can have multiple functional labels. For example, a piRNA can not only eliminate transposons during the ping-pong cycle but also mediate mRNA degradation in late cell stages [21]. Thus, there is a need for a careful investigation and dissection of piRNA functions. In this study, we propose a novel method, MLPPF, designed for multi-label predictions of piRNA functions based on pretrained k-mer embedding, positional embedding, and an improved TextRNN model. First, a benchmark dataset was constructed by processing piRNA-function-annotated data and sequence data. Moreover, pretrained k-mer and positional embedding were applied to achieve biologically significant sequence representation. Finally, an end-to-end model that couples the discriminative power of representation with an improved textRNN was used to implement the piRNA functional label prediction task. Compared with the other three methods, MLPPF performed best and revealed the key factors of piRNA subsequences, thus demonstrating its effectiveness.

2. Materials and Methods

To identify the functional labels of piRNAs, our study builds a benchmark dataset, encodes a piRNA sequence with pretrained k-mer and positional embedding; and treats the piRNA function identification problem as an imbalanced multi-label learning issue by using an improved TextRNN model. The prediction process scheme is shown in Figure 1 and is divided into 4 main steps. They are benchmark dataset construction, piRNA sequence encoding, TextRNN model construction, and performance evaluation, which are explained in detail below.

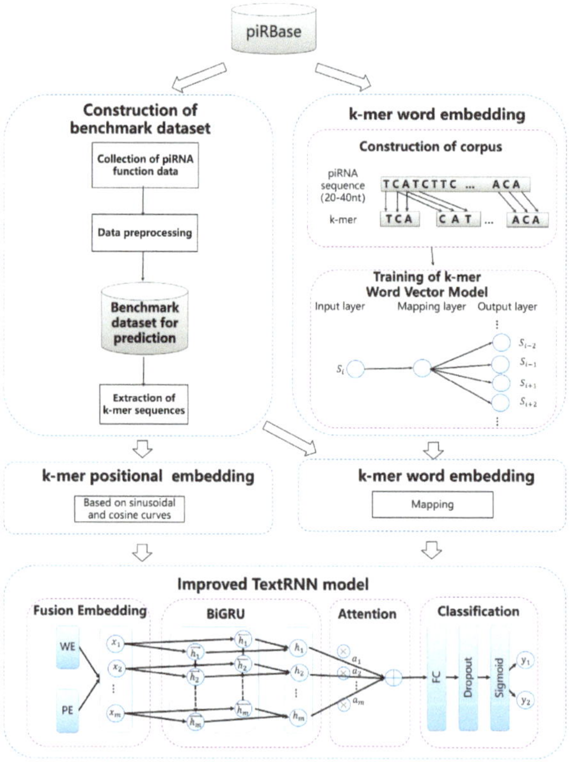

Figure 1. Framework illustration of piRNA functional label prediction.

2.1. Datasets

According to the NONCODE and piRBase databases, Liu et al. [11] constructed the first and most popular benchmark dataset for identifying mouse piRNA functional subsets in 2017, containing 1418 non-piRNA sequences; 709 piRNAs with the function of instructing target mRNA deadenylation; and 709 piRNAs without such a function. In 2020, they improved the dataset by increasing the contents of the three subsets to 798, 1257, and 2068, respectively. Although fruit fly species were added to this improved dataset, most studies still focus on mRNA-related piRNAs and ignore lncRNA-related piRNAs.

In our study, mRNA-related and lncRNA-related piRNAs were considered. The piRNA target data were downloaded in 2022 from piRBase (http://bigdata.ibp.ac.cn/piRBase, accessed on 20 January 2022) and extracted from the published literature [22]. After eliminating redundant data, 2628 non-duplicate piRNA sequences were obtained. In a piRNA target record, piRBase provides a piRBase name linked to detailed information concerning the piRNA, a target gene/transcript ID, a target site, and other relevant information. According to the interaction characteristics of piRNAs, piRNA sequences are marked with functional tags. We focused on two types of functional labels: mRNA-related piRNAs and lncRNA-related piRNAs. The functional labels for specific piRNAs are based on predicted and experimentally validated information about piRNA target sites. piRNA target mRNAs in mouse tissues were extracted from the published literature and used to experimentally verify piRNA target relationships. The prediction of potential piRNA target lncRNAs was performed the same way as piRNA target mRNA cleavage in mouse testes is predicted [4,9,10].If the piRNA only targets an mRNA, the functional label of the piRNA is marked as [1, 0]. If the piRNA only targets a lncRNA, the functional label of the piRNA is marked as [0, 1]. If both piRNA-mRNA and piRNA-lncRNA interactions exist, the functional label of the piRNA is marked as [1, 1]. In the benchmark dataset, the distribution of functional piRNAs reveals that 1806 piRNAs are only related to mRNA, accounting for 68.7%. Additionally, 538 piRNAs are only related to lncRNA, accounting for 20.5%. Furthermore, 284 piRNAs are related to both mRNA and lncRNA, accounting for 10.8%.

2.2. Sequence Embedding

In our study, a fusion of k-mer word embedding and positional embedding was used to obtain a piRNA sequence representation with biological significance, resulting in high accuracy and reliability in the prediction.

2.2.1. k-mer Word Embedding

RNA sequences need to be encoded into a numeric vector before machine learning can take place. Most biological sequence analysis methods use one-hot encoding for their k-mer fragments. While such encoding is popular, it results in high sparsity and does not consider the biological significance of ribonucleic acids. It hardly reflects sequence similarities and differences.

Inspired by studies on natural language processing (NLP), we analogized a piRNA sequence to a sentence and its k-mer subsequence to a word. By using a word-embedding model, representations of piRNA sequences with biological significance were obtained.

Referenced to Zeng et al. [23], a piRNA sequence, S, can be denoted as

$$S = N_1, N_2, \ldots, N_n \tag{1}$$

where N_i is the i-th nucleotide, $N_i \in \{A, G, C, T\}, i = 1, 2, 3, \ldots, n$, and n is the length of the piRNA sequence. The piRNA sequence is stored in a cDNA (complementary DNA) format.

We used a sliding window to extract m k-mer sequence fragments from a piRNA sequence S, as follows:

$$f(S) = S_{1:k}, S_{2:2+k}, \ldots, S_{m:m+k} \tag{2}$$

$$m = n - k + 1 \tag{3}$$

where $S_{i:i+k}$ is the i-th k-mer subsequence, k is the width of the sliding window, and m is the number of k-mer subsequences in the piRNA sequence, S.

Word2vec [24] is a word-embedding technique designed to represent standard words in a corpus as vectors with word semantics. This technique has improved multiple natural language processing tasks. The Skip-gram model is a useful example of a Word2vec model;

it is used to obtain the embedding vectors of k-mers. piRNA sequences in the piRBase database serve as a corpus, and their k-mer sequence fragments, extracted by the sliding window, are used to pretrain vectors with biological meanings in an unsupervised manner. To maximize the probability of the target k-mer and the co-occurrence of the context sequence, the word vector e_i of the k-mer sequence fragment $S_{i:i+k}$ is obtained. The value of k ranged from 2 to 5 in our experiment, and the value selection is discussed in Section 3.1.

The set of m-many k-mer sequence fragments $f(S)$ corresponding to the piRNA sequence S is transformed into a pretrained embedding representation, which is expressed as follows:

$$WE(S) = [e_1, e_2, \ldots, e_m] \tag{4}$$

2.2.2. k-mer Positional Embedding

In natural language processing technology, positional vectors are used to represent the position information of words. To enhance our model in capturing the sequential characteristics of sequences, positional embedding (*PE*) was used to identify piRNA functional labels.

Since the binary representation of position vectors wastes substantial memory, positional embedding generated by sinusoidal and cosine curves of varying frequencies was applied in our study. The positional embedding of the *i*-th k-mer subsequence is a vector determined by both the k-mer position and the component position, calculated as follows:

$$PE_{i,2j} = \sin\left(i/10000^{2j/d}\right) \tag{5}$$

$$PE_{i,2j+1} = \cos\left(i/10000^{2j/d}\right) \tag{6}$$

where i represents the position of the k-mer subsequence in a piRNA, and j represents the component position of the k-mer positional embedding vector. The range of i is [1, m], the range of j is [0, $\left\lfloor \frac{d-1}{2} \right\rfloor$], and d represents the dimension of the positional embedding. $PE_{i,2j}$ and $PE_{i,2j+1}$ denote the value at even and odd component positions in the positional embedding vector of the *i*-th k-mer subsequence, respectively. This positional embedding is based on sinusoidal and cosine curves and provides our model with the ability to model the position of a k-mer subsequence and the distance of every two k-mer subsequences.

2.3. *Improved TextRNN Network*

In NLP, the TextRNN model [25] can capture the most important semantic information in a sentence and improve the performance of multi-label identification tasks. Hence, in our study, an improved TextRNN network was used to systematically recognize piRNA functional labels in four parts: a fusion-encoding layer, a sequence encoder, an attention layer, and a classification layer. The details of the above components are described in the following sections.

2.3.1. k-mer Encoding Layer

In the embedding layer, the final embedding matrix is an aggregate matrix $\boldsymbol{P} \in \mathbb{R}^{m \times d}$, which is accumulated by the k-mer word embedding matrix and the positional embedding matrix. d refers to the dimension of both positional embedding and the pretrained embedding representation. It is computed as follows:

$$\boldsymbol{P} = WE + PE \tag{7}$$

2.3.2. Sequence Encoder

TextRNN [25] is an RNN-based flexible neural network designed for text data processing. In multiple text tests, TextRNN has achieved good results. However, traditional RNNs are likely to face vanishing or exploding gradient problems. As a variant of recurrent neural networks, gated recurrent units (GRUs) [25] can effectively address these problems. By simplifying the gating structure, GRUs become faster than Long Short-Term Memory (LSTM) and can better learn long-term dependencies. Therefore, a GRU can be successfully used to model sequence data in NLP, especially in sequence classification tasks and sequence annotation tasks. Typically, a GRU contains two gates, the update gate and the reset gate, which are used to determine the retention or disposal of information. The update gate z decides how much of the new input should be used to update the hidden state, while the reset gate r determines how much of the previous hidden state should be forgotten. The update gate z_i and reset gate r_i of the i-th hidden unit are computed by

$$z_i = \sigma(W_z x_i + U_z h_{i-1} + b_z) \tag{8}$$

$$r_i = \sigma(W_r x_i + U_r h_{i-1} + b_r) \tag{9}$$

where σ is the sigmoid function, x_i is the vector of the current-position k-mer fragment, and h_{i-1} is the final hidden state of the previous position k-mer fragment. The weight matrices W_z, W_r, U_z, and U_r are learned, and b_z and b_r are biases.

The hidden state h_i and candidate hidden state $\widetilde{h}_i$ of the GRU are computed by

$$h_i = (1 - z_i) \odot h_{i-1} + z_i \odot \widetilde{h}_i \tag{10}$$

$$\widetilde{h}_i = \tanh(W_h x_i + r_i \odot (U_h h_{i-1}) + b_h) \tag{11}$$

where $\odot$ is the dot product, W_h and U_h are weight matrices, and b_h is a bias.

Bi-GRU is a structure-reinforcing GRU neural network and provides the output layer with complete contextual information about the input data at each moment. The input sequence propagates through both a forward GRU and a backward GRU and then concatenates the outputs of both. The calculation process of the final hidden state of the current k-mer fragment, h_i, is as follows:

$$\overrightarrow{h}_i = \overrightarrow{\text{GRU}}\left(x_i, \overrightarrow{h}_{i-1}\right) \tag{12}$$

$$\overleftarrow{h}_i = \overleftarrow{\text{GRU}}\left(x_i, \overleftarrow{h}_{i+1}\right) \tag{13}$$

$$\begin{gathered} h_i = \left[\overrightarrow{h}_i, \overleftarrow{h}_i\right] \\ \boldsymbol{H} = [h_1, h_2, \ldots, h_m] \end{gathered} \tag{14}$$

where $\overrightarrow{h}_i$ and $\overleftarrow{h}_i$ are the forward and backward hidden states of the current k-mer fragment, respectively. $\overrightarrow{h}_{i-1}$ represents the forward hidden state of the previous position k-mer fragment. $\overleftarrow{h}_{i+1}$ represents the backward hidden state of the next position k-mer fragment. Finally, the output of the piRNA sequence encoder, $\boldsymbol{H} \in \mathbb{R}^{m \times h}$, is obtained by consolidating the encoding information from both directions of each k-mer fragment, where h is the dimension of the final hidden state.

2.3.3. Attention Layer

Recent studies have shown that piRNAs degrade mRNAs and lncRNAs through a miRNA-like mechanism. This suggests that a specific sequence fragment at a specific position is required for piRNA functions. The model should selectively focus on specific k-mer piRNA fragments that have biological functions. An attention mechanism can enable neural networks to focus on a subset of their inputs, so an attention layer is used in our model.

The output of the sequence encoder serves as the input to this layer. As referenced by Yang et al. [26], a k-mer-level context vector, u_s, can be introduced, and a normalized importance weights, a_i, can be calculated using a softmax function. To measure the importance of k-mer subsequences, the computation process is as follows:

$$u_i = \tanh(W_s h_i + b_s) \tag{15}$$

$$a_i = \frac{\exp\left(u_i^T u_s\right)}{\sum_i \exp\left(u_i^T u_s\right)} \tag{16}$$

$$\tilde{P} = \sum_{i=1}^{m} a_i h_i \tag{17}$$

where W_s is a trainable weight; b_s is a bias, a_i is the attention weight of the i-th k-mer; and $\tilde{P}$ represents the new weighted representation of the piRNA, as calculated by the sum of element-wise multiplication between attention weights and the input data of that layer.

2.3.4. Classification Layer

We treated this piRNA function prediction task as a multi-label classification problem. We introduced a fully connected layer for linear transformation into the classification layer of the model, allowing each sample to have the possibility of multiple labels. To reduce the model's dependence on specific neurons and improve generalization capabilities, we performed a dropout operation on the output of the fully connected layer. Finally, a sigmoid activation function was used to generate the predicted probability of the corresponding label for each sample, ensuring they are independent of each other.

2.4. *Evaluation Methods*

In our research, 10-fold cross-validation was used to evaluate the performance of the model. Samples were randomly divided into 10 folds. Each fold was used to validate the model, with the remaining data used to train it.

Evaluating the performance of multi-label classification differs from multi-class classification. In multi-class classification, each sample only belongs to one class, and the class labels are mutually exclusive. Predictions can be either entirely correct or incorrect. In multi-label classification, each sample can belong to multiple classes, and evaluating multi-label classification methods is like evaluating of information retrieval methods.

In the present study, the multi-label corpus C is the piRNA sequence set with functional labels, where each sample in this set is represented as (a_i, B_i), $i = 1, 2, \ldots, |C|$, and $|C|$ is the total number of samples in C. a_i is a piRNA sample, B_i is the true associated label set of a_i, and Cl_i is a label set obtained with the prediction method for a_i. L represents the total number of labels.

To evaluate our piRNA function multi-label prediction method, two kinds of metrics were used. One is a sample-based metric, another is a label-based metric. Sample-based metrics include accuracy, precision, recall, F1 score, hamming loss, etc. To better highlight that our study falls within the domain of multi-label classification, we provide explanations for hamming loss, micro_F1, and macro_F1.

- Hamming loss

Hamming loss is used to estimate the incorrect classification ratio, indicating both the failure to predict correct labels and the prediction of incorrect labels. The lower the Hamming loss, the better the performance. The formula is as follows:

$$Hamming\ loss(h, Cl) = \frac{1}{|C|}\sum_{i=1}^{|C|}\frac{|B_i \Delta Cl_i|}{L} \quad (18)$$

where Δ represents the symmetric difference between two sets.

Two label-based metrics are also applied, and they are as follows:

- Micro_F1

Micro_F1 is the harmonic mean of *micro_precision* and *micro_recall*, calculated as follows:

$$Micro\_F1 = \frac{2 \times micro\_precision \times micro\_recall}{micro\_precision + micro\_recall} \quad (19)$$

where micro_precision represents the overall precision of all labels.

- Macro_F1

Macro_F1 is the harmonic mean of among multi-label precision and recall and is calculated as follows:

$$Macro\_F1 = \frac{1}{L}\sum_{j=1}^{L}\frac{2 \times precision_j \times recall_j}{precision_j + recall_j} \quad (20)$$

where $precision_j$ represents the precision of the j-th label.

Apart from the above metrics, the receiver operating characteristic curve (ROC) and the precision–recall curve (PRC) are also used to evaluate the performance of methods.

3. Results

3.1. Hyperparameter Optimization

Many hyperparameters influence prediction performance. The grid search method is used for hyperparameter optimization. The best hyperparameters were selected based on a performance evaluation with the validation set. In the sequence-processing phase, k is a critical parameter of the current task, specifically representing the length of overlapping k-mer fragments obtained through sliding window extraction. If k is too small or too large, the prediction or computation performance is affected. In the pretrained k-mer-embedding phase, we utilized k-mer fragments with lengths ranging from two to five for word vector representation. The impact of the different tested k-mer lengths on performance is shown in Figure 2. The results indicate that F1, Micro_F1, and Macro_F1 slowly grow as k increases. Considering both the prediction performance and computation cost, k is set to 4, and the dimension of the pretrained vectors of k-mer is configured as 64.

In constructing the prediction model, BCEWithLogitsLoss was employed as the loss function, the Adam optimizer was chosen, the batch size was 50, the number of epochs was 10, the learning rate was 0.008, the dropout rate for hidden layers was 0.5, and the hidden layer dimension was set to 256.

3.2. Sequence Embedding Representation Comparison

This section describes four different sequence-encoding methods used to represent overlapping k-mer fragments, including randomly initialized k-mer embedding (Rand_E), pretrained k-mer embedding (Pre_E), randomly initialized k-mer embedding fused with k-mer positional embedding (Rand_E + Pos_E), and pretrained k-mer embedding fused with k-mer positional embedding (Pre_E + Pos_E).

To prove the effectiveness of the Pre_E + Pos_E representation, we compared the proposed method with the other three different embedding methods, as shown in Table 1. Comparing the performance of the Rand_E and Pre_E encoding representations, the overall prediction performance of Pre_E was higher than Rand_E. Using Pos_E as the basis for Pre_E, pretrained k-mer embedding fused with k-mer positional embedding performed best among the seven evaluation metrics. The results indicate that the proposed embedding representation effectively captures the semantic information and relative positional relationships of the k-mer fragments.

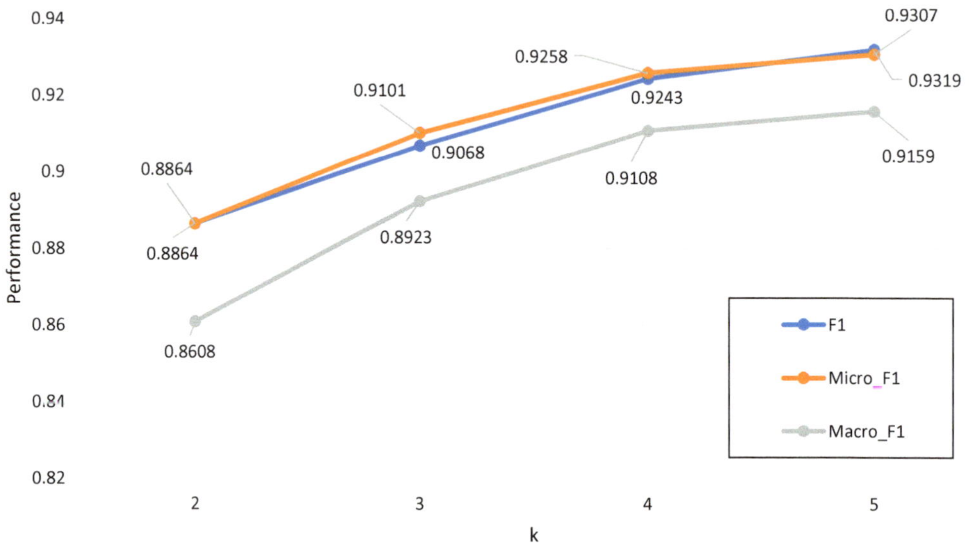

Figure 2. The predictive results with different k-mer lengths.

Table 1. Performance comparison of improved TextRNN model using four sequence-embedding methods.

Representation	Acc	Pre	Recall	F1	HL	Micro_F1	Macro_F1
Rand_E	0.9054	0.9189	0.9256	0.9167	0.0906	0.9185	0.9029
Pre_E	0.9085	0.9197	0.9252	0.9178	0.0854	0.9229	0.9079
Rand_E + Pos_E	0.9098	0.9229	0.9260	0.9196	0.0843	0.9237	0.9083
Pre_E + Pos_E	**0.9134**	**0.9231**	**0.9363**	**0.9243**	**0.0830**	**0.9258**	**0.9108**

Abbreviations: Acc, Accuracy; Pre, Precision; HL, Hamming Loss.

3.3. Performance Comparison

To better evaluate the performance of the improved TextRNN model in predicting piRNA functional multi-labels, we compared it with TextCNN, Transformer and Binary Relevance (BR) using pretrained k-mer embedding fused with positional embedding representation. TextCNN is a text classification model that can capture local sequence correlations well by using convolution cores and pooling operations. Transformer is a classic model proposed by Google, mainly used in NLP to capture the semantic relationships between sequences. Considering that non-deep methods achieve good performance [27], BR which decomposes the multi-label learning problem into multiple independent binary classification tasks is selected in this comparison. Using the BR method, we built an independent SVM model for each class label.

The performance of the four methods is shown in Table 2; seven performance metrics are listed. The results demonstrate that our method achieved the best performance; six indicators were above 90%, and the overall performance was higher than TextCNN, Transformer, or BinaryRelevance. Obviously, our proposed computational method performs better than other methods. In addition, ROC and PRC were used to evaluate classification performance using the Pre_E + Pos_E embedding method, as depicted in Figure 3a,b. Among the four comparison methods, the ROC curve based on the improved TextRNN was significantly higher than the other methods, and its AUC was the highest at 96.58%.

Table 2. Performance comparison of four methods based on pretrained k-mer embedding fused with k-mer positional embedding.

Method	Acc	Pre	Recall	F1	HL	Micro_F1	Macro_F1
BinaryRelevance	0.7584	0.8016	0.7723	0.7774	0.2321	0.7828	0.6536
TextCNN	0.8274	0.8383	0.8719	0.8459	0.1718	0.8495	0.8218
Transformer	0.8132	0.8288	0.8569	0.8329	0.1868	0.8355	0.8022
Improved TextRNN	**0.9134**	**0.9231**	**0.9363**	**0.9243**	**0.0830**	**0.9258**	**0.9108**

Abbreviations: Acc, Accuracy; Pre, Precision; HL, Hamming Loss.

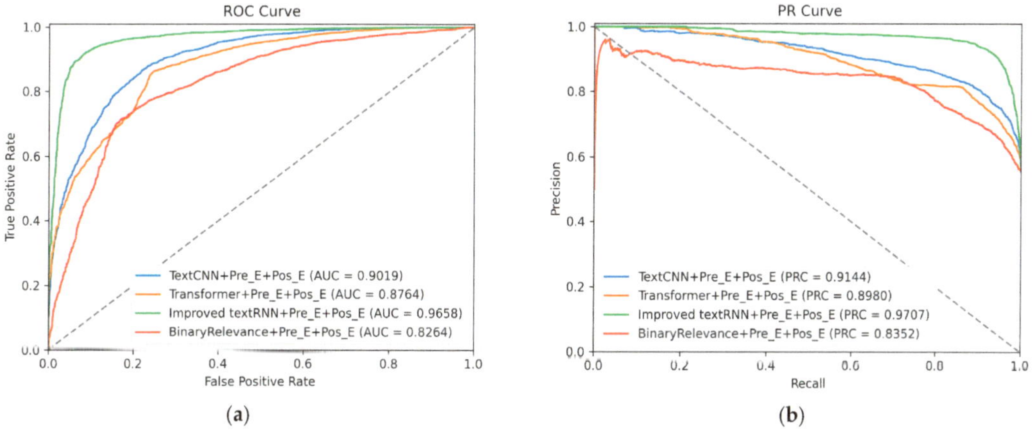

Figure 3. Performance curves of Four methods: (**a**) is the ROC curves of four models; (**b**) is the PRC curves of four models.

In summary, our method had the best predictive performance using the aggregate embedding method and the improved TextRNN model.

3.4. Performance Comparison of RNN Structure

RNN is a flexible network structure. The effects of different RNN structures on model performance are illustrated in Table 3. These structures include unidirectional GRU (UniGRU), bidirectional GRU (BiGRU), unidirectional LSTM (UniLSTM), and bidirectional LSTM (BiLSTM). The results show that the final hidden states obtained by BiGRU contained the most sequence context information and had the best performance among the six evaluation metrics. In UniGRU, the highest precision was achieved at 92.39%.

Table 3. Performance comparison of different RNN structures.

RNN	Acc	Pre	Recall	F1	HL	Micro_F1	Macro_F1
UniGRU	0.9123	**0.9239**	0.9317	0.9226	0.0854	0.9235	0.9068
BiGRU	**0.9134**	0.9231	**0.9363**	**0.9243**	**0.0830**	**0.9258**	**0.9108**
UniLSTM	0.9062	0.9184	0.9285	0.9177	0.0932	0.9167	0.9017
BiLSTM	0.8967	0.9104	0.9193	0.9088	0.1020	0.9086	0.8903

Next, we evaluated the ROC and PRC of our model in the different RNN structures, as shown in Figure 4a,b. To more clearly demonstrate the impact of different RNN structures on model performance, we choose to enlarge the x-axis range from 0.0 to 0.2 and the y-axis range from 0.8 to 1.0 in the ROC curve and enlarge the x-axis range from 0.8 to 1.0 and the y-axis range from 0.8 to 1.0 in the PR curve. The results reveal that all four RNN structures achieved AUC values surpassing 95%. BiGRU reached the highest at 96.58%, followed by UniGRU at 96.03%, UniLSTM at 95.60%, and BiLSTM at 95.58%. Through comparative analysis, we found that GRU performed slightly better than LSTM in predicting piRNA functional labels, and BiGRU proved more effective in capturing the semantic relationships within the piRNA sequences.

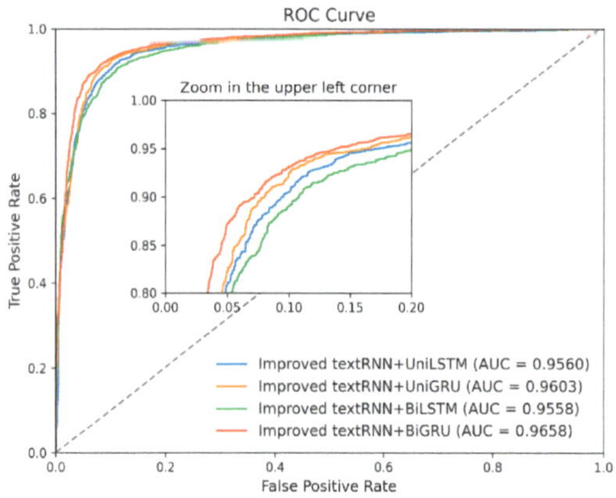

(a)

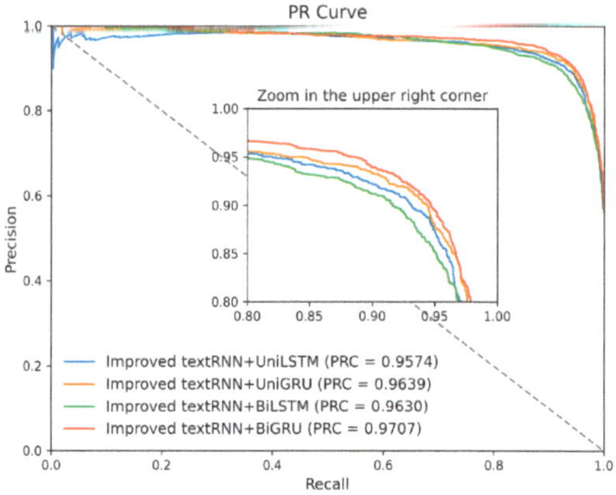

(b)

Figure 4. (**a**) is the ROC curves of four RNN structures; (**b**) is the PRC curves of four RNN structures.

3.5. Attention Layer Analysis

At present, the attention mechanism is widely acknowledged as a crucial part of modern neural networks and has made significant advancements in various tasks. The attention mechanism was introduced to focus on key fragments of the piRNA sequence while ignoring irrelevant information.

First, ablation studies on the attention mechanism were performed, and the results are presented in Table 4. They indicate that the contribution of the attention layer in our model is not significant. Furthermore, we took a close look at the attention weights and plotted heat maps to reveal the key factors that are captured by the model using the attention mechanism. Different colors reflect the model's attention to different k-mer segments. The darker the color, the greater the contribution of the corresponding segment to the prediction task. The results of the piRNA demo are shown in Figure 5. For example, in the first piRNA in Figure 5, it seems that a focus is placed near the 5′ ends of the piRNA, and the k-mer fragment is "CCAG". We believe the attention mechanism helped us to mine key subsequences of functional piRNA as in the above case.

Table 4. Performance comparison of ablation studies on the attention layer.

Method	Acc	Pre	Recall	HL	F1	Micro_F1	Macro_F1
Our model without attention layer	0.9113	0.9229	0.9305	**0.0824**	0.9216	0.9257	**0.9117**
Our model with attention layer	**0.9134**	**0.9231**	**0.9363**	0.0830	**0.9243**	**0.9258**	0.9108

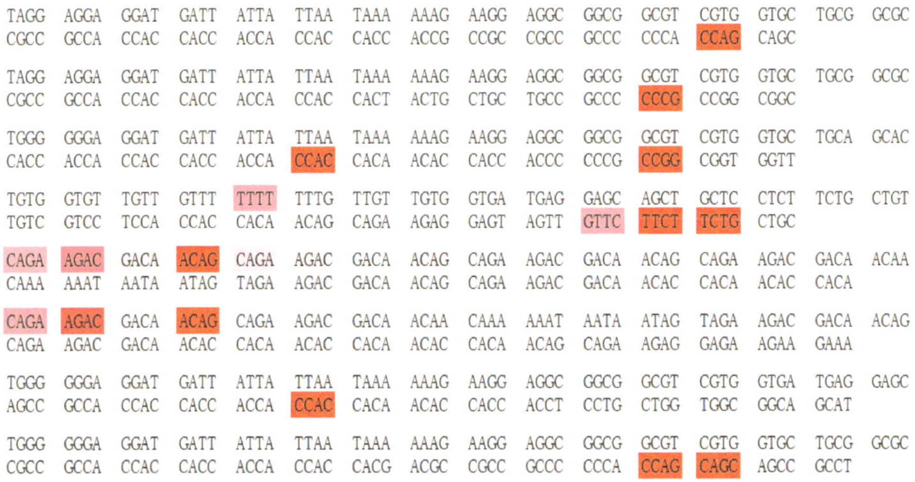

Figure 5. The Heatmap of piRNA sequences.

4. Conclusions and Future Directions

Compared with the prediction results for miRNA and lncRNA functional labels, research related to piRNAs is still in an early phase. In this study, we developed a computational method for predicting functional labels for piRNAs based on pretrained k-mer embedding, positional embedding, and an improved TextRNN model. First, we collected piRNA functional label data and sequence data and then constructed a benchmark dataset via data processing. Moreover, pretrained k-mer and positional embedding were applied to obtain sequence representation with biological significance. Finally, an end-to-end model that couples the discriminative power of representation with the improved textRNN was used to implement the piRNA functional label prediction task. In conclusion, our model can characterize piRNA functional labels and could be beneficial to researchers investigating piRNA functions.

Bioinformatics investigations necessitate extensive data. In contrast to the abundant databases on miRNA-mRNA and miRNA-lncRNA, functional annotated data on piRNA remain limited. Our ongoing studies revolve around a dedicated focus on contemporary advancements in piRNA research and will improve our work in the following future directions:

1. Expand and subdivide the functional labels of piRNA

Due to data limitations, we only focused on two types of functional labels for piRNA in this study. Existing studies have shown that piRNAs can not only degrade mRNA in a miRNA-like manner but also extensively activate mRNA translation. According to these biological facts, we will subdivide piRNA functional labels based on data accumulation. In addition, piRNA functions are diverse, as they can regulate various genetic factors such as transposable elements (TE). For these regulatory objects, we will expand the piRNA functional labels through data accumulation.

2. Identification of functional sites

Based on the transcriptome data, we will identify the functional sites of piRNA and explore piRNAs as potential biomarkers and drug targets using a computational method. This method can characterize the functional sites of piRNAs, helping researchers infer the potential regulatory functions of piRNAs and their binding mechanisms with other genetic factors.

Author Contributions: Conceptualization, Y.L. (Yajun Liu) and R.L.; methodology, software and writing, Y.L. (Yajun Liu), R.L. and Y.L. (Yang Lu); data collection, Z.W.; writing, review and editing, A.L. and W.L. All authors have read and agreed to the published version of the manuscript.

Funding: This work was supported by the Young Scientists Fund of the National Natural Science Foundation of China (Grant No. 62202374), the Natural Science Basic Research Program of Shaanxi Province of China (Program No. 2022JQ-719 and 2021JM-347), the China Postdoctoral Science Foundation (2021M693887).

Data Availability Statement: Denchmark dataset and source code for MLPPF are available at https://github.com/lralrac/MLPPF-master (accessed on 16 December 2023).

Conflicts of Interest: The authors declare no conflict of interest.

References

1. Aravin, A.; Gaidatzis, D.; Pfeffer, S.; Lagos-Quintana, M.; Landgraf, P.; Iovino, N.; Morris, P.; Brownstein, M.J.; Kuramochi-Miyagawa, S.; Nakano, T. A novel class of small RNAs bind to MILI protein in mouse testes. *Nature* **2006**, *442*, 203–207. [CrossRef]
2. Liu, Y.; Li, A.; Zhu, Y.; Pang, X.; Hei, X.; Xie, G.; Wu, F.-X. piRSNP: A Database of piRNA-related SNPs and their Effects on Cancerrelated piRNA Functions. *Curr. Bioinform.* **2023**, *18*, 509–516. [CrossRef]
3. Zhang, S.; Pointer, B.; Kelleher, E.S. Rapid evolution of piRNA-mediated silencing of an invading transposable element was driven by abundant de novo mutations. *Genome Res.* **2020**, *30*, 566–575. [CrossRef]
4. Gou, L.T.; Dai, P.; Yang, J.H.; Xue, Y.C.; Hu, Y.P.; Zhou, Y.; Kang, J.Y.; Wang, X.; Li, H.R.; Hua, M.M.; et al. Pachytene piRNAs instruct massive mRNA elimination during late spermiogenesis. *Cell Res.* **2014**, *24*, 680–700. [CrossRef]
5. Watanabe, T.; Cheng, E.C.; Zhong, M.; Lin, H. Retrotransposons and pseudogenes regulate mRNAs and lncRNAs via the piRNA pathway in the germline. *Genome Res.* **2015**, *25*, 368. [CrossRef]
6. Dai, P.; Wang, X.; Gou, L.-T.; Li, Z.-T.; Wen, Z.; Chen, Z.-G.; Hua, M.-M.; Zhong, A.; Wang, L.; Su, H.; et al. A translation-activating function of MIWI/piRNA during mouse spermiogenesis. *Cell* **2019**, *179*, 1566–1581.e1516. [CrossRef]
7. Ramat, A.; Simonelig, M. Functions of PIWI Proteins in Gene Regulation: New Arrows Added to the piRNA Quiver. *Trends Genet.* **2021**, *37*, 188–200. [CrossRef]
8. Fei, R.; Wan, Y.; Hu, B.; Li, A.; Li, Q. A novel network core structure extraction algorithm utilized variational autoencoder for community detection. *Expert Syst. Appl.* **2023**, *222*, 119775. [CrossRef]
9. Zhang, P.; Kang, J.Y.; Gou, L.T.; Wang, J.J.; Xue, Y.C.; Skogerboe, G.; Dai, P.; Huang, D.W.; Chen, R.S.; Fu, X.D.; et al. MIWI and piRNA-mediated cleavage of messenger RNAs in mouse testes. *Cell Res.* **2015**, *25*, 193–207. [CrossRef]
10. Goh, W.S.S.; Falciatori, I.; Tam, O.H.; Burgess, R.; Meikar, O.; Kotaja, N.; Hammell, M.; Hannon, G.J. piRNA-directed cleavage of meiotic transcripts regulates spermatogenesis. *Genes Dev.* **2015**, *29*, 1032–1044. [CrossRef]
11. Liu, B.; Yang, F.; Chou, K.C. 2L-piRNA: A Two-Layer Ensemble Classifier for Identifying Piwi-Interacting RNAs and Their Function. *Mol. Ther. Nucleic Acids* **2017**, *7*, 267–277. [CrossRef]
12. Li, T.Y.; Gao, M.Y.; Song, R.Y.; Yin, Q.; Chen, Y. Support Vector Machine Classifier for Accurate Identification of piRNA. *Appl. Sci.* **2018**, *8*, 2204. [CrossRef]
13. Khan, S.; Khan, M.; Iqbal, N.; Hussain, T.; Khan, S.A.; Chou, K.C. A Two-Level Computation Model Based on Deep Learning Algorithm for Identification of piRNA and Their Functions via Chou's 5-Steps Rule. *Int. J. Pept. Res. Ther.* **2020**, *26*, 795–809. [CrossRef]
14. Zuo, Y.; Zou, Q.; Lin, J.; Jiang, M.; Liu, X. 2lpiRNApred: A two-layered integrated algorithm for identifying piRNAs and their functions based on LFE-GM feature selection. *RNA Biol.* **2020**, *17*, 892–902. [CrossRef]
15. Khan, S.; Khan, M.; Iqbal, N.; Khan, S.A.; Chou, K.-C. Prediction of piRNAs and their function based on discriminative intelligent model using hybrid features into Chou's PseKNC. *Chemom. Intell. Lab. Syst.* **2020**, *203*, 104056. [CrossRef]
16. John, B.; Enright, A.J.; Aravin, A.; Tuschl, T.; Sander, C.; Marks, D.S. Human MicroRNA targets. *PLoS Biol.* **2004**, *2*, e363. [CrossRef]
17. Yuan, J.; Zhang, P.; Cui, Y.; Wang, J.J.; Skogerbo, G.; Huang, D.W.; Chen, R.S.; He, S.M. Computational identification of piRNA targets on mouse mRNAs. *Bioinformatics* **2016**, *32*, 1170–1177. [CrossRef]
18. Wu, W.S.; Huang, W.C.; Brown, J.S.; Zhang, D.; Song, X.; Chen, H.; Tu, S.; Weng, Z.; Lee, H.C. pirScan: A webserver to predict piRNA targeting sites and to avoid transgene silencing in C. elegans. *Nucleic Acids Res.* **2018**, *46*, W43–W48. [CrossRef]

19. Zhang, D.; Tu, S.; Stubna, M.; Wu, W.S.; Huang, W.C.; Weng, Z.; Lee, H.C. The piRNA targeting rules and the resistance to piRNA silencing in endogenous genes. *Science* **2018**, *359*, 587–592. [CrossRef]
20. Yang, T.-H.; Shiue, S.-C.; Chen, K.-Y.; Tseng, Y.-Y.; Wu, W.-S. Identifying piRNA targets on mRNAs in C. elegans using a deep multi-head attention network. *BMC Bioinform.* **2021**, *22*, 503. [CrossRef]
21. Jensen, S.; Brasset, E.; Parey, E.; Crollius, H.R.; Sharakhov, I.V.; Vaury, C. Conserved Small Nucleotidic Elements at the Origin of Concerted piRNA Biogenesis from Genes and lncRNAs. *Cells* **2020**, *9*, 1491. [CrossRef]
22. Wang, J.; Shi, Y.; Zhou, H.; Zhang, P.; Song, T.; Ying, Z.; Yu, H.; Li, Y.; Zhao, Y.; Zeng, X.; et al. piRBase: Integrating piRNA annotation in all aspects. *Nucleic Acids Res.* **2022**, *50*, D265–D272. [CrossRef]
23. Zeng, M.; Wu, Y.; Lu, C.; Zhang, F.; Wu, F.X.; Li, M. DeepLncLoc: A deep learning framework for long non-coding RNA subcellular localization prediction based on subsequence embedding. *Brief. Bioinform.* **2022**, *23*, bbab360. [CrossRef]
24. Mikolov, T.; Chen, K.; Corrado, G.; Dean, J. Efficient estimation of word representations in vector space. *arXiv* **2013**, arXiv:1301.3781. [CrossRef]
25. Liu, P.; Qiu, X.; Huang, X.J. Recurrent neural network for text classification with multi-task learning. *arXiv* **2016**, arXiv:1605.05101. [CrossRef]
26. Yang, Z.; Yang, D.; Dyer, C.; He, X.; Smola, A.; Hovy, E. Hierarchical attention networks for document classification. In Proceedings of the 2016 Conference of the North American Chapter of the Association for Computational Linguistics: Human Language Technologies, San Diego, CA, USA, 12–17 June 2016; pp. 1480–1489.
27. Xing, L.; Lesperance, M.L.; Zhang, X. Simultaneous prediction of multiple outcomes using revised stacking algorithms. *Bioinformatics* **2020**, *36*, 65–72. [CrossRef]

electronics

MDPI

Article

Personalized Federated Learning Based on Bidirectional Knowledge Distillation for WiFi Gesture Recognition

Huan Geng [1,2], Dongshang Deng [1,2], Weidong Zhang [1,2], Ping Ji [1,2,]* and Xuangou Wu [1,2]

1 School of Computer Science and Technology, Anhui University of Technology, Ma'anshan 243032, China; hgeng@ahut.edu.cn (H.G.); dsdeng@ahut.edu.cn (D.D.); wdzhang@ahut.edu.cn (W.Z.); wuxgou@ahut.edu.cn (X.W.)

2 Anhui Engineering Research Center for Intelligent Applications and Security of Industrial Internet, Ma'anshan 243032, China

* Correspondence: jiping@ahut.edu.cn

Abstract: WiFi-based human gesture recognition has a wide range of applications in smart homes. Existing methods train gesture classification models by collecting large amounts of WiFi signal data in a centralized manner. However, centralized training faces challenges, including high communication overhead and the risk of data privacy leakage. Federated learning (FL) provides an opportunity to collaboratively train and share models without compromising data privacy. One of the main challenges FL faces is data that is non-Independent and Identically Distributed (non-IID) across clients. Specifically, in the gesture recognition scenario, since the transmission of WiFi signals is susceptible to cross-environment and cross-person interference, non-IID mainly manifests itself as a cross-domain problem. Cross-domain makes the knowledge learned between client models incompatible. Therefore, in the cross-domain scenario, effectively extracting and combining the knowledge learned by the client is a challenge. To solve this problem, we propose pFedBKD, a novel personalized federated learning scheme via bidirectional distillation. First, the knowledge that is beneficial to the client is extracted from the shared server model through knowledge distillation in the client, which helps train the personalized model of the client. Second, the server adaptively adjusts the aggregation weights according to the deviation between the shared model and the client's local model so that the server's shared model can extract more public knowledge. We conduct experiments on multiple open-source datasets. Experimental results show that our method is superior to existing methods and effectively alleviates the problem of reduced model recognition accuracy caused by cross-domain challenges.

Keywords: gesture recognition; personalized federated learning; knowledge distillation; cross-domain

1. Introduction

With the continuous development of the intelligent Internet of Things (IoT), WiFi-based gesture recognition is widely being applied in diverse domains such as smart homes [1,2], person recognition [3], and virtual reality [4,5]. Current WiFi-based gesture recognition methods require centralized user data collection to train gesture recognition models [6–10]. In addition, higher data volume requirements are required to achieve better performance of the model. However, collecting data is difficult, data transmission will consume a large amount of communication resources, and sharing data will cause concerns about user privacy [11–15].

Federated learning (FL) [16] emerged as a solution that only requires the client to upload model parameters instead of raw data. The classic FL system mainly consists of a server trusted by all parties and multiple clients. In each round of communication, the aggregated global model parameters are sent by the server to the clients participating in this round of updates. After receiving the parameters, the client performs training locally based on its private data. Then, the client participating in the update sends the updated local model parameters to the server side and performs the aggregation operation on the server side. During the entire process, the server can only access the gradients or model parameters uploaded by participants, thus protecting the client's data privacy to a great extent.

However, one of the main challenges in FL is non-Independent and Identically Distributed (non-IID) [17–20] across client data. In WiFi-based gesture recognition scenarios, non-IID is mainly presented cross-domain: cross-environment [21,22] and cross-person [6,23]. Due to the multipath effect of Channel State Information (CSI) [24,25], cross-environment and cross-person lead to changes in the phase and amplitude of CSI signals, making the collected data features heterogeneous. Cross-domain not only makes the knowledge learned between client models incompatible, but also makes global and local knowledge incompatible. Ultimately, the accuracy of client-side testing of the global model after aggregation will be lower than before aggregation.

In response to the above cross-domain problems, existing research can be mainly divided into two different categories: traditional federated learning, which generates a unified model and personalized federated learning (PFL), which generates its personalized model for each client. Traditional federated learning, exemplified by approaches like FedProx [26] and SCAFFOLD [27], aims to generate a powerful global model that converges to the global optimum and is shared with all clients. On the other hand, PFL endeavours to train a personalized model tailored to perform effectively on each client, as demonstrated by methods such as FedFomo [28], Ditto [29] and pFedSD [30]. However, the methods mentioned above either address the incompatibility issue between local and global knowledge or exclusively concern the incompatibility problem among local knowledge without considering the two jointly.

To address the cross-domain problem, we propose a personalized federated learning approach based on bidirectional knowledge distillation for WiFi gesture recognition (pFedBKD). First, during the local training process of the client, we use knowledge distillation (KD) to extract the knowledge of the global model locally to absorb more beneficial local knowledge. The effects of incompatibility between global and local knowledge are mitigated. Second, we quantify the extent to which the local model deviates from the global distribution by uploading the difference between the labels produced locally by the global and local models. We assign greater weights to local models that exhibit lower deviations from the global distribution. This strategy helps alleviate the effect of incompatibility between local knowledge.

The main contributions of this paper can be summarized as follows:

- We propose pFedBKD to solve the incompatibility problem between knowledge caused by cross-domain challenges by using knowledge distillation on the client side and adjusting the weight of the aggregation model on the server side.
- In order to alleviate the knowledge incompatibility between the global model and the local model due to cross-domain challenges, we integrate global and local knowledge through the KD algorithm during the local training process to generate a personalized model. We then determine the aggregation weights in the aggregation process by evaluating the local and global bias degree using Jensen-Shannon (JS) divergence.
- We conduct extensive experiments on open-source datasets (Widar3.0 [6], and UT-HAR [31] datasets) in multiple cross-domain scenarios. Experimental results show that our proposed method is better than existing methods and improves model recognition accuracy.

The subsequent sections of this work are structured in the following manner: Section 2 provides an overview of the existing research in the field. Section 3 provides an explanation for the motivation. Section 4 provides a clear and concise explanation of the problem formulation for PFL. The system design is outlined in Section 5. Section 6 displays the empirical findings. Ultimately, Section 7 serves as the final conclusion of this paper.

2. Related Work

Recently, FL has thrived as users pay more attention to the privacy and security of their data. However, gesture recognition scenarios often involve multiple users and devices, and the data between different clients is non-IID. Applying the federated averaging algorithm to build a global model cannot guarantee performance. Work on federated learning and WiFi-based action recognition technology is the main emphasis of this section. These kinds of work on federated learning are specifically divided into three types: FL in human activity recognition, federated knowledge distillation and model aggregation in FL.

2.1. Federated Learning in Human Activity Recognition

FL's benefits of protecting privacy and cutting communication costs have led to its widespread use in human activity recognition [32–35]. Sozinov et al. [33] apply FedAvg to human activity recognition for the first time. WiFederated [36] adopts the FL framework to scale the deployment of CSI-based WiFi sensing systems from multiple locations. The introduction of FL in human activity recognition will bring new challenges. Traditional data-centric methods cannot be used directly in FL scenarios because FL transmits model parameters rather than raw data. To address the above challenges, ClusterFL [37] reduces the impact of data heterogeneity through collaborative training between similar nodes. Nevertheless, these approaches ignore the contradiction between global and local knowledge by using the global model in place of the local model while updating the client.

2.2. Federated Learning and Knowledge Distillation

Multiple studies have investigated the integration of FL with KD to tackle the issue of data heterogeneity. By saving model parameters after the last round of local updates, pFedSD [30] extracts previous personalized knowledge into the local model through knowledge distillation in the new round of updates to accelerate recall. FedFTG [38] uses the local model as a discriminator and generates hard samples that can represent the local distribution through adversarial training. Then, KD is used to extract local knowledge to the aggregated model to improve the precision of the global model. pFedDF [39] presents a unified distillation technique for combining models, suitable for heterogeneous scenarios. Our approach addresses cross-domain challenges by reducing the incompatibility between local and global knowledge while mitigating the incompatibility among local knowledge.

2.3. Model Aggregation in Federated Learning

Model aggregation is crucial in combining knowledge from different client devices while minimizing communication costs and improving learning performance in FL. Chen et al. [40] propose a synchronous model learning strategy at the client level and a time-weighted aggregation method at the server side to reduce communication costs and improve FL accuracy. In order to promote similar client collaboration in the model aggregation process, FedAMP [41] introduces a novel federated attention messaging method. Rather than addressing cross-domain issues, the primary goal of these model aggregation solutions is to increase FL's communication efficiency.

3. Analysis and Motivations

In recent years, wireless devices have become an essential part of the IoT fields, such as smart homes, which can use wireless signals to identify user actions. By employing a sophisticated model architecture, the efficacy of the ultimate trained model will be enhanced as the number of users ready to provide private action data increases [42]. However, in real-life scenarios, most users are unwilling to share private data, or the labour and bandwidth costs required to collect data are too high. FL, in this instance, does not necessitate the client to upload sensitive information. Instead, it collectively trains the global model by transmitting parameters to the server. User privacy is ensured, and communication bandwidth is conserved.

Due to the differences in environments or users among different clients, traditional federated averaging (FedAvg) algorithms have mediocre performance [8]. In our trials, we assess the precision of both the local and global models to examine the correlation between these two models, as depicted in Figure 1.

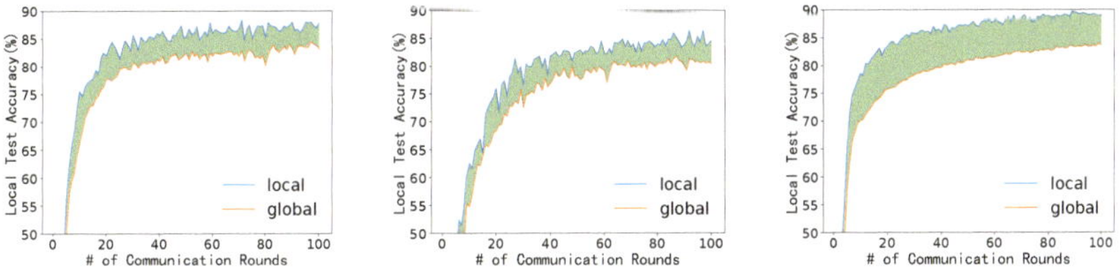

(**a**) Cross-environment (**b**) Cross-person (**c**) Cross-environment and Cross-person

Figure 1. When FedAvg is applied to the Widar3.0 [6] dataset, you can observe the change in client-side test accuracy of the model before and after aggregation (green shaded area). Local models show higher accuracy when cross-environment, cross-person, and both exist.

Our experiments indicate that the precision of model aggregation falls when clients have challenges that span cross-domain. This phenomenon is caused by the incompatibility between global and local knowledge due to cross-domain issues [30]. This occurrence suggests that when the aggregation process takes place, historical local knowledge is abandoned, leading to a decline in the precision of the local model. Therefore, in a new communication round, the client must retrain the local model accuracy to the level of the previous round. The retraining process increases training time and may reduce the final model accuracy. When cross-domain problems become more severe, the phenomenon of accuracy decline becomes more prominent. From this, we judge that the precision of the global aggregation model decreases due to the incompatibility between local knowledge in the aggregation stage. At the same time, due to the incompatibility of global and local knowledge, the client's use of the global model for initialization in a new round of updates will lead to a decrease in accuracy.

Subsequently, we proceed with the training procedures of the classic FedAvg algorithm to conduct a more comprehensive examination of the factors contributing to the decrease in performance. For each communication cycle, a subset of clients denoted as rK, will be chosen to take part in the update, where r is a value between 0 and 1. The chosen client performs E local epochs. The participating client in the current iteration receives the updated model transmitted by the server and utilizes it as the initial reference for a subsequent training iteration. Server-sent models are aggregated from selected clients with different data distributions (such as different environments or users).

Hence, the most recent version of the model downloaded to the client exhibits superior accuracy in global distribution compared to its local distribution [26]. Figure 1 depicts the disparity in accuracy between the global model used for testing and the local model specific to the client following the most recent set of changes. The global model's performance has notably decreased following the latest round of aggregation compared to the accuracy of the model submitted by the customer in the prior round. The performance degradation is caused by the client using the downloaded global model as the starting point for a new round of updates. In real-world environments where cross-domain problems are more severe, this decrease in accuracy will become more apparent.

Assume that in t communication round, the update selects a client that has not been selected in previous rounds of updates, Then, the client will need more local updates to reach the previous performance level. However, the classic federated learning algorithm does not consider this, and the locally updated epochs are consistent. In order to obtain a generalized global model, the classic FedAvg algorithm discards some of the client's interests, especially in scenarios with severe cross-domain problems. Determining how to balance generalization and personalization is a problem that PFL needs to solve. Using the global model in FedAvg to initialize the local model can enhance generalization capabilities, but it is challenging to adapt to different scenarios between clients. At the same time, due to the differences between local data distributions, if the aggregation stage can reduce the impact of different distribution differences, the global model's accuracy after aggregation can be improved.

4. Preliminaries

4.1. Gesture Recognition Technology

In an orthogonal frequency division multiplexing (OFDM) system [43], a wireless sensing device collects a set of S subcarriers from each data packet, which consists of complex values. CSI is described as

$$Z(f_i, t) = |Z(f_i, t)|e^{j\angle Z(f_i, t)}, i \in [1, S] \tag{1}$$

where $|Z(f_i, t)|$ symbolizes the CSI's amplitude of subcarrier f_i at the centre frequency and t timestamp, while $\angle Z(f_i, t)$ represents the phase of CSI.

Doppler Frequency Shift (DFS) [44] occurs due to the relative motion between the transmitter and receiver of a wireless device. According to the Carrier Amplitude and Phase Recovery Method (CARM), the fundamental reason for DFS is the variation in signal propagation paths. It is possible to represent the shift caused by the reflected signals as

$$f_D(t) = -\frac{1}{\overline{\lambda}}\frac{d}{dt}d(t) = -f\frac{d}{dt}\tau(t) \tag{2}$$

where $\overline{\lambda}$ represents the signal's wavelength, f represents the subcarrier frequency, and $\tau(t)$ represents the time it takes for the signal to travel. Also, $d(t)$ represents the distance of the path where there is no direct line of sight.

DFS occurs when volunteers perform gestures that cause various body parts to move at different speeds, especially when the movements are relatively large. Assuming that the vector of velocity $\vec{v}$ at each timestamp causes cumulative DFS, note that for k transmitter-receiver links, the DFS $F_D^k(\vec{v})$ can be calculated using the given formula.

$$F_D^k(\vec{v}) = c_x^k\vec{v}_x + c_y^k\vec{v}_y \tag{3}$$

The location of the transmitter-receiver link determines c_x^k and c_y^k. $\vec{v}_x$ represents the user's facial direction, $\vec{v}_y$ represents the vertical direction [45]. c_x^k and c_y^k can be used to find the optimal solution of $\vec{v}_x$. $\vec{v}_y$ can be separated from the measured DFS using CSI [6]. $\vec{v}_x$ and $\vec{v}_y$ can be used to represent the body velocity distribution (BVP). The same operations can be carried out by several users in various forms.

4.2. Personalized Federated Learning

Below, we first review the traditional FL objective function and then introduce the objective function of PFL. Our empirical observations of performance degradation of global models in PFL and our desire to reduce incompatibilities between local knowledge motivate us to provide pFedBKD.

We generate personalized models for different clients adapted to the client's local data distribution as the ultimate goal. The dataset in this article consists of supervised WiFi-based gesture recognition data. Each client has its data set D_k, with a total of K clients (wireless devices). A piece of data consists of x input and y tags. All client data sets form $D = \bigcup_{k=1}^{K} D_k$. We first review the classic FL system, whose goal is to reduce the total experience loss:

$$\min_{w} F(w) = \sum_{k=1}^{K} \frac{|D_k|}{|D|} F_k(w) \tag{4}$$

The optimization function of client k is expressed as $F_k(w)$, where w represents the global model parameters.

Since the distribution of D_k is very different between different clients, a single global model w is challenging to guarantee to fit the local target $F_k(w)$ of each client. PFL generates a personalized model v_k for client k that is different from other clients and consistent with its local target.

$$\min_{\{v_1,v_2,\cdots,v_K\}} \sum_{k=1}^{K} \frac{|D_k|}{|D|} F_k(v_k) \tag{5}$$

5. Our Solution and Algorithm Description

5.1. Overview

In this section, we divide pFedBKD into two parts to introduce the design of the pFedBKD framework in detail. The details of our method are summarized in Algorithms 1 and 2. Algorithm 1 describes the calculation process of the client, and Algorithm 2 describes the calculation process of the server. Figure 2 shows that the pFedBKD process is based on a client-server framework, where the wireless device is considered a client.

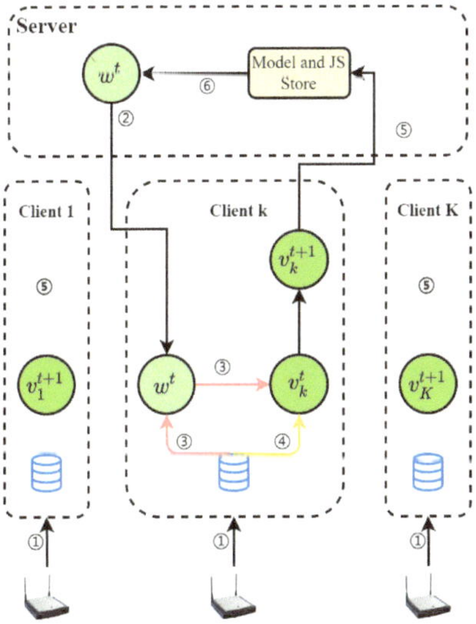

Figure 2. Description of pFedBKD workflow. Each communication round performs data training on the client side and model aggregation on the server side until the termination condition is met. The workflow consists of six steps: ① this is the collection and preprocessing part of CSI data; ② when communication starts, the server sends the initial model w_0; in subsequent updates, sends the aggregated updated global model w^t; ③ trains the local model v_k^t on the client data set, extract the knowledge of w^t to the local through KD; ④ calculates v_k^{t+1} and w^t on the client data set JS value of w^t; ⑤ the client uploads the updated parameter w^{t+1} and JS value to the server; ⑥ the collected JS values are normalized to generate aggregate weights, and then the aggregation model generates a global model w^{t+1}.

Algorithm 1 pFedBKD Algorithm: Client

Input: local traning batch size B, learning rate η, local epochs E
Output: client personalization models $\{v_k\}_{k\in[K]}$

procedure CLIENTUPLOAD(k, w^t)
Download the model from the server
for $i = 1, \ldots, E$ **do**
  $\Phi_k(v_k^t) = F_k(v_k^t) + \lambda \mathcal{L}_{KL}(q(v_k^t)||q(w^t))$
  $v_k^t = v_k^t - \eta \nabla \Phi_k(v_k^t, w_t)$
end for
Store models v_k^t and w^t
Calculate JS divergence L_k^{t+1} ▷ Equation (8)
return local model v_k^t and L_k^{t+1}
end procedure

Algorithm 2 pFedBKD Algorithm: Server

Input: communication rounds T, training participation ratio r
Output: client personalization models $\{v_k\}_{k\in[K]}$

procedure SERVERAGGREGSYION()
Initialize model w^0
for $t = 1, \ldots, T$ **do**
  Extract rK clients to form C^t
  C^t clients downloads global model parameters w^t
  for each client $k \in C^t$ **do**
    $v_k^{t+1}, L_k^{t+1} \leftarrow ClientUpload(k, w^t)$
  end for
  Compute aggregate weights $\beta_t^k = \frac{1/L_k^{t+1}}{\sum_{k=1}^{K} 1/L_k^{t+1}}$
  $w^{t+1} = \sum_{k=1}^{K} \beta_t^k v_k^{t+1}$
end for
end procedure

5.2. Client Model Training and Extract Global Knowledge to Local

When training clients, strike a balance between local and global knowledge. We refrain from replacing the client model with a global model to leverage global knowledge. Instead, we use KD to bring global knowledge to clients. To regulate the amount of mixing between the global and local knowledge, we employ a hyperparameter λ.

Therefore, the client's loss function is

$$\Phi_k(v_k^t) = F_k(v_k^t) + \lambda \mathcal{L}_{KL}(q(v_k^t)||q(w^t)) \quad (6)$$

Here, the degree of local participation in global knowledge is regulated by the hyperparameter λ. The function $F_k(\cdot)$ represents the loss of client k. $\mathcal{L}_{KL}$ represents the KL divergence function between the global model prediction $q(w^t)$ and the current client local prediction $q(v_k^t)$.

In pFedBKD, client k updates client model parameters using function $\Phi_k(v_k^t)$ (instead of $F_k(v_k^t)$). The client model weights v_k are updated via stochastic gradient descent (SGD) as follows:

$$v_k^t = v_k^t - \eta \nabla \Phi_k(v_k^t, w_t) \quad (7)$$

where η represents the learning rate.

We will also calculate the Jensen-Shannon (JS) divergence between the updated client-side local model on its private training set and the predictions of the global model parameters.

$$\mathcal{L}_{JS}(q(v_k^{t+1})||q(w^t)) = \frac{1}{2}\mathcal{L}_{KL}(q(v_k^{t+1})||\frac{q(v_k^{t+1}) + q(w^t)}{2}) + \frac{1}{2}\mathcal{L}_{KL}(q(w^t)||\frac{q(v_k^{t+1}) + q(w^t)}{2}) \quad (8)$$

JS divergence is symmetric compared to KL divergence. Symmetry assumes that there are two probability distributions, P and Q; choosing P as the reference distribution and Q as the reference distribution will have the same result. The calculated JS divergence values and updated client model parameters are subsequently transferred to the server.

5.3. Calculate Aggregated Weights Based on Global and Local Biases

In the traditional FedAvg algorithm, the contribution of each client is measured by the amount of data (in general, the number of client data sets is equal in the experimental environment). Due to the data heterogeneity among the various clients, the data distribution of the client is inconsistent with the global data distribution. When the model weight is aggregated on the server side, a new way to measure the aggregated weight is needed. Due to the limitations of other methods, we use the JS divergence value mentioned in the previous section. The greater the JS value of a particular client, the greater the deviation between its data and global distribution. To mitigate the influence of the local deviation from the global distribution during aggregation, it should give a smaller weight, and the aggregation weight β_t^k is calculated as follows:

$$\beta_t^k = \frac{1/\mathcal{L}_{JS}(q(v_k^{t+1}), q(w^t))}{\sum_{k=1}^{K} 1/\mathcal{L}_{JS}(q(v_k^{t+1}), q(w^t))} \quad (9)$$

To create the next iteration of the global model w^{t+1}, each client submits the revised model parameters, which are then combined on the server side based on the aggregation weight:

$$w^{t+1} = \sum_{k=1}^{K} \beta_t^k v_k^{t+1} \quad (10)$$

6. Experiment Results

The following experiments showcase the efficacy of our approach and investigate the influence of alterations in hyperparameters $\{\lambda, \tau\}$ on performance.

6.1. Dataset

Our experiments used two open-source data sets, Widar3.0 [6] and UT-HAR [31]. We verified that our method performs well in cross-domain situations in Widar3.0. In order to improve the robustness and comprehensiveness of our method, we expanded the scope of the study. We used UT-HAR to verify the effectiveness of our method further.

Widar3.0 [6] contains WiFi data from 17 users and three environments. In Widar3.0, not all users have taken corresponding actions in each environment. Therefore, to better verify various cross-domain challenges, we use six actions, namely push and pull, scan, tap, slide, draw O and zigzag. Widar3.0 makes detailed annotations for each data user and environment. Therefore, we can easily set up various cross-domain (including cross-person and cross-environment) experiments to verify our solution.

UT-HAR [31] is a CSI dataset including six users and seven actions. We use all its data in our experiments. In UT-HAR, we use the Dirichlet distribution [46] to control the degree of heterogeneity, recorded as $Dir(\rho)$. The smaller the ρ, the more heterogeneous the setting.

6.2. Settings

In this article, whenever Widar3.0 appears in the comparison experiment, the experimental data set uses Widar3.0. Otherwise, the data set used is UTHAR. In pFedBKD, we first set up a complex scenario to simulate the natural environment. That is, there is heterogeneity between different client environments, and users also have heterogeneity.

Moreover, we test the performance of our method in cross-environment and cross-person situations, respectively.

We keep the parameter settings consistent with standard work. Unless otherwise stated, each client runs for five epochs per round by default and communicates for 100 rounds. The ratio of training set to test set in the client is 7:3. We use the Adam optimizer in Widar3.0, setting the weight decay to 0, the momentum to 0.9, and the learning rate to 0.001. In the UT-HAR experiment, we used the SGD optimizer with a weight decay 1×10^{-6}. and a learning rate of 0.01.

In Widar3.0 for each task, the training batch size is $B = 128$, while in UT-HAR, the training batch size is $B = 64$. μ_1 is selected for FedProx from {0.001, 0.01, 0.1, 1}. Ditto controls the hyperparameter μ_2 of local update, and we choose among {0.01, 0.1, 0.5, 1, 2}. We choose λ from {0.1, 0.3, 0.5} for our technique, and we modify the temperature τ from $\{1, 10\}$.

Our method is implemented with Python 3.8. The deep learning library of torch v.1.11.0 is used for coding and implementation, and TensorFlow v.2.3 is used as the back-end for the model. The hardware platform we used was a desktop with a 3.40 GHz AMD Ryzen 7 5800 eight-core processor CPU, 48 GB RAM, and an NVIDIA GeForce RTX 3070 GPU.

6.3. Model Structure

This article uses two model structures corresponding to the data sets Widar3.0 and UT-HAR, respectively. Regarding Widar3.0: first, there are two 3×3 convolution blocks for extracting spatial features. Then, there is a 2×2 max pooling layer for feature dimensionality reduction, followed by two fully connected layers. We utilize a gated recurrent unit (GRU) to extract dynamic features from BVP since it is time series data. Compared with long short-term memory (LSTM) [47], GRU can achieve comparable results using fewer parameters. To prevent overfitting, we introduce a dropout layer. To obtain the prediction result, we employ a fully connected layer as a classifier. Lastly, input the softmax classifier. Regarding UT-HAR: here, we use the classic Multilayer Perceptron (MLP), which consists of three fully connected layers. Use the fully connected layer to extract data features, pass through the hidden layer, and finally output the classification prediction result through the output layer.

6.4. Benchmark

We compare pFedBKD with four baselines. We briefly introduce these baselines as follows.

- Widar3.0 [6]: the technique amalgamates the data from all users involved in the training process.
- FedAvg [16]: upload all client model parameters and average to generate a global model.
- FedProx [26]: using l_2 regularization during local updates, the client's update direction is prevented from deviating too much from the global distribution.
- pFedSD [30]: by saving model parameters after the last round of local updates, it extracts previous personalized knowledge into the local model through knowledge distillation in the new round of updates to accelerate recall.
- Diito [29]: by regularizing the global model parameters, a personalized model is generated for the client to improve the fairness and robustness of FL.

6.5. Experimental Analysis

In cases when there are differences between environments and users, each client stores a user's data, and there are cross-environment and cross-person exchanges between clients. There are 21 clients in total. The performance of our method is still better than other solutions when both cross-domain factors exist, as shown in Figure 3. Our method is more effective in this scenario, and the accuracy rate can reach 0.9, which is far better than other methods. The performance of FedAvg is not as good as that of Widar3.0. FedAvg exhibits suboptimal performance in the presence of significant variation in data between clients. Moreover, the performance of FedProx is not good. Simply adding near-end items on the client side cannot handle this cross-domain problem well. Although pFedSD and Ditto have achieved some results, it still has a particular gap with our method because it ignores the incompatibility between local knowledge.

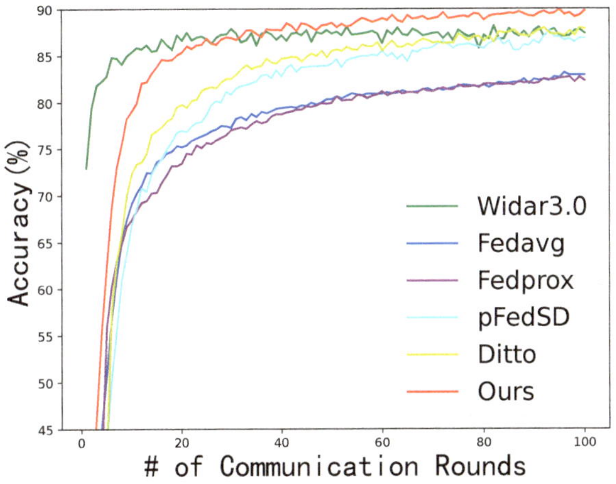

Figure 3. Comparison between pFedBKD and other methods in the case of differences in users and environments.

When there are differences in the environment: Table 1 displays a comparison of different approaches for the same users in different rooms. Furthermore, it is apparent that the precision of the majority of techniques increases with the growing number of individuals involved. As the overall user participation in training diminishes, specifically when the total number of datasets falls, the performance of all approaches also declines. In the case of significant client heterogeneity, the performance performance between FedProx and FedAvg is lower because they ignore the needs of client personalization. Due to the cross-environment advantage of the BVP dataset, most methods are inferior to the training results of Widar3.0, but our method still has advantages. In Widar3.0, there are only three of the same users in room 1 and room 2, namely user 1, user 2, and user 3. To mitigate the impact of user variations, we just utilize these three individuals for experimental purposes. Since the training does not involve many user data, the accuracy of all methods is low in this case.

Table 1. On the data set Widar3.0, the accuracy of different methods is compared when there are cross-environment differences. The client belongs to room 1 or room 2.

User Num	Widar3.0	FedAvg	FedProx	pFedSD	Ditto	Ours
Users = 1	0.805	0.788	0.806	0.832	0.823	0.833
Users = 2	0.844	0.804	0.831	0.851	0.838	0.854
Users = 3	0.851	0.823	0.839	0.855	0.852	0.862

When there are differences in users: the accuracy of pFedBKD in Table 2 can exceed 0.85 in room 1 and reach 0.89 when the number of users reaches 12. Overall, pFedBKD has better performance than other methods. The benefit of pFedBKD diminishes as the level of data heterogeneity diminishes. Conversely, as the level of variation in data rises, the advantages of pFedBKD over alternative methods become increasingly apparent. We can see that the performance of FedAvg and FedProx is average in the experiment. When the number of users participating in training is four and eight, the performance of pFedSD is second only to ours and better than that of other methods. When the number of participants in training reaches 12, Ditto's performance exceeds pFedSD. However, there is still a gap between it and our method. Our method considers the impact of mitigating the incompatibility of global knowledge and local knowledge on the client side and the impact between local knowledge on the server, which makes our method perform better.

Table 2. On the data set Widar3.0, the accuracy of each method is compared when there are cross-person differences. All clients' environments belong to room 1.

User Num	Widar3.0	FedAvg	FedProx	pFedSD	Ditto	Ours
Users = 4	0.819	0.812	0.784	0.845	0.841	0.854
Users = 8	0.853	0.816	0.836	0.87	0.867	0.874
Users = 12	0.856	0.799	0.80	0.852	0.869	0.882

Table 3 shows that the performance of all methods exceeds 0.78. As ρ increases, that is, when data heterogeneity between clients decreases, the performance of all methods improves. According to Table 3, we can observe that the performance improvement of FedProx is limited because it only cares about global performance. The performance of pFedSD and Ditto is similar. FedProx only cares about the global model's performance and ignores the local model's personalised needs. pFedSD and Ditto only consider the incompatibility between the global and local models on the client side. In short, our method still maintains the lead under various ρ values.

Table 3. Accuracy comparison under different ρ values in UT-HAR.

$Dir(\rho)$	FedAvg	FedProx	pFedSD	Ditto	Ours
$Dir(0.01)$	0.783	0.797	0.822	0.819	0.845
$Dir(0.05)$	0.866	0.869	0.893	0.886	0.928
$Dir(0.1)$	0.916	0.889	0.936	0.939	0.954

In Figure 4, we demonstrate the variation of performance under different hyperparameters (coefficient λ and temperature τ). We tested various values of τ from the set {1, 5, 10} and λ from the set {0.1, 0.3, 0.5, 0.7}. Generally, $\tau = 1$ yielded better results. Lower temperature values indicate that negative labels were given less attention during distillation.

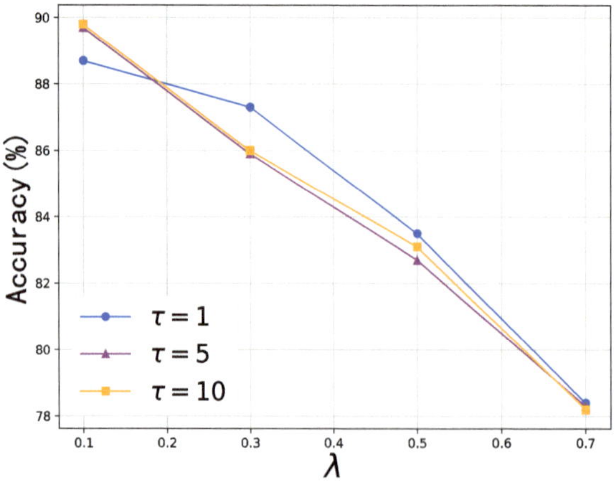

Figure 4. Effects of λ and τ on dataset Widar3.0.

The λ parameter determines the impact of global knowledge on local training, and we maintained a constant value for it throughout our studies. The graph in Figure 4 demonstrates that an increase in the value of λ resulted in a decline in performance. Hence, selecting a modest value for λ is crucial to attain the highest level of accuracy. We also contemplated dynamically modifying the parameter λ by assigning distinct values to clients, contingent upon the global and local model's performance in local test sets.

7. Conclusions

We proposed pFedBKD, an action recognition method based on PFL. To solve the adverse effects of the previous PFL method, pFedBKD designed a method that did not directly use the global model for initialization but indirectly utilized the global knowledge by using KD, avoiding the problem of knowledge forgetting. In the aggregation, the server assigned weights according to the degree of local deviation from the global values, significantly mitigating the influence of data heterogeneity. The experimental results unequivocally demonstrated that pFedBKD effectively mitigated the problem of model accuracy degradation stemming from the heterogeneity of data features among clients.

Author Contributions: Conceptualization, H.G., D.D. and P.J.; methodology, H.G.; software, H.G.; validation, H.G. and W.Z.; formal analysis, H.G.; investigation, H.G.; resources, W.Z.; data curation, H.G.; writing—original draft preparation, H.G.; writing—review and editing, H.G. and D.D.; visualization, H.G.; supervision, X.W.; project administration, X.W.; funding acquisition, X.W. All authors have read and agreed to the published version of the manuscript.

Funding: This research was funded by the National Nature Science Foundation of China, grant number 62172003; the University Synergy Innovation Program of Anhui Province, grant number GXXT-2022-051; the Natural Science Foundation of Anhui Provincial Education Department, grant number YJS20210350.

Data Availability Statement: The Widar3.0 data set used in this study comes from Tsinghua University. The link is http://tns.thss.tsinghua.edu.cn/widar3.0/, and the access date is 2 September 2023; The link of the UT-HAR data set is https://github.com/xyanchen/WiFi-CSI-Sensing-Benchmark, and the access date is 2 September 2023.

Conflicts of Interest: The authors declare no conflict of interest.

References

1. Zou, H.; Zhou, Y.; Yang, J.; Jiang, H.; Xie, L.; Spanos, C.J. WiFi-enabled device-free gesture recognition for smart home automation. In Proceedings of the 2018 IEEE 14th International Conference on Control and Automation (ICCA), Anchorage, AK, USA, 12–15 June 2018; pp. 476–481.
2. Zhang, B.B.; Zhang, D.; Li, Y.; Hu, Y.; Chen, Y. Unsupervised Domain Adaptation for RF-based Gesture Recognition. *IEEE Internet Things J.* **2023**, *10*, 21026–21038. [CrossRef]
3. Shahzad, M.; Zhang, S. Augmenting user identification with WiFi based gesture recognition. *Proc. Acm Interactive Mobile Wearable Ubiquitous Technol.* **2018**, *2*, 1–27. [CrossRef]
4. Fu, Z.; Xu, J.; Zhu, Z.; Liu, A.X.; Sun, X. Writing in the air with WiFi signals for virtual reality devices. *IEEE Trans. Mob. Comput.* **2018**, *18*, 473–484. [CrossRef]
5. Polo, A.; Capra, F.; Lusa, S.; Rocca, P.; Salas-Sánchez, A.Á.; Salucci, M. Machine Learning-based Inversion of Wireless Signals for Real-Time Gesture Recognition. In Proceedings of the 2023 12th International Conference on Modern Circuits and Systems Technologies (MOCAST), Athens, Greece, 28–30 June 2023; pp. 1–3.
6. Zheng, Y.; Zhang, Y.; Qian, K.; Zhang, G.; Liu, Y.; Wu, C.; Yang, Z. Zero-Effort Cross-Domain Gesture Recognition with Wi-Fi. In Proceedings of the 17th Annual International Conference on Mobile Systems, Applications, and Services, New York, NY, USA, 17–21 June 2019; pp. 313–325.
7. Xiao, C.; Lei, Y.; Ma, Y.; Zhou, F.; Qin, Z. DeepSeg: Deep-learning-based activity segmentation framework for activity recognition using WiFi. *IEEE Internet Things J.* **2021**, *8*, 5669–5681. [CrossRef]
8. Li, X.; Song, F.; Luo, M.; Li, K.; Chang, L.; Chen, X.; Wang, Z. Caring: Towards Collaborative and Cross-domain Wi-Fi Sensing. *IEEE Trans. Mob. Comput.* **2023**, *2023*, 1–14. [CrossRef]
9. Liu, S.; Chen, Z.; Wu, M.; Wang, H.; Xing, B.; Chen, L. Generalizing Wireless Cross-Multiple-Factor Gesture Recognition to Unseen Domains. *IEEE Trans. Mob. Comput.* **2023**, *2023*, 1–14. [CrossRef]
10. Zhang, C.; Jiao, W. ImgFi: A High Accuracy and Lightweight Human Activity Recognition Framework Using CSI Image. *IEEE Sens. J.* **2023**, *23*, 21966–21977. [CrossRef]

11. Truex, S.; Baracaldo, N.; Anwar, A.; Steinke, T.; Ludwig, H.; Zhang, R.; Zhou, Y. A Hybrid Approach to Privacy-Preserving Federated Learning. In Proceedings of the 12th ACM Workshop on Artificial Intelligence and Security, New York, NY, USA, 15 November 2019; pp. 1–11.
12. Mothukuri, V.; Parizi, R.M.; Pouriyeh, S.; Huang, Y.; Dehghantanha, A.; Srivastava, G. A survey on security and privacy of federated learning. *Future Gener. Comput. Syst.* **2021**, *115*, 619–640. [CrossRef]
13. Zhang, T.; Xu, C.; Shen, J.; Kuang, X.; Grieco, L.A. How to Disturb Network Reconnaissance: A Moving Target Defense Approach Based on Deep Reinforcement Learning. *IEEE Trans. Inf. Forensics Secur.* **2023**, *18*, 5735–5748. [CrossRef]
14. Zhang, T.; Xu, C.; Zou, P.; Tian, H.; Kuang, X.; Yang, S.; Zhong, L.; Niyato, D. How to mitigate DDOS intelligently in SD-IOV: A moving target defense approach. *IEEE Trans. Ind. Inform.* **2023**, *19*, 1097–1106. [CrossRef]
15. Niknam, S.; Dhillon, H.S.; Reed, J.H. Federated learning for wireless communications: Motivation, opportunities, and challenges. *IEEE Commun. Mag.* **2020**, *58*, 46–51. [CrossRef]
16. McMahan, B.; Moore, E.; Ramage, D.; Hampson, S.; Arcas, B.A.y. Communication-Efficient Learning of Deep Networks from Decentralized Data. In Proceedings of the Machine Learning Research, Proceedings of the 20th International Conference on Artificial Intelligence and Statistics, Seattle, WA, USA, 20–22 April 2017; Volume 54, pp. 1273–1282.
17. Zhao, Y.; Li, M.; Lai, L.; Suda, N.; Civin, D.; Chandra, V. Federated learning with non-iid data. *arXiv* **2018**, arXiv:1806.00582.
18. Sattler, F.; Wiedemann, S.; Müller, K.R.; Samek, W. Robust and communication-efficient federated learning from non-iid data. *IEEE Trans. Neural Netw. Learn. Syst.* **2019**, *31*, 3400–3413. [CrossRef] [PubMed]
19. Wang, H.; Kaplan, Z.; Niu, D.; Li, B. Optimizing federated learning on non-iid data with reinforcement learning. In Proceedings of the IEEE INFOCOM 2020-IEEE Conference on Computer Communications, Virtual Conference, 6–9 July 2020; pp. 1698–1707.
20. Zhu, H.; Xu, J.; Liu, S.; Jin, Y. Federated learning on non-IID data: A survey. *Neurocomputing* **2021**, *465*, 371–390. [CrossRef]
21. Zhang, Y.; Chen, Y.; Wang, Y.; Liu, Q.; Cheng, A. CSI-based human activity recognition with graph few-shot learning. *IEEE Internet Things J.* **2022**, *9*, 4139–4151. [CrossRef]
22. Zhang, X.; Tang, C.; Yin, K.; Ni, Q. WiFi-based cross-domain gesture recognition via modified prototypical networks. *IEEE Internet Things J.* **2021**, *9*, 8584–8596. [CrossRef]
23. Xiao, R.; Liu, J.; Han, J.; Ren, K. OneFi: One-Shot Recognition for Unseen Gesture via COTS WiFi. In Proceedings of the 19th ACM Conference on Embedded Networked Sensor Systems, New York, NY, USA, 15–17 November 2021; pp. 206–219.
24. Wu, K.; Xiao, J.; Yi, Y.; Chen, D.; Luo, X.; Ni, L.M. CSI-based indoor localization. *IEEE Trans. Parallel Distrib. Syst.* **2012**, *24*, 1300–1309. [CrossRef]
25. Yang, Z.; Zhou, Z.; Liu, Y. From RSSI to CSI: Indoor localization via channel response. *ACM Comput. Surv. CSUR* **2013**, *46*, 1–32. [CrossRef]
26. Li, T.; Sahu, A.K.; Zaheer, M.; Sanjabi, M.; Talwalkar, A.; Smith, V. Federated Optimization in Heterogeneous Networks. In *Proceedings of Machine Learning and Systems*; Dhillon, I., Papailiopoulos, D., Sze, V., Eds.; Springer: Berlin/Heidelberg, Germany, 2020; Volume 2, pp. 429–450.
27. Karimireddy, S.P.; Kale, S.; Mohri, M.; Reddi, S.; Stich, S.; Suresh, A.T. SCAFFOLD: Stochastic Controlled Averaging for Federated Learning. In Proceedings of the 37th International Conference on Machine Learning, Online, 13–18 July 2020; Volume 119, pp. 5132–5143.
28. Zhang, M.; Sapra, K.; Fidler, S.; Yeung, S.; Alvarez, J.M. Personalized Federated Learning with First Order Model Optimization. In Proceedings of the International Conference on Learning Representations, Virtual Event, 3–7 May 2021; pp. 1–17.
29. Li, T.; Hu, S.; Beirami, A.; Smith, V. Ditto: Fair and robust federated learning through personalization. In Proceedings of the International Conference on Machine Learning, Virtual Event, 18–24 July 2021; pp. 6357–6368.
30. Jin, H.; Bai, D.; Yao, D.; Dai, Y.; Gu, L.; Yu, C.; Sun, L. Personalized edge intelligence via federated self-knowledge distillation. *IEEE Trans. Parallel Distrib. Syst.* **2023**, *34*, 567–580. [CrossRef]
31. Yang, J.; Chen, X.; Zou, H.; Lu, C.X.; Wang, D.; Sun, S.; Xie, L. SenseFi: A library and benchmark on deep-learning-empowered WiFi human sensing. *Patterns* **2023**, *4*, 1–22. [CrossRef]
32. Chen, Y.; Qin, X.; Wang, J.; Yu, C.; Gao, W. FedHealth: A Federated Transfer Learning Framework for Wearable Healthcare. *IEEE Intell. Syst.* **2020**, *35*, 83–93. [CrossRef]
33. Sozinov, K.; Vlassov, V.; Girdzijauskas, S. Human activity recognition using federated learning. In Proceedings of the 2018 IEEE International Conference on Parallel & Distributed Processing with Applications, Ubiquitous Computing & Communications, Big Data & Cloud Computing, Social Computing & Networking, Sustainable Computing & Communications (ISPA/IUCC/BDCloud/SocialCom/SustainCom), Melbourne, Australia, 11–13 December 2018; pp. 1103–1111.
34. Bettini, C.; Civitarese, G.; Presotto, R. Personalized semi-supervised federated learning for human activity recognition. *arXiv* **2021**, arXiv:2104.08094.
35. Xiao, Z.; Xu, X.; Xing, H.; Song, F.; Wang, X.; Zhao, B. A federated learning system with enhanced feature extraction for human activity recognition. *Knowl. Based Syst.* **2021**, *229*, 107338. [CrossRef]
36. Hernandez, S.M.; Bulut, E. WiFederated: Scalable WiFi Sensing Using Edge-Based Federated Learning. *IEEE Internet Things J.* **2022**, *9*, 12628–12640. [CrossRef]
37. Ouyang, X.; Xie, Z.; Zhou, J.; Huang, J.; Xing, G. ClusterFL: A Similarity-Aware Federated Learning System for Human Activity Recognition. In Proceedings of the 19th Annual International Conference on Mobile Systems, Applications, and Services, New York, NY, USA, 24 June–2 July 2021; pp. 54–66.

38. Zhang, L.; Shen, L.; Ding, L.; Tao, D.; Duan, L.Y. Fine-Tuning Global Model via Data-Free Knowledge Distillation for Non-IID Federated Learning. In Proceedings of the IEEE/CVF Conference on Computer Vision and Pattern Recognition (CVPR), New Orleans, LA, USA, 18–24 June 2022; pp. 10174–10183.
39. Zhang, J.; Guo, S.; Ma, X.; Wang, H.; Xu, W.; Wu, F. Parameterized Knowledge Transfer for Personalized Federated Learning. In *Proceedings of the Advances in Neural Information Processing Systems*; Ranzato, M., Beygelzimer, A., Dauphin, Y., Liang, P., Vaughan, J.W., Eds.; Curran Associates, Inc.: Red Hook, NY, USA, 2021; Volume 34, pp. 10092–10104.
40. Chen, Y.; Sun, X.; Jin, Y. Communication-Efficient Federated Deep Learning with Layerwise Asynchronous Model Update and Temporally Weighted Aggregation. *IEEE Trans. Neural Netw. Learn. Syst.* **2020**, *31*, 4229–4238. [CrossRef] [PubMed]
41. Huang, Y.; Chu, L.; Zhou, Z.; Wang, L.; Liu, J.; Pei, J.; Zhang, Y. Personalized Cross-Silo Federated Learning on Non-IID Data. *Proc. Aaai Conf. Artif. Intell.* **2021**, *35*, 7865–7873. [CrossRef]
42. Jiang, W.; Miao, C.; Ma, F.; Yao, S.; Wang, Y.; Yuan, Y.; Xue, H.; Song, C.; Ma, X.; Koutsonikolas, D.; et al. Towards Environment Independent Device Free Human Activity Recognition. In Proceedings of the 24th Annual International Conference on Mobile Computing and Networking, New Delhi, India, 29 October–2 November 2018; pp. 289–304.
43. Armada, A.G. Understanding the effects of phase noise in orthogonal frequency division multiplexing (OFDM). *IEEE Trans. Broadcast.* **2001**, *47*, 153–159. [CrossRef]
44. Li, X.; Li, S.; Zhang, D.; Xiong, J.; Wang, Y.; Mei, H. Dynamic-MUSIC: Accurate Device-Free Indoor Localization. In Proceedings of the 2016 ACM International Joint Conference on Pervasive and Ubiquitous Computing, Heidelberg, Germany, 12–16 September 2016; pp. 196–207.
45. Qian, K.; Wu, C.; Yang, Z.; Liu, Y.; Jamieson, K. Widar: Decimeter-Level Passive Tracking via Velocity Monitoring with Commodity Wi-Fi. In Proceedings of the 18th ACM International Symposium on Mobile Ad Hoc Networking and Computing, Chennai, India, 10–14 July 2017; pp. 1–10.
46. Lin, T.; Kong, L.; Stich, S.U.; Jaggi, M. Ensemble distillation for robust model fusion in federated learning. *Adv. Neural Inf. Process. Syst.* **2020**, *33*, 2351–2363.
47. Zhang, T.; Xu, C.; Lian, Y.; Tian, H.; Kang, J.; Kuang, X.; Niyato, D. When Moving Target Defense Meets Attack Prediction in Digital Twins: A Convolutional and Hierarchical Reinforcement Learning Approach. *IEEE J. Sel. Areas Commun.* **2023**, *41*, 3293–3305. [CrossRef]

electronics

MDPI

Article

Mobile Sensoring Data Verification via a Pairing-Free Certificateless Signature Secure Approach against Novel Public Key Replacement Attacks

Guilin Wang [1], Hua Shen [2], Liquan Chen [1], Jinguang Han [1] and Ge Wu [1,*]

[1] School of Cyber Science and Engineering, Southeast University, Nanjing 210096, China; wglin@seu.edu.cn (G.W.)
[2] School of Computer Science, Hubei University of Technology, Wuhan 430068, China
* Correspondence: gewu@seu.edu.cn

Abstract: To achieve flexible sensing coverage with low deployment costs, mobile users need to contribute their equipment as sensors. Data integrity is one of the most fundamental security requirements and can be verified by digital signature techniques. In the mobile crowdsensing (MCS) environment, most sensors, such as smartphones, are resource-limited. Therefore, many traditional cryptographic algorithms that require complex computations cannot be efficiently implemented on these sensors. In this paper, we study the security of certificateless signatures, in particular, some constructions without pairing. We notice that there is no secure pairing-free certificateless signature scheme against the super adversary. We also find a potential attack that has not been fully addressed in previous studies. To handle these two issues, we propose a concrete secure construction that can withstand this attack. Our scheme does not rely on pairing operations and can be applied in scenarios where the devices' resources are limited.

Keywords: mobile sensors; data integrity; certificateless signature; public key replacement attack; pairing-free

1. Introduction

Various mobile sensors are utilized in IoT devices to perform real-time data detection. These sensors capture sensitive information such as vehicle status, power system data, and personal health information, among others. Once collected, the data are transmitted to a central server for processing, making data security a critical consideration. To ensure data credibility and reliability, the use of digital signatures for integrity verification and message tracing is imperative for these sensing devices. Given the limited hardware resources of these devices, signature schemes with less complex pairing computations are preferred. Over the last few decades, the public key infrastructure/certificate authority (PKI/CA) system has been extensively employed. Within this system, upper layers issue certificates for lower layers, constructing a chain of trust from the trusted root to individual entities. However, many signature schemes reliant on the PKI/CA system introduce complex certificate management challenges, including distribution, update, and revocation, which are often financially burdensome for sensor devices.

Shamir [1] proposed identity-based cryptography (IBC) as a solution to eliminate the need for certificates. This approach allows users to directly generate their public keys from identity information, such as the IP. The private key generator (PKG) is responsible for holding the system master key and using it to generate all user's private keys. By bypassing the need for certificates, IBC ensures the correctness of public key generation directly from identity information. Despite this advantage, the system's security heavily relies on the PKG. Consequently, a key escrow problem arises, as every private key is generated by the PKG, who then has the capability to arbitrarily compromise the security of the scheme.

Consequently, if the PKG is breached or lacks full trust, the safety of the entire system is compromised, leaving no user immune to potential security breaches.

Al-Riyami and Paterson [2] introduced certificateless public key cryptography (CLPKC) as a solution to the shortcomings of existing systems. In CLPKC, the key generation center (KGC) is responsible for controlling the master private key and differs from traditional PKI/CA systems in that it only generates a portion of the private key for users. Users must independently select and safeguard a secret value, using it to calculate both the complete private key and public key. As a result, the explicit binding of public keys and identity information through certificates is eliminated. Instead, the implicit binding of identity and public key occurs through the use of partial private keys, ensuring that only a valid user can generate a valid private key. Although KGC has ownership of the master private key, the secret values remain unknown. Consequently, CLPKC resolves the issue of key escrow in the IBC and eliminates the need for certificates in PKI/CA systems. Yet, the complexity and power of adversaries increase, posing new challenges. Consequently, there is ongoing research to comprehensively evaluate adversary capabilities and develop a fully secure CLPKC scheme.

1.1. Related Works

In 2003, Al-Riyami and Paterson [2] introduced the CLPKC system, which was based on the IBE scheme proposed by Boneh and Franklin [3] in 2001, and included an adversary model and security definition. However, their signature scheme was compromised by Huang et al. in 2005 [4]. Meanwhile, Yum and Lee developed general secure constructions for signature schemes (CLS) [5] and encryption schemes (CLE) [6] in 2004, which were constructed on a PKI/CA scheme and an IBC scheme. Despite this, subsequent work by Hu et al. [7] and Libert et al. [8] in 2006 demonstrated the insecurity of Yum and Lee's general construction. In response to the threat posed by malicious KGC, Au et al. further fortified the security model of CLPKC in 2006 and determined that a class of schemes with the same key structure may be vulnerable under malicious KGC and unable to address key escrow issues [9]. Building on this, Huang et al. revisited the CLPKC security model in 2007, categorizing adversaries into three levels: Normal, Strong, and Super adversaries. In addition, they proposed a secure CLS scheme specifically designed to withstand super adversaries [10].

A number of CLPKC schemes have been proposed; they aim to address the limitations of pairing operations, which can be expensive and inefficient in lightweight equipment like mobile sensors. Baek et al. [11] introduced the first CLPKC scheme without pairing operations, using the Schnorr signature [12]. However, Sun et al. [13] identified some drawbacks in Baek's approach and subsequently developed a new CLE scheme. Notably, Zhang and Mao [14] also devised a CLS scheme using the RSA signature. Despite this, Xu et al. [15] highlighted a flaw in the CLS scheme proposed by Gowri et al. [16], revealing that their signatures were susceptible to forgery. In response, Xu et al. [15] proposed a secure CLS scheme designed to withstand normal adversaries. Additionally, Karati et al. [17] developed a highly efficient CLS scheme by eliminating the map-to-point hash function, although Zhang et al. [18] later discovered that this scheme was vulnerable to breach through the replacement of the public key. Several other CLS schemes [19–24] were also proposed but were ultimately proven to be weak. More recently, Du et al. [25] and Xiang et al. [26] put forth two super-secure CLS schemes, but their security proofs were found to be incorrect, particularly with regard to the divisor always being calculated as zero when addressing underlying difficulties.

1.2. Motivations

In the CLS secure model, adversaries are categorized into two types. Type I adversaries have the capability to replace the public key with any string. In the security proof, the simulator must provide the correct signature in response to a signature inquiry, irrespective of whether the public key has been replaced. Not only that, the question arises of whether this signature should be valid before or after the replacement. Different levels of adversaries are defined by Huang based on this distinction, namely normal, strong, and super. The primary differentiator among these levels is the validity of the signatures they are able to obtain. A normal adversary may obtain a signature that is valid before the replacement, while a strong adversary may obtain a signature that is valid after the replacement, only if it supplies the corresponding secret values. On the other hand, a super adversary has the ability to replace the public key with a new key and receive a valid signature under the new key. In 2011, Huang introduced the first super security certificateless signature scheme using pairing. Subsequent works attempted to propose a secure CLS scheme without pairing, but the majority failed to achieve security against the super adversary.

Among the proposed pairing-free CLS schemes, the partial private key is typically calculated through Schnorr signature [12], which includes a random number R. It is important to note that this random number should be publicly available in the public key. Consequently, a $TypeI$ adversary has the ability to query for a partial private key and replace the public key, and the order of these two operations is not limited. Furthermore, the presence of super adversaries introduces the potential for them to substitute the private key without providing the new secret value. This vulnerability becomes even more pronounced when the adversary first replaces the random number with a new one and then requests the new partial private key under the new number, rendering existing schemes unable to respond correctly without a new secret value. It is essential to recognize that this vulnerability has been previously overlooked in CLS schemes that do not involve pairing.

1.3. Contributions

- Under the ECDLP assumption, this paper proposes a secure CLS scheme without pairing. Our work includes completing the security proof against super adversaries in the ROM, as shown by [10].
- We fix the weakness that the simulator of the CLS scheme using Schnorr signatures could not answer partial private key queries after replacing the public key. Specifically, we adjusted the structure of the public key to partially restrict these queries
- Our signature scheme breaks away from pairing operations and the signature length is only two group elements, achieving a balance between computational efficiency and transmission costs.

1.4. Structure

In Section 2, we present the outline of CLS schemes and the security model. In Section 3, we introduce our secure CLS scheme without pairing, and in Section 4, we demonstrate its security. Section 5 analyzes the efficiency of our scheme, while Section 6 provides a summary of this paper.

2. Certificateless Signature Schemes

2.1. Construction

A CLS scheme usually involves three parties: the KGC, one user who signs a message, and another user who verifies the signature and consists of six algorithms:

- **Setup(λ).** KGC runs this algorithm with inputting security parameter λ. The final output is the system public parameters PP and the system master secret key msk. KGC publishes PP and keeps msk private.
- **PartialPrivateKey(PP, msk, ID).** KGC runs this algorithm with inputting PP, msk and a user identity ID. Then KGC must distribute the output as user partial private key D_{ID} securely.
- **SecretValue(PP, ID).** A user runs this algorithm by inputting PP and ID. The final output serves as the secret value x_{ID}.
- **PublicKey(PP, ID, x_{ID}, D_{ID}).** A user runs this algorithm with inputting PP, ID, x_{ID} and D_{ID}. The output serves as its public key PK_{ID} and should be published.

- **Sign($PP, m, ID, x_{ID}, D_{ID}$).** A user runs this algorithm with inputting PP, a message m, ID, x_{ID} and D_{ID}. The output serves as the signature σ.
- **Verify($PP, \sigma, m, ID, PK_{ID}$).** A user runs this algorithm with inputting PP, ID, PK_{ID}, m and σ. Then it outputs "1" when validation is successful and otherwise outputs 0.

2.2. Security Models

We consider two types of super adversaries. The $TypeI$ adversaries simulate external attackers who are allowed to replace public keys arbitrarily and get partial private keys and secret values by corrupting some users. The $TypeII$ adversaries simulate the malicious KGC. They own the system master key but are not allowed to replace public keys. In this paper, we prove the security through two games, and the attack ability of adversaries is described by the access to the oracles. Specifically, the following five oracles will be considered.

- ***CreateUser(ID).*** This oracle will reply with a public key. When the ID is queried for the first time, the oracle generates a partial private key, a secret value, and a public key and records all information. It will reply according to records.
- ***PartialPrivateKeyExtract(ID).*** This oracle will reply with a partial private key. When the ID is queried for the first time, the oracle call ***Createuser(ID).*** It will reply according to the records.
- ***SecretValueExtract(ID).*** This oracle will reply with a secret value. When the ID is queried for the first time, the oracle calls ***Createuser(ID).*** It will reply according to the records.
- ***ReplacePublicKey(ID,PK').*** This oracle will change the public key of ID in records. When the ID is queried for the first time, the oracle calls ***Createuser(ID)***. Then it changes the public key to PK' in records.
- ***SuperSign(ID,m).*** The oracle will reply with a legal signature of a message m under the PK and ID in records. Note that the PK may have been replaced and there may be no secret value in records.

Game I : A challenger C interacts with a super $TypeI$ adversary A_1 through Game I. C controls all the oracle and records the interactive information. The complete game processes are as follows:

Init. C runs $Setup$ and transmits PP to A_1.

Query. A_1 can query for the above five oracles adaptively and C must respond correctly.

Forgery. A_1 finally outputs a signature $\sigma*$, a message $m*$, $PK*$ and $ID*$.

If the following equations hold, A_1 wins in Game I.

1. A_1 has not asked for the partial private key of $ID*$,
2. A_1 has not asked for a signature of the message $m*$ under $ID*$ and $PK*$,
3. The signature $\sigma*$ is valid, i.e.,

$$Verify(PP, ID*, PK*, m*, \sigma*) = 1 \tag{1}$$

Game II: The challenger C interacts with a super $TypeII$ adversary A_2 through game II. C controls all the oracle and records the interactive information. The complete game processes are as follows:

Init. C runs the $Setup$ algorithm and transmits both PP and msk to A_2.

Query. A_2 can query for four oracles except for $PartialPrivateKeyExtract(ID)$ adaptively and C must respond correctly. A_2 does not need to ask $PartialPrivateKeyExtract(ID)$ as it knows msk.

Forgery. A_2 finally outputs a signature $\sigma*$, a message $m*$, $PK*$ and $ID*$.

If the following equations hold, A_2 wins in Game II.

1. A_2 has not asked for the secret value of $ID*$,
2. A_2 has not replaced the public key of $ID*$,
3. A_2 has not asked for a signature of $m*$ under $ID*$ and $PK*$,

4. The signature $\sigma*$ is valid, i.e.,

$$Verify(PP, ID*, PK*, m*, \sigma*) = 1 \tag{2}$$

3. Our CLS Scheme

3.1. Security Assumptions

Given an elliptic curve group G of a prime order q, a point P is a generator and another point Q is a random element. The Elliptic Curve Discrete Logarithm Problem (ECDLP) is to calculate $a \in Z_q*$ which satisfies the equation $Q = aP$. Our scheme is secure if the probability of solving the ECDLP is negligible for any probabilistic polynomial-time adversary.

3.2. Scheme Construction

There are six algorithms in our construction.

1. **Setup(λ)**: Inputting a security parameters λ, KGC generates public parameters PP and master secret key msk. First, it randomly generates a prime number q of λ-bits and an elliptic curve group G of order q. It randomly picks a generator $P \in G$, a number $s \in Z_q$ and sets $P_{pub} = sP$. It also selects the cryptography hash functions $< H_0, H_1, H_2, H_3, H_4 >$: $\{0,1\}^* \rightarrow Z_q$. Finally, KGC publishes $PP = \{G, P_{pub}, H_0, H_1, H_2, H_3, H_4\}$ and sets $msk = s$.

2. **PartialPrivateKey(PP, msk, ID)**: When generating the partial private key for ID, KGC inputs PP, msk and ID. Then KGC randomly selects $r, y_{ID} \in Z_q$ and calculates

$$R_{ID} = rP \tag{3}$$

$$d_{ID} = r + sH_1(ID, R_{ID}, P_{pub}) \tag{4}$$

$$Y_{ID} = y_{ID}P \tag{5}$$

$$\pi_{ID} = y_{ID} + sH_0(ID, Y_{ID}, R_{ID}, P_{pub}) \tag{6}$$

The partial private key $D_{ID} =< R_{ID}, d_{ID}, Y_{ID}, \pi_{ID} >$ must be securely transmitted to the user, and its legality can be verified by calculating $h_0 = H_0(ID, Y_{ID}, R_{ID}, P_{pub})$, $h_1 = H_1(ID, R_{ID}, P_{pub})$ and checking whether the equations $d_{ID}P = R_{ID} + h_1P_{pub}$, $\pi_{ID}P = Y_{ID} + h_0P_{pub}$ hold.

3. **SecretValue(PP, ID)**: With inputting PP and ID, the user randomly selects $x_{ID} \in Z_q$ as the secret value.

4. **PublicKey(PP, ID, x_{ID}, D_{ID})**: When generating the public key, the user inputs PP, ID, x_{ID} and D_{ID}. Then it calculates $X_{ID} = x_{ID}P$ and sets public key $PK_{ID} =< R_{ID}, Y_{ID}, X_{ID}, \pi_{ID} >$.

5. **Sign($PP, m, ID, x_{ID}, D_{ID}, PK_{ID}$)**: When signing a message m, the user inputs PP, m, ID, x_{ID} and $D_{ID} =< R_{ID}, d_{ID}, Y_{ID}, \pi_{ID} >$. Then it selects random $t \in Z_q$ and calculates

$$T = tP \tag{7}$$

$$h_2 = H_2(ID, m, PK_{ID}, T) \tag{8}$$

$$h_3 = H_3(ID, m, PK_{ID}, T) \tag{9}$$

$$h_4 = H_4(ID, m, T, PK_{ID}, P_{pub}) \tag{10}$$

$$\tau = t \cdot h_2 + x \cdot h_3 + d_{ID} \cdot h_4 \tag{11}$$

The user sets $\sigma =< T, \tau >$ as the signature.

6. **Verify($PP, m, \sigma, ID, PK_{ID}$)**: When verifying the legitimacy of a message-signature pair, the user inputs PP, m, σ, ID and PK_{ID}. Then it calculates

$$h_1 = H_1(ID, R_{ID}, P_{pub}) \tag{12}$$

$$h_2 = H_2(ID, m, PK_{ID}, T) \tag{13}$$

$$h_3 = H_3(ID, m, PK_{ID}, T) \tag{14}$$

$$h_4 = H_4(ID, m, T, PK_{ID}, P_{pub}) \tag{15}$$

and checks $\tau P = h_2 T + h_3 X_{ID} + h_4(R_{ID} + h_1 P_{pub})$. Finally, it outputs "1" when validation is successful and otherwise outputs "0".

4. Security Proof

Next, we demonstrate the security of our scheme against two super adversaries.

Theorem 1. *In the Random Oracle Model, assuming that ECDLP is difficult in the selected group G, our scheme is existentially unforgeable against super adversaries. This theorem can be obtained from the Lemmas 1 and 2.*

Lemma 1. *Assuming that there exists a super Type-I adversary A_1 who can (ϵ, t)-win $GameI$, then the ECDLP in G must be (ϵ', t')-solved.*

Proof. Given a ECDLP instance $< G, P, Q >$, we construct an algorithm C_1 to (ϵ', t')-calculate a solution by interacting with the adversary A_1. □

H_i are simulated as random oracle and C_1 maintains the tables L_i to record the input *val* and output *res* corresponding to H_i. The $GameI$ runs as follows.

Setup. C_1 randomly selects $ID*$ as the challenge identity, sets $P_{pub} = Q$ and publishes $PP = \{G, P_{pub}, H_0, H_1, H_2, H_3, H_4\}$.

Query. A_1 can adaptively query to C_1 at any time and C_1 will response as follows.

- $Hash_i(val)$. C_1 first checks whether val exists in L_i. If there is a record, C_1 returns $< val, res >$. Otherwise C_1 randomly selects $h_i \in Z_q$, returns $res = h_i$ and insert $< val, res >$ into L_i.
- $CreateUser(ID_i)$. Suppose C_1 queries $CreateUser(ID_i)$ for at most q_u times. It maintains a list L_u and sets a *tag* in L_u to record whether the $< R, Y, \sigma >$ in the public key has been replaced. C_1 returns the public key according to the record if ID_i is found in the list L_u. Otherwise,
  - If $ID_i = ID*$, C_1 randomly selects $r, x, h_1, \pi, h_0 \in Z_q$, calculates $R = rP$, $X = xP$ and sets $H_1(ID, R, P_{pub}) = h_1$, calculates $Y = \pi P - h_0 P_{pub}$ and sets $H_0(ID, Y_{ID}, P_{pub}, R) = h_0$. Then it returns $PK =< R, X, Y, \pi >$ and inserts $< ID*, r, x, h_1, \pi, h_0, R, X, Y, tag = 0 >$ into the table L_u.
  - If $ID_i \neq ID*$, C_1 randomly selects $d, x, h_1, \pi, h_0 \in Z_q$, calculates $R = dP - h_1 P_{pub}, X = xP, Y = \pi P - h_0 P_{pub}$ and sets $H_1(ID, R, P_{pub}) = h_1, H_0(ID, Y, P_{pub}, R) = h_0$. Then return $PK =< R, X, Y, \pi >$ and insert $(ID_i, d, x, y, h_1, \pi, h_0, R, X, Y, tag = 0)$ into the table L_u.
- $PartialPrivateKeyExtract(ID_i)$. Suppose C_1 queries this oracle for at most q_{ppk} times.
  - If $ID_i = ID*$, abort the game.
  - Otherwise, C_1 searches the table L_u for ID_i. If ID_i is found and $tag = 0$, return d according to the record directly. If ID_i is found while the $tag = 1$, C_1 checks whether the public key $PK =< R, X, Y, \pi >$ is legal by $h_0 = H_0(ID_i, Y, R, P_{pub})$, $\pi P = Y + h_0 P_{pub}$. If the public key is still valid, we use the forking lemma on $h_0' = H_0(ID_i, Y, R, P_{pub})$ to get a new $< R_1, Y_1, \pi_1 >$ that satisfies $\pi_1 P = Y_1 + h_0' P_{pub}$. Then we can get $\pi = y + h_0 s$, $\pi_1 = y + h_0' s$ and $s = \frac{\pi - \pi_1}{h_0 - h_0'}$ is the solution

to the ECDLP instance. If the public key is invalid, we return nothing. In addition, if ID_i is not found, call $CreateUser(ID_i)$ and then return d_{ID}.

- $SecretValueExtract(ID_i)$.
  - If $ID_i = ID*$, abort the game.
  - Otherwise, C_1 searches the table L_u for ID_i. If ID_i is found $tag = 0$, C_1 returns x_{ID_i} according to the record directly. If ID_i is found while the public key has been replaced without providing x_{ID_i}, C_1 returns nothing. If ID_i is not found, C_1 calls $CreateUser(ID_i)$ and returns x_{ID_i}.
- $ReplacePublicKey(ID_i, PK')$. C_1 searches the table L_u to find ID_i. If ID_i is found, it replaces $< R, Y, X, \pi >$ with PK'. Otherwise, C_1 calls $CreateUser(ID_i)$ and replaces $< R, Y, X, \pi >$ with PK'. C_1 sets $tag = 1$.
- $SuperSign(ID_i, m)$.
  - If $ID = ID^*$ or $tag = 1$, C_1 randomly selects $\tau, h_3, h_4, h_2 \in Z_q$ and calculates $T = h_2^{-1}(\tau P - h_3X - h_4R - h_4h_1P_{pub})$. Then C_1 set $h_2 = H_2(ID_i, m, PK, T)$, $h_3 = H_3(ID_i, m, PK, T)$, $h_4 = H_4(ID_i, m, T, PK, P_{pub})$ in L_2, L_3, L_4. $< T, \tau >$ is valid signature for

$$h_2T + h_3X + h_4(R + h_1P_{pub}) = \tau P \tag{16}$$

    and note that C_1 does not need to know x,
  - If $ID \neq ID^*$ and $tag = 0$, C_1 searches the table L_u to find ID_i. If ID_i is found, C_1 get $< d, x >$. Then C_1 randomly selects $t, h_2, h_3, h_4 \in Z_q$ and sets $h_2 = H_2(ID_i, m, PK, T)$, $h_3 = H_3(ID_i, m, PK, T)$, $h_4 = H_4(ID_i, m, T, PK, P_{pub})$ in L_i. Finally C_1 calculates $\tau = h_2t + h_3x + h_4d$. $< T, \tau >$ is a valid signature.

Forgery. In the end, A_1 outputs $< T, \tau, m, ID >$. If $ID \neq ID*$, aborts. Otherwise, C_1 searches the table L_u to find ID and verifies the signature:

$$h_1 = H_1(ID, R, P_{pub}) \tag{17}$$

$$h_2 = H_2(ID, m, PK, T) \tag{18}$$

$$h_3 = H_3(ID, m, PK, T) \tag{19}$$

$$h_4 = H_4(ID, m, T, PK, P_{pub}) \tag{20}$$

$$\tau P = h_2T + h_3X + h_4(R + h_0P_{pub}) \tag{21}$$

If $tag = 0$, we use the forking lemma on H_4 to get a new output $< T, \tau', m, ID >$. These outputs satisfy $\tau = h_2t + h_3x + h_4d, \tau' = h_2t + h_3x + h_4'd$ so that C_1 can calculate $d = \frac{\tau - \tau'}{h_4 - h_4'}$. If R is not replaced, C_1 owns r and calculates $s = (d - r)/h_1$. s is the solution to the ECDLP instance. If $tag = 1$, we do the same as in $PartialPrivateKeyExtract(ID_i)$ to get s.

C_1 will solve the ECDLP if the following events occur:

- ϵ_1: C_1 never aborts in $GameI$,
- ϵ_2: A_1 generates a valid forgery $< T, \tau, m, ID >$,
- ϵ_3: In the forgery, $ID = ID^*$

So the probability of C_1 is $Pr[\epsilon_1 \wedge \epsilon_2 \wedge \epsilon_3] = Pr[\epsilon_1] \cdot Pr[\epsilon_2|\epsilon_1] \cdot Pr[\epsilon_3|\epsilon_1 \wedge \epsilon_2]$.

C_1 will abort in the $GameI$ if A_1 extracts the partial private key for any userID^*. So $Pr[\epsilon_1] = (1 - 1/q_u)^{q_{ppk}}$. If C_1 does not abort in the $GameI$, A_1 generates a valid forgery with ϵ. So $Pr[\epsilon_2|\epsilon_1] = \epsilon$. As the ID^* is selected randomly, $Pr[\epsilon_3|\epsilon_1 \wedge \epsilon_2] = 1/q_u$. So the probability is $\epsilon' = Pr[\epsilon_1 \wedge \epsilon_2 \wedge \epsilon_3] = Pr[\epsilon_1] \cdot Pr[\epsilon_2|\epsilon_1] \cdot Pr[\epsilon_3|\epsilon_1 \wedge \epsilon_2] = (1 - 1/q_u)^{q_{ppk}} \cdot 1/q_u \cdot \epsilon$.

Lemma 2. *Assuming that there exists a super Type-II adversary A_2 who can (ϵ, t)-win $GameII$, then the ECDLP must be (ϵ, t)-solved.*

Proof. Given a ECDLP instance $< G, P, Q >$, we construct an algorithm C_2 to (ϵ', t')-calculate a solution by interacting with the adversary A_2 . □

H_i are simulated as random oracle and C_2 maintains the tables L_i to record the input val and output res corresponding to H_i. The $GameII$ runs as follows.

Setup. C_2 randomly selects $ID*$ as the challenge identity and $s \in Z_q$ as the msk. Then calculate $P_{pub} = sP$ and public $PP = \{G, P_{pub}, H_0, H_1, H_2, H_3, H_4\}$.

Query. A_2 can adaptively query to C_2 at any time and C_2 will response as follows.

- $Hash_i(val)$. C_2 first checks whether val exists in L_i. If there is a record, C_2 returns $< val, res >$. Otherwise C_2 randomly selects $h_i \in Z_q$, returns $res = h_i$ and inserts $< val, res >$ into L_i
- $CreateUser(ID_i)$. Suppose it queries $CreateUser(ID_i)$ for at most q_u times. C_2 maintains a list L_u and sets a tag in L_u to record whether the public key has been replaced. C_2 returns the public key if ID_i is in the list. Otherwise,
  - If $ID_i = ID^*$, C_2 randomly selects $r, y_{ID}, h_1, h_0 \in Z_q$, calculates $R = rP, Y = yP, d = r + sh_1, \sigma = y_{ID} + d_{ID}h_0$ and sets $H_1(ID, R, P_{pub}) = h_1, H_0(ID, Y_{ID}, mp, R) = h_0, X = Q$. Then it publishes the public key $PK_{ID_i} =< R, X, Y, \sigma >$ and inserts $< ID*, d, r, y_{ID}, 0, h_1, \sigma, h_0, R, X, Y, tag = 0 >$ into the table L_u.
  - If $ID_i \neq ID^*$, C_2 randomly selects $r, x_{ID}, y_{ID}, h_1, h_0 \in Z_q$, calculates $R = rP, Y = yP, X = xP, d_{ID} = r + sH_1, \sigma = y_{ID} + d_{ID}H_0$ and sets $H_1(ID, R, P_{pub}) = h_1, H_0(ID, Y, P_{pub}, R) = h_0$. Then it publishes the public key $PK_{ID_i} =< R, X, Y, \sigma >$ and inserts $< ID_i, d, x, y, h_1, \sigma, h_0, X, Y, R, tag = 0 >$ into the table L_u.
- $PartialPrivateKeyExtract(ID_i)$. Owning the msk, A_2 can arbitrarily finish this query for any ID_i.
- $SecretValueExtract(ID_i)$. Suppose it queries $ExtractSecretValue(ID_i)$ for at most q_{sv} times.
  - If $ID_i = ID*$, abort the game.
  - Otherwise, C_2 searches the table L_u for ID_i.If ID_i is found, it returns x directly. Otherwise, it calls $CreateUser(ID_i)$ and returns x.
- $ReplacePublicKey(ID_i, PK')$. Suppose it queries $ReplacePublicKey(ID_i, PK')$ for at most q_{rp} times.
  - If $ID_i = ID*$, abort the game.
  - Otherwise, C_2 searches the table L_u for ID_i. If ID_i is found, it replaces $< R, Y, X, \sigma >$ with PK'. Otherwise, C_2 calls $CreateUser(ID_i)$, replaces $< R, Y, X, \sigma >$ with PK' and sets $tag = 1$.
- $SuperSign(ID_i, m)$.
  - If $ID = ID^*$ or $tag = 1$, C_2 randomly selects $\tau, h_3, h_4, h_2 \in Z_q$ and calculates $T = (\tau P - h_3X - h_4R - h_4h_1P_{pub})h_2^{-1}$. Then C_2 sets $h_2 = H_2(ID_i, m, PK, T)$, $h_3 = H_3(ID_i, m, PK, T)$, $h_4 = H_4(ID_i, m, T, PK, P_{pub})$ in L_i. $< T, \tau >$ is a valid signature and note that C_2 does not need to know x.
  - If $ID \neq ID^*$ and $tag = 0$, C_2 searches the table L_u to find ID_i. If ID_i is found, C_2 knows $< d, x >$. Otherwise, C_2 calls $CreateUser(ID_i)$ and gets $< d, x >$ for ID_i. Then C_2 randomly selects $t, h_2, h_3, h_4 \in Z_q$ and sets $h_2 = H_2(ID_i, m, PK, T)$, $h_3 = H_3(ID_i, m, PK, T)$, $h_4 = H_4(ID_i, m, T, PK, P_{pub})$ in L_i. Finally C_2 calculates $\tau = h_2t + h_3x + h_4d$. $< T, \tau >$ is valid signature.

- *Forgery*. In the end, A_2 outputs $< T, \tau, m, ID >$. If $ID \neq ID*$, aborts. Otherwise, C_2 searches the table L_u to find ID and verifies the signature as follows:

$$h_1 = H_1(ID, R, P_{pub}) \tag{22}$$
$$h_2 = H_2(ID, m, PK, T) \tag{23}$$
$$h_3 = H_3(ID, m, PK, T) \tag{24}$$
$$h_4 = H_4(ID, m, T, PK, P_{pub}) \tag{25}$$
$$\tau P = h_2 T + h_3 X + h_4(R + h_0 P_{pub}) \tag{26}$$

Use forking lemma on H_3 to get a new $< T, \tau' >$ so that $\tau' = t \cdot h_2 + x \cdot h_3' + d_{ID} \cdot h_4$. Then calculate $x = \frac{\tau - \tau'}{h_3 - h_3'}$ is the solution to the ECDLP.

C_2 will solve the ECDLP if the following events occur:

1. ϵ_1: C_2 never aborts in the $GameI$,
2. ϵ_2: A_2 generates a valid forgery $< T, \tau, m, ID >$,
3. ϵ_3: In the forgery, $ID = ID^*$

So the probability of C_2 is $Pr[\epsilon_1 \wedge \epsilon_2 \wedge \epsilon_3] = Pr[\epsilon_1] \cdot Pr[\epsilon_2|\epsilon_1] \cdot Pr[\epsilon_3|\epsilon_1 \wedge \epsilon_2]$.

C_2 will abort in the $GameII$ if A_2 extracts the secret value or replaces the public key for the user ID^*. So $Pr[\epsilon_1] = (1 - 1/q_u)^{q_{sv}}(1 - 1/q_u)^{q_{rp}}$. If C_2 does not abort in the $GameII$, A_2 generates a valid forgery with ϵ. So $Pr[\epsilon_2|\epsilon_1] = \epsilon$. As the ID^* is selected randomly, $Pr[\epsilon_3|\epsilon_1 \wedge \epsilon_2] = 1/q_u$. So the probability is $\epsilon' = Pr[\epsilon_1 \wedge \epsilon_2 \wedge \epsilon_3] = Pr[\epsilon_1] \cdot Pr[\epsilon_2|\epsilon_1] \cdot Pr[\epsilon_3|\epsilon_1 \wedge \epsilon_2] = (1 - 1/q_u)^{q_{ppk} + q_{rp}} \cdot 1/q_u \epsilon$.

5. Efficiency Analysis

We analyze the efficiency and security of our CLS scheme and compare it with a series of schemes. Among these schemes, Huang et al. [10] designed a secure CLS scheme against super adversaries but relies on pairing. All other solutions do not require pairing and can not be proven to be safe against the super adversary. We conduct simulation experiments in the environment in Table 1 and choose a type-D pairing which is discovered by [27] and constructed on the curve $y^2 = x^3 + ax + b$ over the field F_q for a 160-bit prime q. So the length of a point x-coordinate in G_1 is roughly the same as 160-bit. The embedding degree is 6 so that the size of finite field in G_2 and G_t is 960-bit. The notations and time of different operations are shown in Table 2. The theoretical analysis of all schemes is shown in Table 3. Here $|G_1|, |G_2|$ and $|Z_q|$ denote the element size in G_1, G_2 and Z_q. To make Table 3 clearer, we ignore the insignificant time of A_1, M_t, I_q, A_q and M_q. The time of different schemes is shown in the Figure 1.

It has been observed that several secure certificateless signature schemes have been introduced without utilizing pairing, yet none of them were able to be proven secure against super adversaries. Some of the schemes, which are based on the Schnorr signature, are unable to respond to the super adversary's query when requesting specific private keys after the replacement of the public key. Our proposed solution not only attains security against super adversaries but also rectifies this minor issue, all the while maintaining a reasonable level of efficiency in signing and verifying. While Huang's scheme also achieves security against super adversaries, it relies on pairing operations, leading to increased computational time and signature size compared to our scheme. Consequently, our scheme effectively enhances both security and efficiency, while also addressing a slight deficiency in the security model.

Table 1. Experiment Environment.

CPU	OS	RAM	Compiler&Library
Inter i7-12700 @4.9 GHz	Ubuntu 20.04.1	32GB DDR5	PBC 0.5.14 & GCC 9.4.0

Table 2. Notation and time of the group operation.

Notation	Operation	Time (ms)
A_1	a point addition in G_1	0.0029
M_1	a scalar multiplication in G_1	0.3552
A_2	a point addition in G_2	0.0145
M_2	a scalar multiplication in G_2	2.8250
M_t	a multiplication in G_t	0.0045
Ex_t	a exponential operation in G_t	0.6497
P	a pairing operation : $G_1 \times G_2 \rightarrow G_t$	2.2532
I_q	a inversion operation in Z_q	0.0028
A_q	a addition in Z_q	0.0007
M_q	a multiplication in $Z_q 1$	0.0006

Table 3. Theoretical Analysis.

Scheme	Sign	Verify	PPK	∣Sign∣	∣PK∣	∣PPK∣	Security
[10]	$M_2 + P + 2M_1$	$2M_2 + A_2 + 2P + Ex_t$	M_1	$\|G_1\| + 2\|Zq\|$	$\|G_2\|$	$\|G_1\|$	Super typeI&II
[26]	M_1	$4M_1$	M_1	$\|G_1\| + \|Zq\|$	$2\|G_1\|$	$\|G_1\| + \|Zq\|$	Strong typeI&II
[24]	M_1	$3M_1$	$2M_1$	$\|G_1\| + \|Zq\|$	$\|G_1\|$	$\|G_1\| + \|Zq\|$	Insecure
[28]	M_1	$3M_1$	M_1	$\|G_1\| + \|Zq\|$	$\|G_1\|$	$\|G_1\| + \|Zq\|$	Insecure
[17]	$2M_1 + M_2$	$2Ex_t + P$	M_1	$\|G_2\| + \|G_1\|$	$\|G_2\| + \|G_1\|$	$2\|G_1\|$	Insecure
[16]	M_1	$3M_1$	M_1	$\|G_1\| + \|Zq\|$	$2\|G_1\|$	$\|G_1\| + \|Zq\|$	Insecure
[25]	M_1	$4M_1$	M_1	$\|G_1\| + \|Zq\|$	$2\|G_1\|$	$\|G_1\| + \|Zq\|$	Strong typeI&II
Ours	M_1	$5M_1$	$2M_1$	$\|G_1\| + \|Zq\|$	$3\|G_1\| + \|Zq\|$	$2\|G_1\| + 2\|Zq\|$	Super typeI&II

* The Sign, Verify and PPK denote the operations in *Sign*,*Verify* and *PartialPrivateKey* algorithms. ∣Sign∣, ∣PK∣, and ∣PPK∣ represent the length of the signature, public key, and partial private key. The Security represents the level of adversary that these schemes can resist.

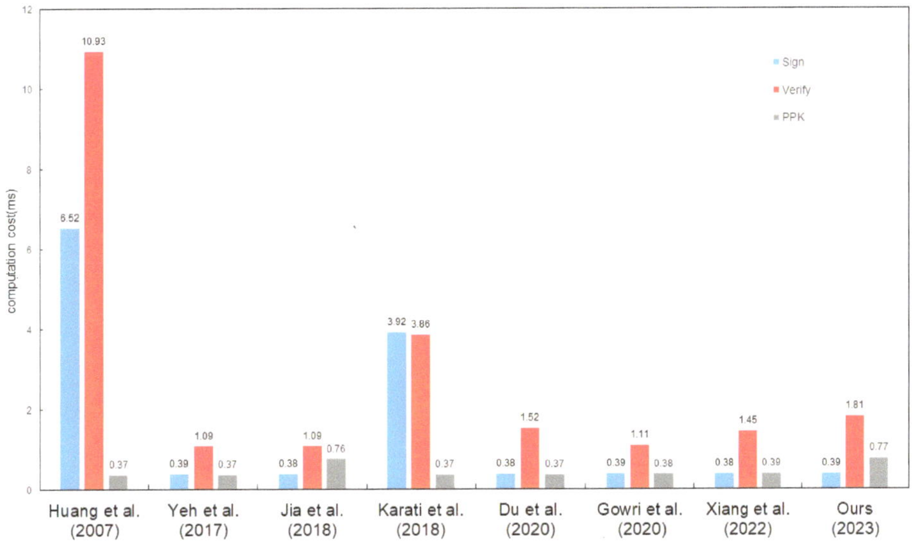

Figure 1. The time of *Sign*,*Verify* and *PartialPrivateKey* algorithms [10,16,17,24–26,28].

6. Conclusions

We find that existing secure CLS schemes against super adversaries often require expensive pairing operations, making them unsuitable for lightweight equipment. Some pairing-free schemes are unable to resist super adversaries and suffer from the issue where the challenger cannot answer partial private key inquiries after replacing the public key. To address these limitations, we have developed a secure CLS scheme against super adversaries without relying on pairing operations, and we have provided comprehensive proof of its security. Experimental testing has demonstrated that our scheme exhibits superior computational efficiency and a smaller signature size compared to schemes offering similar security guarantees.

Author Contributions: Conceptualization, G.W. (Ge Wu); Validation, L.C.; Formal analysis, J.H.; Resources, L.C.; Writing—original draft, G.W. (Guilin Wang); Writing—review & editing, H.S.; Supervision, G.W. (Ge Wu); Project administration, G.W. (Ge Wu). All authors have read and agreed to the published version of the manuscript.

Funding: This work was supported by the National Natural Science Foundation of China (No. 62002058), Natural Science Foundation of Jiangsu Province (No. BK20200391), and Fundamental Research Funds for the Central Universities (No. 2242021R40011).

Institutional Review Board Statement: Not applicable.

Informed Consent Statement: Not applicable.

Data Availability Statement: Data are contained within the article.

Acknowledgments: We would like to thank the anonymous reviewers of this paper for their valuable comments and suggestions.

Conflicts of Interest: The authors declare no conflict of interest.

References

1. Shamir, A. Identity-Based Cryptosystems and Signature Schemes. In Proceedings of the Advances in Cryptology, Proceedings of CRYPTO '84, Santa Barbara, CA, USA, 19–22 August 1984; Blakley, G.R., Chaum, D., Eds.; Lecture Notes in Computer Science; Springer: Berlin/Heidelberg, Germany, 1984; Volume 196, pp. 47–53. [CrossRef]
2. Al-Riyami, S.S.; Paterson, K.G. Certificateless Public Key Cryptography. In Proceedings of the Advances in Cryptology—ASIACRYPT 2003, 9th International Conference on the Theory and Application of Cryptology and Information Security, Taipei, Taiwan, 30 November–4 December 2003; Laih, C., Ed.; Lecture Notes in Computer Science; Springer: Berlin/Heidelberg, Germany, 2003; Volume 2894, pp. 452–473. [CrossRef]
3. Boneh, D.; Franklin, M.K. Identity-Based Encryption from the Weil Pairing. In Proceedings of the Advances in Cryptology—CRYPTO 2001, 21st Annual International Cryptology Conference, Santa Barbara, CA, USA, 19–23 August 2001; Kilian, J., Ed.; Lecture Notes in Computer Science; Springer: Berlin/Heidelberg, Germany, 2001; Volume 2139, pp. 213–229. [CrossRef]
4. Huang, X.; Susilo, W.; Mu, Y.; Zhang, F. On the Security of Certificateless Signature Schemes from Asiacrypt 2003. In Proceedings of the Cryptology and Network Security, 4th International Conference, CANS 2005, Xiamen, China, 14–16 December 2005; Desmedt, Y., Wang, H., Mu, Y., Li, Y., Eds.; Lecture Notes in Computer Science; Springer: Berlin/Heidelberg, Germany, 2005; Volume 3810, pp. 13–25. [CrossRef]
5. Yum, D.H.; Lee, P.J. Generic Construction of Certificateless Signature. In Proceedings of the Information Security and Privacy: 9th Australasian Conference, ACISP 2004, Sydney, Australia, 13–15 July 2004; Wang, H., Pieprzyk, J., Varadharajan, V., Eds.; Lecture Notes in Computer Science; Springer: Berlin/Heidelberg, Germany, 2004; Volume 3108, pp. 200–211. [CrossRef]
6. Yum, D.H.; Lee, P.J. Generic Construction of Certificateless Encryption. In Proceedings of the Computational Science and Its Applications—ICCSA 2004, International Conference, Assisi, Italy, 14–17 May 2004; Proceedings, Part I; Laganà, A., Gavrilova, M.L., Kumar, V., Mun, Y., Tan, C.J.K., Gervasi, O., Eds.; Lecture Notes in Computer Science; Springer: Berlin/Heidelberg, Germany, 2004; Vol. 3043, pp. 802–811. [CrossRef]
7. Hu, B.C.; Wong, D.S.; Zhang, Z.; Deng, X. Key Replacement Attack Against a Generic Construction of Certificateless Signature. In Proceedings of the Information Security and Privacy, 11th Australasian Conference, ACISP 2006, Melbourne, Australia, 3–5 July 2006; Batten, L.M.; Safavi-Naini, R., Eds.; Lecture Notes in Computer Science; Springer: Berlin/Heidelberg, Germany, 2006; Volume 4058, pp. 235–246. [CrossRef]
8. Libert, B.; Quisquater, J. On Constructing Certificateless Cryptosystems from Identity Based Encryption. In Proceedings of the Public Key Cryptography—PKC 2006, 9th International Conference on Theory and Practice of Public-Key Cryptography, New York, NY, USA, 24–26 April 2006; Yung, M., Dodis, Y., Kiayias, A., Malkin, T., Eds.; Lecture Notes in Computer Science; Springer: Berlin/Heidelberg, Germany, 2006; Volume 3958, pp. 474–490. [CrossRef]

9. Au, M.H.; Chen, J.; Liu, J.K.; Mu, Y.; Wong, D.S.; Yang, G. Malicious KGC Attacks in Certificateless Cryptography. *IACR Cryptol. Eprint Arch.* **2006**, 255.
10. Huang, X.; Mu, Y.; Susilo, W.; Wong, D.S.; Wu, W. Certificateless signature revisited. In Proceedings of the Information Security and Privacy: 12th Australasian Conference, ACISP 2007, Townsville, Australia, 2–4 July 2007; Proceedings 12; Springer: Berlin/Heidelberg, Germany, 2007; pp. 308–322.
11. Baek, J.; Safavi-Naini, R.; Susilo, W. Certificateless Public Key Encryption Without Pairing. In Proceedings of the Information Security, 8th International Conference, ISC 2005, Singapore, 20–23 September 2005; Zhou, J.; López, J.; Deng, R.H.; Bao, F., Eds.; Lecture Notes in Computer Science; Springer: Berlin/Heidelberg, Germany, 2005; Volume 3650, pp. 134–148. [CrossRef]
12. Schnorr, C.P. Efficient identification and signatures for smart cards. In Proceedings of the Advances in Cryptology—CRYPTO'89 Proceedings 9, Santa Barbara, CA, USA, 11–15 August 1990; Springer: Berlin/Heidelberg, Germany, 1990; pp. 239–252.
13. Sun, Y.; Zhang, F.; Baek, J. Strongly Secure Certificateless Public Key Encryption Without Pairing. In Proceedings of the Cryptology and Network Security, 6th International Conference, CANS 2007, Singapore, 8–10 December 2007; Lecture Notes in Computer Science; Bao, F., Ling, S., Okamoto, T., Wang, H., Xing, C., Eds.; Springer: Berlin/Heidelberg, Germany, 2007; Volume 4856, pp. 194–208. [CrossRef]
14. Zhang, J.; Mao, J. An efficient RSA-based certificateless signature scheme. *J. Syst. Softw.* **2012**, *85*, 638–642. [CrossRef]
15. Xu, Z.; Luo, M.; Khan, M.K.; Choo, K.R.; He, D. Analysis and Improvement of a Certificateless Signature Scheme for Resource-Constrained Scenarios. *IEEE Commun. Lett.* **2021**, *25*, 1074–1078. [CrossRef]
16. Gowri, T.; Rao, G.S.; Reddy, P.V.; Gayathri, N.B.; Reddy, D.V.R.K. Efficient Pairing-Free Certificateless Signature Scheme for Secure Communication in Resource-Constrained Devices. *IEEE Commun. Lett.* **2020**, *24*, 1641–1645. [CrossRef]
17. Karati, A.; Islam, S.H.; Biswas, G.P. A pairing-free and provably secure certificateless signature scheme. *Inf. Sci.* **2018**, *450*, 378–391. [CrossRef]
18. Zhang, B.; Zhu, T.; Hu, C.; Zhao, C. Cryptanalysis of a Lightweight Certificateless Signature Scheme for IIOT Environments. *IEEE Access* **2018**, *6*, 73885–73894. [CrossRef]
19. Wang, L.; Chen, K.; Long, Y.; Wang, H. An efficient pairing-free certificateless signature scheme for resource-limited systems. *Sci. China Inf. Sci.* **2017**, *60*, 119102. [CrossRef]
20. Gong, P.; Li, P. Further improvement of a certificateless signature scheme without pairing. *Int. J. Commun. Syst.* **2014**, *27*, 2083–2091. [CrossRef]
21. Wang, L.; Chen, K.; Long, Y.; Mao, X.; Wang, H. A Modified Efficient Certificateless Signature Scheme without Bilinear Pairings. In Proceedings of the 2015 International Conference on Intelligent Networking and Collaborative Systems, INCoS 2015, Taipei, Taiwan, 2–4 September 2015; Xhafa, F., Barolli, L., Eds.; IEEE: Piscataway Township, NJ, USA, 2015; pp. 82–85. [CrossRef]
22. Yeh, K.; Tsai, K.; Kuo, R.; Wu, T. Robust Certificateless Signature Scheme without Bilinear Pairings. In Proceedings of the 2013 International Conference on IT Convergence and Security, ICITCS 2013, Macau, China, 16–18 December 2013; IEEE Computer Society: Piscataway Township, NJ, USA, 2013; pp. 1–4. [CrossRef]
23. Yeh, K.; Tsai, K.; Fan, C. An efficient certificateless signature scheme without bilinear pairings. *Multim. Tools Appl.* **2015**, *74*, 6519–6530. [CrossRef]
24. Jia, X.; He, D.; Liu, Q.; Choo, K.R. An efficient provably-secure certificateless signature scheme for Internet-of-Things deployment. *Hoc Netw.* **2018**, *71*, 78–87. [CrossRef]
25. Du, H.; Wen, Q.; Zhang, S.; Gao, M. A new provably secure certificateless signature scheme for Internet of Things. *Hoc Netw.* **2020**, *100*, 102074. [CrossRef]
26. Xiang, D.; Li, X.; Gao, J.; Zhang, X. A secure and efficient certificateless signature scheme for Internet of Things. *Hoc Netw.* **2022**, *124*, 102702. [CrossRef]
27. Member, A.M.; Nakabayashi, M.; Nonmembers, S.T. New Explicit Conditions of Elliptic Curve Traces for FR-Reduction. *Tech. Rep. Ieice Isec* **2001**, *100*, 1234–1243.
28. Yeh, K.; Su, C.; Choo, K.R.; Chiu, W. A Novel Certificateless Signature Scheme for Smart Objects in the Internet-of-Things. *Sensors* **2017**, *17*, 1001. [CrossRef] [PubMed]

electronics

Article

A New DSGRU-Based Intrusion Detection Method for the Internet of Things

Yueling Liu [1], Yingcong Lan [1], Changsong Yang [1,2,3,*], Yong Ding [1,4] and Chunhai Li [1]

1 Guangxi Key Laboratory of Cryptography and Information Security, Guilin University of Electronic Technology, Guilin 541004, China; ylliu@guet.edu.cn (Y.L.); 22032201048@mails.guet.edu.cn (Y.L.); stone_dingy@guet.edu.cn (Y.D.); chunhaili@guet.edu.cn (C.L.)
2 Guangdong Provincial Key Laboratory of Novel Security Intelligence Technologies, Shenzhen 518055, China
3 Guangxi Key Laboratory of Trusted Software, Guilin University of Electronic Technology, Guilin 541004, China
4 Institute of Cyberspace Technology, HKCT Institute for Higher Education, Hong Kong 999077, China
* Correspondence: csyang@guet.edu.cn; Tel.: +86-13397838265

Abstract: The Internet of Things (IoT), a rapidly developing technology, connects entities to the Internet through information sensing devices and networks. Recently, IoT has gained widespread application in daily life and work due to its high efficiency and convenience. However, with the rapid development of IoT, the systems are intruded upon by malicious users and hackers more and more frequently. As a result, intrusion detection has attracted significant attention, and numerous schemes have been proposed that can precisely identify malicious intrusion operations. However, the existing schemes suffer from several severe challenges, such as low accuracy, high computational overhead, and poor real-time performance, in processing large-scale, high-dimensional, and temporally correlated IoT network traffic data. To address these challenges, we propose a new intrusion detection scheme for IoT in this paper. Specifically, we first improve the traditional Gate Recurrent Unit (GRU) and design a novel neural network model, namely, the Deep Supplement Gate Recurrent Unit (DSGRU). This model comprises an Original Gate Recurrent Unit (OGRU), a Decode Gate Recurrent Unit (DGRU), and a Softmax activation function. Compared with the traditional GRU, our proposed DSGRU can more efficiently extract features from IoT network traffic data and reduce the loss of features caused by nonlinear transformations during the learning process. Subsequently, we adopt DSGRU to design a novel intrusion detection scheme for IoT. We also analyze the theoretical computational complexity of the proposed scheme. Finally, we implement our proposed intrusion detection scheme and evaluate its performance based on the UNSW-NB15 and NSL-KDD datasets. The experimental results demonstrate that our proposed DSGRU-based intrusion detection scheme achieves better performance, including in terms of *Accuracy*, *Precision*, *Recall*, *F1_score*, loss value, and efficiency.

Keywords: network security; Internet of Things; intrusion detection; deep learning; deep supplement gate recurrent unit

1. Introduction

The IoT, a rapidly developing and promising technology, connects entities to the internet through information sensing devices (such as infrared sensors, laser scanners, global positioning systems, and others) and a communication network based on agreed-upon protocols, thus forming a network of everything [1–3]. Due to its attractive advantages of high efficiency and convenience, IoT has been widely applied in daily life and work. A report by IoT Analytics showed that the enterprise IoT market reached USD 201 billion at the end of 2022, and will reach USD 483 billion by the end of 2027. However, alongside the rapid development and widespread application of IoT, it is increasingly targeted by hackers, and its security has become a major concern for users [4].

To protect IoT security, plenty of security protection technologies have been applied in the IoT landscape, such as firewalls [5,6], authentication mechanisms [7,8], data encryption [9–11], and so on. Although these technologies can prevent many attacks, they are all passive defenses. That is, they can only protect IoT security when attacks occur. Meanwhile, they lack the capability to actively analyze network behaviors, identify threat patterns, or forecast attacks, thus limiting their effectiveness against a wide array of network attacks [10]. To achieve active defense, intrusion detection systems have been deployed in IoT. By collecting and analyzing network traffic data, these systems can determine whether there are malicious intrusions [12]. Upon detecting intrusions, they can also promptly intercept and respond to the attacks. Additionally, they can inform system administrators of malicious intrusions, thereby assisting them in taking related measures [13].

Recently, thanks to the rapid advancement of artificial intelligence, machine learning and deep learning have been widely applied in intrusion detection, resulting in a substantial body of literature. However, these schemes cannot be directly suitable for IoT because IoT network traffic data are characterized by large-scale, heterogeneous multiple sources, high dimensionality, and temporal correlation [14]. According to a report by IoT Analytics, the number of devices accessing the IoT is expected to reach 22 billion globally by the end of 2025 [2]. Generally, these IoT devices are constantly collecting and sharing data, thus generating large-scale, heterogeneous, high-dimensional, and temporally correlated network traffic data [15,16]. The existing intrusion detection solutions directly applied in the IoT environment will suffer from low accuracy, high computational overhead, and poor real-time performance.

Specifically, in the data processing phase, the existing schemes require a significant computational overhead to process large-scale IoT network traffic data, thus incurring substantial time overhead. As a result, this can greatly affect the overall efficiency of intrusion detection [17]. Meanwhile, to learn and characterize the characteristics of IoT network traffic data, these schemes necessitate numerous matrix calculations and nonlinear transformations, which might lead to feature loss. These issues can diminish the capacity for data characterization and might impair the model's ability to generalize, potentially reducing its applicability and universality. Therefore, the motivation of this paper is to design a novel intrusion detection scheme for IoT, one that can effectively process large-scale, heterogeneous, high-dimensional, and temporally correlated IoT network traffic data.

1.1. Contributions

In this paper, we design a new neural network model and use it to propose an intrusion detection scheme for IoT, which can achieve efficient and accurate intrusion detection. As a consequence, the main contributions of this paper can be summarized as follows:

- We improve the traditional GRU model and design a novel neural network algorithm, namely, DSGRU, which consists of OGRU, DGRU, and the Softmax activation function. Specifically, OGRU is utilized to characterize the learned network traffic data, while DGRU is utilized to decode and recover the features that have been characterized by OGRU. Meanwhile, DSGRU can better characterize the network traffic data and discover the intrinsic connections within the temporally correlated network traffic data. Moreover, DSGRU can greatly reduce feature loss during the nonlinear transformation process through loss compensation, thus effectively enhancing the robustness and generalization ability.
- We adopt DSGRU to propose a novel intrusion detection scheme for the IoT environment, which is ideally suited for large-scale IoT network traffic data characterized by heterogeneous multiple sources, high dimensionality, and temporal correlation. By employing a loss compensation approach, our proposed scheme can reduce feature loss of IoT network traffic data during the model training process. Meanwhile, our scheme can effectively learn the temporal correlation between IoT network traffic data, thus improving intrusion detection accuracy. Moreover, our scheme enhances efficiency by reducing the operations involved in nonlinear transformations.

- We provide the total computational time overhead and theoretical computational complexity analysis to demonstrate the efficiency of our proposed scheme. Meanwhile, we develop a prototype implementation and simulate our proposed scheme. Finally, we test our proposed scheme based on the UNSW-NB15 dataset and NSL-KDD dataset, and provide the overall performance evaluation. The experimental results not only demonstrate that our proposed scheme is suitable for the IoT environment but also demonstrate the practicability and universality of our proposed scheme.

The structure of this article is as follows. Some preliminaries will be described in Section 2. In Section 3, we propose a novel neural network model that will be utilized to establish our intrusion detection scheme. In Section 4, we first describe the system framework and then present the detailed intrusion detection scheme for the IoT environment. We provide the theoretical computational complexity comparison in Section 5. In Section 6, we implement our proposed scheme and provide the performance evaluation. Finally, we present our discussion and conclusion in Sections 7 and 8, respectively.

1.2. Related Works

Intrusion detection was first proposed by Denning in 1987 [18], which provided a general framework for intrusion detection. After that, it has attracted significant attention from both academia and industry, leading to a series of solutions. Generally, over the last decade, probabilistic statistics and deep learning have been widely utilized to achieve intrusion detection.

A lot of the existing solutions utilize classical data classification methods from machine learning to detect intrusion traffic data [19,20]. To detect IoT cyber attacks, Kuang et al. [21] combined Kernel Principal Component Analysis (KPCA) with Improved Chaotic Particle Swarm Optimization (ICPSO) to propose a new Support Vector Machine (SVM) model. Subsequently, they used this new SVM for intrusion detection. By integrating SVM and plain Bayesian feature embedding, Gu et al. [22] designed a new intrusion detection scheme. In their solution, they first performed a plain Bayesian feature transformation based on the original data features. Subsequently, they trained a model based on the data obtained after the transformation and utilized the trained model to reach intrusion detection. By combining an artificial neural network and SVM, Hussain et al. [23] designed a two-stage hybrid intrusion detection scheme. In their scheme, they utilized SVM to achieve anomaly detection and adopted an artificial neural network to complete misuse detection. Lv et al. [24] designed a hybrid kernel function for a limited learning machine and utilized it to establish an intrusion detection scheme. Additionally, they achieved automatic parameter optimization by combining a novel Gravitational Search Algorithm (GSA) with the Differential Evolution (DE) algorithm. Saleh et al. [25] achieved intrusion detection based on an optimized k-nearest neighbor and SVM classifier. However, traditional classification techniques cannot realize automatic parameter optimization during the data pre-processing and feature extraction phases. That is, they require reliance on the expertise of specialists and achieve learning and classification through human involvement. Therefore, they are not able to quickly and accurately process large-scale, heterogeneous, high-dimensional, and temporally correlated IoT network traffic data.

Deep learning, a novel research hotspot in neural networks and artificial intelligence, has been extensively applied in network intrusion detection and has achieved outstanding results [26,27]. In 2018, to satisfy the security requirements of the modern network, Shone et al. [28] designed a novel intrusion detection scheme based on a stacked Non-symmetric Deep Autoencoder (NDAE). Experimental results demonstrated the strong potential of the proposal in modern networks. To achieve intrusion detection in wireless sensor networks, Otoum et al. [29] developed an intrusion detection system based on clustered constrained Boltzmann machines. In 2020, Kasongo and Sun [30] investigated the design of an intrusion detection scheme in a wireless network environment. Subsequently, by combining a Feed-Forward Deep Neural Network (FFDNN) with a Wrapper-Based Feature Extraction Unit (WFEU), they proposed a network intrusion detection scheme, which could improve effectiveness and accuracy. To protect the security of industrial Cyber-Physical Systems (CPSs), Li et al. [31] designed an intrusion detection scheme based on a Convolutional Neural Network (CNN) and GRU. Almutlaq et al. [32] proposed a two-stage intrusion detection method for an intelligent transportation system, which could effectively improve the accuracy and efficiency of intrusion detection.

To improve the performance of intrusion detection in distributed networks, Keshk et al. [33] proposed a new SPIP IoT intrusion detection framework to identify network attacks and explain the model's decisions. Wu et al. [34] presented a hybrid intrusion detection scheme based on Stacked Autoencoders (SAEs) and the Kernel Approximation algorithm. They implemented their proposed scheme and provided a performance evaluation based on the NSL-KDD dataset. The experimental results verify the efficiency and accuracy of their proposal. To achieve intrusion detection in imbalanced datasets, Lee et al. [35] proposed a new intrusion detection method by combining an Autoencoder (AE) with a Generative Adversarial Network (GAN). Specifically, they used GAN to sample a few classes of data and adopted AE to downsize the data, thus improving overall performance. Lo et al. [36] proposed a Long Short-Term Memory (LSTM) algorithm, and then utilized LSTM to establish a new intrusion detection system with a high false alarm rate.

To detect the unbalanced attack types, Imrana et al. [37] proposed a Bidirectional LSTM for intrusion detection and the experiment results showed the effectiveness of Bidirectional LSTM. Aljrees et al. [38] introduced a novel paradigm that synergized efficient data encryption, the Quondam Signature Algorithm (QSA), and federated learning, to effectively detect random attacks in the IoT system. Sook et al. [39] proposed a two-phase network traffic anomaly detection system compatible with the ETSI-NFV standard 5G architecture. Although the above solutions can improve the accuracy of intrusion detection, they need to perform a large number of nonlinear transformations when dealing with large-scale, heterogeneous, high-dimensional, and temporally correlated IoT network traffic data, thus affecting efficiency and real-time performance. Meanwhile, they suffer from the problem of local data feature loss, which can reduce accuracy and generalization ability [40].

2. Preliminaries

To solve the problems of ineffective long-term memory information transfer and gradient vanishing in backpropagation, a new recurrent neural network GRU, which is very similar to the Long Short-Term Memory (LSTM) neural network, has been widely used [41]. GRU can efficiently capture the semantic associations between long sequences, thus mitigating the problems of gradient vanishing and gradient explosion. However, the structure and computation of GRU are both simpler than those of LSTM. GRU mainly consists of two gate structure units: the update gate and the reset gate, as demonstrated in Figure 1.

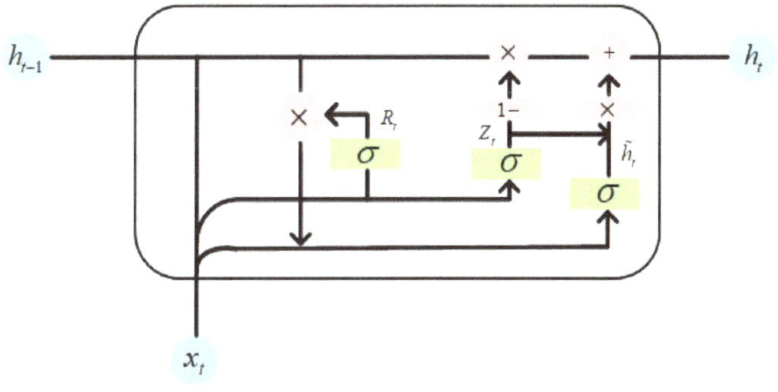

Figure 1. The structure of the GRU model.

In GRU, the reset gate controls the flow of the previous moment's hidden state into the candidate's hidden state of the current moment, which may contain all the historical information about the time series up to that previous moment. Therefore, the reset gate enables the discarding of historical information that is not relevant to the prediction. The update gate controls the extent to which the current moment forgets the content of messages unrelated to the current moment and determines how much of the current candidate's hidden state is retained.

As shown in Figure 1 symbol R_t denotes the reset gate and symbol Z_t denotes the update gate. The GRU model can be described as follows.

Firstly, the reset gate R_t and the update gate Z_t are jointly determined by the past-moment information t and the current-moment information x_t, where x_t is a small batch of inputs at a given moment t. Subsequently, the reset gate R_t and the update gate Z_t can be computed as follows:

$$R_t = \sigma(W_R \cdot [h_{t-1}, x_t]) \tag{1}$$

$$Z_t = \sigma(W_Z \cdot [h_{t-1}, x_t]) \tag{2}$$

where σ is the sigmoid function, and W_R and W_Z are learnable parameters.

Secondly, the candidate's hidden state $\tilde{h}_t$ of GRU at moment t is controlled by the information of the past moment h_{t-1} and current moment x_t. The computational formula is described as follows:

$$\tilde{h}_t = \tanh(W_{\tilde{h}} \cdot [R_t \times h_{t-1}, x_t]) \tag{3}$$

where tanh is the tanh activation function and $W_{\tilde{h}}$ is the learnable parameter.

Finally, when calculating the hidden state h_t at moment t, it is necessary to utilize the update gate Z_t at the current moment to combine the hidden state h_{t-1} and the candidate's hidden state $\tilde{h}_t$. The specific formula is as follows:

$$h_t = (1 - Z_t) \times h_{t-1} + Z_t \times \tilde{h} \tag{4}$$

3. Deep Supplement Gate Recurrent Unit

Although GRU can achieve impressive performance in processing temporally correlated network traffic data, it requires performing numerous nonlinear transformations during the data feature learning process, resulting in feature loss and reduced efficiency. To address these issues, we have improved upon the traditional GRU and designed a novel neural network model called DSGRU. Its construction is demonstrated in Figure 2.

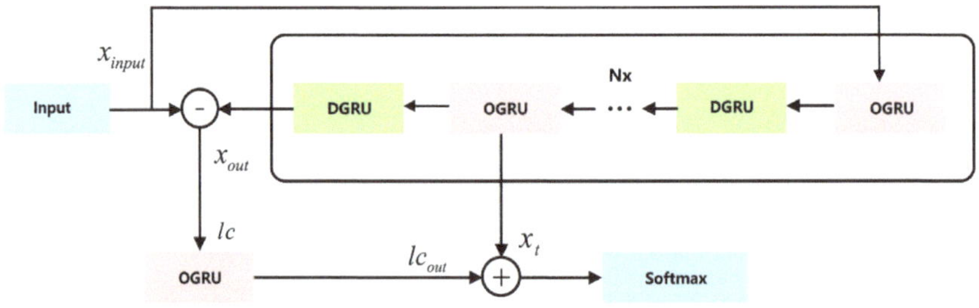

Figure 2. The structure of the DSGRU model.

We can directly see from Figure 2 that the proposed DSGRU consists of two types of GRU, i.e., OGRU and DGRU. Generally, OGRU contains a traditional GRU network and a fully connected layer. Meanwhile, OGRU is primarily utilized to learn data characterization from the input data. Similarly, DGRU consists of a traditional GRU and a fully connected layer, but its main function is to decode and recover the feature data after OGRU has learned the data characterization.

Unlike the traditional GRU, DSGRU is equipped with more hidden layers by deepening the OGRUs and the DGRUs. The deeper OGRUs and DGRUs can learn data features more fully, recover more data features, and lose fewer data features, thus improving the learning characterization ability. At the same time, by increasing the layers of DGRU, it can retain more original data features in data decoding and provide more accurate loss compensation data in subsequent loss compensation. Subsequently, the overall data feature information loss is reduced through accurate loss compensation

In Figure 2, we utilize the symbol x_{input} to represent the input data and x_t to represent the data characterization of the output of OGRU located in the last layer. Moreover, we use x_{out} to denote the decoded data output of the last layer of DGRU, lc to denote the loss data, and lc_{out} to denote the loss compensation data. N_x denotes the number of layers of encoding and decoding. For simplicity, we use $N_x = 2$ as an example to illustrate a specific flow of DSGRU in the following part.

Firstly, x_{input} is assigned to x_{out}, and then x_{out} is encoded and decoded twice. Subsequently, x_t is obtained by the characterization learning executed by the OGRU located in the last layer. At the same time, x_{out} is obtained by the last layer of DGRU decoding, which can be calculated as follows:

$$x_{out} = x_{input} \tag{5}$$

$$x_t = OGRU(x_{out}) \tag{6}$$

$$x_{out} = DGRU(x_t) \tag{7}$$

$$x_t = OGRU(x_{out}) \tag{8}$$

$$x_{out} = DGRU(x_t) \tag{9}$$

Secondly, the loss data, lc, are obtained by subtracting the input data, x_{input}, from the x_{out} data obtained by the DGRU. Therefore, the loss data, l_c, can be computed by using the following formula:

$$lc = x_{input} - x_{out} \tag{10}$$

Finally, the loss compensation data, lc_{out}, are obtained through OGRU representation learning; then, x_t plus lc_{out} are assigned to x_t, and the final result is obtained after a Softmax activation function with the following formula:

$$lc_{out} = OGRU(lc) \tag{11}$$

$$x_t = x_t + lc_{out} \tag{12}$$

4. Our Proposed Scheme

In the following section, we will first describe the system framework of our new intrusion detection scheme. Subsequently, we will introduce the DSGRU-based intrusion detection scheme in detail.

4.1. System Framework

We investigate the design of an intrusion detection scheme for IoT. Recently, with the rapid advancement of information technology, especially in cloud computing, wireless networks, and sensor technology, the popularity and coverage of IoT have progressively increased. At the same time, the practical application of intrusion detection often involves network traffic data characterized by large-scale, heterogeneous multi-source, high dimensionality, and time correlation. These characteristics present many new challenges to previous intrusion detection solutions [42]. To deal with these issues, we design a DSGRU-based intrusion detection scheme, whose system framework is demonstrated in Figure 3. In our system framework, the main constituent parts can be roughly divided into four sections: data processing, model training, model testing, and result analysis.

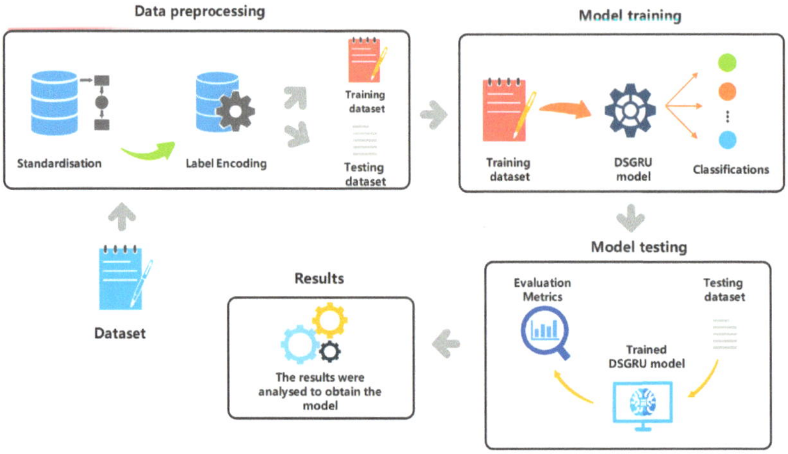

Figure 3. The system framework of our proposed scheme.

The data processing part primarily handles the original input data, i.e., dividing the original data into training and testing datasets, as well as achieving data redundancy elimination, digital encoding, feature extraction, and so on. The model training part focuses on training the DSGRU-based intrusion detection model using the training dataset, while the model testing part tests the trained DSGRU-based intrusion detection model using the testing dataset. That is, the model training part and the model testing part are designed to establish the DSGRU-based intrusion detection scheme, which achieves efficient and accurate intrusion detection in the IoT environment. The result analysis part enables the analysis of intrusion detection results, thereby demonstrating the efficiency, practicability, and accuracy of our proposed DSGRU-based intrusion detection scheme.

To demonstrate the DSGRU-based intrusion detection scheme implementation process more intuitively, the above steps can be summarized into an algorithmic pseudo-code, as shown in Algorithm 1.

Algorithm 1: DSGRU algorithm.

Input: x_{input}
Output: x_t
The dataset constitutes x_{input} data through feature standardization and feature numerical encoding
$x_{out} \leftarrow x_{input}$
for $d = 1$ *to* n **do**
  $x_t \leftarrow OGRU(x_{out})$
  $x_{out} \leftarrow DGRU(x_t)$
$lc \leftarrow x_{input} - x_{out}$
$lc_{out} \leftarrow OGRU(lc)$
return $x_t \leftarrow softMax(x_t + lc_{out})$

4.2. DSGRU-Based Intrusion Detection Scheme

In this subsection, we introduce the DSGRU-based intrusion detection scheme in detail. Note that compared with other neural network algorithms, DSGRU can greatly reduce feature loss through loss compensation, thereby improving robustness and generalization ability, and can better process the potential relation between long-term and short-term dependencies in temporally correlated data. Therefore, our presented DSGRU-based intrusion detection scheme can achieve better performance.

To demonstrate the proposed scheme more clearly, we utilize an algorithm to present the proposed scheme, as demonstrated in Algorithm 2.

Algorithm 2: Intrusion detection algorithm.

Input: Data Feature
Output: Classifications
Load Dataset
Data processing
for *d = 1 to n* **do**
    if *Feature = Nonnumerical* **then**
        Using numerical encoding
    else
        Feature standardization with $Z = \frac{X - X_{\min}}{X_{\max} - X_{\min}}$
Start model training and testing
for *d=1 to n* **do**
    $DSGRU \leftarrow DSGRU_i(X);$
    $result \leftarrow Compare(Y_{real}, Y_{pred})$
Test model on test sets
Calculate DSGRU model performance metrics

In Algorithm 2, we respectively utilize symbol x to represent the attribute features of the data; y to represent the category features of the data; use X to represent the attribute characteristics of the data in standardization. Meanwhile, we denote the minimum value by $X_{\min}$, denote the maximum value by $X_{\max}$, and denote the real situation value by Y_{real}. Moreover, Y_{pred} is utilized to represent the predicted situation value, N_x is used to represent the training epoch, and the symbol *resulting* is adopted to represent the evaluation results. The primary phases of Algorithm 2 can be summarized as follows.

(1) *Data pre-processing.* We process the original network traffic dataset. To be more specific, the original dataset will be transformed into numerical features and then normalized. Subsequently, we utilize the processed dataset to establish an intrusion detection network traffic dataset. The processed dataset will be divided into two parts: a training dataset and a testing dataset. The training dataset is utilized to train the DSGRU-based intrusion detection model and the testing dataset is used to test the intrusion detection performance.

(2) *Model training.* The training dataset is input into the DSGRU-based intrusion detection training model and executes n epochs of training. Subsequently, a trained DSGRU-based intrusion detection model is output.

(3) *Model testing.* The testing dataset is input into the trained DSGRU-based intrusion detection model and then output the intrusion detection results.

(4) *Result analysis.* According to the intrusion detection results output by the trained DSGRU-based intrusion detection model, some related metrics are calculated to evaluate the performance of the proposed scheme.

5. Computational Complexity

In the following part, we will analyze the theoretical computational complexity of the DSGRU-based intrusion detection scheme, SGRU-based intrusion detection scheme [40], GRU-based intrusion detection scheme [41], BiLSTM-based intrusion detection scheme [37], and DAE-BPNN-based intrusion detection scheme [39], as demonstrated in Table 1. For simplicity, symbol m is used to represent the dimensionality of the input data and symbol n is utilized to represent the dimensionality of the hidden layer.

Table 1. Theoretical computational complexity.

Methodology	Total Times of Calculations	Computational Complexity
DSGRU	$T[(2 \times d + 1) \times (3 \times n \times m + 3 \times n^2 + 3 \times n) + 2 \times n + 2 \times m]$	$O(n^2)$
SGRU [40]	$T[3 \times (3 \times n \times m + 3 \times n^2 + 3 \times n) + 2 \times n + 2 \times m]$	$O(n^2)$
GRU [41]	$T(3 \times n \times m + 3 \times n^2 + 3 \times n)$	$O(n^2)$
BiLSTM [37]	$T(2 \times (4 \times n \times m + 4 \times n^2 + 4 \times n))$	$O(n^2)$
DAE-BPNN [39]	$T(3 \times n \times m + 3 \times n^2))$	$O(n^2)$

To compute the time complexity of DSGRU, the time complexity of GRU is analyzed first. According to Formulas (1)–(4) in Section 2, GRU requires maintaining three sets of parameters: the input gate, the forgetting gate, and the candidate state. Therefore, the total computational time overhead of GRU is $T(3 \times n \times m + 3 \times n^2 + 3 \times n)$. That is, the computational complexity of GRU can be denoted as $O(n^2)$. LSTM then requires maintaining four sets of parameters: the input gate, the oblivion gate, the output gate, and the candidate state. Therefore, the total computational time overhead of BiLSTM is $T(2 \times (4 \times n \times m + 4 \times n^2 + 4 \times n))$. That is, the computational complexity of BiLSTM is denoted as $O(n^2)$. Meanwhile, the total computational time overhead of DSGRU is $T[(2 \times d + 1) \times (3 \times n \times m + 3 \times n^2 + 3 \times n) + 2 \times n + 2 \times m]$, where d is the number of layers of OGRU and DGRU. As a consequence, the computational complexity of DSGRU and GRU are the same and both are $O(n^2)$. Moreover, since both DAE and BPNN contain two-layer–fully connected layer structures in our reproduction experiments, the total computational time overhead is $T(3 \times n \times m + 3 \times n^2)$, and the computational complexity can be denoted as $O(n^2)$.

6. Experiments

In the following section, we will implement our proposed scheme and provide the performance evaluation. Specifically, we will provide a detailed description of the experimental environment, experimental dataset, and experimental evaluation metrics. Subsequently, we describe the experimental results, along with a comprehensive analysis.

6.1. Implementation

The proposed scheme will be implemented in the Python programming language using the PyTorch deep learning framework. The Adaptive Moment Estimation (Adam) algorithm is the optimizer used to update the model weights at a learning rate of 0.001. The number of neurons in the OGRU hidden layer is 20 and the number of neurons in the DGRU hidden layer unit is 43; meanwhile, the loss function used in the model is the categorical cross-entropy for multi-class classification. Moreover, the model batch size is set to 512 and the model training epoch is 250. The following two datasets (UNSW-NB15 dataset and NSL-KDD dataset) both match this parameter configuration. As shown in Figure 2, the model first uses an embedding layer to map the inputs to its representation. Then, it provides the embedding to the OGRU and DGRU layers with multilayer processing. The DSGRU output is then fed to the fully connected layer with Softmax as the activation function. Ideally, the fully connected layer learns and compiles the data extracted by the DSGRU layer to form the final output, which is classified by the output layer. Finally, we use loss compensation to reduce the loss of nonlinear transformation.

6.2. Experimental Environment

To simulate our proposed scheme, all the simulation experiments were performed on a desktop computer that was equipped with an Intel Core i5-8300H CPU running at 2.30 GHz, an NVIDIA GeForce GTX 1050 Ti graphics card, and 16 GB of main memory. Meanwhile, the desktop computer was also equipped with a Windows 11 operating system,

CUDA10.0 driver, cuDNN 7.4.2, and a Python 3.7 environment. Moreover, the deep learning framework utilized in the experiments was PyTorch 1.8.

6.3. Experimental Dataset

We utilized UNSW-NB15 and NSL-KDD as the experimental datasets.

6.3.1. UNSW-NB15 Dataset

The UNSW-NB15 dataset was created by the Australian Centre for Cyber Security (ACCS) lab in 2015 [43]. The UNSW-NB15 dataset comprises both real normal traffic data and malicious attack traffic data. Meanwhile, the UNSW-NB15 dataset encompasses normal traffic data and nine types of attack traffic data. The nine types of attack traffic data are backdoor, penetration analysis, denial of service (Dos) attack, vulnerability exploitation, fuzz test, generalized attack, stomp, shellcode, and worm. Generally, the UNSW-NB15 dataset consists of 2,540,044 data samples classified into 10 types, as follows:

- Normal: The normal network traffic data.
- Fuzzers: Attacks that attempt to paralyze a system with randomly generated data from the web.
- Analysis: Web attacks through port scanning, spamming, and file exfiltration.
- Backdoors: Hacking attacks that access computer data by bypassing system security mechanisms.
- DoS: Uninterrupted malicious attacks on the host computer intended to render the computer out of service.
- Exploits: Malicious attacks through the operating system or software security vulnerabilities.
- Generic: Group password hacking attacks.
- Reconnaissance: Attackers gather information related to their target to carry out the attack.
- Shellcode: Attackers use shell commands to control the target host attack methods.
- Worms: An attack method in which an attacker spreads to other computers through self-replication, rendering other computers unable to function properly.

To thoroughly evaluate the effectiveness of DSGRU in intrusion detection for the IoT environment, we carried out the experiments by using a randomized extraction method on a dataset that consisted of 600,000 samples from the UNSW-NB15 dataset. Meanwhile, to achieve proper evaluation, we split the dataset into a training dataset and a testing dataset, at a ratio of 5:1. Specifically, the first 500,000 data samples were utilized as the training dataset, while the remaining 100,000 data samples were designated as the testing dataset. By this rigorous approach, we can rigorously evaluate the overall performance of the DSGRU-based intrusion detection scheme for the IoT environment.

6.3.2. NSL-KDD Dataset

The NSL-KDD dataset is one of the benchmark datasets used for evaluating intrusion detection systems [44]. It is an enhanced form of the KDD Cup 99 dataset. There are five categories in the NSL-KDD dataset: Normal, Denial of Service (DoS) Attack, User to Root Attack (R2L), Remote to Local Attack (U2R), and a Probe attack. The data types are specifically described as follows:

- Normal: Normal network data.
- DoS: Uninterrupted malicious attacks on the host computer to render the computer out of service.
- R2L: Hacker attacks that access computer data by bypassing security system mechanisms.
- U2R: Attacks that attempt to paralyze the system through randomly generated data over the network.
- Probe: Web attacks through port scanning, spamming, and file exfiltration.

The NSL-KDD dataset contains $KDDTrain^{+}$ as a training set for model learning, and $KDDTesn^{+}$ and $KDDTest^{-21}$ as testing sets for the performance evaluations of the trained models [45]. Among them, $KDDTrain^{+}$ has 125,973 traffic samples, $KDDTesn^{+}$ has 22,544 traffic samples, and $KDDTest^{-21}$ has 11,850 samples. Moreover, to simulate the realism of network traffic, the testing dataset includes many attacks that do not appear in the training set. Therefore, except for the 22 attack types in the training set, there are 17 different attack types in the testing set. To better train the model, $KDDTrain^{+}$ is mainly used as the training set and $KDDTest^{+}$ as the testing set in the experiments.

6.4. Evaluation Metrics

To evaluate an intrusion detection scheme, the typical evaluation metrics include accuracy, false alarms, and missed alarms [46]. However, due to the serious imbalance of IoT network traffic data, normal network traffic data account for the vast majority, which would lead to the bias of traditional evaluation metrics. As a result, to guarantee the comprehensiveness of the evaluation, we will comprehensively adopt $Confusion\ Matrix$, $Accuracy$, $Precision$, $Recall$, and $F1\_score$ as evaluation metrics [47].

$TruePositive$ (TP): True positive represents the number of samples that are truly attacks and that have been correctly detected as attacks.

$FalsePositive$ (FP): False positive represents the number of attacks that are misclassified as normal samples.

$TrueNegative$ (TN): True negative represents the number of normal samples that are incorrectly detected as attacks.

$FalseNegative$ (FN): False negative represents the number of normal samples that are accurately detected as normal samples.

$Accuracy$: Accuracy represents the proportion of correctly detected samples to the total number of samples. The calculation formula of accuracy is as follows.

$$Accuracy = \frac{TN + TP}{TP + TN + FP + FN} \tag{13}$$

$Precision$: Precision indicates the proportion of samples detected by the model to be in the positive category that are actually in the positive category. It focuses on the accuracy of the model's predictions. The calculation formula of precision is as follows:

$$Precision = \frac{TP}{TP + FP} \tag{14}$$

$Recall$: Recall represents the proportion of correct detections that are positives in the model, as a proportion of the data that are actually positives. In the experiment, recall refers to the proportion of attacks that are correctly categorized, such as a proportion of the actual attack data, which can be calculated as follows:

$$Recall = \frac{TP}{TP + FN} \tag{15}$$

$F1\_score$: $F1\_score$ is a comprehensive metric that balances precision and recall. $F1\_score$ is used to assess the model's performance by considering both $Precision$ and $Recall$ simultaneously. The $F1\_score$ is a value between 0 and 1; a higher value indicates a better model performance when $Precision$ and $Recall$ are close. The formula for the $F1\_score$ is as follows:

$$F1\_score = 2 \times \frac{precision \times recall}{recall + precision} \tag{16}$$

$Confusion\ Matrix$: The confusion matrix is a table used to evaluate the performance of a classification model. The rows and columns of the matrix, respectively, represent the predicted and actual values. Specifically, TP, FP, TN, and FN can be calculated based on the number of instances in each category of the confusion matrix, and then the evaluation metrics, such as accuracy, precision, recall, and *F1_score* score can be calculated using Formulas (13)–(16).

6.5. Experimental Results

In this subsection, we simulate our proposed scheme and compare the performance with some previous intrusion detection solutions. Specifically, we will compare the performances among our proposed DSGRU-based intrusion detection scheme, SGRU-based intrusion detection scheme [40], GRU-based intrusion detection scheme [41], BiLSTM-based intrusion detection scheme [37], and DAE-BPNN-based intrusion detection scheme [39].

Confusion Matrix. We firstly test the fully trained model and then obtain the confusion matrix, as demonstrated in Figures 4 and 5.

In Figures 4 and 5, the diagonal of the confusion matrix represents the number of correct identifications for each category. For a deep learning model, the training process is a form of self-learning. In other words, deep learning models can learn a significant amount of knowledge from the training dataset and then present the data features. Then, in Figures 4 and 5, the larger the numbers in the diagonal, the more knowledge the model has learned. Because the dataset is extremely unbalanced, categories with more data can achieve higher accuracy, while those with less data tend to have lower accuracy.

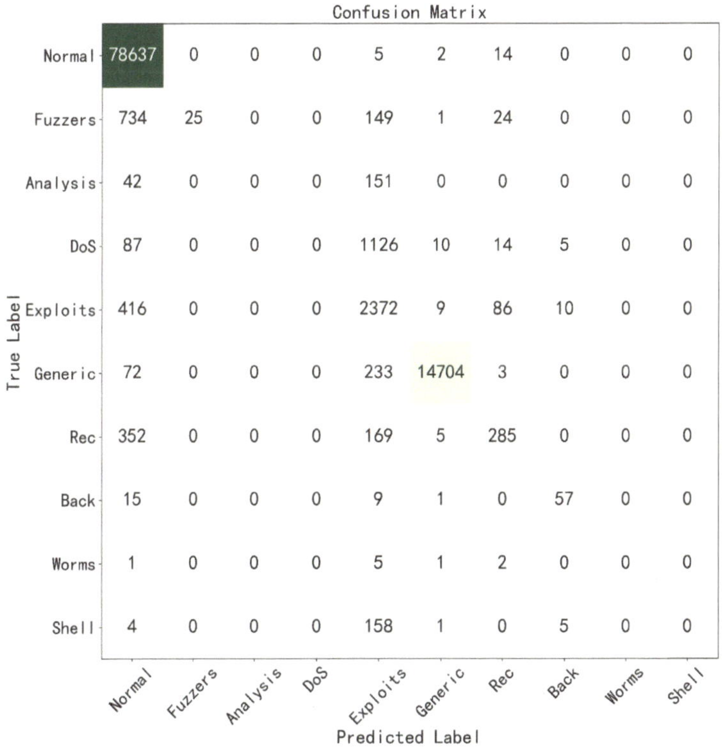

Figure 4. Confusion matrix of DSGRU based on the UNSW-NB15 dataset.

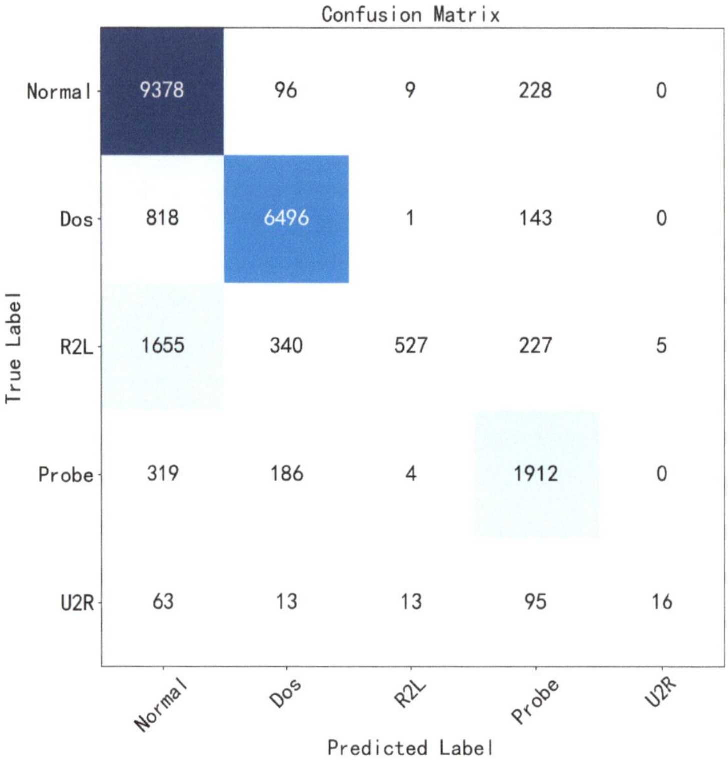

Figure 5. Confusion matrix of DSGRU based on the NSL-KDD dataset.

6.5.1. Model Fit Analysis

To evaluate the model fitting degree, we compare the loss values of the DSGRU-based intrusion detection scheme, SGRU-based intrusion detection scheme [40], GRU-based intrusion detection scheme [41], BiLSTM-based intrusion detection scheme [37], and DAE-BPNN-based intrusion detection scheme [39]. Subsequently, the comparison results are demonstrated in Table 2 and Figure 6.

Table 2. Comparison of loss values.

Dataset		DSGRU	SGRU	GRU	BiLSTM	DAE-BPNN
UNSW-NB15	Loss value	1.55^{-2}	1.62^{-2}	1.97^{-2}	1.95^{-2}	1.87^{-2}
NSL-KDD		1.76^{-3}	2.07^{-3}	1.82^{-3}	2.39^{-2}	3.39^{-3}

From Table 2, we can see that when the dataset is the UNSW-NB15 dataset, the final loss value of the GRU-based intrusion detection scheme [41] is the highest, followed by that of the BiLSTM-based intrusion detection scheme [37], and the loss value of our proposed DSGRU-based intrusion detection scheme is the lowest. However, when the dataset is the NSL-KDD dataset, the final loss value of the DAE-BPNN-based intrusion detection scheme [39] is the highest, followed by that of the BiLSTM-based intrusion detection scheme [37], and the loss value of our proposed DSGRU-based intrusion detection scheme is the lowest. This demonstrates that, compared with the other four previous schemes, our proposed DSGRU-based intrusion detection scheme can achieve a better degree of fit.

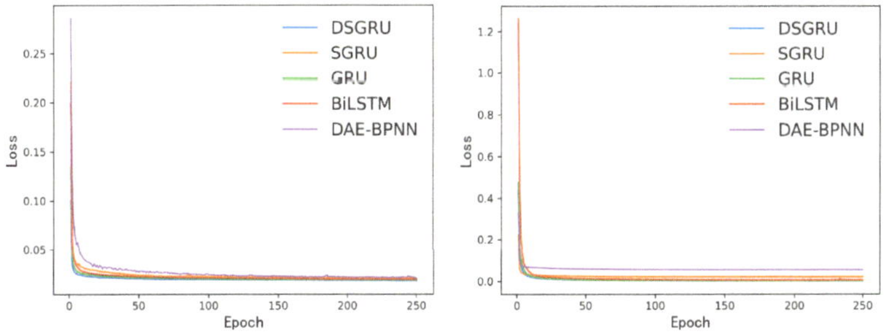

(a) (b)

Figure 6. Comparison of loss values of different methods. (**a**) Loss for the UNSW-NB15 dataset. (**b**) Loss for the NSL-KDD dataset.

From Figure 6, we can obviously detect that our proposed DSGRU-based intrusion detection scheme has a better decline in loss value. In other words, compared with the other four previous solutions, our proposed scheme has a better loss value convergence rate and lower loss value. This is because—compared with the other four previous schemes—DSGRU can learn the temporal correlation of the dataset and achieve loss compensation in the model training process. Meanwhile, DSGRU can better consider the information to be transmitted in the future compared to the other four schemes.

6.5.2. Effectiveness Evaluation

To evaluate the effectiveness, we compare the five different schemes from the metrics of accuracy, precision, recall, and *F1_score* based on the UNSW-NB15 dataset and NSL-KDD dataset. Subsequently, the comparison results are demonstrated in Figure 7.

Figure 7a demonstrates the effectiveness of the comparison results based on the UNSW-NB15 dataset. We can obviously see that, compared with the other four previous intrusion detection schemes, our proposed scheme performs best in accuracy, precision, recall, and *F1_score*. For example, the accuracy of our proposed scheme reaches 96.08%, which is 1.34%, 1.86%, 1.74%, and 1.70% higher than those of the SGRU-based intrusion detection scheme [40], GRU-based intrusion detection scheme [41], BiLSTM-based intrusion detection scheme [37], and DAE-BPNN-based intrusion detection scheme [39], respectively. For another example, the precision of our DSGRU-based intrusion detection scheme reaches 95.52%. However, the precision of the SGRU-based intrusion detection scheme [40] is 92.89%, the precision of the GRU-based intrusion detection scheme [41] is 92.59%, the precision of the BiLSTM-based intrusion detection scheme [37] is 91.59%, and the precision of the DAE-BPNN-based intrusion detection scheme [39] is 90.89%. Meanwhile, the other two metrics (i.e., recall and *F1_score*) of our proposed scheme are both better than those of the other four solutions.

Meanwhile, to illustrate the good generalization ability and robustness of our proposed scheme, we also utilize the NSL-KDD dataset to verify the effectiveness; the comparison results are shown in Figure 7a. From Figure 7b, we can see that our proposed scheme is better than the other four solutions. For accuracy, our proposed scheme reaches 81.10%. However, the accuracies of the SGRU-based intrusion detection scheme [40], GRU-based intrusion detection scheme [41], BiLSTM-based intrusion detection scheme [37], and DAE-BPNN-based intrusion detection scheme [39] are 79.47%, 77.42%, 79.92%, and 78.24%, respectively. Similarly, the other metrics (i.e., precision, recall, and *F1_score*) of our proposed scheme all are better than those of the other four solutions.

From Figure 7, we see that our proposed scheme achieves the best performance among the five solutions, which means that DSGRU can more fully extract the related features from the dataset. Meanwhile, DSGRU can better mine the intrinsic connection between the temporal correlation network traffic data.

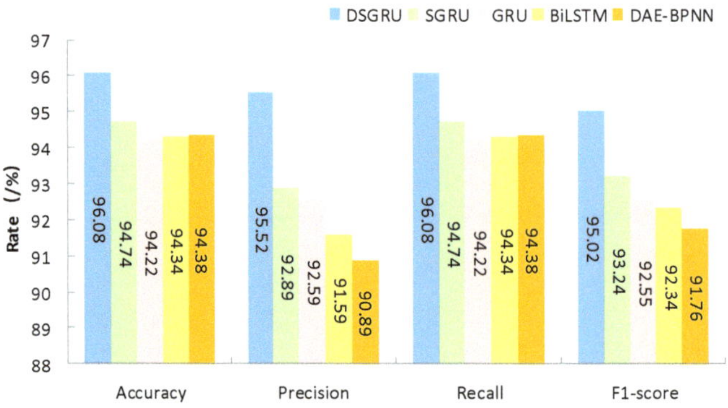

(a)

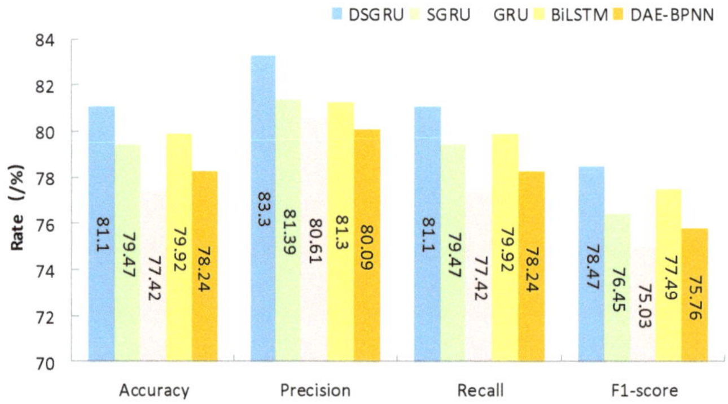

(b)

Figure 7. Comparison of the effectiveness of the five models. (**a**) Results for the UNSW-NB15 dataset. (**b**) Results for the NSL-KDD dataset.

6.5.3. Efficiency Evaluation

In this experiment, we, respectively, measure the total computational time overhead, the model training computational time overhead, and the model testing computational time overhead based on the theoretical computational complexity described in Table 1. Subsequently, the comparison results are demonstrated in Figures 8–10.

Efficiency evaluation based on the UNSW-NB15 dataset. We first measure the total time overhead and model training time overhead based on the UNSW-NB15 dataset, as shown in Figure 8. We can easily discover from Figure 8a that the BiLSTM-based intrusion detection scheme [37] requires the most total computational time overhead, followed by our proposed DSGRU-based intrusion detection scheme. The GRU-based intrusion detection scheme [41] requires the least total computational time overhead. This is because LSTM includes four gate structures, whereas GRU has only three gate structures and fewer parameters. Meanwhile, both DSGRU and SGRU comprise multiple GRUs, resulting in longer total computational time overhead compared to GRU, but still shorter than that of BiLSTM.

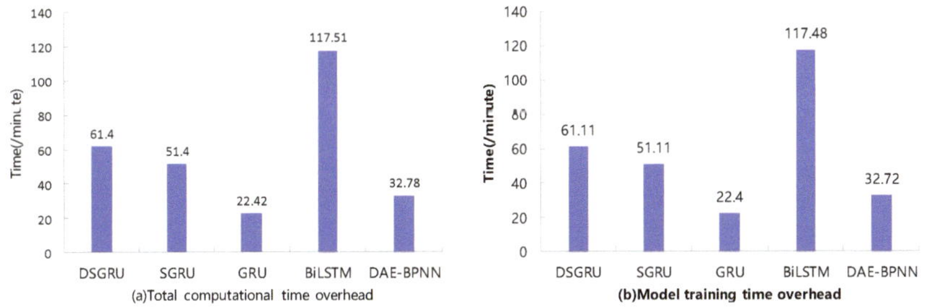

Figure 8. Total time overhead and model training time overhead based on the UNSW-NB15 dataset.

Figure 8b shows the model training time overhead, from which we can directly observe that the ranking of the model training time overhead for the five schemes is the same as that of the total time overhead. Meanwhile, from Figure 8, we see that model training constitutes the majority of the time overhead. For instance, the total computational time overhead of our proposed DSGRU-based intrusion detection scheme based on the UNSW-NB15 dataset is 61.40 min, while the model training requires 61.11 min. For another example, the BiLSTM model training requires 117.48 min, which occupies 99.97% of the total computational time overhead. In the model training process, feature extraction and learning will be completed. These two processes require some complex operations to help the model learn the features, hence they consume most of the time. However, it is important to note that model training is completed offline in advance, so it does not significantly affect efficiency.

To evaluate the real-time intrusion detection, we measure the model testing time overhead, as demonstrated in (Figure 9). From Figure 9, we can see that the BiLSTM-based intrusion detection scheme [37] requires the most model testing time overhead, followed by the DAE-BPNN-based intrusion detection scheme [39] and our proposed DSGRU-based intrusion detection scheme. The GRU-based intrusion detection scheme [41] requires the least model testing time overhead. However, the difference in model testing time overhead is small. For example, our proposed scheme requires 2.1 s to achieve model testing, while the model testing time overhead of the GRU-based intrusion detection scheme [41] is 1.3 s. In other words, the difference in model testing time overhead is so small that it is acceptable. Therefore, we can consider our proposed DSGRU-based intrusion detection scheme to be quite efficient.

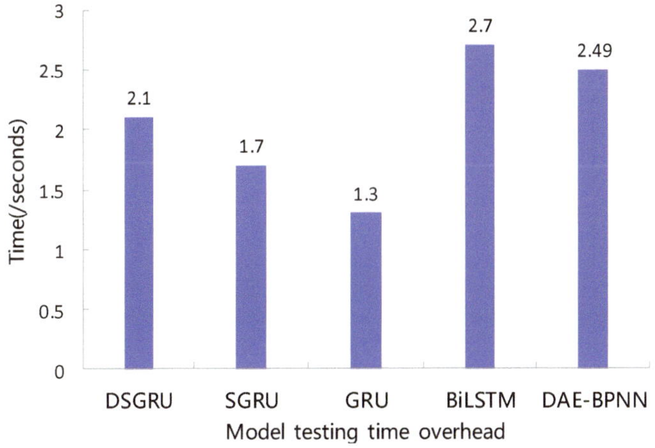

Figure 9. Model testing time overhead based on the UNSW-NB15 dataset.

Efficiency evaluation based on the NSL-KDD dataset. To further verify the efficiency of our proposed scheme, we also measure the time overhead based on the NSL-KDD dataset. Subsequently, the total time overhead and model training time overhead are demonstrated in Figure 10. We can clearly see that the time overhead for all five solutions is less when based on the NSL-KDD dataset compared to those based on the UNSW-NB15 dataset. This is because the number of data items in the NSL-KDD dataset is fewer than in the UNSW-NB15 dataset. Meanwhile, we see that the rankings of the total time overhead and the model training time overhead based on the NSL-KDD dataset are the same as those based on the UNSW-NB15 dataset. That is, the BiLSTM-based intrusion detection scheme [37] requires the most total computational time overhead and model training time overhead, followed by our proposed DSGRU-based intrusion detection scheme. The GRU-based intrusion detection scheme [41] requires the least total computational time overhead and model training computational time overhead.

Moreover, we measure the model testing time overhead based on the NSL-KDD dataset, as shown in Figure 11. From Figure 11, we can see that the DAE-BPNN-based intrusion detection scheme [39] requires the most model testing time overhead, followed by the BiLSTM-based intrusion detection scheme [37], and our proposed DSGRU-based intrusion detection scheme requires the least model testing time overhead. Specifically, in the model testing process, our proposed scheme merely requires 0.31 s, while the DAE-BPNN-based intrusion detection scheme [39] requires 1.08 s, and the BiLSTM-based intrusion detection scheme [37] requires 0.86 s. Meanwhile, the time overhead of our proposed scheme is 0.11 s less than that of the GRU-based intrusion detection scheme [41]. Therefore, we can see that our proposed DSGRU-based intrusion detection scheme is the most efficient in the model testing process based on the NSL-KDD dataset.

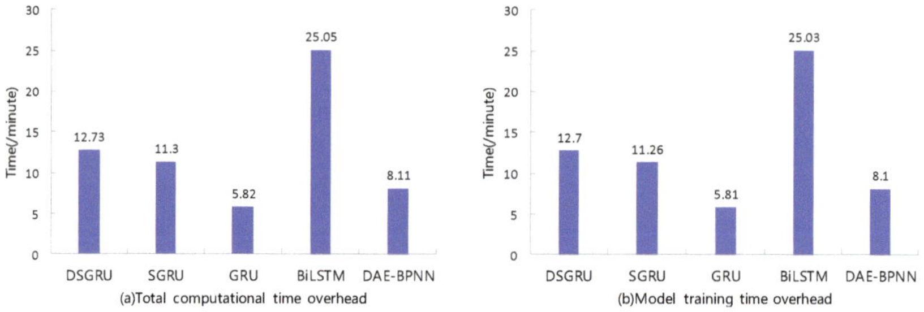

Figure 10. Total time overhead and model training time overhead based on the NSL-KDD dataset.

By analyzing and comparing the theoretical computational costs and computational complexity (which are described in Section 5), we see that although our proposed DSGRU-based intrusion detection scheme requires performing the most operations, the computational complexity of our scheme is the same as the other four previous schemes. Meanwhile, from the experimental results, we can see that our proposed DSGRU-based intrusion detection scheme requires a little more time overhead than the SGRU-based intrusion detection scheme [40] and GRU-based intrusion detection scheme [41]. However, the difference in time overhead is quite small. Moreover, our proposed DSGRU-based intrusion detection scheme can greatly improve the overall performance. Therefore, we can still consider our proposed scheme to be more attractive than the other four previous schemes

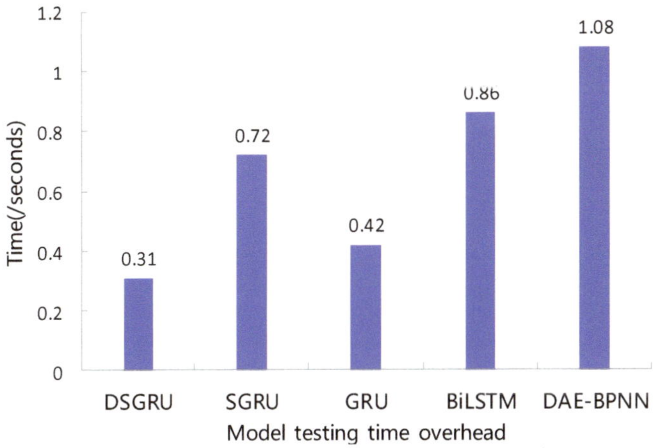

Figure 11. Model testing time overhead based on the NSL-KDD dataset.

7. Discussion

As is well known, there are many neural network models that can achieve intrusion detection. However, in this paper, DSGRU was designed and utilized to propose a novel intrusion detection scheme because DSGRU is perfectly suitable for the IoT environment, where the network traffic data is characterized by large-scale, heterogeneous multiple sources, high-dimensionality, and temporal correlation. In general, the main purpose of our proposed scheme is to attempt to address the following challenging problems.

How can the proposed scheme be suitable for the IoT environment compared to other comparable solutions? In the IoT environment, network traffic data are characterized by large-scale, heterogeneous multiple sources, high dimensionality, and temporal correlation. Traditional intrusion detection schemes require plenty of nonlinear transformations and complex matrix manipulations to process these network traffic data, thus reducing the efficiency and effectiveness. In our proposed scheme, we adopt DSGRU to establish the intrusion detection scheme, which can reduce the nonlinear transformations and matrix manipulations. Meanwhile, DSGRU can effectively find relations within the temporal correlation data. Therefore, by using the advantages of DSGRU, our proposed scheme can improve the overall performance in processing large-scale, heterogeneous multiple sources, high-dimensionality, and temporal correlation network traffic data.

How can the proposed scheme effectively reduce feature loss compared to the other neural network model? In our proposed scheme, we adopt DSGRU as the building block to establish the intrusion detection scheme. Generally, DSGRU consists of ORU, DGRU, and the Softmax activation function. On the one hand, DSGRU can learn more features by improving the number of layers for OGRU and DGRU. On the other hand, in the model training process, DSGRU will execute the loss compensation operation. That is, DSGRU will obtain the loss data and add them to x_t. As a consequence, our proposed scheme can effectively reduce feature loss during the model training process.

How can the proposed scheme greatly improve effectiveness compared to other comparable solutions? Compared with some previous solutions, our proposed scheme can greatly improve the effectiveness of intrusion detection due to the following factors. Firstly, DSGRU can perform loss compensation to reduce feature loss, thus improving the generalization ability of the intrusion detection model. Secondly, by increasing the layers of OGRU and DGRU, DSGRU can learn more feature data from the original dataset. Lastly, DSGRU can effectively reduce the operations of nonlinear transformations, thus reducing feature loss. As a consequence, our proposed scheme can greatly improve effectiveness compared to other comparable solutions.

8. Conclusions and Future Work

In this section, we will first conclude this paper. Subsequently, we will describe the research points that we will study in the future.

8.1. Conclusions

In an IoT environment, the network traffic data are characterized by large-scale, heterogeneous multiple sources, high-dimensionality, and temporal correlation, which could seriously affect the efficiency and accuracy of deep-learning-based intrusion detection schemes. To solve the above challenge, we designed a DSGRU-based intrusion detection scheme for the IoT environment. Specifically, we first designed a new neural network model called DSGRU. Subsequently, we utilized DSGRU to propose a novel intrusion detection scheme for the IoT environment. By using the attractive advantages of DSGRU, our proposed intrusion detection scheme could greatly improve the overall performance. Finally, we implemented our proposed DSGRU-based intrusion detection scheme and provided accurate experimental results based on the UNSW-NB15 dataset and NSL-KDD dataset. Meanwhile, the experimental results show that our proposed DSGRU-based intrusion detection scheme can achieve significant improvements in both effectiveness and efficiency when compared to some previous intrusion detection solutions. Specifically, when the datasets are UNSW-NB15 and NSL-KDD, the accuracies are 96.06% and 81.10%, the precisions are 95.52% and 83.34%, and the model training times are 61 min and 12 min, respectively.

8.2. Future Work

In this paper, we mainly studied the design of the intrusion detection scheme for the IoT environment and proposed a DSGRU-based intrusion detection scheme. Our proposed scheme can improve intrusion detection efficiency and accuracy. However, in practical applications, system administrators not only wish to comprehend the current security situation through intrusion detection but also seek to know the future security situation through intrusion forecasting. Therefore, we will study the solution for intrusion forecasting.

Author Contributions: Conceptualization, Y.L. (Yueling Liu) and C.Y.; methodology, Y.L. (Yueling Liu) and C.Y.; software, C.Y. and Y.L. (Yingcong Lan); validation, Y.L. (Yueling Liu), Y.L. (Yingcong Lan) and Y.D.; investigation, C.L.; resources, Y.D.; data curation, Y.L. (Yingcong Lan); writing—original draft preparation, Y.L. (Yueling Liu); writing—review and editing, Y.L. (Yueling Liu) and C.Y.; visualization, Y.L. (Yueling Liu); supervision, Y.D. and C.L.; project administration, C.L.; funding acquisition, C.Y. and Y.D. All authors have read and agreed to the published version of the manuscript.

Funding: This research was funded by the Key Science and Technology Project of Guangxi (grant no. AA22068067), the Central Guidance on Local Science and Technology Development Fund of Guangxi Province (grant no. ZY23055008), the Guangdong Provincial Key Laboratory of Novel Security Intelligence Technologies (grant no. 2022B1212010005), the Guangxi Key Laboratory of Trusted Software (grant no. KX202329), and the National Natural Science Foundation of China (grant no. 62172119).

Data Availability Statement: The UNSW-NB15 dataset can be downloaded from https://research.unsw.edu.au/projects/unsw-nb15-dataset (accessed on 18 August 2023) and the NSL-KDD dataset can be downloaded from https://www.unb.ca/cic/datasets/nsl.html (accessed on 29 August 2023).

Conflicts of Interest: The authors declare no conflict of interest.

References

1. Xiong, J.; Ma, R.; Chen, L.; Tian, Y.; Li, Q.; Liu, X.; Yao, Z. A personalized privacy protection framework for mobile crowdsensing in IIoT. *IEEE Trans. Ind. Inform.* **2019**, *16*, 4231–4241. [CrossRef]
2. Bag, S.; Gupta, S.; Kumar, S. Industry 4.0 adoption and 10R advance manufacturing capabilities for sustainable development. *Int. J. Prod. Econ.* **2021**, *231*, 107844. [CrossRef]
3. Kou, L.; Wu, J.; Zhang, F.; Ji, P.; Ke, W.; Wan, J.; Liu, H.; Li, Y.; Yuan, Q. Image encryption for Offshore wind power based on 2D-LCLM and Zhou Yi Eight Trigrams. *Int. J. Bio-Inspired Comput.* **2023**, *22*, 53–64. [CrossRef]

4. Roman, R.; Zhou, J.; Lopez, J. On the features and challenges of security and privacy in distributed internet of things. *Comput. Netw.* **2013**, *57*, 2266–2279. [CrossRef]
5. Togay, C.; Kasif, A.; Catal, C.; Tekinerdogan, B. A firewall policy anomaly detection framework for reliable network security. *IEEE Trans. Reliab.* **2022**, *71*, 339–347. [CrossRef]
6. Ren, H.; Xu, G.; Qi, H.; Zhang, T. PriFR: Privacy-preserving Large-scale File Retrieval System via Blockchain for Encrypted Cloud Data. In Proceedings of the 2023 IEEE 9th Intl Conference on Big Data Security on Cloud (BigDataSecurity), IEEE Intl Conference on High Performance and Smart Computing,(HPSC) and IEEE Intl Conference on Intelligent Data and Security (IDS), New York, NY, USA, 6–8 May 2023; IEEE: Piscataway, NJ, USA, 2023.
7. Ning, H.; Zhen, Z.; Shi, F.; Daneshm, M. A survey of identity modeling and identity addressing in Internet of Things. *IEEE Internet Things J.* **2020**, *7*, 4697–4710. [CrossRef]
8. Taparia, A.; Banu, P.K.N. A survey of blockchain: Concepts, applications and challenges. *Int. J. Comput. Sci. Math.* **2023**, *17*, 152–165. [CrossRef]
9. Muhammad, K.; Hamza, R.; Ahmad, J.; Lloret, J.; Wang, H.; Baik, S.W. Secure surveillance framework for IoT systems using probabilistic image encryption. *IEEE Trans. Ind. Inform.* **2018**, *14*, 3679–3689. [CrossRef]
10. Meneghello, F.; Calore, M.; Zucchetto, D.; Polese, M.; Zanella, A. IoT: Internet of threats? A survey of practical security vulnerabilities in real IoT devices. *IEEE Internet Things J.* **2019**, *6*, 8182–8201. [CrossRef]
11. Ren, H.; Li, H.; Liu, D.; Xu, G.; Cheng, N.; Shen, X. Privacy-preserving efficient verifiable deep packet inspection for cloud-assisted middlebox. *IEEE Trans. Cloud Comput.* **2020**, *10*, 1052–1064. [CrossRef]
12. Verma, S.; Kawamoto, Y.; Kato, N. A network-aware Internet-wide scan for security maximization of IPV6-enabled WLAN IoT devices. *IEEE Internet Things J.* **2020**, *8*, 8411–8422. [CrossRef]
13. Arisdakessian, S.; Wahab, O.A.; Mourad, A.; Otrok, H.; Guizani, M. A survey on IoT intru-sion detection: Federated learning, game theory, social psychology, and explainable AI as future directions. *IEEE Internet Things J.* **2022**, *10*, 4059–4092. [CrossRef]
14. Zhang, J.; Wang, Y.; Li, S.; Shi, S. An architecture for IoT-enabled smart transportation security system: A geospatial approach. *IEEE Internet Things J.* **2020**, *8*, 6205–6213. [CrossRef]
15. Zhang, J.; Wang, Y.; Li, S.; Shi, S. POTA: Privacy-Preserving Online Multi-Task Assignment with Path Planning. *IEEE Trans. Mob. Comput.* **2023**, 1–13. . [CrossRef]
16. Hu, C.; Zhang, C.; Lei, D.; Wu, T.; Liu, X.; Zhu, L. Achieving Privacy-Preserving and Verifiable Support Vector Machine Training in the Cloud. *IEEE Trans. Inf. Forensics Secur.* **2023**, *18*, 3476–3491. [CrossRef]
17. Zhang, C.; Hu, C.; Wu, T.; Zhu, L.; Liu, X. Achieving efficient and privacy-preserving neural network training and prediction in cloud environments. *IEEE Trans. Dependable Secur. Comput.* **2022**, *20*, 4245–4257. [CrossRef]
18. Liao, H.J.; Lin, C.H.R.; Lin, Y.C.; Tung, K.Y. Intrusion detection system: A comprehensive review. *J. Netw. Comput. Appl.* **2013**, *36*, 16–24. [CrossRef]
19. Kuang, F.; Xu, W.; Zhang, S. A novel hybrid KPCA and SVM with GA model for intrusion detection. *Appl. Soft Comput.* **2014**, *18*, 178–184. [CrossRef]
20. Mohammadi, M.; Rashid, T.A.; Karim, S.H.T.; Aldalwie, A.H.M.; Tho, Q.T.; Bidaki, M.; Rahmani, A.M.; Hosseinzadeh, M. A comprehensive survey and taxonomy of the SVM-based intrusion detection systems. *J. Netw. Comput. Appl.* **2021**, *178*, 102983. [CrossRef]
21. Kuang, F.; Zhang, S.; Jin, Z.; Xu, W. A novel SVM by combining kernel principal component analysis and improved chaotic particle swarm optimization for intrusion detection. *Soft Comput.* **2015**, *19*, 1187–1199. [CrossRef]
22. Gu, J.; Lu, S. An effective intrusion detection approach using SVM with naïve Bayes feature embedding. *Comput. Secur.* **2021**, *103*, 102158. [CrossRef]
23. Hussain, J.; Lalmuanawma, S.; Chhakchhuak, L. A two-stagehybrid classification technique for network intrusion detection system. *Int. J. Comput. Intell. Syst.* **2016**, *9*, 863–875. [CrossRef]
24. Lv, L.; Wang, W.; Zhang, Z.; Liu, X. A novel intrusion detection system based on an optimal hybrid kernel extreme learning machine. *Knowl.-Based Syst.* **2020**, *195*, 105648. [CrossRef]
25. Saleh, A.I.; Talaat, F.M.; Labib, L.M. A hybrid intrusion detection system (HIDS) based on prioritized k-nearest neighbors and optimized SVM classifiers. *Artif. Intell. Rev.* **2019**, *51*, 403–443. [CrossRef]
26. Zhang, C.; Costa-Pérez, X.P.; Patras, P. Adversarial attacks against deep learning-based network intrusion detection systems and defense mechanisms. *IEEE/ACM Trans. Netw.* **2022**, *30*, 1294–1311. [CrossRef]
27. Xie, G.; Yang, L.T.; Yang, Y.; Luo, H.; Li, R.; Alazab, M. Threat analysis for automotive CAN networks: A GAN model-based intrusion detection technique. *IEEE Trans. Intell. Transp. Syst.* **2021**, *22*, 4467–4477. [CrossRef]
28. Shone, N.; Ngoc, T.N.; Phai, V.D.; Shi, Q. A deep learning approach to network Intrusion detection. *IEEE Trans. Emerg. Top. Comput. Intell.* **2018**, *2*, 41–50. [CrossRef]
29. Otoum, S.; Kantarci, B.; Mouftah, H.T. On the feasibility of deep learning in sensor network intrusion detection. *IEEE Netw. Lett.* **2019**, *1*, 68–71. [CrossRef]
30. Kasongo, S.M.; Sun, Y. A deep learning method with wrapper based feature extraction for wireless intrusion detection system. *Comput. Secur.* **2020**, *92*, 101752. [CrossRef]
31. Li, B.; Wu, Y.; Song, J.; Lu, R.; Li, T.; Zhao, L. DeepFed: Federated deep learning for intrusion detection in industrial cyber–physical systems. *IEEE Trans. Ind. Inform.* **2021**, *17*, 5615–5624. [CrossRef]

32. Almutlaq, S.; Derhab, A.; Hassan, M.M.; Kaur, K. Two-stage intrusion detection system in intelligent transportation systems using rule extraction methods from deep neural networks. *IEEE Trans. Intell. Transp. Syst.* **2022**, 1–15. [CrossRef]
33. Keshk, M.; Koroniotis, N.; Pham, N.; Moustafa, N.; Turnbull, B.; Zomaya, A.Y. An explainable deep learning-enabled intrusion detection framework in IoT networks. *Inf. Sci.* **2023**, *639*, 119000. [CrossRef]
34. Wu, Y.; Lee, W.W.; Gong, X.; Wang, H. A hybrid intrusion detection model combining SAE with kernel approximation in Internet of Things. *Sensors* **2020**, *20*, 5710. [CrossRef] [PubMed]
35. Lee, J.H.; Park, K.H. AE-CGAN model based high performance network intrusion detection system. *Appl. Sci.* **2019**, *9*, 4221. [CrossRef]
36. Lo W.; Alqahtani, H.; Thakur, K.; Almadhor, A.; Chander, S.; Kumar, G. A hybrid deep learning based intrusion detection system using spatial-temporal representation of in-vehicle network traffic. *Veh. Commun.* **2022**, *35*, 100471.
37. Imrana, Y.; Xiang, Y.; Ali, L.; Abdul-Rauf, Z. A bidirectional LSTM deep learning approach for intrusion detection. *Expert Syst. Appl.* **2021**, *185*, 115524. [CrossRef]
38. Aljrees, T.; Kumar, A.; Singh, K.U.; Singh, T. Enhancing IoT Security through a Green and Sustainable Federated Learning Platform: Leveraging Efficient Encryption and the Quondam Signature Algorithm. *Sensors* **2023**, *23*, 8090. [CrossRef]
39. Sood, K.; Nosouhi, M.R.; Nguyen, D.D.N.; Jiang, F.; Chowdhury, M.; Doss, R. Intrusion detection scheme with dimensionality reduction in next generation networks. *IEEE Trans. Inf. Forensics Secur.* **2023**, *18*, 965–979. [CrossRef]
40. Liu, Z.Y.; Yang, C.S.; Xiao, J.; Song, B.W.; Shi, K.X. A Novel Intrusion Detection Method Based on Supplement Gate Recurrent Unit for IoT. *Wirel. Communi-Cations Mob. Comput.* **2022**, *2022*, 3678493. [CrossRef]
41. Ansari, M.S.; Bartoš, V.; Lee, B. GRU-based deep learning approach for network intrusion alert prediction. *Future Gener. Comput. Syst.* **2022**, *128*, 235–247. [CrossRef]
42. Zavrak, S.; İskefiyeli, M. Anomaly-based intrusion detection from network flow features using variational autoencoder. *IEEE Access* **2020**, *8*, 108346–108358. [CrossRef]
43. Moustafa, N.; Slay, J. UNSW-NB15: A comprehensive data set for network intrusion detection systems (UNSW-NB15 network data set). In Proceedings of the 2015 Military Communications and Information Systems Conference, Cracow, Poland, 18–19 May 2015.
44. Tavallaee, M.; Bagheri, E.; Lu, W.; Ghorbani, A.A. A detailed analysis of the KDD CUP 99 data set. In Proceedings of the 2009 IEEE Symposium on Computational Intelligence for Security and Defense Applications, Ottawa, ON, Canada, 8–10 July 2009; IEEE: Piscataway, NJ, USA, 2009.
45. Lee, W.; Stolfo, S.J. A framework for constructing features and models for intrusion detection systems. *ACM Trans. Inf. Syst. Secur. (TiSSEC)* **2000**, *3*, 227–261. [CrossRef]
46. Peres, R.S.; Barata, J.; Leitao, P.; Garcia, G. Multistage quality control using machine learning in the automotive industry. *IEEE Access* **2019**, *7*, 79908–79916. [CrossRef]
47. Chicco, D.; Jurman, G. The advantages of the Matthews correlation coefficient (MCC) over F1 score and accuracy in binary classification evaluation. *BMC Genom.* **2020**, *21*, 6. [CrossRef] [PubMed]

electronics

MDPI

Article

Improving Throughput of Mobile Sensors via Certificateless Signature Supporting Batch Verification

Chuan He[1,2,*], Bo Zhang [1,2], Liang Zhang [3], Zesheng Xi [1,2], Yuan Fang [3] and Yunfan Wang [1,2]

1 State Grid Smart Grid Research Institute Co., Ltd., Beijing 102200, China; zhangbo@geiri.sgcc.com.cn (B.Z.); xizesheng@geiri.sgcc.com.cn (Z.X.); wangyunfan@geiri.sgcc.com.cn (Y.W.)

2 State Grid Key Laboratory of Information & Network, Nanjing 211100, China

3 State Grid Anhui Electric Power Co., Ltd., Information & Telecommunication Branch, Hefei 230061, China; zhangliang@geiri.sgcc.com.cn (L.Z.); fangxuan@geiri.sgcc.com.cn (Y.F.)

* Correspondence: hechuan@geiri.sgcc.com.cn

Abstract: Mobile sensors enjoy the advantages of easy installation and low consumption, which have been widely adopted in many information systems. In those systems where data are generated rapidly, the throughput of the sensors is one of the most fundamental factors that determine the system functionality. For example, to guarantee data integrity, digital signature techniques can be applied. In many practical scenarios, such as the smart grid system, data are generated rapidly and, hence, the signature together with the data must also be transmitted and verified in time. This requires the mobile sensors to support a high-throughput data processing ability. In this setting, how to achieve efficient signature schemes supporting batch verification must be considered. Many signatures, such as the original national cryptographic standard, namely, the SM2 algorithm, do not support batch verification and are in a public-key infrastructure setting. In this paper, we propose a SM2-based certificateless signature scheme with batch verification, which is suitable for the aforementioned environment. The scheme extends the Chinese cryptographic standard SM2 algorithm to the certificateless setting and multiple signatures can be verified simultaneously. Another advantage of this scheme is that its signing phase does not involve any pairing operation. The verification phase only requires a constant pairing operation, which is not related to the number of signatures to be verified. The construction is generic and can be instantiated using any traditional signature scheme.

Keywords: mobile sensor; data integrity; certificateless signature; batch verification; pairing free

1. Introduction

A smart grid is a new type of network based on multiple power devices, which integrates a power data transmission function and power transmission function. These terminal devices often have limited hardware resources while generating mass data. How to increase throughput while ensuring data validation with limited hardware resources is an urgent problem that smart grids face. The validation of power data ensures, on the one hand, the integrity of data. Integrity directly affects the statistical, regulatory, and distribution of the electricity resources. In addition, considering the uncertain work environment of these devices, it is inevitable that sensor equipment malfunctions lead to data anomalies. At this point, it is necessary to quickly locate the device sending the abnormal data. Therefore, tracing the source of the error data is also a function that needs to be implemented. Digital signature technology can protect data from tampering and repudiation, which is sufficient for the data requirements of smart grids.

The earliest digital signature schemes mostly relied on the public-key infrastructure (PKI) setting, which bound user identity and public key information through the issuance of certificates by a CA (a certificate authority). However, this certificate can bring complex certificate management issues to the system and have high requirements for communication bandwidth and storage resources for devices so that it is unsuitable for grid devices. To address this issue, cryptography researchers have proposed identity-based cryptosystems (IBCs) [1,2] that directly use some identifiable information as public keys, such as phone numbers and email addresses. However, the private key comes entirely from the private key generator (PKG) in IBCs. This centralized trust dependency brings serious key escrow problems. Once the PKG center is attacked, it brings security issues to all subordinate devices. The certificateless public-key cryptosystem (CLPKC) inherits the advantages of the previous systems. In the CLPKC, there is neither certificates nor the problem of key escrow. Therefore, the CLPKC is more suitable for smart grid equipment in resource constrained scenarios.

In detail, many smart grid sensors are embedded with sequential numbers in the equipment. The sequential numbers can be treated as identities of the users in the systems and can be used to verify signatures or trace the origin of the message. On the other hand, the identity-based setting is not enough for the smart grid environment since there are large numbers of nodes in the system and it is not easy to select a widely adopted and fully trusted third party as the PKG. Therefore, certificateless cryptography is a prominent candidate for such a system. As is known to all, the pairing operations are comparatively complex and take much more time for computation than other group structures like the elliptic curve setting. However, many certificateless cryptographic schemes share similar algebraic structures to the identity-based constructions and are built upon pairing-friendly groups. Pairing-free certificateless signature schemes have not been widely developed, especially the scheme derived from the national cryptographic standard. To sum up, signature schemes that satisfy the pairing-free, certificateless setting, based on the published standard have many applications in smart grid system. Unfortunately, few constructions have been studied in the literature.

In addition, due to the high real-time requirements of data in the power system, the signature algorithm used must be able to calculate quickly [3]. The terminal node may generate electricity data at any time, and the server will receive multiple data streams from multiple nodes at the same time. The server must be able to quickly process signature verification, which requires the signature algorithm to preferably support batch verification. In these systems, both efficiency [4] and privacy-preserving properties [5] need to be taken into consideration. Signatures that support batch verification can solve this problem. Namely, the signatures on the data collected from various sensors and other equipment can be aggregated in a certain node before being transmitted to the center and can later be verified together. The framework is shown in Figure 1.

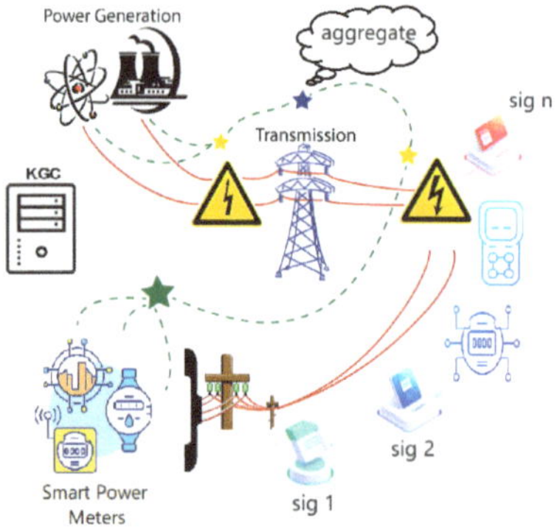

Figure 1. Framework of certificateless signature with batch verification.

1.1. Related Work

The CLPKC was first proposed by Al-Riyami and Paterson [6] to deal with the key escrow problem in the identity-based encryption (IBE) system [2]. They provided the construction of three schemes including encryption, signature, and key agreement. In addition, two basic adversary models in the certificateless cryptosystem were identified, namely, Type I adversary and Type II adversary. Due to the excellent properties of no-certificate, many researchers were attracted and many follow-up work was proposed. Yum and Lee summarized a general secure construction method of the certificateless signature (CLS) scheme [7] and certificateless encryption (CLE) scheme [8]. However, later these constructions were proved to be unsafe by Hu et al. [9] and Libert et al. [10]. In 2005, Huang et al. [11] proved that there was a security risk in the original Al-Riyami and Paterson scheme [6]. Au et al. [12] re-examined the security model of CLPKC and proposed the concept of a new adversary model called the malicious key generation center (KGC). Huang et al. [13] further subdivided each type opponent into three levels based on their attack capabilities and provided a super secure certificateless signature scheme. Among the known models, security against the super-type adversary achieves the most secure level. Nevertheless, the signature length was slightly long and contained three group elements. In recent years, many new shorter certificateless signature schemes and certificateless aggregate signatures [14,15] were proposed. There are also some schemes that have been proven to be insecure. For example, Shim [16] analyzed five recent articles and found that they can all be forged by adversaries. Therefore, how to construct secure certificateless signatures still requires a very rigorous approach. For a comparative survey of certificateless signature, ref. [17] is a good reference for the related studies until 2022. Two other related but earlier surveys can be found in [18,19].

In addition to solving the key escrow problem, compared to IBCs, another major advantage of certificateless cryptosystem is that they can be implemented without pairing. Baek et al. [20] explored the first certificateless encryption scheme without pairing using the Schnorr signature. However, Sun et al. [21] showed that the scheme in [20] did not consider public key attacks. They fixed the problem using a new scheme with a more stringent security model. The certificateless signature scheme without pairing was finished by He et al. [22] in 2010. For the IoT scenario, Gong et al. [23] and Yang et al. [24] designed a certificateless aggregation signature without pairing and Dai et al. [25] proposed a certificateless aggregation signcryption without pairing. Moreover, many certificateless schemes based on other PKI signatures have been studied. Using the RSA signature, Zhang et al. [26] also constructed a CLS scheme. Another study point is constructing CLS schemes based on already-published cryptographic standards. In 2022, Tang et al. [27] proposed a CLS scheme (in Chinese) based on the Chinese national cryptographic standard. The scheme is built upon the identity-based standard, namely, the SM9 (SM stands for the Chinese pinyi "shangmi", which means a commercial cryptography application) algorithm. As a result, it must rely on the pairing operation. Recently, He et al. [28] proposed a new CLS scheme using the SM2 algorithm without pairing. But their scheme requires zero-knowledge proof to verify the user public keys and how to support batch verification remains unknown. For batch verification, the certificateless aggregate signature (CLAS) [15,29] technique can be considered.

1.2. Motivation and Contributions

From the above analysis, we can see the enormous advantages of the certificateless cryptosystem and the feasibility of constructing a certificateless scheme based on the traditional signature scheme. However, current research is mostly limited to the implementation of the most basic signature schemes, while some signature algorithms with special functions have not yet emerged. For example, in systems with high throughput and low latency requirements, batch verification of signatures is also a crucial attribute that directly affects the availability of the entire system. Currently, there is no batch verifiable certificateless signature algorithm based on the national security algorithm. The primary contributions of this study include:

1. We propose a certificateless signature algorithm with batch verification based on the Chinese national cryptographic standards, in particular with the SM2 algorithm;
2. Our scheme supports batch verification of multiple signatures, thereby accelerating the algorithm in high throughput scenarios.

1.3. Technical Overview

From the above analysis, we can see that current studies on certificateless signature (CLS) schemes encounter the limitations of either relying on pairing operations like the scheme [27] built on the SM9 algorithm, or the underlying scheme not being selected as the cryptographic standard. The scheme proposed by He et al. [28] is extended from the SM2 algorithm and does not involve any pairing operation. However, it does not support batch verification. We first review the basic idea of He et al.'s construction. The core technical transformation from a traditional signature scheme to a certificate-based signature scheme is show in Figure 2.

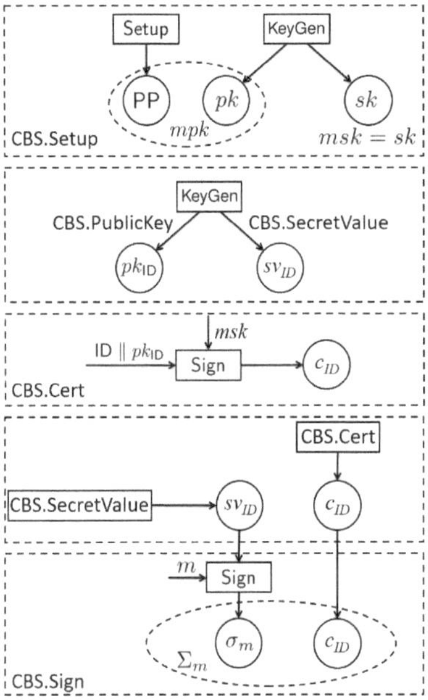

Figure 2. Transformation from traditional signature to certificate-based signature.

A certificateless signature is similar to a certificate-based signature. The main difference is the secret value setting phase. In the CLS scheme, it is not necessary for the user to select a secret value and compute the public key first, before transmitting the public key to the key generation center (KGC) to obtain the partial private key. This means that the user can apply the partial private key from the KGC first; then, generate the secret value and compute the public key later. During the key extraction phase, the user's public key may not yet be generated and, hence, cannot directly use the above transformation. To solve this issue, the user's public key contain two parts: one part is from the key extraction phase, which is similar to the certificate-based setting; the other part is generated by the user itself. These two parts are independently generated but must be used together to sign a message. This paves the way for transforming a traditional signature scheme into a CLS scheme.

As for the zero-knowledge proof part, we use the property of bilinear pairing to replace the complex proof process. Even though this brings the pairing operation into the scheme, it only appears in the verification phase and the signing phase does not involve any pairing operation. For verification, since our scheme supports batch verification, multiple signatures can be verified simultaneously and the number of pairing operations is constant. This means that the additional time cost caused by the pairing operations is a fixed value and, hence, it will not incur too much computational cost during batch verification. The details of batch verification are depicted in Section 4.2.

1.4. Organization

The structure of this article is organized as follows. In Section 2, two preliminaries will be briefly introduced, including CLS and bilinear pairing, and a SM2-based CLS scheme will be reviewed. In Section 3, a new signature scheme with batch verification will be proposed, and in Section 4, the performance of these schemes will be evaluated through simulation experiments. Finally, a conclusion of the entire article is provided in Section 5.

2. Preliminaries

We will describe the definition of two preliminaries, including bilinear pairing and the certificateless signature. We will also review a SM2-based CLS scheme.

2.1. Bilinear Pairing

For three cyclic groups G_1, G_2, G_T of a prime order q, a map $e : G_1 \times G_2 \rightarrow G_T$ is a bilinear pairing if and only if three properties hold:

- Computable: given any $g \in G_1, h \in G_2$, calculating $e(g, h) \in G_T$ is efficient;
- Bilinear: for $x, y \in Z_q$, the equation $e(g^x, h^y) = e(g, h)^{xy}$ always holds;
- Nondegenerate: if g is a generator of G_1 and h is a generator of G_2, $e(g, h)$ will also be a generator of G_T.

2.2. Certificateless Signature

The CLS scheme usually includes six algorithms:

- Setup (1^λ): The Setup algorithm is usually operated by the KGC to initialize the scheme, which receives a security parameter 1^λ. The system master public and secret key pair (mpk, msk) will be generated;
- KeyExt (mpk, msk, ID): The KeyExt algorithm is usually operated by the KGC, which receives the master key pair mpk, msk and a user identity ID. Finally, a partial private key d_{ID} is generated and transmitted to the user;
- SecretValue (mpk, ID): The SecretValue algorithm is usually completed by a user, which receives the master public key mpk and a user identity ID. Finally, a secret value sv_{ID} is generated and returned to the user;
- PublicKey $(mpk, \mathsf{ID}, sv_{\mathsf{ID}})$: The PublicKey algorithm is usually completed by a user, which receives the master public key mpk, a user identity ID, and a secret value sv_{ID}. A user public key pk_{ID} will be output;
- Sign $(mpk, d_{\mathsf{ID}}, sv_{\mathsf{ID}}, m)$: The Sign algorithm is usually completed by a user signing it. They receive the master public key mpk, a partial private key d_{ID}, a secret value sv_{ID}, and a message m. A signature σ_m on the message m will be output;
- Verify $(mpk, \mathsf{ID}, m, \sigma_m)$: The Verify algorithm is usually completed by a user verifying it. They receive the master public key mpk, a user identity ID, a public key pk_{ID}, a message m, and a signature σ_m. If the output is "1", it means the signature is legal; otherwise, the signature is illegal.

2.3. Review a CLS Scheme Based on SM2

The SM2-based CLS scheme designed by He et al. [28] is made up of six algorithms.

- Setup (1^λ): The Setup algorithm receives the security parameter 1^λ as input and uses the SM2 setup algorithm. It chooses an elliptic curve group $(\mathbb{G}, p, P)$ with parameters a, b and coordinates x_P, y_P. Then, it randomly picks $\alpha \in \mathbb{Z}_p$ and computes $P_{pub} = [\alpha]P$. It also selects a hash function H, such as the SM3 algorithm. Finally, the algorithm returns the master public and secret key pair as

$$mpk = (\mathbb{G}, p, P, P_{pub}, H),\ msk = \alpha.$$

- KeyExt (mpk, msk, ID): The KeyExt algorithm receives the master key pair (mpk, msk) and an identity ID as inputs. Firstly, it randomly selects $x \in \mathbb{Z}_p$ and computes

$ppk_{\mathsf{ID}} = [x]P$. Then, it concatenates the identity ID and the partial public key ppk_{ID}. Finally, it runs the SM2 signature algorithm to produce the partial private key.

1. Compute $e = H(\mathsf{ID} \parallel ppk_{\mathsf{ID}})$;
2. Pick $k \in \mathbb{Z}_p$ randomly and calculate $[k]P = (x_1, y_1), r = (e + x_1) \bmod p$;
3. Compute $s = ((1+\alpha)^{-1} \cdot (k - r \cdot \alpha)) \bmod p$.

The partial private key is $d_{\mathsf{ID}} = (r, s, x, ppk_{\mathsf{ID}})$;

- ScretValue (mpk, ID): The ScretValue algorithm receives the master public key mpk and an identity ID. Then, it runs the SM2 key generation algorithm. It randomly selects a $y \in \mathbb{Z}_p$ and sets $sv_{\mathsf{ID}} = (x, y)$ with the random value x received from the KGC. Next, it outputs the secret value sv_{ID};
- PublicKey $(mpk, \mathsf{ID}, sv_{\mathsf{ID}})$: The PublicKey algorithm receives the master public key mpk, an identity ID, and a secret value $sv_{\mathsf{ID}} = (x, y)$. Then, it computes $[y]P$ and generates a noninteractive zero-knowledge proof (NIZKP) π of holding the unique y with respect to $[y]P$. Next, it sets $pk_{\mathsf{ID}} = (ppk_{\mathsf{ID}}, [y]P, \pi)$ and outputs pk_{ID} as the public key;
- Sign $(mpk, d_{\mathsf{ID}}, sv_{\mathsf{ID}}, m)$: The Sign algorithm receives the master public key mpk, a partial private key $d_{\mathsf{ID}} = (r, s, x, ppk_{\mathsf{ID}})$, a secret value $sv_{\mathsf{ID}} = (x, y)$, and a message m. It first concatenates the identity ID and message m. Then, it computes $(x + y) \bmod p$ and runs the SM2 signing algorithm with $(x + y)$ to generate the part signature. In detail,

  1. Compute $e = H(\mathsf{ID} \parallel m)$;
  2. Pick $k \in \mathbb{Z}_p$ randomly and compute $[k]P = (x_1, y_1), r' = (e + x_1) \bmod p$;
  3. Compute $s' = ((1 + (x+y))^{-1} \cdot (k - r' \cdot (x+y)) \bmod p$.

  Next, it outputs the signature $\sigma_m = (r, s, r', s')$;
- Verify$(mpk, \mathsf{ID}, pk_{\mathsf{ID}}, m, \sigma_m)$: The Verify algorithm receives the master public key mpk, an identity ID, a public key $pk_{\mathsf{ID}} = (ppk_{\mathsf{ID}}, [y]P, \pi)$, a message m, and a signature $\sigma_m = (r, s, r', s')$. Then, it runs the SM2 algorithm to verify (r, s) and (r', s') and checks whether π is valid. In detail,

  1. Compute $e_1' = H(\mathsf{ID} \parallel ppk_{\mathsf{ID}}), e_2' = H(\mathsf{ID} \parallel m)$;
  2. Compute $t_1 = (r + s) \bmod p, t_2 = (r' + s') \bmod p$;
  3. Compute $[s]P + [t_1]P_{pub} = (x_1', y_1'), [s']P + [t_2](ppk_{\mathsf{ID}} + [y]P) = (x_2', y_2')$;
  4. Compute $R = (e_1' + x_1'), R' = (e_2' + x_2')$.

  If the proof π is valid and the equations $r = R, r' = R'$ hold, it outputs "1". Otherwise, it outputs "0".

3. A Certificateless Signature Scheme Supporting Batch Verification

3.1. Zero-Knowledge Proof with Pairing

In the above scheme, we need to provide a NIZKP of y in the user public key to avoid adversaries bypassing $[x]P$ by setting $[y]P$. However, zero-knowledge proof requires additional overhead and increases the length of the user public key. We provide an extension scheme that uses bilinear pairing tools to verify the binding relationship between $[x]P$ and $[y]P$. A user who verifies the signature can ensure that the signer knows the y corresponding to Y by calculating $e([x]P, [y]P) = e([xy]P, P)$. The extension scheme is depicted in the following.

3.2. Construction

Next, we describe our new certificateless signature scheme with batch verification based on SM2. Our scheme also consists of six algorithms.

- Setup (1^λ): The Setup algorithm receives a security parameter 1^λ. It generates an elliptic curve group $(\mathbb{G}, p, P)$ with parameters a, b and coordinates x_P, y_P. Then, it picks $\alpha \in \mathbb{Z}_p$ randomly and sets $P_{pub} = [\alpha]P$. Next, it chooses a hash function H, such as the SM3 algorithm. Finally, it outputs the master key pair as

$$mpk = (\mathbb{G}, p, P, P_{pub}, H),\ msk = \alpha.$$

- KeyExt (mpk, msk, ID): The KeyExt algorithm receives the master key pair (mpk, msk) and an identity ID as inputs. It first picks $x \in \mathbb{Z}_p$ randomly and calculates $ppk_{\mathsf{ID}} = [x]P$. Then, it concatenates ID with ppk_{ID}. Next, it runs the SM2 algorithm to generate a partial private key.
  1. Compute $e = H(\mathsf{ID} \parallel ppk_{\mathsf{ID}})$;
  2. Pick $k \in \mathbb{Z}_p$ randomly and compute $[k]P = (x_1, y_1), r = (e + x_1) \bmod p$;
  3. Compute $s = ((1+\alpha)^{-1} \cdot (k - r \cdot \alpha)) \bmod p$.

  It transmits the partial private key $d_{\mathsf{ID}} = (r, s, x, ppk_{\mathsf{ID}})$ to the user safely;
- ScretValue (mpk, ID): The ScretValue algorithm receives the master public key mpk and an identity ID as inputs. Then, it runs the SM2 key generation algorithm. It selects $y \in \mathbb{Z}_p$ randomly and sets $sv_{\mathsf{ID}} = (x, y)$ with the random value x received from KGC. Next, it outputs the secret value sv_{ID};
- PublicKey $(mpk, \mathsf{ID}, sv_{\mathsf{ID}})$: The PublicKey algorithm receives the master public key mpk, a user identity ID, and a secret value $sv_{\mathsf{ID}} = (x, y)$ of the user as inputs. Then, it computes $[y]P$ and $[xy]P$. Next, it sets $pk_{\mathsf{ID}} = (ppk_{\mathsf{ID}}, [y]P, [xy]P)$ and produces the public key pk_{ID};
- Sign $(mpk, d_{\mathsf{ID}}, sv_{\mathsf{ID}}, m)$: The Sign algorithm inputs the master public key mpk, a user partial private key $d_{\mathsf{ID}} = (r, s, x, ppk_{\mathsf{ID}})$, a secret value $sv_{\mathsf{ID}} = (x, y)$, and a message m. It first concatenates the identity ID and the message m. Then, it computes $xy \bmod p$ and runs the SM2 signing algorithm with xy to generate the part signature. In detail,
  1. Compute $e = H(\mathsf{ID} \parallel m)$;
  2. Pick $k' \in \mathbb{Z}_p$ randomly and compute $[k']P = (x_2, y_2), r' = (e + x_2) \bmod p$;
  3. Compute $s' = ((1+xy)^{-1} \cdot (k' - r' \cdot xy) \bmod p$.

  Next, it outputs the signature $\sigma = (r, s, r', s')$;
- Verify $(mpk, \mathsf{ID}, pk_{\mathsf{ID}}, m, \sigma)$: The Verify algorithm receives the master public key mpk, an identity ID, public key $pk_{\mathsf{ID}} = ([x]P, [y]P, [xy]P)$, a message m, and a signature $\sigma = (r, s, r', s)$. It first checks if $e([x]P, [y]P) = e([xy]P, P)$ holds. Then, it runs the SM2 verification algorithm to check the validity of σ_{ID} and σ_m. In detail,
  1. Compute $e_1' = H(\mathsf{ID} \parallel ppk_{\mathsf{ID}}), t_1 = (r + s) \bmod p, [s]P + [t_1]P_{pub} = (x_1', y_1')$, $R = (e_1' + x_1')$. Then check if the equations $R = r$ holds;
  2. Compute $e_2' = H(\mathsf{ID} \parallel m), t_2 = (r' + s') \bmod p, [s']P + [t_2]([xy]P) = (x_2', y_2')$, $R' = (e_2' + x_2')$.Then check if the equations $R' = r'$ holds;
  3. Check if the equations $e([x]P, [y]P) = e([xy]P, P)$ holds

  If all three equations hold, it outputs "1". Otherwise, it outputs "0".

4. Performance Analyses

4.1. Computational Costs

The efficiency performance of the scheme was evaluated by comparing it with Huang's CLS [13] through simulation experiments. We use $T_{add}, T_P, T_{mul}, T_e$ to represent the time of a point addition, a pairing operation, a scalar multiplication in the elliptic curve group, and an exponential operation in the G_T group. G and Z_p represent the elliptic curve group and the group of integers that are modular to a prime number p without an explicit statement. The experimental environment and the results are shown as Table 1 and Table 2, respectively:

Table 1. Experimental environment.

CPU	OS	RAM	Compiler and Library
Intel i7-12700z	Ubuntu 14.04	32 GB DDR5 4800 MHz	GNU C/C++ & PBC 0.5.14

Table 2. Efficiency comparison of the CLS schemes.

Scheme	Signature Length	Sign Computation	Verify Computation	Sign Time (ms)	Verify Time (ms)
He	$4\|Z_p\|$	$3T_{add} + 3T_{mul}$	$6T_{mul} + 7T_{add}$	1.01	4.81
Huang	$1\|G\| + 2\|Z_p\|$	$3T_{mul} + T_P + T_e$	$2T_{mul} + 2T_P + T_e$	4.08	3.63
Our	$4\|Z_p\|$	$3T_{add} + 3T_{mul}$	$6T_{mul} + 7T_{add}$	0.99	5.26

In the above table, $|Z_p|$ and $|G|$ denote the binary length of an element in group Z_p and G, respectively.

4.2. Batch Verification

This scheme requires the pairing operations in the verification algorithm, which consumes a lot of resources. To accelerate the algorithm, we can batch process a large number of signatures from the same user. For example, when multiple signatures from the same user are received consecutively, the received r, s, X, Y must all be consistent. Therefore, the verification equations can be performed once. The following is a simplified validation algorithm:

Batch-Verify $(mpk, \mathsf{ID}, pk_{\mathsf{ID}}, \{m_1, m_2, \ldots, m_n\}, \{\sigma_1, \sigma_2, \ldots, \sigma_n\})$: The verification algorithm inputs the master public key mpk, a user's identity ID, a public key pk_{ID}, n messages $\{m_1, m_2, \ldots, m_n\}$, and n signatures $\{\sigma_1, \sigma_2, \ldots, \sigma_n\}$. The $\{\sigma_i\}_{i\in\{1\ldots n\}}$ is denoted as $\{r_i, s_i, r'_i, s'_i\}$ and the pk_{ID} is denoted as $\{[x]P, [y]P, [xy]P\}$.

1. Compute $e'_{i,1} = H(\mathsf{ID} \parallel ppk_{\mathsf{ID}})$, $t_{i,1} = (r_i + s_i) \bmod p$, $[s_i]P + [t_{i,1}]P_{pub} = (x'_{i,1}, y'_{i,1})$, $R_i = (e'_{i,1} + x'_{i,1})$. Then, check if the equations $R_i = r_i$ holds. For n signatures coming from the same user, the $\{r_i, s_i, [x]P\}$ are the same so that this step only needs to be calculated once for n signatures;
2. Compute $e'_{i,2} = H(\mathsf{ID} \parallel m_i)$, $t_{i,2} = (r'_i + s'_i) \bmod p$, $[s'_i]P + [t_{i,2}]([xy]P) = (x'_{i,2}, y'_{i,2})$, $R'_i = (e'_{i,2} + x'_{i,2})$. Then, check if the equation $R'_i = r'_i$ holds. This step must to be executed for each signature;
3. Check if the equation $e([x]P, [y]P) = e([xy]P, P)$ holds. This step only needs to be calculated once for n signatures.

If all three equations hold, it outputs "1". Otherwise, it outputs "0".

In this way, when verifying n signatures from the same user, step 1 and 3 only need to be performed once and step 2 needs to be performed n times. Thus, the expensive pairing operation only needs to be performed twice.

Multi-User-Batch-Verify $(mpk, \{ID_1, ID_2, \ldots, ID_m\}, \{pk_{ID_1}, pk_{ID_2}, \ldots, pk_{ID_m}\}, \{m_{1,1}, \ldots, m_{1,n}, m_{1,2}, \ldots, m_{m,n}\}, \{\sigma_{1,1}, \sigma_{1,2}, \ldots, \sigma_{1,n}, \ldots, \sigma_{m,n}\})$: The verification algorithm inputs the master public key mpk, m identities $\{\mathsf{ID}_1, \mathsf{ID}_2, \ldots, \mathsf{ID}_m\}$, and m public keys $\{pk_{\mathsf{ID}_1}, pk_{\mathsf{ID}_2}, \ldots, pk_{\mathsf{ID}_m}\}$. The $m_{i,j}$ and $\sigma_{i,j}$ denote the j-th message and signature for i-th user, respectively. The $\sigma_{i,j}$ is denoted as $(r_{i,j}, s_{i,j}, r'_{i,j}, s'_{i,j})$ and the pk_{ID_i} is denoted as $([x_i]P, [y_i]P, [xy_i]P)$.

1. Compute $e'_{i,1} = H(\mathsf{ID}_i \parallel [x_i]P)$, $t_{i,j,1} = (r_{i,j} + s_{i,j}) \bmod p$, $[s_{i,j}]P + [t_{i,j,1}]P_{pub} = (x'_{i,j,1}, y'_{i,j,1})$, $R_{i,j} = (e'_{i,1} + x'_{i,j,1})$. Then, check if the equation $R_{i,j} = r_{i,j}$ holds. This step needs to be calculated once for each user;
2. Compute $e'_{i,j,2} = H(\mathsf{ID}_i \parallel m_{i,j})$, $t_{i,j,2} = (r'_{i,j} + s'_{i,j}) \bmod p$, $[s'_{i,j}]P + [t_{i,j,2}]([xy_i]P) = (x'_{i,j,2}, y'_{i,j,2})$, $R'_{i,j} = (e'_{i,j,2} + x'_{i,j,2})$. Then, check if the equation $R'_{i,j} = r'_{i,j}$ holds. This step must to be calculated for each signature;
3. For all m public keys, calculate $\pi_1 = \prod_{i=1,j=1,i!=j}^{m} e([x_i]P, [y_j]P) = \prod_{i=1}^{m}(\prod_{j=1,j!=i}^{m}(e([x_i]P, [y_j]P))$. This calculation can be completed by a third-party assistant and the results

can be sent to the user. Then, the user calculates $\pi_2 = e(\sum_{i=1}^{m}[x_i]P, \sum_{i=1}^{m}[y_i]P)$ and $\pi_3 = e(\sum_{i=1}^{m}[xy_i]P, P)$. Finally, check if the equation $\frac{\pi_2}{\pi_1} = \pi_3$ holds.

If all equations in the three steps hold, it outputs "1". Otherwise, it outputs "0".

In this way, when verifying the signatures from m users, the pairing operation can be completed twice locally rather than increasing with the number of users.

5. Conclusions and Future Work

To accelerate the verification algorithm, we extended the CLS scheme proposed by He et al. [28] and accelerated the algorithm execution through batch verification. The proposed scheme is still based on the Chinese national cryptographic standard (SM2) algorithm and no pairing operation is required during the signing process. This guarantees both efficiency and the requirement of using the standard cryptographic algorithm. In addition, the noninteractive zero-knowledge proof (NIZKP) of the signature is replaced by verifying an equation. This improvement provides efficient batch verification for multiple signatures. The number of pairing operations is constant regardless of the amount of signatures.

In this paper, we propose a basic certificateless signature scheme derived from the SM2 algorithm without resorting to the use of pairing operations. Signing or verifying a single signature does not involve any pairing operation. In addition, we further show how to improve the scheme to support batch verification. Nevertheless, the verification of multiple signatures requires a constant number of pairing operations. Despite the fact that the number is constant and is independent from the number of signatures in a batch verification, how to achieve a fully pairing-free SM2-based certificateless signature scheme that supports batch verification is worth studying. In addition, the security analysis is based on the random oracle model, which treats the hash function as an oracle. How to construct schemes without random oracles would also improve the security to a greater extent.

Author Contributions: Conceptualization, C.H.; formal analysis, B.Z.; methodology, C.H.; software, Z.X.; Writing—original draft, Y.W.; Writing—review and editing, L.Z. and Y.F. All authors have read and agreed to the published version of the manuscript.

Funding: This research was funded by the science and technology project of State Grid Corporation of China "Research on lightweight cryptographic technology for power IOT terminal" (Grand No. 5700-202255186A-1-1-ZN).

Institutional Review Board Statement: Not applicable.

Informed Consent Statement: Not applicable.

Data Availability Statement: All the related research data are available upon authors request.

Acknowledgments: We would like to thank the anonymous reviewers of this paper for their valuable comments and suggestions.

Conflicts of Interest: The authors declare no conflict of interest.

References

1. Shamir, A. Identity-Based Cryptosystems and Signature Schemes. In *Advances in Cryptology: Proceedings of CRYPTO 84 4*; Lecture Notes in Computer Science; Blakley, G.R., Chaum, D., Eds.; Springer: Berlin/Heidelberg, Germany, 1984; Volume 196, pp. 47–53. [CrossRef]
2. Boneh, D.; Franklin, M.K. Identity-Based Encryption from the Weil Pairing. In Proceedings of the Advances in Cryptology—CRYPTO 2001, 21st Annual International Cryptology Conference, Santa Barbara, CA, USA, 19–23 August 2001; Proceedings; Lecture Notes in Computer Science; Kilian, J., Ed.; Springer: Berlin/Heidelberg, Germany, 2001; Volume 2139, pp. 213–229. [CrossRef]
3. Zhang, C.; Zhao, M.; Zhu, L.; Zhang, W.; Wu, T.; Ni, J. FRUIT: A Blockchain-Based Efficient and Privacy-Preserving Quality-Aware Incentive Scheme. *IEEE J. Sel. Areas Commun.* **2022**, *40*, 3343–3357. [CrossRef]
4. Zhang, C.; Hu, C.; Wu, T.; Zhu, L.; Liu, X. Achieving Efficient and Privacy-Preserving Neural Network Training and Prediction in Cloud Environments. *IEEE Trans. Dependable Secur. Comput.* **2022**, *early access*. [CrossRef]
5. Hu, C.; Zhang, C.; Lei, D.; Wu, T.; Liu, X.; Zhu, L. Achieving Privacy-Preserving and Verifiable Support Vector Machine Training in the Cloud. *IEEE Trans. Inf. Forensics Secur.* **2023**, *18*, 3476–3491. [CrossRef]

6. Al-Riyami, S.S.; Paterson, K.G. Certificateless Public Key Cryptography. In Proceedings of the Advances in Cryptology—ASIACRYPT 2003, 9th International Conference on the Theory and Application of Cryptology and Information Security, Taipei, Taiwan, 30 November–4 December 2003; Lecture Notes in Computer Science; Laih, C., Ed.; Springer: Berlin/Heidelberg, Germany, 2003; Volume 2894, pp. 452–473. [CrossRef]
7. Yum, D.H.; Lee, P.J. Generic Construction of Certificateless Signature. In Proceedings of the Information Security and Privacy: 9th Australasian Conference, ACISP 2004, Sydney, Australia, 13–15 July 2004; Lecture Notes in Computer Science; Wang, H., Pieprzyk, J., Varadharajan, V., Eds.; Springer: Berlin/Heidelberg, Germany, 2004; Volume 3108, pp. 200–211. [CrossRef]
8. Yum, D.H.; Lee, P.J. Generic Construction of Certificateless Encryption. In Proceedings of the Computational Science and Its Applications—ICCSA 2004, International Conference, Assisi, Italy, 14–17 May 2004; Lecture Notes in Computer Science; Laganà, A., Gavrilova, M.L., Kumar, V., Mun, Y., Tan, C.J.K., Gervasi, O., Eds.; Springer: Berlin/Heidelberg, Germany, 2004; Volume 3043, pp. 802–811. [CrossRef]
9. Hu, B.C.; Wong, D.S.; Zhang, Z.; Deng, X. Key Replacement Attack Against a Generic Construction of Certificateless Signature. In Proceedings of the Information Security and Privacy, 11th Australasian Conference, ACISP 2006, Melbourne, Australia, 3–5 July 2006; Lecture Notes in Computer Science; Batten, L.M., Safavi-Naini, R., Eds.; Springer: Berlin/Heidelberg, Germany, 2006; Volume 4058, pp. 235–246. [CrossRef]
10. Libert, B.; Quisquater, J. On Constructing Certificateless Cryptosystems from Identity Based Encryption. In Proceedings of the Public Key Cryptography—PKC 2006, 9th International Conference on Theory and Practice of Public-Key Cryptography, New York, NY, USA, 24–26 April 2006; Lecture Notes in Computer Science. Yung, M., Dodis, Y., Kiayias, A., Malkin, T., Eds.; Springer: Berlin/Heidelberg, Germany, 2006; Volume 3958, pp. 474–490. [CrossRef]
11. Huang, X.; Susilo, W.; Mu, Y.; Zhang, F. On the Security of Certificateless Signature Schemes from Asiacrypt 2003. In Proceedings of the Cryptology and Network Security, 4th International Conference, CANS 2005, Xiamen, China, 14–16 December 2005; Lecture Notes in Computer Science; Desmedt, Y., Wang, H., Mu, Y., Li, Y., Eds.; Springer: Berlin/Heidelberg, Germany, 2005; Volume 3810, pp. 13–25. [CrossRef]
12. Au, M.H.; Chen, J.; Liu, J.K.; Mu, Y.; Wong, D.S.; Yang, G. Malicious KGC Attacks in Certificateless Cryptography. *IACR Cryptol. ePrint Arch.* **2006**, 255.
13. Huang, X.; Mu, Y.; Susilo, W.; Wong, D.S.; Wu, W. Certificateless Signatures: New Schemes and Security Models. *Comput. J.* **2012**, *55*, 457–474. [CrossRef]
14. Zhang, F.; Shen, L.; Wu, G. Notes on the security of certificateless aggregate signature schemes. *Inf. Sci.* **2014**, *287*, 32–37. [CrossRef]
15. Wu, G.; Zhang, F.; Shen, L.; Guo, F.; Susilo, W. Certificateless aggregate signature scheme secure against fully chosen-key attacks. *Inf. Sci.* **2020**, *514*, 288–301. [CrossRef]
16. Shim, K. Design Principles of Secure Certificateless Signature and Aggregate Signature Schemes for IoT Environments. *IEEE Access* **2022**, *10*, 124848–124857. [CrossRef]
17. Hussain, S.; Ullah, S.S.; Ali, I.; Xie, J.; Inukollu, V.N. Certificateless signature schemes in Industrial Internet of Things: A comparative survey. *Comput. Commun.* **2022**, *181*, 116–131. [CrossRef]
18. Housani, H.A.; Baek, J.; Yeun, C.Y. Survey on certificateless public key cryptography. In Proceedings of the 6th International Conference for Internet Technology and Secured Transactions, ICITST 2011, Abu Dhabi, United Arab Emirates, 11–14 December 2011; IEEE: Piscataway, NJ, USA, 2011; pp. 53–58.
19. Chen, Y.; Tso, R. A survey on security of certificateless signature schemes. *IETE Tech. Rev.* **2016**, *33*, 115–121. [CrossRef]
20. Baek, J.; Safavi-Naini, R.; Susilo, W. Certificateless Public Key Encryption without Pairing. In Proceedings of the Information Security, 8th International Conference, ISC 2005, Singapore, 20–23 September 2005; Lecture Notes in Computer Science; Zhou, J., López, J., Deng, R.H., Bao, F., Eds.; Springer: Berlin/Heidelberg, Germany, 2005; Volume 3650, pp. 134–148. [CrossRef]
21. Sun, Y.; Zhang, F.; Baek, J. Strongly Secure Certificateless Public Key Encryption without Pairing. In Proceedings of the Cryptology and Network Security, 6th International Conference, CANS 2007, Singapore, 8–10 December 2007; Lecture Notes in Computer Science; Bao, F., Ling, S., Okamoto, T., Wang, H., Xing, C., Eds.; Springer: Berlin/Heidelberg, Germany, 2007; Volume 4856, pp. 194–208. [CrossRef]
22. He, D.; Chen, J.; Zhang, R. Efficient and provably-secure certificateless signature scheme without bilinear pairings. *IACR Cryptol. ePrint Arch.* **2010**, 632. [CrossRef]
23. Gong, Z.; Gao, T.; Guo, N. PCAS: Cryptanalysis and improvement of pairing-free certificateless aggregate signature scheme with conditional privacy-preserving for VANETs. *Ad. Hoc. Netw.* **2023**, *144*, 103134. [CrossRef]
24. Yang, X.; Wen, H.; Diao, R.; Du, X.; Wang, C. Improved Security of a Pairing-Free Certificateless Aggregate Signature in Healthcare Wireless Medical Sensor Networks. *IEEE Internet Things J.* **2023**, *10*, 10881–10892. [CrossRef]
25. Dai, C.; Xu, Z. Pairing-Free Certificateless Aggregate Signcryption Scheme for Vehicular Sensor Networks. *IEEE Internet Things J.* **2023**, *10*, 5063–5072. [CrossRef]
26. Zhang, J.; Mao, J. An efficient RSA-based certificateless signature scheme. *J. Syst. Softw.* **2012**, *85*, 638–642. [CrossRef]
27. Tang, F.; Gan, N.; Yang, X.; Wang, J. Anti malicious KGC certificateless signature scheme based on blockchain and domestic cryptographic SM9. *Chin. J. Netw. Inf. Secur.* **2022**, *8*, 9–19.

28. He, C.; Zhang, B.; Zhang, L.; Xi, Z.; Fang, Y.; Wang, Y. Pairing-Free Certificateless Signature Scheme based on SM2 Algorithm. In Proceedings of the 2nd International Conference on Network Simulation and Evaluation, NSE 2023, Shenzhen, China, 22–24 November 2023; Springer: Berlin/Heidelberg, Germany, 2023.
29. Gong, Z.; Long, Y.; Hong, X.; Chen, K. Two Certificateless Aggregate Signatures from Bilinear Maps. In *Proceedings of the 8th ACIS International Conference on Software Engineering, Artificial Intelligence, Networking and Parallel/Distributed Computing, SNPD 2007, Qingdao, China, 30 July–1 August 2007*; Feng, W., Gao, F., Eds.; IEEE Computer Society: Washington, DC, USA; pp. 188–193. [CrossRef]

electronics

MDPI

Article

FLIBD: A Federated Learning-Based IoT Big Data Management Approach for Privacy-Preserving over Apache Spark with FATE

Aristeidis Karras [1,*], Anastasios Giannaros [1], Leonidas Theodorakopoulos [2], George A. Krimpas [1], Gerasimos Kalogeratos [2], Christos Karras [1,*] and Spyros Sioutas [1]

[1] Computer Engineering and Informatics Department, University of Patras, 26504 Patras, Greece; giannaros@ceid.upatras.gr (A.G.); krimpas@upatras.gr (G.A.K.); sioutas@ceid.upatras.gr (S.S.)

[2] Department of Management Science and Technology, University of Patras, 26334 Patras, Greece; theodleo@upatras.gr (L.T.); gkalogeratos@upatras.gr (G.K.)

* Correspondence: akarras@ceid.upatras.gr (A.K.); c.karras@ceid.upatras.gr (C.K.)

Abstract: In this study, we introduce FLIBD, a novel strategy for managing Internet of Things (IoT) Big Data, intricately designed to ensure privacy preservation across extensive system networks. By utilising Federated Learning (FL), Apache Spark, and Federated AI Technology Enabler (FATE), we skilfully investigated the complicated area of IoT data management while simultaneously reinforcing privacy across broad network configurations. Our FLIBD architecture was thoughtfully designed to safeguard data and model privacy through a synergistic integration of distributed model training and secure model consolidation. Notably, we delved into an in-depth examination of adversarial activities within federated learning contexts. The Federated Adversarial Attack for Multi-Task Learning (FAAMT) was thoroughly assessed, unmasking its proficiency in showcasing and exploiting vulnerabilities across various federated learning approaches. Moreover, we offer an incisive evaluation of numerous federated learning defence mechanisms, including Romoa and RFA, in the scope of the FAAMT. Utilising well-defined evaluation metrics and analytical processes, our study demonstrated a resilient framework suitable for managing IoT Big Data across widespread deployments, while concurrently presenting a solid contribution to the progression and discussion surrounding defensive methodologies within the federated learning and IoT areas.

Keywords: federated learning; privacy preserving; data poisoning; Big Data systems; Apache Spark; FATE; IoT data management

1. Introduction

Federated Learning (FL) is poised to play an essential role in extending the Internet of Things (IoT) and Big Data ecosystems by enabling entities to harness the computational power of private devices, thus safeguarding user data privacy [1]. Despite its benefits, FL is vulnerable to multiple types of assaults, including label-flipping and covert attacks [2–4]. The label-flipping attack specifically targets the central model by manipulating its decisions for a specific class, which can result in biased or incorrect results. To protect federated learning from data poisoning, researchers have devised techniques like differential privacy, which conceals user data details, and secure multi-party computation, which confidentially processes data across different sources. These methods strengthen FL's defences, preserving both data privacy and integrity [5–8]. To counter these threats, the research community has developed a plethora of privacy-preserving mechanisms and advanced techniques for improved model training, optimisation, and deployment while preserving the accuracy of the central model.

In the context of the Internet of Things and Big Data systems, Federated Learning (FL) has emerged as a vital paradigm for addressing the challenges associated with distributed data processing, privacy preservation, and resource utilisation. FL enables decentralised machine learning on edge devices, facilitating efficient data processing without compromising privacy [9,10]. Federated Learning (FL) stands out as a pivotal approach to addressing the complex issues arising from the integration of the Internet of Things (IoT) with Big Data analytics. In the vast and dynamic landscape of the IoT, where Intelligent Transportation Systems (ITSs) stand as a cornerstone, FL is being adopted to navigate the complexities of privacy and data management. ITSs, which are a quintessential source of Big Data, benefit from FL's decentralised nature, enabling enhanced data privacy without compromising the utility of the information extracted from countless daily transactions [11]. In parallel, FL is advancing the field of healthcare, particularly in the management of Sexually Transmitted Infections (STIs), by providing a framework that respects patient confidentiality while harnessing large datasets for better disease control [12].

The potential of FL extends beyond healthcare into the automotive industry, particularly in the vehicular IoT. The system's ability to harness a multitude of end-user data for local model training makes it a promising alternative to traditional GPS navigation in urban environments. This is because it allows for the collection and processing of data points across diverse vehicular trajectories, thus enabling more-precise and context-aware navigation systems [13]. The privacy-centric design of FL ensures that sensitive user data remain on local devices, thereby reducing the risk of breaches and unauthorised access, a compelling advantage for massive user data applications [14].

Despite its significant advantages, FL is not without its vulnerabilities, with data poisoning attacks representing a salient threat to its security paradigm. These attacks compromise the integrity of learning models by injecting malicious data into the training process. Recent studies have shown that FL systems are susceptible to such threats, prompting an increase in research focused on fortifying these systems against potential breaches [15]. The research presented in [16,17] examined the security vulnerabilities of federated learning within IoT ecosystems and suggested measures to strengthen its security. Ultimately, as FL continues to be integrated across various sectors, ensuring the security of its systems against such attacks is imperative, warranting further investigation and development of sophisticated defence mechanisms, as illustrated by the extensive research in the studies [18–24,26].

In an FL scenario, the label-flipping attack is a significant concern because it can manipulate the central decisions of the model for a specific class, without reducing its overall accuracy. This manipulation can result in biased or incorrect results, which can have far-reaching consequences for businesses and individuals. To address this issue, the research community has developed various countermeasures to mitigate the risk of data poisoning attacks. The results of the experiments described in this paper provide valuable insights into the efficacy of these privacy-preserving mechanisms and their potential to mitigate the risk of data poisoning attacks in FL systems. The findings are particularly relevant for businesses that rely on FL for training machine learning models as they can help ensure the security and integrity of the models while promoting reliable results.

The contribution of this work is to initiate a comprehensive exploration of the security aspects of federated learning within the scope of IoT Big Data management using the perspective of the Federated Adversarial Attack for Multi-Task Learning (FAAMT) algorithm. Within our proposed model framework, we traversed the complex routes of managing large-scale data, ensuring that the inherent privacy features of federated learning are not jeopardised by potential adversarial attacks. Our research clearly outlines the potential vulnerabilities and susceptibilities of federated multi-task learning systems to data poisoning attacks, shedding light on essential insights to strengthen the robustness and security of the FLIBD approach. By integrating the robust, privacy-preserving Big Data management approach with a thorough analysis and mitigation of adversarial attacks via FAAMT and relevant defence mechanisms, this study creates a well-defined, stable foundation that ensures both the efficient management of IoT Big Data and the protection of collaborative, federated learning experiences in multi-task learning environments. Thus, our work presents a balanced combination of efficient data management and enhanced security, driving the implementation of federated learning in real-world IoT and Big Data applications towards a secure, privacy-preserving future.

The remainder of this work is structured as follows. In Section 2, related work in the field of federated learning and data poisoning is surveyed and covered in detail along with state-of-the-art methods and data encryption applications. Section 3 outlines the methodology at both the theory and application levels, while Section 4 delves into the various types of attacks on federated learning. Section 5 highlights the experimental results and their findings. Finally, Section 7 concludes this work, and Section 7.1 provides a roadmap for future research directions.

2. Related Work

Federated Learning (FL) and data poisoning attacks are two crucial areas of research that have garnered significant attention in recent years. This section outlines the current progress and activities in these areas. FL is an innovative architecture designed to protect user privacy in machine learning environments in various areas [25–27]. It is commonly misunderstood, but this section provides examples to better understand its workings. For instance, when different companies aim to collaborate on a machine learning model training process, FL ensures that each company's local data remain internal by using encryption technology to transfer parameters between clients and the central server, thereby leading to the creation of a Global Model while preserving privacy.

Horizontal Federated Learning (HFL) is a subset of federated learning that splits datasets horizontally and removes data for training with the same user features, but different users [28,29]. This increases the number of user samples, but HFL may be vulnerable when the user attributes of two datasets overlap significantly, but the users themselves do not. To reduce private information exposure during the processing and transmission of components, HFL can employ homomorphic encryption systems [30–32], differential privacy mechanisms [33–35], and safe aggregation frameworks [36–38]. Other methods include blockchain-based FL [39,40] and multi-task FL [41,42].

Vertical Federated Learning (VFL) is used when the user attributes of two datasets partially overlap, but the users themselves overlap significantly [43–45]. This involves splitting the datasets vertically along a user/feature axis and removing data when users are identical, but user attributes vary. Approaches for VFL include SecureBoost, which suggests that all members input user attributes to train jointly, and a privacy-protecting logistic regression model based on VFL with parallelising objects for analysis and increased accuracy results [46–48].

Data poisoning attacks are an important topic of study in adversarial machine learning, which try to undermine machine learning algorithms [49,50]. These attacks have been studied on various machine learning models, including support vector machines [51], autoregressive models [52], collaborative filtering based on matrix factorisation [53], and neural networks for graph data [54–56]. In the context of multitask learning, Reference [57] offered a poisoning attack technique that differs from the situation in federated machine learning, where machine learning models are constructed based on datasets spread across various nodes/devices.

Federated machine learning is a rapidly growing field and offers opportunities for collaborative machine learning, but it also raises serious security and privacy concerns. To tackle these challenges, various defence strategies have been explored, including differential privacy, secure and robust aggregation, and outlier detection. Differential privacy has grown into an increasingly standard method for maintaining privacy in federated learning, but it can negatively impact the model's accuracy by introducing random noise to the data. Using secure and robust aggregation methods, such as Median-based aggregation, Trimmed Mean, Krum, and Bulyan, federated learning systems remain secure and robust. Outlier detection methods, such as rejection of adverse effects and Trim, identify and reject adversarial system interference proactively.

2.1. Data Security Encryption in Federated Learning: Relevant Literature and Approaches

Federated learning employs a distributed machine learning approach that facilitates training directly on devices, obviating the need to share sensitive data with a central server. Despite its advantages, concerns about data privacy and security persist in federated learning [58–61]. Various techniques, including homomorphic encryption, have been advanced to address these challenges. Homomorphic encryption is particularly noteworthy as it enables operations on encrypted data without necessitating their decryption, thereby maintaining data confidentiality.

In the study by [58], the researchers combined homomorphic encryption with cryptographic tools, such as masking and local model protection, to counter potential model inversion or reconstruction attacks, common threats in the domain of private financial or business data. Their findings affirmed that their proposed approach meets the data privacy standards. Another research work [59] conceptualised a blockchain-backed federated learning model for the Industrial Internet of Things (IIoT). This study introduced data protection schemes like distributed K-means clustering utilising differential privacy and homomorphic encryption and distributed AdaBoost with homomorphic encryption, emphasising multi-faceted data protection during the data and model sharing phases.

A different approach was presented in [60], where a system-level client selection method called Dubhe was introduced. This method allows clients to actively engage in training while ensuring their data privacy, using homomorphic encryption. The experiments revealed that Dubhe's performance, in terms of classification accuracy, is on par with the optimal greedy method, with minimal encryption and communication costs. Another mention is the study in [61], which offered an overview of challenges in federated learning and evaluated existing solutions, notably featuring homomorphic encryption.

Expanding on recent work in federated learning security, the study conducted by Fan et al. introduced a novel data-sharing scheme to enhance both security and efficiency [62]. Within this framework, three principal entities—the Cloud Service Provider (CSP), Data Provider (DP), and Data Requester (DR)—collaborate. Essentially, the DP uploads private data and potentially a re-encryption key to the CSP, allowing data re-encryption to specific user groups. Subsequently, the DR can request and decrypt this re-encrypted data using its private key. The scheme outlines eight critical algorithms, presenting an approach that holds significant promise for improving data-sharing protocols in FL ecosystems.

Following the exploration into federated learning security, another notable study detailed a sophisticated encryption algorithm tailored for plaintext images [63]. This process commences by segmenting the image into R, G, and B channels, with subsequent encryption operations applied uniformly across these channels. Key steps in this approach include the separation of channels, leveraging the 2D-LCLM complex chaotic system to generate pseudo-random sequences, and employing the Zhou Yi Eight Trigrams encryption rule to finalise the encryption. This method underscores the evolution of encryption techniques suitable for multimedia data in modern research landscapes.

In the context of images, as previously noted, another study delved into the scope of blockchain security by highlighting a traceability model for the DAG blockchain system [64]. As images demand robust encryption methods, blockchains seek dependable verification systems. This model applies a witness mechanism, encompassing everything from unit addition to the blockchain to information retrieval for users. In this context, a "unit" serves as the primary data container, encapsulating vital information such as hash values and the public key of the uploader. A defining feature of this model is its steadfast commitment to data integrity. Once a unit is validated, modifying its content becomes challenging since all interconnected units would require alterations, ensuring that unauthorised changes are nearly impossible.

A study examined adaptable encryption and decryption frameworks for CKKS homomorphic encryption, enabling computation on encrypted data without decryption [65]. The CKKS scheme, reliant on the RLWE problem and approximate arithmetic, encodes real numbers into polynomials for encryption with a public key. After remote computation on encrypted data, the client decrypts the received results with its secret key. The paper highlights the importance of secure key generation and evaluation key creation for homomorphic operations. The proposed architectures aim to enhance the efficiency of CKKS encryption without delving into extensive data security details [65]. In conjunction with adaptable encryption for CKKS, the study expects future research to integrate homomorphic encryption with machine learning, potentially exploring HE-integrated federated learning for enhanced data privacy.

Ultimately, reviews of the literature on data security in federated learning emphasise strategies such as homomorphic encryption and blockchain to protect data in machine learning. Various methods are proposed to safeguard sensitive information, from cryptographic techniques to innovative data-sharing schemes, bolstering security while maintaining efficiency. The aim is to forge robust federated learning systems that guarantee data privacy, with emerging research exploring the integration of these security methods with homomorphic encryption for enhanced machine learning applications.

2.2. Privacy Threats in Federated Learning

Privacy challenges that are inherent within Federated Learning (FL) architectures, particularly pertaining to the extensive interaction across various participating entities, pose significant research concerns [66]. One such crucial threat is the Deep Gradients Leakage attack, which is strategically leveraged by an adversary who acts as an aggregator. Within this attack schema, the adversary capitalises on exploiting the gradients of the model with the underlying intent to extrapolate or infer the private data of the individual participants [67]. This form of attack underscores an intricate manipulation of data and, quite conspicuously, has a direct impact on the inherent privacy of data that are circulated within the FL architecture. Furthermore, the assimilation of Generative Adversarial Network (GAN) attacks within the adversarial framework often sees the attacker using GANs to meticulously generate data, which mirrors the private data of participants [67]. The data generation here is formulated such that it concurrently is metaphorically camouflaged, disguising it as legitimate data and, thus, introducing potential jeopardy to the integrity and confidentiality of the original data.

In conjunction with the previous attacks, the looming threat of poisoning attacks and inference attacks magnifies the privacy dilemma in FL. The former envisages a scenario wherein an adversarial participant malevolently injects data into the training process with the aim to subtly, yet systematically, manipulate the Global Model, consequently propagating erroneous inferences [68]. This perturbation of the learning process is not just detrimental to the model accuracy, but also corrodes the authenticity of predictions, potentially cascading to flawed decision-making processes. On the other hand, inference attacks extrapolate this issue, where an adversary infers the private data of other participants through a strategic exploration of the Global Model [68]. Moreover, range inference attacks refine this adversarial strategy by attempting to ascertain the range of the private data of participants, providing a discreet, yet robust mechanism to violate privacy norms [69]. Thus, these types of attacks lead to a wide and deep invasion of privacy, calling for new and effective strategies to mitigate them.

Addressing privacy threats in Federated Learning (FL) invokes a multilayered approach where technologies like blockchain and Trusted Execution Environments (TEEs) have been significant, yet not entirely impervious to certain attack vectors. The incorporation of blockchain technology serves as a decentralised ledger, which aids in securing transparent record-keeping and transactions, thereby mitigating single-point failures and ensuring a level of accountability within the FL paradigm [67]. Concurrently, TEEs ensure secure computational zones, safeguarding data and models during the computation and offering a protective shield against a spectrum of threats.

However, it is essential to acknowledge that current FL protocols exhibit certain deficiencies in rendering an all-encompassing security framework, thus spotlighting a crucial necessity for more-detailed and in-depth research in this arena [70]. The pressing requirement pivots around designing a security architecture that seamlessly blends robustness and comprehensiveness while also manifesting adaptability to the ever-evolving threat landscape. This ensures sustained, privacy-preserving FL operations among the intricate and dynamic cyber–physical interactions in large-scale IoT systems [71]. This establishes a prolific domain for continuing and prospective research, with a dedicated focus on embedding a sophisticated and well-articulated balance of security and privacy within the FL paradigm. Ensuring that innovative solutions are not merely confined to theoretical frameworks, but extend to practical viability in real-world deployments also stands as a pivotal aspect. Such a pursuit not only enriches the academic discourse around privacy-preserving mechanisms in FL, but also contributes substantively to the operational robustness of FL in large-scale systems where data privacy and security are paramount.

2.3. *Privacy and Security in Federated Learning Systems: State-of-the-Art Defensive Mechanisms*

Federated Learning (FL) emerges as a pivotal methodology, enabling Machine Learning (ML) application directly on devices while safeguarding sensitive and private information from unwarranted disclosure and tracking. Despite its innovative approach, FL's security framework invites further scrutiny, especially within sectors managing exceptionally sensitive data, such as the healthcare industry [72–74]. Vulnerabilities in FL, including susceptibility to model poisoning, data heterogeneity, and model inversion attacks, possess the potential to undermine the efficacy of the Global Model [72–76].

Various defensive tactics have been introduced to counter these threats, such as the implementation of robust aggregation algorithms, deploying Multi-Party-Computation (MPC)-based secure aggregation, and the utilisation of trained autoencoder-based anomaly-detection models [73–75]. Notably, several state-of-the-art defences against model poisoning attacks, including FedCC, Krum, and Trimmed Mean, have been articulated in the existing literature [75,77].

Nevertheless, these strategies often provide solutions that are parallel and non-intersecting with respect to individual attacks or concerns. Moreover, the meticulous orchestration of collusion among malicious participants can subtly reduce the bias triggered in the poisoned local model—minimising disparities from the poison-free model. This subtlety becomes critical in facilitating stealthy backdoor attacks and eluding a myriad of top-tier defence strategies currently available in FL [76]. Thus, a void exists, signalling an exigent need for additional research aimed at devising potent and encompassing defensive mechanisms to bolster the security infrastructure of FL systems.

Romoa stands out in the arena of Federated Learning (FL) as it applies a logarithm-based normalisation strategy, steering clear of the pitfalls associated with scaled gradients that originate from nefarious entities. This strategic model aggregation method acts as a bulwark against model poisoning attacks, a pertinent concern in the FL framework, where several decentralised nodes collaborate in model training. The stabilisation and integrity of the model during its training phase are crucial to ensure the derived insights and applications remain valid and reliable. Hence, Romoa not only addresses the immediate concerns related to malicious activities in FL, but also underscores the necessity of innovatively confronting challenges to uphold the robustness of decentralised learning models.

Concurrently, Robust Federated Aggregation (RFA) demonstrates a divergent, yet equally significant methodology, emphasising the utilisation of a weighted average of gradients to fortify FL systems against Byzantine attacks. The pertinence of resisting such attacks is elevated in sensitive domains, such as healthcare, where the accuracy and reliability of models can directly impact decision-making and outcomes. RFA, through its adept handling of gradients and ensuring the integrity of the aggregation process, helps to sustain the credibility of FL in environments where malicious actors might seek to destabilise the model. Thus, RFA emerges not merely as a defensive mechanism, but as a vital cog ensuring the seamless operation of FL systems, especially where the veracity of aggregated models is critical.

While Romoa and RFA significantly advance the security mechanisms within FL systems, the journey towards a thoroughly secure, decentralised learning environment remains ongoing and necessitates continual research and development. This becomes particularly poignant in the realms of the IoT and Big Data, where large volumes of data are processed and analysed across various nodes. The challenge extends beyond merely defending against known threats to preemptively identifying and mitigating potential future vulnerabilities within the FL paradigm. The continual evolvement of defence mechanisms, in tandem with the evolution of threats, underscores the dynamic and complex nature of securing FL systems. Therefore, it is imperative for the research community to remain engaged in a persistent exploration of innovative strategies and mechanisms to safeguard FL against a spectrum of threats, ensuring its viability and trustworthiness in diverse applications across varied domains.

Navigating through the landscape of defensive mechanisms in federated learning, a variety of strategies have been spotlighted, each exemplifying unique approaches and methodologies towards mitigating adversarial endeavours. The summary presented in Table 1 encapsulates a selection of these mechanisms, illustrating the diversity and specificity with which each strategy is forged and employed. Notably, while strategies like FedCC and Krum emphasise robust aggregation algorithms and server-side defences, respectively, others like FL-WBC introduce client-based strategies to shield the federated learning model from adversarial attacks. This table not only serves as a confluence of varied defensive strategies, but also underscores the multifaceted nature of the challenges that federated learning systems encounter in maintaining model integrity and privacy preservation. Thus, the mechanisms detailed in Table 1 establish a foundation for a more-detailed and -subtle examination of the architectural and functional aspects of these defences, thereby facilitating subsequent research and progression in the spectrum of secure and robust federated learning. This overview of different mechanisms seeks to build a basic understanding, which will help direct future research and development paths in the field.

Table 1. Summary of defensive mechanisms in federated learning systems.

Mechanism	Description	Reference
FedCC	Employs a robust aggregation algorithm, mitigating both targeted and untargeted model poisoning or backdoor attacks, even in non-IID data scenarios.	[75]
Krum	Acts as a server-side defence via an aggregation mechanism, but may be susceptible to Covert Model Poisoning (CMP).	[77]
Trimmed Mean	Server-side aggregation similar to Krum, yet also potentially prone to CMP, aiming to resist model poisoning attacks.	[77]
MPC-Based Aggregation	Mitigates model inversion attacks by employing a trained autoencoder-based anomaly-detection model during aggregation.	[74]
FL-WBC	A client-based strategy that minimises attack impacts on the Global Model by perturbing the parameter space during local training.	[78]
Romoa	Utilises a logarithm-based normalisation to manage scaled gradients from malicious vehicles, resisting model poisoning attacks.	[79]
RFA	Utilises a weighted average of gradients to resist Byzantine attacks, aiming to establish a robust aggregation method.	[80]

2.3.1. Limitations of Current Defensive Mechanisms in Federated Learning

The development and implementation of defensive mechanisms in Federated Learning (FL) have been imperative for ensuring secure and robust model training in decentralised learning environments. Nonetheless, prevailing methods manifest substantial limitations, hampering their optimal functionality and efficacy in practical scenarios.

Computational and Communication Overhead

A significant limitation is the computational burden imposed on Edge Devices (EDs), which often possess restricted computational resources. This limitation arises from the heavy computation overhead, which is further exacerbated when these devices are tasked with conducting complex learning or defensive processes. Concurrently, the communication overhead is another crucial aspect, predominantly related to the uploading of converged local models' parameters to a centralised server, where aggregation is performed. This not only demands substantial communication resources, but also exposes the system to potential communication-related vulnerabilities [81].

Knowledge Preservation and Incremental Learning

Moreover, a crucial challenge is associated with the guarantee of preserved knowledge, especially in the context of incremental learning over new local datasets. The current defensive mechanisms may jeopardise the acquired knowledge due to the absence of a solid framework that ensures the stability and plasticity of the learned models during subsequent learning phases. This issue is particularly prominent when FL systems encounter novel data, and adaptive learning becomes crucial to preserving and updating the Global Model appropriately [82].

Security and Privacy Concerns

Security concerns, including susceptibility to various attacks (such as model poisoning, privacy inference, and Byzantine attacks), underscore another essential limitation. While privacy preservation is a cornerstone of FL, ensuring robust defence against intricate attack strategies, particularly those exploiting the decentralised nature of FL, remains a pressing concern. The vulnerabilities related to privacy inference attacks, which aim to infer sensitive information from the shared model updates, and Byzantine attacks, where malicious actors disseminate falsified updates, are notably challenging to mitigate comprehensively [82]. This notwithstanding, novel approaches, namely Romoa and RFA, have been proposed to address some of these challenges by introducing advanced aggregation methods designed to resist various attacks while ensuring robust model training [81].

2.4. Problem Statement

Navigating the management of voluminous data derived from the Internet of Things (IoT) environment, coupled with ensuring privacy within expansive systems through Federated Learning (FL), highlights a complex and multi-dimensional challenge. Specifically, our discourse pivots on the following predominant axes of difficulties:

- **Massive and rapid IoT data:** IoT environments are characterised by the generation of immense volumes of data (D_i) at an astounding velocity, making effective and efficient data management imperative to prevent systemic bottlenecks and to ensure sustained operational performance.
- **Preserving privacy with FL:** Ensuring the data (D_i and D_t) remain localised and uncompromised during Global Model training in FL demands robust methodologies to prevent leakage or unintended disclosure of sensitive information through model updates (**W**).
- **Label-flipping attacks:** These attacks, wherein labels of data instances are maliciously altered ($\tilde{D}i$ and $\tilde{D}s$), present a pronounced threat to model integrity and efficacy in

FL. Here, the design and implementation of defensive mechanisms that can detect, mitigate, or recover from such attacks is of paramount importance.

$$\mathcal{H}(\tilde{D}i, \tilde{D}s; \mathbf{W}) \to \min_{\mathbf{W}} L(D_i, D_t, \mathbf{W}) \tag{1}$$

where $\mathcal{H}$ is the high-level function that seeks to minimise the loss function L given the perturbed data and weight matrix, ensuring the learned model $\mathbf{W}$ is resilient against the attack.

- **Ensuring scalability:** Addressing the scale, by ensuring the developed FL model not only counters privacy and security threats, but also scales efficiently to manage and process expansive and diverse IoT Big Data.
- **Technological integration and novelty:** While FATE offers a promising federated learning framework and Apache Spark offers fast in-memory data processing, exploring and integrating these technologies in an innovative manner that cohesively addresses IoT Big Data management challenges within an FL paradigm becomes crucial.

$$\mathcal{H}(D_i, D_t; \mathbf{W}, \mathbf{\Omega}) \to \min_{\mathbf{W}, \mathbf{\Omega}} L(D_i, D_t, \mathbf{W}, \mathbf{\Omega}) \tag{2}$$

where $\mathcal{H}$ is aimed at minimising the loss function L concerning the data, the weight matrix $\mathbf{W}$, and the model relationship matrix $\mathbf{\Omega}$, ensuring a harmonised functionality between the integrated technologies and, also, enabling scalable and efficient data processing and model training across federated nodes.

The core objective of FLIBD is to diligently construct a framework that mitigates the identified challenges. This venture not only seeks to resolve current issues, but also aspires to craft a model that leads, moulds, and enhances forthcoming technological and methodological progress within the sphere of privacy-preserving data management in expansive IoT deployments, leveraging federated learning.

2.5. Proposed Architecture

FLIBD formulates an insightful architecture, intending to skilfully manage voluminous IoT-originated data whilst concurrently ensuring meticulous privacy preservation across large-scale systems, achieved by integratively employing Federated Learning (FL), Apache Spark, and FATE. The fundamental layers and their concomitant functionalities are delineated below and represented in Figure 1:

1. **IoT data harvesting and initial processing layer:**
    - Dynamic data acquisition: implements a strategic approach to dynamically harvest, categorise, and preliminarily process extensive IoT data, utilising Apache Spark's proficient in-memory computation to adeptly handle both streaming and batch data.
2. **In situ model training and data privacy layer:**
    - Intrinsic local model training: employs FATE to facilitate localised model training, reinforcing data privacy by ensuring data are processed in situ.
    - Data and model security mechanism: integrate cryptographic and obfuscation techniques to safeguard data and model during communication, thus fortifying privacy and integrity.
3. **Federated learning and secure model consolidation layer:**
    - Privacy-aware federated learning: engages FATE to promote decentralised learning, which encourages local model training and securely amalgamates model updates without necessitating direct data exchange.
    - Model aggregation and resilience: establishes a secure aggregation node that amalgamates model updates and validates them against potential adversarial actions and possible model poisoning.

4. **Global Model enhancement and feedback integration layer:**
   - Deploy, Enhance, and Evaluate: apply the Global Model to enhance local models, instigating a comprehensive evaluation and feedback mechanism that informs subsequent training cycles.
5. **Adaptive scalability and dynamic management layer:**
   - Dynamic scalability management: utilises Apache Spark to ensure adaptive scalability, which accommodates the continuous data and computational demands intrinsic to vast IoT setups.
   - Proactive system management: implements AI-driven predictive management and maintenance mechanisms, aiming to anticipate potential system needs and iteratively optimise for both performance and reliability.

In essence, the FLIBD architecture aspires to function as a robust foundation for upcoming advancements in privacy-preserving data management within the continuously evolving IoT environment. It makes an effort to navigate present challenges with viable solutions, whilst concurrently establishing a robust framework beneficial to encouraging future research and development in privacy-preserving methodologies for managing IoT Big Data across large-scale scenarios.

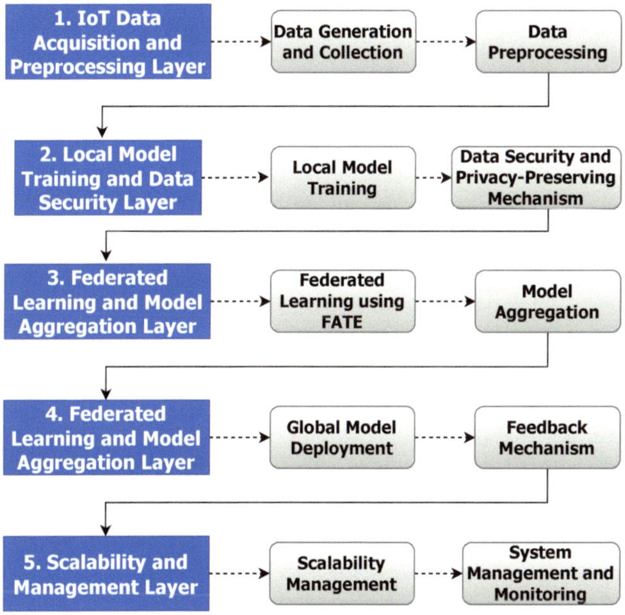

Figure 1. The basic architecture.

3. Methodology

In this section, we provide a comprehensive overview of the steps taken in the data poisoning attack strategies that we propose for federated machine learning. Initially, the concept of federated multi-task learning functions as a general framework for multi-task learning in a federated environment is given. We then present the mathematical formulation of our poisoning attack and describe how to further optimise the model. The abbreviations for the variables used in our work are given in Table 2. To make it simpler for the reader to follow our methodology and comprehend the underlying principles, we introduce and elucidate these notations in depth throughout the paper. Moreover, we provide a representation of our methodology, which includes plots, to help the reader understand the steps involved in our proposed attack.

Table 2. Notation for utilised variables.

Symbol	Interpretation
D_i	Uninfected data for node i
D_t	Uninfected data for target node t
$\tilde{D}i$	Infected data for node i
$\tilde{D}s$	Infected data for attacking node s
$\mathcal{T}$	Set of target nodes
$\mathcal{S}$	Set of attacking nodes
$\mathcal{H}$	Upper level function
$\mathbf{W}$	Weight matrix
$\mathbf{\Omega}$	Model relationship matrix

Objectives of Federated Machine Learning

In this section, we address the issue of data poisoning attacks in federated multi-task learning. We introduce three types of attacks based on real-world scenarios and propose a bilevel formulation to determine the optimal attacks. The goal of the attacker is to degrade the performance of a set of target nodes $\mathcal{T}$ by injecting corrupted or poisoned data into a set of source attacking nodes $\mathcal{S}$. The objective of federated machine learning is to develop a model from data generated by n distinct devices denoted as $\mathcal{D}_i$ with $i \in [n]$, which may have different data distributions. To address this, separate models $\mathbf{w}_1, \ldots, \mathbf{w}_n$ are trained on individual local datasets. The focus of this paper is on a horizontal (sample-based) federated learning model known as federated multi-task learning [83], which is a general multi-task learning framework applied in a federated setting. The federated multi-task learning model can be represented as:

$$\sum_{i=1}^{N}\sum_{j=1}^{M_i} \mathcal{L}i\left(\mathbf{w}i^\top \mathbf{x}i,j,\mathbf{y}i,j\right), \tag{3}$$

regularised by the trace of the product $\mathbf{W\Omega W}^\top$ scaled by λ_1 and the Frobenius norm of $\mathbf{W}$ squared scaled by λ_2:

$$\lambda_1 \mathrm{Tr}\left(\mathbf{W\Omega W}^\top\right) + \lambda_2 |\mathbf{W}|_F^2. \tag{4}$$

The symbol Tr denotes the trace, and $|\mathbf{W}|_F$ denotes the Frobenius norm of $\mathbf{W}$.

Here, $(\mathbf{x}_i^j, \mathbf{y}_i^j)$ is the j-th sample of the i-th device and m_i represents the number of clean samples in the i-th device. The matrix $W \in \mathcal{R}^{d\times n}$, with the i-th column being the weight vector for the i-th device, comprises the weight vectors $\mathbf{w}_1, \ldots, \mathbf{w}_n$. The relationships among the devices are modelled by $\Omega \in \mathcal{R}^{n\times n}$, and the regularisation terms are controlled by the parameters $\lambda_1 > 0$ and $\lambda_2 > 0$.

In the context of federated machine learning, finding the $\mathbf{\Omega}$ matrix can be computed separately from the data, as it is independent of them. A key contribution of [83] was the creation of an effective method for distributed optimisation to update the $\mathbf{W}$ matrix. This was accomplished by incorporating the ideas of distributed primal–dual optimisation, which were previously outlined in [84].

Let $m = \sum_{i=1}^{n} m_i$ and $\mathcal{X} = \mathrm{Diag}(\mathcal{X}1, \ldots, \mathcal{X}n) \in \mathbb{R}^{nd\times m}$. Holding the $\mathbf{\Omega}$ matrix constant, the optimisation problem can be re-expressed in its dual form with the dual variables $\alpha_i \in \mathbb{R}^{m_i}$ as follows:

$$\min \boldsymbol{\alpha}, \mathbf{W}, \mathbf{\Omega} \sum i = 1^n \sum j = 1^{m_i} \mathcal{L}_i\left(-\boldsymbol{\alpha}_i^\top \mathbf{x}_i^j\right) + \lambda_1 \mathrm{Tr}\left(\mathbf{W\Omega W}^\top\right). \tag{5}$$

where Tr denotes the trace function and λ_1 is a hyperparameter. The optimisation process of finding the $\mathbf{\Omega}$ matrix is separable from the data, allowing it to be calculated at a central location. The study by [83] contributed a robust method for distributed optimisation to refine the $\mathbf{W}$ matrix, building upon the concepts of distributed primal–dual optimisation described in [84]. The optimisation involves the conjugate dual function

$\mathcal{L}i^*$ of $\mathcal{L}i$ and the term λ_1 that regularises $\text{Tr}(\mathbf{W}\boldsymbol{\Omega}\mathbf{W}^\top)$. The variable α_i^j in $\oslash \in \mathcal{R}^n$ represents the j-th sample $(\mathbf{x}_i^j, \mathbf{y}_i^j)$ from the i-th device. In this work, we designate $D_i = (\mathbf{x}_i^j, \boldsymbol{\alpha}_i, \mathbf{y}_i^j) \mid \mathbf{x}_i^j \in \mathbb{R}^d, \boldsymbol{\alpha}_i \in \mathbb{R}^{m_i}, \mathbf{y}_i^j \in \mathbb{R}^{m_i}$ as the uncorrupted data in device i. The malicious data injected into node i are represented as:

$$\tilde{D}_i = (\tilde{X}_i, \tilde{\alpha}_i, \tilde{y}_i) \mid \tilde{X}_i \in \mathbb{R}^{d\times\tilde{n}_i}, \tilde{\alpha}_i \in \mathbb{R}^{\tilde{n}_i}, \tilde{y}_i \in \mathbb{R}^{\tilde{n}_i} \tag{6}$$

where $\tilde{n}_i$ is the number of injected samples for node i. If $i \notin \mathcal{S}$, then $\tilde{D}_i = \emptyset$, meaning that $\tilde{n}_i = 0$. The three types of attacks we focused on for FL systems are:

- Direct attack: $\mathcal{T} = \mathcal{S}$. The attacker can directly inject data into all the target nodes, exploiting a vulnerability during data collection. For instance, in the case of mobile phone activity recognition, an attacker can provide counterfeit sensor data to directly attack the target mobile phones (nodes).
- Indirect attack: When no direct data injection is possible into the targeted nodes, symbolised by $\mathcal{T} \cap \mathcal{S} = \emptyset$, the attacker can exert influence on these nodes indirectly. This is achieved by introducing tainted data into adjacent nodes, exploiting the communication protocol to subsequently impact the target nodes. Such an attack leverages the interconnected nature of the network, allowing for the propagation of the attack effects through the established data-sharing pathways.
- Hybrid attack: This form of attack represents a combination of both direct and indirect methods, wherein the aggressor has the capability to contaminate the data pools of both the target and source nodes at once. By employing this dual approach, the attacker enhances the potential to disrupt the network, manipulating data flows and learning processes by simultaneously injecting poisoned data into multiple nodes, thereby magnifying the scope and impact of the attack across the network.

The objective to maximally impair the functioning of the target nodes is structured as a two-tiered optimisation challenge, in line with the model proposed by [55]:

$$\max_{\tilde{D}s|s\in\mathcal{S}} \sum t|t \in \mathcal{T}\mathcal{L}t(D_t, w_t), \text{s.t.,} \quad \min \alpha, \mathbf{W}, \boldsymbol{\Omega} \sum_{\ell=1}^{m} \frac{1}{n_\ell + \tilde{n}\ell} \mathcal{L}\ell(D_\ell \cap \tilde{D}_\ell) + \lambda_1 \mathcal{R}(X\alpha). \tag{7}$$

Here, $\tilde{D}_s|s \in \mathcal{S}$ denotes the set of injected data for the source attacking nodes. The upper-level problem is defined as maximising the performance degradation of the target nodes and is denoted as $\mathcal{H}$. The secondary optimisation issue, addressed by the second condition, concerns a federated multi-task learning scenario in which the training dataset comprises a combination of unaltered and compromised data points.

$$\begin{aligned} &\max_{\tilde{D}_s\subset\mathcal{S}} \sum_{t\in\mathcal{T}} \mathcal{L}_t(D_t, w_t), \\ &\text{s.t.,} \min_{\substack{\alpha,\mathbf{W},\\ \boldsymbol{\Omega}}} \left(\sum_{\ell=1}^{m} \frac{1}{n_\ell + \tilde{n}_\ell} \mathcal{L}_\ell(D_\ell \cup \tilde{D}_\ell, \mathbf{W}) + \lambda_1 \mathcal{R}(X\alpha) + \lambda_2 \|\mathbf{W}\|_F^2 \right), \\ &\|\alpha_i\|_2 \le C, \quad \forall i \in \{1, \dots, n\}. \end{aligned} \tag{8}$$

The adjusted optimisation challenge, as specified in Equation (8), is detailed as follows:

- The aim, symbolised by $\max_{\tilde{D}_s|s\in\mathcal{S}} \sum_{t|t\in\mathcal{T}} \mathcal{L}_t(D_t, w_t)$, seeks to escalate the collective loss for all target nodes within the group $\mathcal{T}$, with $\tilde{D}_s$ representing the data manipulated by the attackers.
- The initial limitation strives to diminish the total loss for all learning tasks under the federation, depicted by $\min_{\alpha,\mathbf{W},\boldsymbol{\Omega}} \left(\sum_{\ell=1}^{m} \frac{1}{n_\ell+\tilde{n}_\ell} \mathcal{L}_\ell(D_\ell \cup \tilde{D}_\ell, \mathbf{W}) + \lambda_1 \mathcal{R}(X\alpha) + \lambda_2 \|\mathbf{W}\|_F^2 \right)$. This includes both the original and tampered data, with $\mathcal{L}_\ell$ denoting the loss for each task ℓ.

- To deter overfitting, which is fitting the model too closely to a limited set of data points, the model includes penalty terms $\lambda_1 \mathcal{R}(X\alpha)$ and $\lambda_2 \|\mathbf{W}\|_F^2$. These terms penalise the model's complexity, balanced by the parameters λ_1 and λ_2.
- A constraint $\|\alpha_i\|_2 \leq C$ ensures that the model's parameters α do not exceed a certain threshold C, maintaining the model's general performance and stability.

In essence, this framework streamlines the complex aspects of federated learning when tasked with handling both unmodified and tampered data, a situation often arising in extensive data settings such as the IoT.

4. Attacks on Federated Learning

This section presents the newly developed FAAMT algorithm, designed to identify the most-strategic approaches for launching attacks within federated learning environments. The algorithm builds upon the commonly used approach in data poisoning attack research, based on related works, and utilises a projected stochastic gradient ascent method to effectively raise the empirical loss of the target nodes, thereby reducing their performance in classification or regression tasks.

In the health IoT domain, a notable innovation is the DPFL-HIoT model, which applies Gradient Boosting Trees (GBTs) to detect healthcare fraud [85]. This method effectively safeguards patient data privacy while still enabling the machine learning model training process. Considering the sensitivity of health information and the difficulties in merging such data, FL emerges as a practical AI-powered tool. It serves the vast amounts of medical data stored in healthcare institutions, crucial for enabling smart health services like telehealth, diagnostics, and ongoing patient monitoring. FL, thus, offers a critical solution that allows for the use of these data while prioritising privacy.

A recent study described a method for executing tensor decomposition while safeguarding privacy within federated cloud systems [86]. This method is detailed extensively, alongside a comprehensive analysis of its complexity. It employs the Paillier encryption scheme and secure multi-party computation to ensure the confidentiality of the decomposition process. Additionally, the paper evaluates the precision of its predictive ratings alongside the computational and communication overhead incurred by users. The analysis of complexity includes the unfolding of tensors, the application of the Lanczos algorithm to these unfolded matrices, the determination of truncated orthogonal bases for tridiagonal matrices, and the construction of the core tensor using encrypted data. The findings within this paper validate the method's efficacy in maintaining privacy while facilitating tensor decomposition in a federated cloud context.

An innovative strategy has been developed to address the complexity of IoT device data and privacy concerns in Recurrent Neural Network (RNN) models [87]. This approach introduces a Differentially Private Tensor-based RNN (DPTRNN) framework dedicated to maintaining the confidentiality of sensitive user information within IoT applications. The proposed DPTRNN model is designed to tackle the challenges of dealing with heterogeneous IoT data and privacy issues in RNN models. Employing a tensor-based algorithm for back-propagation through time, enhanced with perturbation techniques to ensure privacy, the efficacy of the DPTRNN model is evaluated against video datasets. The results indicated that the model surpasses previous methods in terms of accuracy while providing a higher level of privacy protection.

4.1. *Strategies for Attacking via Alternating Minimisation*

The task of refining the attack strategy within bilevel problems presents a significant hurdle, mainly attributed to the intricate and non-convex characteristics of the subordinate problem. In our bilevel construct, the dominant problem is a straightforward primal issue, whereas the subordinate issue reveals a complex, non-linear, and non-convex nature. To navigate these complexities, we adopted an alternating minimisation technique. This method involves a cyclic update of the injected data to amplify the impact on the function $\mathcal{H}$, which quantifies the performance deterioration of the targeted nodes. This technique is instrumental in addressing the challenging non-convexity of the subordinate problem, paving the way for an enhanced attack stratagem tailored to federated learning contexts.

By implementing this alternating minimisation, we capitalise on its inherent flexibility to fine-tune our approach iteratively, aligning our injected data with the optimal points of disruption. Each iteration brings us closer to a strategy that can subtly, yet substantially weaken the model's performance from within. Moreover, this method's iterative nature allows us to monitor and adjust the attack in real-time, reacting to changes and defences put in place by the network, ensuring that our attack remains effective throughout the learning process. Such adaptability makes it an indispensable tool in the arsenal for compromising federated learning systems.

To tackle the non-convex nature of the lower-level problem in the bilevel optimisation of the attack problem, we adopted an alternating minimisation approach, where we optimise the features of the injected data, denoted by $(\tilde{D}_{s,i}, \alpha s, i)$, by fixing the labels of the injected data. The updates to the injected data $\tilde{D}_{s,i}$ are obtained via the projected stochastic gradient ascent method as shown below:

$$\left(\tilde{D}_{s,i}\right)^{k} \leftarrow \text{Proj}\,\mathbf{X}\left(\left(\tilde{D}_{s,i}\right)^{k-1} + \eta_1 \nabla_{\left(\tilde{D}_{s,i}\right)^{k-1}} \mathcal{H}\right), \tag{9}$$

Here, η_1 denotes the learning rate, k indexes the current iteration, and $\mathbf{X}$ defines the set of all permissible injected data, as outlined by the initial restriction in the primary problem $\mathcal{H}$. The projection operator $\text{Proj}\,\mathbf{X}(\cdot)$ ensures that the injected data lie within the ℓ_2-norm ball of radius r. The corresponding dual variable $\alpha s, i$ is updated accordingly as $\tilde{D}_{s,i}$ evolves:

$$\alpha^{k}_{s,i} \leftarrow \alpha^{k-1}_{s,i} + \Delta\alpha_{s,i} \tag{10}$$

where $\Delta(\alpha_{s,i})$ is the step in the dual space that maximises the upper-level problem $\mathcal{H}$. The equation for computing the gradient of the t-th target node in Equation (9) is derived using the chain rule.

$$\nabla_{\hat{x}^t_a} \mathcal{L}t(D_t, w_t) = \nabla w_t \mathcal{L}t(D_t, w_t) \cdot \nabla \hat{x}^{\pm}_a w_t. \tag{11}$$

The gradient of the objective function at the upper level with respect to both $\hat{x}^t_a$ and w_t is given by $\nabla_{\hat{x}^t_a} \mathcal{L}_t(D_t, w_t) = \nabla_{w_t} \mathcal{L}_t(D_t, w_t) \times \nabla_{\hat{x}^t_a} w_t$. The first term on the right-hand side, $\nabla_{w_t} \mathcal{L}_t(D_t, w_t)$, is readily computable as it solely relies on the loss function $\mathcal{L}_t(\cdot)$. Conversely, the second term, $\nabla_{\hat{x}^t_a} w_t$, hinges on the optimal conditions of the lower-level problem as set out in Equation (7).

In order to ascertain $\nabla_{\hat{x}^t_a} w_t$, we commence by fixing the parameter Ω in the lower-level issue to sidestep its constraints, leading us to the dual problem stated as:

$$\min_{\alpha, \mathbf{W}} \sum_{\ell=1}^{m} \frac{1}{n_\ell + \tilde{n}_\ell} \mathcal{L}_\ell(D_\ell \cup \tilde{D}_\ell) + \lambda_1 \mathcal{R}(X\alpha) \tag{12}$$

Considering the optimality conditions of the lower-level problem as constraints within the upper-level problem, we treat Ω as a constant matrix during the gradient determination. Furthermore, given that $\mathcal{R}(X\alpha)$ is continuously differentiable, we correlate $\mathbf{W}$ and α through the relationship $w_\ell(\alpha) = \nabla \mathcal{R}(X\alpha)$. Lastly, we proceed with updating the dual variable α and calculating the ensuing gradients as shown in Equation (9).

To update the dual variable α, we seek to maximise the dual objective with a least-squares loss or hinge loss function by updating each element of α individually. The optimisation problem in Equation (11) can be reformulated into a constrained optimisation problem for node ℓ as:

$$\min_{\alpha} \sum_{\ell=1}^{m} \frac{1}{n_\ell + \hat{n}\ell} \left(\mathcal{L}\ell^{\star}\left(-\alpha^i_\ell\right) + \mathcal{L}\ell^{\star}\left(-\hat{\alpha}\ell^{i'}\right)\right) + \lambda_1 \mathcal{R}^{\star}(X[\alpha_\ell; \hat{\alpha}_\ell]) \tag{13}$$

To enable distributed computation across multiple nodes, the optimisation problem in Equation (10) can be separated into smaller, data-local subproblems. This is achieved by making a quadratic approximation of the dual problem. At each step k, two samples are chosen randomly, one from the original clean data (i.e., $i \in 1, \ldots, n_\ell$) and one from the injected data (i.e., $i' \in 1, \ldots, \hat{n}\ell$). The updates for both α_ℓ^i and $\hat{\alpha}_\ell^{i'}$ in node ℓ can be computed as:

$$\left(\alpha_\ell^i\right)^k = \left(\alpha_\ell^i\right)^{k-1} + \Delta\alpha_\ell^i, \left(\hat{\alpha}\ell^{i'}\right)^k = \left(\hat{\alpha}\ell^{i'}\right)^{k-1} + \Delta\hat{\alpha}_\ell^{i'}, \tag{14}$$

where $\Delta\alpha_\ell^i$ and $\Delta\hat{\alpha}_\ell^{i'}$ are the stepsizes that maximise the dual objective in Equation (15) when all other variables are fixed. To achieve maximum dual ascent, we optimise:

$$\Delta\alpha_\ell^i = \arg\min_{a \in \mathbb{R}} \mathcal{L}^*\ell\left(-\left(\alpha\ell^i + a\right)\right) + a\left\langle w_\ell(\alpha_\ell), x_\ell^i\right\rangle + \frac{\lambda}{2}\left|x_\ell^i a\right| M_\ell^2 \tag{15}$$

$$\Delta\hat{\alpha}\ell^{i'} = \arg\min \hat{a} \in \mathbb{R}\mathcal{L}^*\ell\left(-\left(\hat{\alpha}\ell^{i'} + \hat{a}\right)\right) + \hat{a}\left\langle w_\ell(\hat{\alpha}\ell), x\ell^{i'}\right\rangle + \frac{\lambda}{2}\left|x_\ell^{i'}\hat{a}\right| M_\ell^2 \tag{16}$$

Here, M is a symmetric positive definite matrix and $M_\ell \in \mathbb{R}^{d \times d}$ is the ℓ-th diagonal block of M. The inverse of M is expressed as

$$M^{-1} = \Omega + \frac{\lambda_2}{\lambda_1} I_{md \times md}. \tag{17}$$

where $\Omega := \Omega \otimes I_{d \times d} \in \mathbb{R}^{md \times md}$ and λ_1 and λ_2 are positive constants. For the least-squares loss function, the closed-form solution for $\Delta\alpha_\ell^i$ is:

$$\Delta\alpha_\ell^i = \frac{y_\ell^i - \left(x_\ell^i\right)^\top x_\ell^i \alpha_\ell^i - 0.5\left(\alpha_\ell^i\right)^{k-1}}{0.5 + \lambda_1 \left|x_\ell^i\right| M\ell^2}. \tag{18}$$

For the hinge loss, $\Delta\hat{\alpha}_\ell^{i^r}$ can be computed as follows:

$$\Delta\hat{\alpha}\ell^{i^r} = y\ell^{i^r} \max\left(0, \min\left(1, \frac{1 - \left(x_\ell^{i^r}\right)^\top x_\ell^{i^r}\left(\alpha_\ell^{k-1}\right) y_\ell^{i^r}}{\lambda_1 \left|x_\ell^{i^r}\right| M_\ell^2} + \left(\alpha_\ell^{k-1}\right) y_\ell^{i^r}\right)\right) - \left(\alpha_\ell^{k-1}\right) \tag{19}$$

The gradient associated with each of the injected data $\hat{x}_s^i$ for the corresponding target node t is expressed as:

$$\nabla_{(\hat{x}_s^s)} \mathcal{L}_t\left((w_t)^\top x_t^j, y_t^j\right) = 2\left((w_t)^\top x_t^j - y_t^j\right) x_t^j \cdot \Delta\hat{\alpha}_s^i \Omega(t,s) \tag{20}$$

For the hinge loss, the gradient is:

$$\nabla_{(\hat{x}_s^u)} \mathcal{L}_t\left((w_t)^\top x_t^j, y_t^j\right) = y_t^j x_t^j \cdot \Delta\alpha_s^i \Omega(t,s) \tag{21}$$

The algorithm for the attack on federated learning is given in Algorithm 1.

The Federated Adversarial Attack for Multi-Task Learning (FAAMT) Algorithm 1 is an essential mechanism designed to test the robustness of federated learning systems against malicious attacks. It systematically integrates adversarial samples into a network's nodes, specifically within a multi-task learning setting. Through iterative updates governed by a central learning rate and convergence criteria, FAAMT evaluates the vulnerability of federated learning structures. This assessment is essential for strengthening the defence mechanisms of such systems against advanced adversarial strategies.

Algorithm 1 Federated Adversarial Attack for Multi-Task Learning (FAAMT).

procedure FAAMT($T, S, \hat{n}_s$)
  Randomly initialise the current state $f(\hat{X}_0, \hat{v}_0, \hat{y}_0) \in S$
  Initialise the set of injected data as $\hat{D} = \hat{D}_0$, and set the iteration counter $k = 0$
  Set the global learning rate α and tolerance ϵ for convergence
  while $k <$ maximum number of iterations **and** not converged **do**
    # of parallel computations for each node
    for all nodes $i = 1$ to m in parallel **do**
      Calculate the solution δv_i for node i using Equation (15) or Equation (16)
      Update the local variables $v_i \leftarrow v_i + \alpha \cdot \delta v_i$
      if $i \in S$ **then**
        Calculate the solution $\delta \hat{v}_i$ for node i using Equation (15) or Equation (16)
        Update the adversarial variables $\hat{v}_i \leftarrow \hat{v}_i + \alpha \cdot \delta \hat{v}_i$
      end if
    end for
    Aggregate local updates to update Global Model parameters W_k
    Check for convergence with a predefined criterion, e.g., $||W_k - W_{k-1}|| < \epsilon$
    Increase counter $k \leftarrow k + 1$
    # of injected data point updates for source nodes
    for all source nodes $s = 1$ to S in parallel **do**
      Update the injected data point $\hat{x}_s$ using Equation (7)
    end for
    Update the set of injected data as $\hat{D} \leftarrow \hat{D} \cup \{\hat{x}_s\}_{s=1}^{S}$
  end while
  if converged **then**
    return Successfully converged with adversarial examples $\hat{D}$
  else
    return Algorithm reached maximum iterations without convergence
  end if
end procedure

Further Analysis

To attack the federated learning model, we focused on the bilevel optimisation problem. The upper-level problem aims to find the optimal attack strategy, while the lower-level problem is to update the model weights. The bilevel problem can be expressed as:

$$\max_{\tilde{D}_{s,i}, \alpha s, i} \quad \mathcal{H}(D, W; \tilde{D}_{s,i}, \alpha s, i) \quad \text{subject to} \quad |\tilde{D}_{s,i}|2 \leq r, \quad W = \arg\min W' \mathcal{L}(D \cup \tilde{D}_{s,i}, W'; \alpha s, i) \tag{22}$$

For the non-convex nature of the lower-level problem, we used the alternating minimisation approach to optimise the bilevel problem. We initiate by fixing the labels of the injected data and optimising the features of the injected data, denoted by $(\tilde{D}_{s,i}, \alpha s, i)$, as follows:

$$\left(\tilde{D}_{s,i}\right)^k \leftarrow \text{Proj}\,\mathbf{X}\left(\left(\tilde{D}_{s,i}\right)^{k-1} + \eta_1 \nabla_{\left(\tilde{D}_{s,i}\right)^{k-1}} \mathcal{H}\right), \tag{23}$$

To compute the gradient, we first derive the gradient of the target node loss function $\mathcal{L}_t(D_t, W)$ with respect to the model weights W:

$$\nabla_W \mathcal{L}t(D_t, W) = \sum j = 1^{n_t} \nabla_w \ell(w_t^\top x_t^j, y_t^j), \tag{24}$$

where $\ell(\cdot)$ is the loss function, x_t^j and y_t^j are the j-th data point and its label in the target node dataset, and n_t is the number of data points in the target node dataset. Next, we need to compute the gradient of the upper-level objective with respect to the injected data $\tilde{D}_{s,i}$:

$$\nabla_{\tilde{D}_{s,i}} \mathcal{H} = \sum_{t=1}^{T} \nabla_{\tilde{D}_{s,i}} \mathcal{L}_t(D_t \cup \tilde{D}_{s,i}, W). \tag{25}$$

To calculate this gradient, we utilise the chain rule, obtaining:

$$\nabla_{\tilde{D}_{s,i}} \mathcal{H} = \sum_{t=1}^{T} \nabla_W \mathcal{L}t(D_t, W) \cdot \nabla \tilde{D}_{s,i} W. \tag{26}$$

For the lower-level problem, we update the model weights W using gradient descent with learning rate η_2:

$$W^k \leftarrow W^{k-1} - \eta_2 \nabla_W \mathcal{L}(D \cup \tilde{D}_{s,i}, W^{k-1}; \alpha s, i). \tag{27}$$

After updating the features of the injected data, we fix the features and optimise the labels of the injected data:

$$\alpha s, i^k \leftarrow \text{Proj}\, \mathcal{Y}\left(\alpha s, i^{k-1} + \eta_3 \nabla_{\alpha s, i^{k-1}} \mathcal{H}\right), \tag{28}$$

where Proj $\mathcal{Y}$ projects the labels into the feasible set $\mathcal{Y}$.

To compute the gradient of the upper level objective with respect to the labels of the injected data, we have:

$$\nabla_{\alpha s,i} \mathcal{H} = \sum_{t=1}^{T} \nabla_{\alpha s,i} \mathcal{L}_t(D_t \cup \tilde{D}_{s,i}, W). \tag{29}$$

We apply the chain rule to obtain the following expression:

$$\nabla_{\alpha s,i} \mathcal{H} = \sum_{t=1}^{T} \nabla_W \mathcal{L}t(D_t, W) \cdot \nabla \alpha s, iW. \tag{30}$$

Finally, the alternating minimisation algorithm consists of iterating through these updates for the features of the injected data, the labels of the injected data, and the model weights until convergence. By focusing on the gradients of the loss function, the attacker can effectively manipulate the model's behaviour, leading to a successful attack.

5. Experimental Results

5.1. System Specifications of Experiments

The ensuing experimental design, crucial for substantiating the efficacy of FLIBD, was scrupulously devised to accurately emulate a pragmatic IoT Big Data management context. This, in turn, allows for a discerning evaluation of the approach's potency in safeguarding privacy within expansive systems. In particular, the experiments were enacted within a high-performance computing environment, marked by its robust computational and storage capabilities, thereby being impeccably aligned for navigating through the complexities of resource-demanding federated learning tasks among handling copious IoT Big Data. A comprehensive exposition of the essential system specifications leveraged for the experiments is proffered in Table 3.

The above system was orchestrated to emulate large-scale system scenarios for federated learning with a lens toward IoT Big Data management. The CPU, equipped with an extensive number of cores, alongside the robust RAM, facilitates efficient parallel processing capabilities, ensuring expedited computational procedures. The GPU, boasting a substantive video memory, becomes quintessential in efficiently managing and processing massive datasets, especially under operations requiring enhanced parallelisation, such as model training in federated learning frameworks. The ultra-fast NVMe storage plays a critical role in minimising data retrieval and storage times, thus mitigating potential bottlenecks arising from disk I/O operations. Furthermore, the experiment leveraged Apache Spark with Federated AI Technology Enabler (FATE) to enable secure computations and model training, allowing data privacy preservation through federated learning mechanisms.

Table 3. System specifications for experimental evaluation.

Component	Specification
CPU	AMD 5950X
RAM	64GB DDR4
Storage	2TB NVMe
GPU	3090Ti (24GB VRAM)
Operating System	Ubuntu 18.04 LTS
Network Interface	1GBPS
Software Framework	Apache Spark with FATE

5.2. Experimental Evaluation of Attacking Mechanism

In the ever-expanding domain of Federated Learning (FL), the imperative to guard against adversarial attacks whilst ensuring accurate model predictions has become paramount. The ensuing analysis offers a rigorous examination of the Federated Adversarial Attack for Multi-Task Learning (FAAMT) algorithm (Algorithm 1). This adversarial approach, developed with meticulous attention to the intricacies of multi-task learning, seeks to diminish the predictive accuracy of various federated learning methods, even those that are conventionally recognised for their robustness against adversarial machinations.

To unravel the efficacy of FAAMT, it was assessed against several widely acknowledged federated learning methods and defences, such as the Global Model, Median Model, Trimmed Mean Model, Krum, Bulyan, RFA, and Romoa. Each method typically exhibits substantial resistance to conventional adversarial tactics, establishing them as formidable entities in federated learning defences. However, through the vision of FAAMT, we sought to decipher whether their robustness holds steadfast or gradually attenuates under the sophisticated attack mechanisms unleashed by the algorithm.

The outcomes derived from applying the FAAMT method (Figure 2) show the performance variations among the federated learning mechanisms previously discussed, unmasking their potential susceptibilities. This analytical exploration, thus, enriches our comprehension of the resilience landscape among adversarial challenges within federated learning frameworks, underscoring the specific vulnerabilities and strengths inherent in each approach.

Intriguingly, the derived results emanating from the visual representation expose a compelling narrative pertaining to the potency of the FAAMT mechanism. A discerning glance at the plot elucidates a conspicuous decrement in the predictive accuracies of the defended federated learning methods under attack, reinforcing the assertion that FAAMT has managed to permeate their defensive veils to a certain degree.

Certain defence mechanisms, which previously heralded unwavering resilience in the face of adversarial onslaughts, now showcase perceptible vulnerabilities when entwined with the FAAMT. This not only lays bare latent susceptibilities within these methods, but also accentuates the detail and sophistication embedded within the FAAMT algorithm. Notably, certain defences exhibited a more-pronounced susceptibility, suggesting a hierarchical differentiation in robustness among the examined methods and emphasising the necessity for an incessant evolution in defence strategies.

As the realm of federated learning continues to evolve, so too will the complexity and cunning of adversarial attacks. Thus, the illumination of FAAMT's ability to infiltrate these robust defence mechanisms propels the discourse on the perennial battle between adversarial attacks and defence methods forward. It beckons the scientific community to explore further, excavate deeper, and innovate with a renewed zeal to safeguard federated learning models against progressively shrewd adversarial endeavours. It is within this iterative process of attack and defence that the future robustness and reliability of federated learning models will be forged, ensuring the integrity and durability of decentralised learning mechanisms in real-world applications.

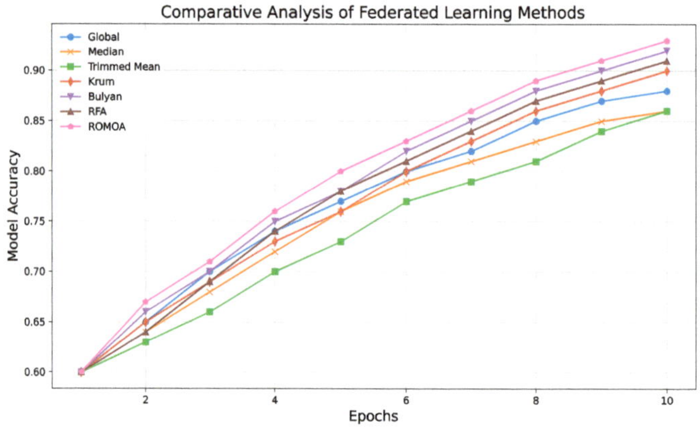

Figure 2. Efficacy assessment of FAAMT against various federated learning defence mechanisms.

5.3. Experimental Evaluation of Defences

This section will analyse the plots produced during the experimental evaluation of the implemented defences based on the proposed attack. In each case, the maximum number of clients was 10 and the number of attackers in the system varied from none to 5 clients, i.e., 50% of the system. A higher percentage than this was not considered as there is no point in implementing a defence on a system that malicious users mostly own. The section will start with the results of the attack on a network using the standard FedAvg aggregation method and then split by the percentage of exposure. For the experiments, we utilised the widely used CIFAR-10 dataset, which contains 32×32 images, which are classified into various object categories like birds, cats, and aeroplanes. The training dataset contains 5000 images for each of the 10 classes. The purpose of this analysis was to determine the effectiveness of the implemented defences against the proposed attack and to identify any vulnerabilities or limitations. The experimental evaluation aimed to provide insights into the defences' strengths and weaknesses under different conditions. The experimental results of this analysis may guide the development of future defences and enhance the security of federated learning systems. We evaluated the methods of the Median, Trimmed Mean, Krum, and Bulyan before the attack and afterwards. Before the label-flipping attack, we observed that a very simple logistic regression model in this task had significant accuracy, approaching 98%. In other words, it is a relatively tractable and simple way to implement this task. This is illustrated in Figure 3a.

From above, we can see the same results as previously, but with the difference that, now, 20% of the users in our system were malicious. We can see from the F1-score that there was a significant decrease in accuracy, which can be catastrophic. In the end, we also provide the F1-score for the case where 50% of the clients were malicious. In Figure 3b, we can see that the Digit 5 class had a significant decrease even with 20% of the clients being malicious. An important by-product of this attack is that the class to which we converted Digit 5 (i.e., Class 2) also had a significant reduction in its F1-score. In Figure 4a, we can observe that the convergence in the F1-score was not as good as in the simple FedAvg method, which started from the third round, while the Median started from the fourth or even fifth round. In Figure 4b, we can see that, even with a method as simple as the Median, we can identify an increase in the F1-score that was immediate. Also, the convergence was similar.

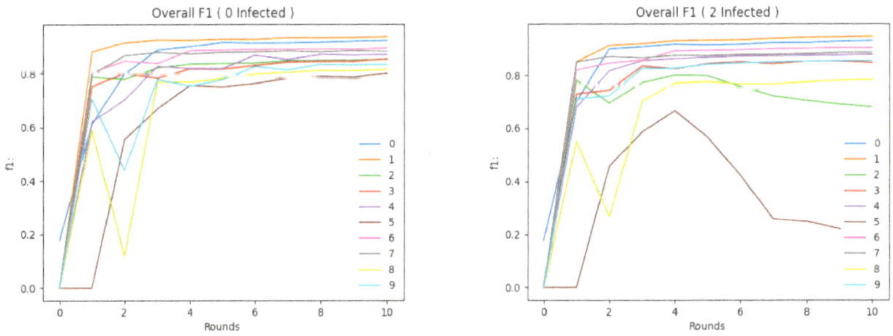

(**a**) F1-score for each digit before attacking. (**b**) F1-score for each digit after attacking.

Figure 3. Performance of the Global Model after each round of FL.

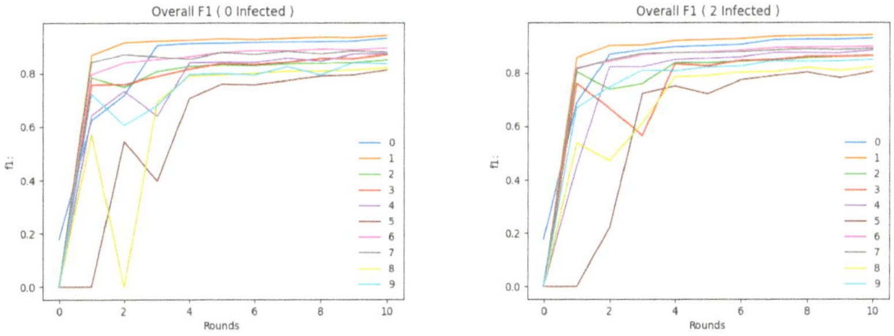

(**a**) F1-score for each digit before attacking. (**b**) F1-score for each digit after attacking.

Figure 4. Performance of the Median Model after each round of FL.

For the Trimmed Mean method, the results are shown in Figure 5a. Similar to the previous method, convergence occurred later. The Trimmed Mean method (Figure 5b) was observed to not perform as well, but this may be attributed to the fact that the customer sample after trimming the edges was small. For the Krum method, the results are shown in Figure 6a. Compared to the previous method, it appeared to have higher convergence. However, after the attack (Figure 6b), it appeared that it lowered while maintaining higher results than the Trimmed Mean method. For the Bulyan method, the results are shown in Figure 7a. Here, the convergence was similar to the Trimmed Mean method, but lower than the Krum model. However, the attack on the model (Figure 7b) appeared to have a more-robust performance.

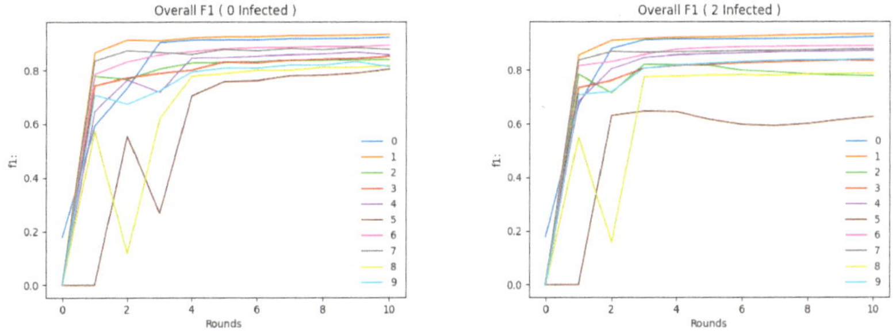

(**a**) F1-score for each digit before attacking. (**b**) F1-score for each digit after attacking.

Figure 5. Performance of the Trimmed Mean Model after each round of FL.

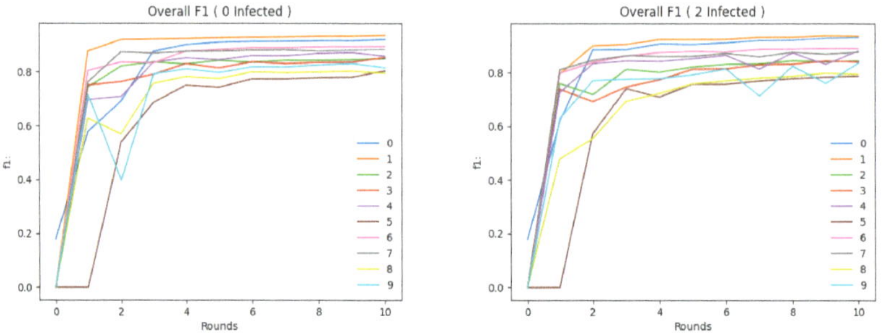

(**a**) F1-score for each digit before attacking. (**b**) F1-score for each digit after attacking.

Figure 6. Performance of the Krum model after each round of FL.

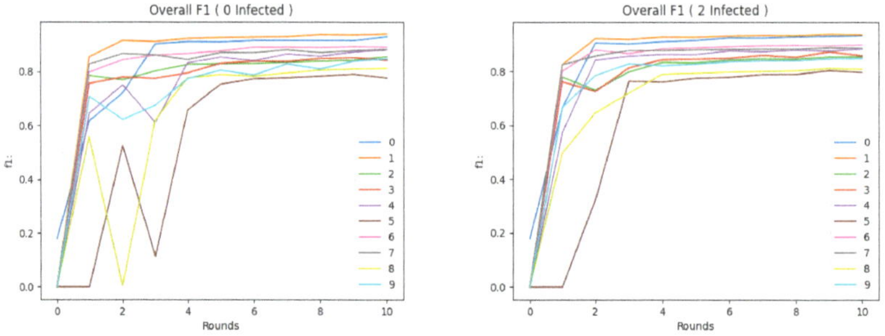

(**a**) F1-score for each digit before attacking. (**b**) F1-score for each digit after attacking.

Figure 7. Performance of the Bulyan model after each round of FL.

Evaluation Metrics:

To rigorously assess the effectiveness of the Federated Adversarial Attack for Multi-Task Learning (FAAMT) and the robustness of various federated learning defensive mechanisms, we employed two pivotal metrics: *accuracy* and the *F1-score*. The accuracy metric gauges the overall performance of the model by evaluating the ratio of correctly predicted instances to the total instances and is defined as

$$\text{Accuracy} = \frac{\text{True Positives (TPs)} + \text{True Negatives (TNs)}}{\text{Total Instances (P+N)}} \tag{31}$$

where TPs and TNs denote the number of true positive and true negative predictions, respectively, and P and N represent the total actual positive and negative instances, respectively. The F1-score, the harmonic mean of precision and recall, offers a balanced perspective, especially pivotal when dealing with imbalanced datasets, and is expressed as:

$$\text{F1-Score} = 2 \times \frac{\text{Precision} \times \text{Recall}}{\text{Precision} + \text{Recall}} \tag{32}$$

where

$$\text{Precision} = \frac{\text{TP}}{\text{TP} + \text{False Positives (FP)}} \tag{33}$$

and

$$\text{Recall} = \frac{\text{TP}}{\text{TP} + \text{False Negatives (FN)}} \tag{34}$$

Utilising these metrics, the ensuing sections deliberate the comprehensive evaluation of the FAAMT and the subjected defence mechanisms, shedding light on their respective strengths and vulnerabilities amidst adversarial incursions.

The results for the proposed attack and defence mechanisms are shown in Table 4, where we assess the accuracy and F1-score for the attack (FAAMT method), as well as the defence mechanism behaviour. Lastly, we evaluated the performance of both the attack and defence on 2 clients infected out of 10.

Table 4. Metrics assessing the performance of attack and defence mechanisms.

Method	Attack (A)		Defence (D)		Affected Clients (D)
	Accuracy	F1-Score	Accuracy	F1 Score	out of 10
Global Model	0.88	0.84	0.85	0.81	2
Median Model	0.86	0.82	0.87	0.83	2
Trimmed Mean Model	0.86	0.81	0.86	0.82	2
Krum	0.90	0.84	0.88	0.83	2
Bulyan	0.93	0.80	0.89	0.83	2

6. Discussion

The experimental analysis presented delved into the complex interactions between various federated learning defence mechanisms and a sophisticated adversarial attack, the FAAMT. The results from the high-performance computational environment underscored the imperative of robust defences in the realm of IoT Big Data management. The experiments revealed that even well-established defences, such as Krum and Bulyan, exhibit vulnerabilities when confronted with the FAAMT, hinting at the subtleties in the defence mechanisms that must be addressed. This observation is crucial, for it demonstrates that the current landscape of federated learning is not impervious to novel attack strategies and must continuously evolve.

Notably, the FAAMT elucidated a significant reduction in the F1-scores of the federated learning models, which was particularly pronounced for certain classes within the CIFAR-10 dataset. This degradation in performance suggests that, while current defences offer a degree of resilience, they are not entirely foolproof against such calculated adversarial intrusions. This is a stark reminder that the security of federated learning models remains a moving target, requiring ongoing research and refinement to mitigate the risk of adversarial exploitation.

The experimental evaluation also offered insights into the performance of various defence strategies post-attack. Methods like the Median and Trimmed Mean, traditionally considered less sophisticated than Krum or Bulyan, displayed a delayed convergence, indicating a slower recovery from adversarial disturbances. This behaviour highlights the need for a balance between the complexity of defence algorithms and their adaptability in the face of adversarial manoeuvres. The nuanced decrease in the performance of the Krum and Trimmed Mean Models post-attack further accentuates the need for dynamic defence strategies capable of coping with the evolving nature of adversarial threats.

In contrast, the Bulyan method showcased a relatively more-robust performance under adversarial conditions, suggesting that certain combinations of defence methodologies may offer enhanced resilience. The experimental results suggested a promising direction for future investigation: examining combined or multi-level defence strategies that could offer stronger protection against adversarial attacks. The field of federated learning, especially within the context of the IoT and Big Data, is, thus, poised at a crucial juncture where the iterative process of developing and testing new defence strategies is not just beneficial, but necessary to safeguard the integrity of decentralised learning models against increasingly sophisticated adversarial tactics.

7. Conclusions

In our investigation, we presented the Federated Adversarial Attack for Multi-Task Learning (FAAMT) algorithm, which significantly exposed the susceptibilities of federated multi-task learning frameworks to data poisoning. Our results provided clear evidence that FAAMT can critically undermine the training process, leading to a noticeable deterioration in model accuracy and performance. This highlights an urgent necessity for the establishment of robust defence strategies within such systems.

As we look to the horizon of federated multi-task learning, it is imperative to address the challenges presented by the FAAMT algorithm. The development and in-depth examination of defence strategies such as secure aggregation, robust outlier detection, and the integration of differential privacy mechanisms are pivotal areas requiring immediate attention. The future landscape should include extensive evaluations of these defences' effectiveness against sophisticated data poisoning tactics with respect to multi-task learning environments.

The fine-tuning of FAAMT can lead to many potential enhancements. Its adaptability could be tested against various data poisoning strategies to assess impacts on user data confidentiality. Furthermore, its extension to other federated learning paradigms, such as federated transfer learning, could provide significant insights. Investigating the resilience of optimisation techniques like gradient clipping related to adversarial interventions in multi-task scenarios could yield beneficial strategies for maintaining system integrity. Additionally, adversarial tactics that specifically target individual tasks or users, while minimising disruption to other system components, could reveal specific system vulnerabilities and build room for the enhancement of privacy-preserving measures.

In summary, this study highlighted a critical and immediate need to reinforce the security and privacy protocols of federated multi-task learning systems. The safe and effective application of these systems in practical settings demands the creation and implementation of robust defence mechanisms. Addressing these open challenges is essential to advancing the adoption of federated multi-task learning, ensuring that it can be confidently deployed to facilitate collaborative learning processes across heterogeneous devices, all while maintaining a steady defence of user privacy in the interconnected ecosystems of the IoT and Big Data.

7.1. Future Work

The prospect of combining Federated Learning (FL) and Automated Machine Learning (AutoML) opens new opportunities for enhancing data privacy and optimising Big Data management. The integration of FL with AutoML, as envisioned in the studies [88,89], provides a robust foundation for the development of the Federated Adversarial Attack for Multi-Task Learning (FAAMT) algorithm. This algorithm aims to address the complexities of multi-task learning within a federated framework, where the goal is to enable the collaborative training of models across multiple tasks while ensuring data privacy and robustness against adversarial attacks. The FAAMT approach could leverage the privacy-preserving nature of FL to protect data across distributed networks and the efficiency of AutoML to optimise learning tasks, thereby ensuring that the integrity of multi-task learning is maintained even in the presence of potential adversarial threats.

The integration of edge intelligence and edge caching mechanisms outlined in the first study with the advanced hyperparameter optimisation techniques from the second study provides the foundational elements necessary for the further development of FAAMT. The algorithm could harness the computational power available at the network edge, alongside sophisticated AutoML methods, to effectively manage the multi-faceted challenges of Big Data in a federated context. This synergy promises to deliver not only more-personalised and immediate data processing at the edge, but also a robust framework for multi-task models that are inherently more resistant to adversarial attacks. In such a way, the FAAMT algorithm has the potential to become a quintessential part of smart, decentralised networks, enabling them to remain resilient in the face of evolving cyber threats while making the most of the vast datasets generated across IoT environments.

The development of the FAAMT algorithm points us in a new direction for research that incorporates the protective features of federated learning with the dynamic fine tuning abilities of AutoML. By utilising both, future work can focus on improving this algorithm to better manage the complex tasks of learning multiple things at once in environments where there may be hostile attempts to disrupt learning. This will include creating better methods to spot and stop such attacks in networks where data are shared across different computers, making algorithms that can learn different tasks more effectively and efficiently, and ensuring that the system can handle the unevenly distributed data that are often found in everyday situations. Further studies can also investigate how to best spread out the work of computing across the edges of the networks, making the most of local computing for AutoML tasks and further protecting the privacy of data within the federated learning setup. As the FAAMT algorithm improves even more, it could be used in many areas, turning multi-task learning in networks where data are shared across many computers into not just a possibility, but a strong method for keeping data private and safe in a world that is more and more connected.

Author Contributions: A.K., A.G., L.T., G.A.K., G.K., C.K. and S.S. conceived of the idea, designed and performed the experiments, analysed the results, drafted the initial manuscript and revised the final manuscript. All authors have read and agreed to the published version of the manuscript.

Funding: This research received no external funding.

Data Availability Statement: The data presented in this study are available upon request from the corresponding author.

Conflicts of Interest: The authors declare no conflict of interest.

References

1. Kairouz, P.; McMahan, H.B.; Avent, B.; Bellet, A.; Bennis, M.; Bhagoji, A.N.; Bonawitz, K.; Charles, Z.; Cormode, G.; Cummings, R.; et al. Advances and open problems in federated learning. *Found. Trends Mach. Learn.* **2021**, *14*, 1–210. [CrossRef]
2. Jebreel, N.M.; Domingo-Ferrer, J.; Sánchez, D.; Blanco-Justicia, A. Defending against the label-flipping attack in federated learning. *arXiv* **2022**, arXiv:2207.01982.
3. Jiang, Y.; Zhang, W.; Chen, Y. Data Quality Detection Mechanism Against Label Flipping Attacks in Federated Learning. *IEEE Trans. Inf. Forensics Secur.* **2023**, *18*, 1625–1637. [CrossRef]
4. Li, D.; Wong, W.E.; Wang, W.; Yao, Y.; Chau, M. Detection and mitigation of label-flipping attacks in federated learning systems with KPCA and K-means. In Proceedings of the 2021 8th International Conference on Dependable Systems and Their Applications (DSA), Yinchuan, China, 5–6 August 2021; pp. 551–559.
5. Cheng, Y.; Liu, Y.; Chen, T.; Yang, Q. Federated learning for privacy-preserving AI. *Commun. ACM* **2020**, *63*, 33–36. [CrossRef]
6. Truex, S.; Baracaldo, N.; Anwar, A.; Steinke, T.; Ludwig, H.; Zhang, R.; Zhou, Y. A hybrid approach to privacy-preserving federated learning. In Proceedings of the 12th ACM Workshop on Artificial Intelligence and Security, 2019; pp. 1–11. Available online: https://arxiv.org/abs/1812.03224 (accessed on 18 October 2023).
7. Wei, K.; Li, J.; Ding, M.; Ma, C.; Yang, H.H.; Farokhi, F.; Jin, S.; Quek, T.Q.; Poor, H.V. Federated learning with differential privacy: Algorithms and performance analysis. *IEEE Trans. Inf. Forensics Secur.* **2020**, *15*, 3454–3469. [CrossRef]
8. Pan, K.; Feng, K. Differential Privacy-Enabled Multi-Party Learning with Dynamic Privacy Budget Allocating Strategy. *Electronics* **2023**, *12*, 658. [CrossRef]
9. Karras, A.; Karras, C.; Giotopoulos, K.C.; Tsolis, D.; Oikonomou, K.; Sioutas, S. Peer to Peer Federated Learning: Towards Decentralized Machine Learning on Edge Devices. In Proceedings of the 2022 7th South-East Europe Design Automation, Computer Engineering, Computer Networks and Social Media Conference (SEEDA-CECNSM), Ioannina, Greece, 23–25 September 2022; pp. 1–9. [CrossRef]
10. Abreha, H.G.; Hayajneh, M.; Serhani, M.A. Federated Learning in Edge Computing: A Systematic Survey. *Sensors* **2022**, *22*, 450. [CrossRef]
11. Kaleem, S.; Sohail, A.; Tariq, M.U.; Asim, M. An Improved Big Data Analytics Architecture Using Federated Learning for IoT-Enabled Urban Intelligent Transportation Systems. *Sustainability* **2023**, *15*, 15333. [CrossRef]
12. Javed, A.R.; Hassan, M.A.; Shahzad, F.; Ahmed, W.; Singh, S.; Baker, T.; Gadekallu, T.R. Integration of blockchain technology and federated learning in vehicular (iot) networks: A comprehensive survey. *Sensors* **2022**, *22*, 4394. [CrossRef]

13. Kong, Q.; Yin, F.; Xiao, Y.; Li, B.; Yang, X.; Cui, S. Achieving Blockchain-based Privacy-Preserving Location Proofs under Federated Learning. In Proceedings of the ICC 2021—IEEE International Conference on Communications, Montreal, QC, Canada, 14–23 June 2021; pp. 1–6. [CrossRef]
14. Math, S.; Tam, P.; Kim, S. Reliable Federated Learning Systems Based on Intelligent Resource Sharing Scheme for Big Data Internet of Things. *IEEE Access* **2021**, *9*, 108091–108100. [CrossRef]
15. Nuding, F.; Mayer, R. Data poisoning in sequential and parallel federated learning. In Proceedings of the 2022 ACM on International Workshop on Security and Privacy Analytics, 2022; pp. 24–34. Available online: https://dl.acm.org/doi/abs/10.1145/3510548.3519372 (accessed on 18 October 2023).
16. Tolpegin, V.; Truex, S.; Gursoy, M.E.; Liu, L. Data poisoning attacks against federated learning systems. In Proceedings of the Computer Security–ESORICS 2020: 25th European Symposium on Research in Computer Security, ESORICS 2020, Guildford, UK, 14–18 September 2020; Springer: Berlin/Heidelberg, Germany, 2020; pp. 480–501.
17. Sun, G.; Cong, Y.; Dong, J.; Wang, Q.; Lyu, L.; Liu, J. Data poisoning attacks on federated machine learning. *IEEE Internet Things J.* **2021**, *9*, 11365–11375. [CrossRef]
18. Li, J.; Guo, W.; Han, X.; Cai, J.; Liu, X. Federated Learning based on Defending Against Data Poisoning Attacks in IoT. *arXiv* **2022**, arXiv:2209.06397.
19. Xu, W.; Fang, W.; Ding, Y.; Zou, M.; Xiong, N. Accelerating Federated Learning for IoT in Big Data Analytics with Pruning, Quantization and Selective Updating. *IEEE Access* **2021**, *9*, 38457–38466. [CrossRef]
20. Fu, A.; Zhang, X.; Xiong, N.; Gao, Y.; Wang, H.; Zhang, J. VFL: A verifiable federated learning with privacy-preserving for big data in industrial IoT. *IEEE Trans. Ind. Inform.* **2020**, *18*, 3316–3326. [CrossRef]
21. Can, Y.S.; Ersoy, C. Privacy-preserving federated deep learning for wearable IoT-based biomedical monitoring. *ACM Trans. Internet Technol. (TOIT)* **2021**, *21*, 1–17. [CrossRef]
22. Zhang, Y.; Zhang, Y.; Zhang, Z.; Bai, H.; Zhong, T.; Song, M. Evaluation of data poisoning attacks on federated learning-based network intrusion detection system. In Proceedings of the 2022 IEEE 24th Int Conf on High Performance Computing & Communications; 8th Int Conf on Data Science & Systems; 20th Int Conf on Smart City; 8th Int Conf on Dependability in Sensor, Cloud & Big Data Systems & Application (HPCC/DSS/SmartCity/DependSys), Hainan, China, 18–20 December 2022; pp. 2235–2242. [CrossRef]
23. Singh, S.; Rathore, S.; Alfarraj, O.; Tolba, A.; Yoon, B. A framework for privacy preservation of IoT healthcare data using Federated Learning and blockchain technology. *Future Gener. Comput. Syst.* **2022**, *129*, 380–388. [CrossRef]
24. Albelaihi, R.; Alasandagutti, A.; Yu, L.; Yao, J.; Sun, X. Deep-Reinforcement-Learning-Assisted Client Selection in Nonorthogonal-Multiple-Access-Based Federated Learning. *IEEE Internet Things J.* **2023**, *10*, 15515–15525. [CrossRef]
25. Yang, Q.; Liu, Y.; Chen, T.; Tong, Y. Federated machine learning: Concept and applications. *ACM Trans. Intell. Syst. Technol. (TIST)* **2019**, *10*, 1–19. [CrossRef]
26. Alam, T.; Gupta, R. Federated Learning and Its Role in the Privacy Preservation of IoT Devices. *Future Internet* **2022**, *14*, 246. [CrossRef]
27. Dhiman, G.; Juneja, S.; Mohafez, H.; El-Bayoumy, I.; Sharma, L.K.; Hadizadeh, M.; Islam, M.A.; Viriyasitavat, W.; Khandaker, M.U. Federated Learning Approach to Protect Healthcare Data over Big Data Scenario. *Sustainability* **2022**, *14*, 2500. [CrossRef]
28. Aono, Y.; Hayashi, T.; Wang, L.; Moriai, S. Privacy-preserving deep learning via additively homomorphic encryption. *IEEE Trans. Inf. Forensics Secur.* **2017**, *13*, 1333–1345.
29. Chen, Y.R.; Rezapour, A.; Tzeng, W.G. Privacy-preserving ridge regression on distributed data. *Inf. Sci.* **2018**, *451*, 34–49. [CrossRef]
30. Fang, H.; Qian, Q. Privacy Preserving Machine Learning with Homomorphic Encryption and Federated Learning. *Future Internet* **2021**, *13*, 94. [CrossRef]
31. Park, J.; Lim, H. Privacy-Preserving Federated Learning Using Homomorphic Encryption. *Appl. Sci.* **2022**, *12*, 734. [CrossRef]
32. Angulo, E.; Márquez, J.; Villanueva-Polanco, R. Training of Classification Models via Federated Learning and Homomorphic Encryption. *Sensors* **2023**, *23*, 1966. [CrossRef]
33. Shen, X.; Jiang, H.; Chen, Y.; Wang, B.; Gao, L. PLDP-FL: Federated Learning with Personalized Local Differential Privacy. *Entropy* **2023**, *25*, 485. [CrossRef]
34. Wang, X.; Wang, J.; Ma, X.; Wen, C. A Differential Privacy Strategy Based on Local Features of Non-Gaussian Noise in Federated Learning. *Sensors* **2022**, *22*, 2424. [CrossRef]
35. Zhao, J.; Yang, M.; Zhang, R.; Song, W.; Zheng, J.; Feng, J.; Matwin, S. Privacy-Enhanced Federated Learning: A Restrictively Self-Sampled and Data-Perturbed Local Differential Privacy Method. *Electronics* **2022**, *11*, 4007. [CrossRef]
36. McMahan, H.B.; Ramage, D.; Talwar, K.; Zhang, L. Learning differentially private recurrent language models. *arXiv* **2017**, arXiv:1710.06963.
37. So, J.; Güler, B.; Avestimehr, A.S. Turbo-Aggregate: Breaking the Quadratic Aggregation Barrier in Secure Federated Learning. *IEEE J. Sel. Areas Inf. Theory* **2021**, *2*, 479–489. [CrossRef]
38. Xu, G.; Li, H.; Liu, S.; Yang, K.; Lin, X. VerifyNet: Secure and Verifiable Federated Learning. *IEEE Trans. Inf. Forensics Secur.* **2020**, *15*, 911–926. [CrossRef]
39. Kim, H.; Park, J.; Bennis, M.; Kim, S.L. Blockchained On-Device Federated Learning. *IEEE Commun. Lett.* **2020**, *24*, 1279–1283. [CrossRef]

40. Mahmood, Z.; Jusas, V. Blockchain-Enabled: Multi-Layered Security Federated Learning Platform for Preserving Data Privacy. *Electronics* **2022**, *11*, 1624. [CrossRef]
41. Liu, H.; Zhou, H.; Chen, H.; Yan, Y.; Huang, J.; Xiong, A.; Yang, S.; Chen, J.; Guo, S. A Federated Learning Multi-Task Scheduling Mechanism Based on Trusted Computing Sandbox. *Sensors* **2023**, *23*, 2093. [CrossRef] [PubMed]
42. Mortaheb, M.; Vahapoglu, C.; Ulukus, S. Personalized Federated Multi-Task Learning over Wireless Fading Channels. *Algorithms* **2022**, *15*, 421. [CrossRef]
43. Du, W.; Atallah, M.J. Privacy-preserving cooperative statistical analysis. In Proceedings of the Seventeenth Annual Computer Security Applications Conference, New Orleans, LA, USA, 10–14 December 2001; pp. 102–110.
44. Du, W.; Han, Y.S.; Chen, S. Privacy-preserving multivariate statistical analysis: Linear regression and classification. In Proceedings of the 2004 SIAM International Conference on Data Mining, Lake Buena Vista, FL, USA, 22–24 April 2004; pp. 222–233.
45. Khan, A.; ten Thij, M.; Wilbik, A. Communication-Efficient Vertical Federated Learning. *Algorithms* **2022**, *15*, 273. [CrossRef]
46. Hardy, S.; Henecka, W.; Ivey-Law, H.; Nock, R.; Patrini, G.; Smith, G.; Thorne, B. Private federated learning on vertically partitioned data via entity resolution and additively homomorphic encryption. *arXiv* **2017**, arXiv:1711.10677.
47. Schoenmakers, B.; Tuyls, P. Efficient binary conversion for Paillier encrypted values. In Proceedings of the Advances in Cryptology-EUROCRYPT 2006: 24th Annual International Conference on the Theory and Applications of Cryptographic Techniques, St. Petersburg, Russia, 28 May–1 June 2006; Springer: Berlin/Heidelberg, Germany, 2006; pp. 522–537.
48. Zhong, Z.; Zhou, Y.; Wu, D.; Chen, X.; Chen, M.; Li, C.; Sheng, Q.Z. P-FedAvg: Parallelizing Federated Learning with Theoretical Guarantees. In Proceedings of the IEEE INFOCOM 2021—IEEE Conference on Computer Communications, Vancouver, BC, Canada, 10–13 May 2021; pp. 1–10. [CrossRef]
49. Barreno, M.; Nelson, B.; Sears, R.; Joseph, A.D.; Tygar, J.D. Can machine learning be secure? In Proceedings of the 2006 ACM Symposium on Information, Computer and Communications Security, Taipei, Taiwan, 21–24 March 2006; pp. 16–25.
50. Huang, L.; Joseph, A.D.; Nelson, B.; Rubinstein, B.I.; Tygar, J.D. Adversarial machine learning. In Proceedings of the 4th ACM Workshop on Security and Artificial Intelligence, Chicago, IL, USA, 21 October 2011; pp. 43–58.
51. Chu, W.L.; Lin, C.J.; Chang, K.N. Detection and Classification of Advanced Persistent Threats and Attacks Using the Support Vector Machine. *Appl. Sci.* **2019**, *9*, 4579. [CrossRef]
52. Chen, Y.; Hayawi, K.; Zhao, Q.; Mou, J.; Yang, L.; Tang, J.; Li, Q.; Wen, H. Vector Auto-Regression-Based False Data Injection Attack Detection Method in Edge Computing Environment. *Sensors* **2022**, *22*, 6789. [CrossRef]
53. Jiang, Y.; Zhou, Y.; Wu, D.; Li, C.; Wang, Y. On the Detection of Shilling Attacks in Federated Collaborative Filtering. In Proceedings of the 2020 International Symposium on Reliable Distributed Systems (SRDS), Shanghai, China, 21–24 September 2020; pp. 185–194. [CrossRef]
54. Alfeld, S.; Zhu, X.; Barford, P. Data poisoning attacks against autoregressive models. In Proceedings of the AAAI Conference on Artificial Intelligence, Phoenix, AZ, USA, 12–17 February 2016; Volume 30.
55. Biggio, B.; Nelson, B.; Laskov, P. Poisoning attacks against support vector machines. *arXiv* **2012**, arXiv:1206.6389.
56. Zügner, D.; Akbarnejad, A.; Günnemann, S. Adversarial attacks on neural networks for graph data. In Proceedings of the 24th ACM SIGKDD International Conference on Knowledge Discovery & Data Mining, 2018; pp. 2847–2856. Available online: https://arxiv.org/abs/1805.07984 (accessed on 18 October 2023).
57. Zhao, M.; An, B.; Yu, Y.; Liu, S.; Pan, S. Data poisoning attacks on multi-task relationship learning. In Proceedings of the AAAI Conference on Artificial Intelligence, New Orleans, LA, USA, 2–7 February 2018; Volume 32.
58. Dhiman, S.; Nayak, S.; Mahato, G.K.; Ram, A.; Chakraborty, S.K. Homomorphic Encryption based Federated Learning for Financial Data Security. In Proceedings of the 2023 4th International Conference on Computing and Communication Systems (I3CS), Shillong, India, 16–18 March 2023; pp. 1–6.
59. Jia, B.; Zhang, X.; Liu, J.; Zhang, Y.; Huang, K.; Liang, Y. Blockchain-Enabled Federated Learning Data Protection Aggregation Scheme With Differential Privacy and Homomorphic Encryption in IIoT. *IEEE Trans. Ind. Inform.* **2022**, *18*, 4049–4058. [CrossRef]
60. Zhang, S.; Li, Z.; Chen, Q.; Zheng, W.; Leng, J.; Guo, M. Dubhe: Towards data unbiasedness with homomorphic encryption in federated learning client selection. In Proceedings of the 50th International Conference on Parallel Processing, Lemont, IL, USA, 9–12 August 2021; pp. 1–10.
61. Guo, X. Federated Learning for Data Security and Privacy Protection. In Proceedings of the 2021 12th International Symposium on Parallel Architectures, Algorithms and Programming (PAAP), Xi'an, China, 10–12 December 2021; pp. 194–197. [CrossRef]
62. Fan, C.I.; Hsu, Y.W.; Shie, C.H.; Tseng, Y.F. ID-Based Multireceiver Homomorphic Proxy Re-Encryption in Federated Learning. *ACM Trans. Sens. Netw.* **2022**, *18*, 1–25. [CrossRef]
63. Kou, L.; Wu, J.; Zhang, F.; Ji, P.; Ke, W.; Wan, J.; Liu, H.; Li, Y.; Yuan, Q. Image encryption for Offshore wind power based on 2D-LCLM and Zhou Yi Eight Trigrams. *Int. J. Bio-Inspired Comput.* **2023**, *22*, 53–64. [CrossRef]
64. Li, L.; Li, T. Traceability model based on improved witness mechanism. *CAAI Trans. Intell. Technol.* **2022**, *7*, 331–339. [CrossRef]
65. Lee, J.; Duong, P.N.; Lee, H. Configurable Encryption and Decryption Architectures for CKKS-Based Homomorphic Encryption. *Sensors* **2023**, *23*, 7389. [CrossRef]
66. Ge, L.; Li, H.; Wang, X.; Wang, Z. A review of secure federated learning: Privacy leakage threats, protection technologies, challenges and future directions. *Neurocomputing* **2023**, *561*, 126897. [CrossRef]
67. Zhang, J.; Zhu, H.; Wang, F.; Zhao, J.; Xu, Q.; Li, H. Security and privacy threats to federated learning: Issues, methods, and challenges. *Secur. Commun. Netw.* **2022**, *2022*, 2886795. [CrossRef]

68. Zhang, J.; Li, M.; Zeng, S.; Xie, B.; Zhao, D. A survey on security and privacy threats to federated learning. In Proceedings of the 2021 International Conference on Networking and Network Applications (NaNA), Lijiang City, China, 29 October–1 November 2021; pp. 319–326. [CrossRef]
69. Li, Y.; Bao, Y.; Xiang, L.; Liu, J.; Chen, C.; Wang, L.; Wang, X. Privacy threats analysis to secure federated learning. *arXiv* **2021**, arXiv:2106.13076.
70. Asad, M.; Moustafa, A.; Yu, C. A critical evaluation of privacy and security threats in federated learning. *Sensors* **2020**, *20*, 7182. [CrossRef]
71. Manzoor, S.I.; Jain, S.; Singh, Y.; Singh, H. Federated Learning Based Privacy Ensured Sensor Communication in IoT Networks: A Taxonomy, Threats and Attacks. *IEEE Access* **2023**, *11*, 42248–42275. [CrossRef]
72. Benmalek, M.; Benrekia, M.A.; Challal, Y. Security of federated learning: Attacks, defensive mechanisms, and challenges. *Rev. Sci. Technol. L'Inform. Série RIA Rev. D'Intell. Artif.* **2022**, *36*, 49–59. [CrossRef]
73. Arbaoui, M.; Rahmoun, A. Towards secure and reliable aggregation for Federated Learning protocols in healthcare applications. In Proceedings of the 2022 Ninth International Conference on Software Defined Systems (SDS), Paris, France, 12–15 December 2022; pp. 1–3.
74. Abdelli, K.; Cho, J.Y.; Pachnicke, S. Secure Collaborative Learning for Predictive Maintenance in Optical Networks. In Proceedings of the Secure IT Systems: 26th Nordic Conference, NordSec 2021, Virtual Event, 29–30 November 2021; Proceedings 26; Springer International Publishing: Berlin/Heidelberg, Germany, 2021; pp. 114–130.
75. Jeong, H.; Son, H.; Lee, S.; Hyun, J.; Chung, T.M. FedCC: Robust Federated Learning against Model Poisoning Attacks. *arXiv* **2022**, arXiv:2212.01976.
76. Lyu, X.; Han, Y.; Wang, W.; Liu, J.; Wang, B.; Liu, J.; Zhang, X. Poisoning with cerberus: Stealthy and colluded backdoor attack against federated learning. In Proceedings of the Thirty-Seventh AAAI Conference on Artificial Intelligence, Washington, DC, USA, 7–14 February 2023.
77. Wei, K.; Li, J.; Ding, M.; Ma, C.; Jeon, Y.S.; Poor, H.V. Covert model poisoning against federated learning: Algorithm design and optimization. *IEEE Trans. Dependable Secur. Comput.* **2023**. [CrossRef]
78. Sun, J.; Li, A.; DiValentin, L.; Hassanzadeh, A.; Chen, Y.; Li, H. Fl-wbc: Enhancing robustness against model poisoning attacks in federated learning from a client perspective. *Adv. Neural Inf. Process. Syst.* **2021**, *34*, 12613–12624.
79. Mao, Y.; Yuan, X.; Zhao, X.; Zhong, S. Romoa: Ro bust Mo del A ggregation for the Resistance of Federated Learning to Model Poisoning Attacks. In Proceedings of the Computer Security–ESORICS 2021: 26th European Symposium on Research in Computer Security, Darmstadt, Germany, 4–8 October 2021; Springer: Berlin/Heidelberg, Germany, 2021; pp. 476–496.
80. Pillutla, K.; Kakade, S.M.; Harchaoui, Z. Robust Aggregation for Federated Learning. *IEEE Trans. Signal Process.* **2022**, *70*, 1142–1154. [CrossRef]
81. Wang, X.; Liang, Z.; Koe, A.S.V.; Wu, Q.; Zhang, X.; Li, H.; Yang, Q. Secure and efficient parameters aggregation protocol for federated incremental learning and its applications. *Int. J. Intell. Syst.* **2022**, *37*, 4471–4487. [CrossRef]
82. Hao, M.; Li, H.; Xu, G.; Chen, H.; Zhang, T. Efficient, private and robust federated learning. In Proceedings of the Annual Computer Security Applications Conference, Virtual Event, 6–10 December 2021; pp. 45–60.
83. Smith, V.; Chiang, C.K.; Sanjabi, M.; Talwalkar, A.S. Federated multi-task learning. *Adv. Neural Inf. Process. Syst.* **2017**, *30*.
84. Shalev-Shwartz, S.; Zhang, T. Accelerated proximal stochastic dual coordinate ascent for regularized loss minimization. In Proceedings of the International Conference on Machine Learning, Beijing, China, 22–24 June 2014; pp. 64–72.
85. Wassan, S.; Suhail, B.; Mubeen, R.; Raj, B.; Agarwal, U.; Khatri, E.; Gopinathan, S.; Dhiman, G. Gradient Boosting for Health IoT Federated Learning. *Sustainability* **2022**, *14*, 16842. [CrossRef]
86. Feng, J.; Yang, L.T.; Zhu, Q.; Choo, K.K.R. Privacy-preserving tensor decomposition over encrypted data in a federated cloud environment. *IEEE Trans. Dependable Secur. Comput.* **2018**, *17*, 857–868. [CrossRef]
87. Feng, J.; Yang, L.T.; Ren, B.; Zou, D.; Dong, M.; Zhang, S. Tensor recurrent neural network with differential privacy. *IEEE Trans. Comput.* **2023**. [CrossRef]
88. Karras, A.; Karras, C.; Giotopoulos, K.C.; Tsolis, D.; Oikonomou, K.; Sioutas, S. Federated Edge Intelligence and Edge Caching Mechanisms. *Information* **2023**, *14*, 414. [CrossRef]
89. Karras, A.; Karras, C.; Schizas, N.; Avlonitis, M.; Sioutas, S. AutoML with Bayesian Optimizations for Big Data Management. *Information* **2023**, *14*, 223. [CrossRef]

electronics

MDPI

Article

Certificateless Encryption Supporting Multi-Ciphertext Equality Test with Proxy-Assisted Authorization

Siyue Dong [1,*,†,‡], Zhen Zhao [1,*,†,‡], Baocang Wang [1], Wen Gao [2] and Shanshan Zhang [3]

1 The State Key Laboratory of Integrated Service Networks, Xidian University, Xi'an 710071, China; bcwang@xidian.edu.cn
2 School of Cyberspace Security, Xi'an University of Posts & Telecommunications, Xi'an 710121, China; gaowen@xupt.edu.cn
3 School of Mathematics and Information Science, Baoji University of Arts and Science, Xi'an 721016, China; sszhang@bjwlxy.edu.cn
* Correspondence: sydong@stu.xidian.edu.cn (S.D.); zzhen@xidian.edu.cn (Z.Z.)
† Current address: No. 2 South Taibai Road, Xi'an 710071, China.
‡ These authors contributed equally to this work.

Abstract: Public key encryption with equality test (PKEET) is a cryptographic primitive that enables a tester to determine, without decryption, whether two ciphertexts encrypted with different public keys generate from the same message. In previous research, public key encryption with equality test (PKEET) was extended to include identity-based encryption with equality test (IBEET), thereby broadening the application of PKEET. Subsequently, certificateless encryption with equality test (CLEET) was introduced to address the key escrow problem in IBEET. However, existing CLEET schemes suffer from inefficiency and potential information leakage when dealing with multiple ciphertexts due to the need for pairwise equality tests. To address this issue, we propose a concept of certificateless encryption supporting multi-ciphertext equality test with proxy-assisted authorization (CLE-MET-PA). CLE-MET-PA incorporates the functionality of the multi-ciphertext equality test into CLEET, enabling a tester to perform a single equality test on multiple ciphertexts to determine whether the underlying plaintexts are equal, without revealing any additional information. This enhances the security of our scheme while significantly reducing the computational overhead compared to multiple pairwise equality tests, making our scheme more efficient. Additionally, our approach integrates proxy-assisted authorization, allowing users to delegate a proxy to grant authorizations for equality tests on their behalf when offline. Importantly, the proxy token used in our scheme does not include any portion of the user's private key, providing enhanced protection compared to traditional PKEET schemes in which the user token is often part of the user's private key. We construct a concrete CLE-MET-PA scheme and prove that it achieves CPA security and attains CCA security through an FO transformation.

Keywords: public key encryption with equality test; certificateless encryption; multi-ciphertext equality test

1. Introduction

Cloud computing provides an efficient solution for transferring the storage and computation burdens from users to cloud servers. In recent decades, the continuous improvement in network bandwidth, the emergence of big data, the Internet of Things, and artificial intelligence have led to the rapid development of cloud technology and its applications [1–4]. Cloud storage, in comparison to traditional local storage, offers several advantages including low cost, high scalability, easy management, and maintenance. With cloud technology, users can select the appropriate storage capacity and service types based on their specific requirements and perform various data operations such as uploading, downloading, backup, archiving, and sharing. As a result, more and more individuals and organizations are utilizing cloud servers to process and store their data. However, due to the sensitive nature of their data and the need for privacy protection, it is common practice to encrypt the data on cloud servers using various cryptosystems. Nevertheless, there is a growing demand for cryptographic technologies that enable processing operations, such as searching, deduplication, classification, and data segmentation, while preserving the confidentiality of the encrypted data.

In the realm of processing encrypted data, researchers have proposed various cryptographic primitives, including searchable encryption [5,6] and fully homomorphic encryption [7]. Expanding upon searchable encryption, Boneh et al. [8] introduced public key encryption with keyword search (PEKS) in 2004. The scheme allows a server to verify, without decryption, whether a ciphertext C is generated from a message M as long as it is in possession of the corresponding tag T_M for that ciphertext and the public key used for message encryption. This property renders it suitable for applications such as the classification of public key ciphertexts.

This scheme, however, has a limitation in that it only allows ciphertext management for a single user, restricting comparison and search to ciphertexts under the same public key. To enable ciphertext equality tests across different public keys, additional primitives are necessary. In 2010, Yang et al. [9] proposed the concept of public-key encryption with equality test (PKEET). In their work, the authors introduced a special public key encryption scheme where an entity can determine whether two ciphertexts correspond to identical plaintexts using an equality test algorithm on two ciphertexts encrypted under different public keys.

1.1. Related Work

In the first PKEET scheme proposed by Yang et al. [9], there is a concern regarding the protection of data privacy for the data owner, as there is no restriction on who can perform an equality test. Consequently, the initial advancements in PKEET schemes were predominantly directed towards achieving fine-grained control over tester authorizations. These efforts [10–14] concentrated on devising methods to authorize testers and defining which ciphertexts they could perform equality tests on once granted authorization. The work proposed by Ma et al. [14] extensively examines and provides a comprehensive overview of diverse authorization mechanisms.

In 2016, Ma [15] and Lee et al. [16] introduced the identity-based encryption (IBE) primitive into PKEET, presenting their respective IBEET schemes. These schemes adopt the benefits of identity-based encryption (IBE) cryptosystems, which allow users to generate public and private key pairs using their identity information without the need for digital certificates, therefore addressing the key management problem in public key encryption cryptosystems. This novel approach sparked significant subsequent research on IBEET [17–28].

Certificateless public key encryption with equality test (CL-PKEET). When it comes to solving the key management problem, identity-based encryption (IBE) relies on a central authority, typically the key generation center (KGC), to generate private keys for users based on their identities. However, this reliance on a central authority means that the KGC has the ability to decrypt messages intended for any user. If the KGC is compromised, coerced, or misused, it can result in unauthorized access to users' encrypted data, which is known as the key escrow problem. To address this issue, Al-Riyami et al. [29] proposed certificateless encryption (CLE). In CLE, the KGC generates partial private keys for users, enabling them to generate their own private and public keys. This approach effectively addresses the key escrow problem. Similarly, IBEET also faces the key escrow problem. In order to tackle this problem in IBEET, Qu et al. [30] introduced CLE into PKEET, creating the initial certificateless public key encryption with equality test (CL-PKEET, referred to as CLEET in this paper for brevity) scheme.

Public key encryption with multi-ciphertext equality test (PKE-MET). Before the introduction of PKE-MET by Susilo et al. [31], all PKEET and IBEET schemes only supported pairwise equality tests. Consider a scenario where a tester receives n ciphertexts from n

different users. With a conventional PKEET scheme, the tester would be required to perform a minimum of $n-1$ equality tests between pairs of ciphertexts to determine the equality of the n ciphertexts. However, in the PKE-MET scheme, a specific parameter s is designated, enabling the tester to test the equality of s ciphertexts in a single equality test. Moreover, this feature of multi-ciphertext comparison significantly reduces additional information leakage in equality tests. For example, when conducting an equality test on ciphertexts from three different users to determine whether the plaintexts corresponding to user A, B, and C's ciphertexts are equal, traditional PKEET test algorithms would inevitably reveal additional information, such as the equality of the underlying plaintexts between user A and user B. By exploiting our multi-ciphertext test feature, the leakage of additional information in equality tests can be greatly mitigated. This improvement leads to better efficiency, heightened security, and reduced computational costs for the tester.

Proxy-assisted authorization. One authorization method employed in our scheme is consistent with the majority of PKEET schemes, known as user authorization. In this method, a user generates a token (also referred to as a trapdoor), and sends it to the tester, enabling the tester to conduct equality tests on the user's ciphertexts. Additionally, we introduce a proxy-assisted authorization method, whereby the user can engage with a proxy through a secure and efficient key exchange algorithm to create a proxy token. This token is then securely stored by the proxy and possesses the same authorization capabilities as the user token. There are two primary advantages to this approach. Firstly, it liberates the user from having to be constantly online to authorize a tester, enhancing the practical application value of the scheme. Secondly, unlike the user token, the proxy token does not compromise any part of the user's private key, thus reducing the risk of privacy exposure.

1.2. Our Contribution

We propose a CLE-MET-PA scheme in this paper, and the contributions of this paper are as follows:

- We introduce the multi-ciphertext equality test into CLEET. Our proposal associates each ciphertext with a designated number s, making it possible to perform equality tests on multiple ciphertexts simultaneously in a single test without revealing any additional information, all while retaining the fundamental attributes of certificateless encryption.
- We incorporate the concept of a proxy into our framework. Users have the flexibility to choose and disclose proxies along with their public keys on the public key server. This enables users to delegate authorization to proxies, allowing them to go offline, which effectively improves the practical application value. Moreover, the use of proxy tokens eliminates the exposure of the user's private key, thus enhancing the security of our scheme. Additionally, our encryption process does not involve proxy information. Hence, when users choose a new proxy, there is no need to reconfigure previous ciphertexts. The disclosed proxy information is only utilized in the equality test, resulting in a more flexible scheme. Furthermore, the key generation algorithm for proxies is identical to that of users, meaning that any user can act as a proxy. This enhances the flexibility and efficiency of our scheme.
- We establish formal security models for our concrete CLE-MET-PA scheme, including five different types of adversaries. Subsequently, our work achieves IND-CPA security against adversaries with the trapdoor of the challenge ciphertext and OW-CPA security against adversaries without the trapdoor of the challenge ciphertext. In the extension section, we employ the Fujisaki–Okamoto (FO) transformation [32,33] to modify the encryption and decryption processes, thereby attaining CCA security for our scheme (i.e., IND-CCA security against adversaries with the trapdoor of the challenge ciphertext and OW-CCA security against adversaries without the trapdoor of the challenge ciphertext).

1.3. Organization

In Section 2, we reviewed the concepts of asymmetric bilinear groups and the BDH assumption; in Section 3, we introduced the system model, definitions and security models of CLE-MET-PA; in Section 4, we presented the concrete construction of CLE-MET-PA and verified its correctness; In Section 5, we proved the security of the scheme; in Section 6, we conducted a performance analysis and discussed the security extension of the scheme; in Section 7, we summarized our work.

2. Preliminary

2.1. Asymmetric Bilinear Groups

Let $\mathcal{G} = (p, \mathbb{G}_1, \mathbb{G}_2, \mathbb{G}_T, e)$ be a bilinear groups ensemble, where $\mathbb{G}_1$, $\mathbb{G}_2$, and $\mathbb{G}_T$ are three multiplicative cyclic groups of order p. $g_1 \in \mathbb{G}_1$, $g_2 \in \mathbb{G}_2$ are two generators. A bilinear map $e : \mathbb{G}_1 \times \mathbb{G}_2 \to \mathbb{G}_T$ has the following properties:

1. *Bilinear:* For any $g_1 \in \mathbb{G}_1, g_2 \in \mathbb{G}_2$ and $a, b \in \mathbb{Z}_p$, $e(g_1^a, g_2^b) = e(g_1, g_2)^{ab}$.
2. *Non-degenerate:* $e(g_1, g_2) \neq 1$.
3. *Computable:* For any $g_1 \in \mathbb{G}_1$ and $g_2 \in \mathbb{G}_2$, there is an efficient algorithm to compute $e(g_1, g_2)$.

Since $\mathbb{G}_1 \neq \mathbb{G}_2$, this is an asymmetric bilinear map. In the asymmetric setting, if there exists an efficient computable isomorphism $\psi : \mathbb{G}_1 \to \mathbb{G}_2$, the pairing e is referred to as a *Type 2 pairing*. Conversely, if no such isomorphism exists, e is categorized as a *Type 3 pairing* [34–37].

2.2. Bilinear Diffie–Hellman (BDH) Assumption in Asymmetric Bilinear Groups

The bilinear Diffie–Hellman (BDH) assumption was initially proposed by Boneh et al. [38] in the context of symmetric bilinear groups. Later, Boyen et al. [39] expanded this assumption to asymmetric bilinear settings.

The BDH problem can be defined as follows: consider a set of bilinear groups in Section 2.1, denoted by $\mathcal{G} = \{p, \mathbb{G}_1, \mathbb{G}_2, \mathbb{G}_T, e\}$. Let $g_1 \in \mathbb{G}_1$ and $g_2 \in \mathbb{G}_2$ be two generators. Given an instance $(g_1, g_1^a, g_1^c, g_2, g_2^a, g_2^b) \in \mathbb{G}_1^3 \times \mathbb{G}_2^3$ where a, b, and c are uniformly random choices from $\mathbb{Z}_p^*$, the task is to compute $e(g_1, g_2)^{abc} \in \mathbb{G}_T$.

The BDH assumption is defined as follows: Given an instance of the aforementioned BDH problem, no probabilistic polynomial-time (PPT) adversary, denoted by $\mathcal{A}$, can compute the value of $e(g_1, g_2)^{abc}$ with non-negligible probability. The advantage of $\mathcal{A}$ is defined as:

$$Adv(\mathcal{A}) = Pr[\mathcal{A}(g_1, g_1^a, g_1^c, g_2, g_2^a, g_2^b) = e(g_1, g_2)^{abc}].$$

3. System Model, Definitions, and Security Models

We present the system model of our certificateless encryption supporting multi-ciphertext equality test with proxy-assisted authorization (CLE-MET-PA) scheme, followed by its formal definition and security models.

3.1. System Model of CLE-MET-PA

The system model of our CLE-MET-PA scheme is depicted in Figure 1. The model comprises seven types of entities as follows:

1. Key generation center (KGC): This entity is responsible for system setup, safeguarding the master secret key, and issuing partial private keys to users based on their identities.
2. Message sender: This entity generates ciphertexts using the public key of the target user and uploads them to the cloud server.
3. Message receiver: This entity, often referred to as the user in this paper, can download ciphertexts for decryption, grant authorization to testers for equality tests, and delegate proxies to provide authorizations on its behalf.

4. Cloud server: This entity stores the ciphertexts generated by message senders and allows message receivers to download them. The cloud server often serves as the tester. To ensure generality, we established a separate entity for test purposes.
5. Proxy: This entity can interact with a message receiver to create a proxy token, granting authorization for equality tests on the message receiver's ciphertexts.
6. Public key server: This entity stores public keys issued by message receivers and proxies. Additionally, it keeps track of the message receiver's choice of proxy and publishes its proxy information.
7. Tester: This entity can perform an equality test on a set of s ciphertexts. To conduct the test, the tester must receive s ciphertexts along with the tokens issued by their respective message receivers or proxies. Each ciphertext is designated with the number s.

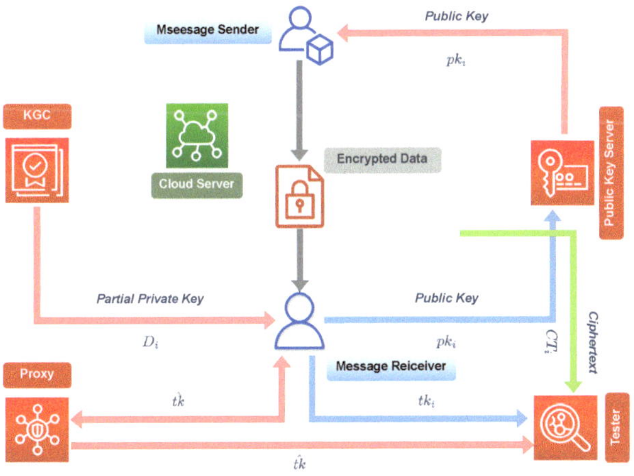

Figure 1. System model of CLE-MET-PA.

The workflow of our proposed CLE-MET-PA scheme is also depicted in Figure 1. The message sender queries the public key server for the necessary public key, encrypts the message using it to obtain the ciphertext, and uploads it to the cloud server. The message receiver can then download the ciphertext from the cloud server, and decrypt it to obtain the message. A message receiver can authorize a tester directly or by a delegated proxy, enabling the tester to perform an equality test on its ciphertexts.

A notable feature of CLE-MET-PA is its multi-ciphertext equality test, illustrated in Figure 2. A tester can conduct a single-test algorithm upon receiving s ciphertexts, each with the designated number s, along with s trapdoors (whether authorized by the user or authorized through user-delegated proxy authorization). The test algorithm outputs 1 if all underlying plaintexts to the ciphertexts are equal, and 0 if at least one underlying plaintext differs from the rest.

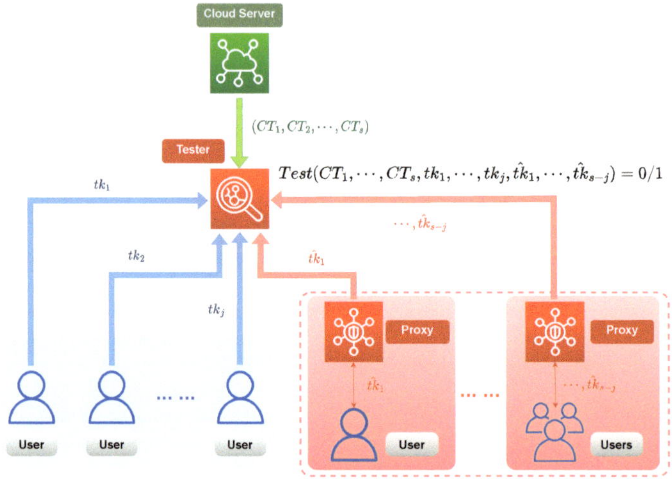

Figure 2. Equality test of CLE-MET-PA.

3.2. *Certificateless Encryption Supporting Multi-Ciphertext Equality Test with Proxy-Assisted Authorization*

A CLE-MET-PA system consists of eleven algorithms as described below:

- Setup(1^λ): This algorithm takes the security parameter λ as input and outputs the system parameter pp and the system master secret key msk.
- Partial-Private-Key-Extract(pp, msk, ID): Given the system parameter pp, a master key msk, and an identifier ID, this algorithm outputs the partial private key D.
- Set-Secret-Value (pp, ID): Given the system parameter pp and an identifier ID, this algorithm outputs a secret value x at random.
- Set-Private-Key (pp, D, x): Given the system parameter pp, a partial private key D, and a secret value x, this algorithm outputs a private key sk.
- Set-Public-Key (pp, x): Given the system parameter pp and a secret value x, this algorithm outputs a public key pk.
- Set-Proxy-Key (pp, ID_P): Given the system parameter pp and a proxy identifier ID_P, this algorithm outputs a proxy public key pk_P and its secret value x_P.
- Enc(pp, pk, M, s): This algorithm outputs a ciphertext CT of a message M, with a designated number s, such that an equality test on CT must be performed with $s-1$ other ciphertexts with the same s.
- Dec(CT, sk): This algorithm outputs the message M or $\perp$.
- Aut(sk): This algorithm outputs a token tk that authorizes the tester to perform an equality test on the ciphertexts of users who own sk.
- Proxy-Aut (pp, sk, sk_P): This protocol outputs a token $\hat{tk}$ issued by the proxy who owns sk_P to the tester, enabling the latter to perform an equality test on the ciphertexts of the users who own sk.
- Test$(CT_1, \cdots, CT_t, \hat{tk}_1, \cdots, \hat{tk}j, tk_1, \cdots, tk_{t-j}$: Given t ciphertexts CT and t tokens, including tokens issued by users and the proxy, this algorithm checks whether $t = s_1 = s_2 = \cdots = s_t$, where s_i is the designated number of CT_i. If not, it outputs $\perp$ and aborts. Otherwise, it outputs 1, implying that the underlying messages of $CT_1, CT_2, \cdots, CT_t$ are equal, or 0, implying that the messages are not equal.

Correctness: We can say that a CLE-MET-PA scheme is correct if the following conditions hold.

(1) For any security parameter λ, any message $M \in \mathcal{M}$, and any number $s \in \mathbb{Z}_p$, we have

$$\Pr\left[\mathsf{Dec}(sk, CT) = M \;\middle|\; \begin{array}{l} pp \leftarrow \mathsf{Setup}(\lambda) \\ D \leftarrow \mathsf{Partial\text{-}Private\text{-}Key\text{-}Extract}(pp, msk, ID) \\ x \leftarrow \mathsf{Set\text{-}Secret\text{-}Value}(pp, ID) \\ sk \leftarrow \mathsf{Set\text{-}Private\text{-}Key}(pp, D, x) \\ pk \leftarrow \mathsf{Set\text{-}Public\text{-}Key}(pp, x) \\ (pk_P, x_P) \leftarrow \mathsf{Set\text{-}Proxy\text{-}Key}(pp, ID_P) \\ CT \leftarrow \mathsf{Enc}(pp, pk, M, s) \end{array}\right] = 1.$$

(2) For any security parameter λ, any message $M \in \mathcal{M}$, any number $t \in \mathbb{Z}_p$, and $i \in \{1, \cdots, t\}$, we have

$$\Pr\left[\begin{array}{l} \mathsf{Test}(CT_1, \cdots, CT_t, \hat{tk}_1, \cdots, \\ \hat{tk}_j, tk_1, \cdots, tk_{t-j}) = 1 \end{array} \;\middle|\; \begin{array}{l} pp \leftarrow \mathsf{Setup}(\lambda) \\ D_i \leftarrow \mathsf{Partial\text{-}Private\text{-}Key\text{-}Extract}(pp, msk, ID_i) \\ x_i \leftarrow \mathsf{Set\text{-}Secret\text{-}Value}(pp, ID_i) \\ sk_i \leftarrow \mathsf{Set\text{-}Private\text{-}Key}(pp, D_I, x_i) \\ pk_i \leftarrow \mathsf{Set\text{-}Public\text{-}Key}(pp, x_i) \\ (pk_P, x_P) \leftarrow \mathsf{Set\text{-}Proxy\text{-}Key}(pp, ID_{P_i}) \\ CT_i \leftarrow \mathsf{Enc}(pp, pk_i, pk_{P_i}, M_i, t) \\ tk_i \leftarrow \mathsf{Aut}(sk_i) \\ \hat{tk}_i \leftarrow \mathsf{Proxy\text{-}Aut}(sk_i) \end{array}\right]$$

is overwhelming.

3.3. Security Models of CLE-MET-PA

We consider five types of adversaries in CLE-MET-PA. Type-I $\sim$ Type-IV exist in CL-PKEET and Type-V in PKE-MET. In CLE, users generate their own pairs of public and private keys. The absence of a certificate in the public key introduces a vulnerability to tampering. We define Type-I and Type-II adversaries as outsiders who possess the capability to replace legitimate public keys. In the context of CLE, where the KGC is not fully trusted, we define Type-III and Type-IV adversaries as curious KGCs who possess the system master secret key msk. For the discussion on the impact of trapdoors needed by the equality tests on system security, we define that Type-II and Type-IV adversaries can acquire all trapdoors in the system, including the trapdoor of the challenge ciphertext. Finally, considering the characteristics of PKE-MET, we define a Type-V adversary. The detailed descriptions are provided below:

- Type-I Adversary: This type of adversary can replace the public key of a user but cannot access the master key. Without the trapdoor of the challenge ciphertext, we define the IND-CPA security model regarding this type of adversary.
- Type-II Adversary: This type of adversary can replace the public key of a user but cannot access the master key. With the trapdoor of the challenge ciphertext, we define the OW-CPA security model regarding this type of adversary.
- Type-III Adversary: This type of adversary cannot replace the public key of a user but can access the master key. Without the trapdoor of the challenge ciphertext, we define the IND-CPA security model regarding this type of adversary.
- Type-IV Adversary: This type of adversary cannot replace the public key of a user but can access the master key. With the trapdoor of the challenge ciphertext, we define the OW-CPA security model regarding this type of adversary.

- Type-V Adversary: This type of adversary attempts to perform an equality test on t ciphertexts $CT_1, \cdots, CT_t$, where all the designated numbers of these ciphertexts are s_i, with $s_i > t$.

We define five games for these five types of adversaries.

Game 1: IND-CPA Game

$$
\begin{gathered}
pp \leftarrow \mathsf{Setup}(1^\lambda);\\
D_i \leftarrow \mathsf{Partial\text{-}Private\text{-}Key\text{-}Extract}(pp, msk, ID_i) \text{ for } 1 \le i \le N;\\
x_i \leftarrow \mathsf{Set\text{-}Secret\text{-}Value}(pp, ID_i)\\
sk_i \leftarrow \mathsf{Set\text{-}Private\text{-}Key}(pp, D_i, x_i)\\
pk_i \leftarrow \mathsf{Set\text{-}Public\text{-}Key}(pp, x_i)\\
(pk_{P_i}, x_{P_i}) \leftarrow \mathsf{Set\text{-}Proxy\text{-}Key}(pp, ID_{P_i})\\
(s^*, pk^*, M_0^*, M_1^*) \leftarrow \mathcal{A}^{\mathcal{O}^{\text{par-key}}(\cdot),\mathcal{O}^{\text{priv-key}}(\cdot),\mathcal{O}^{\text{pub-key}}(\cdot),\mathcal{O}^{\text{pub-rep}}(\cdot),\mathcal{O}^{\text{p-key}}(\cdot),\mathcal{O}^{\text{token}}(\cdot),\mathcal{O}^{\text{p-token}}(\cdot)}(\{pk_i, pk_{P_i}\}_{i=1}^N);\\
CT^* \leftarrow \mathsf{Enc}(pk^*, M_b^*, s^*) \text{ for } b \in \{0,1\}, \text{random } s^*;\\
b' \leftarrow \mathcal{A}^{\mathcal{O}^{\text{par-key}}(\cdot),\mathcal{O}^{\text{priv-key}}(\cdot),\mathcal{O}^{\text{pub-key}}(\cdot),\mathcal{O}^{\text{pub-rep}}(\cdot),\mathcal{O}^{\text{p-key}}(\cdot),\mathcal{O}^{\text{token}}(\cdot),\mathcal{O}^{\text{p-token}}(\cdot)}(\{pk_i, pk_{P_i}\}_{i=1}^N).
\end{gathered}
$$

In Game 1, $\mathcal{O}^{\text{par-key}}(\cdot)$, $\mathcal{O}^{\text{priv-key}}(\cdot)$, $\mathcal{O}^{\text{pub-key}}(\cdot)$, $\mathcal{O}^{\text{pub-rep}}(\cdot)$, $\mathcal{O}^{\text{p-key}}(\cdot)$, $\mathcal{O}^{\text{token}}(\cdot)$, and $\mathcal{O}^{\text{p-token}}(\cdot)$, denote the partial key oracle, the private key oracle, the public key oracle, the public key replace oracle, the proxy key oracle, the token oracle, and the proxy token oracle, respectively. The adversary is not allowed to make private key query, token query, or proxy token query on pk^*. We define the advantage of adversary in winning this game as

$$\mathsf{Adv}_{\mathsf{CLE\text{-}MET\text{-}PA}}^{\mathsf{IND\text{-}CPA,Type\text{-}I}}(\lambda) = \Pr[b' = b] - 1/2.$$

Game 2: OW-CPA Game

$$
\begin{gathered}
pp \leftarrow \mathsf{Setup}(1^\lambda);\\
D_i \leftarrow \mathsf{Partial\text{-}Private\text{-}Key\text{-}Extract}(pp, msk, ID_i) \text{ for } 1 \le i \le N;\\
x_i \leftarrow \mathsf{Set\text{-}Secret\text{-}Value}(pp, ID_i)\\
sk_i \leftarrow \mathsf{Set\text{-}Private\text{-}Key}(pp, D_i, x_i)\\
pk_i \leftarrow \mathsf{Set\text{-}Public\text{-}Key}(pp, x_i)\\
(pk_{P_i}, x_{P_i}) \leftarrow \mathsf{Set\text{-}Proxy\text{-}Key}(pp, ID_{P_i})\\
(s^*, pk^*) \leftarrow \mathcal{A}^{\mathcal{O}^{\text{par-key}}(\cdot),\mathcal{O}^{\text{priv-key}}(\cdot),\mathcal{O}^{\text{pub-key}}(\cdot),\mathcal{O}^{\text{pub-rep}}(\cdot),\mathcal{O}^{\text{p-key}}(\cdot),\mathcal{O}^{\text{token}}(\cdot),\mathcal{O}^{\text{p-token}}(\cdot)}(\{pk_i, pk_{P_i}\}_{i=1}^N);\\
CT^* \leftarrow \mathsf{Enc}(pk^*, M^*, s^*) \text{ for random } M^*, s^*;\\
M' \leftarrow \mathcal{A}^{\mathcal{O}^{\text{par-key}}(\cdot),\mathcal{O}^{\text{priv-key}}(\cdot),\mathcal{O}^{\text{pub-key}}(\cdot),\mathcal{O}^{\text{pub-rep}}(\cdot),\mathcal{O}^{\text{p-key}}(\cdot),\mathcal{O}^{\text{token}}(\cdot),\mathcal{O}^{\text{p-token}}(\cdot)}(\{pk_i, pk_{P_i}\}_{i=1}^N).
\end{gathered}
$$

In Game 2, the adversary is restricted to making a private key query on pk^*. We define the advantage of the adversary in winning this game as

$$\mathsf{Adv}_{\mathsf{CLE\text{-}MET\text{-}PA}}^{\mathsf{OW\text{-}CPA,Type\text{-}II}}(\lambda) = \Pr[M' = M^*].$$

Game 3: IND-CPA Game

$$
\begin{gathered}
pp \leftarrow \mathsf{Setup}(1^\lambda);\\
D_i \leftarrow \mathsf{Partial\text{-}Private\text{-}Key\text{-}Extract}(pp, msk, ID_i) \text{ for } 1 \le i \le N;\\
x_i \leftarrow \mathsf{Set\text{-}Secret\text{-}Value}(pp, ID_i)\\
sk_i \leftarrow \mathsf{Set\text{-}Private\text{-}Key}(pp, D_i, x_i)\\
pk_i \leftarrow \mathsf{Set\text{-}Public\text{-}Key}(pp, x_i)\\
(pk_{P_i}, x_{P_i}) \leftarrow \mathsf{Set\text{-}Proxy\text{-}Key}(pp, ID_{P_i})\\
(s^*, pk^*, M_0^*, M_1^*) \leftarrow \mathcal{A}^{\mathcal{O}^{\text{msk}}(\cdot),\mathcal{O}^{\text{par-key}}(\cdot),\mathcal{O}^{\text{priv-key}}(\cdot),\mathcal{O}^{\text{pub-key}}(\cdot),\mathcal{O}^{\text{p-key}}(\cdot),\mathcal{O}^{\text{token}}(\cdot),\mathcal{O}^{\text{p-token}}(\cdot)}(\{pk_i, pk_{P_i}\}_{i=1}^N);\\
CT^* \leftarrow \mathsf{Enc}(pk^*, M_b^*, s^*) \text{ for } b \in \{0,1\}, \text{random } s^*;\\
b' \leftarrow \mathcal{A}^{\mathcal{O}^{\text{msk}}(\cdot),\mathcal{O}^{\text{par-key}}(\cdot),\mathcal{O}^{\text{priv-key}}(\cdot),\mathcal{O}^{\text{pub-key}}(\cdot),\mathcal{O}^{\text{p-key}}(\cdot),\mathcal{O}^{\text{token}}(\cdot),\mathcal{O}^{\text{p-token}}(\cdot)}(\{pk_i, pk_{P_i}\}_{i=1}^N).
\end{gathered}
$$

In Game 3, the adversary can access the master secret key oracle $\mathcal{O}^{\text{msk}}(\cdot)$, but can no longer access the public key replace oracle. The adversary cannot make a private key, token query, or proxy token query on pk^*. We define the advantage of the adversary in winning this game as

$$\mathsf{Adv}^{\mathsf{IND\text{-}CPA,Type\text{-}III}}_{\mathsf{CLE\text{-}MET\text{-}PA}}(\lambda) = \Pr[b' = b] - 1/2.$$

Game 4: OW-CPA Game

$$\begin{gathered}
pp \leftarrow \mathsf{Setup}(1^\lambda); \\
D_i \leftarrow \mathsf{Partial\text{-}Private\text{-}Key\text{-}Extract}(pp, msk, ID_i) \text{ for } 1 \le i \le N; \\
x_i \leftarrow \mathsf{Set\text{-}Secret\text{-}Value}(pp, ID_i) \\
sk_i \leftarrow \mathsf{Set\text{-}Private\text{-}Key}(pp, D_i, x_i) \\
pk_i \leftarrow \mathsf{Set\text{-}Public\text{-}Key}(pp, x_i) \\
(pk_{P_i}, x_{P_i}) \leftarrow \mathsf{Set\text{-}Proxy\text{-}Key}(pp, ID_{P_i}) \\
(s^*, pk^*) \leftarrow \mathcal{A}^{\mathcal{O}^{\mathsf{msk}}(\cdot), \mathcal{O}^{\mathsf{par\text{-}key}}(\cdot), \mathcal{O}^{\mathsf{priv\text{-}key}}(\cdot), \mathcal{O}^{\mathsf{pub\text{-}key}}(\cdot), \mathcal{O}^{\mathsf{p\text{-}key}}(\cdot), \mathcal{O}^{\mathsf{token}}(\cdot), \mathcal{O}^{\mathsf{p\text{-}token}}(\cdot)}(\{pk_i, pk_{P_i}\}_{i=1}^N); \\
CT^* \leftarrow \mathsf{Enc}(pk^*, M^*, s^*) \text{ for random } M^*, s^*; \\
M' \leftarrow \mathcal{A}^{\mathcal{O}^{\mathsf{msk}}(\cdot), \mathcal{O}^{\mathsf{par\text{-}key}}(\cdot), \mathcal{O}^{\mathsf{priv\text{-}key}}(\cdot), \mathcal{O}^{\mathsf{pub\text{-}key}}(\cdot), \mathcal{O}^{\mathsf{p\text{-}key}}(\cdot), \mathcal{O}^{\mathsf{token}}(\cdot), \mathcal{O}^{\mathsf{p\text{-}token}}(\cdot)}(\{pk_i, pk_{P_i}\}_{i=1}^N).
\end{gathered}$$

In Game 4, the adversary can access the master secret key oracle $\mathcal{O}^{\mathsf{msk}}(\cdot)$, but can no longer access the public key replace oracle. The adversary cannot make a private key query on pk^*. We define the advantage of the adversary in winning this game as

$$\mathsf{Adv}^{\mathsf{OW\text{-}CPA,Type\text{-}IV}}_{\mathsf{CLE\text{-}MET\text{-}PA}}(\lambda) = \Pr[M' = M^*].$$

Game 5: Number Game

$$\begin{gathered}
pp \leftarrow \mathsf{Setup}(1^\lambda); \\
D_i \leftarrow \mathsf{Partial\text{-}Private\text{-}Key\text{-}Extract}(pp, msk, ID_i) \text{ for } 1 \le i \le N; \\
x_i \leftarrow \mathsf{Set\text{-}Secret\text{-}Value}(pp, ID_i) \\
sk_i \leftarrow \mathsf{Set\text{-}Private\text{-}Key}(pp, D_i, x_i) \\
pk_i \leftarrow \mathsf{Set\text{-}Public\text{-}Key}(pp, x_i) \\
(pk_{P_i}, x_{P_i}) \leftarrow \mathsf{Set\text{-}Proxy\text{-}Key}(pp, ID_{P_i}) \\
(s^*, t^*, pk_1^*, \cdots, pk_t^*) \leftarrow \mathcal{A}^{\mathcal{O}^{\mathsf{par\text{-}key}}(\cdot), \mathcal{O}^{\mathsf{priv\text{-}key}}(\cdot), \mathcal{O}^{\mathsf{pub\text{-}key}}(\cdot), \mathcal{O}^{\mathsf{p\text{-}key}}(\cdot), \mathcal{O}^{\mathsf{token}}(\cdot), \mathcal{O}^{\mathsf{p\text{-}token}}(\cdot)}(\{pk_i, pk_{P_i}\}_{i=1}^N), t^* < s^*; \\
(CT_1^*, \cdots, CT_j^*, \cdots, CT_{t^*}^*) \leftarrow \mathsf{Enc}((M_0^*, pk_1^*, s^*), \cdots, (M_0^*, pk_{j-1}^*, s^*), (M_b^*, pk_j^*, s^*), (M_0^*, pk_{j+1}^*, s^*), \cdots, (M_0^*, pk_t^*, s^*)) \\
\text{for random messages } M_0^*, M_1^* \text{ and number } b \in \{0,1\}; \\
b' \leftarrow \mathcal{A}^{\mathcal{O}^{\mathsf{par\text{-}key}}(\cdot), \mathcal{O}^{\mathsf{priv\text{-}key}}(\cdot), \mathcal{O}^{\mathsf{pub\text{-}key}}(\cdot), \mathcal{O}^{\mathsf{p\text{-}key}}(\cdot), \mathcal{O}^{\mathsf{token}}(\cdot), \mathcal{O}^{\mathsf{p\text{-}token}}(\cdot)}(\{pk_i, pk_{P_i}\}_{i=1}^N).
\end{gathered}$$

In Game 5, the adversary cannot make private key queries on $pk_1^*, \cdots, pk_{t^*}^*$. We define the advantage of the adversary in winning this game as

$$\mathsf{Adv}^{\mathsf{Number,Type\text{-}V}}_{\mathsf{CLE\text{-}MET\text{-}PA}}(\lambda) = \Pr[b' = b] - 1/2.$$

4. The Proposed CLE-MET-PA Scheme

In certificateless encryption supporting multi-ciphertext equality test with proxy-assisted authorization (CLE-MET-PA), each ciphertext CT can designate a number s. With this designation, an authorized cloud server is enabled to perform an equality test on s ciphertexts, but only if all the designated numbers of these s ciphertexts are equal to s.

4.1. Our Construction

$\mathsf{Setup}(1^\lambda)$: Taking as input a security parameter λ, the setup algorithm generates a bilinear groups ensemble $\mathcal{G} = (p, \mathbb{G}_1, \mathbb{G}_2, \mathbb{G}_T, e)$, generators $g_1 \in \mathbb{G}_1$, $g_2 \in \mathbb{G}_2$ and five cryptographic hash functions $H_1 : \{0,1\}^* \to \mathbb{G}_2$, $H_2 : \{0,1\}^* \to \mathbb{G}_2$, $H_3 : \{0,1\}^* \to \mathbb{Z}_p$, $H_4 : \{0,1\}^* \to \{0,1\}^{2l}$, $H_5 : \{0,1\}^* \to \{0,1\}^\lambda$, where l is the bit length of a group element in $\mathbb{Z}_p$. Pick a random $\alpha \in \mathbb{Z}_p^*$, $\bar{g} = g_1^\alpha$. It sets the system parameter as

$$pp = \{\mathcal{G}, g_1, g_2, \bar{g}, H_1, H_2, H_3, H_4, H_5\},$$

and the master secret key

$$msk = \alpha.$$

Partial private key extract (pp, msk, ID): Taking as input the system parameter pp, the master key msk, and the identifier ID. The key generation algorithm computes and outputs the partial private key pair

$$D = (D_1, D_2) = (H_1(ID)^{\alpha}, H_2(ID)^{\alpha}).$$

Set-Secret-Value (pp, ID): Taking as input the system parameter pp and an identifier ID. The algorithm picks a value $x \in \mathbb{Z}_q^*$ at random. A proxy secret value corresponding to ID_P is denoted as x_P.

Set-Private-Key (pp, D, x): Taking as input the system parameter pp, a partial private key pair and an secret value x. The algorithm computes the private key pair sk, where

$$sk = (sk_1, sk_2) = (D_1^x, D_2^x) = (H_1(ID)^{\alpha x}, H_2(ID)^{\alpha x}).$$

Set-Public-Key (pp, x): Taking as input the system parameter pp and a secret value x, the algorithm outputs the public key pair

$$pk = (X = \bar{g}^x, Y = g_2^x, Z = g_1^x) = (g_1^{\alpha x}, g_2^x, g_1^x).$$

Set-Proxy-Key (pp, ID_P): The proxy can be any user. A proxy generates the secret value and public key by running Set-Secret-Value (pp, ID_P) and Set-Public-Key (pp, x_P). Output the secret key x_P, and the public key pair

$$pk_P = (X_P = \bar{g}^{x_P}, Y_P = g_2^{x_P}, Z_P = g_1^{x_P}) = (g_1^{\alpha x_P}, g_2^{x_P}, g_1^{x_P}).$$

Enc(pp, pk, M, s): Taking as input the system parameter pp, a user public key pk, check whether $e(X, g_2) = e(\bar{g}, Y)$ and $e(Z, g_2) = e(g_1, Y)$ holds; if not, output $\perp$ and abort. Then, taking as input a message $M \in \mathbb{Z}_p$, and a number $s \in \mathbb{Z}_p$, the encryption algorithm iteratively computes

$$\begin{aligned} &f_0 = H_3(M||s), \quad f_1 = H_3(M||s||f_0), \quad \cdots, \\ &f_{s-1} = H_3(M||s||f_0||\cdots||f_{s-2}) \end{aligned}$$

as illustrated in Figure 3 with $i = s$. Let

$$f(x) = f_0 + f_1 x + f_2 x^2 + \cdots + f_{s-1} x^{s-1}.$$

It randomly chooses $A, r_1, r_2 \in \mathbb{Z}_p$, and outputs the ciphertext $CT = (s, C_1, C_2, C_3, C_4, C_5, C_6)$ as

$$\begin{aligned} &C_1 = g_1^{r_1}, \quad C_2 = H_4(e(X, H_1(ID))^{r_1}) \oplus (M||r_1), \\ &C_3 = g_1^{r_2}, \quad C_4 = Z^{r_2}, \\ &C_5 = H_4(e(X, H_2(ID))^{r_2}) \oplus (A||f(A)), \\ &C_6 = H_5(s||C_1||C_2||C_3||C_4||C_5||e(X, H_2(ID))^{r_2}||f_0||f_1||\cdots||f_{s-1}). \end{aligned}$$

Note that the equality of this ciphertext CT can only be performed as an equality test with other $s-1$ ciphertexts in which all the designated numbers are s.

Dec(CT, sk): Taking as input a ciphertext $CT = (s, C_1, C_2, C_3, C_4, C_5, C_6)$ and a secret key $sk = (H_1(ID)^{\alpha x}, H_2(ID)^{\alpha x})$, the decrypt algorithm computes

$$M'||r_1' = C_2 \oplus H_4(e(C_1, sk_1))$$

It then computes

$$f'_0 = H_3(M'||s), \quad f'_1 = H_3(M'||s||f'_0), \quad \cdots,$$
$$f'_{s-1} = H_3(M'||s||f'_0||\cdots||f'_{s-2})$$

and checks whether the following equations hold or not

$$C_1 = g_1^{r'_1},$$
$$f'(A') = f'_0 + f'_1 A' + \cdots + f'_{s-1} A'^{s-1},$$
$$C_6 = H_5(s||C_1||C_2||C_3||C_4||C_5||e(C_3, sk_2)||f'_0||f'_1||\cdots||f'_{s-1}),$$

where $A'||f'(A') = C_5 \oplus H_4(e(C_3, sk_2))$. If all the equations hold, it returns

$$M = M'.$$

Otherwise, it returns $\perp$.

$\mathsf{Aut}(sk)$: Taking as input a secret key $sk = (sk_1, sk_2) = (H_1(ID)^{\alpha x}, H_2(ID)^{\alpha x})$, the authorization algorithm returns the token as

$$tk = sk_2 = H_2(ID)^{\alpha x}.$$

$\mathsf{Proxy\text{-}Aut}$ (pp, sk, sk_P): Following the algorithm depicted in Table 1, the user receives and publishes $H_2(ID)^{x_P}$ as the proxy information PI,

$$PI = H_2(ID)^{x_P},$$

and the algorithm returns the proxy token as

$$\hat{tk} = H_2(ID)^{\alpha x + x \cdot x_P}.$$

Table 1. Key exchange protocol between the user and proxy.

Key Exchange Protocol
The user checks whether $e(X_P, g_2) = e(\bar{g}, Y_P)$ and $e(Z_P, g_2) = e(g_1, Y_P)$ holds, if not, output $\perp$ and abort.
User $\xleftarrow{H_2(ID)^{x_P}}$ Proxy
The user checks whether $e(Z_P, H_2(ID)) = e(g_1, H_2(ID)^{x_P})$ holds, if not, abort and output $\perp$. Otherwise, the user outputs proxy information $PI = H_2(ID)^{x_P}$, computes $\hat{tk} = sk_2 \cdot (PI)^x = H_2(ID)^{\alpha x + x \cdot x_P}$.
User $\xrightarrow{\hat{tk}}$ Proxy
The proxy receives the proxy token $\hat{tk}$ without revealing x_P and knowing part of sk.

$\mathsf{Test}(CT_1, \cdots, CT_t, \hat{tk}_1, \cdots, \hat{tk}_j, tk_1, \cdots, tk_{t-j})$: Taking as input t ciphertexts $CT_1, \cdots, CT_t$ where $CT_i = (s_i, C_{i,1}, C_{i,2}, C_{i,3}, C_{i,4}, C_{i,5}, C_{i,6})$ and t corresponding tokens including the proxy token and user token: $\hat{tk}_1, \cdots, \hat{tk}_j, tk_1, \cdots, tk_{t-j}$, the test algorithm aborts if the equation $s_1 = \cdots = s_t = t$ does not hold. Otherwise, for each $i \in \{1, \cdots, j\}$:

- With the token authorized by the user, it computes

$$A_i||f_i(A_i) = C_{i,5} \oplus H_4(e(C_{i,3}, tk_i)),$$

- With the proxy token authorized by the proxy, it computes

$$A_i||f_i(A_i) = C_{i,5} \oplus H_4\Big(e(C_{i,3}, \hat{tk}_i)/e(C_{i,4}, PI_i)\Big),$$

where

$$f_i(A_i) = f_{i,0} + f_{i,1}A_i + f_{i,2}A_i^2 + \cdots + f_{i,t-1}A_i^{t-1}.$$

With A_i and $f_i(A_i)$ for $i \in \{1, \cdots, t\}$, we have an equation set as

$$\begin{cases} f_1(A_1) = f_{1,0} + f_{1,1}A_1 + \cdots + f_{1,t-1}A_1^{t-1} \\ f_2(A_2) = f_{2,0} + f_{2,1}A_2 + \cdots + f_{2,t-1}A_2^{t-1} \\ \vdots \\ f_t(A_t) = f_{t,0} + f_{t,1}A_t + \cdots + f_{t,t-1}A_t^{t-1} \end{cases}.$$

Implicitly setting $f_{i,k} = f_{j,k}$ for $i, j \in \{1, 2, \cdots, t\}$ and $k \in \{0, 1, \cdots, t-1\}$, it solves the equation set and obtains a unique solution $f_{i,0}, f_{i,1}, \cdots, f_{i,t-1}$. It checks whether the following equations hold or not for each $i \in \{1, 2, \cdots, j\}$.

$$C_{i,6} = H_5(t||C_{i,1}|| \cdots ||C_{i,5}||e(C_{i,3}, \hat{tk}_i)/e(C_{i,4}, PI_i)||f_{i,0}|| \cdots ||f_{i,t-1}),$$

and for each $i \in \{1, 2, \cdots, t-j\}$.

$$C_{i,6} = H_5(t||C_{i,1}|| \cdots ||C_{i,5}||e(C_{i,3}, tk_i)||f_{i,0}|| \cdots ||f_{i,t-1}).$$

- If all the equations hold, it returns 1, implying that $M_1 = M_2 = \cdots = M_t$.
- Otherwise, it returns 0, implying that the equation $M_1 = M_2 = \cdots = M_t$ does not hold.

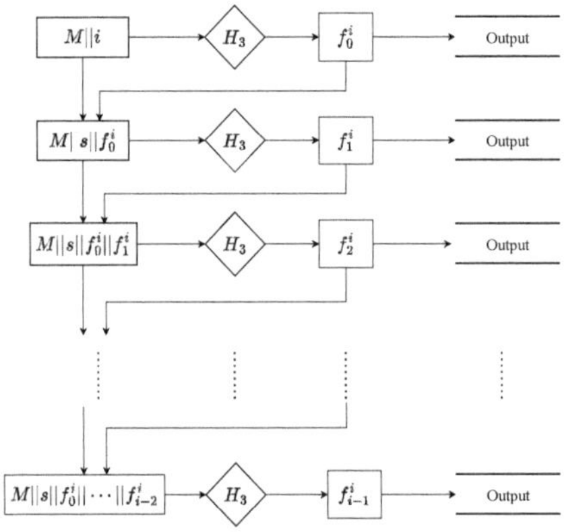

Figure 3. Iteration computation of $\{f_j^n\}_{0 \leq j \leq n-1}$.

4.2. Correctness of CLE-MET-PA

We analyze the correctness of the proposed CLE-MET-PA construction as below.

(1) In the decryption algorithm, denoted by Dec, the decryption process computes the following:

$$\begin{aligned} & C_2 \oplus H_4(sk_1, C_1) \\ =& H_4(e(X, H_1(ID))^{r_1}) \oplus (M||r_1) \oplus H_4(e(sk_1, C_1)) \\ =& H_4(e(g_1^{\alpha x}, H_1(ID))^{r_1}) \oplus (M||r_1) \oplus H_4(e(H_1(ID)^{\alpha x}, g_1^{r_1})) \\ =& M||r_1 \end{aligned}$$

The output M and r_1 satisfy the three listed equations. Subsequently, the decryption algorithm will recover the message M, implying that

$$\Pr\left[\mathsf{Dec}(sk, CT) = M\right] - 1.$$

(2) In the test algorithm, denoted by Test, after implicitly setting $f_{i,k} = f_{j,k}$ for $i, j \in 1, 2, \cdots, t$ and $k \in 0, 1, \cdots, t-1$, we obtain an equation set comprising t equations for t unknown variables. We can then represent the coefficients of this equation set as the following Vandermonde matrix:

$$V = \begin{bmatrix} 1 & A_1 & A_1^2 & \cdots & A_1^{t-1} \\ 1 & A_2 & A_2^2 & \cdots & A_2^{t-1} \\ \vdots & \vdots & \vdots & \vdots & \vdots \\ 1 & A_t & A_t^2 & \cdots & A_t^{t-1} \end{bmatrix}.$$

Thanks to the properties of the Vandermonde matrix, the equation set possesses a unique solution when the determinant of this matrix, denoted by $\det(V)$, satisfies $\det(V) \neq 0$. This determinant is defined as:

$$\det(V) = \prod_{1 \leq i < j \leq t} (A_i - A_j).$$

Since the values of A_i for $i \in 1, \cdots, t$ are randomly chosen from the set $\mathbb{Z}_p$, we can conclude that

$$\det(V) \neq 0$$

holds with overwhelming probability, specifically $\frac{p(p-1)\cdots(p-t+1)}{p^t}$.

Consequently, we obtain a unique solution for the variables $f_{1,0}, f_{1,1}, \cdots, f_{1,t-1}$. Given that $M_1 = \cdots = M_t$, it follows that $f_{i,k} = f_{j,k}$ for $i, j \in 1, 2, \cdots, t$ and $k \in 0, 1, \cdots, t-1$. Thus, the unique solution will satisfy the following equations for $1 \leq i \leq j \leq t$.

$$C_{i,6} = H_5(s||C_{i,1}||\cdots||C_{i,5}||e(C_{i,3}, \hat{tk}_i)/e(C_{i,4}, PI_i)||f_{1,0}||\cdots||f_{1,j})$$
$$C_{i,6} = H_5(s||C_{i,1}||\cdots||C_{i,5}||e(C_{i,3}, tk_i)||f_{1,0}||\cdots||f_{1,t-j+1})$$

Then, we have

$$\mathsf{Test}(CT_1, \cdots, CT, \hat{tk}_1, \cdots, \hat{tk}_j, tk_1, \cdots, tk_{t-j}) = 1$$

will hold with overwhelming probability.

(3) Similarly to the previous step (2), we can obtain a unique solution from the equation set. However, since the equation $M_1 = \cdots = M_t$ does not hold, without a loss of generality, assume that $M_1 \neq M_2 = M_3 = \cdots = M_t$. In this scenario, we then have $f_{1,k} \neq f_{i,k} = f_{j,k}$ for $i, j \in 2, \cdots, t, k \in 0, \cdots, t-1$. Nevertheless, it is evident that the solution cannot simultaneously satisfy the two following equations.

$$C_{1,6} = H_5(t||C_{1,1}||\cdots||C_{1,4}||e(C_{1,3}, \hat{tk}_1)/e(C_{1,4}, PI_1)||f'_{1,0}||\cdots||f'_{1,j})$$
$$C_{2,6} = H_5(t||C_{2,1}||\cdots||C_{2,4}||e(C_{2,3}, \hat{tk}_2)/e(C_{1,4}, PI_2)||f'_{1,0}||\cdots||f'_{1,j})$$

Therefore, the test algorithm will output 0. We have

$$\mathsf{Test}(CT_1, \cdots, CT, \hat{tk}_1, \cdots, \hat{tk}_j, tk_1, \cdots, tk_{t-j}) = 0$$

will hold with overwhelming probability.

5. Security Proof

Our CLE-MET-PA construction is secure due to the hardness of the BDH assumption.

Theorem 1. *For any PPT Type-I adversary, our CLE-MET-PA scheme is IND-CPA-secure based on the BDH assumption in the random oracle model.*

Proof of Theorem 1. Assume there exists an adversary $\mathcal{A}_1$ who can break the IND-CPA security of our scheme with a non-negligible advantage ϵ, we can construct a simulator $\mathcal{B}$ to break the BDH assumption. Given an instance as $(\mathcal{G}, g_1, g_1^a, g_1^c, g_2, g_2^a, g_2^b)$, $\mathcal{B}$ is to compute $e(g_1, g_2)^{abc}$ by running $\mathcal{A}_1$ as a subroutine. $\mathcal{B}$ and $\mathcal{A}_1$ play the following game.

1. *Setup:* $\mathcal{B}$ randomly picks a cryptographic hash function $H_3 : \{0,1\}^* \rightarrow \{0,1\}^\lambda$ and sets the public parameter $pp = \{\mathcal{G}, g_1, g_2, \bar{g}, H_1, H_2, H_3, H_4, H_5\}$, where $\bar{g} = g_1^a$ and H_1, H_2, H_4, H_5 are random oracles. pp is sent to $\mathcal{A}_1$. Lists $L_{H_1}, L_{H_2}, L_{H_4}, L_{H_5}, andL_s$ are initially empty. Assume that $\mathcal{A}_1$ can make $q_{H_1}, q_{H_2}, q_{H_4}, q_{H_5}$ hash queries to $H_1, H_2, H_4, andH_5$, respectively.
2. *Phase 1:* Assume there are n users with identities $ID_1, \cdots, ID_n$ in the system. $\mathcal{B}$ randomly chooses $i^* \in [1, n]$ and performs the following steps.
   - *H_1-query (ID_i):* For i-th query ID_i, $\mathcal{B}$ searches L_{H_1}. If there exists the related item of ID_i as $(u_i, ID_i, H_1(ID_i))$, $\mathcal{B}$ returns $H_1(ID_i)$ to $\mathcal{A}_1$. Otherwise, $\mathcal{B}$ randomly chooses u_i and sets
   $$H_1(ID_i) = \begin{cases} g_2^{u_i}, & if\ i \neq i^*, \\ g_2^{bu_i}, & if\ i = i^*. \end{cases}$$
   $\mathcal{B}$ stores $(u_i, ID_i, H_1(ID_i))$ into L_{H_1} and returns $H_1(ID_i)$ to $\mathcal{A}_1$.
   - *H_2-query (ID_i):* For the i-th query ID_i, $\mathcal{B}$ searches L_{H_2}. If there exists the related item of ID_i as $(v_i, ID_i, H_2(ID_i))$, $\mathcal{B}$ returns $H_2(ID_i)$ to $\mathcal{A}_1$. Otherwise, $\mathcal{B}$ randomly chooses v_i and sets
   $$H_2(ID_i) = \begin{cases} g_2^{v_i}, & if\ i \neq i^*, \\ g_2^{bv_i}, & if\ i = i^*. \end{cases}$$
   $\mathcal{B}$ stores $(v_i, ID_i, H_2(ID_i))$ into L_{H_2} and returns $H_2(ID_i)$ to $\mathcal{A}_1$.
   - *H_4-query (Q_i):* For i-th query Q_i, $\mathcal{B}$ randomly picks $\eta_i \in \{0,1\}^{2l}$, sets $H_4(Q_i) = \eta_i$, stores a new item $(Q_i, H_4(Q_i) = \eta_i)$ into L_{H_4}, and then returns $H_4(Q_i)$ to $\mathcal{A}_1$.
   - *H_5-query (W_i):* For the i-th query W_i, $\mathcal{B}$ randomly picks $\sigma_i \in \{0,1\}^\lambda$, sets $H_5(W_i) = \sigma_i$, stores a new item $(W_i, H_5(W_i) = \sigma_i)$ into L_{H_5}, and then returns $H_5(W_i)$ to $\mathcal{A}_1$.
   - *Partial private key query (ID_i):* For i-th queried identity ID_i, if $ID_i = ID_{i^*}$, $\mathcal{B}$ aborts. Otherwise, if ID_i has not been queried to H_1, $\mathcal{B}$ randomly chooses u_i, sets
   $$H_1(ID_i) = g_2^{u_i},$$
   and stores $(u_i, ID_i, H_1(ID_i))$ into L_{H_1}. If ID_i has not been queried to H_2, $\mathcal{B}$ randomly chooses v_i, sets
   $$H_2(ID_i) = g_2^{v_i},$$
   and stores $(v_i, ID_i, H_2(ID_i))$ into L_{H_2}. $\mathcal{B}$ searches L_{H_1} and L_{H_2} to find the related items of ID_i as $(u_i, ID_i, H_1(ID_i))$ and $(v_i, ID_i, H_2(ID_i))$. $\mathcal{B}$ then computes
   $$D_i = (D_{i,1}, D_{i,2}) = (H_1^\alpha(ID), H_2^\alpha(ID)) = (g_2^{au_i}, g_2^{av_i}),$$
   which can be computed with a known g_2^a, u_i, v_i. $\mathcal{B}$ returns D_i to $\mathcal{A}_1$.
   - *Secret key query (ID_i):* For the i-th queried identity ID_i, $\mathcal{B}$ randomly picks $x_i \in \mathbb{Z}_p$, stores $(ID_i, x_i, -, -)$ into L_s, and returns x_i to $\mathcal{A}_1$.

- *Private key query (ID_i):* For i-th queried identity ID_i, if $ID_i = ID_{i^*}$, $\mathcal{B}$ aborts. Otherwise, if ID_i has not been queried to H_1, $\mathcal{B}$ randomly chooses u_i, sets
$$H_1(ID_i) = g_2^{u_i},$$
and stores $(u_i, ID_i, H_1(ID_i))$ into L_{H_1}. If ID_i has not been queried to H_2, $\mathcal{B}$ randomly chooses v_i, sets
$$H_2(ID_i) = g_2^{v_i},$$
and stores $(v_i, ID_i, H_2(ID_i))$ into L_{H_2}. $\mathcal{B}$ searches L_{H_1} and L_{H_2} to find the related items of ID_i as $(u_i, ID_i, H_1(ID_i))$ and $(v_i, ID_i, H_2(ID_i))$. $\mathcal{B}$ searches L_s and finds the related item of ID_i as $(ID_i, x_i, -, -)$. If the related item of ID_i does exist, $\mathcal{B}$ randomly picks $x_i \in \mathbb{Z}_p$ and computes
$$sk_i = (sk_{i,1}, sk_{i,2}) = (D_1^{x_i}, D_2^{x_i}) = (g_2^{ax_iu_i}, g_2^{ax_iv_i}),$$
which can be computed with known g_2^a, x_i, u_i, v_i. It then stores $(ID_i, x_i, sk_i, -)$ into L_s and returns sk_i to $\mathcal{A}_1$.
- *Public key query (ID_i):* For i-th queried identity ID_i, $\mathcal{B}$ searches L_s, and finds the related item of ID_i as $(ID_i, x_i, -, -)$. If the related item does not exist, $\mathcal{B}$ randomly picks $x_i \in \mathbb{Z}_p$ and computes
$$pk_i = (X_i, Y_i, Z_i) = (g_1^{ax_i}, g_2^{x_i}, g_1^{x_i}),$$
which can be computed with known g_1, g_1^a, g_2, x_i. It then stores $(ID_i, x_i, -, pk_i)$ into L_s and returns pk_i to $\mathcal{A}_1$.
- *Proxy key query (ID_{P_i}):* For a proxy with the related item in L_s as (ID_{P_i}, x_{P_i}), $\mathcal{B}$ performs as *Public key query* step and obtains
$$pk_{P_i} = (X_{P_i}, Y_{P_i}, Z_{P_i}) = \left(g_1^{ax_{P_i}}, g_2^{x_{P_i}}, g_1^{x_{P_i}}\right).$$
which can be computed with known g_1, g_1^a, g_2, x_{P_i}. $\mathcal{B}$ then returns pk_{P_i} and sk_{P_i} to $\mathcal{A}_1$.
- *Public key replace query (ID_i, pk'):* $\mathcal{B}$ changes the public key pk_i corresponding to ID_i to $pk' = (X', Y', Z')$ while receiving (ID_i, pk') if $e(X_i', g_2) = e(\bar{g}_1, Y_i')$ and $e(Z_i', g_2) = e(g_1, Y_i')$ holds.
- *Token query (ID_i):* For a queried ID_i, if $ID_i = ID_{i^*}$, $\mathcal{B}$ aborts. Otherwise, $\mathcal{B}$ searches L_s to find the related item of ID_i as (ID_i, x_i, sk_i), where $sk_i = (sk_1, sk_2)$. If the related item does not exist, $\mathcal{B}$ performs as follows. If ID_i has not been queried to H_1, $\mathcal{B}$ randomly chooses u_i, sets
$$H_1(ID_i) = g_2^{u_i},$$
and stores $(u_i, ID_i, H_1(ID_i))$ into L_{H_1}. If ID_i has not been queried to H_2, $\mathcal{B}$ randomly chooses v_i, sets
$$H_2(ID_i) = g_2^{v_i},$$
and stores $(v_i, ID_i, H_2(ID_i))$ into L_{H_2}. $\mathcal{B}$ searches L_{H_1} and L_{H_2} to find the related items of ID_i as $(u_i, ID_i, H_1(ID_i))$ and $(v_i, ID_i, H_2(ID_i))$. $\mathcal{B}$ searches L_s and finds the related item of ID_i as $(ID_i, x_i, -, -)$. If the related item of ID_i does not exist, $\mathcal{B}$ randomly picks $x_i \in \mathbb{Z}_p$ and computes
$$sk_i = (sk_{i,1}, sk_{i,2}) = (D_1^{x_i}, D_2^{x_i}) = (g_2^{ax_iu_i}, g_2^{ax_iv_i}),$$
which can be computed with known g_2^a, x_i, u_i, v_i. It then stores (ID_i, x_i, sk_i) into L_s. $\mathcal{B}$ returns sk_2 to $\mathcal{A}_1$.

- *Proxy token query* (ID_i, ID_{P_i}): For a queried ID_i, if $ID_i = ID_{i^*}$, $\mathcal{B}$ aborts. Otherwise, $\mathcal{B}$ performs as Aut step except that $\mathcal{B}$ computes $PI_i = H_2(ID_i)^{x_{P_i}} = g_2^{av_i x_i x_{P_i}}$, and the proxy token

$$\hat{tk}_i = H_2(ID)^{\alpha x + x \cdot x_P} = g_2^{av_i x_i + x_i x_{P_i}}$$

with known $g_2, g_2^a, v_i, x_i, x_{P_i}$. $\mathcal{B}$ returns $\hat{tk}_i$ to $\mathcal{A}_1$.

3. *Challenge:* $\mathcal{A}_1$ sends $(s^*, ID^*, M_0^*, M_1^*)$ to $\mathcal{B}$, where s^* represents the designated challenge number, ID^* stands for the challenge identity, and two plaintexts M_0^* and M_1^* are selected from $\{0,1\}^\lambda$ with equal lengths. If $ID^* \neq ID_{i^*}$, $\mathcal{B}$ aborts. Otherwise, it randomly picks $w_1, w_2 \in \mathbb{Z}_p, R_1, R_2 \in \{0,1\}^{2l}, R_3 \in \{0,1\}^\lambda$ and implicitly sets $r_1 = w_1 c, r_2 = w_2 c$. It then computes the challenge ciphertext as

$$\begin{aligned} C_1 &= g_1^{r_1} = g_1^{cw_1}, \\ C_2 &= R_1, \\ C_3 &= g_1^{r_2} = g_1^{cw_2}, \\ C_4 &= g_1^{x_{i^*} r_2} = g_1^{cx_{i^*} w_2}, \\ C_5 &= R_2, \\ C_6 &= R_3. \end{aligned}$$

4. *Phase 2:* $\mathcal{B}$ interacts with $\mathcal{A}_1$ as *Phase 1* with the limitation that ID_{i^*} cannot be queried in *partial private key query*, *secret key query*, *private key query*, *token query*, and *proxy token query*.
5. Guess: $\mathcal{A}_1$ outputs its guess bit $\rho' \in \{0,1\}$.
6. *Solve:* $\mathcal{B}$ randomly chooses an item $(Q_i, H_4(Q_i) = \eta_i)$ from L_{H_4} and sets

$$e(g_1, g_2)^{abc} = Q_i^{\frac{1}{x_{i^*} u_{i^*} w_1}}$$

as the solution to the BDH instance.

7. *Analysis:* To successfully perform the reduction, the simulation should be indistinguishable from the real attack from the point of view of the adversary. As we can see, if the adversary chooses ID_{i^*} as the challenge identity, the simulation will not abort, which means that the simulation is indistinguishable from the real attack. The corresponding probability is $1/n$. Upon the case that the simulation is indistinguishable to the adversary, we have the following analysis. Since the adversary is assumed to break the security with the advantage ϵ, we have that it issues the hash query $e(X_{i^*}, H_1(ID_{i^*}))^{r_1} = e(g_1^{ax_{i^*}}, g_2^{bu_{i^*}})^{cw_1} = e(g_1, g_2)^{abc \cdot x_{i^*} u_{i^*} w_1}$ with probability ϵ. Thus, $\mathcal{B}$ can finally obtain the true solution to the given BDH instance as $e(g_1, g_2)^{abc} = Q_i^{\frac{1}{x_{i^*} u_{i^*} w_1}}$ with a probability of $\frac{\epsilon}{q_{H_4}}$. In conclusion, $\mathcal{B}$ can successfully break the BDH assumption with the probability of

$$\Pr[\mathcal{B} \textit{ chooses the correct hash query} | \textit{the simulation is indistinguishable}] = \frac{\epsilon}{n \cdot q_{H_4}}.$$

□

Theorem 2. *For any PPT Type-II adversary, our CLE-MET-PA scheme is OW-CPA secure based on the BDH assumption in the random oracle model.*

Proof of Theorem 2. Assume there exists an adversary $\mathcal{A}_2$ who can break the OW-CPA security of our scheme with non-negligible advantage ϵ; then, we can construct a simulator

$\mathcal{B}$ to break the BDH assumption. Given an instance as $(\mathcal{G}, g_1, g_1^a, g_1^c, g_2, g_2^a, g_2^b)$, $\mathcal{B}$ is to compute $e(g_1, g_2)^{abc}$ by running $\mathcal{A}_2$ as a subroutine. $\mathcal{B}$ and $\mathcal{A}_2$ play the following game.

1. *Setup:* $\mathcal{B}$ randomly picks a cryptographic hash function $H_3 : \{0,1\}^* \rightarrow \{0,1\}^\lambda$ and sets the public parameter $pp = \{\mathcal{G}, g_1, g_2, \bar{g}, H_1, H_2, H_3, H_4, H_5\}$, where $g = g_1^a$ and H_1, H_2, H_4, H_5 are random oracles. pp is sent to $\mathcal{A}_2$. Lists $L_{H_1}, L_{H_2}, L_{H_4}, L_{H_5}, L_s$ are initially empty. Assume that $\mathcal{A}_2$ can make $q_{H_1}, q_{H_2}, q_{H_4}, q_{H_5}$ hash queries to H_1, H_2, H_4, H_5, respectively.
2. *Phase 1:* Assume there are n users with identities $ID_1, \cdots, ID_n$ in the system. $\mathcal{B}$ randomly chooses $i^* \in [1, n]$ and performs the following steps.
   - *H_1-query (ID_i):* For i-th query ID_i, $\mathcal{B}$ searches L_{H_1}. If there exists the related item of ID_i as $(u_i, ID_i, H_1(ID_i))$, $\mathcal{B}$ returns $H_1(ID_i)$ to $\mathcal{A}_2$. Otherwise, $\mathcal{B}$ randomly chooses u_i and sets
   $$H_1(ID_i) = \begin{cases} g_2^{u_i}, & if\ i \neq i^*, \\ g_2^{bu_i}, & if\ i = i^*. \end{cases}$$
   $\mathcal{B}$ stores $(u_i, ID_i, H_1(ID_i))$ into L_{H_1} and returns $H_1(ID_i)$ to $\mathcal{A}_2$.
   - *H_2-query (ID_i):* For i-th query ID_i, $\mathcal{B}$ searches L_{H_2}. If there exists the related item of ID_i as $(v_i, ID_i, H_2(ID_i))$, $\mathcal{B}$ returns $H_2(ID_i)$ to $\mathcal{A}_2$. Otherwise, $\mathcal{B}$ randomly chooses v_i and sets
   $$H_2(ID_i) = g_2^{v_i}$$
   $\mathcal{B}$ stores $(v_i, ID_i, H_2(ID_i))$ into L_{H_2} and returns $H_2(ID_i)$ to $\mathcal{A}_2$.
   - *H_4-query (Q_i):* For the i-th query Q_i, $\mathcal{B}$ picks $\eta_i \in \{0,1\}^{2l}$ randomly, sets $H_4(Q_i) = \eta_i$, stores a new item $(Q_i, H_4(Q_i) = \eta_i)$ into L_{H_4}, and then returns $H_4(Q_i)$ to $\mathcal{A}_2$.
   - *H_5-query (W_i):* For the i-th query W_i, $\mathcal{B}$ randomly picks $\sigma_i \in \{0,1\}^\lambda$, sets $H_5(W_i) = \sigma_i$, stores a new item $(W_i, H_5(W_i) = \sigma_i)$ into L_{H_5}, and then returns $H_5(W_i)$ to $\mathcal{A}_2$.
   - *Partial private key query (ID_i):* For the i-th queried identity ID_i, if $ID_i = ID_{i^*}$, $\mathcal{B}$ aborts. Otherwise, if ID_i has not been queried to H_1, $\mathcal{B}$ randomly chooses u_i, sets
   $$H_1(ID_i) = g_2^{u_i},$$
   and stores $(u_i, ID_i, H_1(ID_i))$ into L_{H_1}. If ID_i has not been queried to H_2, $\mathcal{B}$ randomly chooses v_i, sets
   $$H_2(ID_i) = g_2^{v_i},$$
   and stores $(v_i, ID_i, H_2(ID_i))$ into L_{H_2}. $\mathcal{B}$ searches L_{H_1} and L_{H_2} to find the related items of ID_i as $(u_i, ID_i, H_1(ID_i))$ and $(v_i, ID_i, H_2(ID_i))$. $\mathcal{B}$ then computes
   $$D_i = (D_{i,1}, D_{i,2}) = (H_1^\alpha(ID), H_2^\alpha(ID)) = (g_2^{au_i}, g_2^{av_i}),$$
   which can be computed with known g_2^a, u_i, v_i. $\mathcal{B}$ returns D_i to $\mathcal{A}_2$.
   - *Secret key query (ID_i):* For the i-th queried identity ID_i, $\mathcal{B}$ randomly picks $x_i \in \mathbb{Z}_p$, stores $(ID_i, x_i, -, -)$ into L_s, and returns x_i to $\mathcal{A}_2$.
   - *Private key query (ID_i):* For the i-th queried identity ID_i, if $ID_i = ID_{i^*}$, $\mathcal{B}$ aborts. Otherwise, if ID_i has not been queried to H_1, $\mathcal{B}$ randomly chooses u_i, sets
   $$H_1(ID_i) = g_2^{u_i},$$
   and stores $(u_i, ID_i, H_1(ID_i))$ into L_{H_1}. If ID_i has not been queried to H_2, $\mathcal{B}$ randomly chooses v_i, sets
   $$H_2(ID_i) = g_2^{v_i},$$

and stores $(v_i, ID_i, H_2(ID_i))$ into L_{H_2}. $\mathcal{B}$ searches L_{H_1} and L_{H_2} to find the related items of ID_i as $(u_i, ID_i, H_1(ID_i))$ and $(v_i, ID_i, H_2(ID_i))$. $\mathcal{B}$ searches L_s and finds the related item of ID_i as $(ID_i, x_i, -, -)$. If the related item of ID_i does not exist, $\mathcal{B}$ randomly picks $x_i \in \mathbb{Z}_p$ and computes

$$sk_i = (sk_{i,1}, sk_{i,2}) = \left(D_1^{x_i}, D_2^{x_i}\right) = \left(g_2^{ax_iu_i}, g_2^{ax_iv_i}\right),$$

which can be computed with known g_2^a, x_i, u_i, v_i. It then stores $(ID_i, x_i, sk_i, -)$ into L_s and returns sk_i to $\mathcal{A}_2$.

- *Public key query (ID_i):* For the i-th queried identity ID_i, $\mathcal{B}$ searches L_s and finds the related item of ID_i as $(ID_i, x_i, -, -)$. If the related item does not exist, $\mathcal{B}$ randomly picks $x_i \in \mathbb{Z}_p$ and computes

$$pk_i = (X_i, Y_i, Z_i) = \left(g_1^{ax_i}, g_2^{x_i}, g_1^{x_i}\right),$$

which can be computed with a known g_1, g_1^a, g_2, x_i. It then stores $(ID_i, x_i, -, pk_i)$ into L_s and returns pk_i to $\mathcal{A}_2$.

- *Proxy key query (ID_{P_i}):* For a proxy with the related item in L_s as (ID_{P_i}, x_{P_i}), $\mathcal{B}$ performs as the *public key query* step and obtains

$$pk_{P_i} = (X_{P_i}, Y_{P_i}, Z_{P_i}) = \left(g_1^{ax_{P_i}}, g_2^{x_{P_i}}, g_1^{x_{P_i}}\right).$$

which can be computed with known g_1, g_1^a, g_2, x_{P_i}. $\mathcal{B}$ then returns pk_{P_i} and sk_{P_i} to $\mathcal{A}_2$.

- *Public key replace query (ID_i, pk'):* $\mathcal{B}$ changes the public key pk_i corresponding to ID_i to $pk' = (X', Y', Z')$ while receiving (ID_i, pk') if $e(X_i', g_2) = e(\bar{g}_1, Y_i')$ and $e(Z_i', g_2) = e(g_1, Y_i')$ holds.

- *Token query (ID_i):* For a queried ID_i, $\mathcal{B}$ searches L_s to find the related item of ID_i as (ID_i, x_i, sk_i), where $sk_i = (sk_1, sk_2)$. If the related item does not exist, $\mathcal{B}$ performs as follows. If ID_i has not been queried to H_1, $\mathcal{B}$ randomly chooses u_i, sets

$$H_1(ID_i) = g_2^{u_i},$$

and stores $(u_i, ID_i, H_1(ID_i))$ into L_{H_1}. If ID_i has not been queried to H_2, $\mathcal{B}$ randomly chooses v_i, sets

$$H_2(ID_i) = g_2^{v_i},$$

and stores $(v_i, ID_i, H_2(ID_i))$ into L_{H_2}. $\mathcal{B}$ searches L_{H_1} and L_{H_2} to find the related items of ID_i as $(u_i, ID_i, H_1(ID_i))$ and $(v_i, ID_i, H_2(ID_i))$. $\mathcal{B}$ searches L_s and finds the related item of ID_i as $(ID_i, x_i, -, -)$. If the related item of ID_i does not exist, $\mathcal{B}$ randomly picks $x_i \in \mathbb{Z}_p$ and computes

$$sk_i = (sk_{i,1}, sk_{i,2}) = \left(D_1^{x_i}, D_2^{x_i}\right) = \left(g_2^{ax_iu_i}, g_2^{ax_iv_i}\right),$$

which can be computed with known g_2^a, x, u_i, v_i. It then stores (ID_i, x_i, sk_i) into L_s. $\mathcal{B}$ returns sk_2 to $\mathcal{A}_2$.

- *Proxy token query (ID_i, ID_{P_i}):* For a queried ID_i, $\mathcal{B}$ performs as Aut step except that $\mathcal{B}$ computes $PI_i = H_2(ID_i)^{x_{P_i}} = g_2^{av_ix_ix_{P_i}}$, and the proxy token

$$\hat{tk}_i = H_2(ID)^{\alpha x + x \cdot x_P} = g_2^{av_ix_i + x_ix_{P_i}}$$

with known $g_2, g_2^a, v_i, x_i, x_{P_i}$. $\mathcal{B}$ returns $\hat{tk}_i$ to $\mathcal{A}_2$.

3. *Challenge:* $\mathcal{A}_2$ sends (s^*, ID^*) to $\mathcal{B}$, where s^* represents the designated challenge number, and ID^* stands for the challenge identity. If $ID^* \neq ID_{i^*}$, $\mathcal{B}$ aborts. Otherwise, it chooses to randomly pick $M^* \in \{0,1\}^\lambda, w_1, w_2 \in \mathbb{Z}_p, R_1 \in \{0,1\}^{2l}$, and

implicitly sets $r_1 = w_1 c, r_2 = w_2 c$. Taking as input M^*, s^*, it then iteratively computes $(f_0, f_1, \cdots, f_{s^*-1})$ and $f(x)$ same as $\mathsf{Enc}(pp, pk, M, s)$ in Section 4.1. Then, it randomly picks $A \in \mathbb{Z}_p$, computes $f(A)$, then outputs the challenge ciphertext as follows:

$$
\begin{aligned}
C_1 &= g_1^{r_1} = g_1^{cw_1},\\
C_2 &= R_1,\\
C_3 &= g_1^{r_2} = g_1^{cw_2},\\
C_4 &= g_1^{x_{i^*} r_2} = g_1^{cx_{i^*} w_2},\\
C_5 &= H_4\Big(e(g_1^{cw_1}, g_2^{av_{i^*} x_{i^*}})\Big) \oplus (A||f(A)),\\
C_6 &= H_5\Big(s^*||C_1^*||C_2^*||C_3^*||C_4^*||C_5^*||e(g_1^{cw_1}, g_2^{av_{i^*} x_{i^*}})||f_0||f_1||\cdots||f_{s^*-1}\Big).
\end{aligned}
$$

4. *Phase 2:* $\mathcal{B}$ interacts with $\mathcal{A}_2$ as *Phase 1* with the limitation that ID_{i^*} cannot be queried in *partial private key query*, *secret key query*, and *private key query*.
5. Guess: $\mathcal{A}_2$ outputs its guess $M' \in \{0,1\}^\lambda$.
6. *Solve:* $\mathcal{B}$ randomly chooses an item $(Q_i, H_4(Q_i) = \eta_i)$ from L_{H_4} and sets

$$e(g_1, g_2)^{abc} = Q_i^{\frac{1}{x_{i^*} u_{i^*} w_1}}$$

as the solution to the BDH instance.

7. *Analysis:* To successfully perform the reduction, the simulation should be indistinguishable from the real attack from the point of view of the adversary. As we can see, if the adversary chooses ID_{i^*} as the challenge identity, the simulation will not abort, which means the simulation is indistinguishable from the real attack. The corresponding probability is $1/n$. Upon the case that the simulation is indistinguishable to the adversary, we have the following analysis. Since the adversary is assumed to break the security with advantage ϵ, we have that it issues the hash query $e(X_{i^*}, H_1(ID_{i^*}))^{r_1} = e(g_1^{ax_{i^*}}, g_2^{bu_{i^*}})^{cw_1} = e(g_1, g_2)^{abc \cdot x_{i^*} u_{i^*} w_1}$ with probability ϵ. Thus, $\mathcal{B}$ finally can obtain the true solution to the given BDH instance as $e(g_1, g_2)^{abc} = Q_i^{\frac{1}{x_{i^*} u_{i^*} w_1}}$ with probability $\frac{\epsilon}{q_{H_4}}$. In conclusion, $\mathcal{B}$ can successfully break the BDH assumption with probability

$$\Pr[\mathcal{B} \textit{ chooses the correct hash query} | \textit{the simulation is indistinguishable}] = \frac{\epsilon}{n \cdot q_{H_4}}.$$

□

Theorem 3. *For any PPT Type-III adversary, our CLE-MET-PA scheme is IND-CPA secure based on the BDH assumption in the random oracle model.*

Proof of Theorem 3. Assume that there exists an adversary $\mathcal{A}_3$ who can break the IND-CPA security of our scheme with the non-negligible advantage ϵ, we can construct a simulator $\mathcal{B}$ to break the BDH assumption. Given an instance as $(\mathcal{G}, g_1, g_1^a, g_1^c, g_2, g_2^a, g_2^b)$, $\mathcal{B}$ is to compute $e(g_1, g_2)^{abc}$ by running $\mathcal{A}_3$ as a subroutine. $\mathcal{B}$ and $\mathcal{A}_3$ play the following game.

1. *Setup:* $\mathcal{B}$ randomly picks a cryptographic hash function $H_3 : \{0,1\}^* \to \{0,1\}^\lambda$, randomly picks $\alpha \in \mathbb{Z}_p^*$, and sets the public parameter pp. $pp = \{\mathcal{G}, g_1, g_2, \bar{g}, H_1, H_2, H_3, H_4, H_5\}$, where $\bar{g} = g_1^\alpha$, H_1, H_2, H_4, H_5 are random oracles. pp is sent to $\mathcal{A}_3$. Lists $L_{H_1}, L_{H_2}, L_{H_4}, L_{H_5}, L_s$ are initially empty. Assume that $\mathcal{A}_3$ can make $q_{H_1}, q_{H_2}, q_{H_4}, q_{H_5}$ hash queries to H_1, H_2, H_4, H_5, respectively.
2. *Phase 1:* Assume there are n users with identities $ID_1, \cdots, ID_n$ in the system. $\mathcal{B}$ randomly chooses $i^* \in [1, n]$ and performs the following steps.
   - *H_i-query (ID_i) ($i = 1, 2, 4, 5$):* $\mathcal{B}$ performs as in the **Proof of Theorem 1**.

- *Master secret key query* (1^λ): $\mathcal{B}$ returns α to $\mathcal{A}_3$.
- *Partial private key query* (ID_i): For i-th queried identity ID_i, if $ID_i = ID_{i^*}$, $\mathcal{B}$ aborts. Otherwise, if ID_i has not been queried to H_1, $\mathcal{B}$ randomly chooses u_i, sets
$$H_1(ID_i) = g_2^{u_i},$$
and stores $(u_i, ID_i, H_1(ID_i))$ into L_{H_1}. If ID_i has not been queried to H_2, $\mathcal{B}$ randomly chooses v_i, sets
$$H_2(ID_i) = g_2^{v_i},$$
and stores $(v_i, ID_i, H_2(ID_i))$ into L_{H_2}. $\mathcal{B}$ searches L_{H_1} and L_{H_2} to find the related items of ID_i as $(u_i, ID_i, H_1(ID_i))$ and $(v_i, ID_i, H_2(ID_i))$. $\mathcal{B}$ then computes
$$D_i = (D_{i,1}, D_{i,2}) = (H_1^\alpha(ID), H_2^\alpha(ID)) = (g_2^{\alpha u_i}, g_2^{\alpha v_i}),$$
which can be computed with known g_2, α, u_i, v_i. $\mathcal{B}$ returns D_i to $\mathcal{A}_3$.
- *Secret key query* (ID_i): For i-th queried identity ID_i, if $ID_i = ID_{i^*}$, $\mathcal{B}$ aborts. Otherwise, $\mathcal{B}$ randomly picks $x_i \in \mathbb{Z}_p$, stores $(ID_i, x_i, -, -)$ into L_s, and returns x_i to $\mathcal{A}_3$.
- *Private key query* (ID_i): For the i-th queried identity ID_i, if $ID_i = ID_{i^*}$, $\mathcal{B}$ aborts. Otherwise, if ID_i was not queried to H_1, $\mathcal{B}$ randomly chooses u_i, sets
$$H_1(ID_i) = g_2^{u_i},$$
and stores $(u_i, ID_i, H_1(ID_i))$ into L_{H_1}. If ID_i has not been queried to H_2, $\mathcal{B}$ randomly chooses v_i, sets
$$H_2(ID_i) = g_2^{v_i},$$
and stores $(v_i, ID_i, H_2(ID_i))$ into L_{H_2}. $\mathcal{B}$ searches L_{H_1} and L_{H_2} to find the related items of ID_i as $(u_i, ID_i, H_1(ID_i))$ and $(v_i, ID_i, H_2(ID_i))$. $\mathcal{B}$ searches L_s and finds the related item of ID_i as $(ID_i, x_i, -, -)$. If the related item of ID_i does not exist, $\mathcal{B}$ randomly picks $x_i \in \mathbb{Z}_p$ and computes
$$sk_i = (sk_{i,1}, sk_{i,2}) = (D_1^{x_i}, D_2^{x_i}) = (g_2^{\alpha x_i u_i}, g_2^{\alpha x_i v_i}),$$
which can be computed with known $g_2, \alpha, x_i, u_i, v_i$. It then stores $(ID_i, x_i, sk_i, -)$ into L_s and returns sk_i to $\mathcal{A}_3$.
- *Public key query* (ID_i): For the i-th queried identity ID_i, if $ID_i \neq ID_{i^*}$, $\mathcal{B}$ searches L_s and finds the related item of ID_i as $(ID_i, x_i, -, -)$. If the related item does not exist, $\mathcal{B}$ randomly picks $x_i \in \mathbb{Z}_p$ and computes
$$pk_i = (X_i, Y_i, Z_i) = (g_1^{\alpha x_i}, g_2^{x_i}, g_1^{x_i}),$$
It then stores $(ID_i, x_i, -, pk_i)$ into L_s and returns pk_i to $\mathcal{A}_3$;
If $ID_i \neq ID_{i^*}$, $\mathcal{B}$ randomly picks $x_i' \in \mathbb{Z}_p$, implicitly sets $x_i = ax_i'$, computes
$$pk_i = (X_i, Y_i, Z_i) = \left(g_1^{\alpha a x_i'}, g_2^{a x_i'}, g_1^{a x_i'}\right),$$
which can be computed with known $g_1^a, g_2^a, \alpha, x_i'$. It then stores $(ID_i, x_i', -, pk_i)$ into L_s and returns pk_i to $\mathcal{A}_3$.
- *Proxy key query* (ID_{P_i}): For a proxy with the related item in L_s as (ID_{P_i}, x_{P_i}), $\mathcal{B}$ performs as a *public key query* step and obtains
$$pk_{P_i} = (X_{P_i}, Y_{P_i}, Z_{P_i}) = \left(g_1^{\alpha x_{P_i}}, g_2^{x_{P_i}}, g_1^{x_{P_i}}\right).$$

which can be computed with known $g_1, \alpha, g_2, x_{P_i}$. $\mathcal{B}$ then returns pk_{P_i} and sk_{P_i} to $\mathcal{A}_3$.

- *Token query (ID_i):* For a queried ID_i, if $ID_i = ID_{i^*}$, $\mathcal{B}$ aborts. Otherwise, $\mathcal{B}$ searches L_s to find the related item of ID_i as (ID_i, x_i, sk_i), where $sk_i = (sk_1, sk_2)$. If the related item does not exist, $\mathcal{B}$ performs as follows. If ID_i has not been queried to H_1, $\mathcal{B}$ randomly chooses u_i, sets

$$H_1(ID_i) = g_2^{u_i},$$

and stores $(u_i, ID_i, H_1(ID_i))$ into L_{H_1}. If ID_i has not been queried to H_2, $\mathcal{B}$ randomly chooses v_i, sets

$$H_2(ID_i) = g_2^{v_i},$$

and stores $(v_i, ID_i, H_2(ID_i))$ into L_{H_2}. $\mathcal{B}$ searches L_{H_1} and L_{H_2} to find the related items of ID_i as $(u_i, ID_i, H_1(ID_i))$ and $(v_i, ID_i, H_2(ID_i))$. $\mathcal{B}$ searches L_s and finds the related item of ID_i as $(ID_i, x_i, -, -)$. If the related item of ID_i does not exist, $\mathcal{B}$ randomly picks $x_i \in \mathbb{Z}_p$ and computes

$$sk_i = (sk_{i,1}, sk_{i,2}) = (D_1^{x_i}, D_2^{x_i}) = (g_2^{\alpha x_i u_i}, g_2^{\alpha x_i v_i}),$$

which can be computed with known g_2^a, x, u_i, v_i. It then stores (ID_i, x_i, sk_i) into L_s. $\mathcal{B}$ returns sk_2 to $\mathcal{A}_3$.

- *Proxy token query (ID_i, ID_{P_i}):* For a queried ID_i, if $ID_i = ID_{i^*}$, $\mathcal{B}$ aborts. Otherwise, $\mathcal{B}$ performs as Aut step except that $\mathcal{B}$ computes $PI_i = H_2(ID_i)^{x_{P_i}} = g_2^{\alpha v_i x_i x_{P_i}}$, and the proxy token

$$\hat{tk}_i = H_2(ID)^{\alpha x + x \cdot x_P} = g_2^{\alpha v_i x_i + x_i x_{P_i}}$$

with known $g_2, \alpha, v_i, x_i, x_{P_i}$. $\mathcal{B}$ returns $\hat{tk}_i$ to $\mathcal{A}_3$.

3. *Challenge:* $\mathcal{A}_3$ sends $(s^*, ID^*, M_0^*, M_1^*)$ to $\mathcal{B}$, where s^* represents the designated challenge number, ID^* stands for the challenge identity, and two plaintexts M_0^* and M_1^* are selected from $\{0,1\}^\lambda$ with equal lengths. If $ID^* \neq ID_{i^*}$, $\mathcal{B}$ aborts. Otherwise, it randomly picks $w_1, w_2 \in \mathbb{Z}_p, R_1, R_2 \in \{0,1\}^{2l}, R_3 \in \{0,1\}^\lambda$ and implicitly sets $r_1 = w_1 c, r_2 = w_2 c$. It then computes the challenge ciphertext as

$$\begin{aligned} C_1 &= g_1^{r_1} = g_1^{c w_1}, \\ C_2 &= R_1, \\ C_3 &= g_1^{r_2} = g_1^{c w_2}, \\ C_4 &= g_1^{x_{i^*} r_2} = g_1^{c x_{i^*} w_2}, \\ C_5 &= R_2, \\ C_6 &= R_3. \end{aligned}$$

4. *Phase 2:* $\mathcal{B}$ interacts with $\mathcal{A}_3$ as *Phase 1* with the limitation that ID_{i^*} cannot be queried in *partial private key query*, *secret key query*, *private key query*, *token query*, and *proxy token query*.
5. Guess: $\mathcal{A}_3$ outputs its guess bit $\rho' \in \{0,1\}$.
6. *Solve:* $\mathcal{B}$ randomly chooses an item $(Q_i, H_4(Q_i) = \eta_i)$ from L_{H_4} and sets

$$e(g_1, g_2)^{abc} = Q_i^{\frac{1}{x_{i^*}^{J} u_{i^*} w_1 \alpha}}$$

as the solution to the BDH instance.

7. *Analysis:* To successfully perform the reduction, the simulation should be indistinguishable from the real attack from the point of view of the adversary. As we can see, if the adversary chooses ID_{i^*} as the challenge identity, the simulation will not abort, which means that the simulation is indistinguishable from the real attack. The corresponding probability is $1/n$. Upon the case that the simulation is indistinguishable to the adversary, we have the following analysis. Since the adversary is assumed to break the security with advantage ϵ, we have that it issues the hash query $e(X_{i^*}, H_1(ID_{i^*}))^{r_1} = e(g_1^{\alpha a x'_{i^*}}, g_2^{b u_{i^*}})^{c w_1} = e(g_1, g_2)^{abc \cdot x'_{i^*} u_{i^*} w_1 \alpha}$ with probability ϵ. Thus, $\mathcal{B}$ finally can obtain the true solution to the given BDH instance as $e(g_1, g_2)^{abc} = Q_i^{\frac{1}{x'_{i^*} u_{i^*} w_1 \alpha}}$ with probability $\frac{\epsilon}{q_{H_4}}$. In conclusion, $\mathcal{B}$ can successfully break the BDH assumption with probability

$$\Pr[\mathcal{B}\ \textit{chooses the correct hash query} | \textit{the simulation is indistinguishable}] = \frac{\epsilon}{n \cdot q_{H_4}}.$$

□

Theorem 4. *For any PPT Type-IV adversary, our CLE-MET-PA scheme is OW-CPA secure based on the BDH assumption in the random oracle model.*

Proof of Theorem 4. Assume there exists an adversary $\mathcal{A}_4$ who can break the IND-CPA security of our scheme with a non-negligible advantage ϵ; we can construct a simulator $\mathcal{B}$ to break the BDH assumption. Given an instance as $(\mathcal{G}, g_1, g_1^a, g_1^c, g_2, g_2^a, g_2^b)$, $\mathcal{B}$ is to compute $e(g_1, g_2)^{abc}$ by running $\mathcal{A}_4$ as a subroutine. $\mathcal{B}$ and $\mathcal{A}_4$ play the following game.

1. *Setup:* $\mathcal{B}$ randomly picks a cryptographic hash function $H_3 : \{0,1\}^* \rightarrow \{0,1\}^\lambda$, randomly picks $\alpha \in \mathbb{Z}_p^*$, and sets the public parameter pp. $pp = \{\mathcal{G}, g_1, g_2, \bar{g}, H_1, H_2, H_3, H_4, H_5\}$, where $\bar{g} = g_1^\alpha$, H_1, H_2, H_4, H_5 are random oracles. pp is sent to $\mathcal{A}_4$. Lists $L_{H_1}, L_{H_2}, L_{H_4}, L_{H_5}, L_s$ are initially empty. Assume that $\mathcal{A}_4$ can make $q_{H_1}, q_{H_2}, q_{H_4}, q_{H_5}$ hash queries to H_1, H_2, H_4, H_5, respectively.
2. *Phase 1:* Assume there are n users with identities $ID_1, \cdots, ID_n$ in the system. $\mathcal{B}$ randomly chooses $i^* \in [1, n]$ and performs the following steps.
   - *H_i-query (ID_i) ($i = 1, 2, 4, 5$):* $\mathcal{B}$ performs as in the **Proof of Theorem 2**.
   - *Master secret key query (1^λ):* $\mathcal{B}$ returns α to $\mathcal{A}_4$.
   - *Partial private key query (ID_i):* For i-th queried identity ID_i, if $ID_i = ID_{i^*}$, $\mathcal{B}$ aborts. Otherwise, if ID_i has not been queried to H_1, $\mathcal{B}$ randomly chooses u_i, sets

     $$H_1(ID_i) = g_2^{u_i},$$

     and stores $(u_i, ID_i, H_1(ID_i))$ into L_{H_1}. If ID_i has not been queried to H_2, $\mathcal{B}$ randomly chooses v_i, sets

     $$H_2(ID_i) = g_2^{v_i},$$

     and stores $(v_i, ID_i, H_2(ID_i))$ into L_{H_2}. $\mathcal{B}$ searches L_{H_1} and L_{H_2} to find the related items of ID_i as $(u_i, ID_i, H_1(ID_i))$ and $(v_i, ID_i, H_2(ID_i))$. $\mathcal{B}$ then computes

     $$D_i = (D_{i,1}, D_{i,2}) = (H_1^\alpha(ID), H_2^\alpha(ID)) = (g_2^{\alpha u_i}, g_2^{\alpha v_i}),$$

     which can be computed with known g_2, α, u_i, v_i. $\mathcal{B}$ returns D_i to $\mathcal{A}_4$.
   - *Secret key query (ID_i):* For i-th queried identity ID_i, if $ID_i = ID_{i^*}$, $\mathcal{B}$ aborts. Otherwise, $\mathcal{B}$ randomly picks $x_i \in \mathbb{Z}_p$, stores $(ID_i, x_i, -, -)$ into L_s, and returns x_i to $\mathcal{A}_4$.
   - *Private key query (ID_i):* For the i-th queried identity ID_i, if $ID_i = ID_{i^*}$, $\mathcal{B}$ aborts. Otherwise, if ID_i has not been queried to H_1, $\mathcal{B}$ randomly chooses u_i, sets

     $$H_1(ID_i) = g_2^{u_i},$$

and stores $(u_i, ID_i, H_1(ID_i))$ into L_{H_1}. If ID_i has not been queried to H_2, $\mathcal{B}$ randomly chooses v_i, sets

$$H_2(ID_i) = g_2^{v_i},$$

and stores $(v_i, ID_i, H_2(ID_i))$ into L_{H_2}. $\mathcal{B}$ searches L_{H_1} and L_{H_2} to find the related items of ID_i as $(u_i, ID_i, H_1(ID_i))$ and $(v_i, ID_i, H_2(ID_i))$. $\mathcal{B}$ searches L_s and finds the related item of ID_i as $(ID_i, x_i, -, -)$. If the related item of ID_i does not exist, $\mathcal{B}$ randomly picks $x_i \in \mathbb{Z}_p$ and computes

$$sk_i = (sk_{i,1}, sk_{i,2}) = (D_1^{x_i}, D_2^{x_i}) = (g_2^{\alpha x_i u_i}, g_2^{\alpha x_i v_i}),$$

which can be computed with known $g_2, \alpha, x_i, u_i, v_i$. It then stores $(ID_i, x_i, sk_i, -)$ into L_s and returns sk_i to $\mathcal{A}_4$.

- *Public key query (ID_i):* For i-th queried identity ID_i, if $ID_i \neq ID_{i^*}$, $\mathcal{B}$ searches L_s and finds the related item of ID_i as $(ID_i, x_i, -, -)$. If the related item does not exist, $\mathcal{B}$ randomly picks $x_i \in \mathbb{Z}_p$ and computes

$$pk_i = (X_i, Y_i, Z_i) = (g_1^{\alpha x_i}, g_2^{x_i}, g_1^{x_i}),$$

It then stores $(ID_i, x_i, -, pk_i)$ into L_s and returns pk_i to $\mathcal{A}_4$;
If $ID_i \neq ID_{i^*}$, $\mathcal{B}$ randomly picks $x_i' \in \mathbb{Z}_p$, implicitly sets $x_i = ax_i'$, and computes

$$pk_i = (X_i, Y_i, Z_i) = \left(g_1^{\alpha a x_i'}, g_2^{a x_i'}, g_1^{a x_i'}\right),$$

which can be computed with known $g_1^a, g_2^a, \alpha, x_i'$. It then stores $(ID_i, x_i', -, pk_i)$ into L_s and returns pk_i to $\mathcal{A}_4$.

- *Proxy key query (ID_{P_i}):* For a proxy with the related item in L_s as (ID_{P_i}, x_{P_i}), $\mathcal{B}$ performs as *public key query* step and obtains

$$pk_{P_i} = (X_{P_i}, Y_{P_i}, Z_{P_i}) = \left(g_1^{\alpha x_{P_i}}, g_2^{x_{P_i}}, g_1^{x_{P_i}}\right).$$

which can be computed with known $g_1, \alpha, g_2, x_{P_i}$. $\mathcal{B}$ then returns pk_{P_i} and sk_{P_i} to $\mathcal{A}_4$.

- *Token query (ID_i):* For a queried ID_i, if $ID_i \neq ID_{i^*}$, $\mathcal{B}$ searches L_s to find the related item of ID_i as (ID_i, x_i, sk_i), where $sk_i = (sk_1, sk_2)$. If the related item does not exist, $\mathcal{B}$ performs as follows. If ID_i has not been queried to H_1, $\mathcal{B}$ randomly chooses u_i, sets

$$H_1(ID_i) = g_2^{u_i},$$

and stores $(u_i, ID_i, H_1(ID_i))$ into L_{H_1}. If ID_i has not been queried to H_2, $\mathcal{B}$ randomly chooses v_i, sets

$$H_2(ID_i) = g_2^{v_i},$$

and stores $(v_i, ID_i, H_2(ID_i))$ into L_{H_2}. $\mathcal{B}$ searches L_{H_1} and L_{H_2} to find the related items of ID_i as $(u_i, ID_i, H_1(ID_i))$ and $(v_i, ID_i, H_2(ID_i))$. $\mathcal{B}$ searches L_s and finds the related item of ID_i as $(ID_i, x_i, -, -)$. If the related item of ID_i does not exist, $\mathcal{B}$ randomly picks $x_i \in \mathbb{Z}_p$ and computes

$$sk_i = (sk_{i,1}, sk_{i,2}) = (D_1^{x_i}, D_2^{x_i}) = (g_2^{\alpha x_i u_i}, g_2^{\alpha x_i v_i}),$$

which can be computed with known $g_2, \alpha, x_i, u_i, v_i$. It then stores (ID_i, x_i, sk_i) into L_s. $\mathcal{B}$ returns sk_2 to $\mathcal{A}_4$.
If $ID_i = ID_{i^*}$, $\mathcal{B}$ searches L_s to find the related item of ID_i as $(ID_i, x_i', -, -)$ and $(v_i, ID_i, H_2(ID_i))$. If the related item of ID_i does not exist, $\mathcal{B}$ randomly picks $x_i' \in \mathbb{Z}_p$ and computes

$$sk_2 = g_2^{\alpha a v_i x_i'},$$

which can be computed with the known g_2^a, α, v_i, x_i', $\mathcal{B}$ returns sk_2 to $\mathcal{A}_4$.

- *Proxy token query* (ID_i, ID_{P_i}): For a queried ID_i, $\mathcal{B}$ performs as Aut step except that $\mathcal{B}$ computes

$$PI_i = H_2(ID_i)^{x_{P_i}} = \begin{cases} g_2^{\alpha v_i x_i x_{P_i}}, & if\ i \neq i^*, \\ g_2^{\alpha a v_i x_i' x_{P_i}}, & if\ i = i^*. \end{cases}$$

$$\hat{tk} = H_2(ID)^{\alpha x + x \cdot x_P} = \begin{cases} g_2^{\alpha v_i x_i + x_i x_{P_i}}, & if\ i \neq i^*, \\ g_2^{\alpha a v_i x_i' + a x_i' x_{P_i}}, & if\ i = i^*. \end{cases}$$

with known $g_2, \alpha, v_i, x_i, x_i', x_{P_i}$.

3. *Challenge:* $\mathcal{A}_4$ sends (s^*, ID^*) to $\mathcal{B}$, where s^* represents the designated challenge number, and ID^* stands for the challenge identity. If $ID^* \neq ID_{i^*}$, $\mathcal{B}$ aborts. Otherwise, it chooses to randomly pick $M^* \in \{0,1\}^\lambda, w_1, w_2 \in \mathbb{Z}_p, R_1 \in \{0,1\}^{2l}$, and implicitly sets $r_1 = w_1 c, r_2 = w_2 c$. Taking as input M^*, s^*, it then iteratively computes $(f_0, f_1, \cdots, f_{s^*-1})$ and $f(x)$ same as $\mathsf{Enc}(pp, pk, pk_P, M, s)$ in Section 4.1. Then, it randomly picks $A \in \mathbb{Z}_p$, computes $f(A)$, before outputting the challenge ciphertext as follows:

$$\begin{aligned} C_1 &= g_1^{r_1} = g_1^{cw_1}, \\ C_2 &= R_1, \\ C_3 &= g_1^{r_2} = g_1^{cw_2}, \\ C_4 &= g_1^{x_{i^*}' r_2} = g_1^{c x_{i^*}' w_2}, \\ C_5 &= H_4\Big(e(g_1^{cw_1}, g_2^{\alpha a v_{i^*} x_{i^*}'})\Big) \oplus (A || f(A)), \\ C_6 &= H_5\Big(s^* || C_1^* || C_2^* || C_3^* || C_4^* || C_5^* || e(g_1^{cw_1}, g_2^{\alpha a v_{i^*} x_{i^*}'}) || f_0 || f_1 || \cdots || f_{s^*-1}\Big). \end{aligned}$$

4. *Phase 2:* $\mathcal{B}$ interacts with $\mathcal{A}_4$ as *Phase 1* with the limitation that ID_{i^*} cannot be queried in *partial private key query*, *secret key query*, and *private key query*.
5. Guess: $\mathcal{A}_4$ outputs its guess $M' \in \{0,1\}^\lambda$.
6. *Solve:* $\mathcal{B}$ randomly chooses an item $(Q_i, H_4(Q_i) = \eta_i)$ from L_{H_4} and sets

$$e(g_1, g_2)^{abc} = Q_i^{\frac{1}{x_{i^*}' u_{i^*} w_1 \alpha}}$$

as the solution to the BDH instance.

7. *Analysis:* To successfully perform the reduction, the simulation should be indistinguishable from the real attack from the point of view of the adversary. As we can see, if the adversary chooses ID_{i^*} as the challenge identity, the simulation will not abort, which means the simulation is indistinguishable from the real attack. The corresponding probability is $1/n$. Upon the case that the simulation is indistinguishable to the adversary, we have the following analysis. Since the adversary is assumed to break the security with advantage ϵ, we have that it issues the hash query $e(X_{i^*}, H_1(ID_{i^*}))^{r_1} = e(g_1^{\alpha a x_{i^*}'}, g_2^{b u_{i^*}})^{c w_1} = e(g_1, g_2)^{abc \cdot x_{i^*}' u_{i^*} w_1 \alpha}$ with probability ϵ. Thus, $\mathcal{B}$ can finally obtain the true solution to the given BDH instance as

$e(g_1, g_2)^{abc} = Q_i^{\frac{1}{x'_{i^*} u_{i^*} w_1 \alpha}}$ with probability $\frac{\epsilon}{q_{H_4}}$. In conclusion, $\mathcal{B}$ can successfully break the BDH assumption with probability

$$\Pr[\mathcal{B} \textit{ chooses the correct hash query} | \textit{the simulation is indistinguishable}] = \frac{\epsilon}{n \cdot q_{H_4}}.$$

□

Theorem 5 (Number Security of CLE-MET-PA). *In the information theoretical sense, no probabilistic polynomial-time adversary has a non-negligible advantage in breaking the number security of our CLE-MET-PA scheme.*

Proof of Theorem 5. In this game of number security, the adversary $\mathcal{A}_5$ tries to determine whether the underlying messages of t^* challenging ciphertexts $CT_1^*, \cdots, CT_{t^*}^*$ are equal or not with all the designated numbers of these ciphertexts, which are s^* and $s^* > t^*$. And, the underlying messages are chosen by $\mathcal{B}$ and they are unknown to $\mathcal{A}_5$. From the setting of our scheme, we have that $\mathcal{A}_5$ has two ways to check whether the underlying messages are equal or not, i.e., extracting M_i or $f_{i,j}$ of CT_i for some $j \in \{0, \cdots, t^* - 1\}$, for each $i \in \{1, \cdots, t^*\}$.

In line with the OW-CPA security proof, $\mathcal{A}_5$ has only a negligible advantage in obtaining the underlying message from the ciphertext under the BDH assumption. To extract a $f_{i,j}$ from the ciphertext $CT_i = (s, C_{i,1}, C_{i,2}, C_{i,3}, C_{i,4}, C_{i,5}, C_{i,6})$, $\mathcal{A}_5$ can make a *token query* or a *Proxy token query* on pk_i and obtain the corresponding token $tk_i = sk_{i,2}$ or $\hat{tk}_i = sk_{i,2} H_2(ID_i)^{x_i x_{P_i}}$ such that it is able to obtain the $A_i || f_i(A_i) = C_{i,5} \oplus H_4(e(C_{i,3}, tk_i))$ or $A_i || f_i(A_i) = C_{i,5} \oplus H_4\left(e(C_{i,3}, \hat{tk}_i) / e(C_{i,4}, PI_i)\right)$, where

$$f_i(A_i) = f_{i,0} + f_{i,1} A_i + \cdots + f_{i,t^*-1} A_i^{t^*-1}$$

and

$$f_{i,j} = H_3(M_i || s || f_{i,0} || \cdots || f_{i,j-1}),\ j \in \{0, \cdots, t^* - 1\}.$$

Obtaining $A_i || f_i(A_i)$ for each $i \in \{1, \cdots, t^*\}$, $\mathcal{A}_5$ has an equation set as

$$\begin{cases} f_1(A_1) = f_{1,0} + f_{1,1} A_1 + \cdots + f_{1,t^*-1} A_1^{t^*-1} \\ f_2(A_2) = f_{2,0} + f_{2,1} A_2 + \cdots + f_{2,t^*-1} A_2^{t^*-1} \\ \quad \vdots \\ f_{t^*}(A_{t^*}) = f_{t^*,0} + f_{t^*,1} A_{t^*} + \cdots + f_{t^*,t^*-1} A_{t^*}^{t^*-1} \end{cases},$$

where A_i for $i \in \{1, \cdots, t^* - 1\}$ are randomly chosen by $\mathcal{C}$. Therefore, after implicitly setting that $f_{i,k} = f_{j,k}$ for $i \in \{1, \cdots, t^* - 1\}, j \in \{0, \cdots, t^* - 1\}$, these $t^* - 1$ equations are nonlinearly correlated with each other by an overwhelming probability such that there are infinite solutions for $\{f_{i,j}\}_{1 \le i \le t^*, 0 \le j \le t^*-1}$. In addition, $\mathcal{A}_5$ has no other information to further ensure whether the underlying messages are equal or not. It can only randomly guess b'. In conclusion, the adversary has a negligible advantage in breaking the number security of the proposed CLE-MET-PA scheme. □

6. Performance Analysis and Extension

6.1. Performance Analysis of CLE-MET-PA

We conducted a visual comparison between our scheme and several existing schemes [15,30,31,40], and the results are presented in Table 2. Among them, Refs. [15,30,40] only support pairwise equality tests. Therefore, in scenarios where we need to test the equality of s ciphertexts, these three schemes require $s - 1$ executions of their test algorithms.

We adopted the commonly used approach for the performance analysis of most PKEET schemes, which involves calculating the complexity of significant algorithms, ciphertext size, and scheme-specific functionalities. This method allows us to evaluate different algorithms using the same standard across various platforms. Initially, we evaluated the complexity of encryption, decryption, and test algorithms, primarily focusing on three metrics: the number of exponential operations, hash operations, and bilinear pairings, denoted by E, H, and P, respectively. We excluded efficient operations such as addition, multiplication, and XOR. Next, we considered additional metrics such as ciphertext size and three functionalities: the anti-key management feature, the anti-key escrow feature, and support for proxy-assisted authorization.

As shown in Table 2, our scheme demonstrates significant advantages in terms of the multi-ciphertext equality test algorithm. In comparison to traditional schemes that support pairwise equality tests, our multi-ciphertext equality test exhibits lower computational complexity than conducting multiple pairwise equality tests. Specifically, even in extreme situations where all tokens are proxy tokens, we only require $2s$ of the most computationally expensive bilinear pairings. This is notably lower than other schemes that support pairwise equality tests. Furthermore, our scheme inherently possesses certificateless encryption properties, effectively addressing the key management problem in PKEET and the key escrow problem in IBEET. This makes our scheme more suitable in scenarios where certificate management is challenging or where anonymous communication is required. Additionally, we introduced the feature of proxy-assisted authorization, enabling users to delegate proxy authorization while they are offline and better protect their private keys. These characteristics make our CLE-MET-PA scheme more competitive for practical use.

Table 2. Comparison among several equality test schemes.

Schemes	[15]	[30]	[40]	[31]	**Ours**
Enc	6E+3H+2P	5E+4H+4P	2E+3H+3P	$(s+2)$E+$(s+3)$H	$(s+3)$E+$(s+5)$H+6P
Dec	4E+3H+2P	2E+4H+2P	1E+2H+3P	$(s+1)$E+$(s+2)$H	$(s-1)$E+$(s+3)$H+2P
Test	$(s-1)$(2E+4P)	$(s-1)$(2H+4P)	$(s-1)$(4H+4P)	sE+ 2sH+SE	2sH+$(s+j)$P+SE
$\lvert CT\rvert$	$5\lvert\mathbb{G}\rvert+\lvert\mathbb{Z}_p\rvert$	$3\lvert\mathbb{G}\rvert+\lvert\mathbb{Z}_p\rvert+\{0,1\}^{\lambda}$	$3\lvert\mathbb{G}\rvert+\lvert\mathbb{Z}_p\rvert$	$2\lvert\mathbb{G}\rvert+5\lvert\mathbb{Z}_p\rvert+\{0,1\}^{\lambda}$	$3\lvert\mathbb{G}\rvert+5\lvert\mathbb{Z}_p\rvert+\{0,1\}^{\lambda}$
AntiKM	✓	✓	✓	×	✓
AntiKE	×	✓	✓	✓	✓
PA	×	×	×	×	✓

E, H, P, and SE represent the computation cost of an exponential operation, hash operation, pairing operation, and solving an equation set, respectively. $\lvert\mathbb{Z}_p\rvert, \lvert\mathbb{G}\rvert$ represent the bit length of a group element in $\mathbb{Z}_p, \mathbb{G}$, respectively. j: number of proxy tokens, $(0 \leq j \leq s)$. s: number of ciphertexts to be verified. AntiKM, AntiKE, and PA represent anti-key management feature, anti-key escrow feature and proxy-assisted authorization feature, respectively. The presence of a checkmark indicates that the feature has been included, while a cross indicates that the feature has not been included.

6.2. Extension

As mentioned before in this paper, our CLE-MET-PA scheme achieves IND-CPA security against adversaries without a trapdoor and OW-CPA security against adversaries with a trapdoor. We extend our scheme to CCA security with FO transformation [32,33] by simple modifications. The improved version of CLE-MET-PA is as follows.

$\mathsf{Setup}(1^{\lambda})$: Almost the same as $\mathsf{Setup}(1^{\lambda})$ in Section 4.1. The difference is that while generating pp and msk, additionally generate a cryptographic hash function $H_6 : \{0,1\}^* \rightarrow \{0,1\}^l$, and add it in pp.

$\mathsf{Partial\text{-}Private\text{-}Key\text{-}Extract}\ (pp, msk, ID)$: Same as $\mathsf{Partial\text{-}Private\text{-}Key\text{-}Extract}(pp, msk, ID)$ in Section 4.1.

$\mathsf{Set\text{-}Secret\text{-}Value}\ (pp, ID)$: Same as $\mathsf{Set\text{-}Secret\text{-}Value}\ (pp, ID)$ in Section 4.1.

$\mathsf{Set\text{-}Private\text{-}Key}\ (pp, D, x)$: Same as $\mathsf{Set\text{-}Private\text{-}Key}\ (pp, D, x)$ in Section 4.1.

$\mathsf{Set\text{-}Public\text{-}Key}\ (pp, x)$: Same as $\mathsf{Set\text{-}Public\text{-}Key}\ (pp, x)$ in Section 4.1.

$\mathsf{Set\text{-}Proxy\text{-}Key}\ (pp, ID_P)$: Same as $\mathsf{Set\text{-}Proxy\text{-}Key}\ (pp, ID_P)$ in Section 4.1.

$\mathsf{Enc}(pp, pk, M, s)$: Taking as input the system parameter pp, a user public key pk, and a proxy public key pk_P, check whether $e(X, g_2) = e(\bar{g}, Y)$ holds; if not, output $\perp$ and abort. Then, taking as input a message $M \in \mathbb{Z}_p$, and a number $s \in \mathbb{Z}_p$, iteratively compute $(f_0, f_1, \cdots, f_{s-1})$ and $f(x)$ same as $\mathsf{Enc}(pp, pk, M, s)$ in Section 4.1.

It randomly chooses $A, r_1, r_2 \in \mathbb{Z}_p$, computes $C_3 = H_4(r_1) \oplus (M||r_1)$, $R = H_3(r_1||M||C_3)$, and outputs the ciphertext $CT = (s, C_1, C_2, C_3, C_4, C_5, C_6, C_7)$ as

$$\begin{aligned}
&C_1 = g_1^R, \quad C_2 = H_6\Big(e(X, H_1(ID))^R\Big) \oplus r_1, \\
&C_3 = H_4(r_1) \oplus (M||r_1), \\
&C_4 = g_1^{r_2}, \quad C_5 = Z^{r_2}, \\
&C_6 = H_4(e(X, H_2(ID))^{r_2}) \oplus (A||f(A)), \\
&C_7 = H_5(s||C_1||C_2||C_3||C_4||C_5||C_6||e(X, H_2(ID))^{r_2}||f_0||f_1||\cdots||f_{s-1}).
\end{aligned}$$

$\mathsf{Dec}(CT, sk)$: Taking as input a ciphertext $CT = (s, C_1, C_2, C_3, C_4, C_5, C_6, C_7)$ and a secret key $sk = (H_1(ID)^{\alpha x}, H_2(ID)^{\alpha x})$, the decrypt algorithm computes

$$r_1' = C_2 \oplus H_6(e(sk_1, C_1)), \;\; M'||r_1' = C_3 \oplus H_4(r_1'), \;\; R' = H_3(r_1'||M'||C_3).$$

It then computes

$$\begin{aligned}
&f_0' = H_3(M'||s), \quad f_1' = H_3(M'||s||f_0'), \quad \cdots, \\
&f_{s-1}' = H_3(M'||s||f_0'||\cdots||f_{s-2}')
\end{aligned}$$

and checks whether the following equations hold or not

$$\begin{aligned}
&C_1 = g_1^{R'}, \\
&f'(A') = f_0' + f_1'A' + \cdots + f_{s-1}'A'^{s-1}, \\
&C_7 = H_5(s||C_1||C_2||C_3||C_4||C_5||C_6||e(sk_2, C_4)||f_0'||f_1'||\cdots||f_{s-1}'),
\end{aligned}$$

where $A'||f'(A') = C_5 \oplus H_4(e(sk_2, C_4))$. If all the equations hold, it returns

$$M = M'.$$

Otherwise, it returns $\perp$.

The structures of the subsequent Aut, Proxy-Aut, and Test algorithms are essentially the same as the relevant algorithms in Section 4.1. Since these algorithms do not affect the security of the scheme, we will not elaborate further.

It is important to highlight that the enhanced scheme offers improved security, albeit with a slight increase in system parameter size, cipher size, and computation for encryption and decryption algorithms. In particular, the system parameters (pp) now incorporate an additional hash function. Furthermore, the cipher size increased by $2|\mathbb{Z}_p|$, and both the encryption and decryption algorithms entail two additional hash operations (denoted by 2H). By definition of FO transformation, our improved CLE-MET-PA scheme achieves IND-CCA security against adversaries without the trapdoor of the challenge ciphertext and OW-CCA security against adversaries with trapdoor of the challenge ciphertext.

7. Conclusions

In this work, we presented the notion of CLE-MET-PA, which integrates the characteristics of solving the key management problem in the public key encryption cryptosystem and addressing the key escrow problem in the IBE cryptosystem. It combines the feature of the multi-ciphertext equality test and supports proxy-assisted authorization, enhancing the practical use of the scheme. We formalized the system model and five security models for CLE-MET-PA, and proved that our scheme achieves OW-CPA/IND-CPA security. Finally, through an FO transformation, we obtained the improved version of CLE-MET-PA, which achieves OW-CCA/IND-CCA security.

Author Contributions: Conceptualization, S.D. and Z.Z.; methodology, S.D. and Z.Z.; writing—original draft preparation, S.D.; writing—review and editing, W.G. and S.Z.; supervision, B.W. All authors have read and agreed to the published version of the manuscript.

Funding: This research was funded by the National Natural Science Foundation of China under Grant 61972457, 62102299, 62002288, U19B2021, 62272362, 62202363, and the Youth Innovation Team of Shaanxi Universities, Science and Technology on Communication Security Laboratory Foundation (61421030202012103).

Data Availability Statement: Data sharing is not applicable.

Conflicts of Interest: The authors declare no conflict of interest.

References

1. Qian, L.; Luo, Z.; Du, Y.; Guo, L. Cloud computing: An overview. In Proceedings of the Cloud Computing: First International Conference, CloudCom 2009, Beijing, China, 1–4 December 2009; Proceedings 1; Springer: Berlin/Heidelberg, Germany, 2009; pp. 626–631.
2. Dillon, T.; Wu, C.; Chang, E. Cloud computing: Issues and challenges. In Proceedings of the 2010 24th IEEE International Conference on Advanced Information Networking and Applications, Perth, WA, Australia, 20–23 April 2010; pp. 27–33.
3. Zhang, C.; Hu, C.; Wu, T.; Zhu, L.; Liu, X. Achieving Efficient and Privacy-Preserving Neural Network Training and Prediction in Cloud Environments. *IEEE Trans. Dependable Secur. Comput.* **2022**, *20*, 4245–4257. [CrossRef]
4. Hu, C.; Zhang, C.; Lei, D.; Wu, T.; Liu, X.; Zhu, L. Achieving Privacy-Preserving and Verifiable Support Vector Machine Training in the Cloud. *IEEE Trans. Inf. Forensics Secur.* **2023**, *18*, 3476–3491. [CrossRef]
5. Goldreich, O.; Ostrovsky, R. Software protection and simulation on oblivious RAMs. *J. ACM (JACM)* **1996**, *43*, 431–473. [CrossRef]
6. Song, D.X.; Wagner, D.; Perrig, A. Practical techniques for searches on encrypted data. In Proceedings of the 2000 IEEE Symposium on Security and Privacy, S&P 2000, Berkeley, CA, USA, 14–17 May 2000; pp. 44–55.
7. Gentry, C. Fully homomorphic encryption using ideal lattices. In Proceedings of the Forty-First Annual ACM Symposium on Theory of Computing, Bethesda, MD, USA, 31 May–2 June 2009; pp. 169–178.
8. Boneh, D.; Di Crescenzo, G.; Ostrovsky, R.; Persiano, G. Public key encryption with keyword search. In Proceedings of the Advances in Cryptology-EUROCRYPT 2004: International Conference on the Theory and Applications of Cryptographic Techniques, Interlaken, Switzerland, 2–6 May 2004; Proceedings 23; Springer: Berlin/Heidelberg, Germany, 2004; pp. 506–522.
9. Yang, G.; Tan, C.H.; Huang, Q.; Wong, D.S. Probabilistic public key encryption with equality test. In Proceedings of the Topics in Cryptology-CT-RSA 2010: The Cryptographers' Track at the RSA Conference 2010, San Francisco, CA, USA, 1–5 March 2010; Proceedings; Springer: Berlin/Heidelberg, Germany, 2010; pp. 119–131.
10. Tang, Q. Public key encryption supporting plaintext equality test and user-specified authorization. *Secur. Commun. Netw.* **2012**, *5*, 1351–1362. [CrossRef]
11. Tang, Q. Towards public key encryption scheme supporting equality test with fine-grained authorization. In Proceedings of the Australasian Conference on Information Security and Privacy, ACISP 2011, Melbourne, Australia, 11–13 July 2011; Springer: Berlin/Heidelberg, Germany, 2011; pp. 389–406.
12. Huang, K.; Tso, R.; Chen, Y.C.; Rahman, S.M.M.; Almogren, A.; Alamri, A. PKE-AET: Public key encryption with authorized equality test. *Comput. J.* **2015**, *58*, 2686–2697. [CrossRef]
13. Ma, S.; Zhang, M.; Huang, Q.; Yang, B. Public key encryption with delegated equality test in a multi-user setting. *Comput. J.* **2015**, *58*, 986–1002. [CrossRef]
14. Ma, S.; Huang, Q.; Zhang, M.; Yang, B. Efficient public key encryption with equality test supporting flexible authorization. *IEEE Trans. Inf. Forensics Secur.* **2014**, *10*, 458–470. [CrossRef]
15. Ma, S. Identity-based encryption with outsourced equality test in cloud computing. *Inf. Sci.* **2016**, *328*, 389–402. [CrossRef]
16. Lee, H.T.; Ling, S.; Seo, J.H.; Wang, H. Semi-generic construction of public key encryption and identity-based encryption with equality test. *Inf. Sci.* **2016**, *373*, 419–440. [CrossRef]
17. Wu, T.; Ma, S.; Mu, Y.; Zeng, S. ID-based encryption with equality test against insider attack. In Proceedings of the Information Security and Privacy: 22nd Australasian Conference, ACISP 2017, Auckland, New Zealand, 3–5 July 2017; Proceedings, Part I 22; Springer: Berlin/Heidelberg, Germany, 2017; pp. 168–183.
18. Wu, L.; Zhang, Y.; Choo, K.K.R.; He, D. Efficient and secure identity-based encryption scheme with equality test in cloud computing. *Future Gener. Comput. Syst.* **2017**, *73*, 22–31. [CrossRef]
19. Alornyo, S.; Asante, M.; Hu, X.; Mireku, K.K. Encrypted traffic analytic using identity based encryption with equality test for cloud computing. In Proceedings of the 2018 IEEE 7th International Conference on Adaptive Science & Technology (ICAST), Accra, Ghana, 22–24 August 2018; pp. 1–4.

20. Li, H.; Huang, Q.; Ma, S.; Shen, J.; Susilo, W. Authorized equality test on identity-based ciphertexts for secret data sharing via cloud storage. *IEEE Access* **2019**, *7*, 25409–25421. [CrossRef]
21. Liao, Y.; Fan, Y.; Liang, Y.; Liu, Y.; Mohammed, R. Cryptanalysis of an identity-based encryption scheme with equality test and improvement. *IEEE Access* **2019**, *7*, 75067–75072. [CrossRef]
22. Ling, Y.; Ma, S.; Huang, Q.; Xiang, R.; Li, X. Group id-based encryption with equality test. In Proceedings of the Information Security and Privacy: 24th Australasian Conference, ACISP 2019, Christchurch, New Zealand, 3–5 July 2019; Proceedings 24; Springer: Berlin/Heidelberg, Germany, 2019; pp. 39–57.
23. Ming, Y.; Wang, E. Identity-based encryption with filtered equality test for smart city applications. *Sensors* **2019**, *19*, 3046. [CrossRef]
24. Susilo, W.; Duong, D.H.; Le, H.Q. Efficient post-quantum identity-based encryption with equality test. In Proceedings of the 2020 IEEE 26th International Conference on Parallel and Distributed Systems (ICPADS), Hong Kong, 2–4 December 2020; pp. 633–640.
25. Alornyo, S.; Zhao, Y.; Zhu, G.; Xiong, H. Identity Based Key-Insulated Encryption with Outsourced Equality Test. *Int. J. Netw. Secur.* **2020**, *22*, 257–264.
26. Ramadan, M.; Liao, Y.; Li, F.; Zhou, S.; Abdalla, H. IBEET-RSA: Identity-based encryption with equality test over RSA for wireless body area networks. *Mob. Networks Appl.* **2020**, *25*, 223–233. [CrossRef]
27. Lin, X.J.; Wang, Q.; Sun, L.; Qu, H. Identity-based encryption with equality test and datestamp-based authorization mechanism. *Theor. Comput. Sci.* **2021**, *861*, 117–132. [CrossRef]
28. Zhu, H.; Xue, Q.; Li, T.; Xie, D. Traceable Scheme of Public Key Encryption with Equality Test. *Entropy* **2022**, *24*, 309. [CrossRef]
29. Al-Riyami, S.S.; Paterson, K.G. Certificateless public key cryptography. In Proceedings of the International Conference on the Theory and Application of Cryptology and Information Security, Taipei, Taiwan, 30 November–4 December 2003; Springer: Berlin/Heidelberg, Germany, 2003; pp. 452–473.
30. Qu, H.; Yan, Z.; Lin, X.J.; Zhang, Q.; Sun, L. Certificateless public key encryption with equality test. *Inf. Sci.* **2018**, *462*, 76–92. [CrossRef]
31. Susilo, W.; Guo, F.; Zhao, Z.; Wu, G. PKE-MET: Public-key encryption with multi-ciphertext equality test in cloud computing. *IEEE Trans. Cloud Comput.* **2020**, *10*, 1476–1488. [CrossRef]
32. Fujisaki, E.; Okamoto, T. Secure integration of asymmetric and symmetric encryption schemes. In Proceedings of the Annual International Cryptology Conference, Santa Barbara, CA, USA, 15–19 August 1999; Springer: Berlin/Heidelberg, Germany, 1999; pp. 537–554. [CrossRef]
33. Fujisaki, E.; Okamoto, T. Secure integration of asymmetric and symmetric encryption schemes. *J. Cryptol.* **2013**, *26*, 80–101. [CrossRef]
34. Boneh, D.; Boyen, X.; Shacham, H. Short group signatures. In Proceedings of the Annual International Cryptology Conference, Santa Barbara, CA, USA, 15–19 August 2004; Springer: Berlin/Heidelberg, Germany, 2004; pp. 41–55.
35. Smart, N.P.; Vercauteren, F. On computable isomorphisms in efficient asymmetric pairing-based systems. *Discret. Appl. Math.* **2007**, *155*, 538–547. [CrossRef]
36. Galbraith, S.D.; Paterson, K.G.; Smart, N.P. Pairings for cryptographers. *Discret. Appl. Math.* **2008**, *156*, 3113–3121. [CrossRef]
37. Chatterjee, S.; Menezes, A. On cryptographic protocols employing asymmetric pairings—The role of Ψ revisited. *Discret. Appl. Math.* **2011**, *159*, 1311–1322. [CrossRef]
38. Boneh, D.; Franklin, M. Identity-based encryption from the Weil pairing. In Proceedings of the Annual International Cryptology Conference, Santa Barbara, CA, USA, 19–23 August 2001; Springer: Berlin/Heidelberg, Germany, 2001; pp. 213–229.
39. Boyen, X.; Mei, Q.; Waters, B. Direct chosen ciphertext security from identity-based techniques. In Proceedings of the 12th ACM Conference on Computer and Communications Security, Alexandria, VA, USA, 7–11 November 2005; pp. 320–329.
40. Zhao, M.; Ding, Y.; Tang, S.; Liang, H.; Yang, C.; Wang, H. Dual-server certificateless public key encryption with authorized equality test for outsourced IoT data. *J. Inf. Secur. Appl.* **2023**, *73*, 103441. [CrossRef]

electronics

Article

An Efficient and Secure Blockchain Consensus Protocol for Internet of Vehicles

Xueming Si [1,2,3], Min Li [1,2,3,*], Zhongyuan Yao [1,*], Weihua Zhu [1,2,3], Jianmei Liu [1] and Qian Zhang [4]

1 Frontier Information Technology Research Institute, Zhongyuan University of Technology, Zhengzhou 450007, China; 9770@zut.edu.cn (X.S.); 9773@zut.edu.cn (W.Z.); 6933@zut.edu.cn (J.L.)
2 Henan International Joint Laboratory of Blockchain and Data Sharing, Zhengzhou 450007, China
3 Henan Key Laboratory of Network Cryptography Technology, Zhengzhou 450007, China
4 College of Computer Science, Zhongyuan University of Technology, Zhengzhou 450007, China; 6382@zut.edu.cn
* Correspondence: 2021116578@zut.edu.cn (M.L.); yaozhongyuan@zut.edu.cn (Z.Y.)

Abstract: Conventional blockchain consensus protocols tailored for the Internet of Vehicles (IoV) usually face low transaction throughput, high latency, and elevated communication overhead issues. To address these issues, in this paper, we propose ESBCP, an efficient and secure blockchain consensus protocol for the IoV environment. Firstly, considering the significant performance differences among nodes in the IoV, we designed a blockchain consensus model for the IoV. Roadside units execute a trust evaluation mechanism to select high-quality vehicle nodes for the consensus process, thereby reducing the likelihood of malicious nodes in the consensus cluster. Secondly, we designed a node partition strategy to adapt to the dynamic feature of the IoV. Finally, addressing the mobility of nodes in the IoV, we introduced a dynamic unique node list. Vehicle nodes can promptly select nodes with high reliability from the list of communicable nodes to join their unique node list, while also promptly removing nodes with low reliability from their unique node list. Combining these strategies, we propose DK-PBFT, an improved Practical Byzantine Fault Tolerance consensus algorithm. The algorithm meets the efficiency and mobility requirements of vehicular networks. Through theoretical analysis, ESBCP could prevent external and internal security risks while reducing communication overhead. Experimental verification demonstrated that ESBCP effectively reduces consensus latency and improves transaction throughput. Our proposed ESBCP can be used in other application scenarios that require high consensus efficiency.

Keywords: blockchain; consensus protocols; IoV; trust evaluation mechanism; node partition strategy; dynamic unique node list

1. Introduction

1.1. Research Backgrounds

The Internet of Vehicles (IoV) is an open and integrated network that collaborates among vehicles, roads, people, and roadside infrastructure. It facilitates timely information sharing and cooperation between vehicles by integrating various information technologies [1]. The IoV plays a crucial role in the real world by enabling real-time communication and information sharing. It significantly contributes to areas such as traffic safety, traffic flow optimization, navigation, and emergency assistance. It brings a multitude of conveniences and improvements to the real-world transportation system. In 2020, German artist S. Weckert manipulated the navigation system of Google by slowly walking through the streets with a cart containing 99 mobile phones, tricking the entire Google navigation network into believing that the area was congested with traffic. This incident highlighted the potential security risks associated with such tactics, as research suggests that hackers could exploit this method to induce changes in traffic flow. Currently, the IoV still faces challenges such as inadequate data security assurance, potential leakage of user privacy, and vulnerability of nodes. These issues indirectly hinder the widespread application and technological development of the IoV. Blockchain has emerged as an effective solution for addressing several such issues. With the technological features of decentralization, anonymity, tamper resistance, and traceability, blockchain provides a solution for solving or alleviating security and device management issues in the IoV. However, the IoV exhibits characteristics such as a large-scale node population, dynamic changes in node locations, and mostly resource-constrained environments. Directly incorporating blockchain technology into the IoV would inevitably impact the efficiency of blockchain consensus, leading to a decrease in overall system performance. This would fail to meet the practical requirements of the IoV for high real-time performance and reliability. Therefore, proposing an efficient and secure blockchain consensus protocol tailored for the IoV environment becomes an urgent and critical issue that needs attention and resolution.

1.2. Related Work

Currently, there is relatively limited research on optimizing blockchain consensus protocols for the IoV. Considering the vulnerability of nodes in the IoV and the presence of malicious behavior, Byzantine Fault Tolerance (BFT) consensus algorithms, which possess Byzantine fault tolerance capabilities, are more suitable for IoV scenarios compared to other algorithms. Although the classical Practical Byzantine Fault Tolerance (PBFT) algorithm allows for a proportion of Byzantine nodes to be less than $1/3$ of all nodes, its efficiency sharply declines as the number of network nodes increases. Therefore, a substantial amount of improvement work has been proposed for PBFT. Generally, optimization strategies for PBFT algorithms can be roughly categorized into three types. The first type is controlling the number of participating consensus nodes. This category selects a subset of all system nodes as a committee. The committee nodes participate in the consensus process and then sends the consensus result to the remaining nodes, reducing communication overhead to enhance system scalability. The second type is optimizing the consensus process. This involves improving the selection method of the primary node or adding node evaluation mechanisms to reduce unnecessary communication, thereby increasing consensus efficiency. The third type is enhancing the consensus structure. This category introduces layered models or grouping concepts to reduce the number of required consensus communications, thereby improving consensus efficiency.

In terms of controlling the number of consensus nodes, ref. [2] proposes the VPBFT (PBFT based on Voting) consensus algorithm. It primarily focuses on categorizing nodes in the network into four types using a voting mechanism and assigning them different permissions to reduce the number of participating nodes in the consensus process. However, it does not consider the issue of communication overhead between nodes. Ref. [3] introduces the EPBFT (Extensible PBFT) consensus algorithm, which is designed for dynamic networks. This algorithm utilizes Verifiable Random Function (VRF) to select a subset of nodes to participate in the consensus process, thereby reducing the communication volume of PBFT. However, it does not address the communication latency issue caused by node mobility. Ref. [4] presents the G-PBFT (Geographic Practical Byzantine Fault Tolerance) consensus algorithm tailored for Internet of Things (IoT) scenarios. It achieves consensus using the geographical information of fixed devices, selecting nodes with relatively stable positions as endorsers to participate in PBFT consensus in order to reduce the cost of validating and recording transactions. However, it relies heavily on nodes with relatively stable positions, which are more susceptible to attacks and pose potential security risks.

In the aspect of optimizing the consensus process, ref. [5] proposes the OBFT (Optimistic Byzantine Fault Tolerance) consensus algorithm, which ensures the security and liveness of the algorithm by dynamically setting timeout periods, thereby improving its efficiency to a certain extent. However, for large-scale vehicular network scenarios, its scalability is limited. Based on SVM and PBFT, ref. [6] introduces a primary node selection strategy and incorporates a dynamically adjustable trust mechanism to enhance the security of the consensus system. However, it does not significantly improve throughput and consensus latency. Ref. [7] categorizes transactions into equal and unequal transactions, only publicly disclosing erroneous transactions, thereby reducing the number of consensus iterations and increasing the efficiency and scalability of blockchain consensus. The consensus coordinator used in this approach is centralized, which may face single point of failure issues. Additionally, when the system fails or restarts, this does not address the recovery of the coordinator. Ref. [8] presents the Improved Multi-Primary-Node Practical Byzantine Fault Tolerance (IMPBFT) consensus algorithm, which selects multiple primary nodes to jointly receive client transactions and introduces a pipeline to achieve concurrent execution of IMPBFT consensus, thus improving consensus efficiency. However, it requires an ample amount of resources, such as memory space and computing power for consensus execution, which is not feasible for the limited resources of vehicular network devices. Ref. [9] employs a reputation mechanism calculated through logistic regression to enhance the PBFT consensus process, In addition, it proposes R-PBFT (Reputed PBFT), a fast and intelligent consensus mechanism algorithm. It does not take into account the impact of a large number of mobile nodes in the network on consensus efficiency.

In terms of improving consensus structures, ref. [10] introduces the K-PBFT consensus mechanism, which employs an enhanced k-medoids clustering algorithm to cluster and hierarchically partition consensus nodes, optimizing the consensus process for large-scale consensus nodes. This allows the blockchain model to be applicable in a wider range of scenarios. Ref. [11] conducts node clustering based on location features and decomposes the consensus task to enhance the PBFT consensus algorithm, reducing the required communication for consensus. However, both Refs. [10,11] may have collusion or malicious behavior among nodes within clusters, posing a security risk to the system. Ref. [12] proposes a parallel consensus mechanism based on the DAG lattice structure, addressing the low efficiency caused by an excessive number of consensus nodes and node mobility of PBFT through network sharing. Nevertheless, maintaining the DAG lattice structure incurs high costs and can significantly impact the overall system performance. The DGBFT (Dynamic Grouping Byzantine Fault Tolerance Mechanism) consensus algorithm from ref. [13] groups nodes based on trust levels, effectively excluding malicious nodes and greatly reducing communication complexity. The SG-PBFT consensus algorithm from ref. [14] further improves system consensus efficiency by grouping nodes based on a scoring system. However, the communication complexity in refs. [13,14] remains unchanged compared with PBFT. When the number of system nodes is too high, their substantial communication overhead can greatly hinder consensus efficiency. Ref. [15] improves the PBFT algorithm by electing delegated agents to participate in local and global consensus based on trust levels, thereby enhancing consensus efficiency. Ref. [16] introduces the CDBFT consensus algorithm, dividing nodes into various organizations and selecting a representative node from each organization. This process involves two stages: intra-organizational consensus and representative node consensus, reducing the number of nodes participating in consensus and lowering communication overhead. Ref. [17] proposes C-PBFT (Concurrent PBFT), a two-tier PBFT consensus mechanism. Through an analysis of historical transactions, it divides supply chain nodes into several clusters. Each cluster's primary node is determined through reputation assessment to reduce communication overhead. However, the communication volume in refs. [15–17] remains at a quadratic level. With a large number of nodes, their consensus efficiency sharply decreases, indicating poor scalability.

The above solutions address some of the shortcomings of the classical PBFT consensus algorithm, to some extent improving the efficiency and scalability of the algorithm. However, current optimization work on PBFT algorithms has largely overlooked the specificity of the IoV environment and has not tailored optimizations according to the dynamic and heterogeneous nodes in the IoV. It is evident that existing work can only provide a research direction for how to propose an efficient and secure blockchain consensus mechanism suitable for the IoV environment. Further research is still needed to comprehensively address these issues.

1.3. Research Contributions

In this paper, we introduce Efficient Security Blockchain Consensus Protocol (ESBCP) tailored for the IoV. The algorithm addresses the issue of untrustworthy interactions when communicating with different neighboring vehicles through the implementation of a trust assessment mechanism. It incorporates a node partition mechanism to enhance the concurrency of consensus tasks, thereby accelerating the speed of the consensus process. Additionally, the dynamic unique node list ensures adaptability to the dynamic nature of IoV, thereby enhancing consensus stability. In light of this, our contributions in this paper are multifold.

(1) We propose a blockchain consensus model suitable for the IoV environment, employing a permissioned chain mechanism involving entities such as Onboard Units (OBUs) and Roadside Units (RSUs). The consensus process is divided into the Pre-prepare, Prepare1, Prepare2, Commit1, and Commit2 phases.
(2) Based on the above consensus model, we introduce the ESBCP consensus protocol tailored for the IoV environment. This protocol integrates various strategies including trust assessment mechanisms, node partition, Dynamic Unique Node List (DUNL), and improved consensus algorithms. It addresses the high latency and difficult adaptability issues present in the classical PBFT algorithm.
(3) We conduct detailed theoretical analysis and comparative experimental validation of the ESBCP consensus protocol. The theoretical analysis demonstrates the effectiveness of ESBCP in preventing external and internal security risks. The communication complexity of ESBCP is O(n). The protocol exhibits excellent scalability. Comparative experiments indicate that, in contrast to the CDBFT and SG-PBFT algorithms, ESBCP achieves lower latency, higher throughput, and is more suitable for large-scale IoV environments.

2. Preliminary Knowledge

2.1. Internet of Vehicles (IoV)

The IoV, also known as Vehicle to Everything (V2X), is a significant application of the Internet of Things (IoT) in the field of intelligent transportation. Through onboard devices, it involves real-time data collection from vehicles, including information on their driving status, speed, route, location, and environmental surroundings. This allows for the supervision of all vehicles, ultimately enhancing traffic efficiency. Leveraging modern information and communication technologies such as 5G [18,19], the IoV enables communication between vehicles and various entities, including Vehicle-to-Vehicle (V2V), Vehicle-to-Person (V2P), Vehicle-to-Road (V2R), Vehicle-to-Network (V2N), and Vehicle-to-Infrastructure (V2I), ultimately leading to connectivity between vehicles and everything. Consequently, the IoV not only connects vehicles to one another but also integrates them with pedestrians, roads, networks, and infrastructure, enabling efficient information perception, intelligent analysis, and secure sharing. The architecture of the IoV is illustrated in Figure 1. The IoV possesses characteristics such as real-time interconnectivity, vehicle sensing and recognition, data sharing and exchange, intelligent traffic management, safety and protection, vehicle autonomy, as well as data privacy and security. These features lay the foundation for achieving intelligent transportation, enhancing traffic safety, and providing more convenient travel experiences [20,21].

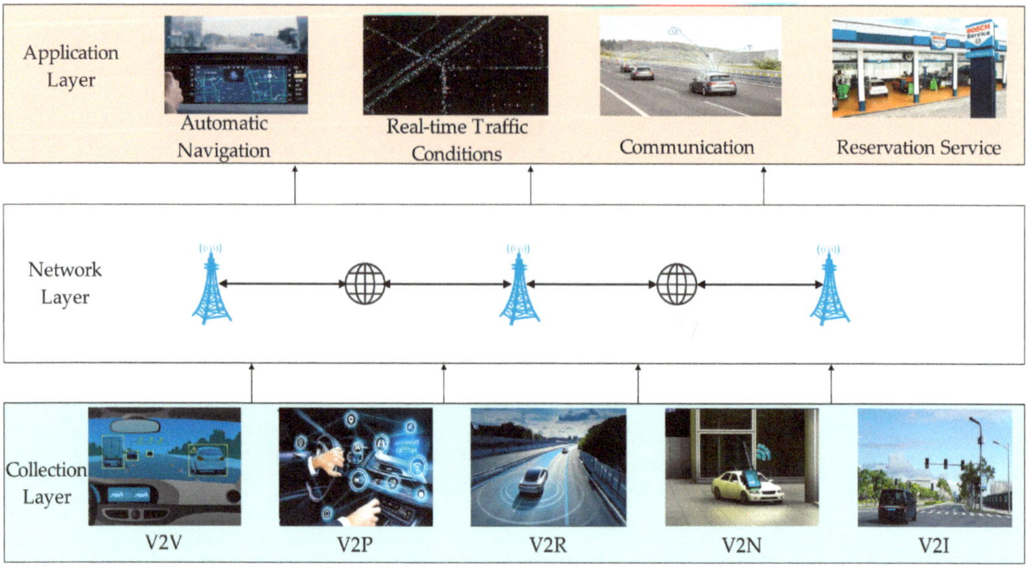

Figure 1. Architecture of the IoV.

2.2. Blockchain

Blockchain technology was initially introduced in a paper entitled "Bitcoin: A Peer-to-Peer Electronic Cash System". The paper was published by a scholar using the pseudonym "Satoshi Nakamoto" in 2008. Blockchain is a novel distributed ledger technology that combines P2P (Peer-to-Peer) networks, smart contracts, consensus mechanisms, cryptography, and other techniques [22–24]. The first block in a blockchain is known as the genesis block. Starting from the genesis block, transaction blocks with timestamps and hash values are linked together in chronological order. Each block records the hash value of its parent block, and contains all transaction information within the current time period. Blocks that have been verified by other nodes in the network are recorded in the blockchain and cannot be modified further. The structure of a blockchain is illustrated in Figure 2.

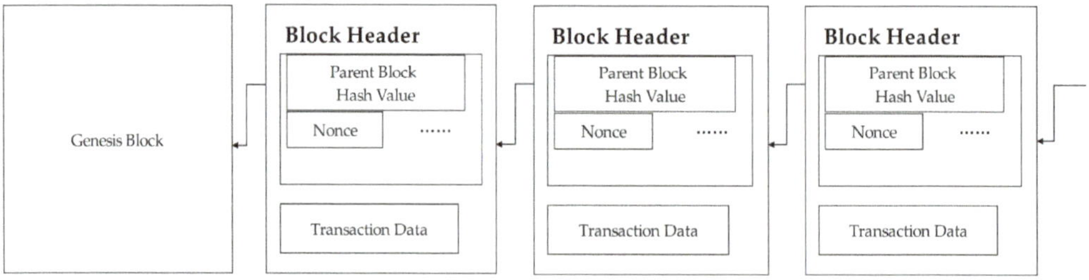

Figure 2. Blockchain structure.

2.3. PBFT Consensus Algorithm

The PBFT (Practical Byzantine Fault Tolerance) consensus algorithm is a Byzantine fault-tolerant algorithm based on state machine replication, designed for achieving consensus in distributed systems. This algorithm primarily consists of two protocols: the consistency protocol and the view-change protocol. Nodes are categorized into three roles: client, leader, and consensus node. It allows for a maximum of $F = (N - 1)/3$ Byzantine nodes, where N is the total number of nodes in the network and F represents the number of Byzantine nodes in the network. The consistency protocol is divided into five phases: request, pre-prepare, prepare, commit, and reply [25–27], as illustrated in Figure 3.

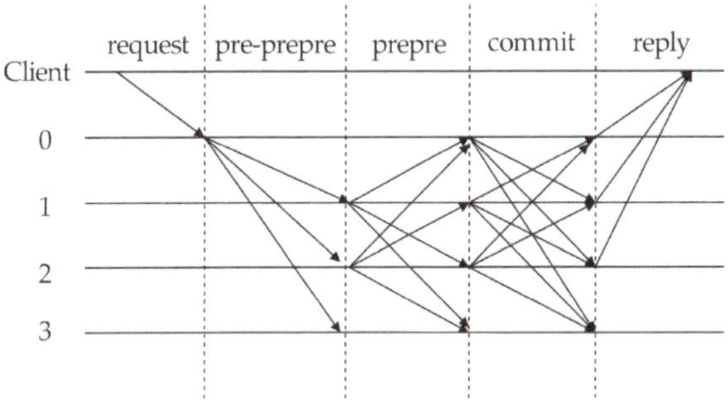

Figure 3. PBFT consensus process.

3. Blockchain Consensus Model for Vehicular Networks

The blockchain consensus model tailored for vehicular networks, as depicted in Figure 4, consists of three main components: the OBU section, the RSU section, and the blockchain section. Each of these components serves specific functions as outlined below:

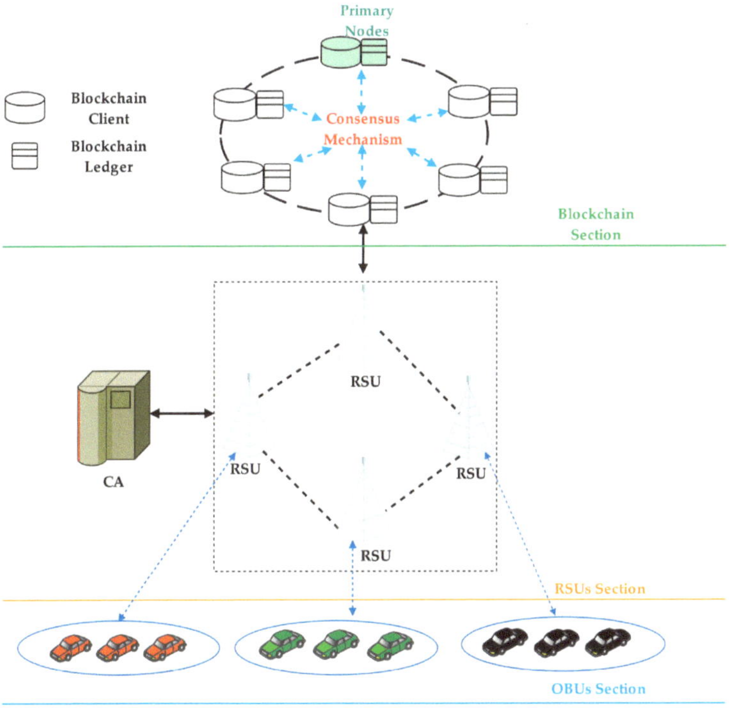

Figure 4. Blockchain consensus model tailored for vehicular networks.

OBU Section: Serving as the communication module of vehicles, it interacts with surrounding vehicles by sharing traffic information collected on the vehicle. It follows the principle of proximity and communicates with the nearest RSUs.

RSU Section: This section is responsible for collecting traffic information sent by vehicles and providing services related to vehicle access and authentication. It interacts with both the blockchain network and vehicle nodes. Additionally, all RSUs collectively maintain a ledger responsible for auditing and verifying the collected transaction information before recording it on the blockchain. Some authorized RSUs can undertake consensus work. Furthermore, RSUs also have the capability to monitor vehicle behavior, assess the credibility of messages sent by vehicles, and update ratings.

Blockchain Section: Based on the proposed blockchain consensus model tailored for vehicular networks, the primary nodes are η_1, which are selected from the RSU section. These primary nodes possess voting rights, block generation rights, and block verification rights. The remaining RSU nodes are responsible for voting and block verification. In the OBU section, high-quality vehicle nodes are selected as ordinary nodes in the consensus process. These nodes only have voting rights.

Based on this consensus model, the ESBCP consensus process is outlined as follows:

(1) RSUs select high-quality vehicle nodes from the OBU section to participate in consensus based on trust assessment algorithms and an improved algorithm using a unique node list.

(2) Node partition algorithm design is carried out by calculating the similarity between nodes based on communication delay, route hops, and distance.

(3) Consensus nodes in the blockchain section proceed with the corresponding partition's DK-PBFT (Dynamic K-medoids Practical Byzantine Fault Tolerance) consensus process. DK-PBFT includes the Pre-prepare, Prepare1, Prepare2, Commit1, and Commit2 phases.

4. ESBCP Consensus Protocol Design and Implementation

To address the challenges posed by the characteristics of large-scale nodes, mobility, and uncertain identities in vehicular network environments to the consensus mechanism in blockchain systems, we propose ESBCP, an efficient and secure blockchain consensus protocol tailored for vehicular networks. The protocol primarily comprises four core algorithms: trust assessment algorithm, node partition algorithm, unique node list improvement algorithm, and DK-PBFT consensus algorithm.

4.1. Trust Assessment Algorithm

The trust assessment algorithm evaluates the trustworthiness of vehicles by assessing their trust values. This resolves the issue of unreliable interactions when communicating with different neighboring vehicles [28]. The process is carried out by RSUs.

Definition: The trust value is an assessment of the credibility of the vehicles. It guides the selection of vehicles for communication based on their level of trustworthiness. The trust value of a vehicle node is primarily determined by two components: the global trust value and the V2V trust value. T represents the trust value of a vehicle node, GT represents the global trust value, and IT represents the trust value of the V2V.

Global Trust Value (GT): It refers to the trust generation set of the target vehicle in the retrospective time period [0, t]. Assuming r rounds of consensus have occurred within the interval [0, t], the calculation formula for the global trust value can be represented by Formulas (1) and (2).

$$GT(i)_r = \frac{1}{1 + e^{(\zeta \sum_{u=1}^{r} d_u + \xi \sum_{u=1}^{r} \omega_u - \psi \sum_{u=1}^{r} \chi_u - \varsigma \sum_{u=1}^{r} c_u)}} \tag{1}$$

$$GT(i)_{cur}^{acc} = (1 - \updownarrow)GT(i)_r + \updownarrow GT(i)_{cur-1}^{acc} \tag{2}$$

where d_u represents the online status of vehicular network nodes in the u-th consensus round, where 1 signifies offline and 0 signifies online. ζ is the penalty coefficient for offline vehicular network nodes. ω_u represents the number of invalid transactions submitted by vehicular network nodes in the u-th consensus round. ξ is the penalty coefficient of malicious transactions. χ_u represents the number of legitimate transactions submitted by vehicular network nodes in the u-th consensus round. ψ is the reward coefficient of real transactions. c_u represents the participation outcome of the vehicular network nodes in the u-th consensus round, where 1 denotes success and 0 denotes failure. ς is the weight coefficient for rewards granted after consensus success. $GT(i)_r$ represents the global trust value of the i-th node in the r-th consensus round. $GT(i)_{cur}^{acc}$ represents the current global trust value of vehicle node i. $GT(i)_{cur-1}^{acc}$ represents the historical global trust value of node i. $\updownarrow$ represents the weight coefficient of historical trust values.

Interactive Trust Value (IT) in V2V: It refers to the comprehensive rating provided by all vehicles within the communication range of the RSUs, based on their interactions with the target vehicle during the time interval [0, t].

The calculation formula for IT can be represented by Formula (3).

$$IT(m,i,t) = \frac{\sum_{\lambda_\mu \in \gamma_g(m,i,t)} y(\lambda_\mu) \cdot f_g}{\sum_{\lambda_\mu \in \gamma_g(m,i,t)} y(\lambda_\mu)} \tag{3}$$

where λ_μ represents the μ-th interaction event, $\gamma_g(m,i,t)$ represents all interaction events collected by RSU m about target vehicle i during time t, and $y(\lambda_\mu)$ represents the deviation coefficient of the evaluation of event λ_μ by the vehicles.

The trust value of the i-th vehicle node is denoted as $T(i)$. The calculation formula for $T(i)$ can be expressed using Formula (4).

$$T(i) = \frac{\delta_G \cdot GT(i)_{cur}^{acc} + \delta_I \cdot IT(m,i,t)}{\sum_{X \in (G,I)} \delta_X} \tag{4}$$

where G and I respectively represent global trust and V2V trust. X represents one of G and I. $\forall X \in (G,I)$, $\delta_X \in [0,\ 1]$; δ_G represents the reliability coefficient of the global trust value, while δ_I represents the reliability coefficient of the V2V trust value.

The pseudocode of the trust value calculation algorithm is shown in Algorithm 1.

Algorithm 1: Trust Value Calculation

Input: $(\lambda_p, L[]), GT(i)_{cur-1}^{acc}, t, t_1$
Output: $T(i)$

set $T(i)_0^{acc} \leftarrow 0$; $Num \leftarrow count(L)$; $r \leftarrow \frac{t}{t_1}$;
  for $i = 0; i < Num; i++$ **do**
    for $u = 1; u < r+1; u++$
      $compute\ GT(i)_r$;
    if $GT(i)_{cur-1}^{acc} = 0$ **then**
      $GT(i)_{cur}^{acc} \leftarrow GT(i)_r$;
    else
      $compute\ GT(i)_{cur}^{acc}$;
    end if
  end for
  $Receive(\gamma_j(m,i,t))$;
  $compute\ IT(m,i,t)$;
  $compute\ T(i)$;
end for

According to Algorithm 1, vehicle i can register with the Certificate Authority (CA) to obtain the initial global trust value, denoted as $T(i)_0^{acc}$. During the process of information sharing, the real-time behavioral attributes of a vehicle node are defined as set $RB = \{d, \omega, \chi, c\}$. This mechanism utilizes RB to dynamically generate a trust value, denoted as $T(i)_{cur}^{acc}$ for vehicle node i. This facilitates the prompt acquisition of the trust value of senders, denoted as $T(i)_{cur}^{acc}$. Additionally, the V2V trust value, denoted as $IT(m,i,t)$, is computed based on the interaction event $\gamma_j(m,i,t)$ collected by RSUs. Finally, the vehicle trust value, denoted as $T(i)$, is derived from both the global trust value and V2V trust value.

As vehicles continue to send messages, $T(i)$ will also undergo continuous changes. This system efficiently achieves trust evaluation, effectively reducing the presence of malicious nodes. In this mechanism, vehicle nodes are not involved in the calculation process, they only engage in message communication. RSUs verify the messages sent by vehicle nodes, and the server completes the corresponding trust value calculation. The trust values of vehicle nodes are transmitted, stored, and maintained within the blockchain network.

4.2. Node Partition Algorithm

In the IoV, there are large numbers of vehicles and devices involved. By partitioning the nodes, consensus tasks can be processed in parallel. The consensus process in different partitions can proceed simultaneously, thus accelerating the overall consensus process and improving its efficiency. The optimization of node partition adapts the consensus algorithm to the specific environment and requirements of the IoV, ensuring an efficient and stable consensus process within the complex IoV network.

K-medoids clustering, an optimization of the k-means clustering algorithm, is a partition-based unsupervised clustering algorithm [29–31]. The k-medoids clustering algorithm attempts to iterate through all sample points within the current cluster, calculating the sum of distances to other sample points, and then selects the optimal point as the new center. To better align the k-medoids clustering algorithm with the PBFT consensus algorithm, efforts are made to assign nodes with lower communication latency and closer distances to the same cluster. Therefore, the similarity between nodes is calculated based on communication latency, routing hop count, and distance.

The communication latency between nodes can be represented by Formula (5).

$$T = \begin{bmatrix} t_{11} & t_{12} & \cdots & t_{1n} \\ t_{21} & t_{22} & \cdots & t_{2n} \\ \vdots & \vdots & \ddots & \vdots \\ t_{n1} & t_{n2} & \cdots & t_{nn} \end{bmatrix} \tag{5}$$

where T represents the matrix of communication latency between nodes, $t_{i,j}$ represents the communication latency between nodes i and j (when i equals j, t_{ij} denotes the latency between the node and itself, which is 0), and n represents the total number of vehicle nodes.

Similarly, the routing hop count between nodes can be expressed using Formula (6).

$$R = \begin{bmatrix} r_{11} & r_{12} & \cdots & r_{1n} \\ r_{21} & r_{22} & \cdots & r_{2n} \\ \vdots & \vdots & \ddots & \vdots \\ r_{n1} & r_{n2} & \cdots & r_{nn} \end{bmatrix} \tag{6}$$

where R represents the matrix of routing hop count between nodes, and $r_{i,j}$ represents the routing hop count between nodes i and j (when i equals j, $r_{i,j}$ denotes the hop count between the node and itself, which is 0).

Similarly, the distance between nodes can be expressed using Formula (7).

$$D = \begin{bmatrix} d_{11} & d_{12} & \cdots & d_{1n} \\ d_{21} & d_{22} & \cdots & d_{2n} \\ \vdots & \vdots & \ddots & \vdots \\ d_{n1} & d_{n2} & \cdots & d_{nn} \end{bmatrix} \tag{7}$$

where D represents the matrix of distances between nodes, and $d_{i,j}$ represents the distance between nodes i and j (when i equals j, d_{ij} denotes the distance between the node and itself, which is 0).

The specific steps for clustering n vehicle nodes into k groups are as follows:

Step 1: Set the current iteration count NI = 0. Select the initial k nodes with the highest trust values from n vehicle nodes.

Step 2: Utilize Formula (8) to calculate the similarity between each non-central point and all central points. Simultaneously, apply the proximity principle to cluster the nodes, thereby forming a collection of clusters, denoted as $\{C_1, C2, \ldots, C_k\}$.

$$Dist(\overline{X_i}, \overline{Y_j}) = \sqrt{t_{ij} r_{ij} d_{ij}} \tag{8}$$

Step 3: Successively, within each cluster, non-central nodes take turns replacing the central node, and the total cost resulting from this substitution is calculated using Formulas (9) and (10). When Cost is less than 0, the node is used to replace the central point; otherwise, it remains unchanged.

$$E = \sum_{i=1}^{k} \sum_{p \in C_i} |p - q_i|^2 \tag{9}$$

$$\text{Cost} = E_{cur} - E_{pre} \tag{10}$$

where p represents the non-central points within the cluster, q_i denotes the central point of cluster C_i, and E signifies the sum of squares of deviations of all nodes within the cluster.

Step 4: After updating the initially generated cluster set and obtaining the optimal cluster set $\{C_1, C2, \ldots, C_k\}$ composed of the best k central points, we partition the remaining vehicle nodes based on the nearest principle. If there are no updates to the cluster set, skip Step 4. If there are too few nodes in a partition, expand the partition range. Conversely, if there are too many nodes in a partition, reduce the partition range. Ensure that the number of nodes in each partition remains within a specified range.

4.3. Improved UNL Algorithm

In applications combining blockchain and the IoV, trustworthiness plays a crucial role. The concept of UNL from the Ripple Protocol Consensus Algorithm (RPCA) can be introduced to enhance the trustworthiness of nodes. However, the original UNL in the RPCA consensus algorithm has some limitations, such as its static nature, meaning nodes cannot be changed once added, and its lack of adaptability, as it cannot dynamically respond to the dynamic changes of vehicle nodes in the IoV [32–36]. To address these issues, we introduce the concept of a Dynamic Unique Node List (DUNL), allowing nodes in the IoV to dynamically select or exclude nodes from the UNL based on their trust values, thus filtering out more reliable nodes for inclusion in the UNL. Building on the previously discussed node partition and trust assessment mechanism, we enhanced the UNL in the RPCA consensus algorithm. Initially, vehicle nodes in their respective partitions exclude any abnormal nodes. Subsequently, they calculate the reliability of nodes in the list of communicable nodes. Based on this reliability, nodes are selected in descending order of trustworthiness to join the UNL, thereby improving the UNL in the RPCA consensus algorithm. The specific formula for calculating reliability is shown in Formula (11).

$$R_{i,j} = (l_1 \times T_{i,j} - l_2 \times v_{i,j} - l_3 \times \tau_{i,j} - l_4 \times \varphi_{i,j}) \times t_{i,j} \tag{11}$$

where $R_{i,j}$ represents the reliability of the j-th node in the list of communicable nodes of the i-th vehicle node. $T_{i,j}$, $v_{i,j}$, $\tau_{i,j}$, $\varphi_{i,j}$ respectively denote the trust value, offline time, number of invalid transactions provided, and delay time of the j-th node in the list of communicable nodes of the i-th vehicle node. l_1 represents the weight coefficient for trust value, l_2 represents the weight coefficient for offline time, l_3 represents the weight coefficient for the number of invalid transactions provided, and l_4 represents the weight coefficient for delay time. $t_{i,j}$ represents the remaining online time of the j-th node in the list of communicable nodes of the i-th vehicle node. In case of equal reliabilities, one is randomly selected to be added to the UNL. Therefore, when i vehicle detects event λ_μ, it sends the event message to the vehicle nodes in the UNL and reports it to the nearest RSUs, reducing event verification time and effectively reducing the likelihood of congestion.

4.4. DK-PBFT Consensus Algorithm

The vehicle nodes in the blockchain network, after undergoing authorization and verification by the CA, join the blockchain network. Simultaneously, they will have trust values and a DUNL. Both the trust values and DUNL will undergo dynamic updates.

In this paper, the nodes participating in the IoV are categorized based on the roles they assume and the functions they perform within the system, as outlined in Table 1.

Table 1. Node descriptions.

Node Type	Node Description	Node Rights
Primary Node	Trusted, selected from RSUs	Voting Rights, Block Generation Rights, Block Verification Rights
General RSU Node	Trusted	Voting Rights, Block Verification Rights
Normal Node	Vehicle nodes ensuring correct and timely message communication	Voting Rights
Abnormal Node	Experiencing malfunction or engaged in malicious behavior	No rights granted

Due to the inherent high trustworthiness of RSUs, a select number of RSUs are chosen as the primary nodes of the consensus group, while the remaining nodes function as regular nodes. The DK-PBFT consensus algorithm, in order to enhance the unpredictability of primary node selection, employs a Verifiable Random Function (VRF) to select multiple primary nodes from the RSUs. Within a partition, the DK-PBFT encompasses a total of N nodes, with η_1 being primary nodes. The client, serving as the initiator of the request, broadcasts the request message to the blockchain network in the form of a transaction request during the request phase. The primary nodes primarily handle the reception of request messages and sort transactions m_s based on timestamps.

Upon receiving a request from the client, the primary nodes engage in the consensus process with the other consensus nodes, as illustrated in Figure 5. Client represents the client; nodes 0 and 5 are primary nodes; nodes 1, 4, and 8 are normal nodes; nodes 2 and 7 are general RSUs nodes; and nodes 3, 6, and 9 are abnormal nodes.

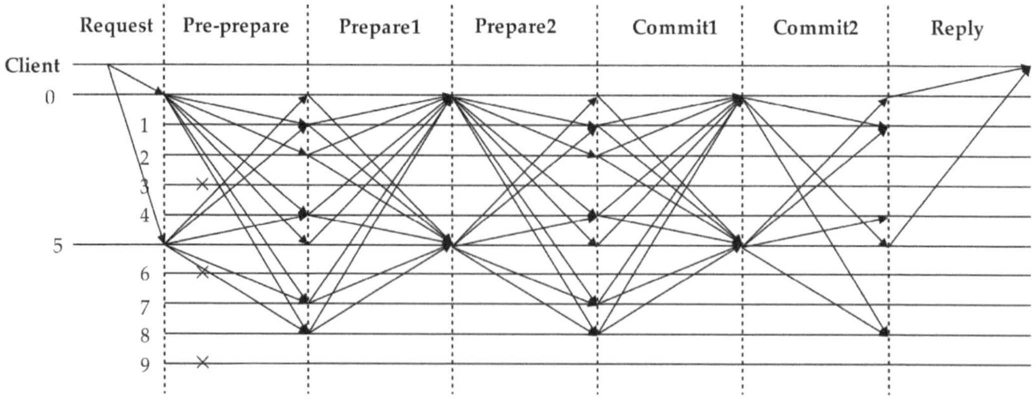

Figure 5. Process of the DK-PBFT consensus algorithm.

After implementing the node partition algorithm, each partition can independently engage in the DK-PBFT algorithm consensus. The pseudocode for the DK-PBFT consensus algorithm is presented in Algorithm 2, and the main process of the optimized DK-PBFT is illustrated in Figure 5. The DK-PBFT consensus mechanism encompasses five phases to complete a round of consensus:

(1) Pre-prepare Phase: After verifying the signature of the received request information $< Request, o, t, sign(o), s >$, each primary node broadcasts a pre-prepare message $<< Pre-prepare, sign(m_s), s >, m_s >$ to other primary nodes. In this message, $Pre-prepare$ identifies the pre-prepare message for consensus, $sign(m_s)$ represents the signature of the primary node on pre-prepare message m_s, s is the sequence number assigned by the primary nodes to message m_s, and message comprises the original transaction request set with the signature of the client. Primary nodes also broadcast pre-prepare messages to the participating consensus nodes in their respective vicinity.

(2) Prepare1 Phase: Upon receiving the Pre-prepare message from the primary nodes, the consensus nodes first verify the signature $sign(m_s)$ and sequence number s of the message. After successful verification, it takes the union of transactions m_s from different primary nodes and sorts them based on timestamps. The resulting transaction set is denoted as M. The consensus node then sends a message $<< Prepare1, H(M), sign(H(M)) >, M >$ to the primary nodes, where $H(M)$ is the hash value of transaction set M.

(3) Prepare2 Phase: When the primary nodes receive the Prepare1 message from more than $\frac{2N}{3}$ nodes, it compares the hash values from each message. If the hash values from more than $\frac{N}{3}$ nodes are the same, the primary nodes broadcast a message $<< Prepare2, Prepare1set, sign(H(M) \parallel Prepare1set >, Prepare1set >$ to all nodes, where $Prepare1set$ represents the collection of $Prepare1$ messages received by the primary nodes.

(4) Commit1 Phase: After receiving the Prepare2 message, normal nodes vote on the message and then send the voting information $Vote(Prepare2)$ back to the primary nodes.

(5) Commit2 Phase: When the master node receives the Commit1 message from over $\frac{2N}{3}$ nodes, it performs a weighted calculation to decide whether to add the information $Vote(Prepare2)$ shared by these vehicle nodes to the blockchain. After successful verification, the primary nodes package these transactions into a block. The primary nodes broadcast this block to all RSU nodes. When the block is validated by all consensus nodes, it signifies the completion of consensus and successful blockchain integration.

RSUs update the trust values and DUNL based on the consensus results.

Algorithm 2: DK-PBFT

Input: *Request*
Output: *result*

$NodePartition();$
while $< Request, o, t, sign(o), s >= True$ **do**
  broadcast $<< Pre-prepare, sign(m_s), s >, m_s >;$
  if $< Pre-prepare >= True$
    $order(m_s);$
    $M = m_1 \cup m_2 \cup \cdots \cup m_s;$
    $send << Prepare1, H(M), sign(H(M)) >, M >;$
  end if
  if $Total(Prepare1) > \frac{2N}{3}$
   if $Total(samehash) > \frac{N}{3}$
     $send << Prepare2, Prepare1set, sign(H(M) \parallel Prepare1set >, Prepare1set >;$
   end if

```
    end if
     if Receive(Prepare2) = True
        Vote(Prepare2);
     end if
      if Total(Commit1) > 2N/3
         Update(T(i));
      end if
      if < Commit2 >= True then
      do < Request, o, t, sign(o), s >;
      reply to the client;
      end if
      VerifyBlock();
      chain(block);
      TrustValueCalculation();
      DUNL();
       return result;
end while
```

5. Theoretical Analysis

In this section, we will analyze ESBCP from two aspects: security and communication overhead.

5.1. Security Analysis

In the scenario of combining blockchain with the IoV, security is of importance. If the blockchain were to be subjected to an attack, it could lead to the exposure of user information, vehicle location data, and other private data, potentially even causing serious consequences such as traffic accidents. In this context, we primarily consider two types of security risks. Firstly, there is the external security risk, where non-members of the IoV may attempt to impersonate existing nodes within the IoV to deceive the system and become part of the network. Secondly, there is the internal security risk, where properly registered and validly signed IoV nodes may become potential security vulnerabilities due to malicious attacks.

To address these two security risks, we employed a permissioned chain mechanism in the constructed blockchain. Every vehicle intending to participate in the IoV must be approved by the CA before being able to join the IoV and utilize shared data. Upon joining the IoV, each vehicle entity possesses its own public–private key pair, and any transaction or message requires the signature of its private key. In this way, when a vehicle receives any message or transaction, the system first verifies if the signature is correct and simultaneously checks if the corresponding public key address is in the permission list. If the signature is incorrect or the sending vehicle is not in the permission list, the message sent will be rejected, effectively preventing these two security risks.

ESBCP further safeguards the security and reliability of the IoV by restricting participation in the consensus to authorized and legitimate vehicles. This approach effectively hinders potential attacks, ensuring the integrity and accuracy of the IoV consensus. In the dynamically changing environment of the IoV, by partitioning nodes and selecting high-quality nodes to participate in the consensus, we can ensure that the consensus algorithm operates efficiently and stably in the complex IoV network.

5.2. Communication Overhead Analysis

Traditional PBFT consensus algorithms consume significant communication resources. To comprehensively evaluate the performance of ESBCP, let us assume there are a total of N nodes in the IoV, with η being the number of RSU nodes, and η_1 being the number of primary nodes. As shown in Figure 5, the DK-PBFT consensus algorithm is divided into five phases. In the pre-prepare phase, each primary node broadcasts the pre-prepare message, resulting in a maximum communication volume of $\eta_1(\mathrm{N}-1)$ in this phase. In the two prepare phases, vehicle nodes communicate with primary nodes, resulting in a total communication volume of up to $2\eta_1(N-1)$. In the first commit phase, vehicle nodes communicate with primary nodes, resulting in a total communication volume of up to $2\eta_1(N-1)$. In the second commit phase, primary nodes communicate with other RSU nodes, with a maximum communication volume of $\eta_1(\eta-1)$.

In this paper, we list the communication overhead required for one round of consensus for the ESBCP, PBFT, SG-PBFT, and CDBFT consensus algorithms according to the consensus stages, as shown in Table 2. It can be observed that the communication complexity of the PBFT, SG-PBFT, and CDBFT consensus algorithms are all $O(N^2)$, while the consensus mechanism proposed in this paper has a communication complexity of O(N). This indicates that the communication overhead of the DK-PBFT consensus algorithm proposed in this paper is much lower than that of the traditional PBFT, SG-PBFT, and CDBFT. Although the DK-PBFT adds two phases and requires RSU nodes to verify blocks in later stages, which consumes additional communication resources, it enhances the security of the system.

Table 2. Byzantine consensus algorithm communication overhead comparison.

Consensus Phase	PBFT	CDBFT	SG-PBFT	ESBCP
Request	1	1	1	η_1
Pre-prepare	$N-1$	$N-1$	$N/2-1$	$\eta_1(N-1)$
Prepare	$(N-1)^2$	$(N-1)^2$	$(N/2-1)(N/2-1)$	$2\eta_1(N-1)$
Commit	$N(N-1)$	$N(N-1)$	$N/2-1$	$\eta_1(N-1)+\eta_1(N-1)$
Reply	N	N	N	η_1
Total	$2N^2-N+1$	$2N^2-N+1$	$N^2/4+N$	$4\eta_1 N-3\eta_1+\eta_1\eta$

6. Experimental Analysis

To comprehensively evaluate the performance of ESBCP, we conducted simulated experiments and compared the performance with existing CDBFT algorithms. The simulation experiments utilized Go to simulate the consensus process of the improved consensus algorithm. The hardware environment consisted of an AMD 2.10 GHz Ryzen 5 5500U processor and 16 GB of memory, running on a 64-bit Windows 11 operating system. The speed of vehicular network nodes, denoted as 'mv', was 12 m per second (12 m/s). These nodes maintained a constant speed throughout the simulation. Dynamic routing was employed in the experiment. This process was simulated without specific content, focusing solely on aspects crucial for the blockchain component. The following assumptions were made about the network environment: (1) sufficient computational power for RSUs; (2) malicious nodes in the network are less than 1/3; (3) the total number of nodes in the network is N, with the actual nodes participating in consensus denoted as N1. Let N1/N = a, where a represents the ratio of actual nodes participating in consensus to the total number of nodes in the network. Considering the differences in transaction quantity per block, input parameters for concurrent transactions by vehicle nodes, and road conditions in each experiment, we conducted each experiment 10 times, taking the average as the final result to reduce errors.

6.1. Consensus Latency

Consensus latency refers to the total duration from the request phase to the reply phase in communication. A consensus algorithm with shorter latency leads to faster transaction confirmation speeds, thus leading to higher efficiency in vehicular networks. In this paper, the consensus latency of the two algorithms was compared under the same latency environment, with node quantities of 100, 200, 300, 400, 500, and 600 tested to observe the impact of node quantity on consensus latency. As shown in Figure 6, with an increase in node quantity, the CDBFT consensus algorithm exhibits an upward trend in consensus latency. In contrast, ESBCP, through a trust evaluation mechanism, comprehensively considers the performance of vehicle nodes and reasonably allocates rights. Additionally, each vehicle node maintains a unique node list, thereby excluding nodes with poor performance or malicious behavior. Ultimately, this stabilizes and maintains the consensus latency at a relatively low and stable level. The CDBFT consensus algorithm only selects nodes to construct blocks based on reputation values without a comprehensive evaluation of node performance. Therefore, the consensus latency of ESBCP is superior to that of the CDBFT consensus algorithm.

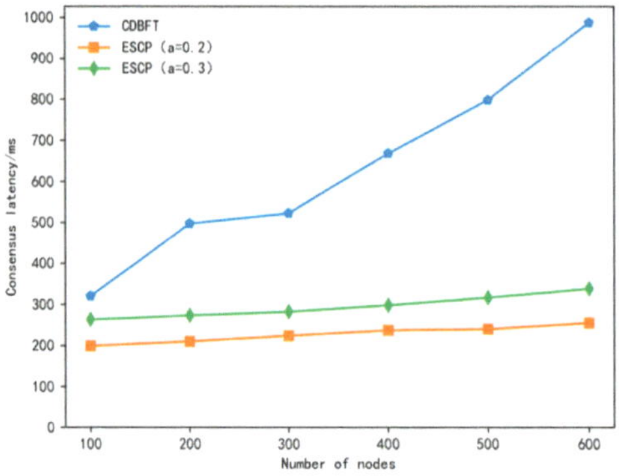

Figure 6. The impact of node quantity on consensus latency.

6.2. Throughput

Throughput, measured in Transactions Per Second (TPS), refers to the quantity of transactions processed by a network within a given unit of time. It quantifies the capability of the consensus algorithm to handle transactional data. The magnitude of TPS reflects the efficiency of this process. The definition of throughput is illustrated in Formula (12).

$$TPS = \frac{SUM}{pe} \tag{12}$$

where pe represents the time interval, while SUM signifies the number of transactions processed within time pe.

In this paper, a comparison of the throughput of the two algorithms was conducted under the same latency environment, with node quantities set at 100, 200, 300, 400, 500, and 600. As shown in Figure 7, the throughput of the CDBFT consensus algorithm exhibits a declining trend as the number of vehicle nodes increases. This is attributed to the significant increase in network bandwidth pressure due to extensive communication overhead between nodes, leading to a notable increase in consensus latency and subsequently a decrease in throughput. ESBCP maintains a relatively stable throughput with a slight decline as the number of nodes increases. This is attributed to the parameter 'a' being set, resulting in a gradual growth of participating vehicle nodes in consensus, which remains at a constant quantity. This significantly alleviates the bandwidth pressure from inter-node communications. Additionally, ESBCP introduces a trusted node list and proposes node partition strategies based on communication latency, routing hops, and distance between nodes to mitigate the impact of offline nodes or malicious behavior on block consensus efficiency. While the CDBFT consensus algorithm completes block consensus through representative nodes, it does not account for the impact of representative vehicle nodes going offline. Therefore, the throughput of the ESBCP consensus algorithm surpasses that of CDBFT.

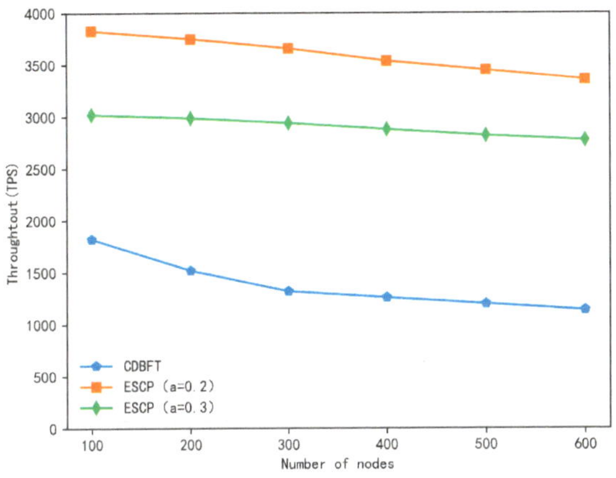

Figure 7. The impact of node quantity on throughput.

6.3. Malicious Node Precision

In this paper, Malicious Node Precision (MNP) refers to the proportion of vehicle nodes identified as malicious among those with low reliability and trust values, utilizing the credit assessment mechanism and dynamic unique node list. It serves as a metric to gauge the accuracy of the vehicular network system in identifying malicious nodes. The calculation formula for MNP in vehicular networks is shown in Formula (13).

$$\text{MNP} = \text{TP}/(\text{TP} + \text{FP}) \tag{13}$$

where TP (True Positive) represents the number of correctly predicted malicious nodes, and FP (False Positive) represents the number of normal nodes incorrectly predicted as malicious.

By selecting node quantities of 100, 200, 300, 400, 500, and 600, with malicious node ratios set at 5%, 10%, 15%, and 20%, the analysis of the impact of malicious node quantity on the precision of ESBCP is presented in Figure 8. It is observed that ESBCP consistently maintains the MNP over 90%. Building upon the PBFT consensus algorithm, the integration of trust assessment mechanisms and UNL effectively detects malicious nodes, thereby enhancing the quality of participating consensus nodes. The trust values between normal and malicious nodes are distinctly differentiated. Consequently, as both the node quantity and malicious node ratio increase, the precision of ESBCP exhibits a slight upward trend.

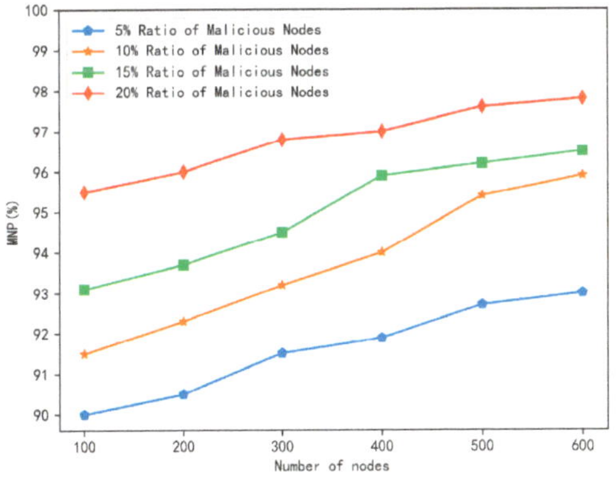

Figure 8. The impact of malicious node ratio on precision.

6.4. Malicious Node Recall

In this paper, Malicious Node Recall (MNR) refers to the proportion of malicious nodes detected among vehicle nodes with low reliability and trust values, utilizing the credit assessment mechanism and DUNL. It measures the performance of system in discovering all malicious nodes. MNR can be calculated using Formula (14).

$$\mathrm{MNR} = \mathrm{TP}/(\mathrm{TP} + \mathrm{FN}) \quad (14)$$

where FN (False Negative) represents the number of samples that are actually malicious nodes but incorrectly predicted as normal nodes.

By selecting node quantities of 100, 200, 300, 400, 500, and 600, with malicious node ratios set at 5%, 10%, 15%, and 20%, the analysis of the impact of malicious node ratio on the MNR of ESBCP is presented in Figure 9. It is observed that as the number of nodes in the network increases, the MNR of ESBCP exhibits an upward trend. However, with an increase in the proportion of malicious nodes, the MNR of ESBCP shows a slight decline. As the number of nodes participating in the network increases, the trust assessment mechanism of ESBCP and DUNL effectively differentiate between normal and malicious nodes, resulting in an increase in MNR. Additionally, as the proportion of malicious nodes gradually increases, ESBCP completes block validation consensus through RSUs, preventing malicious nodes participating in consensus from having the opportunity to launch attacks. This results in their performance during consensus being similar to that of normal nodes, categorizing them as general nodes. As a result, the MNR of ESBCP shows a slight decrease.

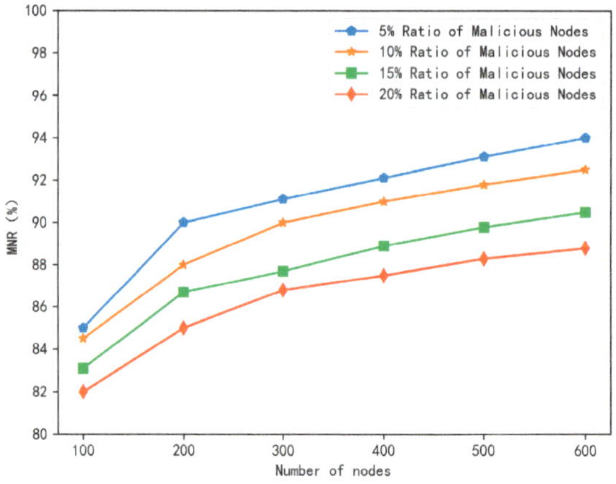

Figure 9. The impact of malicious node proportion on MNR.

7. Conclusions

In this paper, we propose ESBCP, an efficient and secure consensus protocol for blockchain tailored to the IoV. ESBCP features lightweight characteristics and is well-suited for resource-constrained IoV environments, especially in scenarios where vehicle nodes have limited computational and communication capabilities, demonstrating high operational efficiency. By integrating IoV node trust assessment algorithms, node partition algorithms, dynamic unique node list algorithms, and the DK-PBFT consensus algorithm, this protocol effectively reduces consensus latency and enhances system throughput. The theoretical analysis indicated that ESBCP can effectively prevent external and internal security risks, improving the overall security of the IoV system while ensuring good scalability. Experimental validation demonstrated that ESBCP significantly increases throughput and reduces consensus latency.

Author Contributions: Conceptualization, X.S. and M.L.; Data curation, X.S. and J.L.; Formal analysis, Z.Y. and J.L.; Funding acquisition, X.S.; Investigation, M.L. and W.Z.; Methodology, Z.Y. and W.Z.; Project administration, X.S.; Resources, X.S.; Software, M.L.; Supervision, J.L.; Validation, M.L. and Z.Y.; Writing—original draft, M.L.; Writing—review & editing, Z.Y. and Q.Z. All authors have read and agreed to the published version of the manuscript.

Funding: This research was funded by the Major Public Welfare Project of Henan Province, grant number 201300210300; Key Science and Technology Project of Henan Province, grant number 222102210168; Open Fund of Henan Key Laboratory of Network Cryptography Technology, grant number LNCT2021-A14, LNCT2022-A12; Songshan Laboratory Pre-research Project, grant number YYJC032022021; and Postgraduate Research and Innovation Project of Zhongyuan University of Technology, grant number YKY2023ZK52.

Data Availability Statement: The source code in this study is available upon request from the corresponding author.

Conflicts of Interest: The authors declare no conflict of interest.

References

1. Ren, Y.; Zhu, F.; Wang, J.; Sharma, P.K.; Ghosh, U. Novel vote scheme for decision-making feedback based on blockchain in internet of vehicles. *IEEE Trans. Intell. Transp. Syst.* **2021**, *23*, 1639–1648. [CrossRef]
2. Wang, H.Y.; Guo, K.X.; Pan, Q.Q. Byzantine fault tolerance consensus algorithm based on voting mechanism. *J. Comput. Appl.* **2019**, *39*, 1766–1771.
3. Li, Y.; Wang, Z.; Fan, J.; Zheng, Y.; Luo, Y.; Deng, C.; Ding, J. An extensible consensus algorithm based on PBFT. In Proceedings of the 2019 International Conference on Cyber-Enabled Distributed Computing and Knowledge Discovery (CyberC), Guilin, China, 17–19 October 2019; pp. 17–23.
4. Lao, L.; Dai, X.; Xiao, B.; Guo, S. G-pbft: A location-based and scalable consensus protocol for iot-blockchain applications. In Proceedings of the 2020 IEEE International Parallel and Distributed Processing Symposium (IPDPS), New Orleans, LA, USA, 18–22 May 2020; pp. 664–673.
5. Wang, R.H.; Zhang, L.F.; Xu, Q.Q.; Zhou, H. Byzantine fault tolerance algorithm for consortium blockchain. *Appl. Res. Comput.* **2020**, *37*, 3382–3386.
6. Du, N.; Liang, Z.; Huang, Y.; Guo, Z.; Yang, H.; Wang, S. Performance optimisation Method of PBFT Consensus for Supply Chain Integration SVM. In Proceedings of the 2020 7th International Conference on Dependable Systems and Their Applications (DSA), Xi'an, China, 28–29 November 2020; pp. 371–377.
7. Seo, J.; Ko, D.; Kim, S.; Park, S. A Coordination Technique for Improving Scalability of Byzantine Fault-Tolerant Consensus. *Appl. Sci.* **2020**, *10*, 7609. [CrossRef]
8. Ren, X.L.; Zhang, L. Improved multi-primary-node consensus mechanism based on practical Byzantine fault tolerance. *J. Comput. Appl.* **2022**, *42*, 1500–1507.
9. Kumar, A.; Vishwakarma, L.; Das, D. R-PBFT: A secure and intelligent consensus algorithm for Internet of vehicles. *Veh. Commun.* **2023**, *41*, 100609. [CrossRef]
10. Chen, Z.H.; Li, Q. Improved PBFT Consensus Mechanism Based on K-medoids. *Comput. Sci.* **2019**, *46*, 101–107.
11. Liu, W.; Ruan, M.J.; She, W.; Zhang, Z.H.; Tian, Z. PBFT Optimized Consensus Algorithm for Internet of Things. *Comput. Sci.* **2021**, *48*, 151–158.
12. Zhang, X.; Li, R.; Zhao, H. A Parallel Consensus Mechanism Using PBFT Based on DAG-Lattice Structure in the Internet of Vehicles. *IEEE Internet Things J.* **2022**, *10*, 5418–5433. [CrossRef]
13. Yu, G.; Wu, B.; Niu, X. Improved blockchain consensus mechanism based on PBFT algorithm. In Proceedings of the 2020 2nd International Conference on Advances in Computer Technology, Information Science and Communications (CTISC), Suzhou, China, 20–22 March 2020; pp. 14–21.
14. Xu, G.Q.; Bai, H.P.; Xing, J.; Luo, T.; Xiong, N.N.; Cheng, X.C.; Liu, S.Y.; Zheng, X. SG-PBFT: A secure and highly efficient distributed blockchain PBFT consensus algorithm for intelligent Internet of vehicles. *J. Parallel Distrib. Comput.* **2022**, *164*, 1–11. [CrossRef]
15. Duan, J.; Lü, X.; Liu, F. Hierarchical Consensus Optimization of Blockchain Based on Trust Delegation. *Comput. Eng.* **2020**, *46*, 120–130+136.
16. Wang, Y.; Cai, S.; Lin, C.; Chen, Z.; Wang, T.; Gao, Z.; Zhou, C. Study of blockchains's consensus mechanism based on credit. *IEEE Access* **2019**, *7*, 10224–10231. [CrossRef]
17. Xu, X.L.; Zhu, D.W.; Yang, X.X.; Wang, S.; Qi, L.Y.; Dou, W.C. Concurrent practical byzantine fault tolerance for integration of blockchain and supply chain. *ACM Trans. Internet Technol. (TOIT)* **2021**, *21*, 1–17. [CrossRef]
18. Tan, X.D.; Cheng, W.; Huang, H.P.; Jing, T.Y.; Wang, H.Y. Edge-aided searchable data sharing scheme for IoV in the 5G environment. *J. Syst. Archit.* **2023**, *136*, 102834. [CrossRef]

19. Lu, Y.L.; Huang, X.H.; Zhang, K.; Maharjan, S.; Zhang, Y. Blockchain empowered asynchronous federated learning for secure data sharing in internet of vehicles. *IEEE Trans. Veh. Technol.* **2020**, *69*, 4298–4311. [CrossRef]
20. Limbasiya, T.; Das, D. IoVCom: Reliable Comprehensive Communication System for Internet of Vehicles. *IEEE Trans. Dependable Secur. Comput.* **2019**, *18*, 2752–2766. [CrossRef]
21. Su, Z.; Wang, Y.T.; Xu, Q.C.; Zhang, N. LVBS: Lightweight vehicular blockchain for secure data sharing in disaster rescue. *IEEE Trans. Dependable Secur. Comput.* **2020**, *19*, 19–32. [CrossRef]
22. Kamal, M.; Srivastava, G.; Tariq, M. Blockchain-based lightweight and secured v2v communication in the internet of vehicles. *IEEE Trans. Intell. Transp. Syst.* **2020**, *22*, 3997–4004. [CrossRef]
23. Dai, H.N.; Zheng, Z.B.; Zhang, Y. Blockchain for Internet of Things: A survey. *IEEE Internet Things J.* **2019**, *6*, 8076–8094. [CrossRef]
24. Feng, Q.; He, D.B.; Zeadally, S.; Khan, M.K. A survey on privacy protection in blockchain system. *J. Netw. Comput. Appl.* **2019**, *126*, 45–58. [CrossRef]
25. Li, W.Y.; Feng, C.L.; Zhang, L.; Xu, H.; Cao, B.; Imran, M.A. A scalable multi-layer PBFT consensus for blockchain. *IEEE Trans. Parallel Distrib. Syst.* **2020**, *32*, 1146–1160. [CrossRef]
26. Mišić, J.; Mišić, V.B.; Chang, X.L.; Qushtom, H. Adapting PBFT for use with blockchain-enabled IoT systems. *IEEE Trans. Veh. Technol.* **2020**, *70*, 33–48. [CrossRef]
27. Kim, Y.; Park, J. Hybrid decentralized PBFT Blockchain Framework for OpenStack message queue. *Hum. Centric Comput. Inf. Sci.* **2020**, *10*, 31. [CrossRef]
28. Zhang, H.B.; Cao, Y.K.; Liu, K.J.; Wang, R.Y. Distributed trust management scheme based on blockchain in Internet of vehicles. *J. Commun.* **2023**, *44*, 148–157.
29. Wang, D.; Jin, C.J.; Xiao, B.B.; Li, Z.; He, X. Proof-of-activity consensus algorithm based on K-medoids clustering. *Big Data Res.* **2021**, *26*, 100266. [CrossRef]
30. Li, F.; Wang, C. Develop a multi-linear-trend fuzzy information granule based short-term time series forecasting model with k-medoids clustering. *Inf. Sci.* **2023**, *629*, 358–375. [CrossRef]
31. Jia, B.; Zhang, X.S.; Liu, J.W.; Zhang, Y.; Huang, K.; Liang, Y.Q. Blockchain-enabled federated learning data protection aggregation scheme with differential privacy and homomorphic encryption in IIoT. *IEEE Trans. Ind. Inform.* **2021**, *18*, 4049–4058. [CrossRef]
32. Han, R.C.; Shapiro, G.; Gramoli, V.; Xu, X.W. On the performance of distributed ledgers for internet of things. *Internet Things* **2020**, *10*, 100087. [CrossRef]
33. Zheng, Z.B.; Xie, S.A.; Dai, H.N.; Chen, X.P.; Wang, H.M. Blockchain challenges and opportunities: A survey. *Int. J. Web Grid Serv.* **2018**, *14*, 352–375. [CrossRef]
34. Zhang, C.; Zhao, M.; Zhu, L.; Zhang, W.; Wu, T.; Ni, J. FRUIT: A Blockchain-Based Efficient and Privacy-Preserving Quality-Aware Incentive Scheme. *IEEE J. Sel. Areas Commun.* **2022**, *40*, 3343–3357. [CrossRef]
35. Zhang, C.; Hu, C.; Wu, T.; Zhu, L.; Liu, X. Achieving Efficient and Privacy-Preserving Neural Network Training and Prediction in Cloud Environments. *IEEE Trans. Dependable Secur. Comput.* **2023**, *20*, 4245–4257. [CrossRef]
36. Hu, C.F.; Zhang, C.; Lei, D.; Wu, T.; Liu, X.M.; Zhu, L.H. Achieving Privacy-Preserving and Verifiable Support Vector Machine Training in the Cloud. *IEEE Trans. Inf. Forensics Secur.* **2022**, *40*, 3343–3357. [CrossRef]

electronics

MDPI

Article

Towards Privacy-Preserving Federated Neuromorphic Learning via Spiking Neuron Models

Bing Han †, **Qiang Fu** *,† and **Xinliang Zhang** †

China National Institute of Standardization, Beijing 100191, China; hanb@cnis.ac.cn (B.H.); zhangxinliang@cnis.ac.cn (X.Z.)
* Correspondence: fuqiang@cnis.ac.cn
† These authors contributed equally to this work.

Abstract: Federated learning (FL) has been broadly adopted in both academia and industry in recent years. As a bridge to connect the so-called "data islands", FL has contributed greatly to promoting data utilization. In particular, FL enables disjoint entities to cooperatively train a shared model, while protecting each participant's data privacy. However, current FL frameworks cannot offer privacy protection and reduce the computation overhead at the same time. Therefore, its implementation in practical scenarios, such as edge computing, is limited. In this paper, we propose a novel FL framework with spiking neuron models and differential privacy, which simultaneously provides theoretically guaranteed privacy protection and achieves low energy consumption. We model the local forward propagation process in a discrete way similar to nerve signal travel in the human brain. Since neurons only fire when the accumulated membrane potential exceeds a threshold, spiking neuron models require significantly lower energy compared to traditional neural networks. In addition, to protect sensitive information in model gradients, we add differently private noise in both the local training phase and server aggregation phase. Empirical evaluation results show that our proposal can effectively reduce the accuracy of membership inference attacks and property inference attacks, while maintaining a relatively low energy cost. blueFor example, the attack accuracy of a membership inference attack drops to 43% in some scenarios. As a result, our proposed FL framework can work well in large-scale cross-device learning scenarios.

Keywords: federated learning; privacy protection; spiking neural networks

1. Introduction

Multiparty machine learning paradigms are gaining increasing attention recently, as they power many data-driven applications while preserving data privacy [1–4]. Among the many algorithms, a widely adopted paradigm is FL, where multiple participants (or clients) jointly train a shared global model under the coordination of a central server. Since training datasets from each client never leave their holders, a privacy guarantee can be provided in FL. To date, instead of traditional centralized training methods, FL has been broadly implemented in a range of fields, including automatic driving, speech recognition, intelligent medical diagnoses, etc.

However, there remain several challenges to be addressed in FL [5–9]. In this paper, we tackle the problem of privacy protection and computing the energy cost. Many recent works have proven that FL is vulnerable to various kinds of privacy attacks [10,11]. For example, given the local update gradients (or local models), a malicious server can infer whether a specific data point belongs to the training set of a particular client [12]. Moreover, an attacker in the open public environment can precisely reconstruct small batches of training samples [13–15], if the updated gradients are intercepted and the local model architectures are known. Such attacks pose a server privacy threat to FL systems. As a response, many defense methods have been proposed, such as leveraging cryptographic techniques [16,17] or adding differential noise to model gradients [18].

Although these solutions provide effective or provable defenses to FL, they cannot be widely adopted in resource-constrained training scenarios, especially in large-scale and highly distributed FL, e.g., edge computing with massive amounts of unreliable devices. Since current privacy protection techniques incur extra computing overheads and affect model performance [19], data service providers as well as individual users are reluctant to adopt these techniques to ensure data privacy. On the other hand, energy consumption has also become one of the major bottlenecks in promoting FL in Internet of Things (IOT) [20]. Nevertheless, current researchers merely focus on constructing new training protocols to limit resource usage and hardly extend their attention to modifying local models in an energy-efficient manner.

To this end, in this paper, we propose a novel FL framework that offers both theoretically guaranteed privacy protection and low energy consumption. Our proposed framework models the local training in a discrete manner, which is similar to how nerve signals travel in the human brain. Specifically, we leverage spiking neural networks, also known as the third-generation neural network, and differential privacy, a promising technique to protect data privacy, to construct a new local training and server aggregation algorithm. The crux of our framework design lies in how to properly inject differentially private noise into the discontinuous forward propagation process, while maintaining the availability of gradients produced by backpropagation. Our evaluation results demonstrate that our proposal can effectively defend against two common privacy attacks, i.e., membership inference attacks and property inference attacks.

The contributions made in this paper can be summarized as follows.

- We leverage an SNN to tackle the conflict between privacy and efficiency in FL. blue In particular, SNNs enjoy naturally high computing efficiency, with a mathematically traceable computing process. Hence, differential private noise can be added to the training process, while maintaining acceptable model accuracy. Compared to previous works, our proposed framework significantly lowers the hardware requirements for clients.
- To the best of our knowledge, we propose the first FL framework that enjoys both low energy consumption and theoretically guaranteed privacy protection. Our framework protects both the local model and global model by injecting DP noise into the training and transmission process.
- We conduct extensive experiments to evaluate our proposed framework. Empirical evaluation results show that our proposal can effectively defend against common privacy attacks. Moreover, our training scheme can be implemented in large-scale cross-device training, and it does not incur a notable accuracy drop compared to typical FL paradigms with privacy protection.

This paper is organized as follows: Section 2 presents the preliminaries and background of our work, Section 3 formalizes the problem and threat models, Section 4 describes our proposed method, Section 5 shows our empirical evaluation results, Section 6 discusses previous works related to ours, and Section 7 concludes our work.

2. Preliminaries and Background

In this section, we introduce the related preliminaries and background of our work.

2.1. Federated Learning

FL [21] allows multiple participants to cooperatively train a shared global model, while maintaining the confidentiality of their privately held local datasets. Assume that each participant in FL $c_i \in \mathcal{C}$ privately holds a dataset $\mathcal{D}_i \in \mathcal{D}$. Take surprised learning, for example: local dataset $\mathcal{D}_i$ consists of multiple data points d_i, which are characterized by a sample x_i and its corresponding label y_i, i.e., $\{x_i, y_i\} = d_i$. In the canonical FL paradigm, each client locally trains a local model $\mathcal{F}_i(.)$ on $\mathcal{D}_i$ via minimizing a loss function $\mathcal{L}(.)$. This optimization process is typically achieved by gradient decent algorithms. Mathematically,

$$\theta_i^{p+1} \leftarrow \frac{\partial\, \mathcal{L}(\mathcal{D}_i|\theta_i^p)}{\partial\, \theta_i^p}, \tag{1}$$

where p and θ denote the training epoch (or communication round in FL) and weights of local models, respectively. The loss function $\mathcal{L}(.)$ could be predefined before training or dynamically adjusted in the training process, based on practical training goals.

After each client finishes their local training, the central server collects local models from them. A new global model for the next training epoch $\mathcal{F}(.)$ is then created by averaging each local model, i.e.,

$$\mathcal{F}^{p+1}(.) \leftarrow \frac{1}{I}\sum_{c_i} \theta_{c_i}^p. \tag{2}$$

The new global model would be broadcasted to all clients, on which the next local training is based. The local model of each client could be a classical machine learning model or neural network. In this paper, we propose using spiking neuron models, also known as spiking neural networks (SNN), as local models of each client. The authors in [21] have explored the possibility of implementing SNNs in federated learning.

2.2. Spiking Neuron Models

Neuromorphic computing has gained considerable attention in recent years, as it requires lower energy compared to traditional neural networks. A basic model in neuromorphic computing is a spiking neural network (SNN), which is inspired by certain biological principles of the human brain. Different from current artificial neural networks (ANNs), SNNs model the forward propagation process in a discrete manner and are considered to be the third-generation neural network. Specifically, each neuron in the SNN accumulates the incoming spikes and generates a spike when its membrane potential exceeds a threshold. After firing, the membrane potential would be reset to the resting potential. Mathematically, at each time step t, for the i-th neuron, such a process can be modeled as

$$u_i^t = \lambda u_i^{t-1} + \sum_{j\in N} w_{ij} o_j^{t-1} \quad s.t. \quad o_j^{t-1} = \begin{cases} 1 & if\ u_i^{t-1} > v, \\ 0 & otherwise, \end{cases} \tag{3}$$

where u, o, and w_{ij} denote its membrane potential, the output of the previous neuron, and a weight between the i-th and j-th neurons, respectively. $\lambda < 1$ is a constant, indicating the reduction in membrane potential at every time step.

An SNN is typically converted from a well-trained ANN. However, such conversion is time-consuming and the model accuracy cannot be properly persevered. Recent research [22] has proposed Batch Normalization Through Time (BNTT), a novel training method that associates a local learning parameter with each time step. As a result, it is possible to train an SNN without an auxiliary fully trained ANN model. In particular, after the BNTT layer is applied, the forward propagation is modeled as

$$u_i^t = \lambda u_i^{t-1} + \mathrm{BNTT}_{\gamma_i^t}\left(\sum_{j\in N} w_{ij} o_j^t\right) = \lambda u_i^{t-1} + \gamma_i^t \left(\frac{\sum_{j\ N} w_{ij} o_j^t - \mu_i^t}{\sqrt{(\sigma_i^t)^2 + \tau}}\right), \tag{4}$$

where u and σ denote the mean and variance from a batch of samples, and τ is a small constant to ensure numerical stability. A parameter γ can therefore be learnt using backpropagation.

2.3. Differential Privacy

Differential privacy (DP) offers theoretically guaranteed privacy protection to confidential data, while not incurring a significant additional computing cost. The DP-SGD algorithm [23] is the first solution to implement DP in machine learning paradigms, which adds perturbing noise to the stochastic gradient descent. DP-SGD only modifies the training algorithm, not adding noise the dataset itself. As a result, the gradient in the model update (in the case of FL, local models) can be published without privacy leakages. In particular, we have the following definitions.

Definition 1 ([24]). *A randomized mechanism $\mathcal{M}$ with domain D and range $\mathcal{R}$ satisfies (ϵ, δ)-differential privacy if, for any two adjacent inputs $d \in D$, and for any subset of outputs $\mathcal{S} \in \mathcal{R}$, it holds that*

$$\Pr[\mathcal{M}(d) \in S] \leq e^{\epsilon} \Pr[\mathcal{M}(d') \in S]. \tag{5}$$

Under this definition, each output of DP algorithm $\mathcal{M}$ is equally likely on two adjacent databases. The privacy budget, ϵ, controls the amount of the difference between d and d'. A smaller ϵ can provide a stronger privacy guarantee of $\mathcal{M}$. To make the effectiveness of DP measurable, we introduce Renyi Differential Privacy as follows.

Definition 2 ([25]). *A randomized mechanism $\mathcal{M}(d)$ is said to be (α, ϵ)-Renyi differentially private if its distribution over two adjacent inputs d and d' satisfies*

$$D_{\alpha}(\mathcal{M}(d) \| \mathcal{M}(d')) \leq \epsilon, \tag{6}$$

where α tunes the amount of concern placed on unlikely large values of $c(o;\mathcal{M},d,d')$ versus the average value of $c(o;\mathcal{M},d,d')$. Here, $c(o;\mathcal{M},d,d')$ denotes the the privacy loss at an outcome o, which is defined as

$$c(o;\mathcal{M},d,d') = \log \frac{\Pr[\mathcal{M}(d) = o]}{\Pr[\mathcal{M}(d') = o]}. \tag{7}$$

3. Problem Statement and Threat Model

In this paper, our objective is to protect the confidentiality of each participant's local training data. In particular, we consider the following two types of data leakages.

- Membership Leakage. Membership privacy [26,27] concerns indicating whether a specific training sample was involved in the training set. In a membership inference attack (MIA) [28], an attacker manages to obtain black-box access to the target model and query multiple times with its local samples D' to infer which part of D' belongs to the confidential training set. MIA is critical in FL, since each participant as well as the central server can access the shared global model. Moreover, recent researchers [12,28] have proposed more effective MIA pipelines for FL, which significantly increases the risk of privacy leakage.
- Class Leakage. Class leakage exists when the attacker manages to obtain the class distribution of the target dataset. For example, a property inference attack (PIA) [29,30] infers the properties of the training data that are irrelevant to the learning objective. Such properties typically include the proportion of each type of sample in the training set. Similar to MIA, in FL, the shared global model would also cause severe class leakage problems. In particular, with the assistance of a data poisoning attack, an existing attack [30] achieved high accuracy in inferring the general properties of each participant's confidential training dataset.

In FL, since each entity (including the central server) could potentially become compromised, we mainly presume participants to be honest-but-couriers. In other words, each entity would strictly follow the predefined protocol, while trying to infer secret information as much as possible. Therefore, our proposal provides a privacy guarantee in the FL scenario where one or all of the following unexpected conditions are applied.

- (T1) The central server becomes malicious and actively infers confidential information from the received local models. Since the central server has full visibility to all local models, this is the most threatening scenario. Moreover, in order to further extract secret information, the central server could send carefully designed fake global models to a victim participant and infer secret information from their responses.
- (T2) A third party manages to intercept but cannot tamper with the communication between the central server and participants. Likewise, they could actively infer confidential information from updated local models. Different from the malicious central server, the global model is dependable.
- (T3) A number of participants become compromised and cooperatively infer a training set that they do not possess from each training round's global model.

To eliminate these privacy threats, our proposal leverages DP in both local training and server aggregation. Both local models and global models are protected by DP noise, which makes a compromised entity less able to infer sensitive information from the local models and global models.

4. Proposed Method

In this section, we describe our proposed privacy-preserving federated learning by spiking neuron models. A federated learning scheme can generally be divided into two iterative phases: (1) a local search by each participant, denoted by $\mathcal{S}(.)$, and (2) server aggregation, denoted by $\mathcal{A}(.)$. In a communication round, each client firstly performs a local search on their private dataset D, i.e., $\mathcal{F}_i(.) \leftarrow \mathcal{S}(D)$. The trained model $\mathcal{F}(.)$ would be uploaded to a central server, where model aggregation is performed, i.e., $\mathcal{F}(.) \leftarrow \mathcal{A}(\mathcal{F}_1(.)\ldots,\mathcal{F}_i(.),\ldots,\mathcal{F}_c(.))$. In this paper, we design novel local search and server aggregation algorithms for SNNs that provide a privacy guarantee. Figure 1illustrates our proposal at a high level. In the following paragraph, we separately describe our proposed two algorithms.

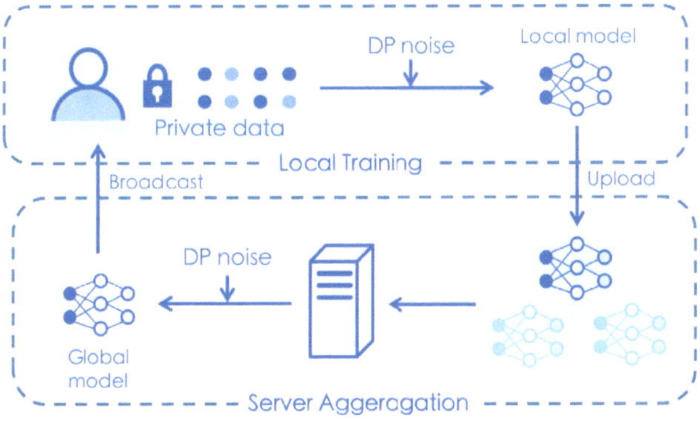

Figure 1. Our proposed training framework at a high level.

4.1. Local Search

In a local search, each client updates their local model by minimizing a loss function $\mathcal{L}(.)$. A widely used loss function is the cross-entropy loss, defined as

$$\mathcal{L}(.) = -\sum_{i} P_A(x_i) log(P_B(x_i)), \tag{8}$$

where P_A and P_B denote two probability distributions. From the accumulated membrane potential, the cross-entropy loss for SNNs can be defined as

$$\mathcal{L}(.) = -\sum_i y_i \log\left(\frac{e^{u_i^T}}{\sum_k e^{u_k^T}}\right). \tag{9}$$

After modeling the discrete propagation process in a continuous manner, i.e., applying surrogate gradient, $\frac{do}{du} = e^{2(u-u_{th})^2}$, gradient descent can be adopted to compute the model updates at each time step. According to the chain rule, the gradient of the corresponding time and layer can be computed as

$$\nabla_w \mathcal{L}(.) = \sum_{t=1}^{T} \frac{\partial \mathcal{L}}{\partial o_i^t} \frac{\partial o_i^t}{\partial u_i^t} \frac{\partial u_i^t}{\partial w_{ij}}. \tag{10}$$

To protect training data privacy, we add Gaussian noise $\mathcal{N}(.)$ to the gradients computed at each training epoch p. As a result, differentially private gradients can be obtained, which makes the attacker less able to extract sensitive information. We provide a privacy guarantee under the framework of GDP theory [31]. In particular, distinguishing between two adjacent datasets D and D' is harder than distinguishing between two Gaussian distributions $\mathcal{N}(0,1)$ and $\mathcal{N}(\kappa,1)$. Therefore, even if a malicious party intercepts the local update gradient or global model, they cannot directly infer or reconstruct the corresponding training set. Mathematically, in the p-th training epoch, the local model for client c is updated by

$$w_c^{p+1} \leftarrow w_c^p - \eta\frac{1}{\mathcal{B}}\left(\left(\mathcal{N}\left(0, \kappa^2 C^2 \mathbf{I}\right) + \nabla_w \mathcal{L}_c^p(.)/\max\left(1, \frac{\left\|\nabla_w \mathcal{L}_c^p(.)\right\|_2}{C}\right)\right) - \nabla_w \mathcal{L}_c^p(.)\right), \tag{11}$$

where η is the learning rate, C is the gradient norm bound, κ is the noise scale, $\mathcal{B}$ is the batch size, and $\mathcal{N}(0, \kappa^2 C^2 \mathbf{I})$ is a normal Gaussian distribution. To avoid privacy leakage, participants usually upload the gradients of each training epoch, instead of uploading the full local model, i.e., $\Delta w_c^{p+1} = \Delta w_c^{p+1} - w_c^p$. This is equal to uploading the full local model, as the central server can directly compute the average on such received gradients.

4.2. Server Aggregation

The central server aggregates all received local updates and forms a new global model. To ensure that all local models have a sufficient impact on the global model, the central server would usually select a subset $\mathbb{S} \in \mathcal{C}$ from all participants. The selection algorithm, for example, could be solving the following maximization problem [32]:

$$\max_{\mathbb{S}} |\mathbb{S}| \quad \text{s.t.} \quad T_{\text{round}} \geq T_{\text{cs}} + T_{\mathbb{S}}^{\text{d}} + \Theta_{|\mathbb{S}|} + T_{\text{agg}}, \tag{12}$$

where $\mathbb{S}$ is the selected client set, T_{round} is the deadline for each round, T_{cs} is the time required for the client selection step, T_{agg} is the time required for the aggregation steps, $T_{\mathbb{S}}^{\text{d}}$ is the time required for global model distribution, and $\Theta_{|\mathbb{S}|}$ is the time for participants in $\mathbb{S}$ required to update and upload the local models.

After client selection, the central server initiates the aggregation process. Denoting the count of non-zero elements of a set by $|.|$, Equation (2) can be expanded as follows:

$$\mathcal{F}^{p+1}(.) \leftarrow \mathcal{F}^p(.) + \frac{1}{\sum_{c\in\mathbb{S}}\left|D_{c_i}^{p+1}\right|} \sum_{c\in\mathbb{S}} \left|D_{c_i}^{p+1}\right| \Delta w_{c_i}^{p+1}. \tag{13}$$

Here, participants with more data samples are given more weight in aggregation, which helps the global model to converge faster. To enhance the privacy of the global model, i.e., defend against third parties intercepting the broadcasted global model, DP noise can be added before it is published:

$$\mathcal{F}^{p+1}(.) \leftarrow \mathcal{F}^{p+1}(.) + \mathcal{N}\left(0, \kappa'^2 C'^2 \mathbf{I}\right). \tag{14}$$

In particular, to limit the performance penalty incurred by adding DP noise, noise is only applicable to model weights that do not change significantly compared to the last training round. The central server also selects some particular training terminal conditions, which indicate when the FL ends. This also helps to reduce the overfitting of the model. The detailed algorithm of our proposed training scheme is shown in Algorithm 1.

Algorithm 1: Privacy-Preserving Federated Neuromorphic Learning

Input : Total communication round $\mathcal{P}$, client set $\mathcal{C}$, local learning rate η, training terminal conditions ϕ, local training batch size $\mathcal{B}$, client selection algorithm $\mathcal{F}_s(.)$,

Initialize: Model parameter of local models w_i^0.

for $p = 1 : \mathcal{P}$ **do**
- $\mathbb{S} \leftarrow \mathcal{F}_s(\mathcal{C})$
- **for** *each* $c_i \in \mathbb{S}$ **do in parallel**
  - $w_{c_i}^{p+1} \leftarrow$ **Equation (11)**
  - $\Delta w_{c_i}^{p+1} = \Delta w_{c_i}^{p+1} - w_{c_i}^{p}$
  - upload $\Delta w_{c_i}^{p+1}$ to central server
- $\mathcal{F}^{p+1}(.) \leftarrow \mathcal{F}^{p}(.) + \frac{1}{\sum_{c\in\mathbb{S}}\left|D_{c_i}^{p+1}\right|}\sum_{c\in\mathbb{S}}\left|D_{c_i}^{p+1}\right|\Delta w_{c_i}^{p+1}$
- $\mathcal{F}^{p+1}(.) \leftarrow \mathcal{F}^{p+1}(.) + \mathcal{N}(0, \kappa'^2 C'^2 \mathbf{I})$
- **if** *training terminal conditions* ϕ *are matched* **then**
  - **return** $\mathcal{F}^{p+1}(.)$

return $\mathcal{F}^{p+1}(.)$

5. Experiments

In this section, we present the empirical evaluation results of our proposal. We test the final accuracy of the well-trained global model, as well as its ability in defending different privacy attacks.

5.1. Settings

Our evaluation is conducted on the PyTorch Framework 3.8. All experiments are conducted 5 times, and the average results are reported. Detailed settings are described as follows.

Dataset and Learning Scale. We conduct experiments to evaluate the performance of our FL framework on the MNIST and CIFAR-10 datasets. MNIST consists of 60,000 training samples and 10,000 test samples, which are 28 × 28 grayscale images. CIFAR-10 consists of 60,000 training samples and 10,000 test samples, which are 32 × 32 RGB images. To simulate three practical learning scenarios [33] (cross-silo FL and cross-device FL), the datasets are split according to the following.

1. cross-silo FL: Participants are different organizations (e.g., hospitals or banks) or geo-distributed data centers. Typically, there are 2–100 participants in this scenario, and all of them are reliable, i.e., no failure or drop out. Our simulation of this scenario splits the dataset with the following settings: (1) *CS_1*: 6 clients, with 10,000 training samples each, (2) *CS_2*: 20 clients, with 2000–5000 samples each, and (3) *CS_3*: 50 clients, with 1000–2000 samples each. All local gradients would aggregated by the central server, i.e., client selection is disabled.
2. cross-device FL: Participants are a very large number of massively parallel mobile or IoT devices, typically up to 10^5. During training, only a small of participants are available at any one time, i.e., some of the participants would have a probability not responding to the central server. Our simulation of this scenario splits the dataset with the following settings: (1) *CD_1*: 200 clients, each with 500 training samples randomly selected from the training set, and (2) *CD_2*: 1000 clients, each with 250 training

samples. randomly selected from the training set. The central server only selects 30 local models for aggregation according to its selection protocol.

Model Architectures. We implement two local model architectures: (1) *M1*, a lightweight fully connected neural network with 5 hidden layers; and (2) *M2*, VGG13, which consists of 10 convolutional filters 3×3 and two fully connected layers with pooling. As a comparison, both architectures would be implemented as an ANN and SNN. The training batch size $\mathcal{B}$ for each participant is 32, and the learning rate η is 0.005. In VGG16, we also use a momentum of 0.9 to avoid falling into local optima. The activation function in ANNs is set with Sigmoid. In each communication round, the local model is trained by 10 epochs before updating the gradients on the central server. The DP noise added in the local training phase and aggregation phase is $\mathcal{N}(0, 0.01)$ and $\mathcal{N}(0, 0.005)$, respectively.

5.2. Training Accuracy

We report the training accuracy of the well-trained global model, as well as the communication rounds needed under different settings, in Table 1 (MNIST) and Table 2 (CIFAR-10). In general, the global model can converge well under both FedAvg and our method. Please note that our method provides privacy protection, which would cause a performance penalty. We will present the evaluation results in defending against privacy attacks in the next subsection.

Table 1. The converged global model accuracy (Acc) and communication rounds (CR) in different settings for the MNIST dataset.

		FedAvg M1		FedAvg M2		Ours M1		Ours M2	
		Acc	CR	Acc	CR	Acc	CR	Acc	CR
CS_1	SNN	98.9%	126	99.1%	178	97.1%	152	97.2%	219
	ANN	99.2%	97	99.6%	169	97.4%	128	97.8%	143
CS_2	SNN	98.8%	134	98.9%	189	97.0%	180	97.4%	269
	ANN	99.2%	106	99.3%	170	97.2%	144	97.6%	178
CS_3	SNN	98.3%	150	98.5%	195	96.3%	208	96.8%	285
	ANN	99.0%	111	99.3%	182	96.8%	160	97.1%	197
CD_1	SNN	96.5%	213	96.9%	245	94.2%	323	94.8%	329
	ANN	97.8%	178	98.0%	190	94.9%	219	95.5%	230
CD_2	SNN	95.7%	256	95.8%	281	93.8%	348	94.4%	367
	ANN	97.1%	220	97.5%	243	94.0%	245	95.2%	277

Table 2. The converged global model accuracy (Acc) and communication rounds (CR) in different settings for the CIFAR-10 dataset.

		FedAvg M1		FedAvg M2		Ours M1		Ours M2	
		Acc	CR	Acc	CR	Acc	CR	Acc	CR
CS_1	SNN	96.2%	186	96.8%	240	95.7%	187	95.9%	199
	ANN	96.6%	170	97.6%	226	96.1%	165	96.3%	186
CS_2	SNN	95.9%	193	96.3%	258	95.2%	196	95.6%	215
	ANN	96.5%	179	97.0%	239	95.5%	173	95.5%	194
CS_3	SNN	95.1%	205	95.9%	262	94.6%	228	94.9%	254
	ANN	95.7%	186	96.5%	245	94.8%	212	94.3%	210
CD_1	SNN	93.2%	240	94.3%	280	94.2%	347	94.6%	363
	ANN	94.1%	210	94.7%	255	93.6%	236	94.7%	274
CD_2	SNN	92.6%	269	93.8%	293	93.3%	366	94.0%	370
	ANN	93.4%	238	94.2%	276	93.4%	250	93.3%	280

From both tables, we can observe that, in both simple and complex network architectures (M1 and M2), our proposed FL scheme can provide a global SNN model with testing accuracy similar to the ANN. In both network architectures, the number of communication rounds for the SNN is 1.5 times more than for the ANN on average, especially in large training scenarios. Moreover, the decrease in model accuracy compared to the ANN does not vary with the learning scale. It can be estimated that, in even larger learning scenarios with more uncertainties, our proposal can achieve a global model that is similar to an ANN in terms of accuracy, while enjoying the unique benefits of SNNs, e.g., low computing energy cost. From Table 2, we can see that the SNN also performs well on RGB images. Next, we report how the global model accuracy increases with the communication rounds in Figure 2. The tested global model accuracies under the setting of M2 CIFAR-10 are shown. For cross-silo training, the global model accuracy increases faster than for cross-device training.

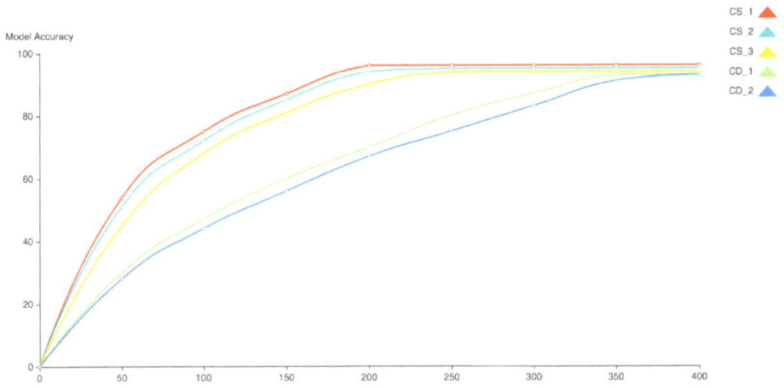

Figure 2. Change in global model accuracy with the increase in communication rounds (CIFAR-10, M2).

5.3. Defense against Privacy Attacks

In this subsection, we present the evaluation results in terms of defending against privacy attacks. As mentioned in Section 3, we mainly consider membership inference attacks and property inference attacks. We posit that (1) the central server or (2) some of the clients are malicious. The MIA follows the implementation of [34], and the attack accuracy is reported in Table 3. The PIA follows the implementation of [35], and the attack accuracy is reported in Table 4. We use the same metric for attack accuracy as in [35].

The MIA accuracy in Table 3 is computed by

$$MA_{\mathcal{A}} = 2\mathbb{P}[\ \mathcal{F}_{\mathcal{A}}(Y_t \mid \boldsymbol{aux}\ ) = \epsilon\ ] - 1, \tag{15}$$

where ***aux*** denotes the information available to the attacker (i.e., attacker's advantage), and $\mathcal{F}_{\mathcal{A}}$ is the chosen attack algorithm. Since a randomly initialized attack algorithm achieves 50% accuracy (random guess), this measurement of the performance of MIA would be more rational. From Table 3, we can observe that our proposed FL framework can effectively prevent MIA in different learning scenarios. The attack accuracy drops significantly (65% in average) in simple and complex datasets. In large models, our proposal can provide even better privacy protection.

As for defense against PIA, our training scheme also achieves similar defense performance compared to the results in MIA. From Table 4, we can observe that the attack accuracy decreases considerably with our training scheme. In different settings, the distribution of only a small portion of confidential data can be inferred by the attacker. From all tables, we can conclude that our proposed training scheme can provide strong privacy protection in different threat models, while only causing a slight drop in model performance and convergence speed.

Table 3. MIA accuracy under FedAvg and our proposed training scheme in MNIST (D1) and CIFAR-10 (D2).

MIA	FedAvg M1		Ours M1		FedAvg M2		Ours M2	
	D1	D2	D1	D2	D1	D2	D1	D2
CS_1	67.3%	61.1%	23.0%	26.6%	69.9%	63.5%	23.5%	25.9%
CS_2	65.9%	61.0%	21.9%	26.3%	68.1%	62.9%	23.2%	25.3%
CS_3	65.1%	60.4%	20.8%	29.5%	67.5%	62.3%	22.7%	24.8%
CD_1	52.1%	48.2%	19.6%	18.6%	59.1%	51.2%	17.6%	20.2%
CD_2	49.3%	42.1%	18.5%	17.9%	58.3%	47.0%	17.1%	19.6%

Table 4. PIA accuracy under FedAvg and our proposed training scheme in MNIST (D1) and CIFAR-10 (D2).

PIA	FedAvg M1		Ours M1		FedAvg M2		Ours M2	
	D1	D2	D1	D2	D1	D2	D1	D2
CS_1	78.6%	75.0%	30.3%	28.7%	73.9%	71.8%	27.4%	25.7%
CS_2	77.2%	74.2%	29.4%	26.6%	73.1%	70.9%	26.7%	25.0%
CS_3	76.4%	73.7%	28.7%	26.0%	72.0%	70.1%	26.1%	24.6%
CD_1	72.1%	71.0%	26.9%	24.9%	67.5%	65.7%	24.0%	22.4%
CD_2	71.2%	69.5%	26.1%	24.0%	64.3%	63.1%	22.9%	21.8%

5.4. Ablation Study

We also conduct an ablation study to further verify the effectiveness of our proposal. We test the defense performance when (1) the scale of added noise is changed, and (2) we only enable DP in local training or server aggregation. We select the most challenging scenario in the cross-silo and cross-device context, respectively, i.e., *CS_3* and *CD_2*. The results are reported in Tables 5 and 6, respectively.

In Table 5, we further show the distribution of DP noise added in local training. We evaluate $\mathcal{N}(0,0.02)$ and $\mathcal{N}(0,0.005)$, and the global model accuracy (Acc), communication rounds (CR), and privacy attack accuracy (PA) are reported. PA reflects the model's general ability in defending against privacy attacks and is computed from the average attack accuracy of MIA and PIA. Generally speaking, adding DP noise with a wider range would cause a penalty in both model accuracy and convergence speed, but provide more powerful privacy protection. In practical training, participants can choose the appropriate scale of noise.

Table 5. Results showing how the scale of added noise in local training impacts global model accuracy (Acc), communication rounds (CR), and privacy attack accuracy (PA). PA equals the average attack accuracy of MIA and PIA.

		CS_3 M1		CD_2 M1		CS_3 M2		CD_2 M2	
		D1	D2	D1	D2	D1	D2	D1	D2
	Acc	96.3%	94.6%	93.8%	93.3%	96.8%	94.9%	94.4%	94.0%
$\mathcal{N}(0,0.01)$	CR	208	228	348	366	285	254	367	370
	PA	24.8%	27.8%	22.3%	21.0%	24.4%	24.7%	20.0%	20.7%
	Acc	95.6%	93.3%	92.9%	92.0%	95.1%	93.7%	92.6%	91.3%
$\mathcal{N}(0,0.02)$	CR	213	237	365	378	298	265	388	386
	PA	23.6%	25.7%	20.9%	19.8%	19.7%	18.9%	16.5%	16.0%
	Acc	97.0%	95.6%	94.4%	94.6%	97.2%	95.8%	95.7%	95.2%
$\mathcal{N}(0,0.005)$	CR	196	207	328	332	250	239	354	348
	PA	27.5%	26.7%	23.9%	23.6%	29.8%	30.6%	28.6%	29.5%

Table 6. Results when only applying DP noise in local training phase or server aggregation phase.

		CS_3 M1		CD_2 M1		CS_3 M2		CD_2 M2	
		D1	D2	D1	D2	D1	D2	D1	D2
DP in local training	Acc	95.1%	93.8%	93.2%	93.0%	95.7%	94.4%	93.9%	93.5%
	CR	187	198	306	328	246	289	345	356
	(PA	34.9%	36.6%	31.7%	32.8%	30.9%	31.7%	30.1%	32.6%
DP in server aggregation	Acc	95.3%	94.5%	93.9%	93.4%	95.7%	95.2%	95.0%	93.7%
	CR	181	196	294	310	239	265	310	327
	PA	32.7%	31.9%	31.3%	31.0%	31.8%	32.0%	31.7%	32.2%

Next, we investigate the model's defense capability when only adding DP noise in local training or server aggregation. In Tables 1 and 6, we can observe that applying DP noise in only the local training phase or server aggregation phase can allow resistance to privacy attacks. However, such privacy protection is weaker than when injecting noise in both phases.

6. Related Work

Our work mainly follows two lines of research: federated learning and spiking neuron models. The following paragraph briefly introduces recent advances in these two areas.

6.1. Federated Learning

Federated learning has quickly become one of the gold standards in privacy-preserving machine learning solutions since it was first introduced by Google in 2016 [19]. The pioneering work in FL typically simply considers all clients to be honest to each other, which makes directly aggregating local gradients possible [36]. However, the existence of malicious clients has prompted the proposal of more secure and robust FL frameworks [18].

Specifically, a number of works have designed different kinds of attacks to manipulate the training process or infer privacy data in FL. Zhu et al. proved that an attacker is able to reconstruct the actual training set of each participant if the local update gradient can be accessed [13]. Similarly, a malicious subset of the participants has been proven to be able to poison the global model by sending model updates derived from mislabeled data [37]. Moreover, FL can also easily be backdoored if the attacker manages to continuously send corrupted gradients to the aggregation server [38].

Nevertheless, in regard to these attacks, a wide range of researchers have provided many defense solutions. For example, Moriai et al. consider using homomorphic encryption to ensure the confidentiality of the whole training process [39]. In order to prevent different kinds of data inference attacks, adding differential noise to the training process has also been considered in a number of secure training schemes [10].

6.2. Spiking Neuron Models

The recent increasing need for the autonomy of machines in the real world has promoted the application of SNNs [40,41]. Inspired by biological neural networks, SNNs leverage plasticity and backpropagation as the main training methods [42]. Despite great advantages in energy consumption and learnability, SNNs are still difficult to train in many cases, since there exist complex dynamics of neurons, and the spike operations are naturally non-differentiable. Recent studies of SNNs can broadly be divided into the following streams.

Research stream 1: Investigating and advancing the connection between neural networks and SNNs. For example, Jason K. et al. explored the delicate interplay between encoding data as spikes and the learning process and investigated how deep learning might move towards biologically plausible online learning [43]. Yufei et al. designed an information maximization loss that aims at maximizing the information flow in the SNN, which ensures sufficient model updates at the beginning and accurate gradients at the end of the training [44].

Research stream 2: Boosting the convergence of SNNs. For example, Fang et al. proposed the spike-element-wise (SEW) ResNet to realize residual learning in deep SNNs, which overcomes the vanishing/exploding gradient problems of spiking ResNet [45]. To overcome the challenge of discrete spikes prohibiting gradient calculation, Yuhang et al. proposed a surrogate gradient approach that serves as continuous relaxation [46]. By encoding the spike trains into a spike representation using (weighted) firing rate coding, Qingyan et al. proposed the differentiation on spike representation method, which provides competitive accuracy to ANNs yet with low latency [47].

Research stream 3: Promoting the practical application of SNNs. For example, Xie et al. designed a novel network structure for SNNs based on neuron receptive fields, which extract information from the pixel and spatial dimensions of traffic signs [48]. Moreover, Viale et al. used an SNN connected to an event-based camera to tackle the classification problem between cars and other objects [49].

7. Conclusions and Future Work

In this paper, we propose the first privacy-preserving FL framework with SNNs. Our proposal can simultaneously provide theoretically guaranteed privacy protection and achieve low energy consumption. Our framework injects DP noise into the training and transmission process. We conducted extensive experiments to evaluate our proposed framework. Empirical evaluation results have shown that our proposal can effectively defend against common privacy attacks. blueFor example, the attack accuracy of membership inference attacks drops to 43% in some scenarios. Moreover, our training scheme can be implemented in large-scale cross-device training, and it does not incur a significant accuracy drop compared to typical FL paradigms with privacy protection.

Author Contributions: Conceptualization, B.H. and Q.F.; methodology, B.H.; software, B.H.; validation, B.H., Q.F. and X.Z.; formal analysis, B.H., Q.F. and X.Z.; writing—original draft preparation, B.H. and Q.F. All authors have read and agreed to the published version of the manuscript.

Funding: This research was funded by the National Key R&D Plan Program, grant number 2021YFF0602203; the State Administration for Market Regulation Science and Technology Plan Project, grant number 2022MK187; and the President Funding Key Project of China National Institute of Standardization, grant number 242022Y-9470.

Data Availability Statement: The data can be shared upon request.

Conflicts of Interest: The authors declare no conflict of interest.

References

1. Hu, C.; Zhang, C.; Lei, D.; Wu, T.; Liu, X.; Zhu, L. Achieving Privacy-Preserving and Verifiable Support Vector Machine Training in the Cloud. *IEEE Trans. Inf. Forensics Secur.* **2023**, *18*, 3476–3491. [CrossRef]
2. Zhang, C.; Hu, C.; Wu, T.; Zhu, L.; Liu, X. Achieving Efficient and Privacy-Preserving Neural Network Training and Prediction in Cloud Environments. *IEEE Trans. Dependable Secur. Comput.* **2023**, *20*, 4245–4257. [CrossRef]
3. Ren, H.; Li, H.; Liu, D.; Xu, G.; Shen, X.S. Enabling Secure and Versatile Packet Inspection with Probable Cause Privacy for Outsourced Middlebox. *IEEE Trans. Cloud Comput.* **2022**, *10*, 2580–2594. [CrossRef]
4. Ren, H.; Li, H.; Liu, D.; Xu, G.; Cheng, N.; Shen, X. Privacy-Preserving Efficient Verifiable Deep Packet Inspection for Cloud-Assisted Middlebox. *IEEE Trans. Cloud Comput.* **2022**, *10*, 1052–1064. [CrossRef]
5. Wang, Y.; Chen, K.; Tan, Y.; Huang, S.; Ma, W.; Li, Y. Stealthy and Flexible Trojan in Deep Learning Framework. *IEEE Trans. Dependable Secur. Comput.* **2023**, *20*, 1789–1798. [CrossRef]
6. Wang, Y.; Tan, Y.; Baker, T.; Kumar, N.; Zhang, Q. Deep Fusion: Crafting Transferable Adversarial Examples and Improving Robustness of Industrial Artificial Intelligence of Things. *IEEE Trans. Ind. Inform.* **2023**, *19*, 7480–7488. [CrossRef]
7. Wang, Y.; Wu, S.; Jiang, W.; Hao, S.; Tan, Y.; Zhang, Q. Demiguise Attack: Crafting Invisible Semantic Adversarial Perturbations with Perceptual Similarity. In Proceedings of the Thirtieth International Joint Conference on Artificial Intelligence, IJCAI 2021, Montreal, QC, Canada, 19–27 August 2021; pp. 3125–3133. [CrossRef]
8. Pan, Z.; Hu, L.; Tang, W.; Li, J.; He, Y.; Liu, Z. Privacy-Preserving Multi-Granular Federated Neural Architecture Search–A General Framework. *IEEE Trans. Knowl. Data Eng.* **2023**, *35*, 2975–2986. [CrossRef]
9. Liu, Z.; Hu, C.; Shan, C.; Yan, Z. ADCaDeM: A Novel Method of Calculating Attack Damage Based on Differential Manifolds. *IEEE Trans. Dependable Secur. Comput.* **2023**, *20*, 4070–4084. [CrossRef]

10. Mothukuri, V.; Parizi, R.M.; Pouriyeh, S.; Huang, Y.; Dehghantanha, A.; Srivastava, G. A survey on security and privacy of federated learning. *Future Gener. Comput. Syst.* **2021**, *115*, 619–640. [CrossRef]
11. Yin, X.; Zhu, Y.; Hu, J. A comprehensive survey of privacy-preserving federated learning: A taxonomy, review, and future directions. *ACM Comput. Surv. (CSUR)* **2021**, *54*, 1–36. [CrossRef]
12. Zhang, J.; Zhang, J.; Chen, J.; Yu, S. Gan enhanced membership inference: A passive local attack in federated learning. In Proceedings of the ICC 2020—2020 IEEE International Conference on Communications (ICC), Dublin, Ireland, 7–11 June 2020; pp. 1–6.
13. Zhu, L.; Liu, Z.; Han, S. Deep leakage from gradients. *Adv. Neural Inf. Process. Syst.* **2019**, *32*, 14774–14784.
14. Huang, W.; Sun, M.; Zhu, L.; Oh, S.K.; Pedrycz, W. Deep fuzzy min–max neural network: Analysis and design. *IEEE Trans. Neural Netw. Learn. Syst.* **2022**, 1–12. [CrossRef] [PubMed]
15. Huang, W.; Xiao, Y.; Oh, S.K.; Pedrycz, W.; Zhu, L. Random Polynomial Neural Networks: Analysis and Design. *IEEE Trans. Neural Netw. Learn. Syst.* **2023**, 1–11. [CrossRef] [PubMed]
16. Zhang, C.; Li, S.; Xia, J.; Wang, W.; Yan, F.; Liu, Y. Efficient homomorphic encryption for {Cross-Silo} federated learning. In Proceedings of the 2020 USENIX Annual Technical Conference (USENIX ATC 20), Virtual, 5–17 July 2020; pp. 493–506.
17. Huang, W.; Zhang, Y.; Wan, S. A sorting fuzzy min-max model in an embedded system for atrial fibrillation detection. *ACM Trans. Multimed. Comput. Commun. Appl. (TOMM)* **2022**, *18*, 1–18. [CrossRef]
18. Wei, K.; Li, J.; Ding, M.; Ma, C.; Yang, H.H.; Farokhi, F.; Jin, S.; Quek, T.Q.; Poor, H.V. Federated learning with differential privacy: Algorithms and performance analysis. *IEEE Trans. Inf. Forensics Secur.* **2020**, *15*, 3454–3469. [CrossRef]
19. Li, Q.; Wen, Z.; Wu, Z.; Hu, S.; Wang, N.; Li, Y.; Liu, X.; He, B. A survey on federated learning systems: Vision, hype and reality for data privacy and protection. *IEEE Trans. Knowl. Data Eng.* **2021**, *35*, 3347–3366. [CrossRef]
20. Shi, D.; Li, L.; Chen, R.; Prakash, P.; Pan, M.; Fang, Y. Towards energy efficient federated learning over 5g+ mobile devices. *IEEE Wirel. Commun.* **2022**, *29*, 44–51. [CrossRef]
21. Bonawitz, K.; Eichner, H.; Grieskamp, W.; Huba, D.; Ingerman, A.; Ivanov, V.; Kiddon, C.; Konečný, J.; Mazzocchi, S.; McMahan, B.; et al. Towards federated learning at scale: System design. *Proc. Mach. Learn. Syst.* **2019**, *1*, 374–388.
22. Kim, Y.; Panda, P. Revisiting batch normalization for training low-latency deep spiking neural networks from scratch. *Front. Neurosci.* **2020**, *15*, 773954. [CrossRef]
23. Abadi, M.; Chu, A.; Goodfellow, I.; McMahan, H.B.; Mironov, I.; Talwar, K.; Zhang, L. Deep learning with differential privacy. In Proceedings of the 2016 ACM SIGSAC Conference on Computer and Communications Security, Vienna, Austria, 24–28 October 2016; pp. 308–318.
24. Dwork, C.; McSherry, F.; Nissim, K.; Smith, A. Calibrating noise to sensitivity in private data analysis. In Proceedings of the Theory of Cryptography Conference, New York, NY, USA, 4–7 March 2006; pp. 265–284.
25. Mironov, I. Rényi differential privacy. In Proceedings of the 2017 IEEE 30th Computer Security Foundations Symposium (CSF), Santa Barbara, CA, USA, 21–15 August 2017; pp. 263–275.
26. Li, N.; Qardaji, W.; Su, D.; Wu, Y.; Yang, W. Membership privacy: A unifying framework for privacy definitions. In Proceedings of the 2013 ACM SIGSAC Conference on Computer & Communications Security, Berlin, Germany, 4–8 November 2013; pp. 889–900.
27. Long, Y.; Bindschaedler, V.; Gunter, C.A. Towards measuring membership privacy. *arXiv* **2017**, arXiv:1712.09136.
28. Zari, O.; Xu, C.; Neglia, G. Efficient passive membership inference attack in federated learning. *arXiv* **2021**, arXiv:2111.00430.
29. Wang, Z.; Huang, Y.; Song, M.; Wu, L.; Xue, F.; Ren, K. Poisoning-assisted property inference attack against federated learning. *IEEE Trans. Dependable Secur. Comput.* **2022**, *20*, 3328–3340. [CrossRef]
30. Xu, M.; Li, X. Subject property inference attack in collaborative learning. In Proceedings of the 2020 12th International Conference on Intelligent Human-Machine Systems and Cybernetics (IHMSC), Hangzhou, China, 22–23 August 2020; pp. 227–231.
31. Dong, J.; Roth, A.; Su, W.J. Gaussian differential privacy. *arXiv* **2019**, arXiv:1905.02383.
32. Nishio, T.; Yonetani, R. Client selection for federated learning with heterogeneous resources in mobile edge. In Proceedings of the ICC 2019—2019 IEEE International Conference on Communications (ICC), Shanghai, China, 20–24 May 2019; pp. 1–7.
33. Kairouz, P.; McMahan, H.B.; Avent, B.; Bellet, A.; Bennis, M.; Bhagoji, A.N.; Bonawitz, K.; Charles, Z.; Cormode, G.; Cummings, R.; et al. Advances and open problems in federated learning. *Found. Trends Mach. Learn.* **2021**, *14*, 1–210. [CrossRef]
34. Salem, A.; Zhang, Y.; Humbert, M.; Berrang, P.; Fritz, M.; Backes, M. Ml-leaks: Model and data independent membership inference attacks and defenses on machine learning models. *arXiv* **2018**, arXiv:1806.01246.
35. Ganju, K.; Wang, Q.; Yang, W.; Gunter, C.A.; Borisov, N. Property inference attacks on fully connected neural networks using permutation invariant representations. In Proceedings of the 2018 ACM SIGSAC Conference on Computer and Communications Security, Toronto, ON, Canada, 15–19 October 2018; pp. 619–633.
36. Li, T.; Sahu, A.K.; Talwalkar, A.; Smith, V. Federated learning: Challenges, methods, and future directions. *IEEE Signal Process. Mag.* **2020**, *37*, 50–60. [CrossRef]
37. Tolpegin, V.; Truex, S.; Gursoy, M.E.; Liu, L. Data poisoning attacks against federated learning systems. In Proceedings of the Computer Security—ESORICS 2020: 25th European Symposium on Research in Computer Security, ESORICS 2020, Guildford, UK, 14–18 September 2020; pp. 480–501.
38. Wang, H.; Sreenivasan, K.; Rajput, S.; Vishwakarma, H.; Agarwal, S.; Sohn, J.Y.; Lee, K.; Papailiopoulos, D. Attack of the tails: Yes, you really can backdoor federated learning. *Adv. Neural Inf. Process. Syst.* **2020**, *33*, 16070–16084.

39. Moriai, S. Privacy-preserving deep learning via additively homomorphic encryption. In Proceedings of the 2019 IEEE 26th Symposium on Computer Arithmetic (ARITH), Kyoto, Japan, 10–12 June 2019; p. 198.
40. Ghosh-Dastidar, S.; Adeli, H. Spiking neural networks. *Int. J. Neural Syst.* **2009**, *19*, 295–308. [CrossRef]
41. Yamazaki, K.; Vo-Ho, V.K.; Bulsara, D.; Le, N. Spiking neural networks and their applications: A Review. *Brain Sci.* **2022**, *12*, 863. [CrossRef]
42. Basu, A.; Deng, L.; Frenkel, C.; Zhang, X. Spiking neural network integrated circuits: A review of trends and future directions. In Proceedings of the 2022 IEEE Custom Integrated Circuits Conference (CICC), Newport Beach, CA, USA, 24–27 April 2022; pp. 1–8.
43. Eshraghian, J.K.; Ward, M.; Neftci, E.; Wang, X.; Lenz, G.; Dwivedi, G.; Bennamoun, M.; Jeong, D.S.; Lu, W.D. Training spiking neural networks using lessons from deep learning. *arXiv* **2021**, arXiv:2109.12894.
44. Guo, Y.; Chen, Y.; Zhang, L.; Liu, X.; Wang, Y.; Huang, X.; Ma, Z. IM-Loss: Information Maximization Loss for Spiking Neural Networks. In *Advances in Neural Information Processing Systems*; Koyejo, S., Mohamed, S., Agarwal, A., Belgrave, D., Cho, K., Oh, A., Eds.; Curran Associates, Inc.: Red Hook, NY, USA, 2022; Volume 35, pp. 156–166.
45. Fang, W.; Yu, Z.; Chen, Y.; Huang, T.; Masquelier, T.; Tian, Y. Deep residual learning in spiking neural networks. *Adv. Neural Inf. Process. Syst.* **2021**, *34*, 21056–21069.
46. Li, Y.; Guo, Y.; Zhang, S.; Deng, S.; Hai, Y.; Gu, S. Differentiable spike: Rethinking gradient-descent for training spiking neural networks. *Adv. Neural Inf. Process. Syst.* **2021**, *34*, 23426–23439.
47. Meng, Q.; Xiao, M.; Yan, S.; Wang, Y.; Lin, Z.; Luo, Z.Q. Training high-performance low-latency spiking neural networks by differentiation on spike representation. In Proceedings of the IEEE/CVF Conference on Computer Vision and Pattern Recognition, New Orleans, LA, USA, 19–20 June 2022; pp. 12444–12453.
48. Xie, K.; Zhang, Z.; Li, B.; Kang, J.; Niyato, D.; Xie, S.; Wu, Y. Efficient federated learning with spike neural networks for traffic sign recognition. *IEEE Trans. Veh. Technol.* **2022**, *71*, 9980–9992. [CrossRef]
49. Viale, A.; Marchisio, A.; Martina, M.; Masera, G.; Shafique, M. Carsnn: An efficient spiking neural network for event-based autonomous cars on the loihi neuromorphic research processor. In Proceedings of the 2021 International Joint Conference on Neural Networks (IJCNN), Shenzhen, China, 18–22 July 2021; pp. 1–10.

electronics

MDPI

Article

PIRB: Privacy-Preserving Identity-Based Redactable Blockchains with Accountability

Yuhua Xu [1] **and Zihan Li** [2,*]

[1] School of Computer Science and Technology, Beijing Institute of Technology, Beijing 100081, China; 1120201967@bit.edu.cn
[2] School of Cyberspace Science and Technology, Beijing Institute of Technology, Beijing 100081, China
* Correspondence: zihanl@bit.edu.cn

Abstract: In this paper, we propose a privacy-preserving identity-based redactable blockchain (PIRB), the first identity-based redactable blockchain that supports flexible policies while maintaining accountability. Based on digital identities, PIRB enables a knowledge owner to set one policy for a batch of users while preserving policy privacy. Furthermore, similar to state-of-the-art solutions, PIRB draws inspiration from the proxy re-encryption technique to enforce user accountability. The design of PIRB entails addressing two primary technical challenges: firstly, achieving a flexible policy while upholding policy privacy; secondly, establishing accountability measures. To tackle the former challenge, we propose an enhanced identity-based encryption scheme that integrates polynomial function techniques. To address the latter challenge, a distinct identifier is generated for each user and subsequently concealed within the user's secret key. Specifically, following existing schemes, we present the first scheme PIRB-I to cater to one-way access control scenarios, empowering owners to define access policies for designated editors. Additionally, recognizing the needs on the editor side for owner selection, we enhance PIRB-I through the introduction of matchmaking encryption, thereby supporting bilateral access control in a framework denoted as the second scheme PIRB-II. Notably, PIRB-I and PIRB-II involve a trade-off between computational and communication complexities. Specifically, when contrasted with PIRB-I, PIRB-II facilitates editors in owner selection, thereby mitigating editors' communication overheads at the cost of increased computational overheads during policy generation and matching. Theoretical analysis demonstrates the inherent trade-off complexity and the resilience exhibited by PIRB-I and PIRB-II against chosen-plaintext attacks. Extensive experimentation on the FISCO blockchain shows that, compared with the state-of-the-art works, PIRB-I and PIRB-II achieve 200 times and 100 times computational efficiency improvements and 50 times and 60 times communication efficiency improvements on average, respectively.

Keywords: redactable blockchains; digital identity; privacy preservation; accountability

1. Introduction

Currently, the growing interest in blockchain has led to its increasing identity-based applications, i.e., authentication [1–3], database service [4–7], and health monitoring [8,9]. In these applications, blockchain techniques introduce essential features such as immutability, anonymity, and traceability. To illustrate, consider a scenario in which Alice and Bob engage in the storage, exchange, and management of data through a blockchain-based digital identity scheme on a database [10–12]. Immutability serves to safeguard the security of the submitted digital assets. Simultaneously, anonymity ensures identity privacy for the submitter. Furthermore, traceability effectively thwarts any malicious attempts at data submission. Hence, it is obvious that blockchain techniques exhibit significant potential in identity-based scenarios.

The imperative requirement of redactability in identity-based blockchains has gained prominence in the realm of data security. This requirement harmonizes with the stringent regulations represented by the General Data Protection Regulation (GDPR) [13,14], aiming to uphold users' right to be forgotten and mitigate the dissemination of malicious data. To elucidate, within the framework of an identity-based blockchain on a knowledge marketplace [15], individuals such as Alice, who are knowledge owners, seek to endow their data with an expiration date, thereby preserving their value and veracity. In addition, in the event of Alice introducing malware into the blockchain, the blockchain administrator, Bob, should possess the capability to revoke Alice's malicious data. Alice also needs the capacity to set flexible access policies for editors while preserving privacy to preclude the misuse of editing privileges. Furthermore, to prevent malicious data erasure or tampering, the scheme must effectively institute mechanisms of accountability. Notably, there is a specific concern that Bob, with edit privileges, may exploit the system by maliciously erasing or altering Alice's data for personal gain. These scenarios underscore the crucial role of redactability and accountability in identity-based blockchains, despite the significant challenges they pose.

To satisfy the requirements of an identity-based redactable blockchain, several schemes have been proposed. Chen et al. [16] presented an identity-based chameleon hash scheme without key exposure. Building upon [16], Zhou et al. [17] introduced an innovative identity-based fine-grained redactable blockchain framework. However, the existing identity-based schemes fail to support one policy for a batch of users, thereby constraining the flexibility of privilege distribution, which results in significant overheads when dealing with a batch of users collectively. Additionally, these schemes lack support for accountability, opening the door to potential malicious behaviors. Consequently, our attention is directed toward attribute-based redactable blockchain schemes that facilitate the implementation of flexible policies. Derler et al. [18] initially introduced the policy-based chameleon hash (PCH) approach, harnessing chameleon hash with ephemeral trapdoors (CHET) and attribute-based encryption (ABE). Seeking to bolster accountability, Xu et al. [19] introduced the identity-based signature with existential unforgeability. The access policies in these schemes achieve high flexibility. Regrettably, none of the existing attribute-based schemes have provisions for the preservation of policy privacy [20], potentially leading to privacy breaches when applying existing attribute-based methodologies directly to identity-based scenarios. Specifically, treating each identity as an attribute, during the edit phases of attribute-based redactable blockchain schemes, the policy matrices must be utilized in plaintext. This not only exposes the policy context and size, thus compromising privacy, but also divulges the identities of suitable users during the match process, which can further cause secret key forgery and information leakage, jeopardizing public trust in the blockchain-based digital identity platform. As an illustrative example, within an identity-based blockchain system designed for medical services, Alice, a patient, stores her medical records on the blockchain. She sets a policy that grants the editing privilege to Bob, the designated doctor responsible for ensuring that the records align with Alice's current health condition. However, a potential vulnerability arises with policy disclosure, wherein Bob's identity becomes susceptible to exposure following an editing action. Specifically, if an attacker gains access to the policy's content, they can extract the list of authorized editors' identities and verify that Bob's identity is among them, which could potentially facilitate fraudulent activities and pose threats to the identity-based system's security. Furthermore, while both the existing identity-based and attribute-based schemes concentrate on one-way access control scenarios, none of them satisfies the need to select suitable owners on the editor side to reduce communication costs. This limitation impedes the broader application of redactable blockchain techniques in bilateral access control scenarios, which has become a practical requirement [21–23]. Hence, as shown in Table 1, the research gap pertains to the proposition of an identity-based redactable blockchain with the support of flexible policies while preserving policy privacy, achieving accountability, and supporting bilateral access control.

Table 1. Comparison with redactable blockchain schemes.

Scheme	Paradigm	Policy Privacy	Accountability	Flexible Policy	Access Control
[24]	public-key-based	✘	✘	✘	one-way
[18]	attribute-based	✘	✘	✔	one-way
[25]	consensus-based	✘	✔	✔	one-way
[26]	attribute-based	✘	✔	✔	one-way
[27]	attribute-based	✘	✔	✔	one-way
[28]	attribute-based	✘	✔	✔	one-way
[29]	attribute-based	✘	✘	✔	one-way
[19]	attribute-based	✘	✔	✔	one-way
[16]	identity-based	✔	✘	✘	one-way
[30]	identity-based	✔	✘	✘	one-way
[31]	identity-based	✔	✘	✘	one-way
[17]	identity-based	✔	✘	✘	one-way
PIRB-I	identity-based	✔	✔	✔	one-way
PIRB-II	identity-based	✔	✔	✔	bilateral

The symbols ✔ and ✘ in Table 1 represent "support" and "not support", respectively.

The realization of a practical identity-based redactable blockchain presents three distinct challenges that need to be addressed. Firstly, integrating redactable blockchain functionality within identity-based scenarios requires the formulation of a scheme that supports flexible access policies while upholding policy privacy. Precisely, the scheme should facilitate one policy for a batch of users. Secondly, to enhance the scheme's integrity, accountability measures must be introduced, thereby enabling the imposition of penalties upon users found engaging in malicious behaviors. Thirdly, to meet the imperative of minimizing editors' communication overhead, it becomes crucial to endow editors with the capability to set policies for owner selection. Consequently, the realization of bilateral access control presents itself as a challenge.

In response to the prevailing challenges, we propose a privacy-preserving identity-based redactable blockchain scheme with accountability. Specifically, we summarize our contributions as follows.

- To tackle the challenges, we present a privacy-preserving identity-based redactable blockchain based on the chameleon hash with ephemeral trapdoors, denoted as PIRB, which contains two schemes, PIRB-I and PIRB-II. With an identity-based encryption scheme introduced, PIRB-I facilitates one-way access control, while PIRB-II achieves bilateral access control while upholding match privacy preservation. Moreover, we leverage the polynomial function technique to support one policy for a batch of users.
- To mitigate the potential misuse of editing privileges for malicious behaviors, the proxy re-encryption technique is introduced as an accountability mechanism.
- A formal theoretical analysis establishes the correctness, security, and complexity of PIRB. Correctness analysis proves the necessary and sufficient conditions for the accurate operation of PIRB, contingent upon the fulfillment of the policy by the identity-based attribute. Security analysis demonstrates that PIRB concurrently upholds trapdoor privacy, identity privacy, policy privacy, and match privacy under the chosen-plaintext attack model. Additionally, complexity analysis presents the computational and communication complexity of both PIRB-I and PIRB-II, comparing them with two existing attribute-based redactable blockchain schemes. Empirical experiments corroborate our scheme's practical efficiency enhancements.

Organization. In this paper, we present a comprehensive overview of our work, organized as follows. The problem formulation, which includes the system model, threat model, problem statement, and design goals, is introduced in Section 2. Next, we introduce the preliminaries, which present the definition of the chameleon hash with ephemeral trapdoors and identity-based encryption, in Section 3. Subsequently, Section 4 is dedicated to the detailed construction of PIRB-I and PIRB-II. In Section 5, a formal theoretical analysis, which thoroughly analyzes the correctness, security, and complexity of PIRB-I and PIRB-II, is provided. In Section 6, we present a thorough performance evaluation. The related works are introduced in Section 7. Finally, we give the conclusions of this paper in Section 8.

2. Problem Formulation

2.1. System Model

Within our system, the central emphasis lies on the consortium blockchain, a framework commonly employed for data sharing. The operation of our system is conducted under the oversight of multiple authoritative nodes, ensuring privacy preservation. As depicted in Figure 1, the system model of PIRB encompasses four primary entities: consortium nodes, knowledge owners, knowledge editors, and service nodes. These entities are elaborated upon as follows.

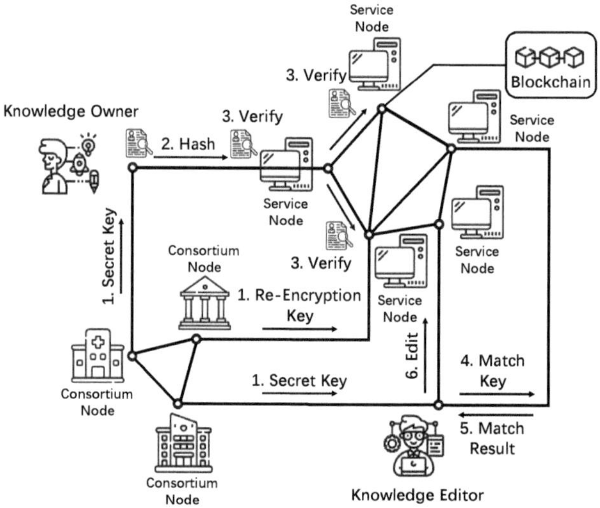

Figure 1. System model of PIRB.

Consortium Node. The responsibility for key generation and the allocation of virtual identities rests with the consortium nodes. These nodes also uphold accountability by managing the association between virtual and actual identities, disclosing such information publicly when required. Typically, these consortium nodes are endowed with authorization due to their representation of prominent enterprises, thereby considered to be fully trusted.

Knowledge Owner. Knowledge owners encompass both entities and individuals who submit data into the blockchain. These proprietors have the authority to grant specific users the edit privilege through the formulation of an identity-based access policy concurrent with the generation of the data hash.

Knowledge Editor. The task of a knowledge editor involves proficiently matching authorized data for editing with corresponding trapdoors of CHET, utilizing service nodes. Subsequently, in finalizing the edit, the knowledge editor calculates a valid message for the edited data, ensuring that all checks hold while maintaining the original data hash.

Service Node. Service nodes are responsible for storing and updating the blockchain, as well as overseeing proxy re-encryption and matching services for knowledge editors. Specifically, these nodes decentralize the storage of the blockchain and, when engaging in edits, they ensure data consistency through a consensus protocol. Importantly, they also preserve the integrity of the original records for accountability.

2.2. Threat Model

The consortium nodes are bestowed with full trust, engaging in interactions solely through secure channels. Functioning as data submitters, the knowledge owners are also fully trusted. The service nodes are honest-but-curious. This implies that these service nodes faithfully execute computations and adhere to protocols yet concurrently harbor an intent to gather privacy-related information from other entities. Specifically, while matching appropriate editors to messages, the service nodes endeavor to attain the ability to modify messages, thereby attempting to procure unwarranted privileges. Additionally, the service nodes strive to ascertain the identities of users along with deducing interrelationships among these users via the outcomes of matches. Notably, the knowledge editors are positioned as untrusted entities. To elaborate, a knowledge editor endeavors to gain editing rights for messages for which the owners have not been granted. Furthermore, even an editor who possesses edit privileges may exhibit malicious behaviors, seeking to evade subsequent repercussions. It is imperative to acknowledge that the service nodes are devoid of collusion capabilities with other entities, as well as any inclination to feign legitimacy as valid knowledge owners or editors.

2.3. Problem Statement and Design Goals

Certain regulations necessitate the redactability of blockchains for effective management. Nonetheless, the inherent structure of hash links imposes substantial constraints on the redactability, striking a balance between security and flexibility. To address this challenge, some solutions have been proposed in the form of attribute-based redactable blockchain schemes. However, within an identity-based framework, the absence of a redactable blockchain scheme remains conspicuous. Moreover, a straightforward adaptation of existing attribute-based schemes is deemed infeasible due to the potential privacy vulnerabilities in identity-based scenarios. Specifically, considering each identity as an attribute, during edit phases in attribute-based redactable blockchain schemes, the utilization of policies for plaintext purposes lacks the preservation of the policy context and size privacy, consequently enabling the potential inference of the suitable editors' identities. Thus, the main challenge lies in devising a privacy-preserving identity-based redactable blockchain solution that encompasses trapdoor privacy, identity privacy, policy privacy, and match privacy, all while upholding accountability. We delineate a set of design goals as follows.

Privacy. The preservation of privacy in PIRB is of paramount importance, encompassing trapdoor privacy, identity privacy, policy privacy, and match privacy. Specifically, regarding trapdoor privacy, PIRB ensures that an editor's access to the trapdoor of CHET from the ciphertext is contingent upon the satisfaction of the owner's requirements by the editor's identity and policy. Concerning identity privacy, PIRB ensures that only the consortium nodes possess the capability to differentiate the actual identity of a participating user from that of their peers. Both users and service nodes remain incapable of distinguishing, in the absence of consortium nodes, the submitting owner or editor from other entities. Turning to policy privacy, PIRB prevents any derivation of the user's policy content or size from the ciphertext. With only a user's ciphertext, discerning a fitting identity for the policy or ascertaining the precise policy dimension becomes an infeasible task. Lastly, match privacy necessitates that service nodes remain devoid of any information in instances where an editor fails to match a message. Within the binary access control scenario, the failure of a match prevents service nodes from distinguishing the fitness of the owner's or editor's identity.

Utility. The design of PIRB should prioritize flexibility and efficiency. It should be capable of accommodating one-way and bilateral access control, while also supporting one policy for a batch of users. The core services within the PIRB framework, i.e., hash generation, match, and edit, should be executed with optimal efficiency. It is crucial that the PIRB system delivers these services accurately, with minimal computational and communication overheads.

Accountability. If a case of malicious editing behavior is identified within the PIRB system, appropriate penalties can be enforced through a traceable process. In the context of such misconduct, the consortium nodes possess the capability to ascertain the actual identity of an anonymous editor.

3. Preliminaries

3.1. Chameleon Hash with Ephemeral Trapdoors

The chameleon hash (CH) [32] empowers a message to be edited without changing its hash. Specifically, the public key and its trapdoor are generated first. To compute the hash of a message m, a randomness r is selected for m, and the hash h can be generated with (m,r). To replace m with m', an editor needs to obtain the trapdoor and compute a new randomness r' for m' where the hash of (m',r') is still h. To improve trapdoor security, the chameleon hash with ephemeral trapdoors (CHET) [33] was proposed. For each message m, a unique ephemeral trapdoor is generated to preserve the edit privilege from the leakage of the long-time trapdoor. The security of CHET is described in detail in [34]. In our constructions, we employ CHET to achieve the desirable property of redactability within the blockchain. The definition of CHET is presented as follows.

Definition 1. *CHET: The scheme CHET consists of five algorithms* (**PPGen**, **KTGen**, **Hash**, **Verify**, **Edit**).

PPGen $\lambda \to \mathsf{pp}_{\mathsf{CHET}}$: *On inputting the security parameter* λ, **PPGen** *outputs the public parameter* $\mathsf{pp}_{\mathsf{CHET}}$.

KTGen $\mathsf{pp}_{\mathsf{CHET}} \to (\mathsf{pk}_{\mathsf{CHET}}, \mathsf{ltd}_{\mathsf{CHET}})$: *On inputting the public parameter* $\mathsf{pp}_{\mathsf{CHET}}$, **KTGen** *outputs the public key* $\mathsf{pk}_{\mathsf{CHET}}$ *and the long-term trapdoor* $\mathsf{ltd}_{\mathsf{CHET}} = d_1$.

Hash $(\mathsf{pk}_{\mathsf{CHET}}, m) \to (\mathsf{etd}_{\mathsf{CHET}}, h, r)$: *On inputting the public key* $\mathsf{pk}_{\mathsf{CHET}} = e$ *and the message* $m \in \mathcal{M}$, **Hash** *outputs the hash* $h = (h_1,h_2)$, *the randomness* $r = (r_1,r_2)$ *and the ephemeral trapdoor* $\mathsf{etd}_{\mathsf{CHET}} = d_2$, *where* $\mathcal{M}$ *is the massage space. Specifically, for* $z \in \{1,2\}$,

$$h_z = G_z(m) r_z^e \bmod N_z,$$

where $G_z : \{0,1\}^* \to \mathbb{Z}^*_{N_z}$, $N_z = p_z q_z$, $ed_z \equiv 1 \bmod (p_z-1)(q_z-1)$.

Verify $(\mathsf{pk}_{\mathsf{CHET}}, m, h, r) \to V$: *On inputting the public key* $\mathsf{pk}_{\mathsf{CHET}}$, *the message* m, *the hash* h *and the randomness* r, **Verify** *outputs the result* $V \in 0,1$.

Edit $(\mathsf{ltd}_{\mathsf{CHET}}, \mathsf{etd}_{\mathsf{CHET}}, m, m', h, r) \to r'$: *On inputting the long-term trapdoor* $\mathsf{ltd}_{\mathsf{CHET}} = d_1$, *the ephemeral trapdoor* $\mathsf{etd}_{\mathsf{CHET}} = d_2$, *the message* m, *the edited message* m', *the hash* h *and the randomness* r, **Edit** *outputs the new randomness* $r' = (r'_1, r'_2)$. *Specifically, for* $z \in \{1,2\}$,

$$r'_z = \left(h_z (G_z(m'))^{-1}\right)^{d_z} \bmod N_z,$$

to ensure that $G_z(m') r'^e_z \bmod N_z = G_z(m) r^e_z \bmod N_z = h_z$. *Therefore,* m *is edited to* m' *without changing the hash* h.

3.2. Identity-Based Encryption

Identity-based encryption (IBE) [35] allows users to set the identity-based access policy for their ciphertexts without the traditional public key so that the need for the certificate authority is mitigated. In our constructions, we utilize IBE to implement an access control mechanism for the trapdoors of CHET. The definition of IBE is presented as follows.

Definition 2. *IBE: The scheme IBE consists of four algorithms* (**Setup**, **KeyGen**, **Encrypt**, **Decrypt**).

Setup $\lambda \rightarrow (\mathsf{pp}_{\mathsf{IBE}}, \mathsf{msk}_{\mathsf{IBE}})$: *On inputting the security parameter λ,* **Setup** *outputs the public parameter $\mathsf{pp}_{\mathsf{IBE}} = (P, sP)$ and the master secret key $\mathsf{msk}_{\mathsf{IBE}} = s$.*

KeyGen $(\mathsf{pp}_{\mathsf{IBE}}, \mathsf{msk}_{\mathsf{IBE}}, ID) \rightarrow (\mathsf{pk}_{\mathsf{CHET}}, \mathsf{sk}_{\mathsf{CHET}})$: *On inputting the public parameter $\mathsf{pp}_{\mathsf{CHET}}$, the master secret key $\mathsf{msk}_{\mathsf{IBE}}$ and a user's identity $ID \in \{0,1\}^*$,* **KeyGen** *outputs the user's secret key $\mathsf{sk}_{\mathsf{ID}} = sQ_{ID}$, where ID is used as a public key.*

Encrypt $(ID, m) \rightarrow c$: *On inputting the user's identity ID and the plaintext $m \in \mathcal{M}$,* **Encrypt** *outputs the ciphertext $c \in \mathcal{C}$ as*

$$c = (c_0, c_1) = (rP, m \oplus e(sP, Q_{ID})^r),$$

where $\mathcal{M}$ is the plaintext space and $\mathcal{C}$ is the ciphertext space.

Decrypt $(\mathsf{sk}_{\mathsf{ID}}, c) \rightarrow m$: *On inputting the user's secret key $\mathsf{sk}_{\mathsf{ID}}$ and the ciphertext c,* **Decrypt** *outputs the the plaintext m' as*

$$m' = c \oplus e(rP, sQ_{ID}) = m,$$

3.3. Polynomial Function

The polynomial function technique allows one policy to match with multiple roots. Specifically, to hide a secret t, the owner selects roots $x_1, x_2, \cdots, x_n$ as the keys of access control and computes

$$f(x) = r\prod_{i=1}^{n}(x - x_i) + t = \sum_{l=0}^{n} a_l x^l,$$

where r is a random value. Subsequently, the owner submits the coefficients $\{a_l\}_{l=0}^{n}$. Then, a user with the root $x_u \in \{x_i\}_{i=0}^{n}$ can compute

$$f(x_u) = \sum_{l=0}^{n} a_l x_u^l = r \prod_{i=1, i\neq u}^{n} (x_u - x_i) \cdot (x_u - x_u) + t = t,$$

to recover the secret t. Otherwise, the user cannot obtain t. In our constructions, we leverage the polynomial function technique to attain flexible policies, wherein one policy can be applied to a batch of users.

4. Proposed Schemes

In this section, we introduce the detailed design of the two schemes of PIRB, PIRB-I and PIRB-II. The notations are summarized in Table 2.

Table 2. Notations and descriptions.

Notation	Description	Notation	Description
Ψ	The description of the bilinear map.	$\mathsf{epk}_{\mathsf{CHET,j}}$	Owner u_j's ephemeral public key ofCHET.
mpk	The master public key.	$\mathsf{etd}_{\mathsf{CHET,j}}$	Owner u_j's ephemeral trapdoor of CHET.
msk	The master secret key.	$\mathsf{rsk}_{\mathsf{k}}$	Editor u_k's edit re-encryption key.
$\mathcal{U}$	The set of all users.	m_j	Owner u_j's message.
$\mathcal{U}_i$	The set of user u_i's authorized editors or interested owners.	h_j	The hash of m_j.
N	The preset maximum policy size.	r_j	The randomness of m_j.
n_i	The number of elements in $\mathcal{U}_i$.	T_j	Owner u_j's match ciphertext.
ID_{u_i}	User u_i's identity.	$T_{j,0}$	Owner u_j's trapdoor ciphertext.
VID_{u_i}	User u_i's virtual identity.	$T_{j,1}$	Owner u_j's search ciphertext.
$\mathsf{sk}_{\mathsf{IBE,i}}$	User u_i's secret key of IBE.	$T_{j,2}$	Owner u_j's return ciphertext.
$\mathsf{rsk}_{\mathsf{IBE,i}}$	User u_i's re-encryption key of IBE.	K_k	Editor u_k's match key.
$\mathsf{pk}_{\mathsf{CHET,j}}$	Owneru_j's long-term public key of CHET.	$R_{k,j}$	Editor u_k's match result with owner u_j.
$\mathsf{ltd}_{\mathsf{CHET,j}}$	Owner u_j's long-term trapdoor of CHET.	R_k	The set of editor u_k's match results.

4.1. Proposed PIRB-I

4.1.1. Main Idea

PIRB-I is a privacy-preserving identity-based redactable blockchain scheme with accountability and one-way access control. The consortium nodes first exchange the identity-based secret keys to the users and the associated re-encryption keys to the service nodes simultaneously as the basis of policy generation. Then, a number of knowledge owners generate the match ciphertext with identity-based policies while computing the hashes and submitting the messages to the service nodes. When a knowledge editor requests the edit privilege, the editor computes the match key and submits it to the service nodes. After receiving the match key, the service nodes operate a match with the re-encryption key and return the match result to the editor. Finally, the editor decrypts the result and computes the new randomness to edit the message without changing the hash.

4.1.2. Detailed Construction

PIRB-I consists of seven phases, i.e., **Setup**, **KeyGen**, **Hash**, **Verify**, **Match**, **Edit**, **Trace**. The workflow of PIRB-I is shown in Figure 2.

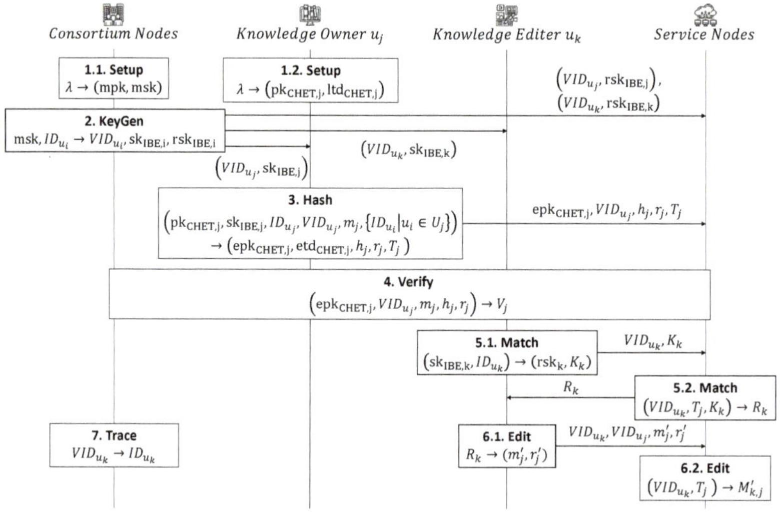

Figure 2. Workflow of PIRB-I.

Setup $\lambda \to (\mathrm{mpk}, \mathrm{msk}, \mathrm{pk}_{\mathrm{CHET,j}}, \mathrm{ltd}_{\mathrm{CHET,j}})$: The consortium nodes cooperate to generate a description of the bilinear map $\Psi = (p, g, \mathbb{G}, \mathbb{G}_T, e)$, where $e : \mathbb{G} \times \mathbb{G} \to \mathbb{G}_T$, and select two hash functions $H_1[\cdot] : \{0,1\}^* \to \mathbb{Z}_p$ and $H_2[\cdot] : \mathbb{G}_T \to \{0,1\}^*$. Subsequently, the consortium nodes select a random value $s \in \mathbb{Z}_p$ as the master secret key msk and select $(g^{\frac{1}{s}}, H_1[\cdot], H_2[\cdot], \Psi)$ as the master public key mpk.

Simultaneously, every knowledge owner generates a long-term trapdoor for chameleon hash with ephemeral trapdoors (CHET). Specifically, knowledge owner u_j selects primes $e_j, p_{j,1}, q_{j,1}$ and set $N_{j,1} = p_{j,1}q_{j,1}$. Then, u_j computes $d_{j,1}$ that $e_j d_{j,1} \equiv 1 \bmod (p_{j,1} - 1)(q_{j,1} - 1)$ as the long-term trapdoor of CHET $\mathrm{ltd}_{\mathrm{CHET,j}}$, chooses a hash function $G_{j,1} : \{0,1\}^* \to \mathbb{Z}^*_{N_{j,1}}$ and selects $(N_{j,1}, e_j, G_{j,1})$ as the long-term public key $\mathrm{pk}_{\mathrm{CHET,j}}$.

KeyGen $(\mathrm{msk}, \{ID_{u_i} | u_i \in \mathcal{U}\}) \to (\{VID_{u_i} | u_i \in \mathcal{U}\}, \{\mathrm{sk}_{\mathrm{IBE,i}} | u_i \in \mathcal{U}\}, \{\mathrm{rsk}_{\mathrm{IBE,i}} | u_i \in \mathcal{U}\})$: For each user in the user set U, including each knowledge owner, the consortium nodes generate a secret key. Specifically, for user $u_i \in U$ with identity ID_{u_i}, the consortium nodes generate a virtual identity VID_{u_i} randomly. Subsequently, the consortium nodes select random value $s_{i,0}$ as u_i's re-encryption key $\mathrm{rsk}_{\mathrm{IBE,i}}$ and compute $g^{s_{i,0} s H_1(ID_{u_i})}$ as u_i's secret key $\mathrm{sk}_{\mathrm{IBE,i}}$. Then, the consortium nodes send $(VID_{u_i}, \mathrm{sk}_{\mathrm{IBE,i}})$ to u_i and $(VID_{u_i}, \mathrm{rsk}_{\mathrm{IBE,i}})$ to the service nodes via a secure channel.

Hash $(\mathrm{pk}_{\mathrm{CHET,j}}, \mathrm{sk}_{\mathrm{IBE,j}}, ID_{u_j}, VID_{u_j}, m_j, \{ID_{u_i} | u_i \in \mathcal{U}_j\}) \to (\mathrm{epk}_{\mathrm{CHET,j}}, \mathrm{etd}_{\mathrm{CHET,j}}, h_j, r_j, T_j)$: For a message of knowledge m_j on the blockchain, the knowledge owner u_j computes the hash value h_j and sets the access policy. Note that the knowledge m_j can be stored either in plaintext or ciphertext, allowing the owner u_j to employ ciphertext as a means to safeguard data privacy. Specifically, u_j selects primes $p_{j,2}, q_{j,2}$ and sets $N_{j,2} = p_{j,2}q_{j,2}$. Compute $d_{j,2}$ that $e_j d_{j,2} \equiv 1 \bmod (p_{j,2}-1)(q_{j,2}-1)$ as the ephemeral trapdoor of CHET $\mathsf{etd}_{\mathsf{CHET,j}}$. Choose a hash function $G_{j,2} : \{0,1\}^* \to \mathbb{Z}^*_{N_{j,2}}$ and select $(e_j, N_{j,1}, G_{j,1}, N_{j,2}, G_{j,2})$ as the ephemeral public key $\mathsf{epk}_{\mathsf{CHET,j}}$. Subsequently, u_j generates the hash of m_j as $h_j = (h_{j,1}, h_{j,2})$, and for $z \in \{1,2\}$,

$$h_{j,z} = G_{j,z}\left(VID_{u_j}, m_j, G_{j,1}, N_{j,1}, G_{j,2}, N_{j,2}\right) r_{j,z}^{e_j} \bmod N_{j,z},$$

where $r_{j,1}, r_{j,2}$ are random values and $r_j = (r_{j,1}, r_{j,2})$. To set the access policy, the knowledge owner u_j selects a random value $t \in \mathbb{Z}_p$ and calculates the trapdoor ciphertext $T_{j,0} = (T_{j,0,1}, T_{j,0,2}) = (d_{j,1} \oplus G_{j,1}(e(g,g)^t), d_{j,2} \oplus G_{j,2}(e(g,g)^t))$. Subsequently, u_j selects a list $\mathcal{U}_j = \{u_1, u_2, \cdots, u_n\}$ with n members who have the adapting right and expands the number of elements to N with fuzzy identities as $\mathcal{U}'_j = \{u_1, u_2, \cdots, u_n, u'_{n+1}, \cdots, u'_N\}$, $\mathcal{U}''_j = \{u_1, u_2, \cdots, u_n, u''_{n+1}, \cdots, u''_N\}$ before the generation of polynomial functions. Note that to weaken the correlation between the two functions, the fuzzy identities of each polynomial function are unique. In addition, the fuzzy identities are selected to avoid affecting the **Match** phase. Then, u_j generates

$$\begin{aligned} f_1(x) =& r_1 \prod_{i=1, u'_i \in \mathcal{U}'_j}^{N} \left(x - H_1\left(ID_{u'_i}\right)\right) = \sum_{l=0}^{N} a_l x^l, \\ f_2(x) =& r_2 \prod_{i=1, u''_i \in \mathcal{U}''_j}^{N} \left(x - H_1\left(ID_{u''_i}\right)\right) + t = \sum_{l=0}^{N} b_l x^l, \end{aligned}$$

where $r_1, r_2 \in \mathbb{Z}_p$ are random values.

Then, u_j computes the search ciphertext $T_{j,1}$ as

$$\begin{aligned} T_{j,1} &= (T_{j,1,N}, T_{j,1,N-1}, \cdots, T_{j,1,1}, T_{j,1,0}), \\ T_{j,1,l} &= g^{\frac{a_l}{s}}, 1 \le l \le N, \\ T_{j,1,0} &= g^{a_0}, \end{aligned}$$

and the return ciphertext $T_{j,2}$ as

$$\begin{aligned} T_{j,2} &= (T_{j,2,N}, T_{j,2,N-1}, \cdots, T_{j,2,1}, T_{j,2,0}), \\ T_{j,2,l} &= g^{\frac{b_l}{s}}, 1 \le l \le N, \\ T_{j,1,0} &= g^{b_0}, \end{aligned}$$

with mpk. Then, u_j sets the match ciphertext $T_j = (T_{j,0}, T_{j,1}, T_{j,2})$.

Finally, u_j sends $(\mathsf{epk}_{\mathsf{CHET,j}}, VID_{u_j}, h_j, r_j, T_j)$ to the service nodes. Note that with the message above, the service nodes cannot obtain ID_{u_j}.

Verify $(\mathsf{epk}_{\mathsf{CHET,j}}, VID_{u_j}, m_j, h_j, r_j) \to V_j$: After the service nodes receive the message, every node can verify the hash. Specifically, with $\mathsf{epk}_{\mathsf{CHET,j}}$, the node checks $h_{j,1} \stackrel{?}{=} G_{j,1}(VID_{u_j}, m_j, G_{j,1}, N_{j,1}, G_{j,2}, N_{j,2}) r_{j,1}^{e_j}$ and $h_{j,2} \stackrel{?}{=} G_{j,2}(VID_{u_j}, m_j, G_{j,1}, N_{j,1}, G_{j,2}, N_{j,2}) r_{j,2}^{e_j}$. If all checks hold, the node returns the result $V_j = 1$ and otherwise returns $V_j = 0$.

Match $(VID_{u_k}, T_j, K_k) \to R_k$: To find the editable message for u_k on the blockchain, the user u_k sends a request to the service nodes, and the service nodes return the message to u_k. Specifically, with $\mathsf{sk}_{\mathsf{IBE,k}} = g^{s_{k,0} s H_1(ID_{u_k})}$, u_k calculates the match key K_k as

$$\begin{aligned} K_k &= (K_{k,N}, K_{k,N-1}, \cdots, K_{k,1}, K_{k,0}), \\ K_{k,m} &= g^{s_k s_{k,0} s H_1(ID_{u_k})^m}, 1 \le m \le N, \\ K_{k,0} &= g^{s_k}, \end{aligned}$$

where s_k is a random value, and it sets the edit re-encryption key $\mathsf{rsk_k} = s_k$. Then, u_k sends K_k to the service nodes. Note that with K_k, the service nodes cannot obtain ID_{u_j}. After receiving K_k, with $T_{j,1}$, the service nodes calculate

$$M_{k,j} = \prod_{l=1}^{N} e\left(T_{j,1,l}, K_{k,l}^{\frac{1}{s_{k,0}}}\right) \cdot e(T_{j,1,0}, K_{k,0})$$

to match u_k with u_j's message and then check $M_{j,k} \stackrel{?}{=} e(g,g)^0$. If $u_k \in U_j$, $M_{j,k} = e(g,g)^0$; otherwise, the service nodes cannot obtain any information from $M_{j,k}$. Then, with $T_{j,2}$, the service nodes calculate

$$\begin{aligned} R_{k,j,0} =& \prod_{l=1}^{N} e\left(T_{j,2,l}, K_{k,l}^{\frac{1}{s_{k,0}}}\right) \cdot e(T_{j,2,0}, K_{k,0}) \\ =& e(g,g)^{s_k t}, \end{aligned}$$

and select $R_{k,j} = (R_{k,j,0}, \mathsf{epk_{CHET,j}}, VID_{u_j}, m_j, h_j, r_j, T_j)$. Finally, the service nodes return the set of match results $R_k = \{R_{k,j} | M_{k,j} = e(g,g)^0\}$ to u_k.

Edit $(\mathsf{rsk_k}, R_k) \to (m'_j, r'_j)$: Receiving the set of match results from the service nodes, u_k obtains the edit privilege. Our constructions provide support for both on-chain storage and hybrid storage approaches. In the interest of conciseness, we will focus on hybrid storage. Specifically, u_k first verifies the hash as the phase of **Verify**. If $V_j = 1$, with $R_{k,j,0} = e(g,g)^{s_k t}$ and the edit re-encryption key $\mathsf{rsk_k} = s_k$, u_k computes $(e(g,g)^{s_k t})^{\frac{1}{s_k}} = e(g,g)^t$ and $T_{j,0,1} \oplus G_{j,1}(e(g,g)^t) = d_{j,1}, T_{j,0,2} \oplus G_{j,2}(e(g,g)^t) = d_{j,2}$. Subsequently, for $z \in \{1,2\}$, u_k computes

$$r'_{j,z} = \left(h_{j,z}\left(G_{j,z}\left(VID_{u_j}, m'_j, G_{j,1}, N_{j,1}, G_{j,2}, N_{j,2}\right)\right)^{-1}\right)^{d_{j,z}} \mod N_{j,z},$$

and sets $r'_j = (r'_{j,1}, r'_{j,2})$ to change m_j to m'_j and then checks $h_{j,1} \stackrel{?}{=} G_{j,1}(VID_{u_j}, m'_j, G_{j,1}, N_{j,1}, G_{j,2}, N_{j,2}) r'^{\,e_j}_{j,1}$ and $h_{j,2} \stackrel{?}{=} G_{j,2}(VID_{u_j}, m'_j, G_{j,1}, N_{j,1}, G_{j,2}, N_{j,2}) r'^{\,e_j}_{j,2}$. Next, u_k sends $(VID_{u_j}, VID_{u_k}, m'_j, r'_j)$ to the service nodes by encapsulating it within a transaction. If all checks hold, the service nodes submit the updated data $(VID_{u_j}, VID_{u_k}, m'_j, r'_j)$ to the blockchain, ensuring that the original data are modified while preserving the integrity of the hash value.

Trace $VID_{u_k} \to ID_{u_k}$: If an editor is found to display malicious behaviors, the consortium nodes will reveal their actual identity to the public for penalties. Specifically, if the malicious behaviors of u_k are found, with the virtual identity VID_{u_k}, the consortium nodes will find the associated actual identity ID_{u_k} and reveal it to the public to stop the service to u_k and impose penalties on the editor.

4.2. Proposed PIRB-II

4.2.1. Main Idea

PIRB-I addresses the challenge in one-way access control scenarios; however, the absence of predetermined owner selection may lead to the excessive influx of messages for editors. In light of this, we introduce PIRB-II, which empowers editors to establish policies for owner selection. This refinement aims to mitigate the issue of message overload for editors, enhancing the overall system's efficiency and functionality. To enable bilateral access control, PIRB-II is different in the **Hash** and **Match** phases from PIRB-I. Specifically, the match key of the owner and the match ciphertext of the editor are also needed in the **Match** phase. To preserve the match privacy, the owner and the editor, respectively, generate the match ciphertext and key with a random value.

4.2.2. Detailed Construction

PIRB-II consists of seven phases, i.e., **Setup**, **KeyGen**, **Hash**, **Verify**, **Match**, **Edit**, **Trace**. We highlight the **Hash** and **Match** phases in PIRB-II, which are different from those in PIRB-I. The workflow of PIRB-II is shown in Figure 3.

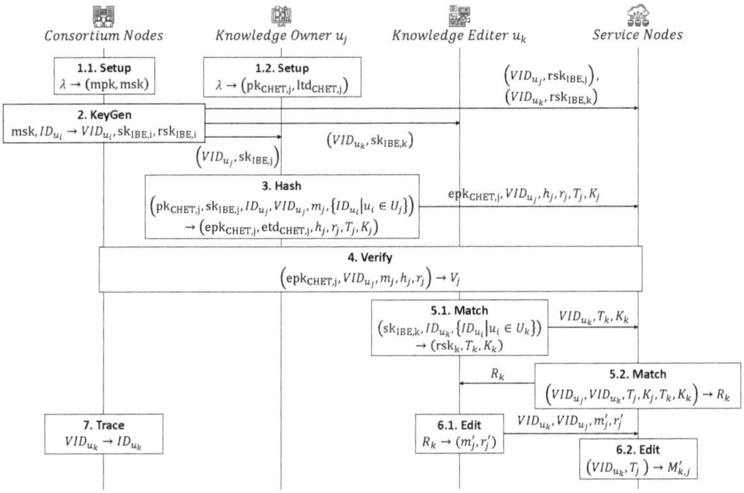

Figure 3. Workflow of PIRB-II.

Setup $\lambda \rightarrow (\mathsf{mpk}, \mathsf{msk}, \mathsf{pk}_{\mathsf{CHET,j}}, \mathsf{ltd}_{\mathsf{CHET,j}})$: The phase of **Setup** is the same as PIRB-I.

KeyGen $(\mathsf{msk}, \{ID_{u_i} | u_i \in \mathcal{U}\}) \rightarrow (\{VID_{u_i} | u_i \in \mathcal{U}\}, \{\mathsf{sk}_{\mathsf{IBE,i}} | u_i \in \mathcal{U}\}, \{\mathsf{rsk}_{\mathsf{IBE,i}} | u_i \in \mathcal{U}\})$: The phase of **KeyGen** is the same as PIRB-I.

Hash $(\mathsf{pk}_{\mathsf{CHET,j}}, \mathsf{sk}_{\mathsf{IBE,k}}, ID_{u_j}, VID_{u_j}, m_j, \{ID_{u_i} | u_i \in \mathcal{U}_j\}) \rightarrow (\mathsf{epk}_{\mathsf{CHET,j}}, \mathsf{etd}_{\mathsf{CHET,j}}, h_j, r_j, T_j, K_j)$: For a message of knowledge m_j in plaintext or ciphertext on the blockchain, the knowledge owner u_j computes the hash value h_j and sets the access policy. Specifically, as in PIRB-I, u_j selects primes $p_{j,2}, q_{j,2}$, computes $N_{j,2}, d_{j,2}$ and chooses a hash function $G_{j,2}$. Then, u_j selects $\mathsf{epk}_{\mathsf{CHET,j}} = (e_j, N_{j,1}, G_{j,1}, N_{j,2}, G_{j,2})$ and $\mathsf{etd}_{\mathsf{CHET,j}} = d_{j,2}$. Subsequently, u_j generates the hash h_j and sets $r_j = (r_{j,1}, r_{j,2})$. To set the access policy, the knowledge owner u_j selects a random value $t \in \mathbb{Z}_p$, calculates the trapdoor ciphertext $T_{j,0}$, selects a list $\mathcal{U}_j$ and expands the number of elements to N with fuzzy identities as $\mathcal{U}_j', \mathcal{U}_j''$ as in PIRB-I before the generation of polynomial functions. Then, u_j generates

$$f_{j,1}(x) = r_1 \prod_{i=1, u_i' \in \mathcal{U}_j'}^{N} \left(x - H_1\left(ID_{u_i'}\right)\right) - s_j = \sum_{l=0}^{N} a_l x^l,$$

$$f_{j,2}(x) = r_2 \prod_{i=1, u_i'' \in \mathcal{U}_j''}^{N} \left(x - H_1\left(ID_{u_i''}\right)\right) + t - s_j = \sum_{l=0}^{N} b_l x^l,$$

where $r_1, r_2, s_j \in \mathbb{Z}_p$ are random values.

Then, u_j computes the search ciphertext $T_{j,1}$ and the return ciphertext $T_{j,2}$ as in PIRB-I, with mpk and sets the match ciphertext $T_j = (T_{j,0}, T_{j,1}, T_{j,2})$. Subsequently, with $\mathsf{sk}_{\mathsf{IBE,k}}$, u_j generates the match key K_j as

$$K_j = (K_{j,N}, K_{j,N-1}, \cdots, K_{j,1}, K_{j,0}),$$
$$K_{j,l} = g^{s_j s_{j,0} s H_1(ID_{u_j})^l}, 1 \leq l \leq N,$$
$$K_{j,0} = g^{s_j},$$

Finally, u_j submits $(\mathsf{epk}_{\mathsf{CHET,j}}, VID_{u_j}, h_j, r_j, T_j, K_j)$ to the blockchain.

Verify $(\mathsf{epk}_{\mathsf{CHET,j}}, VID_{u_j}, m_j, h_j, r_j) \rightarrow V_j$: The phase of **Verify** is the same as in PIRB-I.

Match $(VID_{u_k}, VID_{u_j}, T_j, K_j, T_k, K_k) \rightarrow R_k$: To find the editable message for u_k on the blockchain, the user u_k sends a request to the service nodes, and the service nodes return the message to u_k. Specifically, u_k selects a list $\mathcal{U}_k = \{u_{k,1}, u_{k,2}, \cdots, u_{k,n_k}\}$ with n_k interested owners and expands the number of elements to N with fuzzy identities as $\mathcal{U}'_k = \{u_{k,1}, u_{k,2}, \cdots, u_{k,n_k}, u'_{k,n_k+1}, \cdots, u'_{k,N}\}$ before the generation of polynomial functions. Then, u_k generates

$$f_k(x) = r_3 \prod_{i=1, u'_i \in \mathcal{U}'_k}^{N} \left(x - H_1\left(ID_{u'_i}\right)\right) + s_k = \sum_{m=0}^{N} c_m x^m,$$

where r_3, s_k are random values, and it computes the match ciphertext

$$T_k = (T_{k,N}, T_{k,N-1}, \cdots, T_{k,1}, T_{k,0}),$$
$$T_{k,m} = g^{\frac{c_m}{s}}, 1 \leq m \leq N,$$
$$T_{k,0} = g^{a_0},$$

with mpk. Subsequently, with $\mathsf{sk_{IBE,k}}$, u_k calculates the match key K_k as in PIRB-I and sets the edit re-encryption key $\mathsf{rsk_k} = s_k$. Then, u_k sends (VID_{u_k}, T_k, K_k) to the service nodes. With $\mathsf{rsk_{IBE,k}} = s_{k,0}$ and $\mathsf{rsk_{IBE,j}} = s_{j,0}$, the service nodes calculate

$$M_{k,j} = \prod_{l=1}^{N} e\left(T_{j,1,l}, K_{k,l}^{\frac{1}{s_{k,0}}}\right) \cdot e(T_{j,1,0}, K_{k,0}) \cdot \prod_{m=1}^{N} e\left(T_{k,l}, K_{j,l}^{\frac{1}{s_{j,0}}}\right) \cdot e(T_{k,0}, K_{j,0}),$$

with $T_{j,1}$ to match u_k with u_j's message and check $M_{j,k} \stackrel{?}{=} e(g,g)^{s_k(-s_j)+s_j s_k} = e(g,g)^0$. If $M_{j,k} = e(g,g)^0$, $u_k \in U_j$ and $u_j \in U_k$; otherwise, with the random values s_j, s_k, the service nodes cannot obtain any information from $M_{j,k}$. Then, with $T_{j,2}$, the service nodes calculate

$$\begin{aligned} R_{k,j,0} =& \prod_{l=1}^{N} e\left(T_{j,2,l}, K_{k,l}^{\frac{1}{s_{k,0}}}\right) \cdot e(T_{j,1,0}, K_{k,0}) \cdot \prod_{m=1}^{N} e\left(T_{k,m}, K_{j,m}^{\frac{1}{s_{j,0}}}\right) \cdot e(T_{k,0}, K_{j,0}) \\ =& e(g,g)^{s_k(-s_j)+s_k t} \cdot e(g,g)^{s_j s_k} = e(g,g)^{s_k t}, \end{aligned}$$

and select $R_{k,j} = (R_{k,j,0}, \mathsf{epk_{CHET,j}}, VID_{u_j}, m_j, h_j, r_j, T_j)$. Finally, the service nodes return the set of match results $R_k = \{R_{k,j} | M_{k,j} = e(g,g)^0\}$ to u_k.

Edit $(\mathsf{rsk_k}, R_k) \rightarrow (m'_j, r'_j)$: The phase of **Edit** is the same as in PIRB-I.

Trace $VID_{u_k} \rightarrow ID_{u_k}$: The phase of **Trace** is the same as in PIRB-I.

5. Theoretical Analysis

5.1. Correctness Analysis

We provide a correctness analysis for the **Match** and **Edit** phases in PIRB.

Theorem 1. *In PIRB-I, if and only if* $(u_k \in \mathcal{U}_j)$ *holds, the service node obtains a successful match between the owner* u_j *and the editor* u_k*. Otherwise, the service node cannot obtain any meaningful match result.*

Proof. If $(u_k \in \mathcal{U}_j)$, ID_{u_k} is used to generate the polynomial function f_1. Then, in the **Match** phase, with $T_{j,1}$, K_k and $\mathsf{rsk_{IBE,k}} = s_{k,0}$, the service nodes compute

$$\begin{aligned} M_{k,j} =& \prod_{l=1}^{N} e\left(T_{j,1,l}, K_{k,l}^{\frac{1}{s_{k,0}}}\right) \cdot e(T_{j,1,0}, K_{k,0}) \\ =& \prod_{l=1}^{N} e\left(g^{\frac{a_l}{s}}, g^{s_k s H_1(ID_{u_k})^l}\right) \cdot e(g^{a_0}, g^{s_k}) \\ =& e(g,g)^{s_k\left(\sum_{l=0}^{N} a_l H_1(ID_{u_k})^l\right)}, \end{aligned}$$

and obtain $M_{k,j} = e(g,g)^0$. Similarly, if $(u_k \in \mathcal{U}_j)$, ID_{u_k} is used to generate the polynomial function f_2. Then, with $T_{j,2}$, K_k and $\mathsf{rsk}_{\mathsf{IBE,k}} = s_{k,0}$, the service nodes similarly compute

$$\begin{aligned}
R_{k,j,0} =& \prod_{l=1}^{N} e\left(T_{j,2,l}, K_{k,l}^{\frac{1}{s_{k,0}}}\right) \cdot e(T_{j,2,0}, K_{k,0}) \\
=& \prod_{l=1}^{N} e\left(g^{\frac{b_l}{s}}, g^{s_k s H_1(ID_{u_k})^l}\right) \cdot e\left(g^{b_0}, g^{s_k}\right) \\
=& e(g,g)^{s_k\left(\sum_{l=0}^{N} b_l H_1(ID_{u_k})^l\right)} = e(g,g)^{s_k t},
\end{aligned}$$

and return the match result to the editor u_k. Otherwise, the service nodes cannot obtain $M_{k,j} = e(g,g)^0$ or $R_{k,j,0} = e(g,g)^{s_k t}$. Thus, Theorem 1 is proven. □

Theorem 2. *In PIRB-II, if and only if $(u_k \in \mathcal{U}_j) \wedge (u_j \in \mathcal{U}_k)$ holds, the service nodes obtain a successful match between the owner u_j and the editor u_k. Otherwise, the service nodes cannot obtain any meaningful match result.*

Proof. Similar to Theorem 1, if $(u_k \in \mathcal{U}_j) \wedge (u_j \in \mathcal{U}_k)$, ID_{u_k} is used to generate the polynomial functions $f_{j,1}$ and $f_{j,2}$, and ID_{u_j} is used to generate the polynomial function f_k. Then, in the **Match** phase, with $T_{j,1}$, K_k, $\mathsf{rsk}_{\mathsf{IBE,k}} = s_{k,0}$ and $\mathsf{rsk}_{\mathsf{IBE,j}} = s_{j,0}$, the service nodes compute

$$\begin{aligned}
M_{k,j} =& \prod_{l=1}^{N} e\left(T_{j,1,l}, K_{k,l}^{\frac{1}{s_{k,0}}}\right) \cdot e(T_{j,1,0}, K_{k,0}) \cdot \prod_{m=1}^{N} e\left(T_{k,m}, K_{j,m}^{\frac{1}{s_{j,0}}}\right) \cdot e(T_{k,0}, K_{j,0}) \\
=& \prod_{l=1}^{N} e\left(g^{\frac{a_l}{s}}, g^{s_k s H_1(ID_{u_k})^l}\right) \cdot e(g^{a_0}, g^{s_k}) \cdot \prod_{m=1}^{N} e\left(g^{\frac{c_m}{s}}, g^{s_j s H_1(ID_{u_j})^m}\right) \cdot e(g^{c_0}, g^{s_j}) \\
=& e(g,g)^{s_k\left(\sum_{l=0}^{N} a_l H_1(ID_{u_k})^l\right) + s_j\left(\sum_{m=0}^{N} c_m H_1(ID_{u_j})^m\right)} \\
=& e(g,g)^{s_k(-s_j)} \cdot e(g,g)^{s_j s_k} = e(g,g)^0.
\end{aligned}$$

Then, with $T_{j,2}$, K_k, $\mathsf{rsk}_{\mathsf{IBE,k}} = s_{k,0}$ and $\mathsf{rsk}_{\mathsf{IBE,j}} = s_{j,0}$, the service nodes similarly compute

$$\begin{aligned}
R_{k,j,0} =& \prod_{l=1}^{N} e\left(T_{j,2,l}, K_{k,l}^{\frac{1}{s_{k,0}}}\right) \cdot e(T_{j,2,0}, K_{k,0}) \cdot \prod_{m=1}^{N} e\left(T_{k,m}, K_{j,m}^{\frac{1}{s_{j,0}}}\right) \cdot e(T_{k,0}, K_{j,0}) \\
=& \prod_{l=1}^{N} e\left(g^{\frac{b_l}{s}}, g^{s_k s H_1(ID_{u_k})^l}\right) \cdot e\left(g^{b_0}, g^{s_k}\right) \cdot \prod_{m=1}^{N} e\left(g^{\frac{c_m}{s}}, g^{s_j s H_1(ID_{u_j})^m}\right) \cdot e(g^{c_0}, g^{s_j}) \\
=& e(g,g)^{s_k\left(\sum_{l=0}^{N} b_l H_1(ID_{u_k})^l\right) + s_j\left(\sum_{m=0}^{N} c_m H_1(ID_{u_j})^m\right)} \\
=& e(g,g)^{s_k(-s_j) + s_k t} \cdot e(g,g)^{s_j s_k} = e(g,g)^{s_k t},
\end{aligned}$$

and return the match result to the editor u_k. Otherwise, the service nodes cannot obtain $M_{k,j} = e(g,g)^0$ or $R_{k,j,0} = e(g,g)^{s_k t}$. Thus, Theorem 2 is proven. □

Theorem 3. *In PIRB-I and PIRB-II, if and only if the editor u_k receives the result of a successful match with the owner u_j and has the edit re-encryption key $\mathsf{rsk}_\mathsf{k} = s_k$, u_k obtains u_j's trapdoors (i.e., the long-term trapdoor and the ephemeral trapdoor) of CHET and edits the message m_j to m'_j. Otherwise, the editor cannot obtain the edit privilege.*

Proof. In both PIRB-I and PIRB-II, if the service nodes obtain a successful match between the owner u_j and the editor u_k, the editor u_k receives $e(g,g)^{s_k t}$ from the match result. If u_k has the edit re-encryption key $\mathsf{rsk}_\mathsf{k} = s_k$, u_k computes

$$(e(g,g)^{s_k t})^{\frac{1}{s_k}} = e(g,g)^t.$$

Moreover, with the trapdoor ciphertext $T_{j,0}$, u_k computes

$$T_{j,0,1} \oplus G_{j,1}(e(g,g)^t) = d_{j,1}, T_{j,0,2} \oplus G_{j,2}(e(g,g)^t) = d_{j,2},$$

to obtain the long-term trapdoor $d_{j,1}$ and the ephemeral trapdoor $d_{j,2}$. To edit the message m_j to m'_j, with $d_{j,1}$ and $d_{j,2}$, for $z \in \{1,2\}$, u_k computes

$$r'_{j,z} = \left(h_{j,z}\left(G_{j,z}\left(VID_{u_j}, m'_j, G_{j,1}, N_{j,1}, G_{j,2}, N_{j,2} \right) \right)^{-1} \right)^{d_{j,z}} \bmod N_{j,z},$$

so that

$$r'^{\,e_j}_{j,z} = \left(\left(h_{j,z}\left(G_{j,z}\left(VID_{u_j}, m'_j, G_{j,1}, N_{j,1}, G_{j,2}, N_{j,2} \right) \right)^{-1} \right)^{d_{j,z}} \right)^{e_j} \bmod N_{j,z}$$

$$= h_{j,z}\left(G_{j,z}\left(m'_j, G_{j,1}, N_{j,1}, G_{j,2}, N_{j,2} \right) \right)^{-1} \bmod N_{j,z},$$

$$G_{j,z}\left(m'_j, G_{j,1}, N_{j,1}, G_{j,2}, N_{j,2} \right) r'^{\,e_j}_{j,z} \bmod N_{j,z} = h_{j,z}.$$

Thus, u_k obtains valid randomness r' to edit m_j to m'_j without changing the hash $h_j = (h_{j,1}, h_{j,2})$. Otherwise, u_k cannot obtain the trapdoors of CHET and the valid randomness r'. Thus, Theorem 3 is proven. □

5.2. Security Analysis

In the security analysis, we prove the privacy preservation (i.e., trapdoor, identity, policy, and match privacy) and accountability of PIRB.

Theorem 4. *Our encryption approach is secure under the chosen-plaintext attack model.*

Proof. As shown in Algorithm 1, we provide an experiment between challenger $\mathcal{C}$ and adversary $\mathcal{A}$. Based on the experiment, we define security under the CPA model as

$$\mathsf{Adv}_{\mathcal{A}}^{IND-CPA}(\lambda) = |Pr[b' = b|\mathcal{A}(DB_0, DB_1, T)] - \frac{1}{2}| \leq \epsilon,$$

where ϵ is negligible.

Algorithm 1 An experiment between the adversary and the challenger

Setup: The challenger $\mathcal{C}$ selects a random value $s \in \mathbb{Z}_p$ to denote the master secret key and initializes $(g^{\frac{1}{s}}, H_1[\cdot], H_2[\cdot], \Psi)$ to denote the master public key.
Phase1: The adversary $\mathcal{A}$ applies for the secret key from $\mathcal{C}$. Then, $\mathcal{C}$ selects a random value $s_{A,0} \in \mathbb{Z}_p$ to denote the re-encryption key and generates and then publishes the secret key $g^{s_{A,0} s H_1(ID_A)}$ without $s_{A,0}$.
Challenge: $\mathcal{A}$ chooses the secret key $g^{s_{A,0} s H_1(ID_A)}$ and two databases $DB_0 = (t_{0,1}, t_{0,2}, \cdots, t_{0,n})$ and $DB_1 = (t_{1,1}, t_{1,2}, \cdots, t_{1,n})$, where $\{t_{z,i}\}_{i=0}^n \subseteq \mathbb{Z}_p$ for $z \in \{0,1\}$. $\mathcal{C}$ tosses a random binary coin $b \in \{0,1\}$ beyond the purview of $\mathcal{A}$. Then, $\mathcal{C}$ selects $\{r_i\}_{i=0}^n \subseteq \mathbb{Z}_p$ and generates the polynomial coefficients with the identity policy including the adversary $\mathcal{A}$'s identity. Subsequently, $\mathcal{C}$ encrypts $\{t_{b,i}\}_{i=0}^n \subseteq \mathbb{Z}_p$ to the ciphertexts $T = \{T_i\}_{i=0}^n$ and publishes the ciphertexts.
Guess: $\mathcal{A}$ submits the guess b'.

Assume that $DB_0 = (t_{0,1}, t_{0,2}, \cdots, t_{0,n})$ is the encrypted database. In the **Challenge** phase, for $i \in \{1,2,\cdots,n\}$, the challenger $\mathcal{C}$ picks $r_i \in \mathbb{Z}_p$ and selects the list $\mathcal{U}' = \{u_1, u_2, \cdots, u_n, u'_{n+1}, \cdots, u'_N\}$ where $u \in \mathcal{U}'$. Then, $\mathcal{C}$ generates the polynomial coefficients $\{b_{i,l}\}_{l=0}^N$ where

$$r_i \prod_{l=1,u'_l \in \mathcal{U}'}^{N} \left(x - H_1\left(ID_{u'_l}\right)\right) + t_{0,i} = \sum_{l=0}^{N} b_{i,l} x^l.$$

Subsequently, $\mathcal{C}$ generates

$$T_i = (T_{i,N}, T_{i,N-1}, \cdots, T_{i,1}, T_{i,0}),$$
$$T_{i,l} = g^{\frac{b_l}{s}}, 1 \leq l \leq N,$$
$$T_{i,0} = g^{b_0},$$

and publishes the ciphertexts.

To estimate the encrypted database, the adversary $\mathcal{A}$ selects $s_A \in \mathbb{Z}_p$ and computes

$$K = (K_N, K_{N-1}, \cdots, K_1, K_0),$$
$$K_l = g^{s_A s_{A,0} s H_1(ID_A)^l}, 1 \leq l \leq N,$$
$$K_0 = g^{s_A}.$$

Then, the adversary $\mathcal{A}$ attempts to decrypt the encryption. However, without the re-encryption key $s_{A,0}$, $\mathcal{A}$ must set $s'_{A,0}$ as a random value and compute

$$R' = \prod_{l=1}^{N} e\left(T_{j,2,l}, K_{k,l}^{\frac{1}{s'_{A,0}}}\right) \cdot e\left(T_{j,2,0}, K_{k,0}\right)$$
$$= e(g,g)^{s_A\left(\frac{s_{A,0}}{s'_{A,0}}\left(\sum_{l=1}^{N} b_l H_1(ID_A)^l\right) + b_0\right)},$$

which is not equal to $R = e(g,g)^{s_A t}$. Subsequently, $\mathcal{A}$ computes $R'^{\frac{1}{s_A}}$, which can only be considered as a random value. In addition, if there are two trapdoors $t_{0,i}$ and $t_{0,j}$ in DB_0, with the different random values r_i and r_j, $\mathcal{C}$ returns two different ciphertexts T_i and T_j, which $\mathcal{A}$ cannot distinguish. Then, $\mathcal{A}$ can only select $b' = 0$ or $b' = 1$ at random. Therefore,

$$\mathsf{Adv}_{\mathcal{A}}^{IND-CPA}(\lambda) = |Pr[b' = b|\mathcal{A}(DB_0, DB_1, T)] - \frac{1}{2}| \leq \epsilon,$$

where ϵ is negligible. In addition, without the master secret key s, $\mathcal{A}$ cannot forge other secret keys. Therefore, Theorem 4 is proven. □

Theorem 5. *Our proxy re-encryption approach for the* **Match** *phase is secure under the chosen-plaintext attack model.*

Proof. Similar to Theorem 4, we can establish the security of the proposed proxy re-encryption technique under the chosen-plaintext attack model. Without the edit re-encryption key $s_{A,0}$, $\mathcal{A}$ cannot obtain any information from the ciphertexts or the match results. Therefore, the detailed proof can be omitted. □

Theorem 6. *If Theorems 4 and 5 are proven, for any adversary, the trapdoor, policy, identity, and match privacy will not be disclosed.*

Proof. In our work, the knowledge owner cannot receive any response or data from other entities, and the knowledge editor can only receive the match results from the service nodes. Since the security of our encryption and proxy re-encryption approaches is demonstrated under the chosen-plaintext attack model, the owner and editor cannot obtain other trapdoors with their secret keys but the edit privilege. Since Theorem 5 is proven, the service nodes cannot obtain the trapdoor with the match ciphertext, match key, re-encryption key, and match results. Then, nobody can break the trapdoor privacy. Without the master secret key s and the edit re-encryption key s_A, the service nodes cannot forge secret keys from the received match keys or infer the editor $\mathcal{A}$'s identity. Moreover, without the re-encryption key $s_{A,0}$, the editor $\mathcal{A}$ also cannot forge secret keys from his or her own secret key. Then, the identity privacy is preserved. For the editor or the other entities, it is difficult to infer policy content or the exact policy size from the ciphertext, which preserves policy privacy. In addition, in PIRB-II, it is also difficult to distinguish which identity is unsuitable for the policy as the service nodes must execute the complete **Match** phase to obtain the match results, which preserves the match privacy. Therefore, Theorem 6 is proven. □

Theorem 7. *Any editor with malicious behaviors can be traced in PIRB.*

Proof. An editor can engage in malicious behaviors in the **Match** and **Edit** phases. In the **Match** phase, the editor $\mathcal{A}$ can generate the match key without the random value s_A as

$$K' = (K'_N, K'_{N-1}, \cdots, K'_1, K'_0),$$
$$K'_l = g^{s_{A,0} s H_1(ID_A)^l}, 1 \le l \le N,$$
$$K'_0 = g,$$

to break the trapdoor privacy. Specifically, the service nodes can compute

$$R' = \prod_{l=1}^{N} e\left(T_{j,2,l}, {K'_{k,l}}^{\frac{1}{s_{A,0}}}\right) \cdot e\left(T_{j,2,0}, K'_{k,0}\right)$$
$$= e(g,g)^{\left(\sum_{l=1}^{N} b_l H_1(ID_A)^l + b_0\right)} = e(g,g)^t,$$

to directly obtain the trapdoor. However, since Theorem 6 is proven, $\mathcal{A}$ cannot forge secret keys from his or her own secret key. Then, to execute the *Match* phase, $\mathcal{A}$ must generate the match key with his or her own secret key and provide the virtual identity VID_{u_A} for the associated re-encryption key $s_{A,0}$. With VID_{u_A}, the consortium nodes can trace the editor *mathcalA*. Similarly, if the editor $\mathcal{A}$ displays illegal edit behaviors, $\mathcal{A}$ can still be traced with the virtual identity VID_{u_A}. Therefore, Theorem 7 is proven. □

5.3. Complexity Analysis

In the complexity analysis, we analyze the computational complexity and communication complexity among the consortium blockchain schemes supporting one policy for a batch of users, i.e., DerlerNDSS19, XuTIFS23, PIRB-I and PIRB-II. The complexity analysis results are shown in Table 3.

Table 3. Theoretical computational complexity and communication complexity.

Scheme	Entity	Computational Complexity	Communication Complexity
DerlerNDSS19	Knowledge Owner	$\mathcal{O}(N_P)T_e + \mathcal{O}(1)T_p + \mathcal{O}(N_P)T_h + \mathcal{O}(1)T_{SE}$	$\mathcal{O}(N_P)\lvert 1^\lambda\rvert$
	Service Node	—	$(\phi_o + \phi_s\phi_e)\mathcal{O}(N_P)\lvert 1^\lambda\rvert$
	Knowledge Editor	$\phi_s(\mathcal{O}(N_P)T_e + \mathcal{O}(1)T_p + \mathcal{O}(N_P)T_h + \mathcal{O}(1)T_{SD})$	$\phi_s\mathcal{O}(N_P)\lvert 1^\lambda\rvert$
XuTIFS23	Knowledge Owner	$\mathcal{O}(N_P)T_e + \mathcal{O}(1)T_p + \mathcal{O}(N_P)T_h + \mathcal{O}(1)T_{SE}$	$\mathcal{O}(N_P)\lvert 1^\lambda\rvert$
	Service Node	—	$(\phi_o + \phi_s\phi_e)\mathcal{O}(N_P)\lvert 1^\lambda\rvert$
	Knowledge Editor	$\phi_s(\mathcal{O}(N_P)T_e + \mathcal{O}(1)T_p + \mathcal{O}(N_P)T_h + \mathcal{O}(1)T_{SD})$	$\phi_s\mathcal{O}(N_P)\lvert 1^\lambda\rvert$
PIRB-I	Knowledge Owner	$\mathcal{O}(N)T_e + \mathcal{O}(1)T_p + \mathcal{O}(N)T_h$	$\mathcal{O}(N)\lvert 1^\lambda\rvert$
	Service Node	$\phi_o\phi_e(\mathcal{O}(N)T_e + \mathcal{O}(N)T_p)$	$(\phi_o + \phi_e)\mathcal{O}(N)\lvert 1^\lambda\rvert + \phi_s\phi_e\mathcal{O}(1)\lvert 1^\lambda\rvert$
	Knowledge Editor	$\mathcal{O}(N)T_e + \phi_s(\mathcal{O}(1)T_e + \mathcal{O}(1)T_h)$	$\mathcal{O}(N)\lvert 1^\lambda\rvert + \phi_s\mathcal{O}(1)\lvert 1^\lambda\rvert$
PIRB-II	Knowledge Owner	$1.5\mathcal{O}(N)T_e + \mathcal{O}(1)T_p + \mathcal{O}(N)T_h$	$1.5\mathcal{O}(N)\lvert 1^\lambda\rvert$
	Service Node	$2\phi_o\phi_e(\mathcal{O}(N)T_e + \mathcal{O}(N)T_p)$	$2(\phi_o + \phi_e)\mathcal{O}(N)\lvert 1^\lambda\rvert + \phi'_s\phi_e\mathcal{O}(1)\lvert 1^\lambda\rvert$
	Knowledge Editor	$2\mathcal{O}(N)T_e + \phi_s(\mathcal{O}(1)T_e + \mathcal{O}(1)T_h)$	$2\mathcal{O}(N)\lvert 1^\lambda\rvert + \phi'_s\mathcal{O}(1)\lvert 1^\lambda\rvert$

Notation Introduction. In Table 3, N is the preset maximum policy size in PIRB, and N_P denotes the size of the policy. T_p, T_h, T_e, T_{SE} and T_{SD} denote the time for executing an operation of pairing, hash, exponent, symmetric encryption, and symmetric decryption, respectively. ϕ_o, ϕ_s and ϕ_e denote the number of total knowledge owners, suitable knowledge owners and knowledge editors, respectively. Note that the number of knowledge editors is the number of required knowledge editors for the match and edit service per unit of time. In PIRB-II, the number of suitable knowledge owners is actually lower compared to other schemes, denoted as ϕ_s'. Moreover, the constant coefficients in the complexity analysis of PIRB-II serve the purpose of facilitating a comparative evaluation with PIRB-I.

Complexity Analysis Results. From Table 3, on the knowledge owner side, the computational and communication complexity in PIRB are, respectively, $\mathcal{O}(N)T_e + \mathcal{O}(1)T_p + \mathcal{O}(N)T_h$ and $\mathcal{O}(N)|1^\lambda|$, which is similar to other schemes. On the service node side, the computational and communication complexity in PIRB are, respectively, $\phi_o\phi_e(\mathcal{O}(N)T_e + \mathcal{O}(N)T_p)$ and $(\phi_o + \phi_e)\mathcal{O}(N)|1^\lambda| + \phi_s\phi_e\mathcal{O}(1)|1^\lambda|$, which is slightly higher than other schemes. This is because, in PIRB, to find suitable owners while hiding the policies, we designed the **Match** phase, and the service nodes perform the phase to decrease the overheads of the knowledge editors. On the knowledge editor side, the computational and communication complexity in PIRB are, respectively, $\mathcal{O}(N)T_e + \phi_s(\mathcal{O}(1)T_e + \mathcal{O}(1)T_h)$ and $\mathcal{O}(N)|1^\lambda| + \phi_s\mathcal{O}(1)|1^\lambda|$, which is much lower than DerlerNDSS19 and XuTIFS23. This is because the service nodes bear the overheads of pairing to reduce the computational complexity and perform the **Match** phase to prevent the editors from searching for suitable owners to reduce the communication complexity. Moreover, because the exact number of exponent operations in PIRB is much lower than in DerlerNDSS19 and XuTIFS23, the total overhead in PIRB is also lower. PIRB-I and PIRB-II involve a trade-off between computational and communication complexity.

6. Performance Evaluation

In this section, based on an original model deployed on the FISCO blockchain, we evaluate the performance of our schemes, i.e., PIRB-I and PIRB-II, compared with two recent redactable blockchain schemes, DerlerNDSS19 [18] and XuTIFS23 [19].

6.1. Experimental Configuration

We deploy the FISCO blockchain on a Ubuntu-18.04.6 virtual machine created on the VMware Workstation 16 Pro, with 4 CPUs with 4GB RAM and 20 GB SCSI. Our implementation and execution of the prototype are conducted on a laptop with 64-bit CPU, Windows 10, Intel(R) Core(TM) i7-10510U 1.80 GHz with 16 GB of RAM. In DerlerNDSS19, XuTIFS23 and our own works, we employ the Java programming language and utilize the JPBC library to realize the computational function, choosing the Type A curve with 80-bit security. Note that since PIRB does not rely on a specific curve, the experimental results can be extrapolated to curves with elevated security parameters, despite the trade-off between the security level and efficiency. To ensure statistical robustness, each experiment is executed ten times, and the resultant average running time is computed as the definitive experimental outcome. The policy size, which is a key parameter in DerlerNDSS19 and XuTIFS23, ranges from 10 to 100, aligning with the preset maximum policy size in our constructions.

6.2. Experimental Evaluation

We focus on the computational overheads of the **Hash**, **Match** and **Edit** phases.

On the knowledge owner side. We evaluate the computational and communication costs on the worker side and illustrate the experimental results in Figure 4. Particularly, because the computational and communication overhead is only correlated with the policy size in DerlerNDSS19, XuTIFS23 and the preset maximum policy size in our constructions, we consider the policy size from 10 to 100. The security parameter λ is set to 80. Figure 4a shows that PIRB-I and PIRB-II are more efficient than DerlerNDSS19 and XuTIFS23 regarding the computational costs. This is because an owner executes at least $12N_P$ hash and $12N_P$ exponent operations in DerlerNDSS19 and XuTIFS23; however, an owner executes only N hash and $2N$ exponent operations in PIRB-I and N hash and $3N$ exponent operations in

PIRB-II. In addition, Figure 4a shows that the computational overheads of all four schemes grow linearly with the size of the policies. Figure 4b shows that the four schemes have similar communication costs.

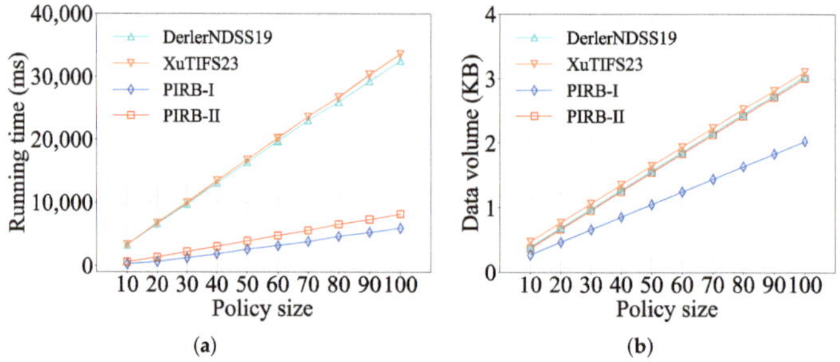

Figure 4. Computational and communication costs with respect to policy size on the owner side. (**a**) Computational costs with respect to policy size on the owner side. (**b**) Communication costs with respect to policy size on the owner side.

On the service nodes. Next, we evaluate the computational costs on the service nodes for an editor and illustrate the experimental results in Figure 5. Specifically, we consider the number of owners from 10 to 100 and set the preset maximum policy size as 10, 20, 50 and 100. As Figure 5 shows, the service nodes execute $\phi_o N + \phi_s N$ and $2\phi_o N + 2\phi_s' N$ exponent and pairing operations in PIRB-I and PIRB-II, respectively, where $\phi_s' < \phi_s$ actually.

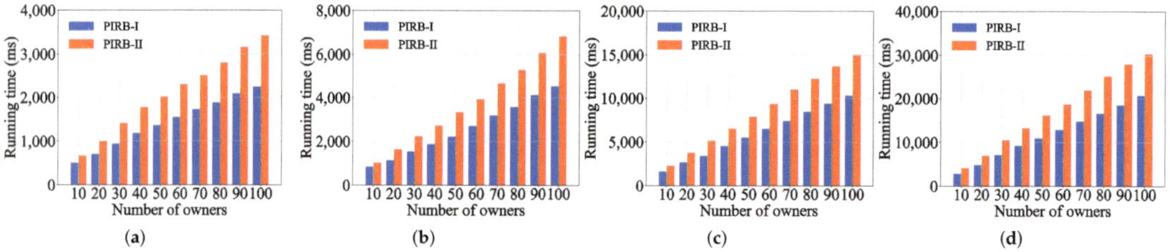

Figure 5. Computational costs with respect to number of owners on the edge devices. (**a**) Computational costs with respect to number of owners with policy size 10. (**b**) Computational costs with respect to number of owners with policy size 20. (**c**) Computational costs with respect to number of workers with policy size 50. (**d**) Computational costs with respect to number of workers with policy size 100.

On the knowledge editor side. Finally, we evaluate the computational and communication costs on the editor side and illustrate the experimental results in Figures 6 and 7. Particularly, because the computational and communication overhead is correlated with the policy size, the suitable owner number in DerlerNDSS19 and XuTIFS23 and the preset maximum policy size, the suitable owner number, in our constructions, we consider the policy size from 10 to 100 and set the number of suitable owners as 10, 20, 50 and 100. Notably, the number of suitable owners in PIRB-II is actually less than in other schemes. Therefore, we set the number of suitable owners as 5, 10, 25 and 50. The security parameter λ is set to 80. Figure 6 shows that PIRB-I and PIRB-II have better computational performance than DerlerNDSS19 and XuTIFS23. This is because an editor executes at least $12\phi_s N_P$ hash and $12\phi_s N_P$ exponent operations in DerlerNDSS19 and XuTIFS23; however, an owner executes only ϕ_s hash and $N + \phi_s$ exponent operations in PIRB-I and ϕ_s hash and $2N + \phi_s$ exponent operations in PIRB-II. Figure 7 shows that PIRB-I and PIRB-II have lower communication costs than DerlerNDSS19 and XuTIFS23. This is because, in DerlerNDSS19 and XuTIFS23, the communication costs are $80\phi_s(3N_P + 2)$ and $80\phi_s(3N_P + 4)$, respectively, which brings overheads proportional to the number of suitable owners ϕ_s. However, in PIRB-I and PIRB-II, with the **Match** phase to decrease the communication costs, the communication costs are $80(N + 4\phi_s)$ and $80(2N + 4\phi'_s)$, respectively, where $\phi'_s < \phi_s$ actually. Notably, Figures 6 and 7 show that PIRB-I and PIRB-II involve a trade-off between computational and communication overheads. Specifically, while PIRB-I demonstrates superior computational efficiency compared to PIRB-II, PIRB-II exhibits a distinct advantage in terms of communication overhead. This is due to the growing number of suitable owners, leading to a situation where the advantage of PIRB-I's uncomplicated policy format is outweighed by the editors' policy functionality in PIRB-II, which effectively minimizes the number of returned match results.

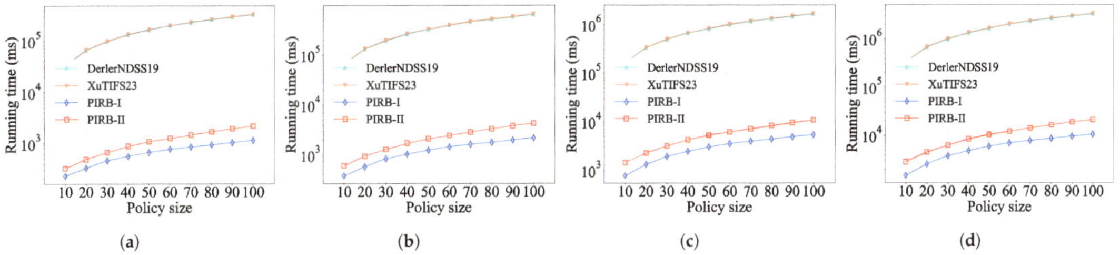

Figure 6. Computational costs with respect to policy size on the editor side. (**a**) Computational costs with respect to policy size with 10 suitable owners. (**b**) Computational costs with respect to policy size with 20 suitable owners. (**c**) Computational costs with respect to policy size with 50 suitable owners. (**d**) Computational costs with respect to policy size with 100 suitable owners.

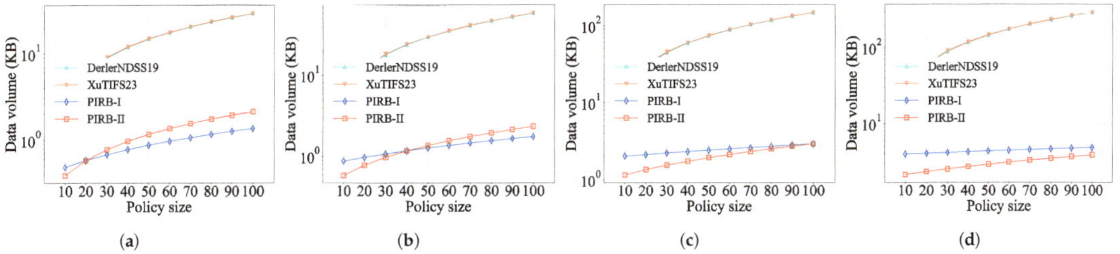

Figure 7. Communication costs with respect to policy size on the editor side. (**a**) Communication costs with respect to policy size with 10 suitable owners. (**b**) Communication costs with respect to policy size with 20 suitable owners. (**c**) Communication costs with respect to policy size with 50 suitable owners. (**d**) Communication costs with respect to policy size with 100 suitable owners.

7. Related Works

This section introduces the related works on redactable blockchain and identity-based encryption.

In recent years, several redactable blockchain schemes have been proposed. For identity-based scenarios, Ateniese et al. [36] introduced the pioneering concept of an identity-based chameleon hash. However, this scheme exhibits susceptibility to key exposure unless an identity is never reused. Addressing this concern, Chen et al. [16] presented an identity-based chameleon hash scheme without key exposure in the random oracle model, and Bao et al. [37] subsequently proposed a hierarchical extension. Seeking to enhance the security, Xie et al. [30] devised an identity-based chameleon hash scheme within the standard model. Expanding upon this, Li et al. [31] formulated an efficient identity-based chameleon hash scheme to optimize the size of public parameters and reduce computational complexity. Building upon this groundwork [16], Zhou et al. [17] introduced an identity-based fine-grained redactable blockchain. However, the aforementioned identity-based schemes are limited in their capacity to support flexible policies and to implement bilateral access control.

Hence, we then focus on policy-based redactable blockchain schemes that offer the capacity for flexible policies. Ateniese et al. [24] introduced the pioneering redactable blockchain leveraging chameleon hash techniques, securing the trapdoor through public key infrastructure for trapdoor access control. However, this scheme suffers from limitations such as inflexible privilege management due to a single fixed public key, compromising modifier identity privacy and susceptibility to collision vulnerabilities. Moreover, the scheme grants the modifier excessive rewriting power at the block level, failing to accommodate finer-grained transaction-level needs. Seeking enhanced security and flexibility, Derler et al. [18] devised the policy-based chameleon hash (PCH) framework, integrating chameleon hash with ephemeral trapdoors (CHET) and attribute-based encryption (ABE). CHET introduces a safeguard against collisions by combining long-term and ephemeral trapdoors, while ABE imparts flexibility and privacy preservation through the linear secret-sharing scheme. Subsequently, Tian et al. [26] extended PCH with black-box accountability, yet this introduced inadvertent susceptibility to semi-trusted modifiers due to key leakage. To bolster accountability, Xu et al. [19] introduced identity-based signatures with existential unforgeability and proposed an attribute-based traitor tracing scheme. Moreover, Xu et al. [27] introduced number resistance and expiration dates to govern rewriting privileges, enforced through double-authentication preventing signatures, supplemented by a monetary penalty system to deter malicious behavior. For permissionless settings, Deuber et al. [25] devised an efficient redactable blockchain employing consensus-based voting. Notably, this solution entails traversing transaction logs for redaction validation and voting, incurring time costs. In decentralized settings, Jia et al. [28] proposed a decentralized chameleon hash for redactable blockchains, collaboratively generating keys across untrusted blockchain nodes. Ma et al. [29] introduced a decentralized policy-based chameleon hash employing multi-authority attribute-based encryption to manage editing privileges. However, the two approaches in [28,29] neglect data and policy privacy and incur substantial communication overheads for intricate policies. Regrettably, none of the above schemes preserves policy privacy. Guo et al. [38] proposed a decentralized policy-hidden fine-grained redactable blockchain. Moreover, in cases involving bilateral access control scenarios, none of these schemes offer viable solutions.

The encryption of trapdoors in the CHET framework necessitates the use of an identity-based encryption scheme. The pioneering work by Boneh et al. [35] introduced the first identity-based encryption scheme utilizing the Weil pairing, achieving chosen-ciphertext security within the random oracle model. Subsequent efforts by Boneh et al. [39,40] yielded two distinct schemes, enhancing chosen-ciphertext security within the selective identity model and the full identity model, respectively. Despite these advancements, concerns regarding efficiency persist. Waters et al. [41] proposed an efficient identity-based encryption scheme, ensuring chosen-ciphertext security in the full identity model, albeit relying on numerous public parameters. To mitigate this parameter proliferation, Gentry et al. [42] presented a practical identity-based encryption scheme. Moreover, efforts to augment the capabilities of identity-based encryption led to the conception of tightly secure identity-based encryption [43] and function-private identity-based encryption [44]. However, a notable limitation among the aforementioned schemes is their inability to achieve one policy for a batch of users. This gap was addressed by Sun et al. [45] through the introduction of efficient matchmaking encryption, leveraging polynomial functions to facilitate flexible data sharing. Nevertheless, for editors, the absence of an effective matching mechanism [6,46] introduces the potential for superfluous communication overheads in the endeavor to select appropriate ciphertexts.

8. Conclusions

In this paper, we have introduced a novel privacy-preserving identity-based redactable blockchain (PIRB), which leverages the combined techniques of identity-based encryption and chameleon hash with ephemeral trapdoors. The PIRB scheme specifically addresses the need for redactable blockchains in identity-based scenarios, ensuring the preservation of trapdoor, identity, policy, and match privacy. Notably, PIRB employs a polynomial function technique to achieve one identity-based policy for a batch of users, offering both one-way (PIRB-I) and bilateral (PIRB-II) access control paradigms. Moreover, accountability is upheld through the utilization of virtual identities. Our constructions have been rigorously validated through correctness analysis, affirming the successful execution of match and edit operations. The security analysis under a chosen-plaintext attack attests to the robust preservation of trapdoor, identity, policy, and match privacy, while also ensuring accountability. The detailed complexity analysis, along with empirical evidence from a prototype implementation, underscores the tangible efficiency enhancements that our constructions bring to practical deployment. As a direction for future exploration, we envision augmenting our constructions with fine-grained privilege management encompassing read, use, and edit privileges, thereby enhancing the adaptability of blockchain technology across emerging applications.

Author Contributions: Conceptualization, Y.X.; Formal analysis, Z.L.; Investigation, Y.X.; Methodology, Y.X.; Software, Z.L.; Supervision, Z.L.; Writing—original draft, Y.X.; Writing—review and editing, Z.L. All authors have read and agreed to the published version of the manuscript.

Funding: This research was funded by the "National Key R&D Program of China" (Grant Nos. 2021YFB2700500 and 2021YFB2700503), the National Natural Science Foundation of China (Grant No. 62232002), and the Shandong Provincial Key Research and Development Program (Grant No. 2021CXGC010106).

Conflicts of Interest: The authors declare no conflict of interest.

References

1. Zhou, B.; Li, H.; Xu, L. An Authentication Scheme Using Identity-based Encryption & Blockchain. In Proceedings of the 2018 IEEE Symposium on Computers and Communications (ISCC 2018), Natal, Brazil, 25–28 June 2018; pp. 556–561.
2. Babu, E.S.; Dadi, A.K.; Singh, K.K.; Nayak, S.R.; Bhoi, A.K.; Singh, A. A distributed identity-based authentication scheme for internet of things devices using permissioned blockchain system. *Expert Syst. J. Knowl. Eng.* **2022**, *39*, e12941. [CrossRef]
3. Huang, C.; Wang, W.; Liu, D.; Lu, R.; Shen, X. Blockchain-Assisted Personalized Car Insurance with Privacy Preservation and Fraud Resistance. *IEEE Trans. Veh. Technol.* **2023**, *72*, 3777–3792. [CrossRef]
4. Xue, J.; Xu, C.; Zhao, J.; Ma, J. Identity-based public auditing for cloud storage systems against malicious auditors via blockchain. *Sci. China Inf. Sci.* **2019**, *62*, 32104:1–32104:16. [CrossRef]
5. Yuan, Y.; Zhang, J.; Xu, W.; Li, Z. Identity-based public data integrity verification scheme in cloud storage system via blockchain. *J. Supercomput.* **2022**, *78*, 8509–8530. [CrossRef]
6. Li, Y.; Zhao, M.; Li, Z.; Zhang, W.; Dong, J.; Wu, T.; Zhang, C.; Zhu, L. Achieving a Blockchain-based Privacy-preserving Quality-aware Knowledge Marketplace in Crowdsensing. In Proceedings of the 20th IEEE International Conference on Embedded and Ubiquitous Computing (EUC 2022), Wuhan, China, 9–11 December 2022; pp. 90–97.
7. Ren, H.; Li, H.; Liu, D.; Xu, G.; Cheng, N.; Shen, X. Privacy-Preserving Efficient Verifiable Deep Packet Inspection for Cloud-Assisted Middlebox. *IEEE Trans. Cloud Comput.* **2022**, *10*, 1052–1064. [CrossRef]
8. Sharma, P.; Moparthi, N.R.; Namasudra, S.; Shanmuganathan, V.; Hsu, C. Blockchain-based IoT architecture to secure healthcare system using identity-based encryption. *Expert Syst. J. Knowl. Eng.* **2022**, *39*, e12915. [CrossRef]
9. Ren, H.; Xu, G.; Qi, H.; Zhang, T. PriFR: Privacy-preserving Large-scale File Retrieval System via Blockchain for Encrypted Cloud Data. In Proceedings of the 2023 IEEE 9th Intl Conference on Big Data Security on Cloud (BigDataSecurity), IEEE Intl Conference on High Performance and Smart Computing (HPSC) and IEEE Intl Conference on Intelligent Data and Security (IDS), New York, NY, USA, 6–8 May 2023; pp. 16–23.
10. Hu, C.; Zhang, C.; Lei, D.; Wu, T.; Liu, X.; Zhu, L. Achieving Privacy-Preserving and Verifiable Support Vector Machine Training in the Cloud. *IEEE Trans. Inf. Forensics Secur.* **2023**, *18*, 3476–3491. [CrossRef]
11. Zhang, C.; Hu, C.; Wu, T.; Zhu, L.; Liu, X. Achieving Efficient and Privacy-Preserving Neural Network Training and Prediction in Cloud Environments. *IEEE Trans. Dependable Secur. Comput.* **2022**, *20*, 4245–4257. [CrossRef]
12. Huang, C.; Liu, D.; Yang, A.; Lu, R.; Shen, X. Multi-client Secure and Efficient DPF-based Keyword Search for Cloud Storage. *IEEE Trans. Dependable Secur. Comput.* **2023**, 1–18. [CrossRef]
13. Regulation, P. General data protection regulation. *Intouch* **2018**, *25*, 1–5.
14. Wu, W.; Li, M.; Qu, K.; Zhou, C.; Shen, X.; Zhuang, W.; Li, X.; Shi, W. Split Learning Over Wireless Networks: Parallel Design and Resource Management. *IEEE J. Sel. Areas Commun.* **2023**, *41*, 1051–1066. [CrossRef]

15. Zhang, C.; Zhao, M.; Zhu, L.; Zhang, W.; Wu, T.; Ni, J. FRUIT: A Blockchain-Based Efficient and Privacy-Preserving Quality-Aware Incentive Scheme. *IEEE J. Sel. Areas Commun.* **2022**, *40*, 3343–3357. [CrossRef]
16. Chen, X.; Zhang, F.; Susilo, W.; Tian, H.; Li, J.; Kim, K. Identity-Based Chameleon Hash Scheme without Key Exposure. In Proceedings of the Information Security and Privacy—15th Australasian Conference (ACISP 2010), Sydney, Australia, 5–7 July 2010; Lecture Notes in Computer Science; Steinfeld, R., Hawkes, P., Eds.; Springer: Berlin/Heidelberg, Germany, 2010; Volume 6168, pp. 200–215.
17. Zhou, G.; Ding, X.; Han, H.; Zhu, A. Fine-Grained Redactable Blockchain Using Trapdoor-Hash. *IEEE Internet Things J.* **2023**, 1. [CrossRef]
18. Derler, D.; Samelin, K.; Slamanig, D.; Striecks, C. Fine-Grained and Controlled Rewriting in Blockchains: Chameleon-Hashing Gone Attribute-Based. In Proceedings of the 26th Annual Network and Distributed System Security Symposium (NDSS 2019), San Diego, CA, USA, 24–27 February 2019; The Internet Society: Reston, VA, USA, 2019.
19. Xu, S.; Huang, X.; Yuan, J.; Li, Y.; Deng, R.H. Accountable and Fine-Grained Controllable Rewriting in Blockchains. *IEEE Trans. Inf. Forensics Secur.* **2023**, *18*, 101–116. [CrossRef]
20. Ren, H.; Li, H.; Liu, D.; Xu, G.; Shen, X.S. Enabling Secure and Versatile Packet Inspection with Probable Cause Privacy for Outsourced Middlebox. *IEEE Trans. Cloud Comput.* **2022**, *10*, 2580–2594. [CrossRef]
21. Zhang, C.; Zhao, M.; Wu, T.; Zhang, W.; Fan, Q.; Zhu, L. Towards Secure Bilateral Friend Query with Conjunctive Policy Matching in Social Networks. In Proceedings of the IEEE Intl Conf on Parallel & Distributed Processing with Applications, Big Data & Cloud Computing, Sustainable Computing & Communications, Social Computing & Networking (ISPA/BDCloud/SocialCom/SustainCom 2022), Melbourne, Australia, 17–19 December 2022; pp. 98–105.
22. Zhang, C.; Zhao, M.; Xu, Y.; Wu, T.; Li, Y.; Zhu, L.; Wang, H. Achieving fuzzy matching data sharing for secure cloud-edge communication. *China Commun.* **2022**, *19*, 257–276. [CrossRef]
23. Wu, W.; Chen, N.; Zhou, C.; Li, M.; Shen, X.; Zhuang, W.; Li, X. Dynamic RAN Slicing for Service-Oriented Vehicular Networks via Constrained Learning. *IEEE J. Sel. Areas Commun.* **2021**, *39*, 2076–2089. [CrossRef]
24. Ateniese, G.; Magri, B.; Venturi, D.; Andrade, E.R. Redactable Blockchain—or—Rewriting History in Bitcoin and Friends. In Proceedings of the 2017 IEEE European Symposium on Security and Privacy (EuroS&P 2017), Paris, France, 26–28 April 2017; pp. 111–126.
25. Deuber, D.; Magri, B.; Thyagarajan, S.A.K. Redactable Blockchain in the Permissionless Setting. In Proceedings of the 2019 IEEE Symposium on Security and Privacy (SP 2019), San Francisco, CA, USA, 19–23 May 2019; pp. 124–138.
26. Tian, Y.; Li, N.; Li, Y.; Szalachowski, P.; Zhou, J. Policy-based Chameleon Hash for Blockchain Rewriting with Black-box Accountability. In Proceedings of the ACSAC '20: Annual Computer Security Applications Conference, Austin, TX, USA, 7–11 December 2020; ACM: New York, NY, USA, 2020; pp. 813–828.
27. Xu, S.; Ning, J.; Ma, J.; Huang, X.; Deng, R.H. K-Time Modifiable and Epoch-Based Redactable Blockchain. *IEEE Trans. Inf. Forensics Secur.* **2021**, *16*, 4507–4520. [CrossRef]
28. Jia, M.; Chen, J.; He, K.; Du, R.; Zheng, L.; Lai, M.; Wang, D.; Liu, F. Redactable Blockchain From Decentralized Chameleon Hash Functions. *IEEE Trans. Inf. Forensics Secur.* **2022**, *17*, 2771–2783. [CrossRef]
29. Ma, J.; Xu, S.; Ning, J.; Huang, X.; Deng, R.H. Redactable Blockchain in Decentralized Setting. *IEEE Trans. Inf. Forensics Secur.* **2022**, *17*, 1227–1242. [CrossRef]
30. Xie, Z.; Shen, Q.; Li, C.; Dong, J.; Fang, Y. Identity-Based Chameleon Hash without Random Oracles and Application in the Mobile Internet. In Proceedings of the ICC 2021—IEEE International Conference on Communications, Montreal, QC, Canada, 14–23 June 2021; pp. 1–6.
31. Li, C.; Shen, Q.; Xie, Z.; Dong, J.; Fang, Y.; Wu, Z. Efficient Identity-Based Chameleon Hash for Mobile Devices. In Proceedings of the IEEE International Conference on Acoustics, Speech and Signal Processing (ICASSP 2022), Singapore, 23–27 May 2022; pp. 3039–3043.
32. Krawczyk, H.; Rabin, T. Chameleon Signatures. In Proceedings of the Network and Distributed System Security Symposium (NDSS 2000), San Diego, CA, USA, 3–4 February 2000; The Internet Society: Reston, VA, USA, 2000.
33. Camenisch, J.; Derler, D.; Krenn, S.; Pöhls, H.C.; Samelin, K.; Slamanig, D. Chameleon-Hashes with Ephemeral Trapdoors—And Applications to Invisible Sanitizable Signatures. In Proceedings of the Public-Key Cryptography—PKC 2017—20th IACR International Conference on Practice and Theory in Public-Key Cryptography, Amsterdam, The Netherlands, 28–31 March 2017; Proceedings, Part II; Lecture Notes in Computer Science; Fehr, S., Ed.; Springer: Berlin/Heidelberg, Germany, 2017; Volume 10175, pp. 152–182.
34. Samelin, K.; Slamanig, D. Policy-Based Sanitizable Signatures. In Proceedings of the Topics in Cryptology—CT-RSA 2020—The Cryptographers' Track at the RSA Conference 2020, San Francisco, CA, USA, 24–28 February 2020; Lecture Notes in Computer Science; Jarecki, S., Ed.; Springer: Berlin/Heidelberg, Germany, 2020; Volume 12006, pp. 538–563.
35. Boneh, D.; Franklin, M.K. Identity-Based Encryption from the Weil Pairing. In Proceedings of the Advances in Cryptology—CRYPTO 2001, 21st Annual International Cryptology Conference, Santa Barbara, CA, USA, 19–23 August 2001; Lecture Notes in Computer Science; Kilian, J., Ed.; Springer: Berlin/Heidelberg, Germany, 2001; Volume 2139, pp. 213–229.
36. Ateniese, G.; de Medeiros, B. Identity-Based Chameleon Hash and Applications. In Proceedings of the Financial Cryptography, 8th International Conference (FC 2004), Key West, FL, USA, 9–12 February 2004; Revised Papers; Lecture Notes in Computer Science; Juels, A., Ed.; Springer: Berlin/Heidelberg, Germany, 2004; Volume 3110, pp. 164–180.

37. Bao, F.; Deng, R.H.; Ding, X.; Lai, J.; Zhao, Y. Hierarchical Identity-Based Chameleon Hash and Its Applications. In Proceedings of the Applied Cryptography and Network Security—9th International Conference, ACNS 2011, Nerja, Spain, 7–10 June 2011; Lecture Notes in Computer Science; López, J., Tsudik, G., Eds.; Volume 6715, pp. 201–219.
38. Guo, H.; Tao, X.; Zhao, M.; Wu, T.; Zhang, C.; Xue, J.; Zhu, L. Decentralized Policy-Hidden Fine-Grained Redaction in Blockchain-Based IoT Systems. *Sensors* **2023**, *23*, 7105. [CrossRef] [PubMed]
39. Boneh, D.; Boyen, X. Efficient Selective-ID Secure Identity-Based Encryption without Random Oracles. In Proceedings of the Advances in Cryptology—EUROCRYPT 2004, International Conference on the Theory and Applications of Cryptographic Techniques, Interlaken, Switzerland, 2–6 May 2004; Lecture Notes in Computer Science; Cachin, C., Camenisch, J., Eds.; Springer: Berlin/Heidelberg, Germany, 2004; Volume 3027, pp. 223–238.
40. Boneh, D.; Boyen, X. Secure Identity Based Encryption without Random Oracles. In Proceedings of the Advances in Cryptology—CRYPTO 2004, 24th Annual International CryptologyConference, Santa Barbara, CA, USA, 15–19 August 2004; Lecture Notes in Computer Science; Franklin, M.K., Ed.; Springer: Berlin/Heidelberg, Germany, 2004; Volume 3152, pp. 443–459.
41. Waters, B. Efficient Identity-Based Encryption without Random Oracles. In Proceedings of the Advances in Cryptology—EUROCRYPT 2005, 24th Annual International Conference on the Theory and Applications of Cryptographic Techniques, Aarhus, Denmark, 22–26 May 2005; Lecture Notes in Computer Science; Cramer, R., Ed.; Springer: Berlin/Heidelberg, Germany, 2005; Volume 3494, pp. 114–127.
42. Gentry, C. Practical Identity-Based Encryption without Random Oracles. In Proceedings of the Advances in Cryptology—EUROCRYPT 2006, 25th Annual International Conference on the Theory and Applications of Cryptographic Techniques, St. Petersburg, Russia, 28 May–1 June 2006; Lecture Notes in Computer Science; Vaudenay, S., Ed.; Volume 4004, pp. 445–464.
43. Chen, J.; Wee, H. Fully, (Almost) Tightly Secure IBE and Dual System Groups. In Proceedings of the Advances in Cryptology—CRYPTO 2013—33rd Annual Cryptology Conference, Santa Barbara, CA, USA, 18–22 August 2013; Proceedings, Part II; Lecture Notes in Computer Science; Canetti, R., Garay, J.A., Eds.; Springer: Berlin/Heidelberg, Germany, 2013; Volume 8043, pp. 435–460.
44. Boneh, D.; Raghunathan, A.; Segev, G. Function-Private Identity-Based Encryption: Hiding the Function in Functional Encryption. In Proceedings of the Advances in Cryptology—CRYPTO 2013—33rd Annual Cryptology Conference, Santa Barbara, CA, USA, 18–22 August 2013; Proceedings, Part II; Lecture Notes in Computer Science; Canetti, R., Garay, J.A., Eds.; Springer: Berlin/Heidelberg, Germany, 2013; Volume 8043, pp. 461–478.
45. Sun, J.; Xu, G.; Zhang, T.; Yang, X.; Alazab, M.; Deng, R.H. Privacy-Aware and Security-Enhanced Efficient Matchmaking Encryption. *IEEE Trans. Inf. Forensics Secur.* **2023**, *18*, 4345–4360. [CrossRef]
46. Zhang, C.; Zhao, M.; Zhu, L.; Wu, T.; Liu, X. Enabling Efficient and Strong Privacy-Preserving Truth Discovery in Mobile Crowdsensing. *IEEE Trans. Inf. Forensics Secur.* **2022**, *17*, 3569–3581. [CrossRef]

electronics

MDPI

Article

Privacy-Preserving Fine-Grained Redaction with Policy Fuzzy Matching in Blockchain-Based Mobile Crowdsensing

Hongchen Guo [1], Haotian Liang [2], Mingyang Zhao [2], Yao Xiao [2], Tong Wu [2,*], Jingfeng Xue [1] and Liehuang Zhu [2]

[1] School of Computer Science and Technology, Beijing Institute of Technology, Beijing 100081, China; guohongchen@bit.edu.cn (H.G.); xuejf@bit.edu.cn (J.X.)

[2] School of Cyberspace Science and Technology, Beijing Institute of Technology, Beijing 100081, China; haotianl@bit.edu.cn (H.L.); mingyangz@bit.edu.cn (M.Z.); 3120195529@bit.edu.cn (Y.X.); liehuangz@bit.edu.cn (L.Z.)

* Correspondence: tracy_tongw@163.com

Abstract: The redactable blockchain has emerged as a promising technique in mobile crowdsensing, allowing users to break immutability in a controlled manner selectively. Unfortunately, current fine-grained redactable blockchains suffer two significant limitations in terms of security and functionality, which severely impede their application in mobile crowdsensing. For security, the transparency of the blockchain allows anyone to access both the data and policy, which consequently results in a breach of user privacy. Regarding functionality, current solutions cannot support error tolerance during policy matching, thereby limiting their applicability in various situations, such as fingerprint-based and face-based identification scenarios. This paper presents a privacy-preserving fine-grained redactable blockchain with policy fuzzy matching, named PRBFM. PRBFM supports fuzzy policy matching and partitions users' privileges without compromising user privacy. The idea of PRBFM is to leverage threshold linear secret sharing based on the Lagrange interpolation theorem to distribute the decryption keys and chameleon hash trapdoors. Additionally, we have incorporated a privacy-preserving policy matching delegation mechanism into PRBFM to minimize user overhead. Our security analysis demonstrates that PRBFM can defend against the chosen-ciphertext attack. Moreover, experiments conducted on the FISCO blockchain platform show that PRBFM is at least 7.8 times faster than existing state-of-the-art solutions.

Keywords: blockchain; fine-grained redaction; policy fuzzy matching; privacy preservation; mobile crowdsensing

1. Introduction

With the increasing prevalence of intelligent terminals, particularly in light of contemporary trends such as "Industrie 4.0" [1] and the IoT, mobile crowdsensing has emerged as a promising application that leverages smart devices in mobile networks to utilize idle resources for sensing tasks effectively [2]. However, the current mobile crowdsensing paradigms primarily rely on centralized platforms that are not entirely trustworthy in practice and give rise to issues such as fraud, security vulnerabilities, and the single point of failure [3]. Consequently, the adoption of blockchain techniques has become widespread as a means to address these challenges. In essence, the immutability of blockchain serves as a critical measure against any manipulation of registered objects for illicit gains [4,5].

However, the immutability of blockchain may impede the application of the blockchain. Nowadays, the blockchain ecosystem is plagued by the presence of inappropriate materials, such as fake news, copyrighted content, and sensitive data [6–9]. Researchers have discovered that individuals with malicious intent can upload objectionable material (such as malware or pornographic links) onto the Bitcoin blockchain [7]. Regrettably, no effective methods currently exist to prevent the dissemination of this harmful content throughout the Bitcoin network. Participants on the chain may be concerned about being associated with illegal issues, discouraging their involvement in and use of the chain. Furthermore, certain blockchain systems have faced the issue of illicit transactions in practical scenarios. For instance, a well-known incident called the "The DAO" attack took place in Ethereum due to the presence of susceptible smart contracts [9]. This attack even necessitated a hard fork to mitigate the resulting adverse consequences. Additionally, various data regulations and requirements, such as the General Data Protection Regulation (GDPR) [10] and the concept of "the right to be forgotten" [11], empower individuals to manage their personal data [12–14]. However, because of the immutability of blockchain, it is evident that the information stored on the chain cannot be altered [15].

In order to break the immutability of the blockchain in a controlled manner selectively, the idea of the redactable blockchain was introduced by Ateniese et al. [16]. However, their method is on the basis of the policy-based chameleon hash (PCH) [6] that inherits the limitations of traditional attribute-based encryption (ABE) [17]. To address this problem, Tian et al. [18] proposed a novel implementation of attribute-based traitor tracing (ABTT) [19,20] that utilizes Hierarchical Identity-Based Encryption (HIBE) and one-time signature schemes. However, this proposed scheme only provides limited accountability. Therefore, Xu et al. [21] proposed a novel scheme of PCH with black-box accountability (PCHA) to overcome this challenge. Moreover, to satisfy the growing need in real-world scenarios, various redactable blockchain schemes have been proposed with necessity characters: dynamism [22], verifiability [23], and flexibility [24].

Unfortunately, these aforementioned redactable blockchain schemes all fall short in the aspects of security and functionality. For security, the data and policy can be accessed by any entity because of the transparency of the blockchain, which may result in potential privacy leakage. When it comes to functionality, existing works lack support for error tolerance during policy matching [25]. For instance, in some real-world scenarios such as fingerprint identification [26] or face recognition [27], it is almost impossible to achieve a 100% perfect match. To sum up, there is an urgent need for a fine-grained redactable blockchain with policy fuzzy matching in a privacy-preserving manner. Hence, four challenges arise:

1. How to enable fine-grained redactable blockchain with fuzzy policy matching;
2. How to conceal the policy based on fuzzy policy matching;
3. How to ensure data privacy while maintaining privilege downward compatibility (i.e., allowing redactable users to access the data) through policy concealment;
4. How to minimize user overhead in a privacy-preserving paradigm.

1.1. Contribution

In this paper, we provide a positive answer to the aforementioned problems by proposing a privacy-preserving fine-grained redactable blockchain with fuzzy policy matching (PRBFM). Specifically, PRBFM supports fuzzy policy matching and partitions users' privileges without compromising user privacy. The main contributions are illustrated below.

- We introduce a novel privacy-preserving fine-grained redactable blockchain with fuzzy policy matching for mobile crowdsensing scenarios. Concretely, to achieve data privacy preservation and fuzzy matching for the redactable blockchain, we leverage the Lagrange interpolation theorem-based secret sharing to distribute the data decryption keys and chameleon hash trapdoors.
- To further satisfy the requirement of privacy-preserving policy matching and reduce the user overhead, we design a privacy-preserving policy matching delegation mechanism for PRBFM.
- A formal security analysis is provided to demonstrate the security of PRBFM against chosen-ciphertext attacks in a random oracle model. Subsequently, we employ a real-world dataset to perform experiments on the FISCO blockchain platform. The experimental results demonstrate that our schemes outperform related existing solutions, with a speed improvement of a minimum of 7.8×.

1.2. Roadmap

The structure of this paper is shown in Figure 1. Section 2 details the system model, threat model, and problem formulation. Proceeding further, Section 3 presents the preliminaries utilized in PRBFM. Subsequently, in Section 4, we formalize our scheme by presenting the definition and detailed construction of PRBFM, while the analysis and applications are discussed in Section 5. Several experiments based on the FISCO blockchain and the real-world dataset are conducted in Section 6. Finally, we discuss several related works about the redactable blockchain in Section 7 before reaching the conclusion in Section 8.

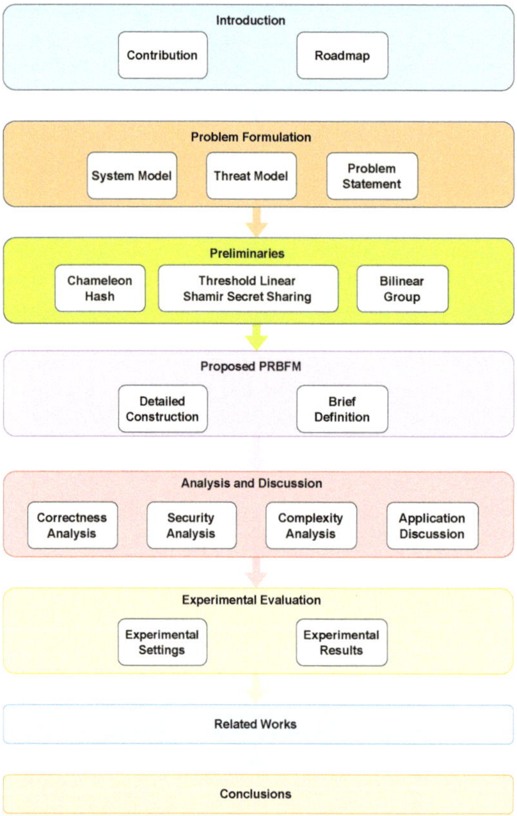

Figure 1. The structure of this paper.

2. Problem Formulation

2.1. System Model

In this section, we formulate the problem addressed by the proposed PRBFM scheme. This scheme involves three different types of entities: *nodes*, *users*, and *data owners*. The nodes are responsible for storing the data of corresponding owners and executing data queries from users with permission. Notably, the nodes can be divided into three main types: privilege nodes (i.e., consortium nodes), storage nodes (i.e., cloud nodes), and computation nodes (i.e., edge nodes). The users usually represent requesters in realistic mobile crowdsensing scenarios. According to their attributes and the policy of the data owner, they can be split into three roles: unauthorized users, authorized users, and authorized modifiers. Unauthorized users are unable to perform any actions on the uploaded data. Authorized users have read-only access to the uploaded data. On the other hand, authorized modifiers can both access and modify the contents of the uploaded data. Similar to the users, the data owners mainly represent individuals or organizations in real-world mobile crowdsensing scenarios. Their prior task is to crowdsense raw data, then encrypt and upload them to the blockchain. The system model is presented in Figure 2.

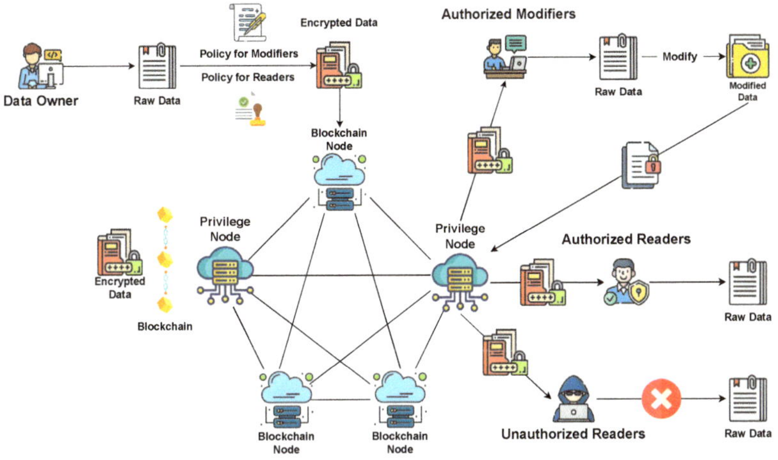

Figure 2. System model of our scheme.

2.2. Threat Model

In blockchain-based mobile crowdsensing scenarios, it is assumed that the privileged nodes, such as the government, organization administrators, and manufacturers, are trustworthy entities as they regulate the blockchain and authorize user privileges [28–30]. Conversely, other entities such as users, data owners, storage nodes, and computation nodes are semi-honest. Though they are expected to follow protocols faithfully, they have the curiosity to probe others' private data, which may lead to unwanted inferences [7,31]. Additionally, users may maliciously collude with other entities except for the privileged nodes, resulting in attacks such as privilege escalation and privacy eavesdropping. We summarize the potential attacks below.

- **Unauthorized access attack:** Since encrypted data submitted by corresponding owners may contain commercially sensitive or private details, they become a prime target of potential adversaries. One such threat is the unauthorized access attack, whereby individuals without authorization may attempt to read or modify the data.
- **Eavesdropping attack:** An unauthorized party may eavesdrop on data transmitted through public channels in an attempt to deduce sensitive details from the intercepted ciphertext.
- **User inferring attack:** Attributes and policies may contain specific characteristics of individuals, such as their occupation, rank, or identity. An attack that expert adversaries may use to elicit sensitive information without knowing personal identifiers, such as the user identity or type of encrypted data, is known as the user inferring attack.
- **Identity disguising attack:** Access to encrypted data is determined based on specific attributes of individual users, including their identity. As a result, identity disguising attacks occur when unauthorized entities attempt to appear as authorized readers or modifiers. These attacks may involve disguising the encryption key with unauthorized attributes or attaching unauthorized attributes to obtained ciphertexts to mislead other entities. In some instances, unauthorized actors may alter or tamper with the message to deceive other parties.
- **Collusion attack:** Unauthorized entities may collaborate to perform various attacks, including those outlined above. For example, unauthorized users may pool their secret keys to recover encrypted data without proper authorization. They may also ex-

change keys to obtain encrypted data without proper authorization from the specified sender's attributes.

2.3. Problem Statement and Design Goals

The problem addressed in this paper is as follows: a data owner encrypts plaintext message m based on a readability policy $\mathcal{P}r$ and an editability policy $\mathcal{P}e(\mathcal{P}r \subset \mathcal{P}e)$. The resulting encryption (C, H) is then submitted to blockchain nodes. Simultaneously, a user with attributes σ exists. The design goal of PRBFM is to *achieve a secure redactable blockchain in which the user can read m only when $\mathcal{P}r \subset \sigma$ and can edit only if $\mathcal{P}e \subset \sigma$ while maintaining the confidentiality of sensitive data, including data from owners, user attributes, and owner policies, to avoid exposure to other parties.*

3. Preliminaries

3.1. Chameleon Hash

Ateniese et al. [16] proposed the chameleon hash. A chameleon hash system typically comprises five algorithms that can be executed in polynomial time. These definitions are illustrated below:

- **PPGen(1^λ)**. This algorithm's input is the security parameter λ. The output of this algorithm is the public parameters PP. Notably, we implicitly assume that mpk is the input for the subsequent algorithms.
- **KeyGen(PP)**. This algorithm uses the public parameters PP as input and generates the public key pk and secret key sk as output.
- **HashGen(pk, m)**. This algorithm takes the public key pk and plaintext message m as input, and outputs the hash h and random value r.
- **Verify(pk, m, r, h)**. This algorithm takes the public key pk, plaintext message m, random value r, and hash h as input, and generates the decision result d as output. Specifically, d is equal to 1 if the hash is valid, and 0 otherwise.
- **Adapt(sk, m, m', r, h)**. This algorithm takes the secret key sk, plaintext message m, alternate message m', random value r, and hash h as input, and generates the alternate random value r' as output.

We make the assumption, without loss of generality, that the *Adapt* algorithm always requires the hash h for verification. If h is invalid, the algorithm outputs $\perp$ instead of the alternate random value r'.

3.2. Threshold Linear Shamir Secret Sharing

In [32], Shamir proposed a Lagrange interpolation theorem-based secret sharing scheme. Given k points $(x_1, y_1), \cdots, (x_k, y_k)$ on the 2-D plane where the values of x_i are distinct, there is one and only one interpolation polynomial $q(x)$ of degree $k-1$ that satisfies:

$$y_i = q(x_i), \forall i = 1, 2, \cdots, k. \tag{1}$$

Without loss of generality, we can assume that the confidential data D are a number. To divide D into n shares, denoted as D_i, $i = 1, 2, \cdots, n$, a random polynomial $q(x)$ of degree $k-1$ is selected as:

$$q(x) = a_0 + a_1 x + \cdots + a_{k-1} x_{k-1}, \tag{2}$$

where $a_0 = D$. For $i = 1, 2, \cdots, n$, the corresponding piece D_i is computed as $D_i = q(i)$.

Using the Lagrange interpolation technique, the coefficient of f can be computed when given any subset of k shares from D_i. The secret data D can be obtained by calculating $D = q(0)$. Note that if we have fewer than k shares, D cannot be reconstructed. Specifically, having only $k-1$ or fewer shares does not reveal any information about D.

3.3. Bilinear Group

Definition 1. *(Bilinear Group). Suppose $\mathbb{G}_1, \mathbb{G}_2$, and $\mathbb{G}_T$ are three bilinear groups. There exists a binlinear map $e : \mathbb{G}_1 \times \mathbb{G}_2 \rightarrow \mathbb{G}_T$, where $|\mathbb{G}_1| = |\mathbb{G}_2| = |\mathbb{G}_T| = p$.*

Let these three groups have the same prime order p. The generators of $\mathbb{G}_1$ and $\mathbb{G}_2$ are g and h, respectively. The map e has the following two properties: Binlinearity and Non-degeneration.

If $\mathbb{G}_1 = \mathbb{G}_2$, it is called symmetric pairing. Otherwise, two different types of asymmetric pairing exist based on the existence of the isomorphism function that from $\mathbb{G}_2$ to $\mathbb{G}_1$.

Then, we present the computationally intractable problem that is utilized in this paper.

Definition 2. *(Decisional Modified Bilinear Diffie-Hellman Problem (MBDFH). Let g_i^a, g_j^b, g_k^c and $e(g_1, g_2)^z$ evaluate whether $e(g_1, g_2)^{\frac{ab}{c}} = e(g_1, g_2)^z$, where $i, j, k \in \{1, 2\}$. Suppose there exists an algorithm that generates the group as $\mathcal{G}$, the distribution D is defined as follows:*

$$\begin{aligned} \mathbb{G} &\stackrel{def}{=} (q, \mathbb{G}_1, \mathbb{G}_2, \mathbb{G}_T, g_1, g_2, e) \leftarrow \mathcal{G}, a, b, c, z \in \mathbb{Z}_q, \\ D &\stackrel{def}{=} (G; g_1, g_2, g_i^a, g_j^b, g_k^c, i, j, k \in \{1, 2\}). \end{aligned} \tag{3}$$

Suppose $\mathcal{A}$ represents a probabilistic polynomial-time (PPT) adversary breaking the MBDH problem.

$$Adv_{\mathcal{A}}^{MBDH}(\lambda) \stackrel{def}{=} |Pr[\mathcal{A}(D, e(g_1, g_2)^{\frac{ab}{c}})] - Pr[\mathcal{A}(D, e(g_1, g_2)^z)]| \tag{4}$$

is negligible for the security parameter λ.

4. Proposed PRBFM

The primary objective of PRBFM is to utilize two techniques. The first technique involves employing Lagrange secret sharing and a chameleon hash, which allow us to create a redactable blockchain having privilege downward compatibility and fuzzy matching while still maintaining privacy. Meanwhile, the second technique involves designing a privacy-preserving matching delegation mechanism, which minimizes user overhead.

4.1. Brief Definition

Before illustrating the details of PRBFM, we will first provide a brief definition:

Definition 3. *PRBFM comprises eight polynomial-time algorithms:* **Setup**, **KeyGen**, **Encrypt**, **Verify**, **TrGen**, **Match**, **Read**, *and* **Edit**.

- **Setup** ($\lambda \rightarrow (mpk, msk)$). *The algorithm yields the master secret key msk and master public key mpk when given a security parameter λ. For simplicity, mpk is implicitly assumed to be taken as input by all other algorithms.*
- **KeyGen** ($(msk, \sigma) \rightarrow sk$). *The algorithm takes σ and msk as inputs and produces the user's secret key sk.*
- **Encrypt** ($(m, x, \mathcal{P}_r, \mathcal{P}_e) \rightarrow (C, H)$). *The algorithm takes message $m \in \mathcal{M}$, Chameleon hash trapdoor x, readability policy $\mathcal{P}_r$, and editability policy $\mathcal{P}_e (\mathcal{P}_r \subset \mathcal{P}_e)$ as inputs and outputs ciphertext C along with the corresponding hash value $H = (h, r_h)$.*
- **Verify** ($(C, H) \rightarrow d_v$). *The algorithm produces a verification result d_v by validating the pair (C, H), with $d_v \in 0, 1$.*
- **TrGen** ($sk \rightarrow T$). *The algorithm takes the secret key sk as input to generate the trapdoor T, which is composed of T_1 and T_{2,i_i^σ}.*
- **Match** ($(T, C) \rightarrow d_m$). *Given the trapdoor T and the ciphertext C, the algorithm outputs a match result $d_m \in 0, 1, 2$ to indicate different levels of access. Specifically, (C^1, H) is returned when $d_m = 1$, and (C^2, H) is returned when $d_m = 2$.*

- **Read** $((C^1, sk) \rightarrow m|\perp)$. *Given the ciphertext C^1 and the secret key sk as inputs, the algorithm retrieves the message m only if $\sigma \subset \mathcal{P}_r$. Otherwise, the algorithm returns an error symbol $\perp$.*
- **Edit** $((C^2, sk, m', \mathcal{P}_r', \mathcal{P}_e') \rightarrow (C', H'))$. *Given the ciphertext C^2, secret key sk, and new message m' along with their respective policies $(\mathcal{P}_r', \mathcal{P}_e')$, the algorithm generates a new ciphertext C' and hash value $H' = (h, r_h')$. Importantly, the editability feature preserves the correspondence of on-chain hashes and off-chain data.*

4.2. Detailed Construction

We now describe the detail of PRBFM.

Setup $\lambda \rightarrow (mpk, msk)$: Based on the decentralized key generation protocol, multiple privilege nodes cooperate to generate the system parameters.

- Generate the description of bilinear map $\Gamma = (p, g, \mathbb{G}, \mathbb{G}_T, e)$, where $e : \mathbb{G} \times \mathbb{G} \rightarrow \mathbb{G}_T$. Subsequently, assume the attribute universe as $\mathcal{U}$ and the size of $\mathcal{U}$ as n. Set the threshold of policy matching as d. Next, generate n random values $\{r_i\}^n$. Then, compute $\{R_i = g^{r_i}\}^n$. Next, select a random value $\alpha \in \mathbb{Z}_p$ and a hash function $H[\cdot] : \mathbb{G}_T \rightarrow \{0,1\}^*$.
- Generate the master secret key $msk = (\{r_i\}^n, \alpha)$ and the master public key $mpk = (\{R_i\}^n, g^\alpha, H, \Gamma)$.

KeyGen $(msk, \sigma) \rightarrow sk$: A user selects a privilege node for registration, and the privilege node combines the user's attribute set to generate the secret key.

- Randomly generate a $(d-1)$-degree polynomial $q(x) = \alpha + a_1 x + a_2 x^2 + \cdots + a_{d-1} x^{d-1}$, where $q(0) = \alpha$. Then, for each attribute $i \in \sigma$, compute $q(i)$. Subsequently, utilize the Lagrange interpolation theorem to compute the Lagrange parameters $\{\Delta_{i,\sigma}(0)\}_i^\sigma$.
- Generate the secret key $sk = \{sk_i = g^{\frac{q(i)\Delta_{i,\sigma}(0)}{r_i}}\}_i^\sigma$. Then, return sk to the user.

Encrypt $(m, x, \mathcal{P}_r, \mathcal{P}_e) \rightarrow (C, H)$: based on readability and editability policies, a user generates the ciphertext and hash value.

- Select two random values $d_1 \in \mathbb{Z}_p$ and $d_2 \in \mathbb{Z}_p$. Generate the readability policy $\mathcal{P}_r$. Compute $\{C_{1,i} = R_i^{d_1}\}_i^{\mathcal{P}_r}$ and $\{C_{2,i} = R_i^{d_2}\}_i^{\mathcal{P}_r}$. Subsequently, compute $C_3 = g^{\alpha d_2}$ and $C_m = m \oplus H[e(g,g)^{\alpha d_1}]$.
- Select two random values $d_3 \in \mathbb{Z}_p$ and $d_4 \in \mathbb{Z}_p$, and the chameleon secret key x. Generate the editability policy $\mathcal{P}_e$. Subsequently, compute $\{C_{4,i} = R_i^{d_3}\}_i^{\mathcal{P}_e}$, $\{C_{5,i} = R_i^{d_4}\}_i^{\mathcal{P}_e}$, $C_6 = g^{\alpha d_4}$, and $C_7 = g^x$. To guarantee the right downward compatibility, compute $C_x = x \oplus H[e(g,g)^{\alpha d_1}] \oplus H[e(g,g)^{\alpha d_3}]$.
- Select a random value $r_h \in \mathbb{Z}_p$ to compute the chameleon hash $h = g^{C_m} g^{x r_h}$.
- Generate the ciphertext $C = (\{C_{1,i}\}_i^{\mathcal{P}_r}, \{C_{2,i}\}_i^{\mathcal{P}_r}, C_3, \{C_{4,i}\}_i^{\mathcal{P}_e}, \{C_{5,i}\}_i^{\mathcal{P}_e}, C_6, C_7, C_m, C_x)$ and hash value $H = (h, r_h)$.
- Send the pair (C, H) to computation nodes and the chameleon hash h to the blockchain. Next, computation nodes upload the pairs to storage nodes.

Verify $(C, H) \rightarrow d_v$: computation nodes verify the validity of the pair (C, H) and output a verification result.

- Check the equation $h \stackrel{?}{=} g^{C_m} C_7^{r_h}$. If the equation holds, output d_v as 1. Otherwise, output d_v as 0 prompts the storage nodes that the pair (C, H) is invalid.

TrGen $sk \rightarrow T$: a user leverages the secret key to generate a trapdoor and sends it to computation nodes.

- Select a random value $t \in \mathbb{Z}_p$ and compute $T_1 = g^t$. Then, utilize sk to compute $\{T_{2,i} = sk_i^t\}_i^\sigma$.
- Generate the trapdoor $T = (T_1, \{T_{2,i}\}_i^\sigma)$ and send T to computation nodes.

Match $(C, T) \rightarrow d_m$: computation nodes utilize the ciphertext and trapdoor to perform policy verification without compromising user privacy.

- Obtain ciphertexts from the storage nodes. Based on the threshold d, respectively select d values from $\{C_{2,i}\}_i^{\mathcal{P}_r}$ and $\{T_{2,i}\}_i^{\sigma}$ to conduct a set $\mathcal{P}_{r,j}$. Then, for each $\mathcal{P}_{r,j}$, check the equation $\Pi_{i=1}^{\mathcal{P}_{r,j}} e(C_{2,i}, T_{2,i}) \stackrel{?}{=} e(C_3, T_1)$.
- If the equation does not hold for all $\mathcal{P}_{r,j}$, computation nodes output $d_m = 0$. Otherwise, record the set $\mathcal{P}_{r,j}$ and computation nodes output $d_m = 1$. In addition, it means that the user is an authorized reader of this message.
- If d_m equals to 1, computation nodes further select d values from $\{C_{5,i}\}_i^{\mathcal{P}_e}$ and $\{T_{2,i}\}_i^{\sigma}$ to conduct a set $\mathcal{P}_{e,j}$. Then, for each $\mathcal{P}_{e,j}$, check the equation $\Pi_{i=1}^{\mathcal{P}_{e,j}} e(C_{5,i}, T_{2,i}) \stackrel{?}{=} e(C_6, T_1)$. If this equation holds, computation nodes output $d_m = 2$, and it means that the user is an authorized modifier for this message. Then, record the set $\mathcal{P}_{e,j}$.
- If d_m equals to 1, return $C^1 = (\mathcal{P}_{r,j}, \{C_{1,i}\}_i^{\mathcal{P}_r}, C_m)$ to the user. If d_m equals to 2, return $C^2 = (\mathcal{P}_{r,j}, \mathcal{P}_{e,j}, \{C_{1,i}\}_i^{\mathcal{P}_r}, \{C_{4,i}\}_i^{\mathcal{P}_e}, C_m, C_x)$ to the user.

Read $(C^1, sk) \to m$: receiving the data from the computation nodes, the user utilizes his/her secret key to recover the message.

- Compute $R = \Pi_{i=1}^{\mathcal{P}_{r,j}} e(C_{1,i}, sk_i) = e(g,g)^{\alpha d_1}$. Recover the message $m = C_m \oplus H[R]$.

Edit $(C^2, sk, m', \mathcal{P}_r', \mathcal{P}_e') \to (C', H')$: based on the secret key, the user read and edit the message.

- Perform the **Read** algorithm to recover the message m.
- Compute $E = \Pi_{i=1}^{\mathcal{P}_{e,j}} e(C_{4,i}, sk_i) = e(g,g)^{\alpha d_3}$. Recover the message $x = C_x \oplus H[E] \oplus H[R]$. If the user attempts to edit the message, generate a new message m'. Subsequently, generate new readability policy $\mathcal{P}_r'$ and editability policy $\mathcal{P}_e'$ and compute the ciphertext $C' = (\{C_{1,i}'\}_i^{\mathcal{P}_r'}, \{C_{2,i}'\}_i^{\mathcal{P}_r'}, C_3', \{C_{4,i}'\}_i^{\mathcal{P}_e'}, \{C_{5,i}'\}_i^{\mathcal{P}_e'}, C_6', C_7, C_m', C_x')$. Next, compute $r_h' = \frac{C_m - C_m'}{x} + r_h$ and generate $H' = (h, r_h')$.
- Send the new pair (C', H') to computation nodes.

The workflow of PRBFM is shown in Figure 3.

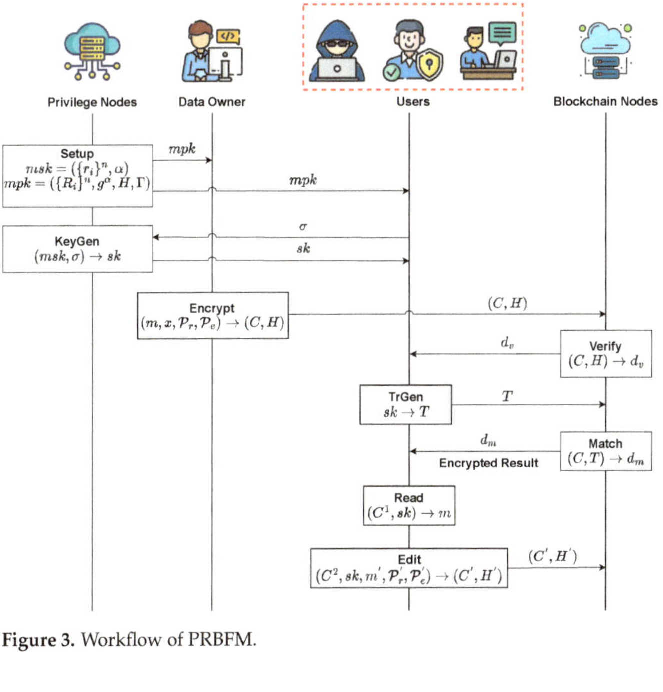

Figure 3. Workflow of PRBFM.

5. Analysis and Discussion

5.1. Correctness Analysis

Theorem 1. *In PRBFM, if and only if an attribute set σ of the user satisfies the policy of the data owner for readers, i.e., $\mathcal{P}_r \subset \sigma$, the $d_m = 1$ and the user is an authorized reader.*

Proof. From the **Encrypt** step, the data owner generates the ciphertext $C = (\{C_{1,i}\}_i^{\mathcal{P}_r}, \{C_{2,i}\}_i^{\mathcal{P}_r}, C_3, \{C_{4,i}\}_i^{\mathcal{P}_e}, \{C_{5,i}\}_i^{\mathcal{P}_e}, C_6, C_7, C_m, C_x)$ and hash value $H = (h, r_h)$. Then, we concentrate on the correctness in the **Match** and the **Read** step. In the **Match** step, after receiving the trapdoor $T = (T_1, \{T_{2,i}\}_i^{\sigma})$, the computation nodes first respectively select d values from $\{C_{2,i}\}_i^{\mathcal{P}_r}$ and $\{T_{2,i}\}_i^{\sigma}$ to conduct a set $\mathcal{P}_{r,j}$ according to the threshold d. Then, for each $\mathcal{P}_{r,j}$, the computation nodes compute

$$\begin{aligned}
\Pi_{i=1}^{\mathcal{P}_{r,j}} e(C_{2,i}, T_{2,i}) &= \Pi_{i=1}^{\mathcal{P}_{r,j}} e(R_i^{d_2}, sk_i^t) \\
&= \Pi_{i=1}^{\mathcal{P}_{r,j}} e(g^{d_2 \cdot r_i}, g^{\frac{q(i)\cdot\Delta_{i,\sigma}(0)\cdot t}{r_i}}) \\
&= e(g,g)^{d_2 \cdot t \cdot \Sigma_{i=1}^{\mathcal{P}_{r,j}} (q(i)\cdot\Delta_{i,\sigma}(0))} \\
&= e(g^{\alpha d_2}, g^t) \\
&= e(C_3, T_1).
\end{aligned} \tag{5}$$

Therefore, in the **Match** step, the correctness of PRBFM holds. In the **Read** step, a user gets $C^1 = (\mathcal{P}_{r,j}, \{C_{1,i}\}_i^{\mathcal{P}_r}, C_m)$, and H from the computation nodes. Next, based on his/her secret key sk, the user computes

$$\begin{aligned}
& C_m \oplus H[\Pi_{i=1}^{\mathcal{P}_{r,j}} e(C_{1,i}, sk_i)] \\
&= C_m \oplus H[\Pi_{i=1}^{\mathcal{P}_{r,j}} e(g^{d_1 \cdot r_i}, g^{\frac{q(i)\Delta_{i,\sigma}(0)}{r_i}})] \\
&= C_m \oplus H[e(g,g)^{d_1 \cdot \Sigma_{i=1}^{\mathcal{P}_{r,j}} (q(i)\cdot\Delta_{i,\sigma}(0))}] \\
&= m \oplus H[e(g,g)^{\alpha d_1}] \oplus H[e(g,g)^{\alpha d_1}] \\
&= m.
\end{aligned} \tag{6}$$

On the basis of the Lagrange interpolation theorem, if and only if the policy $\mathcal{P}_r$ satisfies $\mathcal{P}_r \subset \sigma$, the message m can be recovered and Equations (5) and (6) hold. Therefore, Theorem 1 is proven. □

Theorem 2. *In PRBFM, if and only if an attribute set σ of the user satisfies the policy of the data owner for modifiers, i.e., $\mathcal{P}_e \subset \sigma$, the $d_m = 2$ and the user is an authorized modifier.*

Proof. Similar to Theorem 1, we first prove the correctness of evaluating whether a given user is an authorized modifier in the **Match** step. Concretely, the computation nodes first select d values from $\{C_{5,i}\}_i^{\mathcal{P}_e}$ and $\{T_{2,i}\}_i^{\sigma}$ to conduct a set $\mathcal{P}_{e,j}$. Then, for each $\mathcal{P}_{e,j}$, the computation nodes compute

$$\begin{aligned}
\Pi_{i=1}^{\mathcal{P}_{e,j}} e(C_{5,i}, T_{2,i}) &= \Pi_{i=1}^{\mathcal{P}_{e,j}} e(g^{d_4 \cdot r_i}, g^{\frac{q(i)\cdot\Delta_{i,\sigma}(0)\cdot t}{r_i}}) \\
&= e(g,g)^{d_4 \cdot t \cdot \Sigma_{i=1}^{\mathcal{P}_{e,j}} (q(i)\cdot\Delta_{i,\sigma}(0))} \\
&= e(C_6, T_1).
\end{aligned} \tag{7}$$

Then, in the **Edit** step, if and only if $\mathcal{P}_e \subset \sigma$, the user can recover the chameleon secret key x as follows:

$$C_x \oplus H[E] \oplus H[R] = C_x \oplus H[e(g,g)^{d_3 \cdot \Sigma_{i=1}^{\mathcal{P}_{e,j}}(q(i)\cdot\Delta_{i,\sigma}(0))}] \oplus H[R]$$
$$= C_x \oplus H[e(g,g)^{\alpha d_3}] \oplus H[e(g,g)^{\alpha d_1}] \tag{8}$$
$$= x.$$

where $E = \Pi_{i=1}^{\mathcal{P}_{e,j}} e(C_{4,i}, sk_i)$ and $R = \Pi_{i=1}^{\mathcal{P}_{r,j}} e(C_{1,i}, sk_i)$. Next, based on the x recovered according to Equation (8), the user computes $r_h' = \frac{C_m - C_m'}{x} + r_h$. Notably, if and only if r_h' is calculated as mentioned above, the following equation holds:

$$g^{C_m} \cdot C_7^{r_h} \stackrel{?}{=} g^{C_m'} \cdot C_7^{r_h'}. \tag{9}$$

Otherwise, the x is not valid, and the modification is recognized as illegal. Therefore, Theorem 2 is proven. □

5.2. Security Analysis

The security properties of PRBFM are formally defined based on its construction. These include privacy security, which encompasses data privacy, policy privacy, and attribute privacy, as well as user collusion resistance and collision resistance. The security model follows the oracle model and is indistinguishable under a chosen-ciphertext attack (IND-CCA). The experiment involves a PPT adversary $\mathcal{A}$ and a challenger $\mathcal{C}$ and is depicted in detail in Figure 4.

Setup: The challenger $\mathcal{C}$ runs the **Setup** step to generate the master secret key $msk = (\{r_i\}^n, \alpha)$ and master public key $mpk = (\{R_i\}^n, g^\alpha, H, \Gamma)$. Next, the challenger $\mathcal{C}$ publishes mpk to the adversary $\mathcal{A}$.
Phase 1: The challenger $\mathcal{C}$ permits adversary $\mathcal{A}$ to request the secret keys. In particular, the adversary $\mathcal{A}$ sends the attributes σ to $\mathcal{C}$. The challenger $\mathcal{C}$ randomly generates a $(d-1)$-degree polynomial $q(x)$ and obtains the secret key $sk = \{g^{\frac{q(i)\Delta_{i,\sigma}(0)}{r_i}}\}_i^\sigma$.
Challenge: Adversary $\mathcal{A}$ selects the target user and two messages m_0 and m_1, where $|m_0| == |m_1|$. The challenger $\mathcal{C}$ flips a fair binary coin $b \in \{0,1\}$ outside of the view of $\mathcal{A}$. $\mathcal{C}$ encrypts m_0 and sends (C_0, H_0) to the adversary $\mathcal{A}$ if $b = 0$. Otherwise, m_1 is encrypted, and (C_1, H_1) is sent to $\mathcal{A}$. Notably, the secret key of the target user is not able to be requested in ***Phase 1***.
Phase 2: The challenger $\mathcal{C}$ performs similarly as it did in ***Phase 1***, but $\mathcal{A}$ is able to request the secret key of the target user in ***Phase 2***.
Guess: The adversary $\mathcal{A}$ will submit a guess b' of b, and its advantage to win the experiment can be represented as $Adv_{\mathcal{A}[b'=b]}$.

Figure 4. The experiment played between $\mathcal{A}$ and $\mathcal{C}$.

Theorem 3. *For two multiplicative groups $(\mathbb{G}, \mathbb{G}_T, e)$, and a bilinear map $e : \mathbb{G} \times \mathbb{G} \rightarrow \mathbb{G}_T$, if the Decisionla MBDH problem is hard in $(\mathbb{G}, \mathbb{G}_T, e)$, any PPT adversaries are not able to violate the read-only ciphertext indistinguishability by adopting the chosen-ciphertext attack in the random oracle model.*

Proof. We here assume that if simulator $\mathcal{B}$ has the tuple $(A, B, C, Z) = (g^a, g^b, g^c, e(g,g)^z)$, he will manage to distinguish whether $e(g,g)^z$ is equal to $e(g,g)^{\frac{ab}{c}}$ in the simulation. The detailed process of the simulation is illustrated as follows:

Game 0. Game 0 is the original game, where nothing is different from the original scheme.

Game 1. Game 1 differs from Game 0 in the **Setup** step. For any $i \in \sigma$: $R_i = g^{\frac{1}{\zeta_i}}$; for $i \notin \sigma$: $R_i = g^{\frac{1}{\omega_i}}$. Next, simulator $\mathcal{B}$ gives the public parameters to adversary $\mathcal{A}$. From adversary $\mathcal{A}$'s view, the received public parameters are indistinguishable from the ones in

Game 0. The adversary $\mathcal{A}$ will terminate the game and return fail if it can tell the difference with the advantage ε_{DL}.

Game 2. Game 2 differs from Game 0 in the **KeyGen** step. Adversary $\mathcal{A}$ requests for the secret key of the user. For any $i \in \sigma$: $sk_i = C^{\zeta_i q(i)\Delta_{i,\sigma}(0)}$; for $i \notin \sigma$: $sk_i = C^{\omega_i q(i)\Delta_{i,\sigma}(0)}$. Next, simulator $\mathcal{B}$ gives the secret key sk to adversary $\mathcal{A}$. The adversary $\mathcal{A}$ will terminate the game and return fail if it can tell the difference with the advantage ε_{DL}.

Game 3. Game 3 differs from Game 2 in terms of the hash oracle $\mathcal{O}_H$. Simulator $\mathcal{B}$ submits the message m to $\mathcal{O}_H$ and receives the requested hash value. During the i-th request, simulator $\mathcal{B}$ generates the hash value $H(i) = msg_i$ and stores $H(i)$ as $|msg_i| = |m|$. The adversary $\mathcal{A}$ will terminate the game and return fail if it can tell the difference with the advantage ε_H.

Game 4. Game 4 differs from Game 3 in terms of **Challenge**. The adversary $\mathcal{A}$ submits two challenge messages m_0 and m_1 to simulator $\mathcal{B}$, where $|m_0| = |m_1|$. The simulator $\mathcal{B}$ flips a coin b and returns a challenge encryption C_b. Then, for $i \in \sigma$, simulator $\mathcal{B}$ computes

$$\begin{aligned} C_{m^*} &= m \oplus H[Z] \\ C^*_{1,i} &= B^{d_1} \\ C^*_{2,i} &= C^{d_2} \\ C^*_3 &= A^{\eta_i}. \end{aligned} \tag{10}$$

For $i \notin \varepsilon$, $\mathcal{B}$ computes

$$\begin{aligned} C_{m^*} &= m \oplus H[Z] \\ C^*_{1,i} &= B^{\frac{\mu_{i,1}}{\omega_i}} \\ C^*_{2,i} &= C^{\frac{\mu_{i,2}}{\omega_i}} \\ C^*_3 &= A^{\eta_i}. \end{aligned} \tag{11}$$

If $Z = e(g,g)^{\frac{ab}{c}}$ and $\alpha' = \frac{b}{c}$, we then obtain $C_{m^*} = m \oplus H[Z] = m \oplus H[e(g,g)^{\frac{ab}{c}}] = m \oplus H[e(g,g)^{a\alpha'}]$, $C^*_3 = A^{\eta_i} = g^{a\eta_i}$. For $i \in \sigma$, $C^*_{1,i} = B^{d_1} = g^{bd_1}$ and $C^*_{2,i} = C^{d_2} = g^{cd_2}$; for $i \notin \sigma$, $C^*_{1,i} = B^{\frac{\mu_{i,1}}{\omega_i}} = g^{b\frac{\mu_{i,1}}{\omega_i}}$ and $C^*_{2,i} = C^{\frac{\mu_{i,2}}{\omega_i}} = g^{c\frac{\mu_{i,2}}{\omega_i}}$.

If $Z = e(g,g)^Z$, because z is randomly selected, Z will be random from the view of the adversary $\mathcal{A}$. The game will be terminated if $\mathcal{A}$ can tell the difference between Game 4 and Game 3. Otherwise, $\mathcal{B}$ is able to solve the MBDH problem. Concretely, if $Z = e(g,g)^z$, $Pr[b' = b|Z = e(g,g)^z] = Pr[b' \neq b|Z = e(g,g)^z] = \frac{1}{2}$. If $Z = e(g,g)^{\frac{ab}{c}}$, the adversary $\mathcal{A}$ has an advantage ε' to break the game. Next, the possibility of $\mathcal{A}$'s guess $b = b'$ is $Pr[b' = b|Z = e(g,g)^{\frac{ab}{c}}] = \frac{1}{2} + \varepsilon'$. Therefore, the overall advantage of the simulator $\mathcal{B}$ for breaking the MBDH game is $Adv^{MBDH}_{\mathcal{B}}[b' = b] = |\frac{1}{2}Pr[b' = b|Z = e(g,g)^z]$ $+\frac{1}{2}Pr[b' = b|Z = e(g,g)^{\frac{ab}{c}}] - \frac{1}{2}| = \frac{1}{2}\varepsilon'$.

Game 5. The adversary $\mathcal{A}$ and the simulator $\mathcal{B}$ play the game as mentioned before, except $\sigma \neq \sigma^*$. If adversary $\mathcal{A}$ can tell the difference between **Game 4** and **Game 5**, simulator $\mathcal{B}$ has the advantage ε_{DL} to break the discrete logarithm (DL) problem. Therefore, we obtain $Adv_{\mathcal{A}}[b' = b] = 2\varepsilon_{DL} + \epsilon_H + \frac{1}{2}\varepsilon'$ as the advantage for the adversary $\mathcal{A}$ to win the game. Because the MBDH problem is hard, the components in $Adv_{\mathcal{A}}[b' = b]$ are all negligible. Hence, the $Adv_{\mathcal{A}}[b' = b]$ is also negligible. Next, (C^*_0, H^*_0) and (C^*_1, H^*_1) are indistinguishable from the view of the adversary $\mathcal{A}$. Hence, the PRBFM scheme is able to defend against the chosen-ciphertext attack, and Theorem 3 is proven. □

Theorem 4. *The security of PRBFM includes data privacy, attribute privacy, and policy privacy.*

Proof. Obviously, the security of PRBFM includes data privacy. When it comes to attribute privacy, because the communication channel is secure, the user's attribute set σ can be prevented from being exposed to other entities except for selected privilege nodes during the **KeyGen** step. Next, in the **Match** step, the attribute privacy means the indistinguishability of $T_0 = (T_{0,1}, \{T_{0,2,i}\}_i^{\sigma_0})$ and $T_1 = (T_{1,1}, \{T_{1,2,i}\}_i^{\sigma_1})$. In particular, the simulator $\mathcal{B}$ first selects a random value $\alpha \in \mathbf{Z}_p$. Then, it computes $T_b = (T_{b,0} = g^{\alpha}, \{T_{b,1,i} = g^{sk_i^{\alpha}}\}^{\sigma_b})$ and sends T_b to adversary $\mathcal{A}$. Next, the adversary $\mathcal{A}$ has a negligible advantage ε to guess whether $b = b'$ as follows:

$$Adv_{\mathcal{A}}^{Attr-Pri}[b' = b|\mathcal{A}(\sigma_0, \sigma_1, T_b)] \leq \varepsilon. \tag{12}$$

Hence, adversary $\mathcal{A}$ is not able to violate the attribute privacy during the **Match** step. For other steps such as **Setup**, **Encrypt**, **Verify**, **Read**, and **Edit**, the adversary $\mathcal{A}$ is not able to get information related to the secret key *sk*. Therefore, attribute privacy in PRBFM is guaranteed.

For policy privacy, adversary $\mathcal{A}$ can violate it in two ways. The first is obtaining policies $(\mathcal{P}_r, \mathcal{P}_e)$ from the ciphertext C generated by the data owner. If the adversary $\mathcal{A}$ is able to obtain $(\mathcal{P}_r, \mathcal{P}_e)$ from C, similar to Theorem 3, simulator $\mathcal{B}$ has the ability to perform a PPT algorithm to break the MBDH problem. However, it is evident that the MBDH problem is hard. Thus, adversary $\mathcal{A}$ is not able to violate the policy privacy from the ciphertext C. □

Theorem 5. *If the correctness of the Lagrange interpolation theorem-based secret sharing scheme [32] holds and Theorem 3 is proven, PRBFM can defend against the user collusion attack.*

Proof. Here, we assume that the user may colludes with other users, but there is no collusion with the blockchain nodes. In the **KeyGen** step, the privilege node randomly generates a Lagrange polynomial $q(x)$. Then, it calculates $q(i)$ and the Lagrange parameters $\{\Delta_{i,\sigma}(0)\}_i^{\sigma}$ for each attribute $i \in \sigma$. In PRBFM, only the privilege nodes can obtain $\{q(i)\}_i^{\sigma}$ and $\{\Delta_{i,\sigma}\}_i^{\sigma}$. Suppose an unauthorized user with $q'(1)\Delta'_{1,\sigma}(0)$ collude with $d-1$ unauthorized users who have $\{q'(i)\Delta'_{i,\sigma}(0)\}_{i=1}^{d}$, and their aim is to violate the readability governance in PRBFM. According to Equation (6), $m = C_m \oplus H[\Pi_{i=1}^{\mathcal{P}_{r,j}} e(C_{1,i}, sk_i)]$. Next, the unauthorized user computes

$$\begin{aligned} &C_m \oplus H[\Pi_{i=1}^{\mathcal{P}_{r,j}} e(C_{1,i}, sk_i)] \\ &= C_m \oplus H[\Pi_{i=1}^{\mathcal{P}_{r,j}} e(g^{d_1 \cdot r_i}, g^{\frac{q'(i)\Delta'_{i,\sigma}(0)}{r_i}})] \\ &= C_m \oplus H[e(g,g)^{d_1 \cdot \Sigma_{i=1}^{\mathcal{P}_{r,j}}(q'(i)\cdot\Delta'_{i,\sigma}(0))}]. \end{aligned} \tag{13}$$

On the basis of the correctness of the Lagrange interpolation theorem-based secret sharing scheme, we can indicate that $\Sigma_{i=1}^{\mathcal{P}_{r,j}}(q'(i) \cdot \Delta'_{i,\sigma}(0))$ is not equivalent to the secret value α. Hence, the user cannot violate the readability governance. The user collusion resistance of the editability governance can also be proved in a similar way as the proof of the readability analyzed above. □

Theorem 6. *If the chameleon hash [16] satisfies the collision resistance, PRBFM can defend against hash collision in the random oracle model.*

Proof. In PRBFM, the Lagrange interpolation theorem is utilized to enhance the chameleon hash-based redactable blockchain with PRBFM and bilateral access control. Thus, the collision resistance problem of PRBFM is equivalent to the collision resistance of the chameleon hash. Hence, Theorem 6 is proven. □

5.3. Complexity Analysis

In Table 1, we present the comparison among some recently proposed schemes and PRBFM from the aspects of computational complexity and space complexity, where l is the size of the identity space in Xu et al.'s [21] scheme.

Table 1. Comparison table of some recently proposed schemes.

Scheme	Computational Complexity				Space Complexity			
	KeyGen	Encrypt	Verify	Edit	System Parameter	Encryption Key	Decryption Key	Ciphertext
Derler et al.'s [6] scheme	$\mathcal{O}(2\sigma)$	$\mathcal{O}(\sigma^2)$	$\mathcal{O}(1)$	$\mathcal{O}(\sigma^2+2\sigma)$	$\mathcal{O}(1)$	$\mathcal{O}(\sigma)$	$\mathcal{O}(2\sigma)$	$\mathcal{O}(3\sigma)$
Ma et al.'s [7] scheme	$\mathcal{O}(\sigma)$	$\mathcal{O}(2\sigma)$	$\mathcal{O}(1)$	$\mathcal{O}(6\sigma)$	$\mathcal{O}(1)$	$\mathcal{O}(\sigma)$	$\mathcal{O}(2\sigma)$	$\mathcal{O}(4\sigma)$
Xu et al.'s [21] scheme	$\mathcal{O}(\sigma+l)$	$\mathcal{O}(\sigma^2)$	$\mathcal{O}(1)$	$\mathcal{O}(l^2+3l)$	$\mathcal{O}(1)$	$\mathcal{O}(\sigma)$	$\mathcal{O}(\sigma)$	$\mathcal{O}(2\sigma)$
PRBFM	$\mathcal{O}(\sigma)$	$\mathcal{O}(\mathcal{P}_r+\mathcal{P}_e)$	$\mathcal{O}(1)$	$\mathcal{O}(3\sigma)$	$\mathcal{O}(1)$	$\mathcal{O}(\mathcal{P}_r+\mathcal{P}_e)$	$\mathcal{O}(\sigma)$	$\mathcal{O}(\mathcal{P}_r+\mathcal{P}_e)$

For computational complexity, PRBFM is comparable to that of Xu et al.'s and Ma et al.'s schemes and significantly outperforms that of Derler et al.'s scheme. PRBFM's key generation step has a computational complexity of $\mathcal{O}(\sigma)$ because its privilege nodes randomly select one Lagrange polynomial and perform operations. The computational complexity of the encryption algorithm is about the number of attributes and the size of the policy rather than their multiplication. For the verification steps, it only calculates one equation instead of processing more verification steps in Ma et al.'s scheme and Derler et al.'s scheme, which makes its complexity $\mathcal{O}(1)$. When it comes to the **Read** and **Edit** step, the computational complexity of PRBFM is also comparable to other schemes as it is only related to the size of the policy and the number of attributes.

The space complexity of PRBFM's system parameter is fixed because of the utilization of collision-resistant hash functions, making it comparable with other schemes. The space complexity of the **Encrypt**, **Read**, and **Edit** processes are also influenced by the policy size and number of attributes, respectively. Additionally, since they are determined by the size of the policy and the number of attributes, the space complexity of the ciphertext and the trapdoor is comparable to others.

5.4. Application Discussion

This part explores the potential applications of PRBFM in real-world scenarios. As previously demonstrated, PRBFM successfully addresses limitations in terms of security and functionality. Consequently, PRBFM can be applied in diverse and intricate real-world scenarios while ensuring data privacy preservation.

- **Smart Medical:** Drug testing in the smart medical scenario, based on mobile crowdsourcing, can utilize various sensors. Typically, access to these medical data is limited to patients with specific symptoms. However, attaining a 100% match using patients' physiological data is not feasible, considering the variability of these numerical values. Furthermore, since these physiological data belong to the patients themselves, it is crucial to protect their privacy. Consequently, based on its characters, PRBFM can be applied in this scenario to overcome these challenges.
- **Smart Transportation:** Some companies may employ vehicles equipped with sensors to collect and update transportation data for the purpose of offering predictive services. However, to alleviate the server load, only vehicles in specific conditions (e.g., traffic jams) would be granted access to these prediction data, as using the strict match rule to judge the satisfaction of the conditions is unrealistic. Thus, in this scenario, there is a significant need for fuzzy matching with data privacy preservation, making it conducive to adopting PRBFM.

6. Experimental Evaluation

6.1. Experimental Settings

6.1.1. Setup

We have implemented a prototype system to evaluate the experimental performance of PRBFM. The system programming was carried out in Java, utilizing the Java Pairing-Based Cryptography (JPBC) library. Then, the Type A curve with 80-bit security was selected as the symmetric pairing (Type-I). For the blockchain system, we opted for the FISCO blockchain because of its reliability. To test our schemes, we employed five cloud servers with eight CPUs and 32 GB RAM as blockchain nodes. Of these nodes, two were chosen to be the privilege nodes. To simulate users and data owners, volunteers utilized PCs with 16 GB RAM to communicate with the blockchain nodes. We assumed each user would select a maximum of 100 attributes (i.e., affiliation, occupation, and gender) without loss of generality. Each experiment was conducted ten times, and the average cost was recorded as the final result.

6.1.2. Dataset

To show the efficacy of our proposed schemes, we deployed the MHN dataset, which holds millions of published news headlines sourced from the Australian Broadcasting Corporation. In the course of the experiments, the data owner chooses a headline randomly and uploads it to the blockchain nodes.

6.1.3. Baselines for Comparison

We conducted an assessment of the effectiveness of our proposed PRBFM model by comparing it with other recent fine-grained redactable blockchain schemes, including Derler et al.'s scheme [6], Ma et al.'s scheme [7], and Xu et al.'s scheme [21].

6.1.4. Metrics

To more fully evaluate the performance of PRBFM, we will measure it by four types of metrics:

- The running time for key generation;
- Time consumption on the data owner side;
- Time consumption on the user side;
- Consumption on the blockchain node side.

6.2. Experimental Results

First, we measure the performance of the **KeyGen** step on the privilege node regarding computational costs. We varied the number of attributes from 10 to 100, and the results are displayed in Figure 5. The experimental results indicate that the PRBFM schemes are more efficient in comparison to other schemes. For instance, when the size of attributes is set to 100, PRBFM takes only 1 s to complete key generation, while Derler et al.'s scheme, Ma et al.'s scheme, and Xu et al.'s scheme require 17s, 6s, and 10s, respectively. The reason for this disparity is that the privilege nodes in PRBFM only select one Lagrange polynomial randomly and perform operations with $\mathcal{O}(\sigma)$ complexity. In contrast, the three other proposed schemes require pairing operations or hash calculations to obtain the secret key.

To measure the time consumption on the data owner side, we set the policy range from 10 to 100, as shown in Figure 6. Derler et al.'s scheme and Xu et al.'s scheme incur larger time consumption due to extra exponent operations. In contrast, Ma et al.'s scheme and PRBFM exhibit better performance. Additionally, the Adapt step in Ma et al.'s scheme requires extra pairing operations for policy matching, resulting in larger time consumption for Ma et al.'s scheme than PRBFM.

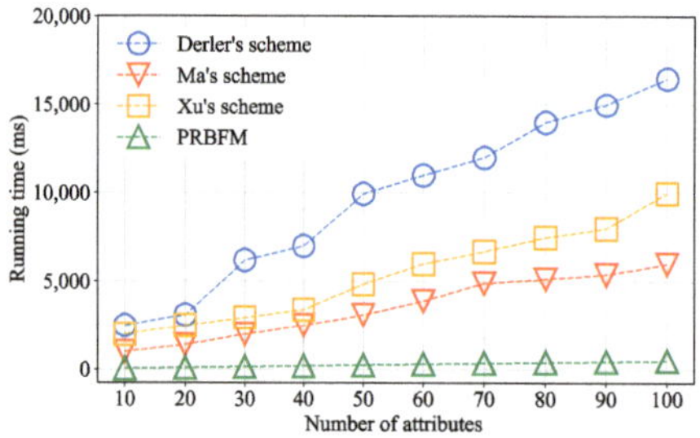

Figure 5. Running time for key generation.

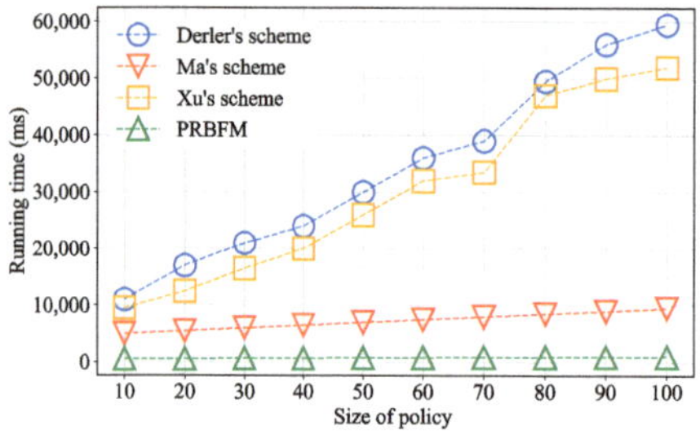

Figure 6. Time consumption on the data owner side.

Regarding Figure 7a, the time consumption is evaluated with the policy size ranging from 10 to 100. The practicality of the **Verify** step in all schemes for real-world scenarios is evident. Notably, PRBFM only needs to verify the generic trapdoor, while Derler et al.'s scheme and Ma et al.'s scheme are required to verify both the generic and ephemeral trapdoor. Therefore, the time consumption for Derler et al.'s and Ma et al.'s schemes is comparatively higher than PRBFM's. Additionally, Xu et al.'s scheme requires more time-consuming operations during the verification step, resulting in it having a higher time consumption than any other scheme.

We then evaluate the time consumption of the trapdoor generation in terms of the user and blockchain nodes. More specifically, we randomly select multiple policy sets with varying data sizes. We denote the total number of policy sets as A_p. Initially, the user is required to obtain the trapdoor related to their attributes, with the number of requests ranging from 10 to 50. Figure 7b indicates that when a user sends 50 data requests to PCBR with $A_p = 5$, the time consumption is 26 s, which is considered practical for real-world scenarios.

During the **Match** stage, we experimented with varying the size of the policy between 10 and 100. To illustrate the results of the experiment for the readability and editability policy match, Figure 8a,b, respectively, display the outcomes. We observed that as the size of the policy increased, the time taken to complete the process increased as well for both readability and editability policy match. Moreover, both matching processes took less than 2 s, indicating the viability of PRBFM. Notably, implementing some cryptographic techniques, such as those presented in [33,34], may improve the efficiency of our proposed strategies. Due to space constraints, we reserve the investigation of streamlining our techniques for future research.

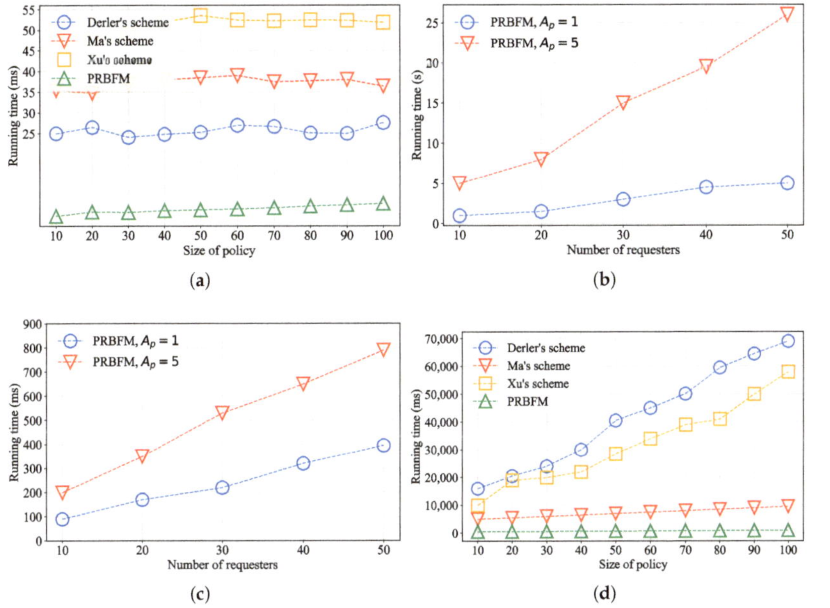

Figure 7. Time consumption on the user side. (**a**) Running time for verification; (**b**) Running time for trapdoor generation; (**c**) Running time for authorized readers; (**d**) Running time for authorized modifiers.

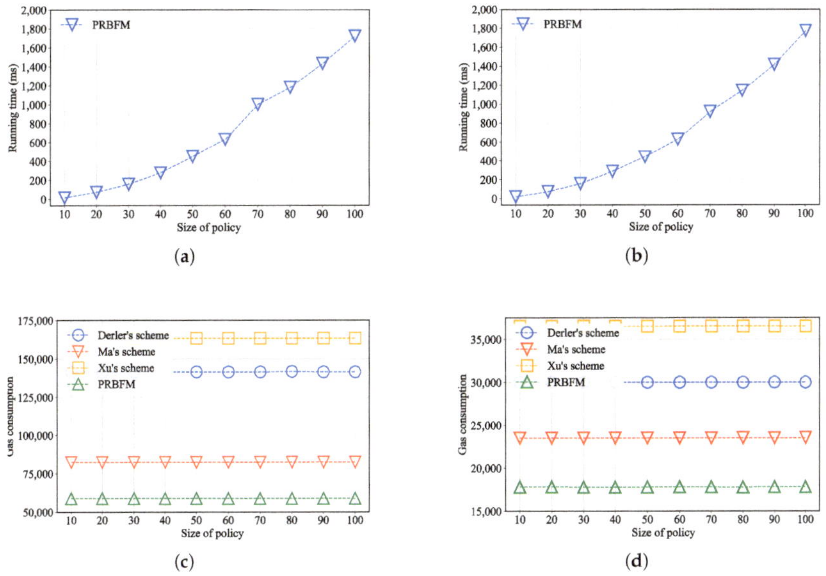

Figure 8. Consumption on blockchain node side. (**a**) Running time for readability policy matching; (**b**) Running time for editability policy matching; (**c**) Gas consumption for hash upload; (**d**) Gas consumption for hash request.

Next, we evaluate the time consumption for the **Read** step in terms of authorized readers. In Figure 7c, the number of requesters ranges from 10 to 50, while the value of

A_p is set at 1 and 5. Since in the PRBFM scheme, the set $\mathcal{P}r, j$ is utilized by authorized readers to recover the message with linear complexity while delegating the policy-matching process to the blockchain nodes, the time consumption for message reading is relatively low. As illustrated in Figure 7c, even with five separate policy sets ($Ap = 5$) and 50 requests, an authorized reader can read messages within 0.8 s.

In this part, we assessed the time consumption among Derler et al.'s scheme, Ma et al.'s scheme, Xu et al.'s scheme, and PRBFM for authorized modifiers. As demonstrated in Figure 7d, PRBFM is more effective than the other schemes when it comes to message editing. This outcome is due to the better performance of PRBFM in the two significant operations (i.e., chameleon secret key recovery and the **Encrypt** step) of the **Edit** step.

Finally, we evaluated the proposed schemes' performance in terms of costs (i.e., gas) on the FISCO blockchain. We varied the policy size from 10 to 100, and the experimental results are exhibited in Figure 8c,d. As illustrated, the gas cost for PRBFM is lower than that of the other schemes. This result is due to PRBFM exclusively updating or requesting one hash value, whereas Ma et al.'s scheme, Derler et al.'s scheme, and Xu et al.'s scheme involve 2, 4, and 6 values, respectively.

7. Related Works

In this section, we introduce the existing studies of the redactable blockchain.

Ateniese et al. [16] proposed the idea of a redactable blockchain. Their scheme uses a permissioned blockchain that needs a central authority to grant rewriting privileges to a designated party, referred to as the "modifier." The designated modifier could coordinate and delete specific content from the blockchain by utilizing a large-scale MPC protocol. This protocol enables block-level rewriting with coarse-grained control, achieved through the use of public key infrastructure (PKI), and an enhanced collision-resistant chameleon hash [31]. The enhanced collision-resistant chameleon hash facilitates modification of the hash link between block headers, while the PKI ensures the sealing of the chameleon hash trapdoor.

Derler et al. [6] introduced a permissioned redactable blockchain that allows for flexible rewriting of privileges through transaction-level rewriting controlled at a fine-grained level. Unlike the research conducted in [16], the authors of [6] employed chameleon hash to hash the transactions during the computation of the Merkle root. To formalize their solution, they presented a new concept called policy-based chameleon hash (PCH), which is derived from chameleon hashes with ephemeral trapdoors (CHET) [35] and attribute-based encryption (ABE) [36].

Deuber et al. [37] presented a permissionless block-level redactable blockchain that eliminates the requirement for a trusted central authority through the use of consensus-based voting. In their approach, the block header is modified to include two hash links. If a proposal for modification garners enough votes, it is approved by breaking one of the links while leaving the other intact. However, this scheme has the drawback of providing weak accountability, as the identity of the modifier can be traced from the proposed pool. Furthermore, this redactable blockchain inherits the vulnerability of consensus-based voting algorithms, rendering it susceptible to bribing and selfish mining attacks.

Regarding the revocability of the redactable blockchain, Panwar et al. [38] introduced a permissioned redactable blockchain that incorporates dynamic group signature schemes (DGSS) and revocable FAME (RFAME) to achieve traceability and revocability. Traceability ensures the life cycle of all transactions is honestly recorded in the blockchain for assisting in tracking history transactions, while revocability can be used to revoke the editing authority of malicious modifiers. However, traceability offers limited accountability, as accountability is to identify who made a particular transaction or redaction, which is more complicated than traceability. Moreover, the secure assignment of the updated secret key is crucial. To address this challenge, Xu et al. [8] introduced the concept of revocable policy-based chameleon hash (RPCH) and implemented it to facilitate efficient privilege revocation. The cost of implementing revocability in RPCH is almost insignificant compared to FAME [36].

To address the requirement for accountability in a redactable blockchain, Tian et al. [18] were the first to explore accountability using a policy-based chameleon hash (PCH). However, their solution only supports weak accountability. Specifically, it could only link the modified transaction while lacking the ability to identify potential key leakage. To address these issues, Xu et al. [21] presented a novel design of PCH called black-box accountability (PCHA) and introduced a practical attribute-based traitor tracing (ABTT) scheme with adaptive security.

For rewriting authorization in a decentralized environment, Zhang et al. [17] presented a multi-authority policy-based chameleon hash (MPCH), and Ma et al. [7] introduced a decentralized policy-based chameleon hash (DPCH). Both MPCH and DPCH employ CHET for data rewriting management and utilize multi-authority attribute-based encryption (MA-ABE) to handle rewriting privileges. However, their schemes do not support dynamic nodes, as the departure of participants would result in a single point of failure. Therefore, Zhang et al. [22] propose a novel dynamic and decentralized attribute-based chameleon hash (DACH) to enable the blockchain history's mutability. By leveraging DACH, their scheme achieves a decentralized, secure, and dynamically redactable blockchain (SDRchain).

Xu et al. [39] introduced a novel redactable blockchain named k-time modifiable and epoch-based redactable blockchain (KERB), which draws inspiration from the double-authentication preventing signature (DAPS) to regulate rewriting privileges. However, due to the restrictions on the number of k-times and epochs, it is necessary to combine customized k-times and epochs, which has yet to be accomplished. To tackle this challenge, Liu et al. [24] selected times and epochs as the controlling factors, restricting users from invoking the credential show method based on customized times within each epoch established by the certificate authority. In their approach, users can redact their credentials to achieve selective disclosure.

Shen et al. [23] propose a verifiable and redactable blockchain that allows for full editing operations, thus supporting verifiability. Their scheme successfully combines the complete editability of block objects and the verifiability of the blockchain state with reasonable additional costs. Specifically, the authors have built a redactable blockchain using a double trapdoor chameleon hash family, which allows for computationally efficient block editing while maintaining resistance against key exposure. However, these presented schemes ignore the privacy of sensitive data and do not support error tolerance during policy matching. Thus, the PRBFM scheme proposed in this paper is designed for fine-grained redactable blockchain with policy fuzzy matching in a privacy-preserving manner.

8. Conclusions

In this paper, we proposed a novel privacy-preserving fine-grained redactable blockchain with fuzzy policy matching for mobile crowdsensing scenarios. Firstly, we presented the PRBFM scheme utilizing Lagrange secret sharing and chameleon hash. Then, we combined the policy paradigm in PRBFM to further design a privacy-preserving policy matching delegation mechanism to protect policy privacy and reduce user overhead. Additionally, we formally analyzed the security of our scheme under IND-CCA, and also provided a detailed complexity analysis in terms of computational and special. Finally, we implemented and measured our scheme on the FISCO blockchain and demonstrated that our scheme outperforms existing works. For future work, we intend to further reduce user overhead with the use of bilateral access control and provide more fine-grained permission management (e.g., usability, readability, and editability).

Author Contributions: Methodology, M.Z.; Software, Y.X.; Formal analysis, T.W.; Investigation, M.Z.; Writing—original draft, H.L.; Supervision, H.G., J.X. and L.Z.; Project administration, H.G. and L.Z. All authors have read and agreed to the published version of the manuscript.

Funding: This research was funded by the National Natural Science Foundation of China (Grant Nos. 62202051, 62102027, and 62172042), China Postdoctoral Science Foundation (Grant Nos. 2021M700435 and 2021TQ0042), Guangdong Provincial Key Laboratory of Novel Security Intelligence Technologies

(Grant No. 2022B1212010005), Shandong Provincial Key Research and Development Program (Grant No. 2021CXGC010106), Major Scientific and Technological Innovation Projects of Shandong Province (2020CXGC010116), and Beijing Institute of Technology Research Fund Program for Young Scholars.

Conflicts of Interest: The authors declare no conflict of interest.

References

1. Zou, S.; Xi, J.; Wang, H.; Xu, G. CrowdBLPS: A blockchain-based location-privacy-preserving mobile crowdsensing system. *IEEE Trans. Ind. Inform.* **2019**, *16*, 4206–4218. [CrossRef]
2. Huang, J.; Kong, L.; Dai, H.N.; Ding, W.; Cheng, L.; Chen, G.; Jin, X.; Zeng, P. Blockchain-based mobile crowd sensing in industrial systems. *IEEE Trans. Ind. Inform.* **2020**, *16*, 6553–6563. [CrossRef]
3. Wang, W.; Yang, Y.; Yin, Z.; Dev, K.; Zhou, X.; Li, X.; Qureshi, N.M.F.; Su, C. BSIF: Blockchain-based secure, interactive, and fair mobile crowdsensing. *IEEE J. Sel. Areas Commun.* **2022**, *40*, 3452–3469. [CrossRef]
4. Zhang, C.; Zhao, M.; Zhu, L.; Zhang, W.; Wu, T.; Ni, J. FRUIT: A blockchain-based efficient and privacy-preserving quality-aware incentive scheme. *IEEE J. Sel. Areas Commun.* **2022**, *40*, 3343–3357.
5. Zhang, C.; Zhao, M.; Zhu, L.; Wu, T.; Liu, X. Enabling efficient and strong privacy-preserving truth discovery in mobile crowdsensing. *IEEE Trans. Inf. Forensics Secur.* **2022**, *17*, 3569–3581. [CrossRef]
6. Derler, D.; Samelin, K.; Slamanig, D.; Striecks, C. Fine-grained and controlled rewriting in blockchains: Chameleon-hashing gone attribute-based. *Cryptol. Eprint Arch.* **2019**.
7. Ma, J.; Xu, S.; Ning, J.; Huang, X.; Deng, R.H. Redactable blockchain in decentralized setting. *IEEE Trans. Inf. Forensics Secur.* **2022**, *17*, 1227–1242. [CrossRef]
8. Xu, S.; Ning, J.; Ma, J.; Xu, G.; Yuan, J.; Deng, R.H. Revocable policy-based chameleon hash. In Proceedings of the Computer Security—ESORICS 2021: 26th European Symposium on Research in Computer Security, Darmstadt, Germany, 4–8 October 2021; Proceedings, Part I 26; Springer: Cham, Switzerland, 2021; pp. 327–347.
9. Jia, M.; Chen, J.; He, K.; Du, R.; Zheng, L.; Lai, M.; Wang, D.; Liu, F. Redactable Blockchain From Decentralized Chameleon Hash Functions. *IEEE Trans. Inf. Forensics Secur.* **2022**, *17*, 2771–2783. [CrossRef]
10. Voigt, P.; Von dem Bussche, A. The eu general data protection regulation (gdpr). In *A Practical Guide*, 1st ed.; Springer International Publishing: Cham, Switzerland, 2017; Volume 10, pp. 10–5555.
11. Alfonsín, J.M.L. Argentina: The right to be forgotten. In *The Right to Be Forgotten: A Comparative Study of the Emergent Right's Evolution and Application in Europe, the Americas, and Asia*; Springer: Cham, Switzerland, 2020; pp. 239–248.
12. Li, C.; Guan, L.; Wu, H.; Cheng, N.; Li, Z.; Shen, X.S. Dynamic Spectrum Control-Assisted Secure and Efficient Transmission Scheme in Heterogeneous Cellular Networks. *Engineering* **2022**, *17*, 220–231. [CrossRef]
13. Zhang, C.; Hu, C.; Wu, T.; Zhu, L.; Liu, X. Achieving Efficient and Privacy-Preserving Neural Network Training and Prediction in Cloud Environments. *IEEE Trans. Dependable Secur. Comput.* 2022, *early access*. [CrossRef]
14. Hu, C.; Zhang, C.; Lei, D.; Wu, T.; Liu, X.; Zhu, L. Achieving Privacy-Preserving and Verifiable Support Vector Machine Training in the Cloud. *IEEE Trans. Inf. Forensics Secur.* **2023**, *18*, 3476–3491. [CrossRef]
15. Li, J.; Ma, H.; Wang, J.; Song, Z.; Xu, W.; Zhang, R. Wolverine: A Scalable and Transaction-Consistent Redactable Permissionless Blockchain. *IEEE Trans. Inf. Forensics Secur.* **2023**, *18*, 1653–1666. [CrossRef]
16. Ateniese, G.; Magri, B.; Venturi, D.; Andrade, E. Redactable blockchain–or–rewriting history in bitcoin and friends. In Proceedings of the 2017 IEEE European Symposium on Security and Privacy (EuroS&P), Paris, France, 26–28 April 2017; IEEE: New York, NY, USA, 2017; pp. 111–126.
17. Zhang, Z.; Li, T.; Wang, Z.; Liu, J. Redactable transactions in consortium blockchain: Controlled by multi-authority CP-ABE. In Proceedings of the Information Security and Privacy: 26th Australasian Conference, ACISP 2021, Virtual Event, 1–3 December 2021; Proceedings 26; Springer: Cham, Switzerland, 2021; pp. 408–429.
18. Tian, Y.; Li, N.; Li, Y.; Szalachowski, P.; Zhou, J. Policy-based chameleon hash for blockchain rewriting with black-box accountability. In Proceedings of the Annual Computer Security Applications Conference, Austin, TX, USA, 7–11 December 2020; pp. 813–828.
19. Liu, Z.; Cao, Z.; Wong, D.S. Blackbox traceable CP-ABE: How to catch people leaking their keys by selling decryption devices on ebay. In Proceedings of the 2013 ACM SIGSAC Conference on Computer & Communications Security, Berlin, Germany, 4–8 November 2013; pp. 475–486.
20. Liu, Z.; Cao, Z.; Wong, D.S. Traceable CP-ABE: How to trace decryption devices found in the wild. *IEEE Trans. Inf. Forensics Secur.* **2014**, *10*, 55–68.
21. Xu, S.; Huang, X.; Yuan, J.; Li, Y.; Deng, R.H. Accountable and Fine-Grained Controllable Rewriting in Blockchains. *IEEE Trans. Inf. Forensics Secur.* **2022**, *18*, 101–116. [CrossRef]
22. Zhang, D.; Le, J.; Lei, X.; Xiang, T.; Liao, X. Secure Redactable Blockchain With Dynamic Support. *IEEE Trans. Dependable Secur. Comput.* 2023, *early access*. [CrossRef]
23. Shen, J.; Chen, X.; Liu, Z.; Susilo, W. Verifiable and Redactable Blockchains with Fully Editing Operations. *IEEE Trans. Inf. Forensics Secur.* **2023**, *18*, 3787–3802. [CrossRef]

24. Liu, Y.; He, D.; Feng, Q.; Luo, M.; Choo, K.K.R. PERCE: A Permissioned Redactable Credentials Scheme for a Period of Membership. *IEEE Trans. Inf. Forensics Secur.* **2023**, *18*, 3132–3142. [CrossRef]
25. Zhang, C.; Zhao, M.; Xu, Y.; Wu, T.; Li, Y.; Zhu, L.; Wang, H. Achieving fuzzy matching data sharing for secure cloud-edge communication. *China Commun.* **2022**, *19*, 257–276. [CrossRef]
26. Yin, X.; Zhu, Y.; Hu, J. Contactless fingerprint recognition based on global minutia topology and loose genetic algorithm. *IEEE Trans. Inf. Forensics Secur.* **2019**, *15*, 28–41. [CrossRef]
27. Boutros, F.; Damer, N.; Kirchbuchner, F.; Kuijper, A. Elasticface: Elastic margin loss for deep face recognition. In Proceedings of the IEEE/CVF Conference on Computer Vision and Pattern Recognition, New Orleans, LA, USA, 18–24 June 2022; pp. 1578–1587.
28. Kumar, R.; Kumar, P.; Tripathi, R.; Gupta, G.P.; Islam, A.N.; Shorfuzzaman, M. Permissioned Blockchain and Deep Learning for Secure and Efficient Data Sharing in Industrial Healthcare Systems. *IEEE Trans. Ind. Inform.* **2022**, *18*, 8065–8073. [CrossRef]
29. Shen, B.; Dong, C.; Minner, S. Combating copycats in the supply chain with permissioned blockchain technology. *Prod. Oper. Manag.* **2022**, *31*, 138–154. [CrossRef]
30. Wu, L.; Lu, W.; Xue, F.; Li, X.; Zhao, R.; Tang, M. Linking permissioned blockchain to Internet of Things (IoT)-BIM platform for off-site production management in modular construction. *Comput. Ind.* **2022**, *135*, 103573. [CrossRef]
31. Hunhevicz, J.; Dounas, T.; Hall, D.M. The promise of blockchain for the construction industry: A governance lens. In *Blockchain for Construction*; Springer: Singapore, 2022; pp. 5–33.
32. Shamir, A. How to Share a Secret. *Commun. ACM* **1979**, *22*, 612–613. [CrossRef]
33. Falzon, F.; Markatou, E.A.; Espiritu, Z.; Tamassia, R. Range Search over Encrypted Multi-Attribute Data. *Proc. VLDB Endow.* **2022**, *16*, 587–600. [CrossRef]
34. Servan-Schreiber, S.; Langowski, S.; Devadas, S. Private approximate nearest neighbor search with sublinear communication. In Proceedings of the 2022 IEEE Symposium on Security and Privacy (SP), San Francisco, CA, USA, 22–25 May 2022; IEEE: New York, NY, USA, 2022; pp. 911–929.
35. Camenisch, J.; Derler, D.; Krenn, S.; Pöhls, H.C.; Samelin, K.; Slamanig, D. Chameleon-Hashes with Ephemeral Trapdoors: And Applications to Invisible Sanitizable Signatures. In Proceedings of the Public-Key Cryptography—PKC 2017: 20th IACR International Conference on Practice and Theory in Public-Key Cryptography, Amsterdam, The Netherlands, 28–31 March 2017; Proceedings, Part II 20; Springer: Cham, Switzerland, 2017; pp. 152–182.
36. Agrawal, S.; Chase, M. FAME: Fast attribute-based message encryption. In Proceedings of the 2017 ACM SIGSAC Conference on Computer and Communications Security, Dallas, TX, USA, 30 October–3 November 2017; pp. 665–682.
37. Deuber, D.; Magri, B.; Thyagarajan, S.A.K. Redactable blockchain in the permissionless setting. In Proceedings of the 2019 IEEE Symposium on Security and Privacy (SP), San Francisco, CA, USA, 19–23 May 2019; IEEE: New York, NY, USA, 2019; pp. 124–138.
38. Panwar, G.; Vishwanathan, R.; Misra, S. ReTRACe: Revocable and traceable blockchain rewrites using attribute-based cryptosystems. In Proceedings of the 26th ACM Symposium on Access Control Models and Technologies, Virtual, 16–18 June 2021; pp. 103–114.
39. Xu, S.; Ning, J.; Ma, J.; Huang, X.; Deng, R.H. K-time modifiable and epoch-based redactable blockchain. *IEEE Trans. Inf. Forensics Secur.* **2021**, *16*, 4507–4520. [CrossRef]

electronics

MDPI

Article

PKGS: A Privacy-Preserving Hitchhiking Task Assignment Scheme for Spatial Crowdsourcing

Peicong He, Yang Xin *, Bochuan Hou and Yixian Yang

School of Cyberspace Security, Beijing University of Posts and Telecommunications, Beijing 100876, China; hepeicong@bupt.edu.cn (P.H.); houbochuan@bupt.edu.cn (B.H.); yxyang@bupt.edu.cn (Y.Y.)
* Correspondence: yangxin@bupt.edu.cn

Abstract: Privacy-preserving task assignment is vital to assign a task to appropriate workers and protect workers' privacy or task privacy for spatial crowdsourcing (SC). Existing solutions usually require each worker to travel to the task location on purpose to perform this task, which fails to consider that workers have specific trajectories and carry out the task on their way in a hitchhiking manner. To this end, this paper proposes a privacy-preserving hitchhiking task assignment scheme for SC, named PKGS. Specifically, we formulate the privacy-preserving hitchhiking task assignment as a decision problem of the relationship between dot and line under privacy protection. In particular, we present a privacy-preserving travel distance calculation protocol and a privacy-preserving comparison protocol through the Paillier cryptosystem and the SC framework. Results of theoretical analysis and experimental evaluation show that PKGS can not only protect the location privacy of both each worker and the task simultaneously but also assign the task to the worker holding a minimum travel distance. In contrast to prior solutions, PKGS outperforms in the computation of travel distance and task assignment.

Keywords: spatial crowdsourcing; task assignment; privacy-preserving; Paillier homomorphic encryption

1. Introduction

Spatial crowdsourcing (SC) [1,2] has been widely applied in our daily life, such as crowdsourcing taxis (Uber, DiDi, Didachuxing, etc.) crowdsourcing logistics, and crowdsourced take-out delivery. In these applications, task assignment is an essential requirement for SC. As shown in Figure 1, the task assignment is to tackle how to assign a crowdsourcing task to appropriate workers. For example, an appropriate worker has a minimum travel distance. The task publishers are called task requesters (TRs), and the task completers are called task workers (TWs).

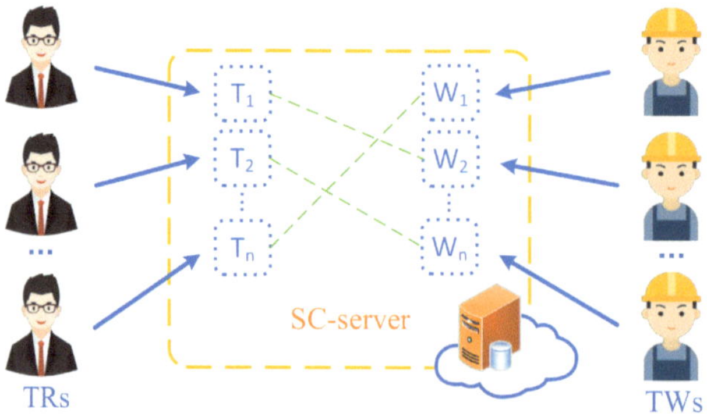

Figure 1. Working Models in SC.

Privacy concerns are widespread in various scenarios in cloud environments, such as neural network training and prediction [3] and support vector machine training in the cloud [4]. It is also a key barrier faced by task assignment of SC. Task assignment of SC always needs to utilize the location both of TWs and task to perform task assignment. However, in terms of TWs and TRs, location data are sensitive information, which involves location privacy [5]. Thus, TWs may refuse to take part in the crowdsourcing task due to privacy concerns. If all TWs do not participate in any crowdsourcing task, the SC paradigm fails to tackle any task by the capability of crowds. On the other hand, in terms of an SC platform, it suffers from high penalties due to disclosing collected TWs' locations and task locations. For example, DiDi is fined $1.28 billion, and Uber is fined $148 million.

Privacy-preserving task assignment simultaneously resolves the task assignment and privacy concerns of SC. Privacy-preserving task assignment is to assign the crowdsourcing task to TWs without compromising any TW or task privacy. Privacy-preserving task assignment has become a research hotpot, and a number of solutions have been proposed. In existing solutions, encryption-based and differential privacy (DP)-based are common methods to protect the privacy of TWs' locations or task locations. DP-based solutions have an advantage over efficiency but are weak in accuracy. In contrast, encryption-based solutions can perform accurate computations but face high computation burdens. Although there are abundant solutions to enable privacy-preserving task assignment, hardly any existing scheme supports the privacy-preserving hitchhiking paradigm, in which each worker has a specific trajectory and is allowed to perform a task on her way without scarifying location privacy of any worker and task. Privacy-preserving hitchhiking task assignment faces with following technical challenges.

The first challenge is how to compute the travel distance without knowing any TW location and task location. The travel distance is the distance between TW's location and a task location. The travel distance is usually measured by Euclidean distance or Manhattan distance. However, whether it is Euclidean distance or Manhattan distance, computing them is not straightforward when the worker's location and the task location are unknown. Technically, it requires computing the travel distance over encrypted or obscured locations. The second challenge is how to estimate reachability without compromising privacy. An SC task is spatiotemporal dependent, thus, and it requires not only computing the travel distance but also estimating whether a TW can reach the task location or not under the time constraint. Intuitively, if all TWs' locations and task locations as well as their temporary information are known, it is easy to estimate whether a TW can reach the location on schedule. However, to protect privacy, a privacy-preserving task assignment solution fails to learn any TW and task spatiotemporal sensitive information. The third challenge is how to search for an optimal worker under privacy protection. The task assignment is usually regarded as an optimization problem, such as searching for the minimum travel distance under multiple constraints. The challenge for privacy-preserving task assignment is to resolve the optimization problem under all data being encrypted or obscured.

To tackle the above challenges, in this paper, we propose a privacy-preserving hitchhiking task assignment solution for SC, called PKGS (PKGS comes from a Privacy-preserving hitchhiKing task assiGnment solution for spatial crowdSourcing). Specifically, we first formulate the privacy-preserving hitchhiking task assignment as a decision problem of the relationship between dot and line within privacy protection. We then adopt the Paillier cryptosystem that enables computation over encrypted data to encrypt the worker and task spatiotemporal information and protect their privacy. To enable the Paillier cryptosystem supporting operations of privacy-preserving task assignment, including computation of traveling distance, accessibility estimation, and optimization under constraints, we carefully design a privacy-preserving travel distance calculation protocol and a privacy-preserving comparison protocol. Our contributions are three-fold as follows.

(1) We formulate a privacy-preserving hitchhiking task assignment. To the best of our knowledge, this paper formulates a privacy-preserving hitchhiking task assignment as

a decision problem of the relationship between dot and line under privacy protection for the first time.

(2) We present two privacy-preserving computation protocols. To enable privacy protection and computation over encrypted data, we present a privacy-preserving travel distance calculation protocol to measure the Manhattan distance between a TW and a task. We also present a privacy-preserving comparison protocol to estimate the accessibility and search for the TW holding a minimum travel distance.

(3) We propose a privacy-preserving hitchhiking task assignment solution and evaluate its effectiveness and efficiency. Based on the proposed two privacy-preserving computation protocols, we construct a privacy-preserving hitchhiking task assignment solution, which can search for the optimal TW with a minimum travel distance within several seconds.

The rest of this paper is organized as follows. We introduce the related work in Section 2. In Section 3, we describe the system model, security model, Paillier cryptosystem, and problem formulation. In Section 4, we introduced Scheme PKGS in detail, including how to select potential TWs and how to select optimal TW. In Section 5, we analyze the security of PKGS. Section 6 reports and evaluates the experimental results. Finally, we draw a conclusion in Section 7.

2. Related Work

In recent research, task assignment protecting user privacy can be roughly divided into two types. One is to protect user privacy by processing user-uploaded information or query feedback information. The other is to achieve the purpose by encrypting this information. The first type mainly builds a cloaking region by processing information data. Intuitively, anonymous and perturbation techniques can do this. Based on k-anonymity [6] and l-diversity [7], a lot of anonymous task assignments have been proposed [8–11]. In [8], Kazemi et al. proposed the PiRi scheme, in which multiple users co-create anonymous zones and send requests to the SC server through anonymous zones, thus achieving privacy protection. Users in the anonymous zone share the results of requests to the SC server. Vu et al. [9] partition at least k adjacent users into a group with locality-sensitive hashing (LSH) that maintains both localization and k-anonymity. They design an algorithm for kNN querying based on this partition. Pournajaf et al. [10] study a spatial task assignment method when workers utilize spatial cloaking to obfuscate their locations, which assigns tasks by managing location regions with resource constraints. Based on Pournajaf's work, Hu et al. [11] consider the extent to which a worker is willing to move so that the worker's position in a task assignment is an area of activity. Like the anonymous technique, perturbation techniques can protect users' privacy by modifying values, such as differential privacy or perturbation of geographical position [12–15]. To et al. [12] utilize a trusted third party to preprocess data and then utilize differential privacy protection to protect the worker's location. After that, they tackle the moving TWs challenge by continuously sending privacy-preserving location information and reducing the noise generated in this way by Kalman filter-based post-processing technique [15]. Based on [12], Gong et al. [13] introduced reputation parameters for quality assessment. In a similar framework, Zhang et al. [14] use contour plots to characterize the distribution of workers and thus have less noise generation than others.

Cryptographic systems to encrypt data are the other way to protect the user's privacy [16–21]. Without further consideration of efficiency, the method is strongly theoretically supported for security. These schemes for encrypting data require the construction of protocols that conform to that encryption method to accomplish the assignment of tasks. Zhao et al. [16] propose the iTAM scheme that achieves multiple constrained exact matching of TR and TW by Paillier. However, the full ciphertext comparison leads to the need to compare all the candidates. Although Shu et al. [17] achieve bidirectional privacy-preserving task assignment through proxy re-encryption, their proposed solution requires additional servers such as proxy servers or fog nodes. Then they proposed pMatch [18], that is, a mechanism based on Shamir secret sharing that solves the problem of needing a proxy in privacy-preserving task assignment. Wang et al. [19] provided a personalized privacy-preserving task assignment mechanism PWSM that uses fuzzy location information to assign tasks to the maximum probability worker closest to the task. In [20], Ni et al. proposed the SPOON scheme, which recruits workers based on user location and protects privacy through proxy re-encryption and BBS+ signature. Liu et al. [21] proposed a range search retrieval method that can perform ciphertext retrieval in a small area, thus improving efficiency, but did not propose a corresponding range determination and scaling method. The encryption scheme has the advantage of accurate retrieval, but its retrieval matching process is time-consuming. Workers need to wait for a long matching time after completing a task before they can be assigned the next task. Therefore, we propose a hitchhiking scheme that enables workers to complete tasks within an existing trip, thus increasing their motivation.

3. Problem Formulation and Preliminaries

3.1. System Model

As depicted in Figure 2, our system model consists of Task Requesters (TRs), Task Workers (TWs), Key Generation Center (KGC), and CS server. The CS server is an online platform provided by a service provider (SP) where it matches the TRs and TWs according to their requirement. In other words, it receives task requests from TRs as well as TWs and matches them online. KGC is a trusted organization for secret key generation and distribution. The TRs are the users of SP who want to find a suitable worker to help them complete a task within space-time by the platform. Similarly, the TWs are the other kind of users of SP who want to find a job satisfying their requirements. In our system, the whole task assignment process is divided into four main steps as follows.

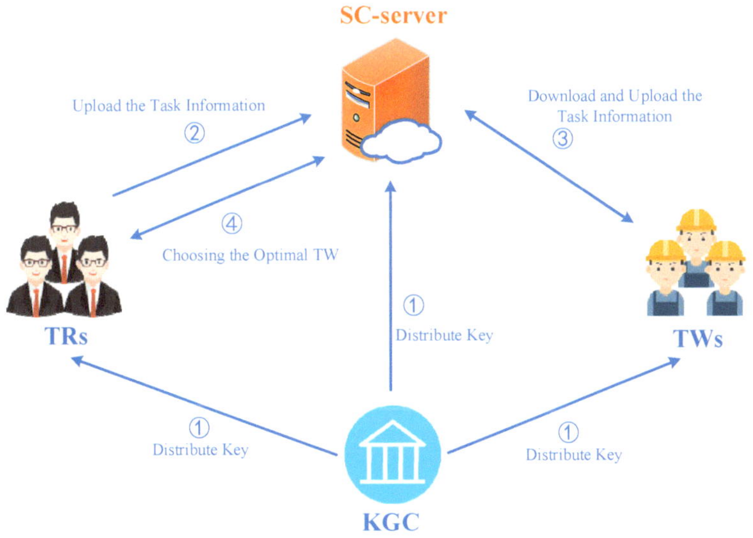

Figure 2. System Model of PKGS.

In ①, KGC generates public and private keys and manages them for TRs, TWs, and the SC server.

In ②, TRs use public keys to encrypt key task information and upload task descriptions and encrypted task information to the SC server.

In ③, TWs download the information about the task they want to perform and upload their work information to the SC server with the same public key encryption.

In ④, the SC server cooperates with the TR issued the task to complete the selection of the optimal worker without revealing private information.

3.2. Security Model

In SC, due to the strongly spatiotemporal properties of tasks, the task request of both TRs and TWs includes much personal sensitive information. This information reveals the current approximate location and needs of a TR or TW to a certain extent, and it has also become the target that the adversary wants to obtain. We assume a strong adversary $\mathcal{A}$ in our model, who has the following capabilities.

(1) $\mathcal{A}$ can disguise as a legal TR or TW and communicate with the SC server to obtain information.
(2) $\mathcal{A}$ can eavesdrop on the communication channel between TRs or TWs and CS server to capture communication information.
(3) $\mathcal{A}$ can compromise the SC server to obtain some information of an unselected TW stored on it.

As Figure 2 shows, the potential threats mainly come from TRs, TWs, and the SC server. Here, we assume that the SC server is semi-honest. In other words, the SC server is honest-but-curious, which follows the protocol but wants to snoop on the user's privacy. This assumption is reasonable because a formal service provider needs to register when releasing its products, and it will provide services under the pre-agreed agreement. However, it also wants to optimize and promote its products by collecting user information, but the collected user information is harmful to users. So, we need to face security threats from these aspects of them, not just adversaries but curious users or the CS server. We should avoid the three of them casually viewing the plaintext of task request information of TRs and TWs. This can prevent an adversary from pretending to be a legal user to obtain the task information of TRs or TWs by his task requirement.

3.3. Paillier Cryptosystem

As a homomorphic public key cryptosystem, the Paillier cryptosystem [22] is widely used for secure multiparty computer protocols.

Key generation: p and q are large prime numbers independently, set $N = pq$ and $\lambda = lcm(p-1, q-1)$, and select random integer $g \in \mathbb{Z}^*_{N^2}$, and then compute $\mu = (L(g^\lambda \mathrm{mod} N^2))^{-1} \mathrm{mod} N$, where the function L is defined as $L(x) = \frac{x-1}{N}$. The public key is $pk = (g, N)$ and the private key is $sk = (\lambda, \mu)$.

Encryption: Given a message $m \in \mathbb{Z}_N$ to be encrypted with the public key pk, $C = [\![m]\!]_{pk} = g^m \cdot r^N \mathrm{mod} N^2$, where r is a selected random integer $r \in \mathbb{Z}^*_N$.

Decryption: Given the ciphertext C to be decrypted with the private key sk, $m = D_{sk}(C) = L(C^\lambda \mathrm{mod} N^2) \cdot \mu \mathrm{mod} N$.

Let $x, y \in \mathbb{Z}_N$, its homomorphic properties are described below.

(1) Additive homomorphism:

$$[\![x]\!] \cdot [\![y]\!] = [\![x + y]\!]. \tag{1}$$

(2) Scalar-multiplicative homomorphism:

$$[\![x]\!]^y = [\![x \cdot y]\!]. \tag{2}$$

3.4. Problem Formulation

In PKGS, we try to help TWs with an existing itinerary to match a suitable task. A TW has her/his departure time, departure location, and destination location. A TR publishes a task that requires someone to complete the specified task at the agreed place at the specified time. To transform the real problem into a mathematical problem, we formulate Task, TW, Travel Distance, and Task Assignment. For the convenience of description, we use *loc* instead of specific coordinates (x, y).

Definition 1 (Task). *A Task denoted by* $T = \{loc_R, T_{Rstart}, T_{task}, TD\}$ *requires a TW to travel to the physical location* loc_R *to perform the task. The task start time is* T_{Rstart}*, and the time required to complete the task is* T_{task}*, TD is a task description without involving privacy of the task.*

Definition 2 (TW). *A TW denoted by* $W = \{loc_S, loc_D, T_{Wstart}, T_{Wend}, v\}$ *starts from point* loc_S *to point* loc_D *, her/his departure time is* T_{Wstart} *, the cutoff time to reach* loc_D *is* T_{Wend} *, and the travel speed is* v*.*

Definition 3 (Travel Distance). *Travel distance is Manhattan Distance (MD) denoted by* $m(A, B)$ *that is a new metric in which the distance between two points is the sum of the absolute differences of their cartesian coordinates and is also known as city block distance or taxicab geometry. Assuming there are two points* $A(x_1, y_1)$ *and* $B(x_2, y_2)$ *, their Manhattan distance is calculated as follows.*

$$m(A, B) = |x_1 - x_2| + |y_1 - y_2| \tag{3}$$

Compared with Euclidean distance, Manhattan distance is more suitable for calculating the distance between two points in the city. As we know, it is not possible to get from point A to point B in a city directly through a building, which is why it is called city block distance or taxicab geometry.

Definition 4 (Task Assignment). *Task assignment is a set of conditions matching TR and TW. As Figure 3 shows, the TW plans to go from* loc_S *to* loc_D *. The task location is* loc_R *. Task assignment requires the following conditions to be met. For the TW, she/he needs to reach* loc_D *before* T_{Wend} *. For the TR, the task needs to start at moment* T_{Rstart} *. The time taken by the TW to travel from* loc_S *to* loc_R *and from* loc_R *to* loc_D *is* T_1 *and* T_2*, respectively. So, the task assignment needs to fulfill the following conditions.*

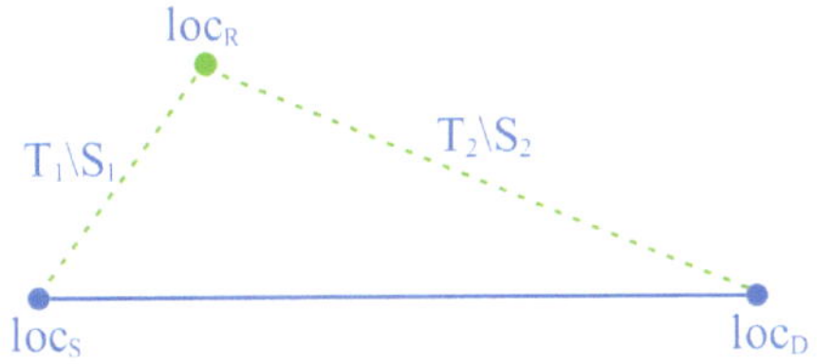

Figure 3. Task Assignment Constraint.

$$\begin{cases} T_{Wstart} + T_1 + T_{task} + T_2 \le T_{Wend} \\ T_{Wstart} + T_1 \le T_{Rstart} \end{cases} \tag{4}$$

To make the matching condition satisfy the homomorphic cryptosystem, we do a little trick with it. We transform a comparison of time into a comparison of distance. Assume there is a TR's task denoted by $T = \{loc_R, T_{Rstart}, T_{task}, TD\}$ and a TW denoted by $W = \{loc_S, loc_D, T_{Wstart}, T_{Wend}, v\}$. If the following constraints are met

$$\begin{cases} S_1 + S_2 \le S \\ S_1 \le S' \end{cases} \tag{5}$$

the TW can perform the TR's task. In this set of equations, $S_1 = m(loc_R, loc_S)$, $S_2 = m(loc_R, loc_D)$, $S = (T_{Wend} - T_{Wstart} - T_{task}) * v$, $S' = (T_{Wstart} - T_{Rstart}) * v$.

Remark 1. *The distance of the TW from the starting point to the task point is denoted as* S_1*. The distance from the task point to the end point of the TW is denoted as* S_2*. The farthest moving distance of the TW under the premise of completing the task is recorded as* S*. This is the product of the time* *the TW can spend moving and his or her speed. Before the task starts, the maximum distance that the TW can move is recorded as S'. Its rationale is like that of S. $S_1+S_2 \leq S$ means that the TW can go to the mission point to complete the mission without delaying his original journey. $S_1 \leq S'$ means that the TW can reach the task point before the task needs to be started.*

Task allocation needs to consider not only whether the task will be completed on time, but also who is the optimal TW. The set of candidate TWs is denoted by $\mathbb{W}= \{W_1, W_2, \ldots, W_n\}$, and the set of S_1 of each TW is denoted by $\mathbb{W}_{S_1}= \{W_1S_1, W_2S_1, \ldots, W_nS_1\}$. A TW is an optimal worker if he satisfies the following conditions.

$$WS_1 = min(\mathbb{W}_{S_1}) \tag{6}$$

As we know, S_1 is the distance of the TW from the start point to the task point. Equation (6) means that WS_1 is the nearest worker to the task point. If the TW is closer, the probability is higher that the TW will arrive at the task point as early as possible to start working.

4. Design of PKGS

4.1. Overview of PKGS

We have a preliminary understanding of PKGS through the previous system model, and now we will introduce its scheme process in detail. In Figure 4, we illustrate the process of PKGS with an example where a TR matches TWs for clarity. This situation can be seen as a case where, among the many TRs tasks, this group of TWs chose this task at the same time.

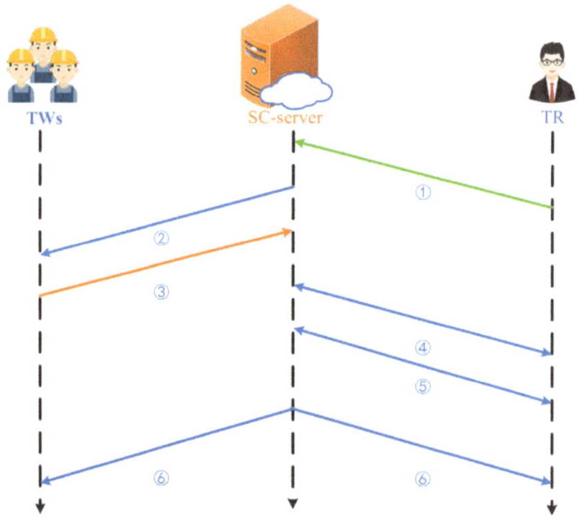

Figure 4. Scheme Process of PKGS.

In ①, a TR sends a request to the SC server to find a suitable TW to complete her/his CS task. As mentioned in Section 3.4, the TR's task is denoted by $T = \{loc_R, T_{Rstart}, T_{task}, TD\}$. To make it easier for TWs to choose, he uploads the encrypted location information loc_R and the time required to complete the task T_{task}, as well as the unencrypted task start time T_{Rstart} and task description TD to the SC server.

In ②, TWs select a task on the SC server and download the task information from it.

In ③, each TW adds their encrypted information to the downloaded encrypted task information and sends the encrypted information back to the SC server.

In ④, the SC server figures out candidate TWs who met the constraints with the help of TR.

In ⑤, the SC server finds the optimal TW from the candidate TWs with TR's assistance.

In ⑥, finally, the SC server establishes a connection between them.

Note that according to the descriptions in Sections 3.4 and 4.1, there are mainly two difficult problems to be solved. The travel distance is calculated from the encrypted task information and the encrypted travel distance is compared. Given this, we will focus on these two types of challenges and address two solutions detailed in the following two subsections.

4.2. Privacy-Preserving Comparison Protocol

Both absolute value symbol removal and constraint judgment require a comparison operation on the ciphertext. In this subsection, we propose a PC (privacy-preserving comparison) protocol to solve the comparison of encrypted information.

The SC server owns the computed ciphertext but cannot get the size relation because it does not have the private key. So, it needs the help of TR. However it cannot send the ciphertext directly to the TR because the TR has the private key and the location of the task. If the ciphertext is sent directly to the TR, then the TR can project the location of the TWs. So, as shown in Figure 5, the SC server performs a perturbation operation before transmission, and the TR decrypts the received message and returns the size relation to the SC server. The details are described below.

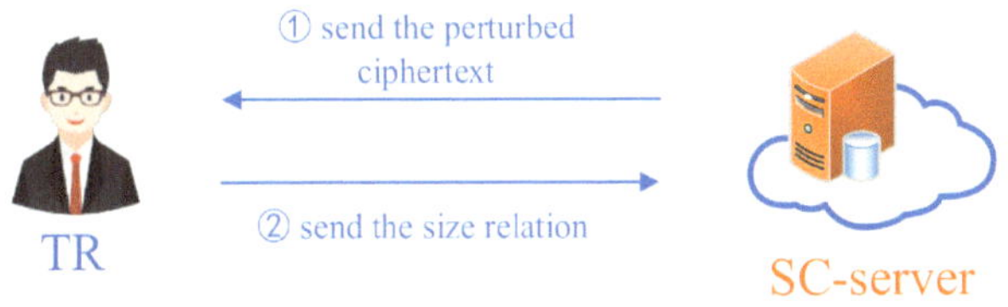

Figure 5. Process of PC.

Assume the length of a public key (N) is L and the encrypted numbers to be compared are recorded as $m = [\![A - B]\!]$. For security purposes, a typical public key length needs to be greater than or equal to 256 bits. Therefore, the number of bits in the values of A, B is much smaller than L. Let the perturbation value be $m_i' = [\![2^{L/2}]\!] \cdot [\![A - B]\!]^{x_i}$. x_i is a random integer for perturbing, ranging from -64 to 64 without 0. Since it is all positive integers in the Paillier cryptosystem, here, we add $2^{L/2}$ to the difference to avoid an overflow situation. The TR compares the sizes of $D_{sk}(m_i')$ and $2^{L/2}$. If $D_{sk}(m_i') > 2^{L/2}$, $R = 1$, if $D_{sk}(m_i') < 2^{L/2}$, $R = -1$, if $D_{sk}(m_i') = 2^{L/2}$, $R = 0$. Then, the SC server can determine the size relationship of A, B based on the values of R and x_i as shown in the following equation.

$$\begin{cases} x_i * R > 0 \ \Rightarrow \ A > B \\ x_i * R < 0 \ \Rightarrow \ A < B \\ x_i * R = 0 \ \Rightarrow \ A = B \end{cases} \tag{7}$$

Remark 2. *$[\![A - B]\!]^{x_i}$ is a number. When we add $2^{L/2}$ to it, if the result is greater than $2^{L/2}$, it means that $[\![A - B]\!]^{x_i}$ is a positive number, if it is less than $2^{L/2}$ then $[\![A - B]\!]^{x_i}$ is negative, and if it is equal to $2^{L/2}$, then $[\![A - B]\!]^{x_i}$ is equal to 0. There are two levels of perturbation of xi. On the one hand, there is its sign, which denotes $A - B$ if it is positive and $B - A$ if it is negative. on the other hand, we amplify the result of $A - B$ by a factor of x_i. The result of $|x_i|$ is the number of times the result of $A - B$. After the perturbation process, the TR can still determine $[\![2^{L/2}]\!]$ and $[\![A - B]\!]^{x_i}$ in relation to each other, but cannot infer one value of A, B from the other. With $R = 1$ and $x_i > 0$, we get $A - B > 0$; with $R = 1$ and $x_i < 0$, we get $A - B < 0$; with $R = -1$ and $x_i > 0$, we get $A - B < 0$; with $R = -1$ and $x_i < 0$, we get $A - B > 0$; with $R = 0$, we get $A = B$. So, we can get the above equation. With this, we can easily complete the comparison operation of encrypted data without revealing private information.*

4.3. Privacy-Preserving Travel Distance Calculation Protocol

In this subsection, we propose a privacy-preserving travel distance calculation protocol based on PC. Denote the PC operation as *P(A,B)*. *A* and *B* are the ciphertexts to be compared and the return value is the size relationship between *A* and *B*. Now, we design the protocol that implements steps ④ and ⑤. In ④, the goal is to find candidate TWs who meet the requirements. In ⑤, the goal is to find the optimal TW. To satisfy the judgment condition of the task assignment, as shown in Equation (5), we need to calculate S_1, S_2, S , S' . Assume that the coordinates of loc_R, loc_S, loc_D are (lat_R, lng_R), (lat_S, lng_S), (lat_D, lng_D), respectively. We can expand these equations as follows.

$$S_1 = m(loc_R, loc_S) = |lat_R - lat_S| + |lng_R - lng_S| \tag{8}$$

$$S_2 = m(loc_R, loc_D) = |lat_R - lat_D| + |lng_R - lng_D| \tag{9}$$

We convert the time point to the number of minutes elapsed so that the time can be converted into an integer for operation.

$$S = (T_{Wend} - T_{Wstart}) * v - T_{task} * v \tag{10}$$

$$S' = (T_{Wstart} - T_{Rstart}) * v \tag{11}$$

To protect privacy, we encrypt this information with TR's Paillier public key. We use $[\![x_1]\!]$ to denote the Paillier encryption ciphertext of x_1. According to the Paillier cryptosystem, we can use the following equation with the encryption task information to calculate the desired distance cipher.

$$\begin{aligned} [\![S_1]\!] &= [\![m(loc_R, loc_S)]\!] \\ &= |[\![lat_R - lat_S]\!]| + |[\![lng_R - lng_S]\!]| \\ &= |[\![lat_R]\!] \cdot [\![lat_S]\!]^{-1}| + |[\![lng_R]\!] \cdot [\![lng_S]\!]^{-1}| \end{aligned} \tag{12}$$

$$\begin{aligned} [\![S_2]\!] &= [\![m(loc_R, loc_D)]\!] \\ &= |[\![lat_R - lat_D]\!]| + |[\![lng_R - lng_D]\!]| \\ &= |[\![lat_R]\!] \cdot [\![lat_D]\!]^{-1}| + |[\![lng_R]\!] \cdot [\![lng_D]\!]^{-1}| \end{aligned} \tag{13}$$

In ①, a TR sends the $[\![lat_R]\!]$, $[\![lng_R]\!]$, $[\![T_{\text{task}}]\!]$, T_{Rstart}, and TD to the SC server.

In ②, TWs select a task on the SC server based on the task description and task start time as well as download the task information from it.

In ③, each TW adds their encrypted information to the downloaded encrypted task information and sends the encrypted information back to the SC server, as $[\![lat_R]\!] \cdot [\![lat_S]\!]^{-1}$, $[\![lng_R]\!] \cdot [\![lng_S]\!]^{-1}$,$[\![lat_R]\!] \cdot [\![lat_D]\!]^{-1}$, $[\![lng_R]\!] \cdot [\![lng_D]\!]^{-1}$,$[\![(T_{Wend} - T_{Wstart}) * v]\!]$, $[\![T_{task}]\!]^{-v}$, $[\![(T_{Wstart} - T_{Rstart}) * v]\!]$.

In ④, the SC server performs a perturbation operation on the values to be compared and the following operations with the assistance of TR: PC($([\![lat_R]\!] \cdot [\![lat_S]\!]^{-1})'$,$[\![2^{L/2}]\!]$), PC($([\![lng_R]\!] \cdot [\![lng_S]\!]^{-1})'$,$[\![2^{L/2}]\!]$), PC($([\![lng_R]\!] \cdot [\![lng_D]\!]^{-1})'$,$[\![2^{L/2}]\!]$), PC($([\![lng_R]\!] \cdot [\![lng_D]\!]^{-1})'$, $[\![2^{L/2}]\!]$). Based on the well-judged size relation, the server can compute $[\![S_1]\!]$, $[\![S_2]\!]$, and calculate $[\![S]\!]$, $[\![S']\!]$ according to the following equation.

$$\begin{aligned} [\![S]\!] &= [\![(T_{Wend} - T_{Wstart}) * v - T_{task} * v]\!] \\ &= [\![(T_{Wend} - T_{Wstart}) * v]\!] \cdot [\![T_{task}]\!]^{-v} \end{aligned} \tag{14}$$

$$[\![S']\!] = [\![(T_{Wstart} - T_{Rstart}) * v]\!] \tag{15}$$

The SC server figures out candidate TWs who meet the constraints based on the following PC operations: PC($([\![S]\!] \cdot [\![S_1]\!]^{-1} \cdot [\![S_2]\!]^{-1})'$,$[\![2^{L/2}]\!]$), PC($([\![S']\!] \cdot [\![S_1]\!]^{-1})'$,$[\![2^{L/2}]\!]$).

In ⑤, the SC server puts the TWs who passed the judgment in ④ into set $\mathbb{W}$ and puts their corresponding S_1 into set $\mathbb{W}_{S_1}$. PC operations are performed continuously in the set $\mathbb{W}_{S_1}$ until the optimal TW is selected and the algorithm is described as follows (Algorithm 1).

Algorithm 1: Find Optimal TW

Input: $\mathbb{W}_{S_1}$
Output: The number of WS_{min}
Initialize min = 1;
for i = 1 to n − 1 **do** //n = $\mathbb{W}_{S_1}$.length
$PC((\llbracket W_i S_1 \rrbracket \cdot \llbracket W_{i+1} S_1 \rrbracket^{-1})', \llbracket 2^{L/2} \rrbracket)$,
min = get the number of the small WS_1
Return min;

In ⑥, finally, the SC server establishes a connection between them according to the number.

5. Security Analysis

In this section, we analyze the security of PKGS in the process of task constraint determination and choosing optimal TW. In other words, PC and travel distance calculation protocol is secure as same as Paillier.

Theorem 1. *If the Paillier cryptosystem is secure, then the PC protocol is secure.*

Proof. For the SC server, the data are always in the form of ciphertext to be computed during the comparison process. Since it has no private key, it cannot decrypt the encrypted data. In other words, if the Paillier is secure, then the server cannot get the user's location information during the comparison process. For the TR, even though she/he has the private key to decrypt the ciphertext, the ciphertext has been perturbed. This also prevents the TR from obtaining the TWs' location information. Since the TR has the private key and the ciphertext is meaningless to him, we next analyze it in plaintext. In the process of perturbation, we randomly disturbed the position of the subtractor and the subtracted number and subjected the result of calculations to random magnification. This makes it impossible for the TR to distinguish the actual difference and to know the exact magnitude relationship, thus making it impossible to speculate on the location of the workers. □

Theorem 2. *If the Paillier cryptosystem is secure, then the travel distance calculation protocol does not reveal the location.*

Proof. In the previous theorem, it was shown that the TR cannot infer the location of TWs from the PC protocol. Next, we analyze the security for TWs and the SC server in the travel distance calculation protocol. For TWs, since they do not have the private key, they cannot decrypt the ciphertext, and no result is returned after they add the encrypted message. If the Paillier cryptosystem is secure, the TWs cannot guess the location of the task. For the SC server, it performs operations on the ciphertext, but the result of the computation is still the ciphertext. Moreover, it has no private key, so it cannot decrypt the ciphertext. The TR decrypts the ciphertext and returns the size relation instead of the specific result of the calculation. That is, if the Paillier cryptosystem is secure, it cannot get the location information of any party. □

6. Performance Analysis

6.1. Experiment Setting

In this section, we will test the performance of our proposed scheme through a series of experiments. As in previous work [16], we used the addition of simulated fields to the real dataset to complete the experiment. In this paper, we use the real Gowalla dataset and select 30 data entries in the range of latitude 37.75431 to 37.80062 and longitude −122.42691 to −122.39382. We choose 10 check-in data as the TWs and add departure time, task working time, and speed attributes at the original latitude of the data. The remaining 20 pieces of data are used as the TRs. Similarly, we add task start time and task need time to it. We assume 10 tasks have been assigned to TWs. In this way, each worker has a certain itinerary. TWs have three transportation tools, walking (90 m/min), bicycles (240 m/min), and cars (660 m/min).

We simulate the SC server with a computer with i7cpu and 16 GB of RAM. We simulate the users with a smartphone with a Kirin 990 core and 8 BG of RAM. We evaluate the performance of the scheme from the two aspects of the total time to complete all tasks and the total distance to complete all tasks.

6.2. Evaluation Results

We choose the related study [16] to complete the comparative experiment. In the experiment, there are 10 TWs with matched 10 tasks. So, each TW has a certain itinerary. We assign the remaining 10 tasks to them. In [16], TWs need to complete tasks and then select new tasks according to their task assignment scheme. In PKGS, we directly match the remaining 10 tasks to the 10 TWs with our task assignment scheme. We reselect 30 recordings and repeat the experiment 10 times. The total task completion time includes the time it takes to get to the task location and the time it takes to complete the task. The total distance traveled to complete all tasks includes the total distance the worker must travel. As shown in Figures 6 and 7, the results of the experiments show that the PKGS has less mission completion time and mission total distance.

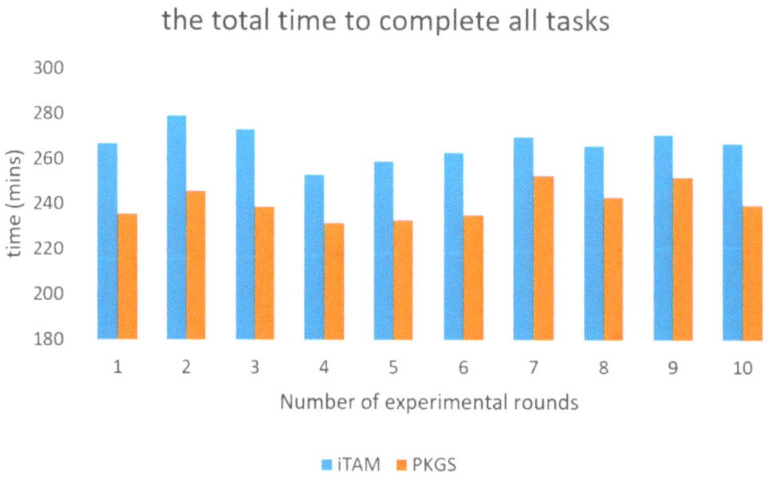

Figure 6. Time of All Tasks Completed.

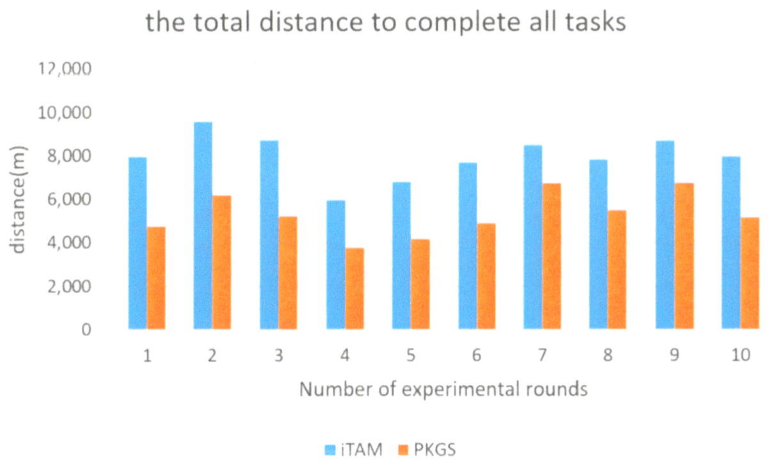

Figure 7. Distance of All Tasks Completed.

7. Conclusions

In this paper, we propose a privacy-preserving hitchhiking task assignment solution for SC, called PKGS, that can help TWs with existing travel trajectories to match with the appropriate TR. Since it can allocate tasks based on the TW's original trajectory under the premise of protecting user privacy. This greatly increases the speed of task completion and reduces the extra distance workers need to travel to complete additional tasks. In future work, we will consider the optimal solution problem of how to package and assign multiple tasks to a single TW.

Author Contributions: Conceptualization, P.H.; methodology, P.H.; software, P.H. and B.H.; validation, P.H.; investigation, P.H. and B.H.; resources, Y.X. and Y.Y.; writing—original draft preparation, P.H.; writing—review and editing, P.H.; supervision, Y.X. and Y.Y.; All authors have read and agreed to the published version of the manuscript.

Funding: This research was funded by the National Key R&D Program of China (No. 2020YFB1805403) and the Foundation of Guizhou Provincial Key Laboratory of Public Big Data (No. 2017BDKFJJ015, No. 2018BDKFJJ008, No. 2018BDKFJJ020, No. 2018BDKFJJ021).

Data Availability Statement: In this paper, we use the Gowalla dataset, the URL of the dataset is https://snap.stanford.edu/data/loc-gowalla.html (accessed on 16 November 2021).

Conflicts of Interest: The authors declare no conflict of interest.

References

1. Feng, W.; Yan, Z.; Zhang, H.; Zeng, K.; Xiao, Y.; Hou, T. A survey on security, privacy, and trust in mobile crowdsourcing. *IEEE Internet Things J.* **2017**, *5*, 2971–2992. [CrossRef]
2. Tong, Y.; Zhou, Z.; Zeng, Y.; Chen, L.; Shahabi, C. Spatial crowdsourcing: A survey. *VLDB J.* **2020**, *29*, 217–250. [CrossRef]
3. Zhang, C.; Hu, C.; Wu, T.; Zhu, L.; Liu, X. Achieving efficient and privacy-preserving neural network training and prediction in cloud environments. *IEEE Trans. Dependable Secur. Comput.* **2022**. Available online: https://ieeexplore.ieee.org/abstract/document/9899726 (accessed on 28 July 2023). [CrossRef]
4. Hu, C.; Zhang, C.; Lei, D.; Wu, T.; Liu, X.; Zhu, L. Achieving Privacy-Preserving and Verifiable Support Vector Machine Training in the Cloud. *IEEE Trans. Inf. Forensics Secur.* **2023**, *18*, 3476–3491. [CrossRef]
5. Zhang, C.; Zhu, L.; Xu, C.; Ni, J.; Huang, C.; Shen, X. Location privacy-preserving task recommendation with geometric range query in mobile crowdsensing. *IEEE Trans. Mob. Comput.* **2021**, *21*, 4410–4425. [CrossRef]
6. Sweeney, L. k-anonymity: A model for protecting privacy. *Int. J. Uncertain. Fuzziness Knowl.-Based Syst.* **2002**, *10*, 557–570. [CrossRef]
7. Machanavajjhala, A.; Kifer, D.; Gehrke, J.; Venkitasubramaniam, M. L-diversity: Privacy beyond k-anonymity. *ACM Trans. Knowl. Discov. Data (TKDD)* **2007**, *1*, 3-es. [CrossRef]

8. Kazemi, L.; Shahabi, C. A privacy-aware framework for participatory sensing. *ACM Sigkdd Explor. Newsl.* **2011**, *13*, 43–51. [CrossRef]
9. Vu, K.; Zheng, R.; Gao, J. Efficient algorithms for k-anonymous location privacy in participatory sensing. In Proceedings of the 2012 Proceedings IEEE INFOCOM, Orlando, FL, USA, 25–30 March 2012; IEEE: Piscataway, NJ, USA, 2012; pp. 2399–2407.
10. Pournajaf, L.; Xiong, L.; Sunderam, V.; Goryczka, S. Spatial task assignment for crowd sensing with cloaked locations. In Proceedings of the 2014 IEEE 15th International Conference on Mobile Data Management, Brisbane, Australia, 14–18 July 2014; IEEE: Piscataway, NJ, USA, 2014; Volume 1, pp. 73–82.
11. Hu, J.; Huang, L.; Li, L.; Qi, M.; Yang, W. Protecting location privacy in spatial crowdsourcing. In Proceedings of the Asia-Pacific Web Conference, Guangzhou, China, 18–20 September 2015; Springer: Cham, Swizerland, 2015; pp. 113–124.
12. To, H.; Ghinita, G.; Shahabi, C. A framework for protecting worker location privacy in spatial crowdsourcing. *Proc. VLDB Endow.* **2014**, *7*, 919–930. [CrossRef]
13. Gong, Y.; Zhang, C.; Fang, Y.; Sun, J. Protecting location privacy for task allocation in ad hoc mobile cloud computing. *IEEE Trans. Emerg. Top. Comput.* **2015**, *6*, 110–121. [CrossRef]
14. Zhang, L.; Lu, X.; Xiong, P.; Zhu, T. A differentially private method for reward-based spatial crowdsourcing. In *International Conference on Applications and Techniques in Information Security*; Springer: Berlin/Heidelberg, Germany, 2015; pp. 153–164.
15. To, H.; Ghinita, G.; Fan, L.; Shahabi, C. Differentially private location protection for worker datasets in spatial crowdsourcing. *IEEE Trans. Mob. Comput.* **2016**, *16*, 934–949. [CrossRef]
16. Zhao, B.; Tang, S.; Liu, X.; Zhang, X.; Chen, W.-N. iTAM: Bilateral privacy-preserving task assignment for mobile crowdsensing. *IEEE Trans. Mob. Comput.* **2020**, *20*, 3351–3366. [CrossRef]
17. Shu, J.; Jia, X.; Yang, K.; Wang, H. Privacy-preserving task recommendation services for crowdsourcing. *IEEE Trans. Serv. Comput.* **2018**, *14*, 235–247. [CrossRef]
18. Shu, J.; Yang, K.; Jia, X.; Liu, X.; Wang, C.; Deng, R.H. Proxy-free privacy-preserving task matching with efficient revocation in crowdsourcing. *IEEE Trans. Dependable Secur. Comput.* **2018**, *18*, 117–130. [CrossRef]
19. Wang, Z.; Hu, J.; Lv, R.; Wei, J.; Wang, Q.; Yang, D.; Qi, H. Personalized privacy-preserving task allocation for mobile crowdsensing. *IEEE Trans. Mob. Comput.* **2018**, *18*, 1330–1341. [CrossRef]
20. Ni, J.; Zhang, K.; Xia, Q.; Lin, X.; Shen, X.S. Enabling strong privacy preservation and accurate task allocation for mobile crowdsensing. *IEEE Trans. Mob. Comput.* **2019**, *19*, 1317–1331. [CrossRef]
21. Liu, A.; Li, Z.X.; Liu, G.F.; Zheng, K.; Zhang, M.; Li, Q.; Zhang, X. Privacy-Preserving Task Assignment in Spatial Crowdsourcing. *J. Comput. Sci. Technol.* **2017**, *32*, 905–918. [CrossRef]
22. Paillier, P. Public-key cryptosystems based on composite degree residuosity classes. In Proceedings of the International Conference on the Theory and Applications of Cryptographic Techniques, Prague, Czech Republic, 2–6 May 1999; Springer: Berlin/Heidelberg, Germany, 1999; pp. 223–238.

electronics

Article

FRIMFL: A Fair and Reliable Incentive Mechanism in Federated Learning

Abrar Ahmed and Bong Jun Choi *

School of Computer Science and Engineering, Soongsil University, Seoul 06978, Republic of Korea; abrar@soongsil.ac.kr

* Correspondence: davidchoi@soongsil.ac.kr

Abstract: Federated learning (FL) enables data owners to collaboratively train a machine learning model without revealing their private data and sharing the global models. Reliable and continuous client participation is essential in FL for building a high-quality global model via the aggregation of local updates from clients over many rounds. Incentive mechanisms are needed to encourage client participation, but malicious clients might provide ineffectual updates to receive rewards. Therefore, a fair and reliable incentive mechanism is needed in FL to promote the continuous participation of clients while selecting clients with high-quality data that will benefit the whole system. In this paper, we propose an FL incentive scheme based on the reverse auction and trust reputation to select reliable clients and fairly reward clients that have a limited budget. Reverse auctions provide candidate clients to bid for the task while reputations reflect their trustworthiness and reliability. Our simulation results show that the proposed scheme can accurately select users with positive contributions to the system based on reputation and data quality. Therefore, compared to the existing schemes, the proposed scheme achieves higher economic benefit encouraging higher participation, satisfies reward fairness and accuracy to promote stable FL development.

Keywords: federated learning; client selection; reverse auction; incentive mechanism

1. Introduction

Federated learning is a promising machine learning technique that aims to preserve the privacy of data owners as they collaboratively train a global model without exposing their raw data [1]. Its potential to assist artificial intelligence in achieving unprecedented success is phenomenal in solving user privacy problems and data islands. As shown in Figure 1, each data owner downloads a global model from a server and trains it locally using its private data samples and computational resources. After local data training, the parameters of locally trained models are aggregated with the server's global model [2] using the model averaging (FedAvg) algorithm. This process continues for multiple training rounds until the desired accuracy or objective function is achieved. Since there is no upload of raw data, FL drastically improves data privacy and security issues. FL's salient privacy-preserving feature and numerous high system characteristics have gained attention and research in academia and industry [3], enabling its broad applicability in various fields such as finance, IoT, health care, and telecommunication. For instance, Google adopted FL in its keyboard application GBoard to improve the performance [4].

Despite its numerous advantages, federated learning still faces significant challenges. Most existing studies assume that all data owners participate unconditionally [5] and honestly contribute data [6]. But this assumption is impractical due to communication and computational resource costs incurred by inevitable training [7]. Simultaneously, clients might face additional barriers of privacy threats and information leakages. Therefore, self-interested individuals will hesitate to participate in model training [8] without any incentives and not serve for free [9]. Hence, without any rewards, individuals will not remain in the FL system, leading to untenable performance. Meanwhile, some data owners might exhibit undesirable behaviors by deceptively training results via submitting poor models intentionally or unintentionally to improve their utilities; the server may need to be fully aware of their computational resources, amount, and data quality. Participants may launch poisoning attacks [10] or malicious updates affecting the global model learning performance. They might also launch free-riding attacks to trick the system and obtain the rewards [11]. Fairness in an emerging trustworthy FL pillar demands a multidisciplinary approach [12,13]. Unfairness exists during client selection [14], model optimization [15], contribution evaluation stages, and incentive distribution [3] that can adversely impact the FL server and clients if not appropriately addressed. Current research in incentive mechanisms lacks fairness in the aggregation phase to weigh individual updates according to their performances [16] and the reward phase in distributing models/payoffs according to their contribution [17]. Clients might be discouraged from enrolling in FL training by unfair treatment. However, equal treatment for all clients without considering their potential contributions can reduce server capability to attract high-quality users, leading to poorly generalized FL models [18]. Moreover, the studies are ineffective in coupling reliable client selection with fair incentive mechanisms, as evaluating client behaviors is inefficient. The clients are inconsistent and have no motivation to participate. Hence, designing an efficient and reliable incentive mechanism in FL is crucial to stimulate clients to contribute quality work and promote stable FL development.

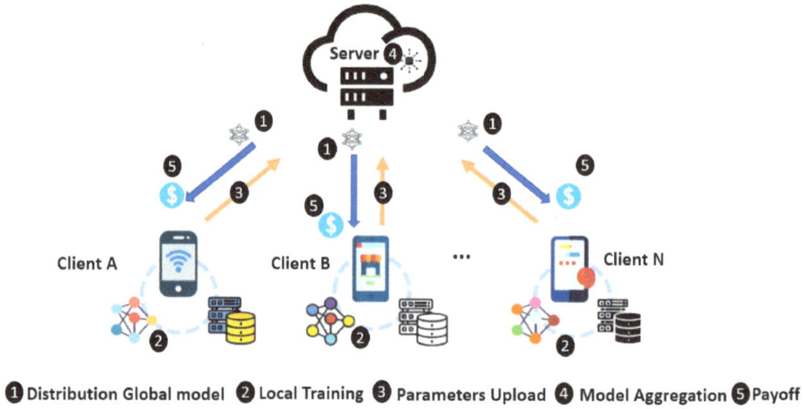

Figure 1. Workflow of incentive distribution in FL.

In this study, we propose an incentive mechanism based on reverse auctions for pricing and reputation trust to encourage clients towards active participation and permit model owners to receive high-quality results. Reverse auctions effectively model training costs and encourage users to participate truthfully. Reputation measures useful updates through trust metrics to reflect an individual's reliability. Client behaviors to manipulate the training process are simulated with at least 60% of malicious poisoning data that lead to slow model convergence and performance in the test environment. To evaluate reputation, we propose a quality-aware selection to examine and differentiate high-quality workers. The server stores and updates candidates' information in the incentive module.

To summarize, our contributions are as follows:

- We proposed a reliable FL incentive scheme (FRIMFL) that combines reverse auction and reputation to incentivize clients.
- We constructed a weighted trust assessment method to reflect clients' reliability considering the quality of model updates.

- We introduced Shapley method to derive the per-round marginal contributions of participants. FRIMFL incorporates reputation (computed from trust and contribution measures) in fair reward allocation to participants.
- The simulation analysis regarding social welfare, contribution fairness, and accuracy shows that our proposed mechanism is compatible, individually rational, and budget feasible.

The remainder of this paper is organized as follows. Section 2 presents related works. Section 3 elaborates on the taxonomy of incentive schemes. Section 4 provides materials and methods consisting of details of the proposed FRIMFL mechanism that distributes incentives using quality, trust, and contribution assessments. Section 5 presents a theoretical analysis to show the economic properties of the proposed mechanism. Section 6 includes the performance evaluation in terms of economic benefits, client selection performance, model accuracy, and fairness. Finally, Section 7 provides discussions, and Section 8 concludes the paper.

2. Related Work

McMahan et al. [1] proposed a FedAvg algorithm that calculates the local model weights accordingly to the client data amount. However, clients may act as free riders or perform malicious attacks like data poisoning attacks. Incentive schemes were proposed to remedy these problems. Client selection, contribution evaluation, and payment allocation are the fundamental building components for incentive mechanisms [19], where optimal reward strategies for both FL servers and clients are computed through objective optimization functions. Kang et al. [20] presented an FL incentive scheme based on a combination of contract theory and reputation using a subjective logic model (SLM). Cong et al. [21] proposed an incentive design in mobile networks using contract theory to tackle the information asymmetry issue for attracting high-quality workers. Similarly, Ye et al. [22] introduced a 2D contract based on client quality and computational capabilities to determine the rewards in a monopolist system. However, the workers' pricing cost for training remains an open question before incentivizing.

Fairness in FL is examined as resource distribution and model optimization using personalization techniques [15]. Ezzeldin et al. [23] proposed a group fairness strategy to mitigate bias in FL models. In [24], a federated dropout pruning approach was presented to customize client models. However, these works only focus on selection and group fairness notions [18]. For context, to deal with fairness from the contribution notion, Zhang et al. [25] measured client contributions based on self-reported information in hierarchical FL. The information includes quality, quantity, communication capabilities, and data collection costs for joining the system. In [26], the authors introduced a mutual evaluation approach where each client receives points based on local credibility protected by differential privacy and blockchain. Michieli and Ozay [16] proposed FairFL for the uniform treatment of users based on their contributions via fair aggregation of model weights. Le et al. [27] adopted auctions using self-reporting where the server evaluates bid information for contribution and winner determination. Cong et al. [28] proposed a Vickey–Clarke–Grove (VCG) scheme to incentivize participants to report costs and quality truthfully. However, self-reported information does not guarantee truthfulness in practice. Zheng et al. [29] introduced a multi-dimensional auction scheme to motivate high-quality workers to participate. Still, there is no assurance that selected individuals would work according to the bidding agreement.

Nishio et al. [14] proposed an FedCS protocol for high-quality client selection with restricted resources. They overshadowed the reliability and data accuracy aspects by considering only computational and communication costs. Zhang et al. [17] proposed a scheme based on auction and reputation to incentivize clients instead of self-reporting. The reputation depends on the contribution evaluation via cosine similarity between the client and global models. However, this might not be reliable for clients with highly imbalanced distribution. Moreover, the formulation of trust through Gompertz's function as a static non-linear mathematical model does not take into account subjective beliefs. It models the trust in a smooth sigmoidal curve, which might not always hold in real-world scenarios. Reputation is an essential metric in FL incentive schemes. Rehman et al. [30] presented a reputation-based blockchain system for client selection. However, the proposed scheme lacks a comprehensive consideration of client contributions to model updates.

The above-mentioned notable works drive client selection and reward systems under threshold-based approaches, thus resulting in the disinterest of FL participants. It is crucial to strike a balance between the interests of all entities in the FL system. Therefore, to address the fairness and reliable evaluation of client performance, our scheme (FRIMFL), based on a reputation mechanism with subjective trust quality, federated Shapley contribution, and reverse auctions, promotes quality performance and ensures contribution fairness during both the client selection and contribution evaluation stages.

3. Taxonomy of Incentive Mechanisms

Incentives motivate data owners to continue participating in the federated learning environment. They can be classified as positive and negative incentives. Positive incentives quest to motivate participants by recognizing the positive impact of contributions and encouraging rewards. Negative incentives intend to avoid malicious attackers or negative participation through reputation, penalty loss, etc. Current studies to incentivize workers can be classified into settings, stages, methods, and research challenges, as described in the following subsections. Figure 2 illustrates the taxonomy of incentive mechanisms.

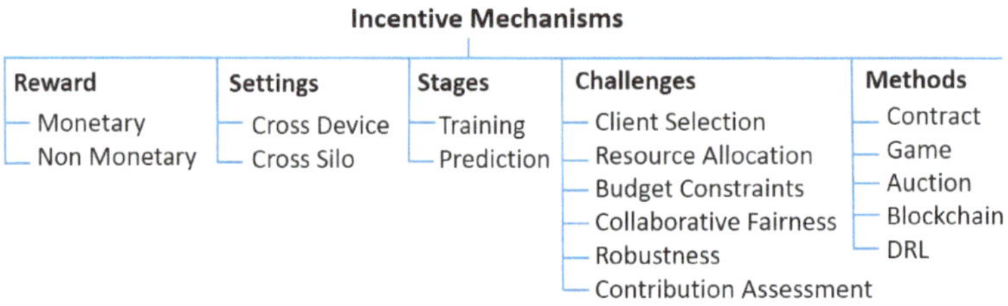

Figure 2. Taxonomy of incentive mechanisms in FL.

3.1. Reward

3.1.1. Monetary Incentives

Monetary incentives deal with the direct distribution of payoffs to FL clients and tend to motivate them to actively participate. This leads to better model training and, thus, high-quality contributions. Data owners and users of FL final models are assumed to be separate entities where data owners care more about their economic preferences.

3.1.2. Non-Monetary Incentives

Non-monetary incentives motivate clients by distributing different FL models or satisfying psychological needs such as reputation or virtual credit. Based on their work quality, such rewards are suitable in scenarios (1) unavailability of monetary budget, (2) clients value the final model more than the monetary incentive.

3.2. Settings

Incentives can be applied to both cross-device and cross-silo FL scenarios. Cross-device FL comprises many data owners, such as mobile or edge devices. In contrast, cross-silo FL has a relatively small number of data owners, such as medical hospitals or financial companies that collaboratively train a global model [31]. Recently, studies [32,33] have addressed cross-silo FL. In this methodology, our incentive scheme is designed for cross-device FL.

3.3. Stages

Figure 1 shows that the complete FL process includes model training and prediction. The training aims to obtain a high-quality global model, while prediction focuses on the good test performance of the designed system.

3.4. Challenges

- Client management to select qualified workers to join and remain in the training process.
- Resource allocation for clients based on the amount of work and data quality.
- Contribution evaluation to measure the contribution of each participant.
- Budget constraints due to the time-consuming commercialization and training of models or unavailability.
- Collaborative fairness corresponding to participant rewards should fairly reflect different levels of contributions.
- Robustness to targeted and untargeted attacks by malicious workers.

3.5. Methods

3.5.1. Contract Theory

Like economics, an FL contract is designed between a server (employer) and data owners (employees). The server cannot always be assumed to know the data owner's resources, data size, and quality. To overcome this issue of information asymmetry, the studies in [20,21,34] adopted contract theory to attract high-quality users. Contract-based selection can enhance participation and model quality; however, it only focuses on optimizing the user's utility/reward.

3.5.2. Game Theory

Game theory involves strategic interactions between rational participants. The goal is to determine the optimal strategy for a client's payoff in relation to other clients' strategies. The Stackelberg game is a game theoretic model with interaction between a leader (server) and follower (client) [35]. The central server gives a set of rules for participants to devise optimal strategies. This iterates until reaching the Nash equilibrium, where no player can improve its payoff by changing their strategy. However, this method is inefficient amid information asymmetry, undesirable behaviors, and non-i.i.d. data to incorporate multiple factors to design incentive schemes.

3.5.3. Blockchain

Blockchain is a decentralized digital ledger in peer-to-peer networks that records each user's encrypted transaction. This allows the features of robust and tamper-proof FL; thus, modern studies adopted it to provide privacy-preserving FL [36,37]. This security advantage can be a transparent record environment to store candidates' information. However, scalability due to time delays can occur in the blockchain FL system.

3.5.4. Auction Theory

Auction theory is an effective mathematical tool for task allocation and cost pricing. Auctions can be classified into forward and reverse auctions. In a forward auction, a seller displays an item, and bidders place the bid price. For our FL incentive scheme, we use the reverse auction where the server acting as a buyer requests a required service/task, and data owners acting as potential sellers perform the task. Le et al. [38] adopted auctions in wireless networks considering computational resources. In general, an auction scheme not only guarantees truthfulness or efficiency but also reduces the computation latency.

3.5.5. Deep Reinforcement Learning

Deep reinforcement learning (DRL) under FL consists of multiple agents performing actions under an environment to maximize rewards and privacy [39]. Incomplete information about clients' decisions and contribution concerns create a challenge in formulating an ideal scheme. Therefore, Zhang et al. [40] adopted DRL with game theory to compute optimal trade pricing and tackle information asymmetry. The authors in [41] designed a hierarchical game to maintain a trade-off between maximizing payment and minimizing the learning rate through DRL. It focused on reducing the training time and determining a strategy based on experience.

4. Materials and Methods

4.1. Proposed Mechanism (FRIMFL)

We consider a collaborative horizontal FL environment with many potential candidates and model owner. Candidates serve as data owners and can be IoT or edge devices. The model owner broadcasts a training task anytime and recruit candidates to participate. Interested data owners examine their data quality and quantity, weigh the cost prices with reward possibility, and formulate strategies to submit bid prices to the server. The server combines their bids and reputation status for client selection and pays for their rewards. Figure 3 illustrates the overall workflow of our architecture.

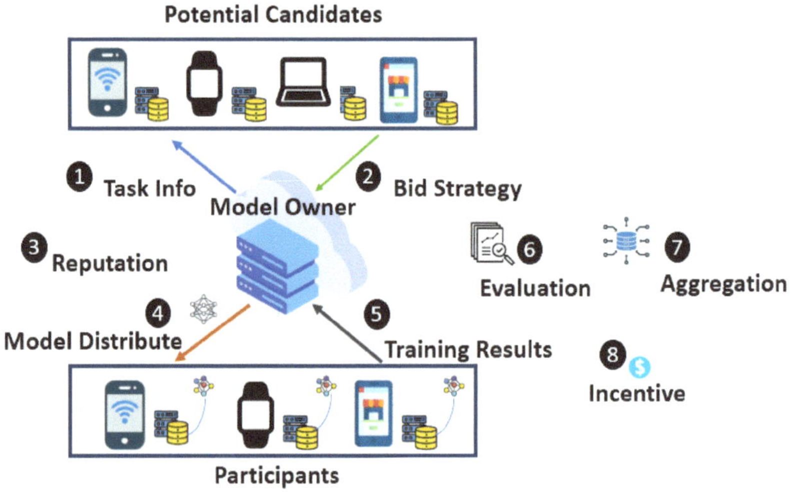

Figure 3. Architecture of FRIMFL.

The processes involved in each step are described below:

1. The server broadcasts the task information to N candidates, describing the budget and model requirements.
2. Interested candidates devise their bidding strategy based on data quantity or computational resources and submit their bid prices B_i^p to the server.
3. The server examines the candidates' reputation in all associated tasks and applies reverse auctions for global model distribution.
4. Selected participants from the candidates receive the initial global model and train local models iteratively on their local dataset.
5. The participants send their training results to the server.
6. The model owner collects training results, receives gradients, and executes quality detection through marginal loss evaluation.
7. The server aggregates quality models corresponding quality weights and measures participant contribution via a federated Shapley assessment and reputation to distribute payoffs.
8. Finally, participants are rewarded as per their level of reputation.

4.2. Reverse Auction-Based Optimal Client Selection

The assessment and selection of highly reputed candidates for any task are reflected by reverse auction design. The utility function of the auction is to maximize social surplus (SS) defined as a composite utility of all participants (P^u) and server (S^u) formulated as:

$$\max_{SS} \sum_{i=1}^{N} P_i^u + S^u, \tag{1a}$$

$$\text{s.t.} \sum_{i=1}^{N} x_i p_i \leq B, \tag{1b}$$

$$x_i v_i \leq p_i. \tag{1c}$$

where x_i is a binary variable as if candidate i is selected to participate, $x_i = 1$, otherwise $x_i = 0$. The utility of participant i is expressed as the difference between its payoff incentive and cost calculated as $P_i^u = (p_i - v_i)$. After global aggregation, the server obtains a final global performance and distributes incentives. Thus, the server utility is calculated as $S^u = [B - \sum_{i=1}^{n} p_i]$. Here, Equation (1b) guarantees that the participant payoff p_i satisfies the budget feasibility, and Equation (1c) guarantees that the participant i should not be compensated less than its true cost v_i.

4.3. Design Properties

Since task requesters and clients are rational, FRIMFL must satisfy the following economic properties:

- Incentive Compatibility (IC) : The auction process satisfies incentive compatibility when all the participants obtain a maximum payoff by reporting bids truthfully.
- Individual Rationality (IR): When the participating users receive positive utility, the mechanism achieves incentive rationality.
- Budget Feasibility: The total incentive amount paid to participants does not exceed the model owners' budget.
- Computational Efficiency: The scheme can be computationally efficient if the winner determination and incentive distribution are computed within polynomial time.
- Aggregation Fairness: Each participant's aggregated weight shall correspond to its performance quality.
- Reward Fairness: Each participant shall be fairly rewarded, corresponding to their contribution levels for the task.

4.4. Quality Trust Assessment

With the ease of accessibility and lack of standard evaluation in the FL system, the participation influence cannot be fully ensured. The client's behavior can be classified as

- Positive Clients: These clients participate honestly, provide reliable model updates without malicious activity, and bid truthful data to complete training tasks.
- Negative Clients: These clients intend to have deceptive behavior, by either data poisoning through incorrect/sign-flip labels to decrease data accuracy or model poisoning to manipulate training performance [42,43].

An inherent way to achieve this is to evaluate the loss of the client model or update that exceeds a predetermined threshold [5]. But determining the threshold might be challenging where the performance of local models might improve in later training rounds if the threshold decreases, respectively. Therefore, we proposed a marginal error loss-based method executed by the server. A local model i is included in the global model m, and the loss l^m of this model is computed on a validation set. Likewise, this local model i is excluded, to make global model m' and loss $l_i^{m'}$ be computed. When a high-quality local model (M_i^l) is aggregated, the loss of the global model is reduced.

We define the threshold quality value ψ to accept the local model ($\psi_i < \psi$) as

$$\psi_i = l_i^{m'} - l^m. \tag{2}$$

In Vanilla FL [1], clients with large amounts of data receive higher weights. In FairFL [16], they receive equal weights. However, this might be an unfair way for an honest client to have a small amount of data with good quality. The existence of free riders can amplify the data size, and client heterogeneity can significantly affect the weights in model aggregation. Hence, it is necessary to aggregate local model weights passing the quality detection. Therefore, the aggregated weight (α_i) for participant i can be computed as

$$\alpha_i = \frac{\psi_i}{\sum_i \psi_i}. \tag{3}$$

Accordingly, the new aggregated global model (G_m) in round t can be determined as

$$G_m = \sum_i \alpha_i M_i^l. \tag{4}$$

The proposed weighted quality detection in FRIMFL is stated in Algorithm 1. Line 1 initializes an empty track of participants (R^t) kept by the model owner, followed by the loss calculation on the global model m. Lines (3–5) describe the evaluation process to compute for a marginal loss impact on all clients using Equation (2). Lines (6–12) present quality detection; for successful detection, (n_i^p) increases and vice versa. Finally, lines (13–16) describe the quality of the local weight used in the final global model aggregation.

Algorithm 1 FRIMFL quality detection

Input: R^t, ψ
Output: n_i^p, n_i^f, G_m
1: $R^t = \varnothing$
2: calculate l^m on global model m
3: **for** each client $i \in N$ **do**
4: calculate $l^{m'}$ on global model m'
5: calculate ψ_i using Equation (2)
6: **if** $\psi_i > \psi$ **then**
7: $R^t \leftarrow R^t \cup \{i\}$
8: $n_i^p{++}$
9: **else**
10: $n_i^f{++}$
11: **end if**
12: **end for**
13: **for** each client $i \in R^t$ **do**
14: calculate α_i using Equation (3)
15: **end for**
16: calculate G_m using Equation (4)
17: **return** n_i^p, n_i^f, G_m

4.5. Contribution Assessment

Fairness is an important parameter to evaluate contributions to attract and retain high-performing users in FL. We propose a per round evaluation method leverage through the Shapley value (SV) method [32,44]. It provides a fair reward distribution to participants as per their marginal contributions to calculate individual utility and encourages high-quality ones to join as early as possible. For instance, three clients, i.e., client 1, client 2, and client 3, collaborate on a task, given a characteristic evaluation function $V(.)$, such that $V(1) = 40$, $V(2) = 60$, $V(3) = 80$, $V(1,2) = 70$, $V(1,3) = 75$, $V(2,3) = 85$, and $V(1,2,3) = 90$. Table 1 depicts all possible combinations to quantify the contribution of all individuals. For any subset S, it is defined as

$$c_i = \frac{1}{N!} \sum_{S \subseteq N \setminus i} |S|!(N - |S| - 1)![V(S \cup i) - V(S)]. \tag{5}$$

Thus, the collective contribution by participant i from round 1 to T can be expressed as

$$c_i = \sum_{t=1}^{T} c_i^t. \tag{6}$$

The contribution quantification in FL is coherent with the following properties.

- Fairness: Participants with similar models or updates shall receive similar contribution values. The contribution scale is correlated with the reward.
- Availability: The contribution value by negative clients shall be 0, as they have no impact on the global model in the current round.
- Additivity: With each cycle of global updates, both long- and short-term contributions are additive to the overall FL process.

We analyze fairness using the Pearson correlation coefficient. Let contributions on x axis such as $x = \{c_1, c_2, \ldots, c_n\}$, rewards on y axis such as $y = \{p_1, p_2, \ldots, p_n\}$ and average of x and y as $\{\hat{x}, \hat{y}\}$. The fairness correlation is given as

$$f_c = \frac{\sum_{i=1}^{n} (x_i - \hat{x})(y_i - \hat{y})}{n s_x s_y}, \tag{7}$$

where $\{s_x, s_y\}$ denote the standard deviations of x and y, respectively. The range of the correlation coefficient is $[-1, 1]$. The larger f_c value suggests high fairness (positive correlation), whereas the negative coefficient implies unfairness (negative correlation). The rewards for quality workers are positively correlated with contributions and reputation. If worker i performs higher than worker j ($c_i > c_j$), then $p_i > p_j$. The analysis and evaluation of f_c are discussed in the following sections.

Table 1. An example of the contribution evaluation in different coalitions.

Client	1-2-3	1-3-2	2-1-3	2-3-1	3-1-2	3-2-1	SV
1	40	40	10	5	0	5	16.67
2	30	15	60	60	10	5	30
3	20	35	20	25	80	80	20

4.6. Reputation Measurement

A reputation mechanism indirectly reflects a participant's credibility and reliability leveraged through client selection and the reward distribution mechanisms. The effective and accurate reputation calculation is crucial for trustworthy FL because high-reputation clients with high performances play a crucial role in model training. The model owner manages the reputation of each participant i based on its contribution and the trust notion associated with quality detection. The trust value for each participant i is computed as

$$t_i = \frac{\omega n_i^p}{\omega n_i^p + (1 - \omega) n_i^f}. \tag{8}$$

where ω denotes the weight on the interaction events. The positive events n_i^p increase the trust score of the participants, and vice versa. To refrain from quality evaluation failure, negative events n_i^f are given a higher weight than positive events. Combining Equations (6) and (8), the reputation of any participant in round t can be stated as

$$r_i = t_i c_i. \tag{9}$$

4.7. Client Selection Reward Module

To achieve any desirable task, the model owner can select different types of participants based on their data quality, bid price, and performance. The participant's reward density is computed as

$$r_i^d = B_i^p / r_i. \tag{10}$$

Hence, to pick the early contributors (highly reputed), the participant set is arranged in the order of increasing reward density as

$$r_1^d < r_2^d < \ldots < r_n^d. \tag{11}$$

The incentive price p_i for different quality participants in the ranking is

$$p_i = \begin{cases} r_i^d + 1, & \text{if } r_i \geq 0.85 \quad \text{(high reputed)}; \\ r_i^d + 0.5, & \text{if } 0.70 < r_i < 0.85 \quad \text{(moderate high reputed)}; \\ r_i^d, & \text{if } 0.6 < r_i < 0.70 \quad \text{(moderate low reputed)}; \\ 0, & \text{if } r_i \leq 0.6 \quad \text{(low reputed)}. \end{cases} \tag{12}$$

This shows that reputation performance can add an extra incentive of 1 or 0.5 to the user's overall payoff (Algorithm 2).

Algorithm 2 FRIMFL incentive allocation.

Input: $B, x_i, w, P = \{P_1, P_2, \ldots, P_n\}$
Output: p_i
$p_i = 0, \ x_i = 1$
for each client $i \in P$ **do**
  Calculate c_i using Equation (6)
  Calculate t_i using Equation (8)
  Calculate r_i using Equation (9)
  Calculate r_i^d using Equation (10)
  Sort all using Equation (11)
  while $\sum_{i=1}^{n} x_i p_i \leq B$ **do**
    Calculate p_i using Equation (12)
  end while
end for
return p_i

5. Theoretical Analysis

Theorem 1 (FRIMFL achieves aggregation fairness). *FRIMFL gives the aggregation weight to each participant update based on its performance corresponding quality.*

Proof. The local model weight passing the quality detection is computed based on the performance instead of the amount of data, i.e., $\alpha_i = \frac{\psi_i}{\sum_i \psi_i}$. □

Theorem 2 (FRIMFL achieves reward fairness). *FRIMFL fairly distributes rewards to individuals based on their performance contribution.*

Proof. To quantify fairness, f_c is $\frac{\sum_{i=1}^{n}(x_i-\hat{x})(y_i-\hat{y})}{ns_x s_y}$. For performers, bringing $y_i = p_i = t_i \frac{c_i}{\sum c_j} = t_i \frac{x_i}{\sum x_j}$ and assuming similar trust values $t_i = t_j$ into Equation (8), we obtain

$$
\begin{aligned}
f_c &= \frac{\sum_{i=1}^{n}(x_i - \frac{1}{n}\sum x_i)(t_i\frac{x_i}{\sum x_j} - \frac{1}{n}\sum t_i \frac{x_i}{\sum x_j})}{ns_x s_y} \\
&= \frac{\sum_{i=1}^{n} x_i(t_i\frac{x_i}{\sum x_j}) - x_i(\frac{1}{n}\sum t_i\frac{x_i}{\sum x_j}) - \frac{1}{n}\sum x_i(t_i\frac{x_i}{\sum x_j}) + \frac{1}{n}\sum x_i(\frac{1}{n}\sum t_i\frac{x_i}{\sum x_j})}{ns_x s_y} \\
&= \frac{\frac{t_i}{\sum x_j}\sum_{i=1}^{n}(x_i^2 - \frac{1}{n}\sum x_i x_i - \frac{1}{n}\sum x_i x_i + \frac{1}{n}\sum x_i \frac{1}{n}\sum x_i)}{ns_x(t_i\frac{x}{\sum x_j})} \\
&= \frac{\frac{t_i}{\sum x_j}\frac{1}{n}\sum_{i=1}^{n}(x_i - \frac{1}{n}\sum x_i)^2}{ns_x(t_i\frac{x}{\sum x_j})} \\
&= 1.
\end{aligned}
$$

□

Theorem 3 (FRIMFL satisfies individual rationality). *Each individual can receive positive utility.*

Proof. The utility for a selected individual i is computed as $u_i = x_i(p_i - v_i)$. If unselected, its utility is zero. Since the incentive is proportional to the contribution, $u_i \geq 0$. □

Theorem 4 (FRIMFL is budget feasible). *The total amount paid to the participating users does not exceed the server's budget.*

Proof. The scheme determines and rewards n participants subjected to $\sum_{i=1}^{n} x_i p_i \leq B$. For the winner i, the incentive is p_i, and for the loser i, the incentive is 0. □

6. Results

6.1. Experimental Settings

We evaluated the performance of the proposed FRIMFL incentive scheme using MNIST [45], Fashion MNIST [46], and CIFAR10 [47] image datasets. The MNIST dataset consists of handwritten digits [0–9], with 60,000 training and 10,000 test samples. Each image has 28 × 28 pixels, and the pixel channel is grayscale. The Fashion MNIST dataset consists of clothing images with 70,000 samples belonging to 10 categories. The image pixel size, channel, and division of training and test set are identical to the MNIST. The CIFAR10 dataset comprises different object images with 60,000 samples and 32 × 32 pixels belonging to 10 categories. For i.i.d. settings, the dataset is uniformly distributed among participants, each with equal random samples, denoted as (UNI). The dataset is randomly partitioned among participants for non-i.i.d. settings and client heterogeneity. To illustrate, five participants own {50, 100, 150, 200, 250} samples, denoted as (IMB). The model comprises a simple convolutional neural network (CNN) with two fully connected layers. Table 2 shows the parameter settings. We introduced negative or malicious behaviors in the FL system as

- Poison clients [42]: They perform training with some percentage of incorrect noisy labels to represent a degree of unreliability.
- Sign-flip clients [48]: They perform training with some percentage of flip labels to represent a degree of unreliability.

We compare our proposed FRIMFL mechanism with the following baselines.

- VFL [1]: It performs standard vanilla FL to randomly select fraction n individuals and calculates aggregation weights based on local dataset sizes.

- FairFL [16]: It gives equal weights to all clients for aggregating local models.
- Greedy: A mechanism always prefers candidates with lower bid prices only. It does not contain reputation and contribution assessment methods.
- RRAFL [17]: An auction and reputation (RRAFL)-based incentive scheme, primarily suited to uniform settings only. The reputation, quality-detection, and reward distributions are different from FRIMFL.

We compare the performances regarding the reverse auction, reputation-based selection, model convergence accuracy, robustness, and contribution fairness. The performance of the reverse auction shows the economic benefits and checks whether the proposed scheme satisfies IR and IC design properties. The performance of reputation-based selection shows how well the scheme can select participants with good data quality. The performance of model accuracy shows the convergence speed and the stability of the scheme. The robustness through cumulative rewards reflects the effectiveness of quality–reputation-based selection to promote positive participation and eliminate negative participation. Lastly, the performance of contribution fairness shows how well the scheme promotes contributions from individual participants.

Table 2. Parameter settings for simulation results.

Parameter	Value
Number of participants (n)	5–20
Bid price (B_i^p)	5–10
Budget (B)	100–300
Learning rate (η)	0.05
Batch size ($\mathcal{B}$)	100
Loss quality threshold (ψ)	−0.03

6.2. Performance of Reverse Auction

Figure 4 compares the three schemes in terms of economic perspective. With 20 participants and a budget of 250, FRIMFL distributes higher payoffs and achieves a 7% higher surplus than RRAFL and Greedy. This is due to an increase in the selection probability of clients and their willingness to participate. Similarly, we compare the payments and cost value sum of all clients to join the training, and the results show that FRIMFL satisfies IR and IC design properties. This provides significant economic benefit for users to participate and makes the overall trade market more stable than both Greedy and RRAFL.

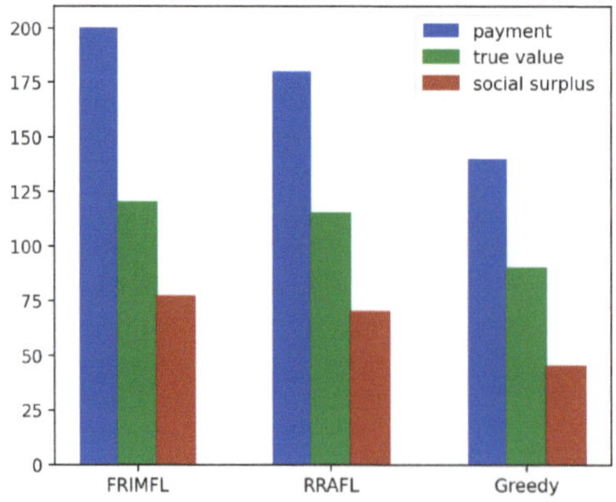

Figure 4. Comparison of economic benefit.

6.3. Performance of Reputation-Based Selection

We evaluate the reputation performance of truthful participants with different data quality rates. Table 3 shows the impact of the data accuracy level (p) on the average reputation for both schemes. Assuming honest participants with at least 60% true quality data, we can observe that the reputation reduces as the individual data accuracy rate decreases with non-linearity. For example, for the clients with a quality rate of 1 (i.e., a dataset containing all accurate labels) and a quality rate of 0.8 (i.e., a dataset containing 80% accurate labels and 20% incorrect labels), FRIMFL gives a higher reputation than RRAFL to those participants with higher quality rates. The reputation of FRIMFL is relatively higher than that of RRAFL due to the fair estimation of contributions. This shows that clients with good-quality data can receive a higher reputation for better incentives.

Table 3. Reputation analysis with different data quality rates.

	1		0.8		0.7		0.6	
Dataset	RRAFL	FRIMFL	RRAFL	FRIMFL	RRAFL	FRIMFL	RRAFL	FRIMFL
MNIST	0.965	**0.974**	0.698	**0.742**	0.588	**0.635**	0.431	**0.508**
CIFAR10	0.951	**0.959**	0.638	**0.711**	0.504	**0.601**	0.416	**0.494**
FMNIST	0.962	**0.970**	0.664	**0.737**	0.581	**0.640**	0.425	**0.510**

The evaluation of the model accuracy under the existence of different reputed clients is illustrated in Figure 5. For datasets [MNIST, CIFAR10, FMNIST], the highest accuracies [0.979, 0.801, 0.981] are observed in the presence of highly reputed (i.e., positive) clients, whereas the lowest accuracies [0.914, 0.722, 0.920] were reported with low reputed clients after 10 global epochs. The low-reputed participants had greater influence than the medium reputed participants on model convergence as they exhibit negative behavior by the falsified quality and lesser contribution towards the global model update. This also shows that slow model convergence is not guaranteed after 10 epochs and could create a loss to the model owner regarding payoff and system performance. With positive and medium clients, model convergence is not only fast but overall useful for model owners.

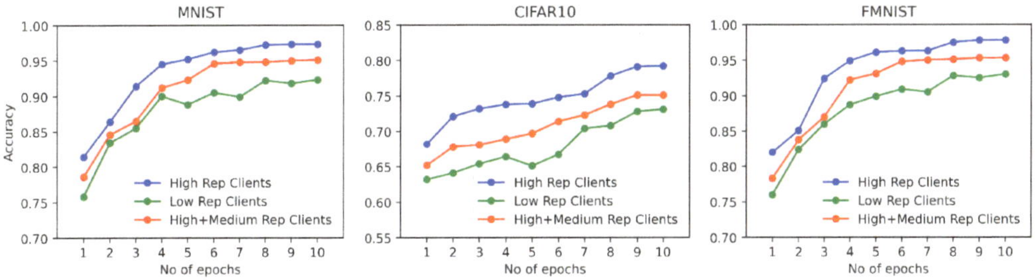

Figure 5. Effect on model accuracy by different reputed clients.

Table 4 shows the percentage of reliable participants selected in all four schemes on three datasets. Overall, FRIMFL selects the most participants, which means that it has effectively encouraged participation. For example, in CIFAR10, the proportion of client selection with good data quality is 0.94 in FRIMFL, significantly higher than 0.92 in RRAFL, 0.62 in VFL, and 0.40 in Greedy. Therefore, FRIMFL can benefit the model owners by providing higher chances to select users with better data quality.

Table 4. Participant selection probability in all four schemes.

Dataset	VFL	Greedy	RRAFL	FRIMFL
MNIST	0.61	0.41	0.93	**0.95**
CIFAR10	0.62	0.40	0.92	**0.94**
FMNIST	0.61	0.41	0.92	**0.95**

Figure 6 compares the accuracy of the final aggregated model in all four schemes. FRIMFL not only filters malicious behaviors through quality detection but also fairly aggregates weights to enhance the model accuracy than all three FairFL, RRAFL, and VFL at the end of task completion. Among the baselines, FairFL achieves a relatively higher performance in terms of convergence and stability than both RRAFL and VFL. This suggests that aggregation fairness handling data heterogeneity can make the global model more accurate and indicates that all reliable participants selected by FRIMFL have a positive effect on the global model accuracy, reaching [0.981, 0.812, 0.988] in three datasets [MNIST, CIFAR10, FMNIST], respectively, at the earliest.

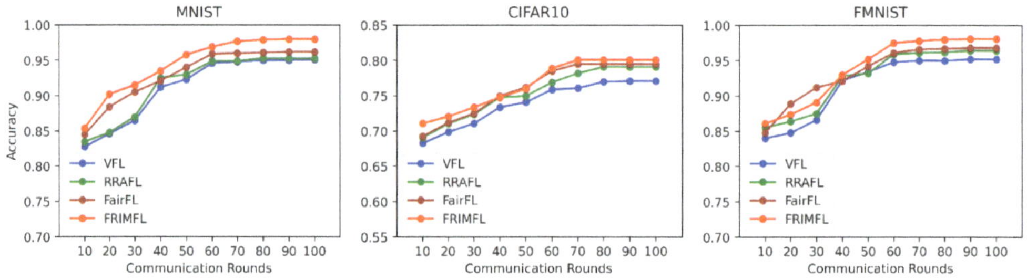

Figure 6. Performance of model accuracy.

The advantage of FRIMFL in an unreliable federation is shown in Figure 7. The x axis represents communication iterations, and the y axis represents the global model accuracy. The percentage of sign-flip and poison clients is equal to 75% to demonstrate untrustworthiness. The combination of such clients causes damage to the global model on all three datasets. The malicious behavior not only slows down the convergence speed but also requires three times more iterations to reach a stable accuracy of 0.812. In contrast, the honest behavior achieves a convergence accuracy of 0.963 approximately at 20 communication iterations. Therefore, the damage caused by malicious activity increases with a higher proportion of faulty labels and training updates.

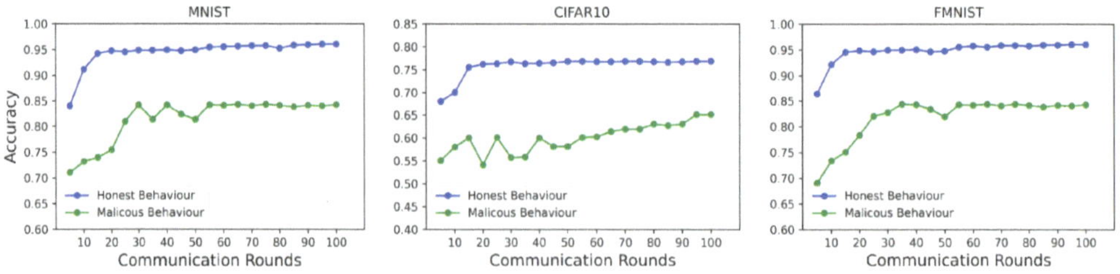

Figure 7. Model convergence under client behaviours.

6.4. *Performance of Model Accuracy*

Figure 8 shows the individual accuracy performance by five data owners in each training round for all three datasets. The participant's local accuracy rate is normal as they join the training coalition with a true data quality. With positive behavior and reliable updates, the server detects and compares local models for global model aggregation. It can be seen that the local accuracy saturates after five communication rounds.

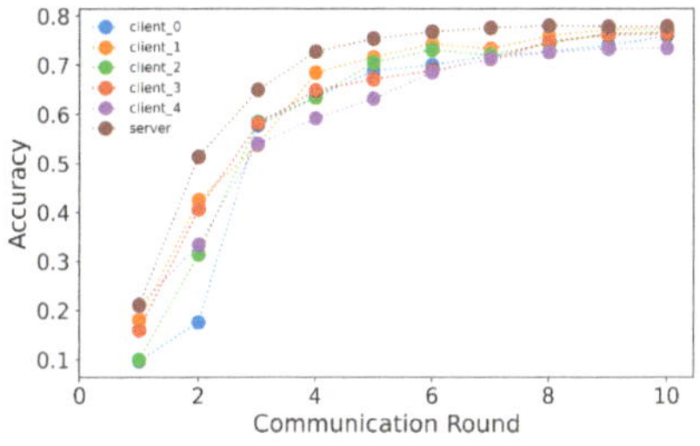

(**a**) MNIST

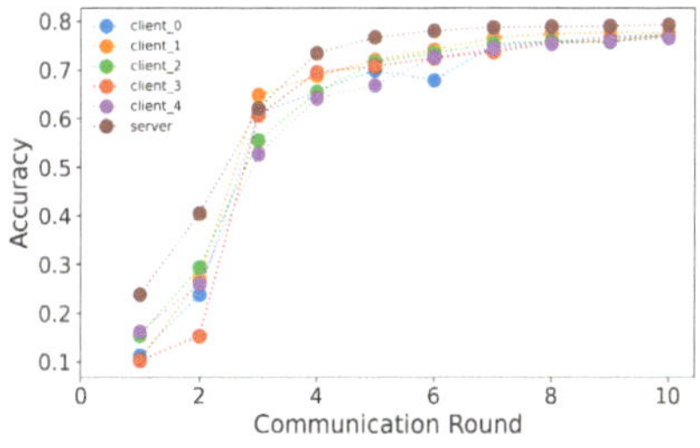

(**b**) CIFAR10

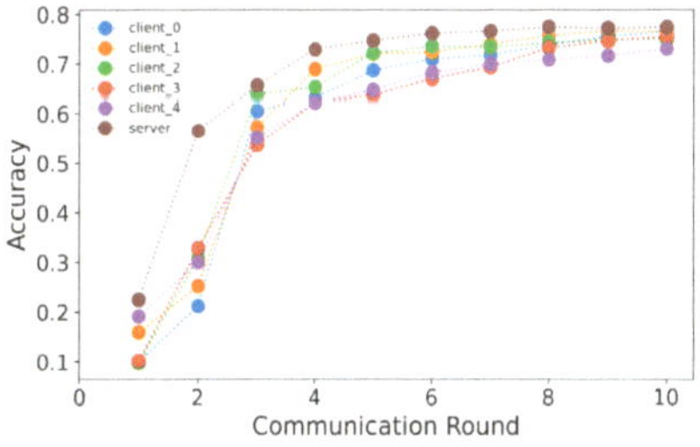

(**c**) FMNIST

Figure 8. Performance of accuracy by 5 different clients.

6.5. Performance of Contribution Fairness

Figure 9 shows the individual contribution level by five data owners in each training round for all three datasets. Initially, the contributions were different for all clients. At training round 3, the highest contributions were observed. Client 0 appears to be the highest in all three datasets, whereas clients 3 and 4 contributed the least. Similar influence by participants in later training rounds demonstrates that FRIMFL promotes early contributions by all data owners.

For three datasets, we compare FRIMFL with the RRAFL baseline in terms of fairness measured through the Pearson correlation coefficient, as shown in Table 5. The highest f_c was obtained in uniform settings (UNI) in both mechanisms. The performance of RRAFL is lower because the contribution measurement via cosine similarity is not ideal for capturing data heterogeneity where clients might provide similar updates to improve their performance.

Table 5. Calculation of Pearson correlation coefficient.

	MNIST		CIFAR10		FMNIST	
Scheme	UNI	IMB	UNI	IMB	UNI	IMB
RRAFL	0.989	0.972	0.979	0.960	0.987	0.973
FRIMFL	**0.992**	**0.988**	**0.985**	**0.973**	**0.993**	**0.986**

The robustness of FRIMFL in fair reward distribution is shown in Figure 10. The x axis represents communication iterations and the y axis represents participants' cumulative incentive, where pf is the proportion of data owners' unreliable (poison-flip) data. The reward values vary with different pf values. Reputed clients with quality data (low pf) are considered collaborators and thus receive rewards. This shows that rewards are positively related to quality and contributions. Clients with malicious data (high pf) who have malicious interactions (bad reputation) are considered to be negative participants and hence punished by the server for obtaining rewards.

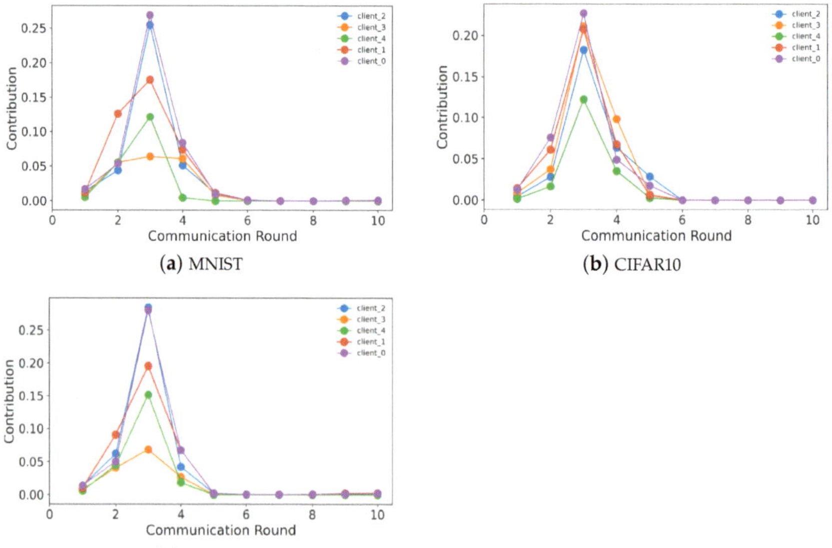

(a) MNIST
(b) CIFAR10
(c) FMNIST

Figure 9. Performance of contribution by 5 different clients.

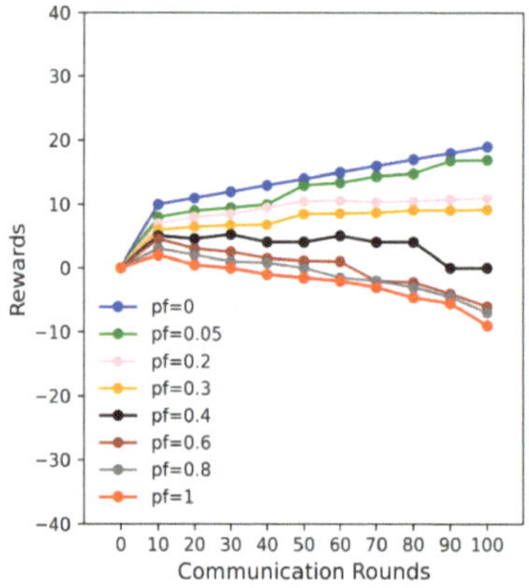

Figure 10. Cumulative rewards of participants with different data.

7. Discussion

The social surplus is relatively higher in the proposed mechanism due to increased participants' desire to select reverse auction. The cost–benefit makes the FL service more active. The Shapley method allows the measuring of client contributions and their impact on the overall performance of the model. Our mechanism implicitly assumes a predetermined incentive budget. However, this might not hold in practice in later training periods [12]. As for future works, a reimbursement option with dynamic incentivizing for long-term participation in diverse scenarios could be investigated. Additionally, the budget restriction only applies to the payments that the system employs to hold truthfulness. The convergence of the model is affected by the influence of negative/malicious clients since they produce misleading gradients. Spoofing attacks with robust defense can also be explored to complete the definition of security in incentive schemes.

8. Conclusions

In this paper, we proposed a fair and reliable incentive mechanism (FRIMFL) for federated learning services between FL model owners and heterogeneous clients. We designed our scheme considering client selection and the reward fairness of truthful clients. First, we adopted reverse auctions to estimate the model training costs and motivate clients to participate. Second, we introduced a reputation mechanism to detect and differentiate client behaviors. Participants' reputation is formulated by combining trust via quality detection and the contribution evaluation via the Shapley method. Finally, by integrating the reverse auction with reputation, we designed a selection and reward mechanism to distribute incentives to individuals for their overall performances. FRIMFL fairly allocates the incentive reward to positive participants and prevents negative ones from damaging the quality model. Through the theoretical analysis, web proved that FRIMFL satisfies individual rationality, incentive compatibility, aggregation fairness, and budget feasibility. Experimental results have shown that our scheme selects the best combination of clients to maximize the social surplus in the FL trading marketplace. The proposed FRIMFL can significantly enhance the economic benefit by 7% based on higher client selection and the model accuracy of FL tasks from 0.9451 to 0.9832 with faster convergence, hence encouraging active participation for the stable development of the FL ecosystem and thus can be a feasible option to incentivize clients.

Author Contributions: Conceptualization, A.A. and B.J.C.; Methodology, A.A.; Software, A.A.; Validation, A.A.; Formal Analysis, A.A.; Investigation, A.A. and B.J.C.; Resources, A.A.; Data Curation, A.A.; Writing—Original Draft Preparation, A.A.; Writing—Review and Editing, B.J.C.; Visualization, A.A.; Supervision, B.J.C.; Project Administration, B.J.C.; Funding Acquisition, B.J.C. All authors have read and agreed to the published version of the manuscript.

Funding: This research was supported by the MSIT Korea under the NRF Korea (NRF-2022R1A2C4001270), the Innovative Human Resource Development for Local Intellectualization support program (IITP-2023-RS-2022-00156360) supervised by the IITP, and the KIAT grant funded by the Korean government (MOTIE) (P0017123, The Competency Development Program for Industry Specialist). This research was also supported by the National Research Foundation (NRF) of Korea (NRF-2020K1A3A1A68093469), funded by the Ministry of Science and ICT (MSIT) Korea, and by the Department of Biotechnology (India) (DBT/IC-12031(22)-ICD-DBT).

Data Availability Statement: MNIST, FMNIST, and CIFAR10 datasets used in this article are publicly available and can be found at [45–47]. The code used to evaluate FRIMFL is available at https://github.com/Abrar-Ahmed-96/incentivefl, accessed on 24 July 2023.

Conflicts of Interest: The authors declare no conflict of interest.

Abbreviations

The following abbreviations are used in this manuscript:

α_i	Local model weight by participant i
B	Federation budget
B_i^p	Bid price of participant i
c_i	Contribution of participant i
CNN	Convolutional neural network
DRL	Deep reinforcement learning
f_c	Fairness correlation coefficient
FL	Federated learning
IC	Incentive compatibility
IR	Individual rationality
l_i^m	Loss of model with participant i
$l_i^{m'}$	Loss of model without participant i

n_i^p	Number of passing detections for participant i
n_i^f	Number of failing detections for participant i
p	Data quality rate
p_i	Payoff of participant i
P_i^u	Utility of participant i
R^t	Record of quality detection
r_i^d	Reward density of participant i
r_i	Reputation of participant i
S_i^u	Server i utility
SS	Social surplus
SV	Shapley value
t_i	Trust on participant i
x_i	Selection flag for participant i

References

1. McMahan, H.B.; Moore, E.; Ramage, D.; Arcas, B.A.Y. Federated Learning of Deep Networks using Model Averaging. *arXiv* **2016**, arXiv:1602.05629.
2. Yang, Q.; Liu, Y.; Chen, T.; Tong, Y. Federated Machine Learning: Concept and Applications. *ACM Trans. Intell. Syst. Technol.* **2019**, *10*, 1–19. [CrossRef]
3. Zhan, Y.; Zhang, J.; Hong, Z.; Wu, L.; Li, P.; Guo, S. A Survey of Incentive Mechanism Design for Federated Learning. *IEEE Trans. Emerg. Top. Comput.* **2022**, *10*, 1035–1044. [CrossRef]
4. Yang, T.; Andrew, G.; Eichner, H.; Sun, H.; Li, W.; Kong, N.; Ramage, D.; Beaufays, F. Applied Federated Learning: Improving Google Keyboard Query Suggestions. *arXiv* **2018**, arXiv:1812.02903.
5. Shayan, M.; Fung, C.; Yoon, C.J.M.; Beschastnikh, I. Biscotti: A Ledger for Private and Secure Peer-to-Peer Machine Learning. *arXiv* **2018**, arXiv:1811.09904.
6. Yu, H.; Liu, Z.; Liu, Y.; Chen, T.; Cong, M.; Weng, X.; Niyato, D.T.; Yang, Q. A Fairness-aware Incentive Scheme for Federated Learning. In Proceedings of the AAAI/ACM Conference on AI, Ethics, and Society, New York, NY, USA, 7–8 February 2020.
7. Zhou, Z.; Liu, P.; Feng, J.; Zhang, Y.; Mumtaz, S.; Rodriguez, J. Computation Resource Allocation and Task Assignment Optimization in Vehicular Fog Computing: A Contract-Matching Approach. *IEEE Trans. Veh. Technol.* **2019**, *68*, 3113–3125. [CrossRef]
8. Dinh, C.T.; Tran, N.H.; Nguyen, M.N.H.; Hong, C.S.; Bao, W.; Zomaya, A.Y.; Gramoli, V. Federated Learning Over Wireless Networks: Convergence Analysis and Resource Allocation. *IEEE/ACM Trans. Netw.* **2021**, *29*, 398–409. [CrossRef]
9. Yang, D.; Xue, G.; Fang, X.; Tang, J. Incentive Mechanisms for Crowdsensing: Crowdsourcing with Smartphones. *IEEE/ACM Trans. Netw.* **2016**, *24*, 1732–1744. [CrossRef]
10. Biggio, B.; Nelson, B.; Laskov, P. Poisoning Attacks against Support Vector Machines. In Proceedings of the ICML, Edinburgh, UK, 26 June–1 July 2012.
11. Lin, J.; Du, M.; Liu, J. Free-riders in Federated Learning: Attacks and Defenses. *arXiv* **2019**, arXiv:1911.12560.
12. Kairouz, P.; McMahan, H.B.; Avent, B.; Bellet, A.; Bennis, M.; Nitin Bhagoji, A.; Bonawitz, K.; Charles, Z.; Cormode, G.; Cummings, R.; et al. Advances and Open Problems in Federated Learning. *Found. Trends Mach. Learn.* **2021**, *14*, 1–210. [CrossRef]
13. Zhang, J.; Shu, Y.; Yu, H. Fairness in Design: A Framework for Facilitating Ethical Artificial Intelligence Designs. *Int. J. Crowd Sci.* **2023**, *7*, 32–39. [CrossRef]
14. Nishio, T.; Yonetani, R. Client Selection for Federated Learning with Heterogeneous Resources in Mobile Edge. In Proceedings of the ICC 2019—2019 IEEE International Conference on Communications (ICC), Shanghai, China, 20–24 May 2019; pp. 1–7. [CrossRef]
15. Li, T.; Hu, S.; Beirami, A.; Smith, V. Ditto: Fair and Robust Federated Learning Through Personalization. In Proceedings of the International Conference on Machine Learning, Virtual Event, 13–18 July 2020.
16. Michieli, U.; Ozay, M. Are All Users Treated Fairly in Federated Learning Systems? In Proceedings of the 2021 IEEE/CVF Conference on Computer Vision and Pattern Recognition Workshops (CVPRW), Nashville, TN, USA, 19–25 June 2021; pp. 2318–2322. [CrossRef]
17. Zhang, J.; Wu, Y.; Pan, R. Incentive Mechanism for Horizontal Federated Learning Based on Reputation and Reverse Auction. In Proceedings of the Web Conference 2021 (WWW '21), Ljubljana, Slovenia, 19–23 April 2021; Association for Computing Machinery: New York, NY, USA, 2021; pp. 947–956. [CrossRef]
18. Shi, Y.; Yu, H.; Leung, C. A Survey of Fairness-Aware Federated Learning. *arXiv* **2021**, arXiv:2111.01872.
19. Zeng, R.; Zeng, C.; Wang, X.; Li, B.; Chu, X. A Comprehensive Survey of Incentive Mechanism for Federated Learning. *arXiv* **2021**, arXiv:2106.15406.
20. Kang, J.; Xiong, Z.; Niyato, D.T.; Xie, S.; Zhang, J. Incentive Mechanism for Reliable Federated Learning: A Joint Optimization Approach to Combining Reputation and Contract Theory. *IEEE Internet Things J.* **2019**, *6*, 10700–10714.

21. Kang, J.; Xiong, Z.; Niyato, D.; Yu, H.; Liang, Y.C.; Kim, D.I. Incentive Design for Efficient Federated Learning in Mobile Networks: A Contract Theory Approach. In Proceedings of the 2019 IEEE VTS Asia Pacific Wireless Communications Symposium (APWCS), Singapore, 28–30 August 2019; pp. 1–5. [CrossRef]
22. Ye, D.; Yu, R.; Pan, M.; Han, Z. Federated Learning in Vehicular Edge Computing: A Selective Model Aggregation Approach. *IEEE Access* **2020**, *8*, 23920–23935. [CrossRef]
23. Ezzeldin, Y.H.; Yan, S.; He, C.; Ferrara, E.; Avestimehr, A.S. FairFed: Enabling Group Fairness in Federated Learning. *Proc. AAAI Conf. Artif. Intell.* **2023**, *37*, 7494–7502. [CrossRef]
24. Horváth, S.; Laskaridis, S.; Almeida, M.; Leontiadis, I.; Venieris, S.; Lane, N. FjORD: Fair and Accurate Federated Learning under heterogeneous targets with Ordered Dropout. In *Advances in Neural Information Processing Systems*; Ranzato, M., Beygelzimer, A., Dauphin, Y., Liang, P., Vaughan, J.W., Eds.; Curran Associates, Inc.: Red Hook, NY, USA, 2021; Volume 34, pp. 12876–12889.
25. Zhang, J.; Li, C.; Robles-Kelly, A.; Kankanhalli, M. Hierarchically Fair Federated Learning. *arXiv* **2020**, arXiv:2004.10386.
26. Lyu, L.; Yu, J.; Nandakumar, K.; Li, Y.; Ma, X.; Jin, J.; Yu, H.; Ng, K.S. Towards Fair and Privacy-Preserving Federated Deep Models. *IEEE Trans. Parallel Distrib. Syst.* **2019**, *31*, 2524–2541. [CrossRef]
27. Thi Le, T.H.; Tran, N.H.; Tun, Y.K.; Nguyen, M.N.H.; Pandey, S.R.; Han, Z.; Hong, C.S. An Incentive Mechanism for Federated Learning in Wireless Cellular Networks: An Auction Approach. *IEEE Trans. Wirel. Commun.* **2021**, *20*, 4874–4887. [CrossRef]
28. Cong, M.; Yu, H.; Weng, X.; Qu, J.; Liu, Y.; Yiu, S.M. A VCG-based Fair Incentive Mechanism for Federated Learning. *arXiv* **2020**, arXiv:2008.06680.
29. Zeng, R.; Zhang, S.; Wang, J.; Chu, X. FMore: An Incentive Scheme of Multi-dimensional Auction for Federated Learning in MEC. In Proceedings of the 2020 IEEE 40th International Conference on Distributed Computing Systems (ICDCS), Singapore, 29 November–1 December 2020; pp. 278–288. [CrossRef]
30. Rehman, M.H.; Salah, K.; Damiani, E.; Svetinovic, D. Towards Blockchain-Based Reputation-Aware Federated Learning. In Proceedings of the IEEE INFOCOM 2020—IEEE Conference on Computer Communications Workshops (INFOCOM WKSHPS), Toronto, ON, Canada, 6–9 July 2020; pp. 183–188.
31. Li, T.; Sahu, A.K.; Talwalkar, A.S.; Smith, V. Federated Learning: Challenges, Methods, and Future Directions. *IEEE Signal Process. Mag.* **2020**, *37*, 50–60. [CrossRef]
32. Pandey, S.R.; Nguyen, L.D.; Popovski, P. FedToken: Tokenized Incentives for Data Contribution in Federated Learning. *arXiv* **2022**, arXiv:2209.09775.
33. Deng, Y.; Lyu, F.; Ren, J.; Chen, Y.C.; Yang, P.; Zhou, Y.; Zhang, Y. FAIR: Quality-Aware Federated Learning with Precise User Incentive and Model Aggregation. In Proceedings of the IEEE INFOCOM 2021—IEEE Conference on Computer Communications, Vancouver, BC, Canada, 10–12 May 2021; pp. 1–10. [CrossRef]
34. Ding, N.; Fang, Z.; Huang, J. Incentive Mechanism Design for Federated Learning with Multi-Dimensional Private Information. In Proceedings of the 2020 18th International Symposium on Modeling and Optimization in Mobile, Ad Hoc, and Wireless Networks (WiOPT), Volos, Greece, 15–19 June 2020; pp. 1–8.
35. Feng, S.; Niyato, D.T.; Wang, P.; Kim, D.I.; Liang, Y.C. Joint Service Pricing and Cooperative Relay Communication for Federated Learning. In Proceedings of the 2019 International Conference on Internet of Things (Things) and IEEE Green Computing and Communications (GreenCom) and IEEE Cyber, Physical and Social Computing (CPSCom) and IEEE Smart Data (SmartData), Halifax, NS, Canada, 30 July–3 August 2018; pp. 815–820.
36. Weng, J.; Weng, J.; Zhang, J.; Li, M.; Zhang, Y.; Luo, W. DeepChain: Auditable and Privacy-Preserving Deep Learning with Blockchain-Based Incentive. *IEEE Trans. Dependable Secur. Comput.* **2021**, *18*, 2438–2455. [CrossRef]
37. Bao, X.; Su, C.; Xiong, Y.; Huang, W.; Hu, Y. FLChain: A Blockchain for Auditable Federated Learning with Trust and Incentive. In Proceedings of the 2019 5th International Conference on Big Data Computing and Communications (BIGCOM), Qingdao, China, 9–11 August 2019; pp. 151–159. [CrossRef]
38. Le, T.H.T.; Tran, N.H.; Tun, Y.K.; Han, Z.; Hong, C.S. Auction based Incentive Design for Efficient Federated Learning in Cellular Wireless Networks. In Proceedings of the 2020 IEEE Wireless Communications and Networking Conference (WCNC), Seoul, Republic of Korea, 25–28 May 2020; pp. 1–6. [CrossRef]
39. Qi, J.; Zhou, Q.; Lei, L.; Zheng, K. Federated Reinforcement Learning: Techniques, Applications, and Open Challenges. *arXiv* **2021**, arXiv:2108.11887.
40. Zhan, Y.; Li, P.; Qu, Z.; Zeng, D.; Guo, S. A Learning-Based Incentive Mechanism for Federated Learning. *IEEE Internet Things J.* **2020**, *7*, 6360–6368. [CrossRef]
41. Zhan, Y.; Zhang, J. An Incentive Mechanism Design for Efficient Edge Learning by Deep Reinforcement Learning Approach. In Proceedings of the IEEE INFOCOM 2020—IEEE Conference on Computer Communications, Toronto, ON, Canada, 6–9 July 2020; pp. 2489–2498. [CrossRef]
42. Tolpegin, V.; Truex, S.; Gursoy, M.E.; Liu, L. Data Poisoning Attacks Against Federated Learning Systems. In Proceedings of the ESORICS, Guildford, UK, 14–18 September 2020.
43. Shejwalkar, V.; Houmansadr, A. Manipulating the Byzantine: Optimizing Model Poisoning Attacks and Defenses for Federated Learning. In Proceedings of the NDSS, Virtually, 21–25 February 2021.
44. Wang, G.; Dang, C.X.; Zhou, Z. Measure Contribution of Participants in Federated Learning. In Proceedings of the 2019 IEEE International Conference on Big Data (Big Data), Los Angeles, CA, USA, 9–12 December 2019; pp. 2597–2604. [CrossRef]

45. Deng, L. The MNIST Database of Handwritten Digit Images for Machine Learning Research [Best of the Web]. *IEEE Signal Process. Mag.* **2012**, *29*, 141–142. [CrossRef]
46. Xiao, H.; Rasul, K.; Vollgraf, R. Fashion-MNIST: A Novel Image Dataset for Benchmarking Machine Learning Algorithms. *arXiv* **2017**, arXiv:1708.07747.
47. Krizhevsky, A. *Learning Multiple Layers of Features from Tiny Images*; University of Toronto: Toronto, ON, Canada, 2009.
48. Fung, C.; Yoon, C.J.M.; Beschastnikh, I. The Limitations of Federated Learning in Sybil Settings. In Proceedings of the International Symposium on Recent Advances in Intrusion Detection, San Sebastian, Spain, 14–18 October 2020.

electronics

MDPI

Article

Enabling Efficient and Privacy-Preserving Task Allocation with Temporal Access Control for Mobile Crowdsensing

Fuyuan Song [1,2], Yiwei Liu [3,*], Siyao Ma [4], Qin Jiang [1], Xiang Zhang [1] and Zhangjie Fu [1,2]

1 School of Computer Science, Nanjing University of Information Science and Technology, Nanjing 210044, China; fysong@nuist.edu.cn (F.S.); qin1_jiang@outlook.com (Q.J.); zhangxiang@nuist.edu.cn (X.Z.); fzj@nuist.edu.cn (Z.F.)
2 State Key Laboratory of Integrated Services Networks, Xidian University, Xi'an 710071, China
3 Defence Industry Secrecy Examination and Certification Center, Beijing 100089, China
4 Beijing Urban Construction Design & Development Group Co., Limited, Beijing 100032, China; masiyao@bjucd.com
* Correspondence: yiweiliu_disecc@163.com

Abstract: The increasing proliferation of GPS-enabled mobile devices, including Unmanned Aerial Vehicles (UAVs), smartphones, and laptops, has resulted in a significant upsurge in the outsourcing of spatial data to cloud servers for storage and computation purposes, such as task allocation and location-based services. However, the reliance on untrusted cloud servers introduces the risk of privacy breaches, as these servers possess the ability to deduce and access users' private information based on task content and query requirements. Existing privacy-preserving task-allocation schemes offer only coarse-grained and non-temporal access control, which restricts their applicability in scenarios involving multiple users and time-series data, such as trajectory and time-related routes. To overcome these challenges, this paper proposes an Efficient and Privacy-Preserving Task Allocation with Temporal Access Control (EPTA-T) scheme for mobile crowdsensing. By leveraging the techniques of Gray code and randomizable matrix multiplication, EPTA-T achieves efficient and privacy-preserving task allocation in mobile crowdsensing. Specifically, EPTA-T supports fine-grained and temporal access control through the utilization of an attribute-based access tree and function integration. The formal security analysis demonstrated that EPTA-T effectively guarantees data privacy and query privacy throughout the task allocation process. Extensive experiments conducted using a real-world dataset indicated that the EPTA-T scheme surpassed the performance of the state-of-the-art scheme.

Keywords: privacy-preserving; task allocation; temporal access control; mobile crowdsensing

1. Introduction

Recently, with the increasing proliferation of task allocation in mobile crowdsensing, it notably enhances the crowdsensing paradigm capability of helping requesters find workers to complete location-aware tasks. This enables requesters to specify task requirements that can be matched with workers based on their respective locations. However, in the mobile crowdsensing environment, the crowdsensing paradigm is inherently untrusted, creating the potential for the capture or inference of task information and workers' locations [1,2]. A prevailing method is to encrypt the spatial data and task content before outsourcing to the crowdsensing paradigm [3], which alleviates the privacy concerns, but incurs limited query functionality and query performance. In addition, the presence of time-related spatial data necessitates the implementation of Temporal Access Control (TAC) in task allocation. For instance, in a Didi Chuxing-based task allocation scenario, if a driver is situated near a requester between the hours of 9:00 and 10:00, the requester can find the driver at any time within that time range, such as 9:30; otherwise, he/she cannot match the driver. Theoretically speaking, a worker's spatial data can only be accessed at the current time

l_c if and only if t_c falls within the worker's time constraint interval $[t_1, t_2]$. Unfortunately, existing task-allocation schemes do not support temporal access control.

Challenge 1: How to design an Efficient and Privacy-Preserving Task Allocation (EPTA) scheme that supports Temporal Access Control (TAC). In mobile crowdsensing, workers' spatial data are typically associated with time-series objects, while requesters' attributes also contain timestamps. To achieve effective and accurate task allocation, TAC needs to be considered and integrated into the mobile crowdsensing system. However, directly combining existing EPTA schemes [1,2,4] with TAC schemes [5,6] may result in privacy breaches and an excessive burden of key management. EPTA and TAC are performed separately. To this end, the cloud server knows which worker meets the task requirements regardless of whether he/she can be accessed, which reveals the worker's timestamp and the worker's location. Moreover, the crowdsensing paradigm can deduce which workers satisfy the task requirements by observing the accessed spatial data, thereby leaking the access pattern. Unfortunately, access pattern leakage can lead to significant privacy issues, such as the disclosure of home addresses, preferences, and behaviors. Additionally, existing approaches have employed attribute-based encryption to enable fine-grained data sharing with access control [7]. However, this introduces computational overhead in terms of data encryption and task allocation. To improve search performance, some symmetric-encryption-based task-allocation schemes [1,8] have been designed. Nevertheless, in multi-user task allocation models, clients are required to share the same secret key, which may lead to key privacy leakage and key management concerns.

Challenge 2: How to provide an arbitrary geometric range query while achieving a fast search. In task allocation, requesters often submit irregular geometric query ranges to find suitable workers located within specific areas for task assignments. However, existing schemes [9,10] only support single or limited geometric ranges, such as circular, rectangular, or triangular ranges. While homomorphic encryption offers a viable approach for secure geometric range queries [11], the computational overhead associated with it is often unacceptable in practical scenarios. To achieve a fast search, Searchable Symmetric Encryption (SSE) [12–14] is commonly employed to enable secure and efficient retrieval of ciphertexts. Unfortunately, SSE fails to support complex query functions such as geometric range queries and lacks flexible key management for multi-user task allocation scenarios. In particular, some works have explored schemes for k-Nearest Neighbor (kNN) queries [15] and skyline queries [16] with privacy guarantees. However, these schemes cannot be directly applied to geometric range queries.

In this paper, we aimed to address the above challenging issues. Specifically, we propose an Efficient and Privacy-Preserving Task Allocation with Temporal Access Control (EPTA-T) scheme for mobile crowdsensing, which efficiently allocates tasks while preserving privacy and incorporating temporal access control. EPTA-T is specifically designed to address the limitations of existing schemes in supporting both task allocation and temporal access control. The main contributions are summarized as follows:

- We utilized Gray code to encode spatial data into vectors. These encoded vectors were then encrypted using randomizable matrix multiplication, enabling us to achieve efficient and privacy-preserving task allocation. This approach significantly reduced the computational overhead associated with data encryption and task allocation, while eliminating the need for key sharing among users.
- To support temporal access control, we leveraged the techniques of function differentiation and function integration. By incorporating these techniques into ciphertext-policy Attribute-Based Encryption (ABE), we constructed an access-tree-based policy. This policy enables precise control over temporal access to the encrypted data. Additionally, the secret involved in the data encryption is treated as the secret of the access policy, ensuring access pattern privacy protection.
- Formal security analysis proves that EPTA-T ensures the confidentiality of data and queries under an Indistinguishability under Selective Chosen-Plaintext Attacks (IND-SCPA) model. The experimental results over a real-world dataset indicated that the

running time of EPTA-T outperformed the state-of-the-art scheme in terms of index encryption, trapdoor generation, and task allocation.

The remainder of this paper is organized as follows. Section 2 presents an overview of related works on privacy-preserving task-allocation schemes. In Section 3, we outline the system model, threat model, design goals, and problem definition of EPTA-T. In Section 4, we provide the necessary background knowledge. Then, in Section 5, we present the detailed construction and technical aspects of the proposed scheme. In Section 6, we prove the security of the proposed scheme. In Section 7, we evaluate and analyze the performance of EPTA-T via experiments. Finally, we conclude our work in Section 8.

2. Related Work

In this section, we mainly focus on the related works on secure task allocation for mobile crowdsensing, including privacy-preserving task allocation and privacy-preserving range query.

2.1. Privacy-Preserving Task Allocation

Currently, privacy-preserving task allocation has received great attention in academia and industry [1,2,4,17,18]. To address the problem of privacy preservation in task allocation, Song et al. [1] proposed an efficient and privacy-preserving task-recommendation scheme by utilizing predicate encryption and randomizable matrix multiplication. Different from randomizable-matrix-based task allocation, Wang et al. [18] utilized a planar Laplace distribution to perturb tasks and workers' locations to protect their location privacy. However, using perturbed locations for task allocation can lead to a decrease in the effectiveness of the task assignments. Thus, Xia et al. [19] presented a probabilistic method to quantify the accessibility between workers and requesters and reduced the effect of the perturbed location on task allocation. To achieve task privacy protection, Zhou et al. [20] designed a tree-based privacy-preserving task-allocation system that addresses the task-allocation problem based on the combinatorial multi-armed slot machine problem. To the balance of user privacy and the usability of task allocation, Wang et al. [18] employed differential privacy to protect location privacy and proposed a multi-task assignment scheme for perturbing the available location information. Xu et al. [21] proposed a privacy-preserving task-allocation scheme using inner-product-based encryption to protect the privacy of task information and workers' locations. However, the schemes in [18–21] do not support temporal access control, i.e., deciding whether the requesters' temporal attributes satisfy a designed time-based access policy.

In summary, how to design an efficient and privacy-preserving task-allocation scheme that supports temporal access control is a crucial issue that needs to be addressed in mobile crowdsensing.

2.2. Privacy-Preserving Range Query

Searchable Symmetric Encryption (SSE) [12–14,22–24] is an effective cryptographic method for secure range query. Based on SSE, Li et al. [25] proposed a tree-aid indistinguishable index structure, which can only support one-dimensional range query. To achieve multi-dimensional range query, several works [1,8] employed an asymmetric scalar-product-preserving encryption approach. For strong security in range query, homomorphic encryption [11,15,26–29] is applied to realize the direct operations over ciphertext, but the computational cost is heavy and unacceptable. Furthermore, Several schemes have explored the limitations and weaknesses of SSE, which significantly balances security and efficiency effectively. Moreover, Wang et al. [9,10] proposed SSE-based schemes for geometric range query, but these schemes have some limitations such as a single geometric query type, inefficient search performance, and a low-dimensional space. To address these issues, Wang et al. [30] proposed a DSSE-based spatial keyword query scheme for dynamic updates. It is worth noting that the above schemes failed to support accurate and efficient geometric range query and temporal access control.

In a word, how to design an efficient and privacy-preserving geometric range query scheme that achieves an arbitrary geometric range query with a fast search is a significant problem that needs to be solved in the spatial data query.

Compared with the existing works, our proposed EPTA-T has three strong aspects: (1) our EPTA-T scheme achieves efficient and privacy-preserving task allocation with temporal access control in mobile crowdsensing; (2) our EPTA-T scheme supports an efficient and privacy-preserving geometric range query with a fast search in a multi-user setting; (3) our EPTA-T scheme guarantees the confidentiality of the data and queries under the IND-SCPA model.

3. Problem Formulation

In this section, we introduce the system model, threat model, design goals, and problem definition of EPTA-T.

3.1. System Model

As shown in Figure 1, the architecture of our mobile crowdsensing system consists of four entities, i.e., a trusted authority ($\mathcal{TA}$), a service provider ($\mathcal{SP}$), multiple workers ($\mathcal{W}$s), and multiple data requesters ($\mathcal{DR}$s).

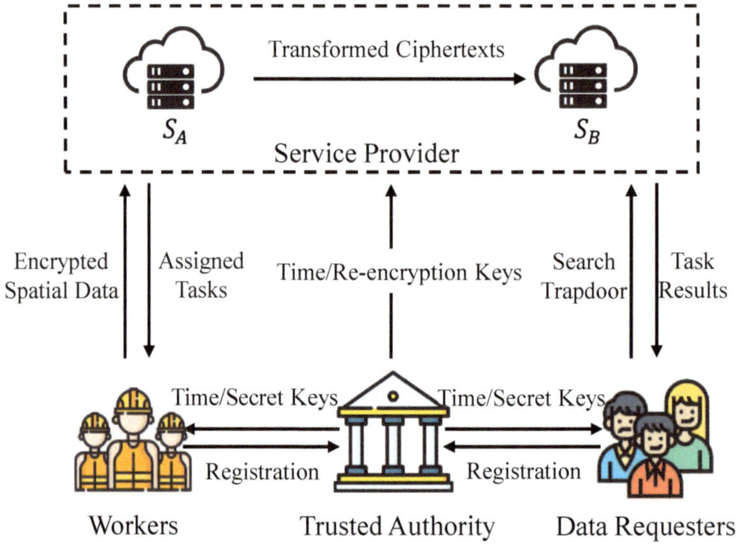

Figure 1. System model.

- Trusted Authority ($\mathcal{TA}$): The $\mathcal{TA}$ is responsible for initializing the system and distributing the secret keys. Initially, the $\mathcal{TA}$ sets up the system to provide registration services for both workers and data requesters and generates encryption keys and re-encryption keys for participating entities.
- Service Provider ($\mathcal{SP}$): The $\mathcal{SP}$ is a crowdsourcing service provider that receives and stores the task content from data requesters. Additionally, the $\mathcal{SP}$ allocates the task requirements to suitable workers. In this model, two non-colluding cloud servers S_A and S_B are introduced to serve as the service provider.
- Workers ($\mathcal{W}$s): Workers encrypt their locations and send the ciphertexts to the service provider. Based on the locations of the workers, the $\mathcal{SP}$ allocates the task requirements to the proper workers. After that, the workers accomplish the task and return the task results to the service provider.

- Data Requesters ($\mathcal{DR}s$): Before publishing the tasks, data requesters encrypt their task requirements. To find suitable workers who satisfy the query constraints, the $\mathcal{DR}s$ generate search trapdoors for their task requirements and submit the search trapdoors along with the encrypted task content to the $\mathcal{SP}$.

In our task allocation model, the $\mathcal{W}$ encrypts his/her spatial data according to the designated access policies, constructs encrypted indexes for task allocation, and transmits both the encrypted spatial data and indexes to the $\mathcal{SP}$. Prior to the $\mathcal{DR}$ releasing a task to the $\mathcal{SP}$, the $\mathcal{DR}$ generates a search trapdoor based on the task requirements and submits it to the $\mathcal{SP}$. Upon receiving the search trapdoor from the $\mathcal{DR}$, the $\mathcal{SP}$ initially converts the $\mathcal{DR}$'s privileged time trapdoor into the trapdoor associated with the current time t_c, but only if the t_c falls within the $\mathcal{DR}$'s privileged time range. Subsequently, the $\mathcal{SP}$ employs EPTA and TAC for task allocation, concurrently verifying whether the $\mathcal{DR}$'s attributes satisfy the access policy and if the search trapdoor corresponds to the appropriate worker index. If these conditions are met, the $\mathcal{SP}$ dispatches the task requirements to the suitable worker. Following the reception of the task results from the selected worker, the $\mathcal{SP}$ returns the results to the $\mathcal{DR}$.

3.2. Threat Model

In our task recommendation, the $\mathcal{TA}$ is fully trusted in the system, and all communications between the $\mathcal{TA}$ and other entities are secure. The $\mathcal{W}$ and $\mathcal{DR}$ are considered to be fully trusted, which means they keep their private keys secret. They would not leak or sell their keys to the $\mathcal{SP}$ for profits. The $\mathcal{SP}$ is considered as semi-honest (i.e., honest-but-curious), which means the $\mathcal{SP}$ will honestly perform the designed protocols to provide the task recommendation services, but the $\mathcal{SP}$ may try to derive private information from encrypted locations and search trapdoors. Based on the information that $\mathcal{SP}$ may derive, we considered the following two attacks:

- *Ciphertext-only attack*: The $\mathcal{SP}$ observes a number of ciphertexts including encrypted locations, encrypted tasks, and search trapdoors, but the $\mathcal{SP}$ cannot obtain their corresponding plaintexts.
- *Chosen-plaintext attack*: Except knowing the encrypted locations and trapdoors, the $\mathcal{SP}$ can oracle access the task recommendation protocols to obtain some plaintext–ciphertext pairs.

Generally, we assumed that there is no collusion between two cloud servers. This assumption is reasonable, as cloud servers are expected to maintain their reputations and protect their own interests [8]. It is worth noting that the no-collusion assumption has been widely adopted in numerous research works within the security community, particularly in the context of the two-server model [8,15,31].

3.3. Design Goals

The design goals of EPTA-T are summarized as follows:

- Privacy protection: The privacy of workers and data requesters should be protected in our EPTA-T scheme. It is not difficult to see that, in task allocation applications that involve more sensitive user data such as workers' locations, requesters' queries, and task results, revealing these data can easily violate user privacy.
- Temporal access control: The EPTA-T scheme should achieve temporal access control for the time-series data (e.g., trajectory data, validity period, and hours of services) in task allocation.
- Efficiency: The computational overhead and communication overhead on the worker and publisher side should be minimized, since the mobile devices are resource-limited. The proposed EPTA-T scheme should achieve efficient data encryption and task allocation.

3.4. Problem Definition

In this paper, our objective was to achieve Efficient and Privacy-Preserving Task Allocation (EPTA) with Temporal Access Control (TAC) for handling massive spatial data comprising temporal and non-temporal attributes. Each spatial datum L_i is encoded as spatial point p_i with a private identity of the worker id_ϱ. The worker's identity id_ϱ is encrypted using a secret key s under an access policy $\mathcal{T}_\varrho$, which encompasses both temporal and non-temporal access attributes. Specifically, the spatial data can only be accessed within the valid time period defined by $at[t_1, t_2] \in \mathcal{T}_\varrho$. Let $\mathsf{IndexEnc}$ be the index encryption algorithm executed by $\mathcal{W}$. Based on the $\mathsf{IndexEnc}$ algorithm, each spatial datum L_i is encrypted as $\widehat{C_{I_i}}$ by using the $\mathcal{W}$'s secret key sk_i, i.e., $\mathsf{IndexEnc}(L_i, sk_i) \rightarrow \widehat{C_{I_i}}$. Let $\mathsf{IndexTran}$ be the index transformation algorithm executed by the $\mathcal{SP}$. In the $\mathsf{IndexTran}$ algorithm, the $\mathcal{SP}$ utilizes the corresponding re-encryption keys RK_A and RK_B to transform the encrypted ciphertext, i.e., $\mathsf{IndexTran}(\widehat{C_{I_i}}, RK_A, RK_B) \rightarrow C_{I_i}$. Let $\mathsf{TrapGen}$ be the trapdoor-generation algorithm executed by $\mathcal{DR}$. When the $\mathcal{DR}$ with an attribute set $S = \{at_1, at_2, \cdots, at_i[t_1', t_2'], \cdots, at_{|S|}\}$ submits a geometric range R_q of task requirements to the $\mathcal{SP}$ at the current time t_c, the search trapdoor $\widehat{T_Q}$ is generated for the geometric range by using the $\mathcal{DR}$'s secret key sk_q, i.e., $\mathsf{TrapGen}(R_q, sk_q) \rightarrow \widehat{T_Q}$. When the $\mathcal{SP}$ receives the search trapdoor $\widehat{T_Q}$ from the $\mathcal{DR}$, using the $\mathsf{TrapTran}$ algorithm, the $\mathcal{SP}$ transforms the $\mathcal{DR}$'s privileged time trapdoor into the search trapdoor linked to the current time t_c when the t_c falls within the privileged time range of $\mathcal{DR}$, i.e., $\mathsf{TrapTran}(\widehat{T_Q}, RK_A, RK_B) \rightarrow T_Q$. Upon receiving the transformed trapdoor T_Q, the $\mathcal{SP}$ performs the task allocation to search the proper workers who satisfy the access policy $\mathcal{T}_\varrho(S, t_c) = 1$ and the geometric range query condition simultaneously. Here, $\mathcal{T}_\varrho(S, t_c) = 1$ means the current time t_c belongs to a valid time period of access policy and the access attribute set, and the $\mathcal{DR}$'s attributes satisfy the designed access policy $\mathcal{T}_\varrho$, i.e., $(t_c \in [t_1, t_2] \cap [t_1', t_2']) \bigwedge (\mathcal{T}_\varrho(S) = 1)$. Let $\mathsf{TAC}(\cdot)$ be the temporal access control function; we have

$$\mathsf{TAC}(\mathcal{T}_\varrho, S, t_c) = \begin{cases} [\![s]\!], & if\ \mathcal{T}_\varrho(S, t_c) = 1; \\ 0, & otherwise, \end{cases} \tag{1}$$

where $[\![s]\!]$ denotes the encrypted secret. Let $\mathsf{EPTA}(\cdot)$ be the efficient and privacy-preserving task allocation primitive function; we have

$$\mathsf{EPTA}(C_{I_i}, T_Q, t_c, [\![s]\!]) = \begin{cases} 1, & if\ tr(C_{I_i} T_Q) = 0; \\ 0, & otherwise. \end{cases} \tag{2}$$

Based on the above problem statement, we give the definition of EPTA-T as follows.

Definition 1 (EPTA-T). *For a worker with the spatial data L_i encrypted under the access policy $\mathcal{T}_\varrho$, the worker is considered as an accessible and suitable one for a $\mathcal{DR}$ who possesses an attribute set S and submits a geometric range R_q of task requirements at the current time t_c, if and only if both conditions $TAC(\mathcal{T}_\varrho, S, t_c) = [\![s]\!]$ and $EPTA(C_{I_i}, T_Q, t_c, [\![s]\!]) = 1$ are met.*

4. Preliminaries

In this section, we review some building blocks that are used in our proposed scheme, including Gray code [6], the access tree [22], and polynomial functions [4].

4.1. Gray Code

The process of converting a binary number $d_1 d_2 \cdots d_n$ into its corresponding binary reflected Gray code involves iterating from right to left. Starting with the rightmost digit d_n, if the preceding digit d_{n-1} is 1, we replace d_n with $1 - d_{n-1}$. If d_{n-1} is 0, we leave d_n unchanged. We then proceed to the next digit d_{n-1} and repeat the process until we reach the first digit d_1, which remains the same as d_0 was assumed to be 0. The resulting sequence $g_1 g_2 \cdots g_n$ represents the binary reflected Gray code. To convert a binary reflected Gray code $g_1 g_2 \cdots g_n$ back to a binary number, we start with the n-th digit and compute the equation as follows:

$$\Sigma_n = \sum_{i=1}^{n-1} g_i (mod 2). \quad (3)$$

If $\Sigma_n = 1$, replace g_n by $1 - g_n$; otherwise, leave it unchanged. Next, we compute

$$\Sigma_{n-1} = \sum_{i=1}^{n-2} g_i (mod 2). \quad (4)$$

By applying the above calculation, we obtain that the binary number $d_1 d_2 \cdots d_n$ corresponds to the initial binary reflected Gray code.

Therefore, the Gray code for $d+1$ bits can be represented as

$$G_{d+1} = (0||g_1, \cdots, 0||g_{2^d}, 1||g_{2^d}, \cdots, 1||g_1),$$

where $||$ denotes the concatenation operator. For example, $G_1 = (0,1)$, $G_2 = (00, 01, 11, 10)$. When using Gray code to encode a $d \times d$ grid, the length of each binary code representing a cell is $2 \cdot 2^{\lceil \log_2 d \rceil}$.

4.2. Access Tree

Consider a tree $\mathcal{T}$ that represents an access policy. In this tree, each non-leaf node represents a threshold gate. The node is defined by its children and a threshold value. The threshold value k_x of a node x is such that $0 < k_x \leq \text{num}_x$, where num_x represents the number of children of node x. On the other hand, each leaf node x in $\mathcal{T}$ represents an attribute at_x, where the threshold value k_x is set to 1.

Let $\mathcal{T}_x$ denote the subtree of $\mathcal{T}$ rooted at node x. If x is a non-leaf node, $\mathcal{T}_x(S) = 1$ if and only if it contains at least k_x children x_i $i \in [1, k_x]$ for which $\mathcal{T}_{x_i}(S) = 1$. In other words, $\mathcal{T}_x(S)$ is true if there are enough child nodes satisfying $\mathcal{T}_{x_i}(S) = 1$ according to the threshold value k_x.

If x is a leaf node, $\mathcal{T}_x(S) = 1$ if and only if the attribute at_x is present in the attribute set S. In other words, $\mathcal{T}_x(S)$ is true if the attribute at_x is a member of S.

4.3. Polynomial Function

The polynomial function relates the coefficients of a polynomial to the sums and products of its roots. Let $f(x)$ be a polynomial function of degree n, i.e., $f(x) = a_n x^n + \cdots + a_1 x + a_0$, where the coefficient of x^i is a_i, and $a_n \neq 0$. Based on the property of the polynomial function, we have

$$f(x) = a_n x^n + \cdots + a_1 x + a_0 = a_n (x - x_n) \cdots (x - x_1),$$

where $x_1, \cdots, x_n$ are the roots of $f(x)$. According to the construction of the polynomial function $f(x)$, we can calculate any subproducts of the roots. For any $i \in [0, n]$, the $(n-i)$-th coefficient a_{n-i} is associated with a signed sum of all possible subproducts of the roots, as shown in Equation (5).

$$\sum_{1 \leq k_1 \leq \cdots \leq k_i \leq n} x_{k_1} x_{k_2} \cdots x_{k_i} = (-1)^i \frac{a_{n-i}}{a_n}. \quad (5)$$

5. The Proposed Scheme

In this section, we first introduce the overview of EPTA-T. After that, we give the detailed construction of EPTA-T. In our EPTA-T, it mainly consists of seven algorithms: System Setup (SystSetup), Key Generation (KeyGen), Index Encryption (IndexEnc), Index Transformation (IndexTran), Trapdoor Generation (TrapGen), Trapdoor Transformation (TrapTran), and task allocation (Query). Finally, we analyzed the correctness of EPTA-T.

5.1. Overview

Since EPTA-T supports secure task allocation in multi-worker multi-requester settings without key sharing, the main idea of EPTA-T is to encode and encrypt the index of the spatial data and the search trapdoor of the task requirement into a matrix-trace-based matching operation, such that TAC can be implemented by the same encryption mechanism without involving additional computational overhead.

Transforming the geometric-range-based task allocation into the inner-product-based matching operation. To enable task allocation based on the geometric ranges of the task requirements, the space is divided into uniform cells with dimensions $L \times L$. The task allocation conditions, specifying the spatial data of workers located within the geometric range defined by the data requester, are encoded using Gray code, where 0 and 1 are represented by two positive integers, X and Y, respectively. Each spatial datum L_i is encoded as spatial point p_i by using Gray code and further expanded into a spatial vector $\overrightarrow{\mathsf{p}_i}$ by padding it with additional entries, including -1. The geometric query range R_q is encoded as the aggregated query code q_i, which represents the combination of the codes for the cells encompassed by the geometric range R_q. Subsequently, the aggregated range query vector $\overrightarrow{\mathsf{q}_i}$ is generated by padding the query code with additional entries, including the sum of the squares of the code values. Specifically, the aggregated query code is generated by replacing the different entries with 0 to reduce the scale of codes in the query range. Consequently, if the inner product between the spatial vector $\overrightarrow{\mathsf{p}_i}$ and the query vector $\overrightarrow{\mathsf{q}_i}$ is 0 (i.e., $\overrightarrow{\mathsf{p}_i} \circ \overrightarrow{\mathsf{q}_i} = 0$), this indicates that the spatial data L_i of the worker are located within the geometric query range R_q. Otherwise, if the inner product is non-zero, this signifies that the spatial data are located outside the query range.

As shown in Figure 2, we give an example of the encoding procedure and geometric range query. In Figure 2, the spatial space is uniformly split into 4×4 cells. The spatial point p_i is encoded as $g_{\mathsf{p}_i} = YYXX$ and further extended as spatial vector $\overrightarrow{\mathsf{p}_i} = (Y, Y, X, X, -1)$. In addition, the geometric query range (green domain) is encoded as $g_{\mathsf{q}_1} = XYXX \vee XYXY \vee YYXX \vee YYXY = 0YX0$ and $g_{\mathsf{q}_2} = YYYY$. After that, the corresponding query vectors are further extended as $\overrightarrow{\mathsf{q}_1} = (0, Y, X, 0, Y^2 + X^2)$ and $\overrightarrow{\mathsf{q}_2} = (Y, Y, Y, Y, 4Y^2)$, respectively. Therefore, the inner product between $\overrightarrow{\mathsf{p}_i}$ and $\overrightarrow{\mathsf{q}_1}$ is 0, which means that the spatial point p_i is located in the geometric query range R_{q_1}.

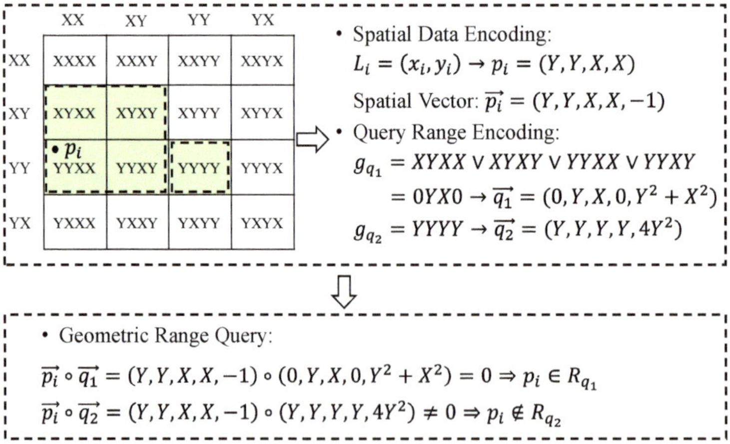

Figure 2. An Encoding Example of Spatial Data and Query Range and Geometric Range Query.

Secure matrix-trace-based task allocation mechanism. In EPTA-T, we encrypt the spatial data L_i as $\widehat{C_{I_i}}$ and transform them as C_{I_i} by calling IndexEnc and IndexTran, respectively. In addition, we encrypt the geometric query range R_q of task allocation as $\widehat{T_Q}$ and transform it as T_Q by calling TrapGen and TrapTran, respectively. After that, we call the Query protocol to calculate the matrix trace (i.e., $tr(C_{I_i} T_Q)$) to retrieve proper workers for task allocation. If the worker $\mathcal{W}_i$ is the proper one, his/her spatial data are located in the geometric range of the task requirement, i.e., $L_i \in R_q$, then $tr(C_{I_i} T_Q) = 0$.

Secure temporal access control. To achieve EPTA with TAC, the key idea is to perturb the search results of EPTA with the access policy by employing a secret used in IndexEnc as the secret of the access policy to encrypt the corresponding spatial data. To this end, privacy-preserving task allocation is correctly performed only when the spatial data are accessible.

To achieve temporal access control, we add time validity to a secret associated with the spatial data and correlate the encrypted secret with an access time period. Only when a data requester has attributes that satisfy the defined access policy and a secret that corresponds to the accessible time period can the data requester access the spatial data.

For TAC, we constructed a hierarchical temporal access tree $\mathcal{T}$ and utilized its leaf nodes to denote different time attributes $at[t_1, t_2]$. In addition, when the $\mathcal{DR}$ can access the spatial data, the $\mathcal{DR}$'s privileged time period $at[t'_1, t'_2] \in S$ should be satisfied. If the current time t_c satisfies $t_c \in [t_1, t_2] \cap [t'_1, t'_2]$, we utilize the polynomial function property to transform the time-related derivation function $f(t)$ associated with $[t_1, t_2]$ and $[t'_1, t'_2]$ into the original function $F(t)$ related to t_c. If $at_x \in S$, we calculate the original function $F_x(t)$ as shown in Equation (6).

$$F_x(t)|_{t=t_c} = a \int_{t_1}^{t_2} \int_{t'_1}^{t'_2} f_x(t) dt dt' = e(g_p, H)^{a y_x(0)}, \tag{6}$$

where a represents a unique entry used to differentiate between different data requesters ($\mathcal{DR}$) selected by the $\mathcal{TA}$, x is a leaf node of the hierarchical temporal access tree, and $y_x(0)$ is the secret share of s for the leaf node x. The entry s is regarded as the secret of the hierarchical temporal access tree $\mathcal{T}$'s root node, which is used to encrypt the private identity of the worker id_i. When the $\mathcal{DR}$'s attributes satisfy the defined access policy at the current time t_c, we have $F_{root} = e(g_p, H)^{as}$.

In our EPTA-T, $\mathcal{SP}$ should first execute TAC by checking whether the $\mathcal{DR}$'s attributes satisfy the defined access policy tree $\mathcal{T}$ at the current time t_c. If the $\mathcal{SP}$ calculates that $F_{root} = e(g_p, H)^{as}$ holds, this indicates that the $\mathcal{DR}$ can access the spatial data. After that, the $\mathcal{SP}$ performs EPTA to calculate $tr(C_{I_i} T_Q)$. If $tr(C_{I_i} T_Q) = 0$ holds, the accessible spatial data satisfy the geometric query range, and the $\mathcal{SP}$ selects the worker identity id_Q as the proper worker and sends the task to this target one.

Remark 1. *To the best of our knowledge, EPTA-T is the first work to support fine-grained and temporal access control in privacy-preserving task allocation, which achieves efficient geometric range query and IND-SCPA security in the multi-worker multi-requester setting without key sharing.*

5.2. The Detailed Construction of EPTA-T

Based on the above overview, we describe the detailed construction of EPTA-T:

(1) **SystSetup** $(1^\lambda) \rightarrow (pp, msk)$. Given a security parameter λ, the $\mathcal{TA}$ generates the master key msk, which consists of two $(n+1) \times (n+1)$ random invertible matrices $\{M_1, M_2\}$, a hash function $h : \{0,1\}^* \rightarrow \mathbb{Z}_p^*$, which hashes any spatial vector and query vector to positive values in $\mathbb{Z}_p^*$ and converts the attribute string to a group element, respectively, a random symmetric key K, and a random permutation $\pi : \mathbb{Z}_p^{n+1} \rightarrow \mathbb{Z}_p^{n+1}$. In addition, $\mathcal{TA}$ generates a composite order bilinear system $\mathbb{S} = (\mathbb{G}, \mathbb{G}_T, e)$ of order $n = p \times r$ and generators $g_p \in \mathbb{G}_p$, $g_r \in \mathbb{G}_r$. Additionally, the $\mathcal{TA}$ randomly selects an entry $\theta \in \mathbb{Z}_p$ and calculates $H = g_p^\theta g_r^\theta$. Namely, the masker secret key can be denoted as $msk = \{M_1, M_2, \pi, h\}$, and the public parameters are generated as $pp = \{\mathbb{S}, g_p, g_r, h, H\}$.

(2) **KeyGen** $(msk, \mathcal{W}_i, \mathcal{DR}_q) \rightarrow (sk_i, sk_q, RK_A, RK_B)$. For a worker $\mathcal{W}_i$, the $\mathcal{TA}$ first chooses two random $(n+1) \times (n+1)$ matrices $\{M_{i,1}, M_{i,2}\}$. Then, $\mathcal{TA}$ computes $M'_{i,1} = M_1 M_{i,1}^{-1}$ and $M'_{i,2} = M_1 M_{i,2}^{-1}$. For a data requester $\mathcal{DR}_q$, the $\mathcal{TA}$ randomly selects two $(n+1) \times (n+1)$ $\{M_{q,1}, M_{q,2}\}$, and then, the $\mathcal{TA}$ computes $M'_{q,1} = M_{q,1}^{-1} M_1^{-1}$ and $M'_{q,2} = M_2^{-1} M_{q,2}^{-1}$. Finally, the $\mathcal{TA}$ sends the secret key $sk_i = \{M_{i,1}, M_{i,2}, \pi, h\}$ to the worker $\mathcal{W}_i$ and the secret key $sk_q = \{M_{q,1}, M_{q,2}, \pi, h, K\}$ to the data requester

$\mathcal{DR}_q$, and the $\mathcal{TA}$ distributes the re-encryption key $RK_A = \{M'_{i,1}, M'_{q,2}\}$ to S_A and the re-encryption key $RK_B = \{M'_{i,2}, M'_{q,1}\}$ to S_B. To distinguish different $\mathcal{DR}$s, the $\mathcal{TA}$ chooses a unique element $a \in \mathbb{Z}_p$ for a certain $\mathcal{DR}$'s attribute set S.

(3) **IndexEnc** $(L_i, sk_i) \rightarrow \widehat{C_{I_i}}$. Given a worker $\mathcal{W}_i$'s spatial data $L_i = (x_i, y_i)$, $\mathcal{W}_i$ encrypts his/her spatial data and outsources it to $\mathcal{SP}$ as follows:

Step 1: Firstly, the $\mathcal{W}_i$ encodes the spatial data L_i as a spatial vector $\overrightarrow{p_i} = (b_1, b_2, \cdots, b_d) \leftarrow Gray(L_i)$, where b_i $(i \in [1, d-1])$ is a value of X or Y, and $b_d = -1$.

Step 2: For the spatial vector $\overrightarrow{p_i} = (b_1, b_2, \cdots, b_d)$, the $\mathcal{W}_i$ transforms $\overrightarrow{p_i}$ to a positive integer $v_i = \sum_{l=1}^{d} b_l \cdot 2^{d-l}$. After that, the workers have a collection of integers, i.e., $\{v_1, v_2, \cdots, v_m\}$, where m denotes the number of workers in the mobile crowdsensing system.

Step 3: To protect the privacy of the transformative integer v_i, the $\mathcal{W}_i$ maps the integer with the one-way hash function h and obtains the hash value $h(v_i)$. Then, the $\mathcal{W}_i$ calculates different powers for the hash value $h(v_i)$ to generate an $(n+1)$-dimensional vector $I_i = (h(v_i)^0, h(v_i)^1, \cdots, h(v_i)^n)$.

Step 4: Next, the $\mathcal{W}_i$ generates a one-time random positive number α and embeds it into the vector I_i. That is, the $\mathcal{W}_i$ obtains the random vector $\overline{I_i} = (\alpha h(v_i)^0, \alpha h(v_i)^1, \cdots, \alpha h(v_i)^n)$.

Step 5: After that, the $\mathcal{W}_i$ permutes the random vector $\overline{I_i}$ to another vector $\widehat{I_i}$ by using the permutation π, i.e., $\widehat{I_i} = \pi(\overline{I_i})$. Then, the $\mathcal{W}_i$ transforms the permuted vector $\widehat{I_i}$ to a corresponding diagonal matrix $\widehat{D_{I_i}}$ with the diagonal being $\widehat{I_i}$.

Step 6: Finally, the $\mathcal{W}_i$ generates a random $(n+1) \times (n+1)$ upper triangular matrix $\mathcal{U}_i$, where the main diagonal entries are 1, and the remainder of the non-zero entries are one-time random values. Then, the $\mathcal{W}_i$ uses his/her secret key sk_i to encrypt $\widehat{D_{I_i}}$ as shown in Equation (7). After this operation, the $\mathcal{W}_i$ sends the encrypted location $\widehat{C_{I_i}}$ to S_A.

$$\widehat{C_{I_i}} = M_{i,1}\mathcal{U}_i\widehat{D_{I_i}}M_{i,2} \tag{7}$$

Specifically, to protect identity privacy, the worker $\mathcal{W}_i$ encrypts the identity id_ϱ as c_ϱ via the standard encryption algorithm (e.g., AES) and encrypts the hierarchical temporal access tree as follows:

- Firstly, the worker $\mathcal{W}_i$ selects the entry s as the secret of the root node of the hierarchical temporal access tree $\mathcal{T}_\varrho$.
- Then, the worker $\mathcal{W}_i$ calculates the secret shares of s for each leaf node x as $y_x(0)$.
- Finally, for each leaf node x, if x is represented as a temporal attribute $at_x[t_1, t_2]$, the $\mathcal{W}_i$ splits $y_x(0)$ into $y_x(0)', y_x(0)''$, which should guarantee that $y_x(0) = y_x(0)' + y_x(0)''$ holds. Thus, $\mathcal{W}_i$ encrypts the leaf node x as $C_x = (H^{y_x(0)'}, h(at_x)^{y_x(0)'}, H^{y_x(0)''}, h(at_x)^{y_x(0)''})$; otherwise, $\mathcal{W}_i$ encrypts it as $C_x = (g_p^{y_x(0)}, h(at_x)^{y_x(0)})$.

To achieve secure task allocation, $\mathcal{W}_i$ outsources the ciphertexts $(c_\varrho, \widehat{C_{I_i}}, C_x)$ to S_A.

(4) **IndexTran** $(c_\varrho, \widehat{C_{I_i}}, C_x, RK_A, RK_B) \rightarrow C_{I_i}$. Upon receiving the encrypted index $\widehat{C_{I_i}}$, S_A uses the corresponding re-encryption key $M'_{i,1}$ to re-encrypt $\widehat{C_{I_i}}$ as shown in Equation (8).

$$\begin{aligned}\widetilde{C_{I_i}} &= M'_{i,1}\widehat{C_{I_i}} \\ &= M'_{i,1}M_{i,1}\mathcal{U}_i\widehat{D_{I_i}}M_{i,2} \\ &= M_1\mathcal{U}_i\widehat{D_{I_i}}M_{i,2}.\end{aligned} \tag{8}$$

Then, S_A sends $\widetilde{C_{I_i}}$ to S_B. After receiving converted ciphertext $\widetilde{C_{I_i}}$, S_B re-encrypts it with the re-encryption key $M'_{i,2}$ as shown in Equation (9).

$$\begin{aligned}C_{I_i} &= \widetilde{C_{I_i}}M'_{I,2} \\ &= M_1\mathcal{U}_i\widehat{D_{I_i}}M_{i,2}M'_{i,2} \\ &= M_1\mathcal{U}_i\widehat{D_{I_i}}M_2.\end{aligned} \tag{9}$$

Finally, S_B stores the converted ciphertext C_{I_i}, the encrypted identity c_Q, and the encrypted access tree C_x:

(5) **TrapGen** $(R_q, sk_q) \rightarrow \widehat{T_Q}$. The data requester $\mathcal{DR}_q$ designated the geometric range of the task requirement as $R_q = (R_{q,ll}, R_{q,lu}, R_{q,rl}, R_{q,ru})$, where ll, lu, rl, ru denote left-lower, left-upper, right-lower, and right-upper of the geometric range bound, respectively. Then, the $\mathcal{DR}_q$ encodes geometric query range R_q into the query vector $\overrightarrow{q}$ based on the Gray code. After that, the data requester $\mathcal{DR}_q$ performs the following operations to generate the search trapdoor:

Step 1: Firstly, $\mathcal{DR}_q$ encodes the geometric range R_q of the task requirement to query vector $\overrightarrow{q}$ as shown in Equation (10) by using the Gray code method.

$$\overrightarrow{q} = (q_1, q_2, \cdots, q_d), \tag{10}$$

where q_i $(i \in [1, d-1])$ is one of X, Y, or 0 and $q_d = \sum_{i=1}^{d-1} q_i^2$.

Step 2: Secondly, to protect the privacy of the query vector, the $\mathcal{DR}_q$ transforms the query vector $\overrightarrow{q}$ into an n-dimensional vector $v_q = (v_{q,1}, v_{q,2}, \cdots, v_{q,n})$ by using the same transformation $v_{q,i} = \sum_{i=1}^{d} q_i \cdot 2^{d-i}$ as mentioned in IndexEnc, where each entry $v_{q,i}$ $(i \in [1, n])$ is a positive integer value.

Step 3: After that, the $\mathcal{DR}_q$ hashes the integer vector v_q as shown in Equation (11) by using the hash function h.

$$h(v_q) = (h(v_{q,1}), h(v_{q,2}), \cdots, h(v_{q,n})). \tag{11}$$

Step 4: To further protect the privacy of the mapping-based task requirement, the $\mathcal{DR}_q$ constructs a polynomial function $f(q)$ of the task requirement with the degree being n, as shown in Equation (12).

$$\begin{aligned} f(q) &= \prod_{i=1}^{n} (q - h(v_{q,i})) \\ &= a_0 + a_1 q + \cdots + a_n q^n. \end{aligned} \tag{12}$$

Step 5: Subsequently, the $\mathcal{DR}_q$ extracts the coefficients of the task function to construct the coefficient vector as $Q = (a_0, a_1, \cdots, a_n)$. Then, the $\mathcal{DR}_q$ embeds a one-time random positive number β into the coefficient vector Q and generates the random vector $\overline{Q} = (\beta a_0, \beta a_1, \cdots, \beta a_n)$.

Step 6: Next, the $\mathcal{DR}_q$ permutes the random vector $\overline{Q}$ as $\hat{Q} = \pi(\overline{Q})$, and then, the $\mathcal{DR}_q$ transforms $\hat{Q}$ into the corresponding diagonal matrix $\widehat{D_Q}$ with the diagonal being $\hat{Q}$.

Step 7: Finally, the $\mathcal{DR}_q$ generates a random $(n+1) \times (n+1)$ upper triangular matrix $\mathcal{P}_q$ with the main diagonal being $(1, 1, \cdots, 1)$ and encrypts the diagonal matrix $\widehat{D_Q}$ by using the secret key sk_q and the $\mathcal{DR}_q$ as shown in Equation (13). After that, the $\mathcal{DR}_q$ sends the encrypted task $Enc_K(\mathcal{T})$ and search trapdoor $\widehat{T_Q}$ to S_A, where Enc denotes symmetric encryption (e.g., AES), and $\mathcal{T}$ is the plaintext of $\mathcal{DR}_q$'s task.

$$\widehat{T_Q} = M_{q,2} \widehat{D_Q} \mathcal{P}_q M_{q,1}. \tag{13}$$

(6) **TrapTran** $(\widehat{T_Q}, RK_A, RK_B) \rightarrow T_Q$. Upon receiving the search trapdoor $\widehat{T_Q}$, S_A utilizes the corresponding re-encryption key $M'_{q,2}$ to re-encrypt $\widehat{T_Q}$, as shown in Equation (14).

$$\begin{aligned} \widetilde{T_Q} &= M'_{q,2} \widehat{T_Q} \\ &= M'_{q,2} M_{q,2} \widehat{D_Q} \mathcal{P}_q M_{q,1} \\ &= M_2^{-1} \widehat{D_Q} \mathcal{P}_q M_{q,1}. \end{aligned} \tag{14}$$

After that, S_A sends $\widetilde{T_Q}$ to S_B. Subsequently, S_B finds the requester $\mathcal{DR}_q$'s re-encryption key $M'_{q,1}$ and re-encrypts $\widetilde{T_Q}$ to T_Q as shown in Equation (15).

$$\begin{aligned} T_Q &= \widetilde{T_Q} M'_{q,1} \\ &= M_2^{-1} \widehat{D_Q} \mathcal{P}_q M_{q,1} M'_{q,1} \\ &= M_2^{-1} \widehat{D_Q} \mathcal{P}_q M_1^{-1}. \end{aligned} \tag{15}$$

(7) **Query** $(c_Q, C_x, t_c, C_{I_i}, T_Q) \to \mathcal{R}_i$. Upon receiving the search trapdoor T_Q, for each encrypted object $\mathsf{EO} = (c_Q, C_x, C_{I_i})$, S_B first checks whether the $\mathcal{DR}_q$'s attribute set S satisfies the defined access policy $\mathcal{T}_Q$ based on Definition 1. If not, S_B outputs $\perp$; otherwise, S_B executes the following Query procedure for task allocation.

Step 1: For each leaf node x in hierarchical temporal access tree $\mathcal{T}_Q$, if $at_x \notin S$, S_B outputs $\perp$. If $at_x \in S$ and $t_c \in [t_1, t_2] \cap [t'_1, t'_2]) \bigwedge (\mathcal{T}_Q(S) = 1)$, S_B utilizes the ciphertext C_x and time-related derivation function to calculate $F_x = a \int_{t_1}^{t_2} \int_{t'_1}^{t'_2} f_x(t) dt dt' = e(g_p, H)^{a y_x(0)}$; otherwise, S_B outputs $\mathsf{TAC}(\mathcal{T}_Q, S, t_c) = 0$. By doing this, we have $F_{root} = e(g_p, H)^{as}$ in the root node of the temporal access tree.

Step 2: Then, S_B checks whether the worker $\mathcal{W}_i$ is a suitable one via the corresponding matrix trace between the $\mathcal{W}_i$'s index C_{I_i} and $\mathcal{DR}_q$'s search trapdoor T_Q, which is equivalent to checking whether the inner product of spatial vector $\overrightarrow{\mathsf{p}_i}$ and query vector $\overrightarrow{\mathsf{q}}$ is equal to 0. By doing this, S_B can determine whether the spatial data L_i of the $\mathcal{W}_i$ are located in the geometric query range R_q of the task requirement by calculating the trace $tr(C_{I_i} T_Q)$ as shown in Equation (16).

$$\begin{aligned} tr(C_{I_i} T_Q) &= tr(M_1 \mathcal{U}_i \widehat{D_{I_i}} M_2 M_2^{-1} \widehat{D_Q} \mathcal{P}_q M_1^{-1}) \\ &= tr(M_1 \mathcal{U}_i \widehat{D_{I_i}} \widehat{D_Q} \mathcal{P}_q M_1^{-1}) \\ &= \overline{I_i} \circ \overline{Q} \\ &= \alpha\beta\Big(a_0 h(v_i)^0 + a_1 h(v_i)^1 + \cdots + a_n h(v_i)^n\Big). \end{aligned} \tag{16}$$

If $tr(C_{I_i} T_Q) = 0$ holds, the worker $\mathcal{W}_i$'s spatial data L_i are located in the geometric query range R_q of the task requirement. Thus, $\mathsf{EPTA}(C_{I_i}, T_Q, t_c, C_x, c_Q) = \mathcal{R}_i = 1$ holds, which means the $\mathcal{W}_i$ is an accessible and proper worker at the current time t_c and adds $\{c_Q, F_{root}\}$ to the search result $\mathcal{R}$. Otherwise, S_B chooses another re-encrypted spatial datum and performs the above secure task allocation procedure until all encrypted spatial data are searched.

5.3. Correctness Analysis

From linear algebra, we have the following theorem about the correctness of EPTA-T.

Theorem 1 (Correctness of EPTA-T). In EPTA-T, $\mathsf{EPTA\text{-}T.Query}(C_{I_i}, T_Q, t_c, C_x, c_Q) \to \mathcal{R}_i = 1$ is correct if and only if both $F_{root} = e(g_p, H)^{as}$ and $tr(C_{I_i} T_Q) = 0$ are satisfied.

Proof. To demonstrate the correctness of EPTA-T, we should prove that both the data requester $\mathcal{DR}_q$'s attribute set S satisfies the temporal access policy $\mathcal{T}_Q$ at the current time t_c and the worker $\mathcal{W}_i$'s location L_i is located in the geometric range R_q of the task requirement when $tr(C_{I_i} T_Q) = 0$ are satisfied.

For the temporal access control constraint, since $y_x(0) = y_x(0)' + y_x(0)''$ and $C_x = (H^{y_x(0)'}, h(at_x)^{y_x(0)'}, H^{y_x(0)''}, h(at_x)^{y_x(0)''})$, we have Equations (17) and (18).

$$F'_x = \frac{e(g_p^a h(at_x)^a, H^{y_x(0)'})}{e(H^a, h(at_x)^{y_x(0)'})} = e(g_p, H)^{a y_x(0)'}. \tag{17}$$

$$F_x'' = \frac{e(g_p^a h(at_x)^a, H^{y_x(0)''})}{e(H^a, h(at_x)^{y_x(0)''})} = e(g_p, H)^{ay_x(0)''}. \tag{18}$$

Based on Equations (17) and (18), we can calculate that $F_x = F_x' \cdot F_x'' = e(g_p, H)^{ay_x(0)}$. Similarly, for the non-leaf node x in $\mathcal{T}_Q$, we also can calculate F_x in a recursive way. To this end, we have $F_root = e(g_p, H)^{as}$, which means the $\mathcal{DR}_q$'s attribute set S satisfies the defined access policy $\mathcal{T}_Q$ at the current time t_c. Therefore, the correctness of TAC is demonstrated.

For the EPTA constraint, note that $C_{I_i}T_Q = M_1\mathcal{U}_i\widehat{D_{I_i}}\widehat{D_Q}\mathcal{P}_q M_1^{-1}$. According to the similarity transformation in linear algebra, we have $tr(C_{I_i}T_Q) = tr(\mathcal{U}_i\widehat{D_{I_i}}\widehat{D_Q}\mathcal{P}_q)$. Since $\mathcal{U}_i$ and $\mathcal{P}_q$ are upper triangular matrices with the main diagonals being $(1, 1, \cdots, 1)$, both $\mathcal{U}_i\widehat{D_{I_i}}$ and $\widehat{D_Q}\mathcal{P}_q$ are upper triangular matrices with the main diagonals being $\widehat{I_i}$ and $\widehat{Q}$. Additionally, by using the same permutation π, $\overline{I_i}$ and $\overline{Q}$ are permuted to $\widehat{I_i}$ and $\widehat{Q}$, respectively. Therefore, we have

$$\begin{aligned} tr(C_{I_i}T_Q) &= \widehat{I_i} \circ \widehat{Q} \\ &= \overline{I_i} \circ \overline{Q} \\ &= \alpha\beta\Big(a_0 h(v_i)^0 + a_1 h(v_i)^1 + \cdots + a_n h(v_i)^n\Big), \end{aligned} \tag{19}$$

where $\widehat{I_i} \circ \widehat{Q}$ denotes the inner product between $\widehat{I_i}$ and $\widehat{Q}$. In Equation (19), since both α and β are two one-time positive values, if $tr(C_{I_i}T_Q) = 0$ holds, the equation $a_0 h(v_i)^0 + a_1 h(v_i)^1 + \cdots + a_n h(v_i)^n = 0$ is satisfied, which means the hash value $h(v_i)$ is the root of the polynomial function $f(q)$ constructed by the requester $\mathcal{DR}_q$. Since $h(v_i)$ and $h(v_q)$ are derived from the spatial vector $\overrightarrow{p_i}$ and $\overrightarrow{q}$, we have $\overrightarrow{p_i} \circ \overrightarrow{q} = 0$. That is, the $\mathcal{W}_i$'s spatial data L_i are located in the geometric query range R_q of the task requirement, i.e., $\mathcal{R}_i = 1$. Therefore, the correctness of EPTA-T is demonstrated. □

Discussion: Our EPTA-T achieves secure task allocation and temporal access control simultaneously. By using randomizable matrix multiplication, EPTA-T can resist the IND-SCPA in multi-user setting. In addition, EPTA-T supports temporal access control by leveraging function differentiation and integration, along with CP-ABE, to regulate access to tasks over time. Our EPTA-T considers the locations of the workers, which is not sufficient for accurate task allocation. In practical task allocation scenarios, workers' keywords are also significant for task matching. To provide a detailed discussion on the advantages and challenges of EPTA-T, we discuss both the functionality and efficiency of EPTA-T as follows:

- Functionality: Our EPTA-T scheme can support task allocation in multi-user settings without key sharing. This is made possible by leveraging proxy re-encryption, which allows the transformation of ciphertexts from an asymmetric key environment to re-encrypted ciphertexts in a symmetric key setting. As a result, even when workers and requesters employ different keys, secure task allocation can still be achieved by utilizing different types of ciphertexts.
- Efficiency: Our EPTA-T scheme provides significant reductions in computational overhead for both the data encryption and task allocation processes. By utilizing randomizable matrix multiplication and matrix decomposition techniques, our EPTA-T scheme avoids heavy cryptographic operations such as fully homomorphic encryption, Paillier encryption, exponential operations, and secure circuits. This design choice leads to a notable improvement in the performance of data encryption and task allocation, as the computational burden is reduced.

6. Security Analysis

Since CPA is stronger than COA, if EPTA-T can resist CPA, it logically follows that it can also provide resistance against COA. Therefore, in this section, we mainly analyzed how EPTA-T can protect the confidentiality of spatial data, workers' identity, the geometric query of the task requirements, and the task results under an Indistinguishability under Selective Chosen-Plaintext Attacks (IND-SCPA) model. Before demonstrating the security of EPTA-T under the IND-SCPA model, we give the definitions of the secure simulation-based experiment between a computationally bounded adversary $\mathcal{A}$ and a challenger $\mathcal{C}$ as follows.

Definition 2 (IND-SCPA data privacy of EPTA-T). *Let $\prod$ be a privacy-preserving task-allocation scheme with temporal access control over a security parameter λ. A security game of data privacy between a challenger $\mathcal{C}$ and an adversary $\mathcal{A}$ is defined as follows:*

- *Initialization: Given a security parameter λ, $\mathcal{A}$ generates two spatial databases $DB_0 = \{L_{0,1}, L_{0,2}, \cdots, L_{0,m}\}$, and $DB_1 = \{L_{1,1}, L_{1,2}, \cdots, L_{1,m}\}$, and sends them to $\mathcal{C}$.*
- *Setup: $\mathcal{C}$ performs the* Setup *algorithm and the*KeyGen *algorithm to generate a master key, public parameter, secret key, and re-encryption key and sends the public parameter to $\mathcal{A}$*
- *Phase 1: $\mathcal{A}$ adaptively submits several encrypted data and trapdoor requests, where each request is one of the following types:*
    1. ***Encrypted data request**: Upon the j-th encrypted data request, $\mathcal{A}$ outputs a spatial dataset $L'_j = \{L'_{j,1}, L'_{j,2}, \cdots, L'_{j,m}\}$. $\mathcal{C}$ responds with encrypted spatial data $\widehat{C'_{I_i}} \leftarrow IndexEnc(L'_j, sk_i)$.*
    2. ***Search trapdoor request**: Upon the j-th search trapdoor request, $\mathcal{A}$ generates a geometric range query R_q and sends it to $\mathcal{C}$. After that, $\mathcal{C}$ responds with a search trapdoor $T_{Q_j} = TrapGen(R_{q_j}, sk_q)$. Here, R_{q_j} is subject to $\mathcal{L}(DB_0, R_{q_j}) = \mathcal{L}(DB_1, R_{q_j})$, where $\mathcal{L}$ is a leakage function obtaining all the information leaked during the task allocation process:*
- *Challenge: With DB_0 and DB_1 selected from the initialization, $\mathcal{C}$ flips a coin $b \in \{0,1\}$, executes* IndexEnc *to calculate the encrypted spatial data $\widehat{C'_{I_i}}$, and sends them to $\mathcal{A}$.*
- *Phase 2: $\mathcal{A}$ runs Phase 1 again and adaptively selects several spatial data, then issues them to $\mathcal{C}$.*
- *Guess: $\mathcal{A}$ outputs his/her guess b' of b. If $b' = b$ holds, $\mathcal{A}$ wins the security game; otherwise, $\mathcal{A}$ fails.*

$\prod$ is secure against IND-SCPA on data privacy if, for any polynomial-time adversary $\mathcal{A}$ in the above security game, $\mathcal{A}$ has at most a negligible advantage as follows:

$$Adv_{\prod,\mathcal{A}}^{IND-SCPA,Data} = |Pr(b' = b) - \frac{1}{2}| \leq negl(\lambda),$$

where $negl(\lambda)$ is a negligible function.

Definition 3 (IND-SCPA query privacy of EPTA-T). *Let $\prod$ be a privacy-preserving task-allocation scheme with temporal access control over a security parameter λ. A security game of query privacy between a challenger $\mathcal{C}$ and an adversary $\mathcal{A}$ is defined as follows:*

- *Initialization: $\mathcal{A}$ submits two geometric range queries R_{q0} and R_{q1} with the same dimensional space to $\mathcal{C}$.*
- *Setup: $\mathcal{C}$ runs the* KeyGen *algorithm to generate a secret key for trapdoor encryption.*
- *Phase 1: $\mathcal{A}$ adaptively submits a series of requests to $\mathcal{C}$. After that, $\mathcal{C}$ responds with encrypted spatial data and trapdoor. Each request is one of the following two types:*
    1. ***Encrypted data request**: Upon the j-th encrypted data request, $\mathcal{A}$ outputs a spatial dataset $L'_j = \{L'_{j,1}, L'_{j,2}, \cdots, L'_{j,m}\}$. Then, $\mathcal{C}$ responds with encrypted spatial data $\widehat{C'_{I_i}} = IndexEnc(L'_j, sk_i)$, where $\widehat{C'_{I_i}}$ is subject to $\mathcal{L}(\widehat{C'_{I_i}}, R_{q0}) = \mathcal{L}(\widehat{C'_{I_i}}, R_{q1})$.*
    2. ***Search trapdoor request**: Upon the j-th trapdoor request, $\mathcal{A}$ outputs a geometric query request R_{q_j}. Then, $\mathcal{C}$ responds with a search trapdoor $\widehat{T_{Q_j}} \leftarrow TrapGen(R_{q_j}, sk_q)$:*

- *Challenge: With R_{q_0} and R_{q_1} selected in the initialization, $\mathcal{C}$ flips a coin $b \in \{0,1\}$ and calculates $\widehat{T_{Q_{b,j}}}$. After that, $\mathcal{C}$ sends it back to $\mathcal{A}$.*
- *Phase 2. $\mathcal{A}$ adaptively selects a series of trapdoor requests and sends them to $\mathcal{C}$, which are still subject to the same restrictions in Phase 1.*
- *Guess: $\mathcal{A}$ outputs his/her guess b' of b. If $b' = b$ holds, $\mathcal{A}$ wins the security game; otherwise, $\mathcal{A}$ fails.*

$\prod$ is secure against IND-SCPA regarding query privacy if, for any polynomial-time adversary $\mathcal{A}$ in the above security game, $\mathcal{A}$ has at most a negligible advantage:

$$Adv_{\prod,\mathcal{A}}^{IND-SCPA,Query} = |Pr(b' = b) - \frac{1}{2}| \leq negl(\lambda).$$

6.1. Data Privacy and Identity Privacy

Theorem 2. *Our EPTA-T scheme guarantees IND-SCPA data privacy and identity privacy.*

Proof. To prove the IND-SCPA data privacy of EPTA-T, we should demonstrate that $\mathcal{A}$ cannot distinguish the ciphertext $\widehat{C_{I_{0,j}}}$ and $\widehat{C_{I_{1,j}}}$ based on the security game defined in Definition 2, even though $\mathcal{A}$ has oracle access to IndexEnc.

Considering that the $\mathcal{W}_i$'s spatial data L_i are firstly encoded as spatial vector $\overrightarrow{p_i}$ by using Gray code, then $\mathcal{W}_i$ transforms $\overrightarrow{p_i}$ into a positive integer v_i and obtains a hash value by using the hash function h. After that, the $\mathcal{W}_i$ calculates an $(n+1)$-dimensional vector I_i based on the hash value $h(v_i)$. In addition, the $\mathcal{W}_i$ permutes the random vector $\overline{I_i}$ to $\widehat{I_i}$ with the random permutation π. Following this, the permuted vector $\widehat{I_i}$ is transformed into a corresponding diagonal matrix $\widehat{D_{I_i}}$. Finally, the spatial data L_i are encrypted as $\widehat{C_{I_i}} = M_{i,1}\mathcal{U}_i\widehat{D_{I_i}}M_{i,2}$. Since $\mathcal{A}$ has no idea about the one-time random value α, the random permutation π, and the random triangular matrix $\mathcal{U}_i$, it is hard to recover the secret key sk_i. Additionally, $\mathcal{A}$ can obtain several plaintext–ciphertext pairs, but it is difficult for $\mathcal{A}$ to launch a linear analysis attack.

In Phase 1 and Phase 2 of Definition 2, $\mathcal{A}$ can adaptively select different spatial data $\{L_j'\}_{j=1}^m$ and obtain the corresponding ciphertexts $\{\widehat{C_{I_j}}\}_{j=1}^m$. Unfortunately, both $\overline{I_i}$ and $\mathcal{U}_i$ are a one-time random vector and matrix determined by $\mathcal{C}$, and the ciphertexts $\{\widehat{C_{I_j}}\}_{j=1}^m$ are random according to $\mathcal{A}$. That is, for the given ciphertexts $\widehat{C_{I_{0,j}}}$ and $\widehat{C_{I_{1,j}}}$ selected by $\mathcal{A}$, $\mathcal{A}$ cannot distinguish which spatial data are actually encrypted. Therefore, even though $\mathcal{A}$ has oracle access to IndexEnc, it has a random guess b' of b with a negligible advantage:

$$Adv_{\prod,\mathcal{A}}^{IND-SCPA,Data} = |Pr(b' = b) - \frac{1}{2}| \leq negl(\lambda).$$

For the identity privacy in EPTA-T, since the worker's identity id_{ϱ} is encrypted as c_{ϱ} by using AES and the secret key of AES is kept private to $\mathcal{A}$, the identity privacy can be well protected. □

6.2. Query Privacy and Result Privacy

Theorem 3. *Our EPTA-T scheme guarantees IND-SCPA query privacy and result privacy.*

Proof. Based on Definition 3, to prove the query privacy, we should demonstrate that $\mathcal{A}$ cannot obtain any sensitive information from the encrypted trapdoor $\widehat{T_Q}$, encrypted attribute set C_x, and matrix trace $tr(C_{I_i}T_Q)$. Similar to the operation in IndexEnc, $\mathcal{A}$ can adaptively select different geometric query range $\{R_{q_j}\}_{j=1}^m$ and observe the corresponding trapdoor $\{\widehat{T_{Q_j}}\}_{j=1}^m$. However, both $\overline{Q}$ and $\mathcal{P}_q$ are a one-time random vector and matrix determined by $\mathcal{C}$, and the encrypted trapdoor $\{\widehat{T_{Q_j}}\}_{j=1}^m$ is random according to $\mathcal{A}$. Therefore, for the given trapdoors $\widehat{T_{Q_{0,j}}}$ and $\widehat{T_{Q_{1,j}}}$ selected by $\mathcal{A}$, even though $\mathcal{A}$ has oracle access to

TrapGen, $\mathcal{A}$ only has a random guess b' of b for the geometric query range with a negligible advantage:

$$Adv_{\prod,\mathcal{A}}^{IND-SCPA,Query} = |Pr(b' = b) - \frac{1}{2}| \leq negl(\lambda).$$

In addition, $\mathcal{A}$ can obtain $F_{root} = e(g_p, H)$ and $tr(C_{I_i} T_Q)$ for temporal access control and task allocation, respectively. However, the privacy of the temporal access tree can be well guaranteed by using Bilinear Diffie–Hellman Assumption (DBDH). Furthermore, the query result only reveals whether $tr(C_{I_i} T_Q)$ is equal to 0 or not, and no more sensitive information of the geometric query can be obtained by $\mathcal{A}$. Therefore, our EPTA-T scheme can well guarantee IND-SCPA query privacy and result privacy. □

7. Performance Evaluation

In this section, we provide a thorough experimental evaluation of the EPTA-T scheme. We first depict the configuration of the experimental environment and selection of parameters. Since our EPTA-T scheme is the first work to support fine-grained and temporal access control in privacy-preserving task allocation, we present the comparison of EPTA-T with Privacy-Preserving Boolean Range Query with Temporal Access Control (PBRQ-T) [6] in terms of the computational overhead on IndexEnc, TrapGen, and Query.

7.1. Implementation Settings

Experimental environment. We implemented our EPTA-T scheme and PBRQ-T with JAVA and utilized the JDK library to implement cryptographic primitives such as AES. We conducted experiments on a laptop with a 2.8 GHz, Intel Core i7, 16 GB RAM as $\mathcal{SP}$ and an Android phone with 8G RAM and Octa-core Processors as $\mathcal{W}$ and $\mathcal{DR}$. In order to precisely measure the computational cost of the $\mathcal{SP}$, $\mathcal{W}$, and $\mathcal{DR}$, all experiments were performed on the same devices. Furthermore, all the reported running times were the average of 100 experiments.

Dataset. We randomly selected 10,000 spatial data from the Yelp dataset (https://www.yelp.com/dataset (accessed on 19 May 2023)) as the test dataset, where each spatial datum included the spatial location and attributes. The number of attributes was 44 in the test dataset.

Parameter setting. To compare with PBRQ-T, all primes were set as 60 bits. In addition, we divided the space into 1000 × 1000 cells; the dimension of the spatial vector was 100; the geometric query range R_q was set as a 64 × 64 square. In our experimental evaluation, we set the number of the $\mathcal{DR}$'s attributes and system attributes as 10, and we assumed that there was only one temporal attribute in the task allocation system.

We compared our EPTA-T scheme with the state-of-the-art PBRQ-T scheme [6]. Note that the PBRQ-T scheme does not support task recommendation in mobile crowdsensing systems. To test the cost domination of our EPTA-T over different database sizes m and dimension vectors n, we mainly evaluated the complexity of index encryption, index transformation, trapdoor generation, trapdoor transformation, and query between $\mathcal{W}$, $\mathcal{DR}$, and $\mathcal{SP}$, respectively.

7.2. Evaluation and Comparison

Performance evaluation of IndexEnc and IndexTran. The cost of IndexEnc was dominated by the database size m. As shown in Figure 3a, when the database size was 10,000, the index encryption time of EPTA-T was about 3 s, while that of PBRQ-T was more than 2500 s. The reason is that our EPTA-T scheme only executes randomizable matrix multiplication for data privacy protection, while PBRQ-T conducts bilinear mapping and exponentiation operations, which have a more-expensive computational cost than our scheme. Therefore, with the increase of the database's size, EPTA-T can save more computational costs on the worker side. Since PBRQ-T does not involve the index transformation operation, we only evaluated our EPTA-T on IndexTran with varying vector dimensions (i.e., n). As shown in Figure 3b, we noticed that our proposed EPTA-T increased linearly with the variable vector dimension n. In addition, the IndexTran costs over different database sizes m were almost close in the lower-dimensional setting.

Performance evaluation of TrapGen and TrapTran. From Figure 3c, we can notice that our EPTA-T had less computational cost for TrapGen and slightly increased with the variable number d of trapdoors, and it was at least 10× faster than PBRQ-T. The underlying reason is that the number of trapdoors had little effect on the calculation of the matrix multiplication. As shown in Figure 3d, we can notice that the TrapTran computational cost of EPTA-T linearly grew with the variable n. Specifically, when the vector dimension achieved 100, the time cost of TrapTran was only 0.7 s, even though the $\mathcal{DR}$ submitted 10 geometric queries at one time.

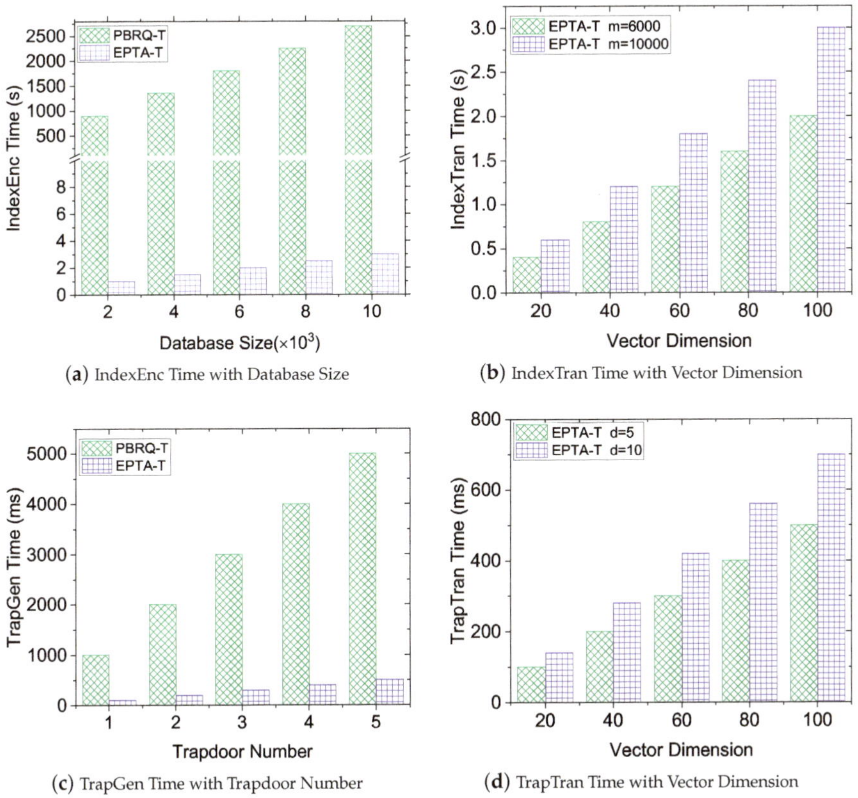

(**a**) IndexEnc Time with Database Size (**b**) IndexTran Time with Vector Dimension

(**c**) TrapGen Time with Trapdoor Number (**d**) TrapTran Time with Vector Dimension

Figure 3. Performance Evaluation of IndexEnc, IndexTran, TrapGen, and TrapTran.

Performance evaluation of Query. To comprehensively evaluate the query cost, we ran the experiments on the database with different sizes and vectors with different dimensions. As shown in Figure 4, the query overhead was scarcely influenced by the database size and the vector dimension. From Figure 4a, we can notice that the query time of both EPTA-T and PBRQ-T increased linearly with m, and the query performance of EPTA-T outperformed that of PBRQ-T. The query time of EPTA-T was about 500× faster than that of PBRQ-T, which indicates that the calculation operations of matrix trace and functional integration were more efficient than those of exponent arithmetic and bilinear mapping. From Figure 4b, we can notice that a higher vector dimension had a greater query time cost with EPTA-T. The underlying logic is that the increase of the vector dimension d caused the number of matrix dimensions to grow and the computational cost of the matrix-trace-based operation to increase.

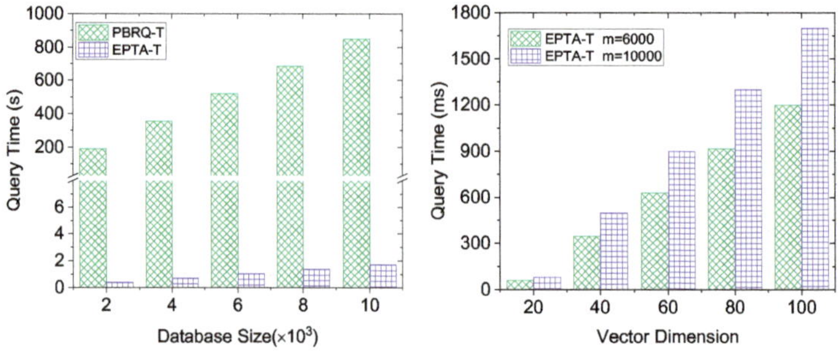

(**a**) Query Time with Database Size (**b**) Query Time with Vector Dimension

Figure 4. Performance Evaluation of Query.

8. Conclusions

In this paper, we investigated and studied the problem of privacy-preserving task allocation with temporal access control for mobile crowdsensing. Specifically, we proposed an Efficient and Privacy-Preserving Task Allocation with Temporal Access Control (EPTA-T) scheme that efficiently achieved secure task allocation in multi-user settings by using Gray code and randomizable matrix multiplication. Moreover, EPTA-T incorporates temporal access control by leveraging function differentiation and integration, along with CP-ABE, to regulate access to tasks over time. Furthermore, formal security analysis and experimental evaluations demonstrated that EPTA-T protects data privacy and query privacy and achieves efficient task allocation compared with the state-of-the-art scheme. Regarding open problems, privacy-preserving spatial-keyword-based task allocation is still a challenging issue that needs to be resolved. For future work, we will further consider additional constraints in privacy-preserving task allocation, such as workers' interests and incentives.

Author Contributions: Conceptualization, F.S. and Y.L.; methodology, F.S.; software, F.S. and S.M.; validation, F.S., Y.L. and Q.J.; writing—original draft preparation, F.S. and Y.L.; writing—review and editing, Q.J., X.Z. and Z.F. All authors have read and agreed to the published version of the manuscript.

Funding: This research was funded by the Defense Industrial Technology Development Program (No. JCKY2021602B002), the National Natural Science Foundation of China (Nos. U20A20174, U22B2062, 62202051, 62202234, and 42001247), the National Key R&D Projects (No. 2021YFB00900 and No. 2018YFB0704000), and the China Postdoctoral Science Foundation (No. 2021M700435 and No. 2021TQ0042).

Data Availability Statement: The data presented in this study are available upon request from the corresponding authors. The data are not publicly available due to the privacy requirements of the project.

Conflicts of Interest: The authors declare no conflict of interest. The funders had no role in the design of the study; in the collection, analyses, or interpretation of the data; in the writing of the manuscript; nor in the decision to publish the results.

References

1. Song, F.; Qin, Z.; Liu, D.; Zhang, J.; Lin, X.; Shen, X. Privacy-preserving task matching with threshold similarity search via vehicular crowdsourcing. *IEEE Trans. Veh. Technol.* **2021**, *70*, 7161–7175. [CrossRef]
2. Ni, J.; Zhang, K.; Xia, Q.; Lin, X.; Shen, X. Enabling strong privacy preservation and accurate task allocation for mobile crowdsensing. *IEEE Trans. Mob. Comput.* **2019**, *19*, 1317–1331. [CrossRef]
3. Liang, J.; Qin, Z.; Xiao, S.; Ou, L.; Lin, X. Efficient and secure decision tree classification for cloud-assisted online diagnosis services. *IEEE Trans. Dependable Secur. Comput.* **2019**, *18*, 1632–1644. [CrossRef]
4. Shu, J.; Jia, X.; Yang, K.; Wang, H. Privacy-preserving task recommendation services for crowdsourcing. *IEEE Trans. Serv. Comput.* **2018**, *14*, 235–247. [CrossRef]

5. Zhu, Y.; Hu, H.; Ahn, G.J.; Huang, D.; Wang, S. Towards temporal access control in cloud computing. In Proceedings of the INFOCOM, Orlando, FL, USA, 25–30 March 2012; pp. 2576–2580.
6. Tong, Q.; Li, X.; Miao, Y.; Liu, X.; Weng, J.; Deng, R.H. Privacy-preserving Boolean range query with temporal access control in mobile computing. *IEEE Trans. Knowl. Data Eng.* **2022**, *35*, 5159–5172. [CrossRef]
7. Deng, H.; Qin, Z.; Wu, Q.; Deng, R.H.; Guan, Z.; Hu, Y.; Li, F. Achieving fine-grained data sharing for hierarchical organizations in clouds. *IEEE Trans. Dependable Secur. Comput.* **2022**, *20*, 1364–1377. [CrossRef]
8. Zhang, C.; Zhu, L.; Xu, C.; Ni, J.; Huang, C.; Shen, X. Location privacy-preserving task recommendation with geometric range query in mobile crowdsensing. *IEEE Trans. Mob. Comput.* **2021**, *21*, 4410–4425. [CrossRef]
9. Wang, B.; Li, M.; Wang, H. Geometric range search on encrypted spatial data. *IEEE Trans. Inf. Forensics Secur.* **2015**, *11*, 704–719. [CrossRef]
10. Wang, B.; Li, M.; Xiong, L. FastGeo: Efficient geometric range queries on encrypted spatial data. *IEEE Trans. Dependable Secur. Comput.* **2017**, *16*, 245–258. [CrossRef]
11. Zhang, S.; Ray, S.; Lu, R.; Guan, Y.; Zheng, Y.; Shao, J. Efficient and Privacy-Preserving Spatial Keyword Similarity Query over Encrypted Data. *IEEE Trans. Dependable Secur. Comput.* 2022, *early access*. [CrossRef]
12. Song, F.; Qin, Z.; Xue, L.; Zhang, J.; Lin, X.; Shen, X. Privacy-preserving keyword similarity search over encrypted spatial data in cloud computing. *IEEE Internet Things J.* **2021**, *9*, 6184–6198. [CrossRef]
13. Liang, J.; Qin, Z.; Ni, J.; Lin, X.; Shen, X. Practical and secure SVM classification for cloud-based remote clinical decision services. *IEEE Trans. Comput.* **2020**, *70*, 1612–1625. [CrossRef]
14. Song, F.; Qin, Z.; Zhang, J.; Liu, D.; Liang, J.; Shen, X. Efficient and privacy-preserving outsourced image retrieval in public clouds. In Proceedings of the GLOBECOM, Taipei, Taiwan, 7–11 December 2020; pp. 1–6.
15. Zheng, Y.; Lu, R.; Zhang, S.; Guan, Y.; Wang, F.; Shao, J.; Zhu, H. PRkNN: Efficient and Privacy-Preserving Reverse kNN Query Over Encrypted Data. *IEEE Trans. Dependable Secur. Comput.* 2022, *early access*. [CrossRef]
16. Zhang, S.; Ray, S.; Lu, R.; Guan, Y.; Zheng, Y.; Shao, J. Toward Privacy-Preserving Aggregate Reverse Skyline Query with Strong Security. *IEEE Trans. Inf. Forensics Secur.* **2022**, *17*, 2538-2552. [CrossRef]
17. Zhang, C.; Hu, C.; Wu, T.; Zhu, L.; Liu, X. Achieving Efficient and Privacy-Preserving Neural Network Training and Prediction in Cloud Environments. *IEEE Trans. Dependable Secur. Comput.* 2022, *early access*. [CrossRef]
18. Wang, H.; Wang, E.; Yang, Y.; Wu, J.; Dressler, F. Privacy-Preserving online task assignment in spatial crowdsourcing: A graph-based approach. In Proceedings of the INFOCOM, Virtual Conference, 2–5 May 2022; pp. 570–579.
19. Xia, Y.; Zhao, B.; Tang, S.; Wu, H.T. Repot: Real-time and privacy-preserving online task assignment for mobile crowdsensing. *Trans. Emerg. Telecommun. Technol.* **2021**, *32*, e4035. [CrossRef]
20. Zhou, P.; Chen, W.; Ji, S.; Jiang, H.; Yu, L.; Wu, D. Privacy-preserving online task allocation in edge-computing-enabled massive crowdsensing. *IEEE Internet Things J.* **2019**, *6*, 7773–7787. [CrossRef]
21. Xu, Z.; Wu, L.; Qin, C.; Li, S.; Zhang, S.; Lu, R. PPTA: Privacy-Preserving Task Assignment Based on Inner Product Functional Encryption in SAM. *IEEE Internet Things J.* **2022**, *10*, 254–267. [CrossRef]
22. Xue, L.; Liu, D.; Huang, C.; Shen, X.; Zhuang, W.; Sun, R.; Ying, B. Blockchain-Based Data Sharing with Key Update for Future Networks. *IEEE J. Sel. Areas Commun.* **2022**, *40*, 3437–3451. [CrossRef]
23. Huang, C.; Liu, D.; Yang, A.; Lu, R.; Shen, X. Multi-client secure and efficient dpf-based keyword search for cloud storage. *IEEE Trans. Dependable Secur. Comput.* 2023, *early access*. [CrossRef]
24. Song, F.; Qin, Z.; Liang, J.; Lin, X. An efficient and privacy-preserving multi-user multi-keyword search scheme without key sharing. In Proceedings of the ICC, Montreal, QC, Canada, 14–23 June 2021; pp. 1–6.
25. Li, R.; Liu, A.X.; Wang, A.L.; Bruhadeshwar, B. Fast and scalable range query processing with strong privacy protection for cloud computing. *IEEE/ACM Trans. Netw.* **2015**, *24*, 2305–2318. [CrossRef]
26. Liu, D.; Wu, H.; Huang, C.; Ni, J.; Shen, X. Blockchain-based credential management for anonymous authentication in sagvn. *IEEE J. Sel. Areas Commun.* **2022**, *40*, 3104–3116. [CrossRef]
27. Li, S.; Zhang, Y.; Xu, C.; Cheng, N.; Liu, Z.; Du, Y.; Shen, X. HealthFort: A Cloud-Based Ehealth System with Conditional Forward Transparency and Secure Provenance via Blockchain. *IEEE Trans. Mob. Comput.* 2022, *early access*. [CrossRef]
28. Ren, H.; Li, H.; Liu, D.; Xu, G.; Shen, X. Enabling Secure and Versatile Packet Inspection with Probable Cause Privacy for Outsourced Middlebox. *IEEE Trans. Cloud Comput.* **2021**, *10*, 2580–2594. [CrossRef]
29. Hu, C.; Zhang, C.; Lei, D.; Wu, T.; Liu, X.; Zhu, L. Achieving Privacy-Preserving and Verifiable Support Vector Machine Training in the Cloud. *IEEE Trans. Inf. Forensics Secur.* 2023, *early access*. [CrossRef]
30. Wang, X.; Ma, J.; Liu, X.; Miao, Y.; Liu, Y.; Deng, R.H. Forward/backward and Content Private DSSE for Spatial Keyword Queries. *IEEE Trans. Dependable Secur. Comput.* 2022, *early access*. [CrossRef]
31. Chen, D.; Zhang, N.; Cheng, N.; Zhang, K.; Qin, Z.; Shen, X. Physical layer based message authentication with secure channel codes. *IEEE Trans. Dependable Secur. Comput.* **2018**, *17*, 1079–1093. [CrossRef]

electronics

MDPI

Article

Verifiable Privacy-Preserving Outsourced Frequent Itemset Mining on Vertically Partitioned Databases

Zhen Zhao [1,2,*], Lei Lan [1], Baocang Wang [1,*] and Jianchang Lai [3]

[1] State Key Laboratory of Integrated Service Networks, Xidian University, Xi'an 710071, China
[2] Henan Key Laboratory of Network Cryptography Technology, Zhengzhou 450001, China
[3] School of Cyber Science and Engineering, Southeast University, Nanjing 211189, China
* Correspondence: zzhen@xidian.edu.cn (Z.Z.); bcwang@xidian.edu.cn (B.W.)

Abstract: In the data era, to simultaneously relieve the heavy computational burden of mining data information from data owners and protecting data privacy, privacy-preserving frequent itemset mining (PPFIM) is presented and has attracted much attention. In PPFIM, data owners and miners outsource the complex task of data mining to the cloud server, which supports strong storage and computing power, and the cloud server cannot extract additional data privacy other than that which is shown by data owners or miners. However, most existing solutions assume that cloud servers will honestly perform the mining process and return the correct results, whereas cloud services are usually provided by a charging third party that may in practice return incorrect results due to computation errors, malicious or criminal activities, etc. To solve this problem, in this paper, we present a verifiable PPFIM protocol on vertically partitioned databases to support the verifiability of the integrity of the mining results, where data owners can authorize the cloud server to perform federated mining on vertically partitioned databases without leaking data information and detect dishonest behaviors in the cloud server from the returned results. We adopt a dual cloud setting to enable data owners to be offline after uploading their encrypted databases to the cloud server, which further relieves the burden on data owners. We implement our protocol and give a detailed analysis in terms of verification accuracy, which shows that the dishonest behaviors of the cloud server can be detected with a probability close to 1 and a sacrifice of only a 1% increase in database size.

Keywords: frequent itemset mining; privacy-preserving; Paillier homomorphic encryption; vertically partitioned databases

1. Introduction

In the era of big data, data mining technology has attracted much attention since it enables the extraction of valuable information from data. As the core technology of association rule mining, frequent itemset mining (FIM) [1–3] is used to find frequent co-occurrence data items in large transaction databases. It has been widely used in market basket analysis [4], healthcare [5], intrusion detection [6], network traffic management [7], and bioinformatics [8]. Taking the most classic supermarket basket as an example, and given a transaction database, FIM can find the commodity combinations that are more frequently added to the same shopping list. Wal-Mart found that beer and diapers are often bought together because American husbands often buy two bottles of beer to themselves when they buy diapers for their children. Such information can help retailers optimize shelf placement and carry out selective marketing, thus increasing sales.

Due to extensive computation costs, data miners usually choose to outsource the task of mining to cloud servers that possess powerful storage and computation capacity. This greatly relieves the computation burden on the local devices of miners as well as exposes the data information of owners since the data will be uploaded to the cloud for mining. Privacy exposure, especially that of sensitive information, may even lead to huge economic losses or even more terrible consequences, such as the leakage of gene banks. This problem on the FIM has also received a substantial amount of attention, and the concept of privacy-preserving FIM (PPFIM) was proposed correspondingly [9,10]. PPFIM can mine the frequent itemsets among the databases while protecting the privacy security of data and mining results against curious cloud servers which, in practice, are often used by charging third parties.

To be realistically usable in further applications, subsequent research on PPFIM has also paid attention to supporting multiple data owners [11–13], where the mining is performed on a joint database that consists of the transactions collected from multiple users. In the literature, the joint database can be divided into horizontally partitioned databases and vertically partitioned databases. A horizontally partitioned database can be divided into multiple tables belonging to different users, where each table contains the same number of columns and different numbers of rows. Conversely, a vertically partitioned database can be split into multiple tables, each containing the same number of rows but different columns. For example, let us consider two tables with the same service types for two different companies, each consisting of transaction rows that identify the ordered services from different customers. We can create a horizontally partitioned database by simply adding the transactions of one table to another. On the other hand, if the two companies provide different service types for the same group of customers, we can obtain a vertically partitioned database by attaching the transactions of a user in one table with the corresponding user in another table.

In particular, as in our example, for a common scenario where, in reality, different merchants that sell different goods in the same region want to plan a joint sales promotion to stimulate consumption, vertically partitioned databases are more suitable. In this scenario, the merchants jointly mine the frequent itemsets with the help of a third cloud server and accordingly cooperate with the related stores to start the sales promotion. However, most existing PPFIM protocols assume that cloud servers can honestly perform a required mining job and correctly return the mining results. However, typically cloud servers cannot be fully trusted in practice, i.e., they may return incorrect results to the merchants to increase profit, engage in malicious activities, or due to some uncontrolled calculation errors, without any risk of being caught. Incorrect mining results may lead to a failed promotion or even substantial financial loss.

Contributions. In this paper, to solve the aforementioned problem, we propose a verifiable PPFIM protocol on vertically partitioned databases to support the checking of the integrity of returned mining results from the cloud. Our FIM protocol provides both privacy protection and verifies the integrity of the results, which is practically needed for data owners and miners who cooperate with not-fully trusted third parties.

In our protocol, prior to uploading their databases to the cloud, merchants, i.e., data owners, add artificial itemsets that are different from the original itemsets to the transactions, applying the technique proposed in [14]. Data owners can then check the integrity of returned results by detecting the malicious actions of cloud servers on these artificial itemsets. To resist the frequency analysis attack, merchants further adopt the algorithm proposed in [15] to insert fictitious transactions into their database. Merchants encrypt their databases and upload them to the cloud, and the cloud then performs mining on the joint encrypted database, following the improved FIM protocol [11] by applying the Paillier [16] algorithm in our solution. Compared with [11], we utilize a dual-cloud setting, instead of a single-cloud setting, such that the merchants do not need to stay online after outsourcing the data. We finally implement our solution and depict the computation costs, which shows that the verification accuracy increases along with the increase in the number of dishonest behaviors in the cloud and the proportion of fictitious itemsets. Particularly, as both the proportion of itemsets affected by the CSP's dishonest behaviors reaches 0.6% and the artificial itemsets proportion in the mining results reaches 1%, the data owner can capture dishonest behaviors from the CSP with a probability close to 100%.

Organization

The rest of this paper is organized as follows. In Section 2, we introduce the literature on PPFIM and verifiable PPFIM. In Section 3, we describe the preliminaries of our solution. Then, we introduce the system model, security model, and design goals of this paper in Section 4. In Section 5, we present our PPFIM scheme based on vertically partitioned databases. The security and experimental analysis of our protocol is shown in Section 6.

2. Related Work

Privacy-preserving frequent itemset mining (PPFIM). Due to the traditional involvement of FIM, the raw data of data owners may cause direct privacy leakage problems in practice; thus, PPFIM is presented [9,10,12] to protect data privacy in the mining process. PPFIM can be generally classified into randomization-based solutions and cryptography-based solutions, among which the former [15,17] hides the original data information through data perturbation techniques so that data mining can be performed without exposing original data values, and the latter protects data by encrypting them prior to uploading them to clouds. In cryptographic-based solutions, as we explained above, data are usually partitioned with two approaches: vertical [10,11,18] and horizontal [9,19]. In the literature on cryptographic-based PPARM algorithms, many studies [11–13,20] have been based on homomorphic encryption schemes [16] to support computations on encrypted data.

Verifiable PPFIM. In most PPFIM protocols, the cloud servers are supposed to honestly execute the mining process and will return correct results. Wong et al. [14] designed an audit environment in which the data owners add artificial data items that originally did not exist in the outsourced database, where data owners can verify the correctness and integrity of the mining results by checking the integrity of artificial data items. However, Ref. [14] does not change the frequency of data items in the original database, which allows the cloud server with some background knowledge to distinguish the real data items from the artificial data items by frequency analysis. Chen et al. [21] applied the BLS signature [22] to verify data integrity and ensure data reliability, which requires more computation costs in terms of checking the integrity than that in [14]. Furthermore, in their scheme, data are encrypted with the homomorphic encryption for higher security, which leads to a larger computation cost and an additional cloud server for auxiliary decryption. In this paper, we improve the technique proposed by [14] to realize an efficient PPFIM protocol, which provides the integrity verification and resists frequency analysis attacks. As shown in Table 1, we compare the contribution of our protocol with the verifiable FIM protocols presented in [14,21].

Table 1. Comparison of contributions.

Scheme	[14]	[21]	Ours
Verifiability	√	√	√
Data Privacy	×	√	√
Against frequency analysis attack	×	√	√
Number of third-party cloud servers	2	3	2
Data encryption	–	Homomorphic encryption	Substitution cipher Homomorphic encryption

3. Preliminaries

In this section, we introduce the building blocks that are applied to our protocol, including the Paillier homomorphic encryption [16], an improved secure comparison protocol (SCP) based on [13,16], the substitution cipher, and some definitions of FIM [14]

3.1. Paillier Homomorphic Encryption

We recall the Paillier homomorphic encryption [16] as below. Note that the Paillier encryption is an additively homomorphic encryption scheme.

Paillier.KeyGen: Taking two large prime numbers p, q as input, it computes $N = pq$ and $\lambda = lcm(p-1, q-1)$, where $lcm(\cdot)$ denotes the least common multiple functions. It selects a random number $g \in \mathbb{Z}^*_{N^2}$ that satisfies $gcd(L(g^\lambda \mod N^2), N) = 1$, where $gcd(\cdot)$ denotes the greatest common divisor function and $L(x) = (x-1)/N$ with $x \in \mathbb{Z}_{N^2}$ and $x \equiv 1 \mod N$. It outputs the public key $pk = \{N, g\}$ and the private key $sk = \lambda$.

Paillier.Enc: Taking as input a message $m \in \mathbb{Z}_N$, it selects a random number $r \in \mathbb{Z}^*_{N^2}$ and computes the ciphertext as $c = [m]_{pk} = g^m r^N \mod N^2$.

Paillier.Dec: Taking as input a ciphertext c, it computes the message with the private key λ as $m = \frac{L(c^\lambda \mod N^2)}{L(g^\lambda \mod N^2)} \mod N$.

Paillier.Add: Taking as input two ciphertexts $[m_1]_{pk}$ and $[m_2]_{pk}$, we have

$$[m_1]_{pk} \cdot [m_2]_{pk} = [m_1 + m_2]_{pk}.$$

This is because

$$\begin{aligned}[m_1]_{pk} \cdot [m_2]_{pk} &= g^{m_1} r_1^N \mod N^2 \cdot g^{m_2} r_2^N \mod N^2 \\ =& g^{m_1+m_2} r_1 + r_2{}^N \mod N^2 \\ =& [m_1 + m_2]_{pk}.\end{aligned}$$

Paillier.Mult: With the additive homomorphic property, we can easily have that given a ciphertext $[m_1]_{pk}$ and a message $m_2 \in \mathbb{Z}_N$,

$$([m_1]_{pk})^{m_2} = [m_1 \cdot m_2]_{pk}.$$

In our protocol, we use Paillier encryption to encrypt 0 and 1, and the corresponding ciphertexts are $r^N \mod N^2$ and $gr^N \mod N^2$, where r is the randomly chosen number, $N = pq$, and g is one of the public key pk of the user.

3.2. Substitution Cipher

Substitution cipher protects the privacy of a single unit but it does not change the frequency of items. This means that every ciphertext and the corresponding item appear at the same frequency. As such, the substitution cipher is vulnerable to frequency analysis attacks. If attackers have some knowledge of the frequencies of the items in raw transactions, they can recover the plaintext by frequency analysis. For example, an attacker knows that bread is the most sold commodity and milk is the second. Once they acquire the transactions database encrypted by substitution cipher, they can find the ciphertexts for bread and milk by counting the frequencies of ciphertexts. We counter frequency analysis by adding fictitious transactions to hide the accuracy frequency of items.

3.3. FIM

We first recall the definition of FIM [23]. Let $I = \{i_1, i_2, \cdots, i_n\}$ be the item domain and a transaction database be $D = \{t_1, t_2, \cdots, t_n\}$, where a transaction t_i is a subset of I. We say that a transaction t_i contains an itemset x if and only if $x \subseteq t_i$. Given a transaction database D, the support of itemset x, denoted by $supp(x)$, is the number of transactions that the itemset x contains in D. Given a support threshold $s\%$, the itemset x is a frequent itemset if and only if $supp(x) > |D| \times s\%$, where $|D|$ is the total number of transactions in D. We also refer to $|D| \times s\%$ as $supp_{min}$. FIM serves to find all frequent itemsets in a given database D.

In our protocol, artificial transactions are inserted into data owners' transaction datasets to verify the integrity of the mining results [14]. To better understand this, we recall the related definitions and theorems below. First of all, a correct mining result must be a valid return.

Definition 1. *(Valid Return) Given a returned FIM result R from the miner, we said that R is valid if* $\forall y \in R, \forall x \subset y$ *and* $x \neq \emptyset \Rightarrow x \in R$ *and* $supp(x) \geq supp(y)$*. We refer to this property as the "monotonicity property" which states that any subset of a frequent itemset must be frequent.*

Then, we introduce the concepts of a positive border and a negative border. Given an item domain I, let L be a set of frequent itemsets that satisfy the monotonicity property.

Definition 2. *(Positive Border) The positive border of L, denoted by* $B^+(L)$*, is the set of all frequent itemsets with a maximal length in L, i.e.,* $B^+(L) = \{x \mid \forall x \in L \text{ and } \forall x \subset y, y \notin L\}$*.*

Definition 3. *(Negative Border) The negative border of L, denoted by* $B^-(L)$*, is the set of all infrequent itemsets with minimal length with respect to L, i.e.,* $B^-(L) = \{x \mid \forall x \subset I \text{ and } x \notin L \text{ and } \forall y \subset x, \text{ where } y \neq \emptyset, \ y \in L\}$*.*

Theorem 1. *Let a set of frequent itemsets* L' *be a valid return from the miner while the real set of frequent itemsets is L. No infrequent itemset is inserted into L if and only if all itemsets in* $B^+(L')$ *are frequent. No frequent itemset is deleted from L if and only if all itemsets in* $B^-(L')$ *are infrequent. Proof of this theorem can be found in [14].*

The inserted artificial itemsets should satisfy the following requirements.

Definition 4. *(Valid Pattern) Let I be a set of unique items in the transaction database D and* I_A *be a set of artificial items. Assume that* $I_A \cap I = \emptyset$*. Given the support threshold s%, we generate a set of artificial frequent itemsets named* AFI *and a set of artificial infrequent itemsets named* AII*. We say that the itemset pattern* (AFI, AII) *is a s-valid pattern if there exists a transaction database* T_A *in which all itemsets in* AFI *are frequent and all itemsets in* AII *are infrequent with the support threshold s%.*

When generating artificial transactions, we insert itemsets belonging to AFI into transactions and try to avoid inserting itemsets belonging to AII. However, if a transaction contains multiple itemsets of AFI, it may contain one or more itemsets of AII. Such a situation is called a "conflict" between the itemsets in AFI. If such "conflicts" never occur in the same transaction, the itemsets of AII will not be included in any transaction.

Definition 5. *(Conflict in AFI) Let* x_i, x_j *be two itemsets belonging to* AFI*,* $i \neq j$*. We say that* x_i *conflicts with* x_j *if and only if there exists* $z \in AII$ *satisfying* $(z - x_i) \cap x_j \neq \emptyset$ *and* $(z - x_j) \cap x_i \neq \emptyset$*. If a transaction t of the artificial database* T_A *contains both* x_i *and* x_j *while* x_i *conflicts with* x_j*, the corresponding itemset z may be included in transaction t.*

Definition 6. *(Conflict Index) Let graph* $G = (V, E)$ *represent the conflict relationships of itemsets in* AFI*. Each node in graph G represents an itemset in* AFI*. An edge* (n_1, n_2) *in graph G represents the conflict between* n_1 *and* n_2*. The conflict index of node n, denoted by* c_n*, is the number of neighbor nodes of n, i.e., the number of itemsets in* AFI *in conflict with n. The conflict index of graph G, denoted by* $CI(G)$*, is equal to the maximum value of the conflict index of nodes in G, i.e.,* $CI(G) = max_{n \in V} c_n$*.*

Theorem 2. *Given an artificial itemset pattern* (AFI, AII) *while* AFI *and* AII *satisfy the monotonicity,* (AFI, AII) *is an* $s - valid$ *pattern if* $CI(G) \leq \frac{1}{s\%} - 1$. *Proof of this theorem can be found in [14].*

4. Models and Design Goals

In this section, we depict the system model, security model, and design goals of our protocol.

4.1. System Model

As shown in Figure 1, our system model consists of two cloud servers (CSP and Evaluator) and multiple data owners.

- *CSP* integrates the vertically partitioned databases from different data owners to generate a joint database. With the help of the Evaluator, CSP mines frequent itemsets in the joint database and returns the mining results to the relevant data owners.
- *Evaluator* is responsible for generating and distributing public/private key pairs (pk, sk) of Paillier encryption for data owners. Additionally, Evaluator assists the CSP in performing FIM.
- *Data owners* sell different goods. They take commodities as items and transform customers' purchase records in the store into digital transactions. By generating a unique identifier TID for each transaction according to the user's bank card, contact information, and other related information, each data owner finally obtains a private transaction database. After inserting artificial data items and fictitious transactions into their own transaction database, data owners encrypt it and then send it to the CSP for PPFIM. It is worth noting that there is no intersection between itemsets among different data owners' databases.

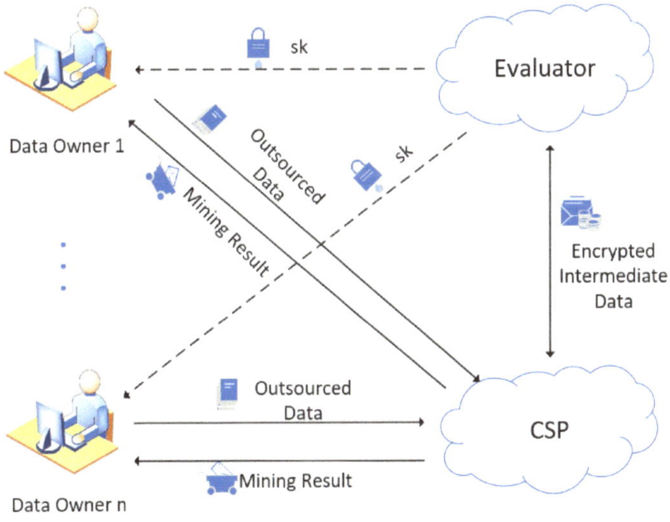

Figure 1. System model.

4.2. Security Model

In our system, we assume the following.

- The CSP is dishonest and curious. Due to saving costs in terms of computation, making illegal profits, or unexpected errors, the CSP may behave dishonestly or erroneously by returning inaccurate mining results to data owners. In addition to that, the CSP is curious about the original transaction information and mining results.

- The Evaluator is honest but curious. If the Evaluator is dishonest, the user can still detect errors in the mining results and confirm whether the CSP or Evaluator performs dishonestly, which is the same for data owners since cloud servers are dishonest. We therefore assume that the Evaluator is honest and curious. The CSP and Evaluator are set to not collude, or else the cloud servers can extract all the underlying messages of encrypted data.
- Data owners are set to not collude with the CSP. In a vertically partitioned data mining scenario, data owners cooperate to send an encrypted transaction database to the CSP to mine frequency itemsets. They ultimately benefit from the correct mining results. Therefore, data owners are not supposed to collude with the CSP.

Note that each data owner should know the items in other owners' transaction databases but have limited knowledge of the TIDs therein in practical applications. Our protocol is more meaningful when there are many common TIDs in data owners' databases, such as those for stores in the same community.

4.3. Design Goals

We design a verifiable privacy-preserving outsourced FIM protocol on vertically partitioned databases to ensure the following:

- *Security of private information.* The original transactions of the encrypted database should be kept secret from the CSP and Evaluator. Data owners should also learn as little information as possible about other owners' databases. The support and threshold should be concealed as they may be used to infer information about raw databases [24]. The CSP and Evaluator should not obtain accurate mining results. Each data owner can only obtain frequent itemsets that contain items in their own transaction database.
- *Verifiability of the integrity of mining results.* Data owners should be able to verify the integrity of mining results, which means that data owners can detect inaccurate results if the CSP performs dishonestly in the mining.

5. PPFIM Protocol

Our protocol can be divided into three phases. First, data owners insert artificial transactions into their own private transaction databases to achieve verifiable integrity in their mining results. Then, data owners process and encrypt their transactions and send the encrypted databases to the CSP. Then, CSP integrates the databases from multiple data owners to generate a joint database and performs FIM on it. Data owners can finally obtain encryption-related mining results from the CSP.

5.1. Artificial Transaction Insertion

For a data owner, given its private transaction database T and support threshold $s\%$, these generate a set of artificial frequent itemsets AFI and a set of artificial infrequent itemsets AII. Upon the corresponding artificial database T_A, the data owner merges T_A and T into a new database D. We divide this process into two main steps: artificial itemset generation and artificial transaction generation.

5.1.1. Artificial Itemset Generation

We adopt the scheme proposed in [14] to generate the artificial frequent itemsets AFI and artificial infrequent itemsets AII that satisfy the requirement of an s-valid pattern. The execution process of artificial itemset generation can be seen in Figure 2 and the details are as follows.

Note that the itemsets belonging to AFI and AII should be satisfied with the demand for the monotonicity property and the conflicting itemsets in AFI jeopardize correctness. We describe the conflicting relationship among AFI by a conflict graph G. (AFI, AII) should be an s-valid pattern (see Theorem 2) such that the data owner could generate the corresponding artificial database $T_A = \{t_1, t_2, \cdots, t_n\}$ in which each itemset in AFI is frequent and each itemset in AII is infrequent.

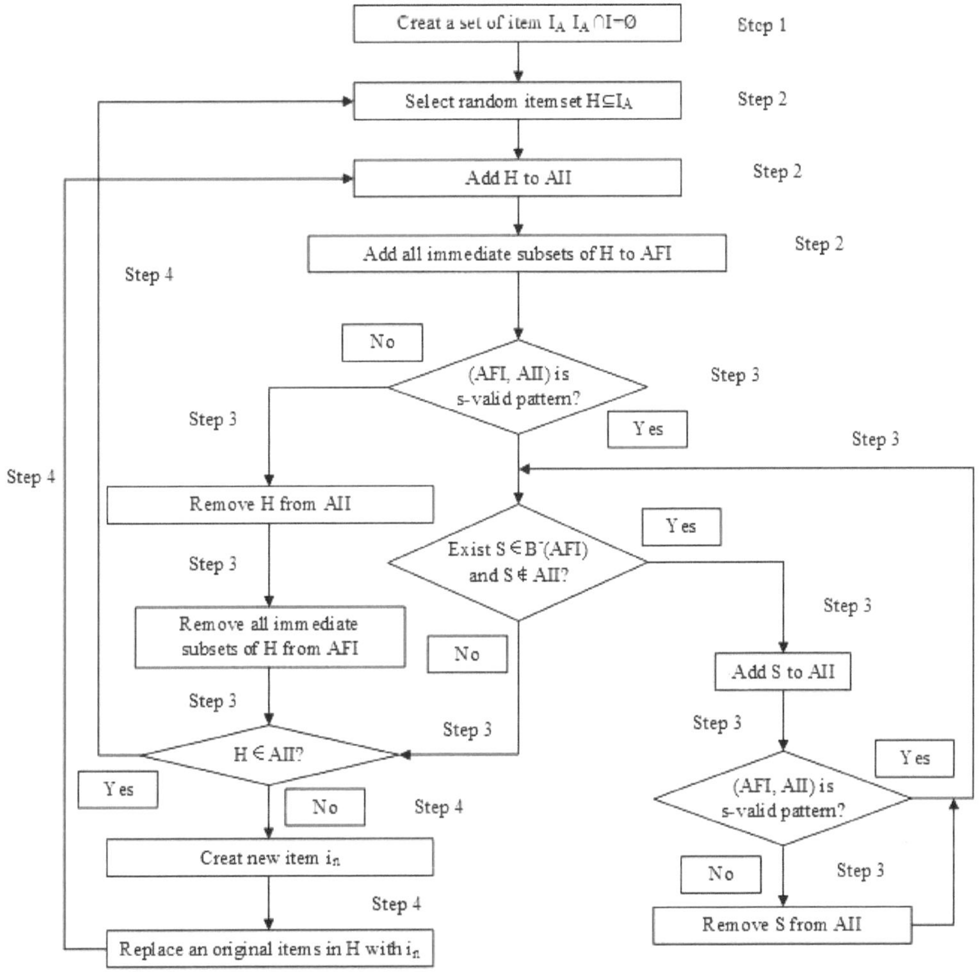

Figure 2. Artificial Itemset Generation.

Step 1: The data owner creates a set of artificial items I_A satisfying $I_A \cap I = \emptyset$, where I represents the item domain of T. The size of AII is denoted as the initial size of I_A.

Step 2: The data owner randomly selects an itemset $H \subseteq I_A$ satisfying $H \notin AII$. It then adds H to AII and all immediate subsets of H to AFI. For example, if $H = ABC$, the data owner adds $\{ABC\}$ to AII and $\{AB, BC, AC\}$ to AFI.

Step 3: The data owner updates the conflict graph G of AFI. If the obtained (AFI, AII) is not an s-valid pattern, it rolls back the addition operation performed in step 2 and goes to step 4. If (AFI, AII) is an s-valid pattern, the data owner calculates $B^-(AFI)$. If there exists an itemset S satisfying $S \in B^-(AFI), S \notin AII$, it adds S to AII. Otherwise, go to step 4. After the addition, the data owner updates G and checks whether (AFI, AII) is an s-valid pattern. If not, it rolls back the insertion.

Step 4: If H is successfully added to AII, repeat steps 2 and 3 until the sizes of AFI and AII meet the requirements. Otherwise, $H \notin AII$, the data owner creates a new artificial item i_n, adds i_n to I_A, replaces an original item in H with i_n, and tries to add H to AII again (step 2).

Suppose the size of H is k, then after a maximum of k attempts, H will be replaced with a completely new itemset which must be successfully inserted into AII. Thus, the algorithm can be successfully executed in finite time. The procedure tries to add itemsets to AFI and AII until they are both big enough. We refer to Section 6 for the relationship between the size of (AFI, AII) and verification accuracy.

5.1.2. Artificial Transaction Generation

In this phase, the data owner generates the artificial transaction database T_A corresponding to (AFI, AII). Recalling the requirements of the artificial database that each itemset of AFI is frequent in T_A and each itemset of AII is infrequent in T_A, we tend to add the AFI itemsets into the transactions without inserting any AII itemsets to avoid jeopardizing correctness. In other words, conflicting AFI itemsets should not be added to the same transaction. We depict the artificial transaction generation process in Figure 3 and the details are as follows.

Step 1: The data owner generates an array f_{AFI}, the size of which is set to be equal with that of AFI. $f_{AFI}[i]$ records the number of times that the i-th itemsets in AFI is added to the artificial transactions.

Step 2: The data owner generates artificial transactions by adding non-conflicting AFI itemsets. It maintains two initially empty sets S^+, S^-, randomly selects an itemset $U \in AFI$, adds U to S^+, and then adds all neighbor nodes of U in the conflict graph G to S^-. Recall that the neighbor nodes of U in G represent itemsets that are in conflict with U.

Step 3: Repeat step 2 until $AFI = S^+ \cup S^-$. Itemsets in S^+ are conflict-free and each itemset in S^- conflicts with at least one itemset in S^+. The first transaction to be generated is the union of all itemsets in S^+. Update f_{AFI}.

Step 4: Remove all itemsets existing in S^+ from AFI and remove all corresponding nodes and related edges in graph G to obtain the conflict graph G' corresponding to S^-. Since each itemset in S^- conflicts with at least one itemset in S^+, $CI(G') \leq CI(G) - 1$.

Step 5: Set $G = G'$, repeat steps 2–4 until $CI(G') = 0$. Take the itemsets left in AFI as an artificial transaction since they are conflict-free. A maximum of $CI(G) + 1$ transactions can be generated in this process.

Step 6: If all values in f_{AFI} are greater than the support threshold, i.e., $f_{\mathsf{AFI}}[i] > \mathsf{Supp}_{min}$, return all artificial transactions as the artificial database T_A. Otherwise, reset the set U and graph G and return to step 2. The data owner merges the original database T with T_A to obtain a new database D. For the following processing and mining, we give an example of database D in Table 2.

Table 2. Data Owners' Transaction Databases.

Alice's Database		**Bob's Database**	
TID	Transaction	TID	Transaction
1	A B C	2	E F
2	A B	3	D E
4	B C	6	F

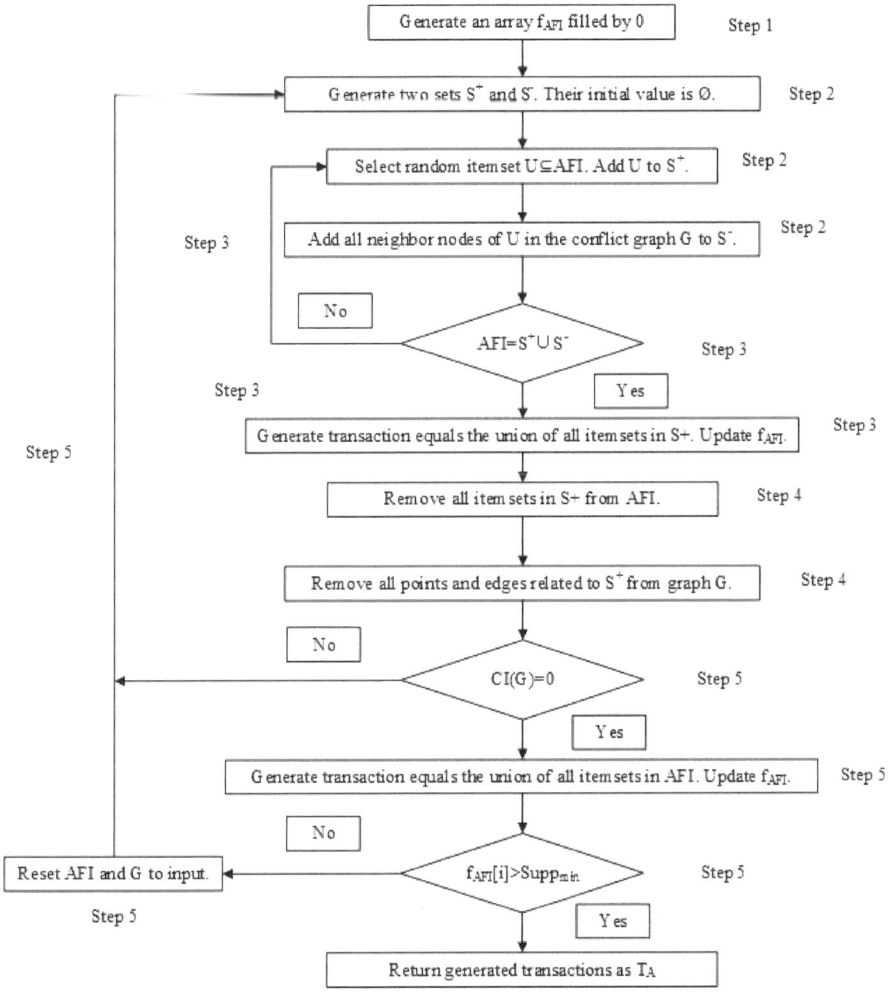

Figure 3. Artificial Transaction Generation.

5.2. Encryption of Databases

In this phase, each data owner encrypts their own transaction database.

Step 1: The Evaluator generates a public/private key pair (pk, sk) of Paillier encryption and sends sk to data owners.

Step 2: In order to counter frequency analysis attacks, we adopt the algorithm proposed in [15] to insert fictitious transactions into database D to obtain a database Z. Note that fictitious transactions are different from artificial transactions, where fictitious transactions are inserted to resist frequency analysis attacks and artificial transactions are inserted to realize the verifiability of the integrity of mining results. In Z, each item has the same frequency of occurrence as at least $k-1$ other items, where k is a number negotiated by data owners.

Step 3: In order to eliminate the influences of fictitious transactions on the mining results, each data owner tags each transaction in Z with an encrypted realness value ERV. The underlying realness values RV of ERV for a transaction in D is 1 and that of a fictitious transaction is 0, which means that $ERV \in \{[1]_{pk}, [0]_{pk}\}$. Since Paillier encryption is a probabilistic encryption cryptosystem, the CSP cannot distinguish the original and fictitious transactions from ERV.

Step 4: With a cryptographic hash function H, data owners replace the transaction's unique identifier TID with $H(TID)$. Each data owner then encrypts the items in database Z according to a substitution alphabet. Note that data owners use different private substitution alphabets, which do not influence the mining since the items belonging to different owners are different. An example of the encrypted databases is shown in Table 3.

Step 5: Each data owner outsources the encrypted database to the CSP.

Table 3. Data Owners' Encrypted Databases.

	Alice's Database			Bob's Database	
TID	Transaction	ERV	TID	Transaction	ERV
H(1)	S_A(A) S_A(B) S_A(C)	[1]	H(2)	S_B(E) S_B(F)	[1]
H(2)	S_A(A) S_A(B)	[1]	H(3)	S_B(D) S_B(E)	[1]
H(3)	S_A(A)	[0]	H(4)	S_B(D)	[0]
H(4)	S_A(B) S_A(C)	[1]	H(6)	S_B(F)	[1]
H(5)	S_A(C)	[0]			

$H(\cdot)$: Hash value of original TID. $S(\cdot)$: The item encrypted by substitution cipher $[\cdot]$: RV encrypted by Paillier.

5.3. Frequent Itemset Mining

The frequent itemset mining is shown below.

Step 1: Data owners negotiate a shared support threshold $supp_{min}$ and send the encrypted support threshold $T_s = [supp_{min}]_{pk}$ to the CSP.

Step 2: The CSP aggregates all data owners' databases based on $H(TID)$ to generate a joint database, where the transaction corresponding to a certain $H(TID)$ consists of that related to $H(TID)$ in all owners' databases. Table 4 gives the joint database of databases listed in Table 3.

Table 4. Joint Database.

TID	Alice's Partition	Bob's Partition	Alice's ERV	Bob's ERV
H(1)	S_A(A) S_A(B) S_A(C)	NULL	[1]	NULL
H(2)	S_A(A) S_A(B)	S_B(E) S_B(F)	[1]	[1]
H(3)	S_A(A)	S_B(D) S_B(E)	[0]	[1]
H(4)	S_A(B) S_A(C)	S_B(D)	[1]	[0]
H(5)	S_A(C)	NULL	[0]	NULL
H(6)	NULL	S_B(F)	NULL	[1]

Step 3: The CSP runs the classical FIM algorithm Eclat to find all frequent itemsets in the joint database. The Eclat algorithm outputs a set of $H(TID)$ that is related to the frequent itemsets in the mining result. It is worth noting that since we add artificial transactions to databases, some itemsets with less support than the support threshold are mistakenly returned as frequent itemsets. In other words, the frequent itemsets returned by the Eclat algorithm are only "seemingly frequent", which obviously contains all real frequent itemsets.

Step 4: For a "seemingly frequent" itemset S, suppose that its actual support is $supp(S)$. As mentioned before, the Eclat algorithm will return the $H(TID)$ set of S-related transactions $T(S)$. The items contained in S may come from multiple data owners, and we denote the set of these users as $D(S)$. In other words, the items contained in S all come from the data owner in $D(S)$, while each data owner has at least one item in itemset S. The i-th transaction i in $T(S)$ consists of transactions from one or more data owners, and we denote the set of these owners as $D(S,i)$. Let $ERV_{i,j}$ represent the ERV of the j-th data owner's partition in the i-th transaction. The CSP then computes the encrypted support of S as

$$[supp(S)]_{pk} = \prod_{i \in T(S)} \left[SC\left(\prod_{j \in D(S,i)} ERV_{i,j}, |D(S,i)| \right)\right],$$

where the secure comparison protocol $SC\left(\sum_{j \in D(S,i)} ERV_{i,j}, |D(S,i)| \right)$ will output a ciphertext of 1 if and only if every data owner in $|D(S,i)|$ has a real partition in the i-th transaction and it outputs 0 otherwise.

Step 5: For a "seemingly frequent" itemset S, the CSP computes the encrypted frequent realness value of S as

$$EFRV(S) = SC\left([supp(S)]_{pk}, T_s \right), \quad (1)$$

where $T_s = [supp_{min}]$ is the encrypted support threshold. If S is a real frequent itemset, $EFRV(S)$ is the ciphertext of 1. Otherwise, it is a ciphertext of 0. CSP sends every "seemingly frequent" itemset S and $EFRV(S)$ to all the data owners in $D(S)$.

Step 6: Data owners decrypt the received $EFRV$ of the "seemingly frequent" itemsets with *sk* to determine the real frequent itemsets. Each data owner can extract the related itemsets in its partition associated with the real frequent itemsets using the substitution cipher.

Step 7: Data owners verify the integrity of the mining results by checking: (1) whether the CSP returned any itemsets in AII; and (2) whether the CSP returned all the itemsets in AFI and their subsets. If (1) happens or (2) does not happen, owners can determine whether dishonest behaviors have occurred.

Step 8: Although data owners cannot directly obtain the related frequent itemsets of other owners, they can know which owners share the same frequent itemset. Data owners can interact with each other to line up willing partnerships and then share the real related itemsets with each other for the next commercial cooperation.

6. Performance Evaluation

6.1. Security Analysis

We analyze the security of this protocol against the CSP and Evaluator below. In our model, the CSP is set to be dishonest and curious, such that it will return incorrect mining results and try to extract the information of data owners' original transactions and the underlying mining results. For the misbehaviors of the CSP, the correctness and security of adding artificial itemsets protect the successfully tracing of the CSP.

In our protocol, the items of the transactions in the database are protected by a substitution cipher that is more secure but vulnerable to frequency analysis attacks. Furthermore, to further resist this type of attack, we apply the technique proposed in [15] to hide an item into at least a set of k items with the same frequency. The security of the technique was proven in [15]. In this protocol, data owners attach an ERV that is a Paillier ciphertext of 1 or 0 to each transaction, which obviously does not help the CSP distinguish the items through the indistinguishability of Paillier encryption. In conclusion, the security of adding artificial itemsets, hiding itemset techniques, and Paillier encryption prevent the CSP from extracting data owners' original transactions.

Next, regarding the security of mining results, we first prove the security of the improved secure comparison protocol below. Suppose that x_i is the input of party P_i, y_i is the input of party P_i, and $\Pi_i(\pi)$ is P_i's execution image of protocol π. We say that the protocol π is secure if $\Pi_i(\pi)$ can be simulated from x_i and y_i such that the distribution of the simulated image $\Pi_i^s(\pi)$ is computationally indistinguishable from $\Pi_i(\pi)$. The Evaluator's execution image of the SC protocol is denoted as $\Pi_{Evaluator}(SC) = \{(w, W), d\}$ where w is the decryption of W. If $t = 0$, then $w = r_1 \cdot (x - y) + r_2$, and if $t = 1$, then $w = r_1 \cdot (y - x) + r_2$. Recall that t is a random number from $(0,1)$ and r_1, r_2 are randomly selected from $\{1, \cdots, 2^l\}$. In addition, d is the comparison result from w. We assume that the simulated image of the Evaluator is $\Pi^s_{Evaluator}(SC) = \{(w', W'), d'\}$ where (w', W') are randomly selected from $\mathbb{Z}_N$ and d' is a random number from $(0,1)$. As Paillier is proven to be semantically secure, (w, W) is computationally indistinguishable from (w', W'). Furthermore, t is randomly selected from $(0,1)$, so d and d' are either 0 or 1 with equal probability. Thus, d is computationally indistinguishable from d'. In summary, the $\Pi_{Evaluator}(SC)$ is computationally indistinguishable from $\Pi^s_{Evaluator}(SC)$. Similarly, $\Pi_{CSP}(SC) = \{X, Y, Z, W, [d]_{pk}, [e]_{pk}\}$ is the execution image of CSP. The simulated image of CSP is $\Pi^s_{CSP}(SC) = \{X', Y', Z', W', \alpha, \beta\}$, where $\{X', Y', Z', W', \alpha, \beta\}$ are random numbers from $\mathbb{Z}_N$. Since Paillier is semantically secure, $\{X', Y', Z', W', \alpha, \beta\}$ are computationally indistinguishable from $\{X, Y, Z, W, [d]_{pk}, [e]_{pk}\}$. Thus, we can claim that $\Pi^s_{CSP}(SC)$ is computationally indistinguishable from $\Pi_{CSP}(SC)$. As a result, we can conclude that the secure comparison protocol is secure.

The CSP can obtain the mining results of the Eclat mining algorithm, the encrypted real support of itemsets, and the encrypted frequent realness value of itemsets. However, since the additional fictitious transactions, the mining results of the Eclat algorithm are actually "seemingly frequent" itemsets that contain infrequent itemsets. Furthermore, the itemsets are also encrypted with a substitution cipher. Due to the security of the secure comparison protocol and Paillier encryption, the CSP can only obtain a set of Paillier ciphertexts without knowing the underlying messages such that it also cannot extract the mining results.

6.2. Experimental Analysis

In this section, we implement our protocol and give the analysis in terms of verification accuracy and computational complexity. Our simulation experiments are performed on a computer with a 64-bit Windows 10 system, an Intel(R) Core(TM) i3-8100 CPU @ 3.60 GHz, and 4.00 GB of RAM. The Paillier algorithm is implemented in Java with a large integer N a length of 1024 bits and a safety parameter λ of 80 bits.

Verification Accuracy. We generate 10 random databases with the same set of data items [25]. The number of data items in each database is 1000, represented by integers from 1 to 1000. The average length of transactions is 10, and the number of transactions in the databases varies from 10,000 to 100,000. For simplicity, the frequent itemsets in these transaction databases are identical, but their support is different. This means that the support thresholds of these databases are different, while the frequent itemsets in mining results are identical. The exact mining result is denoted as L, the number of artificial frequent itemsets is $|AFI| = v \cdot |L|$, and the number of artificial infrequent itemsets is $|AII| = v \cdot |B^-(L)|$. We assumed that the cloud performs $e \cdot (|L| + |B^-(L)|)$ dishonest behavior to the mining results, and the probability that the data owner captures the dishonest behavior of the cloud is p. We randomly delete, add, or replace the frequent itemsets in the mining results and repeat the experiment 1000 times for each database, counting the average probability that these modifications to the experimental results are captured. The experimental results are shown in Figure 4.

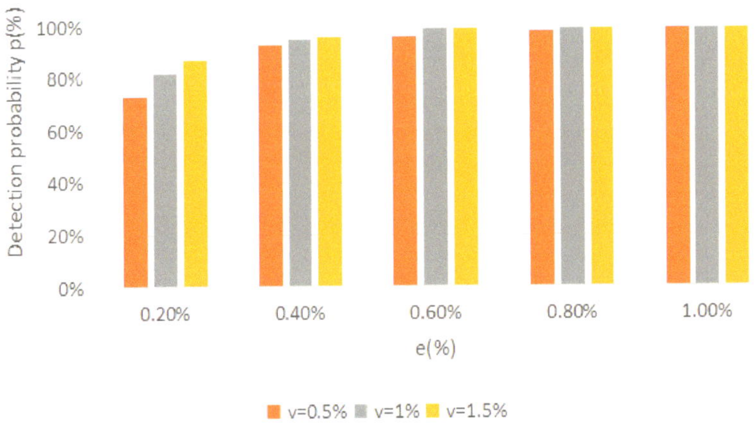

Figure 4. Probability of detecting the dishonest CSP.

As shown in Figure 4, the verification accuracy increases along with the increase in the number of dishonest behaviors in the cloud and the proportion of artificial itemsets. As e represents the proportion of itemsets affected by the CSP's dishonest behaviors and v represents the proportion of artificial itemsets in the mining results which reaches 1%, the data owner can capture dishonest behaviors from the CSP with a probability close to 100%.

Computational complexity. We evaluate the computational complexity of our protocol by computation costs. To be realistic, we test the performance of our solution using the retail database from [25] for mining. To simulate t data owners, we partition the retail database into t vertically partitioned databases. In this experiment, we fix t to 2 and the proportion of artificial itemsets to the mining results to 1%. In our experiment, we assume that the data owners and the two cloud servers are run with identical hardware conditions. We set different support thresholds for PPFIM with our scheme for the retail database. The running time of the Eclat algorithm and the number of frequent itemsets in mining results are shown in Table 5. We also measure the running time of the data owner, CSP, and Evaluator during the FIM of the retail dataset under different thresholds, as shown in Figure 5.

Table 5. Mining result and running time of Eclat.

Support Threshold	**200**	**500**	**1000**	**2000**	**4000**
Number of frequent itemsets	2191	468	135	45	16
Running time of Eclat	2319 ms	1139 ms	857 ms	970 ms	834 ms

As shown in Table 5, the number of frequent itemsets significantly decreases as the threshold value increases. The computation cost of the CSP and Evaluator also decreases along with the increase in support threshold, i.e., the reduction in frequent itemsets in the mining results, as depicted in Figure 5. This can be naturally deduced since more frequent itemsets also imply more operations in mining. Taking Table 5 and Figure 5 together, we have that the vast majority of the computation costs are spent on ciphertext-based operations for the CSP and Evaluator and on encryption and decryption operations for both the data owner and the Evaluator. A secure and more efficient homomorphic encryption algorithm can effectively improve the execution efficiency of our protocol.

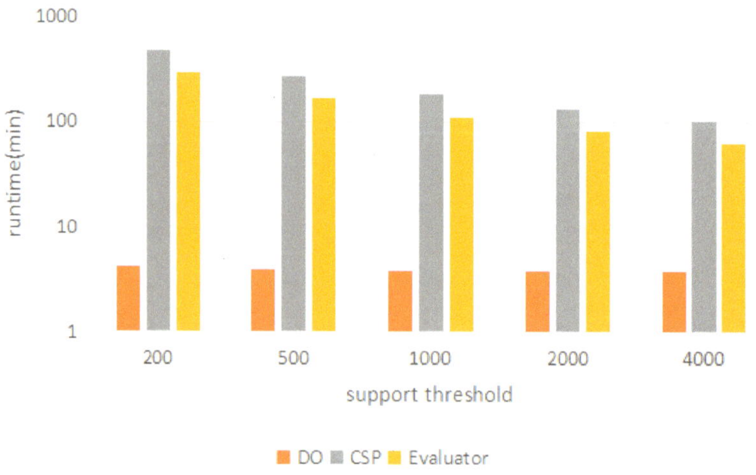

Figure 5. Computational costs of DO, CSP, and Evaluator.

We compare our protocol with the privacy-preserving frequent mining protocols [12,13], which also support multi-user settings [11] in terms of functions, as shown in Table 6. Note that the protocol of [11] that we based ours upon has been proven to be insecure since the security of the applied symmetric homomorphic encryption scheme therein is completely broken [26]—we omit the related comparison in this table. As shown, only our protocol can resist the malicious cloud server, i.e., realizing the verifiability of the integrity of the mining results. In [12], the Evaluator who also owns the private key as our protocol can finally know the final result of the secure comparison protocol and whether a mining itemset is frequent, which obviously leaks the privacy of mining results. This problem was solved in [13] and in our scheme. In addition, the protocols in [12,13] performed mining on horizontally partitioned databases and our protocol is performed on vertically partitioned databases.

Table 6. Comparison of functions.

Scheme	[11]	[12]	[13]	Ours
FIM	√	√	√	√
Data privacy	Partial	√	√	√
Verifiability of mining result integrity	×	×	×	√
Mining result privacy protection	√	×	√	√
Offline	×	√	√	√

7. Conclusions

Based on the Paillier encryption, we propose a verifiable PPFIM protocol on vertically partitioned databases. Our protocol can provide privacy-preserving outsourced mining across multiple data owners with vertically partitioned databases and can further allow data owners to check the integrity of results that are returned from the cloud. The verifiability in the field of privacy-preserving frequent itemset mining is quite significant since the outsourced clouds are usually not fully trusted in practice. However, particular data owners can be offline after they upload their encrypted database to the cloud, which is convenient for data owners and is practical in real applications. As a trade-off, we add artificial transactions in the proposed protocol, which increases the size of the databases and the cost of computation. Experimental analysis shows that a 100% probability of verification accuracy in our protocol in addition to a 1% increased artificial itemset proportion is an acceptable trade-off for small databases. However, when dealing with a database with big data, such as tens of millions of data, the additional 1% increased itemsets will cause a large computational load. Therefore, to efficiently support the verification of the integrity of the mining results without increasing the database size and computation cost can be listed as our future work.

Author Contributions: Conceptualization, Z.Z. and L.L.; methodology, B.W.; software, L.L.; validation, Z.Z., B.W. and J.L.; writing—original draft preparation, Z.Z. and L.L.; writing—review and editing, B.W. and J.L. All authors have read and agreed to the published version of the manuscript.

Funding: This research was funded by the National Natural Science Foundation of China under Grant Nos. 62102299, 62272362, and U19B2021, the Henan Key Laboratory of Network Cryptography Technology under Grant No. LNCT2022-A05, the Fundamental Research Funds for the Central Universities under Grant No. ZYTS23169, and the Youth Innovation Team of Shaanxi Universities.

Data Availability Statement: The data presented in this study are available on request from the corresponding authors. The data are not publicly available due to privacy requirements of the project.

Conflicts of Interest: The authors declare no conflict of interest. The funders had no role in the design of the study; in the collection, analyses, or interpretation of data; in the writing of the manuscript; or in the decision to publish the results.

References

1. Agrawal, R.; Srikant, R. Fast Algorithms for Mining Association Rules in Large Databases. In Proceedings of the VLDB'94, Santiago de Chile, Chile, 12–15 September 1994; pp. 487–499.
2. Han, J.; Pei, J.; Yin, Y.; Mao, R. Mining Frequent Patterns without Candidate Generation: A Frequent-Pattern Tree Approach. *Data Min. Knowl. Discov.* **2004**, *8*, 53–87. [CrossRef]
3. Zaki, M.J. Scalable Algorithms for Association Mining. *IEEE Trans. Knowl. Data Eng.* **2000**, *12*, 372–390. [CrossRef]
4. Brijs, T.; Swinnen, G.; Vanhoof, K.; Wets, G. Using Association Rules for Product Assortment Decisions: A Case Study. In Proceedings of the SIGKDD, San Diego, CA, USA, 15–18 August 1999; pp. 254–260.
5. Brossette, S.E.; Sprague, A.P.; Hardin, J.M.; Waites, K.B.; Jones, W.T.; Moser, S.A. Research Paper: Association Rules and Data Mining in Hospital Infection Control and Public Health Surveillance. *J. Am. Med. Inform. Assoc.* **1998**, *5*, 373–381. [CrossRef] [PubMed]
6. Lee, W.; Stolfo, S.J. Data Mining Approaches for Intrusion Detection. In Proceedings of the USENIX, San Antonio, TX, USA, 26–29 January 1998.
7. Estan, C.; Varghese, G. New directions in traffic measurement and accounting: Focusing on the elephants, ignoring the mice. *ACM Trans. Comput. Syst.* **2003**, *21*, 270–313. [CrossRef]
8. Creighton, C.; Hanash, S. Mining gene expression databases for association rules. *Bioinformatics* **2003**, *19*, 79–86. [CrossRef] [PubMed]
9. Kantarcioglu, M.; Clifton, C. Privacy-Preserving Distributed Mining of Association Rules on Horizontally Partitioned Data. *IEEE Trans. Knowl. Data Eng.* **2004**, *16*, 1026–1037. [CrossRef]
10. Vaidya, J.; Clifton, C. Privacy preserving association rule mining in vertically partitioned data. In Proceedings of the SIGKDD, Edmonton, AB, Canada, 23–26 July 2002; pp. 639–644.
11. Li, L.; Lu, R.; Choo, K.R.; Datta, A.; Shao, J. Privacy-Preserving-Outsourced Association Rule Mining on Vertically Partitioned Databases. *IEEE Trans. Inf. Forensics Secur.* **2016**, *11*, 1847–1861. [CrossRef]
12. Qiu, S.; Wang, B.; Li, M.; Liu, J.; Shi, Y. Toward Practical Privacy-Preserving Frequent Itemset Mining on Encrypted Cloud Data. *IEEE Trans. Cloud Comput.* **2020**, *8*, 312–323. [CrossRef]
13. Liu, L.; Su, J.; Chen, R.; Liu, X.; Wang, X.; Chen, S.; Leung, H. Privacy-Preserving Mining of Association Rule on Outsourced Cloud Data from Multiple Parties. In Proceedings of the ACISP, Wollongong, NSW, Australia, 11–13 July 2018; Volume 10946, pp. 431–451.
14. Wong, W.K.; Cheung, D.W.; Hung, E.; Kao, B.; Mamoulis, N. An Audit Environment for Outsourcing of Frequent Itemset Mining. *Proc. VLDB Endow.* **2009**, *2*, 1162–1172. [CrossRef]
15. Giannotti, F.; Lakshmanan, L.V.S.; Monreale, A.; Pedreschi, D.; Wang, W.H. Privacy-Preserving Mining of Association Rules From Outsourced Transaction Databases. *IEEE Syst. J.* **2013**, *7*, 385–395. [CrossRef]
16. Paillier, P. Public-Key Cryptosystems Based on Composite Degree Residuosity Classes. In Proceedings of the EUROCRYPT '99, Prague, Czech Republic, 2–6 May 1999; Volume 1592, pp. 223–238.
17. Wong, W.K.; Cheung, D.W.; Hung, E.; Kao, B.; Mamoulis, N. Security in Outsourcing of Association Rule Mining. In Proceedings of the 33rd International Conference on Very Large Data Bases, Vienna, Austria, 23–27 September 2007; pp. 111–122.

18. Lamba, J.; Venkaiah, V.C. Privacy-preserving frequent itemset mining in vertically partitioned database using symmetric homomorphic encryption scheme. *Int. J. Inf. Priv. Secur. Integr.* **2020**, *4*, 203–225. [CrossRef]
19. Domadiya, N.H.; Rao, U.P. Privacy Preserving Approach for Association Rule Mining in Horizontally Partitioned Data using MFI and Shamir's Secret Sharing. In Proceedings of the ICIISIEEE, Piscataway, NJ, USA, 1–2 December 2018; pp. 217–222.
20. Ma, C.; Wang, B.; Jooste, K.; Zhang, Z.; Ping, Y. Practical Privacy-Preserving Frequent Itemset Mining on Supermarket Transactions. *IEEE Syst. J.* **2020**, *14*, 1992–2002. [CrossRef]
21. Chen, Y.; Zhao, Q.; Duan, P.; Zhang, B.; Hong, Z.; Wang, B. Verifiable privacy-preserving association rule mining using distributed decryption mechanism on the cloud. *Expert Syst. Appl.* **2022**, *201*, 117086. [CrossRef]
22. Boneh, D.; Lynn, B.; Shacham, H. Short Signatures from the Weil Pairing. In Proceedings of the ASIACRYPT, Gold Coast, Australia, 9–13 December 2001; pp. 514–532.
23. Agrawal, R.; Imielinski, T.; Swami, A.N. Mining Association Rules between Sets of Items in Large Databases. In Proceedings of the SIGMOD, Washington, DC, USA, 26–28 May 1993; pp. 207–216.
24. Rozenberg, B.; Gudes, E. Association rules mining in vertically partitioned databases. *Data Knowl. Eng.* **2006**, *59*, 378–396. [CrossRef]
25. Fournier-Viger, P.; Gomariz, A.; Gueniche, T.; Soltani, A.; Wu, C.; Tseng, V.S. SPMF: A Java open-source pattern mining library. *J. Mach. Learn. Res.* **2014**, *15*, 3389–3393.
26. Wang, B.; Zhan, Y.; Zhang, Z. Cryptanalysis of a Symmetric Fully Homomorphic Encryption Scheme. *IEEE Trans. Inf. Forensics Secur.* **2018**, *13*, 1460–1467. [CrossRef]

MDPI AG
Grosspeteranlage 5
4052 Basel
Switzerland
Tel.: +41 61 683 77 34

Electronics Editorial Office
E-mail: electronics@mdpi.com
www.mdpi.com/journal/electronics

www.ingramcontent.com/pod-product-compliance
Ingram Content Group UK Ltd.
Pitfield, Milton Keynes, MK11 3LW, UK
UKHW061014121026
15625UKWH00069B/608